National Security for a New Era

GLOBALIZATION AND GEOPOLITICS AFTER IRAQ

Third Edition

Donald M. Snow

Professor Emeritus
University of Alabama

PEARSON
Longman

New York   San Francisco   Boston
London   Toronto   Sydney   Tokyo   Singapore   Madrid
Mexico City   Munich   Paris   Cape Town   Hong Kong   Montreal

Acquisitions Editor: Vikram Mukhija
Associate Marketing Manager: Sasha Anderson-Smith
Production Manager: Donna DeBenedictis
Project Coordination, Text Design,
  and Electronic Page Makeup: GGS Book Services
Cover Design Manager: Wendy Ann Fredericks
Cover Designer: Bernadette Skok
Cover Photo: Alexander Nemenov/AFP/Getty Images
Senior Manufacturing Buyer: Dennis J. Para
Printer and Binder and Cover Printer: R.R. Donnelley & Sons Company/Crawfordsville

Library of Congress Cataloging-in-Publication Data
Snow, Donald M., 1943–
  National security for a new era: globalization and geopolitics after Iraq/Donald
M. Snow.—3rd ed.
    p. cm.
  Includes index.
  ISBN 978-0-205-62225-2
 1. National security—United States.   2. United States—Military policy.
 3. World politics—21st century.   I. Title.
  UA23.S5253 2008
  355'.033073—dc22

                                                          2008003329

Please visit us at www.pearsonhighered.com

ISBN-13: 978-0-205-62225-2
ISBN-10: 0-205-62225-9

1 2 3 4 5 6 7 8 9 10—DOC—11 10 09 08

Brief Contents

Contents

Preface

On October 10, 2007, U.S. Secretary of Defense Robert Gates delivered an address to the annual convention of the Association of the United States Army (AUSA), a group comprised of both active duty and retired Army personnel. In that speech, he suggested that the landscape in which the United States uses military force has changed and that unconventional (or asymmetrical) wars will "remain the mainstay of the contemporary battlefield for some time." In addition to historical "warfighting" missions, the Army will be deeply involved in a variety of noncombat roles that are cumulatively known as state building. As someone who has been arguing this same point in print (including earlier editions of this book) and before classes (including the classes of 1990 and 1991 of the U.S. Army War College) for nearly two decades, I felt vindicated by Gates's "revelation." The pages that follow in large measure explain the implications of his suggestion that future American military involvements will more resemble Iraq and Afghanistan than the traditional battlegrounds of World War II.

This new edition represents the current point in an odyssey both for the author and for the subject matter, American national security policy. My first excursion into this subject matter came with the publication of the first edition of the predecessor of this text, *National Security*, in 1985. That text reflected the situation at the time, which remained fixated on deterring a nuclear third world war with the Soviet Union. How far we have come since then! When the first edition of *National Security for a New Era* appeared in 2003, there were new influences to add, notably the impact of international religious terrorism and nontraditional influences like globalization. As suggested in the subtitle of this edition, the impact of the Iraq War now has, at least for a time, become the overriding influence and the context in which American security policy will evolve and in which it can most fully be understood for the upcoming years.

Some of the discussion about the impact of Iraq on the future must, of course, be conditioned by the fact that the war has not ended for the United States. From the perspective of early 2008, when these words are written, two things about that ending seem clear: the American people want the war terminated as soon as possible, and American politicians (including the leading pretenders for the presidency in 2008) lag behind the public in their anticipation of what "as soon as possible" means. Residual involvement could stretch out for several years, and if it does, the result will almost certainly be politically poisonous and probably accentuate the negative impacts suggested in these pages. In the inimitable words of former Secretary of Defense Donald Rumsfeld, we are likely to move from the realm of "knowing what we do not know" to the realm of "not knowing what we do not know." It will certainly be an adventure.

FEATURES

This book is organized, as its predecessor editions have been, in three parts designed to provide comprehensive introductions to national security topics and thus to function as a core text in national security courses. The table of contents is discussed in the next section, but the organization moves from Part I, which provides historical and conceptual context for the study of U.S. national security, to Part II's concerns with current political and military realities, to Part III's emphasis on ongoing security issues (especially those raised by Gates in his AUSA address) and the application of the discussion to likely futures.

An effort has been made to make the text as reader-friendly and easy to follow as possible. Each part, for instance, begins with a brief discussion and rationale of the chapters in that part of the book, and each chapter begins with a preview that provides a glimpse of the material in that particular chapter. Each individual chapter also contains recurring features: a set of Amplification and Challenge! boxes that expand on materials discussed and raise question for reader consideration; a set of Study/Discussion questions drawn from the text; and a Selected Bibliography of materials the author considers relevant and understandable for undergraduate readers.

NEW TO THIS EDITION

Like its predecessor, this text has evolved as well. The first edition appeared in 2003, as the events of September 11, 2001, had cast an increasingly encompassing cloud over the relatively tranquil (at least in retrospect) 1990s. That decade had been dominated by the forces of growing economic globalization, which was then overshadowed by the new geopolitics of combating international religious terrorism. Because both forces remained prominent aspects of the global mix, the first edition was subtitled *Globalization and Geopolitics*. The subtitle was meant to suggest a competition between these two mostly dissimilar approaches as the dominant paradigm for national security, and the subtitle remained unchanged for the second edition.

The subtitle—and with it, much of the thematic emphasis—has changed for this third edition. The new subtitle, *Globalization and Geopolitics After Iraq*, was chosen because of the extraordinary impact the author believes the Iraq War will have on American thinking about and actions on matters of national security for the next five to ten years or even possibly beyond. The author believes there will be an "Iraq hangover" similar in context, if not necessarily in content, to Vietnam. Domestically, there will be a great debate about how to rebuild American armed forces (especially the Army, Marines, and Reserves), stressed to or beyond the breaking point by Iraq, as well as a debate about the kinds of circumstances in which those rejuvenated forces will be used in the future. Like the post-Vietnam period, there will be great pressure to limit their employment and to avoid what the American public has overwhelmingly decided was the promiscuous use of force in Iraq. A major outcome of the "lessons learned" from Iraq will be "No More Iraqs" and the question will be what that means and whether that lesson is more enduring than it was after Vietnam. This emphasis and analytical concern permeates the text, but is most pronounced in Parts II and III, which examine contemporary and future policy. Chapter 10 ("The Legacies of Iraq") is devoted entirely to this concern, and Chapters 11–13 deal with specific issues (asymmetrical warfare, terrorism, and state building) raised by the Iraq experience.

If the reaction to Iraq represents the major concern of contemporary national security policy, there are also other sources of continuity and change. The essential historical and conceptual contexts of security policy remain unchanged, and thus Chapters 3 and 4 (holdovers from the original text) remain largely unchanged, as does Chapter 7 on American interests. Chapters 1 ("The Changing Problem of National Security") and 2 ("Fault Lines: World Politics in a New Millennium") have been updated to encompass the impact of Iraq. Chapters 5 ("The Nature, End, and Consequences of the Cold War") and 6 ("Globalization and Beyond: New Influences on National Security") have been expanded to encompass post–Cold War Russian resurgence and to include factors (e.g., energy) beyond globalization that affect national security. Part II ("The Changing World") includes Chapter 7 on changing American interests in the world ("Security, Interests, and Power"), Chapter 8 ("The Domestic Environment"), and Chapter 9 on ongoing U.S. military problems ("Traditional Military Problems"), in addition to Chapter 10 on Iraq. Part III ("New Challenges") includes the chapters on asymmetrical warfare (Chapter 11), terrorism (Chapter 12), peacekeeping and state building (Chapter 13), and the application of the accumulated discussion of the lesson of Iraq (Chapter 14).

ACKNOWLEDGMENTS

No work of this magnitude is accomplished alone. During the drafting and redrafting of this text, I have benefited from the useful comments and suggestions of a number of reviewers whose suggestions strengthened the effort. They include Valentine J. Belfiglio, *Texas Women's University*; David Benjamin, *University of Bridgeport*; Charles Cushman, *George Washington University*; Gary L. Guertner, *University of Arizona*; Joe D. Hagan, *West Virginia University*; Patrick Haney, *Miami University*; Christopher Jones, *Northern Illinois University*; Richard J. Kilroy Jr., *East Carolina University*; Lawrence Korb, *Center for American Progress*; Edward G. Moore, *University of Texas at Brownsville*; Linda Petrou, *High Point University*; J. Patrick Plumlee, *University of North Florida*; Philip Schrodt, *University of Kansas*; Michael E. Smith, *Georgia State University*; and Chris Van Aller, *Winthrop University*. Any remaining errors are, of course, my own.

Donald M. Snow
Professor Emeritus, University of Alabama

CHAPTER 1

The Changing Problem of National Security

PREVIEW

The United States is arguably at a crossroads about national security as the increasingly unpopular Iraq War moves slowly toward an uncertain conclusion. It has been a turbulent period for the United States, as it was faced with the end of the Cold War and buffeted by the terrorist attacks of September 11, 2001. In this situation, it is natural to ask questions about the amount of change that has occurred in the national security environment and what those changes mean for the United States. This chapter introduces these concerns and the added impact that the Iraq War will have on how the United States thinks about and implements national security policy.

The past two decades have been trying for American national security policy and for those who make, implement, and study that policy and the strategies and plans that carry it out. Two special and largely unpredicted and unprecedented events have served as the benchmarks of change from what now seems (but certainly did not at the time) the relative stability, even tranquility, of the Cold War to the current imbroglio. The first of these was the end of the Cold War, which, in retrospect, began with the succession of Mikhail S. Gorbachev in the former Soviet Union in 1984 and culminated with the formal demise of that state with the last tick of the clock in Moscow at the end of 1991. The balance of the 1990s would witness the remarkably peaceful disappearance of the Soviet-led Communist half of the bipolar politico-military competition that was the touchstone of the four decades of the Cold War competition that defined the American national security problem. The Soviet implosion would be followed by the adjustment to a world with only one standing military superpower.

1

The second event, of course, was the attacks of September 11 and the introduction of international religious terrorism as a continuing anchor of U.S. security concern. It is instructive that the Cold War is now referred to as the "long peace," signifying the absence of systemwide military trauma on the scale of the world wars that distinguish mankind's most violent century, the twentieth. It is also instructive that national security practitioners and analysts increasingly refer to the post–September 11 period as the "long war," suggesting the long-term endurance of the competition with international religious terrorism. The Iraq War, which it will be argued in the pages that follow will act as a traumatic defining influence on American security concerns in a way similar to Vietnam, is one controversial punctuation point in this "long war."

Since the tragic events of September 11, 2001, American concern for national security has been almost totally focused on, some might argue transfixed by, the problem of international terrorism and its likely recurrence on American soil. In the immediate wake of the airplane hijackings that ended with those airplanes being used as missiles against highly visible and symbolic American economic (the World Trade Center towers) and military (the Pentagon) targets, the reaction was of an astonished world fundamentally transformed by the acts of Usama bin Laden and his terrorist organization, Al Qaeda. The United States launched a military campaign to overthrow the Afghani government, which had provided the terrorists sanctuary, and began a manhunt for the elusive bin Laden and his cohorts that continues to this day. The national security establishment reoriented itself to a primary emphasis on suppressing terrorism and preventing its recurrence. The invasion and conquest of Iraq by the United States and its "coalition partners" in 2003 was largely justified as part of the terrorist campaign as well.

The transition has been difficult. Partly, the reason has to do with the nature of the new challenge: *terrorism*. Although terrorism is certainly nothing very new, its application by foreigners on American soil is novel. Domestic terrorist acts have certainly occurred sporadically during American history—the assassination of American presidents, for instance, and the bombing of the Murrah Federal Building in Oklahoma City in 1995 come to mind. Although not widely recognized at the time, the first attack on the World Trade Center in 1993 was indeed an opening gambit of international religious terrorism punctuated by September 11. At the same time, Americans overseas have been the victims of terrorist attacks; during the 1990s, the same Al Qaeda network that committed the September 11 acts was implicated in attacks against the American embassies in Dar es Salaam, Tanzania, and Nairobi, Kenya, in 1998 and against an American warship, the USS *Cole*, moored in a Yemeni port in 2000, for instance. The September 11 attacks dwarfed these previous actions physically and conceptually: nearly three thousand people were killed in the shocking events, which were committed by foreigners acting on our own soil.

Part of the ensuing confusion was conceptual as well. Although a small community of analysts (some of whom are noted in the readings at the end of this chapter) has studied the problem and likelihood of terrorist activity for years, the subject of terrorism had not previously caught the public attention. There is, for instance, a high degree of disagreement about what exactly constitutes terrorism; after September 11, definitions became expansive, with more and more phenomena defined as acts of terrorism. Part of the problem was there is little agreement on what is and is not terrorism (Iraq stands as a seminal example). In the near hysteria of the post–September 11 environment, policy became both riveted to and grounded around the global war on terrorism (GWOT), which became a centerpiece of national security policy.

The Iraq War is, of course, related to the trauma of September 11. It is conceptually of a lower order of importance than either the end of the Cold War or the terrorist attacks, but its impact has eroded the public perceptions of the uses of American force in ways not seen since the reaction to the Vietnam war in the latter half of the 1970s. Whether there will be an "Iraq hangover" of the nature and quality of the reaction to Vietnam is conjectural and controversial and will be examined in more detail in Chapter 10. How the United States responds to the end of the Iraq military experience will, at a minimum, help shape the future of the American national security debate, whether it concerns how American military forces are rebuilt or the ways in which those forces are employed to wage the war against terrorism or to realize other and unrelated national ends. Conceptually, Iraq occupies a position within the "long war" similar to that occupied by Vietnam within the Cold War: essentially a sideshow to the central competition but justified by its arguable contribution to that central competition. The latter assertion will doubtless be controversial itself, especially among supporters of President Bush's continued assertion that "victory" in Iraq is "vital" to American success in the GWOT.

To look at the national security problem—to begin thinking about national security—two directions, outlined here, recur as primary emphases in the chapters that follow. One of these emphases is the theme of change, and it has two aspects in light of the September 11 events. The first is the extent and depth of change that the terrorist attacks introduce into the calculus of national security. The second regards changed dynamics of the environment in light of critical events in the past decade or more. Chief among those influences is the changing nature and profundity of threat. The other emphasis is on the basic nature of the national security environment, and this book introduces and examines two fundamental depictions: an environment dominated by, among other things, international economic growth and expansion (globalization) and one dominated by military threats and what to do about them (geopolitics). Partly because the global impact of globalization has not been uniformly positive it has receded (but not disappeared) as an influence. Other factors like energy and environment have been added to the list of factors now considered as part of national security.

THE NATURE OF CHANGE

The question of change is really two questions: How much has the environment truly been altered by events such as those of September 11, and what dominant characteristics of the national security environment have resulted from those changes? Because of the proximity of some of the events, there is no consensus on either of these matters. This chapter introduces perspectives that will be elaborated in the rest of the text and is intended to assist readers in reaching personal judgments on these matters.

How Much Has Changed?

Immediately after the trauma of September 11, the almost universal reaction of Americans and many overseas was that the change wreaked by the suicide air bombers was profound: that everything (at least figuratively) had changed. But was such a radical interpretation correct? The other way to think about September 11 was that the roots of change were present before the bombers struck and that those influences remain as prominent aspects of an environment. From this perspective, the underlying dynamics had not so much changed as had the vivid demonstrations of some of the most dramatic, traumatic implications of those dynamics. Each perspective deserves at least brief elaboration.

The popular view of the impact of September 11 on the national security environment is that it represents a fundamental, encompassing alteration of the problems facing the United States in the world and how these problems must be confronted. Partially born of the sheer magnitude and audacity of the attacks on the World Trade Center and the Pentagon and their vivid, relentless depiction on television, the initial reaction was that everything had changed, a perception largely reinforced both by the volume and emphasis of the news media and by political figures. The terrorist acts were so dramatic that it was easy to view this as a "new kind of war," one that Americans had difficulty understanding.

Two related elements stood out from the initial shock. The first was the realization of physical vulnerability facing Americans. As pointed out in Chapter 4, one of the unique and favorable parts of the American historical experience has been the virtual invulnerability of American soil to foreign attack. The last time there was an organized physical assault on American soil was during the War of 1812. Granted that Soviet nuclear forces were capable of destroying the United States physically during the Cold War (see Chapter 4), American soil has seldom been threatened, and the integrity of the American homeland has rarely been a source of major concern. The terrorist breach of American invulnerability was thus particularly shocking. Although international terrorists did not (and do not) threaten American existence in the way that Soviet rockets did, American vulnerability to harm (if not extinction) was established by the events of September 11.

The second, related aspect was the continuing nature of vulnerability and the realization that the problem would not dissipate soon. This "new kind of war" would not be climactically decided on some major battlefield where the perpetrators would be decisively vanquished. Rather, the "war on terrorism" would be a long and difficult *campaign* (to borrow the description of French President Jacques Chirac) that would take considerable time and vigilance—a long war, in contemporary language.

The contending interpretation suggests that less has really changed than was presumed immediately after the tragedy. The assertion that not a great deal has changed emphasizes continuities in the pre– and post–September 11 environments.

It suggests, for instance, that the basic sources of instability in the international system before the event came from the most unstable countries of the developing world and that they still do. During the 1990s, the manifestations of this instability were largely chaotic civil conflicts, where the policy question was whether these were important enough for American involvement. Contemporary conflicts continue in some of these states, and those states are the same kinds of places that provide the apparent breeding grounds for terrorism, the eradication of which is the current underlying policy rationale. In the 1990s, the United States joined an international humanitarian effort in Kosovo; in 2001, the United States assisted in the overthrow of the Taliban government on the grounds of denying sanctuary for terrorists, followed by "regime change" in Iraq in 2003, a simple description of our involvement that was vastly more complicated and complex than the name suggested. For these efforts ultimately to succeed, it is now evident that the United States will have to engage in state-building activities so that the target countries will emerge as stable places that eschew violence and terrorists. Is that a sign of change?

At the same time, terrorism was a problem before September 11, and it continues to be a problem. Usama bin Laden had attacked Americans before his most spectacular foray, and he remains a potential menace. The antiterrorism community had been warning of possible terrorist attacks directly against the United States for years, but their warnings had largely gone unheeded (at least partly because those previous warnings had proven false). While it is true that essentially no one had predicted the scale, exact nature, or audacity of the attacks that did occur, it is equally true that terrorism did not come into existence on September 11.

New Dynamics in the Environment?

The years since 1991 have been an especially dynamic period in the evolution of American national security. As argued primarily in Chapter 4, the first two hundred years of the republic was marked by two major periods in national security terms. The first was what I call the formative period, lasting from the birth of the republic through World War II. This period was distinguished by a relatively low order of priority for national security concerns and relatively low commitments to defense matters, with "spikes" of concern when the country was thrust into war situations, followed by a return to the normalcy of peacetime. The second was the Cold War, from the latter 1940s until the implosion of Soviet Communism in 1991. This period was distinguished from its predecessor because it was the first major American sustained involvement in national security affairs, when the United States developed and maintained large standing armed forces in peacetime and when the prevailing paradigm was the national security state (the situation in which preserving the integrity of the state is a major defining purpose of government). It was also the first time the existence of the United States became a matter of concern because Soviet nuclear weapons could physically destroy the United States as a functioning society, admittedly with terrible likely consequences for the Soviet Union as well.

The period from the beginning of the downfall of Communist regimes in Europe in 1989 until the terrorist events of 2001 produced large changes in the American national security problems. Two major events—fault lines—have largely defined those perceived changes. As a result of the second change in particular, there has also been a growing belief that the nature of warfare itself may be changing.

Fault Lines. What is a *fault line* as used in this text? The main idea of the analogy is that fault lines represent traumatic events—akin to the rupture of physical fault lines on the earth's surface accompanying earthquakes—that alter the environment and require an adjustment in the posttraumatic period. The notion is fundamentally compatible with the concept of tectonic shifts that Graham T. Allison Jr. introduced over a decade ago to describe the impact of the implosion of Communist rule.

Two of these fault lines emerged in the decade and a half since 1989 and altered the national security environment in more or less fundamental ways. Both are discussed extensively in Chapter 2 and elsewhere throughout the text but briefly introduced here. The first fault line was the end of the Cold War, symbolized by the peaceful demise of the Soviet Union and the fall, in most cases peacefully, of Communist regimes there and elsewhere. The net result was the end of both the military and the ideological competition between the Communist states, led by the Soviet Union and to some extent China, and the West, led by the United States. Only four states in the world remain technically Communist today, and two of those—China and Vietnam—have renounced Marxist economics, a major underpinning of the ideology. (Only North Korea and Cuba remain staunchly communist, and Cuba's continuing allegiance to the ideology will likely be challenged with the passing of Fidel Castro.) In systemic terms, this fault line is the more consequential of the two because it affects the very nature of the operation of the international system and the basic threats to that system's existence.

The second fault line, of course, is the emergence of international terrorism through the events of September 11, 2001. As noted, those events and their aftermath have had their main impact on the United States (many other states had already experienced this phenomenon and made whatever adjustments they could to it). The impact of this traumatic event has been to raise awareness of vulnerabilities not previously acknowledged and to mobilize government and society to try to reduce that vulnerability.

The impact of Iraq fits into this conceptual structure. The U.S. invasion, conquest, occupation, and eventual withdrawal from Iraq does not rise to the status of a fault line. Unlike the end of the Cold War, its effects are not so largely systemic. The demise of the Cold War fundamentally altered the distribution of power within the world system and altered the structure of the system generally. The aftermath of Iraq will primarily affect how the United States conceptualizes and uses force in the foreseeable future; it will likely have derivative systemic impacts to the extent that American use of force is promoted or—more likely—constrained by its process of self-examination. Unlike September 11, Iraq was not an unanticipated, surprise event that shocked and, in some ways, transformed the international system. Rather, it was the result of a conscious policy decision by the Bush administration, the wisdom of which is part of the emerging debate over post-Iraq American national security policy.

Within the framework of the fault lines (or Allison's tectonic plates) analogy, the Iraq experience can be thought of as an aftershock, an upsetting occurrence related to the original earthquake created by the September 11 fault line shift. How well this analogy holds up depends in some large measure on the extent to which the Iraq decision was the result of actual circumstances set in motion by the GWOT (the position of war supporters) or to which the relationship was non-existent and manufactured (the position of critics). Regardless of which position is most accurate (a debate discussed in Chapter 10), there almost certainly would have been no Iraq War without the events of September 11, a causal—or at least temporal—sequence of sorts.

A comparison of the two fault lines is not without irony, particularly when the measure is the impact of the two on threats, which are the major concern of national security planning. Threats (promises to do harm in the absence of compliance with some demand) can be usefully viewed on two criteria: their likelihood of being carried out and the consequences of their actualization. Likelihood can range from virtually zero (when threats are false—bluffs—or the threatener cannot carry them out) to virtual certainty. Consequences, on the other hand, range from the ability of a threatening party to do more or less great *harm* by carrying out a threat to being able to imperil the *physical existence* of the state by carrying out the threat.

National security environments and the impact of lacerations of the fault lines can usefully be categorized in these terms. During the Cold War, the stakes were exceedingly high, certainly much higher than they are now. The reason was that the potential consequences of war between the superpowers and their allies (planning for which was the central national security problem of the era) included an all-out nuclear exchange that could culminate such a war. That the Cold War could escalate to a nuclear hot war was plausible in an environment of ideological and political competition for predominance in the world.

As the Cold War evolved, however, those very consequences contributed to a gradually lowering likelihood of war. As time passed and arsenal sizes and deadliness increased, both sides increasingly realized that a hot war could effectively destroy them both, leaving no winner. The result was a *necessary peace* (the title of a 1987 book by the author) in which both sides avoided war not because of any mutual empathy but because of fear of the consequences of war. That realization contributed to the perceptions leading to the end of the Cold War.

Exposure of the first fault line—the end of the Cold War—obviously changed the nature of the threat environment. Russia, as the major successor state of the defunct Soviet Union, maintained the nuclear power to destroy the United States, but the death of Communism left it without any plausible ideological reason to use such weapons against a former adversary that was gradually becoming a friend and even ally. Although the arsenal sizes remain formidable, arms control agreements culminating in 2002 have reduced their size on both sides. Thus, the period ushered in by the end of the Cold War (roughly the 1990s) saw both a reduction in the likelihood of major threats being carried out and a gradual lowering of the consequences. Actions by the Putin regime in Russia in recent years have suggested some return to authoritarian rule and at least the possibility of renewed rivalry (see the discussion in Chapter 5).

Exposure of the second fault line further changes the threat calculus in different ways. Al Qaeda, and probably other groups in the future, shows a very high level of willingness to carry out threats that, as argued in Chapter 12, probably cannot all be eliminated in advance: some will succeed. Thus, the likelihood of threats being carried out, in this case by international terrorists, has increased from the Cold War and post–Cold War periods, although it is impossible to specify how much in quantitative terms. While the drama and scope of the September 11 attacks serve as stark testimony to the willingness to do as much harm as possible, the consequences of terrorist threats are considerably less great than would have been the case had the Soviet Union launched a nuclear strike during the Cold War. The threat posed by terrorists, in other words, is to do harm, not to threaten the basic integrity of the American state. Should terrorists come into possession of some of the weapons of mass destruction (WMD, including nuclear, biological, and chemical weapons), as many fear and predict, the amount of harm they could do would increase; it is hard to imagine their development of a capability that threatens the integrity of the United States.

The quality of the threat environment has thus evolved. The Cold War—the memory of which is slipping from our consciousness—created a very deadly threat environment (enormous consequences of war) but one that became less dangerous (lower likelihood threats would be carried out) as time passed. The end of the Cold War gradually reduced the deadliness of threats both psychologically (the reduction of motivation) and physically (arms control; reductions of arsenal sizes) and reduced dangerousness as well, since threats gradually dissipated. The exception to the absence of plausible threats came from international terrorism, specifically from the threats of Usama bin Laden and his Al Qaeda adherents. Unless his capacity to do physical harm increases dramatically, however, such threats will remain at a much lower level of deadliness than was the case during the Cold War. These dynamics suggest several other changes in the environment as well.

The Changing Nature of War? Reaction to the terrorist attacks and subsequent analyses, which include the American campaigns in Afghanistan and Iraq, have raised a popular notion that warfare may be changing, in the sense both that the terrorists are practicing a new kind of war and that, in the future, traditional, conventional forms of warfare may have to be altered or may become obsolete. Traditional warfare, also known as symmetrical warfare may be replaced by its opposite, asymmetrical warfare, as the dominant form of fighting the United States will face in the future. That prospect was likely even before American involvement in Afghanistan and Iraq. The experience of American opponents in both those theaters, but especially in Iraq, reinforces and makes even more likely that prospect.

The term *asymmetrical warfare* has previously been used more or less interchangeably with several other terms to describe irregular warfare and is newer than the dynamic it purports to capture. In fact, the term refers to a form and approach to warfare as old as war itself. At its base, asymmetrical warfare is defined as the situation in which both (or all) sides do not accept or practice the same methods of warfare. Asymmetry can extend both to the methods opposing sides use to conduct military operations and to the rules of warfare to which they adhere. Guerrilla warfare, which the United States encountered in Vietnam through the use of irregular enemy soldiers engaging in tactics such as ambushes, is one form of asymmetrical warfare. Terrorism is another, as are the methods used by the various insurgent groups in Iraq. Those fighting asymmetrically may also reject the rules of war favored by their opponents; consciously targeting civilians is an example.

The concept of asymmetrical warfare implies its opposite, symmetrical warfare. Symmetrical warfare occurs when both sides adopt and fight in the same basic ways and follow the same basic rules. In the contemporary environment, symmetrical warfare generally refers to fighting between traditional, European-style armed forces (armies, navies, air forces) where both sides agree to be bound by the same rules of engagement, basically as specified in the various Geneva Conventions on war. A synonym for symmetrical warfare is *traditional western war* (western in the sense that it is warfare fought along the lines of European-style combat that evolved over time). World War II was the epitome of symmetrical warfare (even if some isolated combatants fought asymmetrically). In the American and European tradition, it is the acceptable, "honorable" way of war.

Why would someone in effect break the accepted conventions and rules on war and fight asymmetrically (a synonym for which is *dishonorably* to some)? The historical answer is clear: what is now called asymmetrical warfare is the approach of a weaker foe trying to overcome the advantages of a force that is superior in whatever the accepted, conventional forms of warfare of the time prescribe. If you know that you will lose if you play by the opponent's rules, then it only makes sense to reject those rules in ways that may turn your weakness into strength and negate your opponent's strengths. There is certainly nothing new or novel about this; in fact, it may be the only thing that makes sense for a weaker party.

Those who are stronger by conventional standards will always decry the resort to asymmetrical means. The U.S. Army would always prefer that its opponents face it in massed formations on conventional battlefields where overwhelming American firepower can be brought to bear to destroy the opponent. An inferior opponent would be foolhardy to cooperate in its own destruction by fighting the way the Americans prefer to fight. Thus, they adopt other means. The various opponents of the United States in Iraq have been prime examples.

Those who argue that asymmetrical warfare is becoming the norm may have a point, although they seldom acknowledge the irony of why they are correct. Since the end of the Cold War, the gap between American conventional (symmetrical) military capability and that of any conceivable foes has progressively widened. This gap was first demonstrated in the Persian Gulf War of 1990–1991, and it has since increased. In 2002, for instance, the defense budget of the United States stood at about $350 billion out of a worldwide total of about $800 billion (including the American total). American military expenditures for 2002 were greater than the expenditures of the next fourteen largest-spending states combined. The budget increases for 2003 pushed the U.S. portion to over one-half of the global total, meaning the United States spent more on defense *than the rest of the world combined*. Admittedly inflated by expenditures in Iraq, that proportion continues to hold.

The result is a conventional, symmetrical military situation in which, effectively, *no state or probable combination of states can successfully confront and fight the United States symmetrically*, using conventional methods and rules. The very success of the American military machine has the effect of negating its own advantage. Any potential adversaries contemplating fighting the Americans can only conclude that the only chance they have of winning is to change the rules to negate the American advantage. In an act that amounts to an unconscious self-fulfilling prophecy, the United States has created the situation in which its future will almost certainly be in opposition to opponents fighting asymmetrically.

The American experiences in Afghanistan and Iraq reinforce this situation, if in slightly different ways. The U.S. interest in Afghanistan arose because the Taliban government of Afghanistan was providing physical sanctuary for Al Qaeda (with whom they were allied in the 1980s effort to expel the Soviet Union from the country) and refused to relinquish the Al Qaeda leadership to U.S. custody. Intent on destroying Al Qaeda, the United States thus found common cause with insurgents (the Northern Alliance) who were engaged in a conventional civil war to overthrow the Taliban. Although largely a guerrilla war, the campaign was symmetrical in the sense that both sides fought by the same rules.

The United States entered the fray with strategic air power and special forces (largely used as target spotters) against the Taliban. The Taliban were forced to stand and fight, incurring devastating losses, because to flee and avoid the bombers would also have ceded the field to the Northern Alliance. Overwhelming American conventional force was thus demonstrated as the Taliban were routed from power. After the overthrow, however, the remaining elements of the Taliban and their Al Qaeda allies reverted to mountain-based asymmetrical warfare and have continued to evade capture or destruction by Afghan and American forces.

The situation in Iraq was similar. Based on their experience in the Persian Gulf War of 1991, the Iraqis knew a conventional, symmetrical defense against an American invasion was suicidal. Thus, they offered only a token resistance that allowed the Americans to sweep through the country with apparent ease. Once the American occupation began, however, elements of the Iraqi armed forces began an asymmetrical campaign against the invaders and their Iraqi collaborators that continued to frustrate the American attempt to pacify the country. Future possible opponents of the United States have undoubtedly taken solace and possible inspiration from the Iraqi and Afghani asymmetrical efforts. The American failure to achieve decisely successful outcomes to either situation (if for different reasons) has to embolden future opponents to conclude that adopting asymmetrical approaches and borrowing Iraqi and Afghani tactics at least give them a chance against the Americans.

The Homeland Security Emphasis. The changed environment induced by September 11 has also produced institutional change within the U.S. government. The trauma of the terrorist onslaught created an atmosphere ripe for proactive approaches to the apparently changed environment, and revelations that the government was not organized optimally to deal with the crisis only added to the clamor for change. The outgrowth of these factors was the institutionalization of homeland security.

The spotlighting of homeland security is, of course, much older than the function it purports to serve. Keeping the homeland secure from foreign enemies is a basic part of national security and has always been implicit in the problem of national security. For almost two centuries before September 11, however, the need to directly secure the homeland had not been an immediate, pressing matter because the United States was effectively immune (or invulnerable) to attack, a point elaborated in Chapter 4. Al Qaeda burst the myth of invulnerability and sent us scurrying for ways to protect ourselves from evidently capable violators of our safety.

The result has been an institutionalization of and emphasis on homeland security as a prominent aspect of American national security. It began within weeks of the disaster when, by executive order, President Bush created the Homeland Security Council and appointed former Pennsylvania Governor Tom Ridge as its director. In 2002, the Homeland Security Act was passed, creating the Department of Homeland Security (DHS) as a Cabinet-level agency and attempting to bring a number of functions related to dealing with threats to security (notably terrorism) under one governmental roof. In 2005, legislation recommended by the 9/11 Commission was enacted to reorganize the intelligence community.

The homeland security emphasis remains a work in progress and one that serves as a useful bellwether to exactly how seriously the government takes the problem. While some functions dealing with the problem have indeed been transferred to DHS, many have not; congressional oversight is a hopeless tangle of committees that overlap and contradict one another; and the reorganization of the intelligence community is still not completed or the "turf wars" surmounted. Chapter 8 explores this evolution and asks whether homeland security word and deed match, and if not, what that says about the actual, as opposed to rhetorical, commitment to the problem.

GLOBALIZATION AND GEOPOLITICS

The other major theme of this volume is the competition between conceptualizations of the international system centered on the dynamics of globalization and geopolitics. Which of these basic dynamics has dominated across time? Which is the paradigm that most accurately depicts the national security situation?

Raising the distinction in this manner reflects the odyssey international politics has traveled over the last decade and a half or more. Geopolitics, the perspective that views military conflict (or its potential) in a hostile environment as the centerpiece of international concern, is the historically dominant perspective. That perspective, captured in some detail in Chapter 3 in the form of the realist paradigm, was clearly the central perspective during the Cold War, and it has returned to a position of central importance since September 11, 2001, with the GWOT and the related mission in Iraq. During the Cold War, this perspective emphasized "godless Communism" as the geopolitical enemy; now, it is international religious terrorism and the "axis of evil."

The 1990s represented an interlude between geopolitical ascendancies. Between the end of the Cold War and September 11, the forces of economic globalization—the spread of market democracies and a gradually expanding economic prosperity globally—took hold and spread as the major dynamic of international life. This period coincided with a receding threat environment for the major powers, and specifically for the United States. The implosion of Communism meant there was no major challenger to western-style market democracy, ideologically or physically. The violence in the system was concentrated in the poorest parts of the developing world, and while it was often ghastly and gruesome, it did not threaten the integrity of the international system or compel military action. In this environment, the so-called American model of development reigned supreme. At the same time, discussions of security expanded to include not only economic security, but also concerns like energy and environmental security.

Casting a major thrust of the discussion in terms of these two forces helps focus the direction of the present national security environment. It is not an either/or question, since both geopolitics and globalization coexisted before and continue to operate. The threat environment that is the central concern of geopolitics was present during the 1990s in the form of forces such as those led by bin Laden, but they were less prominent and compelling. Similarly, the machinations of globalization continue in the post–September 11 atmosphere but at a lower level of visibility. For example, the meetings of the Group of Eight (G-8) economic world leaders continue to be held and receive much public attention. The meetings of organizations like the Asia-Pacific Economic Cooperation (APEC), which President Clinton attended annually with much ado, have faded from center stage, however. President Bush's attendance at the November 2005 APEC summit in South Korea demonstrated that globalization has not left the agenda altogether. At the same time, other concerns such as global warming continue to creep into worldwide discussions about what keeps mankind, and thus Americans, safe and prosperous.

The two dynamics also contradict one another, reflecting different worldviews on the parts of adherents of one force or the other. Globalization represents a highly internationalist approach to the world, placing global concerns and the reconciliation of international differences through international efforts at the center of national concerns. It raises idealist concerns with improving the human condition through international cooperation to a high priority and tends to view geopolitics through a more cooperative, multilateralist lens than does traditional geopolitics.

The geopolitical perspective is inherently more conservative and suspicious of the international environment. Reflecting its grounding in traditional realism and its skeptical view of human nature, the geopolitical perspective emphasizes *national* security as its central value (as opposed to international security) and thus is more inward looking and prone to unilateral as opposed to multilateral solutions to problems.

Which of these competing worldviews will dominate the early twenty-first century? In the immediate aftermath of the September 11, 2001, terrorist events, geopolitics enjoyed a renaissance as the United States responded to the activation of real threats that had been festering outside the spotlight of the 1990s. Support for globalization was eroding at the time as the world economy slowed and was further buffeted by revelations of corporate malfeasance in the United States and the subsequent downturn of the world's stock markets. The Bush administration's GWOT was a clear expression of a geopolitical direction from a president who had campaigned in 2000 as a free trade advocate (one of the central values of globalization). The American reaction to the Iraq War suggested another turn away from the geopolitical orientation (although a distorted variant in the eyes of traditional realists) that allowed that involvement to occur.

CONCLUSION: WHERE FROM HERE?

This brief introduction featuring the two emphases of the nature of change and the conceptual competition between globalization and geopolitics helps frame the material that follows. Because this book is intended as a core text for national security courses that tend to emphasize the military, geopolitical side of national security, the text will do so as well. At the same time, it is clear that what makes the country safe is more than the clash or balance of arms, and the umbrella of globalization and other concerns will facilitate exploring those other aspects of what makes Americans secure.

The basic thesis that will be explored in the following pages can be stated summarily here. Because of unique attributes of the American experience chronicled in Chapter 4, the United States has not through most of its history required a constant, vigilant commitment to national security, and the result has been a fluctuation of interest and emphasis between the dictates of realist pessimism and non-involvement. American isolation from global geopolitics has, of course, ceased to exist, but the contrary impulses of security activism and tranquility have not. The United States enthusiastically retreated from the geopolitical dictates of the Cold War to the globalization-driven prosperity and comparative peace of the 1990s. September 11 returned geopolitics to center stage, where it has remained.

Has the souring of the Iraq War repelled the pendulum of concern away from the pole of geopolitics back toward some new (or renewed) equilibrium? The thesis here is that it clearly has, although the exact nature and effects of change are as yet unclear. What *is* clear is that a post-Iraq world will be, at least for a time, one in which the United States is less willing to employ military force in pursuit of its goals than it was before Iraq. Partly that is true because American armed forces need rebuilding after the Iraq interlude; partly it will be the result of serious questions about the utility of force in the contemporary world.

The reaction to Iraq will occur in a world that is at least as dangerous as it was before the American invasion occurred. Most obviously, international religious terrorism is still present and is arguably more dangerous than ever. How will the United States react in the event of another major terrorist attack against it? What if an important American ally like Pakistan destabilizes? What will the United States do in a dangerous world?

STUDY/DISCUSSION QUESTIONS

1. Why have the last twenty-five years been described as particularly trying for American security policy? What events have contributed to that change? How?
2. What are fault lines? How do they contribute to a changed international environment for security policy? How does the Iraq War fit into this framework? Rate the fault lines in terms of their impact.

3. How has warfare changed? What is asymmetrical warfare, and why has it become the dominant form of violence the United States faces? How does Iraq reinforce this change?
4. Define and discuss the concepts of globalization and geopolitics and how they have competed as the dominant form of international paradigm.

Selected Bibliography

Allison, Graham T., Jr. "Testing Gorbachev." *Foreign Affairs* 67, 1 (Fall 1998), 18–32.

Bloom, Mia. *Dying to Kill: The Allure of Suicide Terror.* New York: Columbia University Press, 2005.

Byford, Grenville. "The Wrong War." *Foreign Affairs* 81, 4 (July/August 2002), 34–43.

Campbell, Kurt M. "Globalization's First War?" *Washington Quarterly* 25, 1 (Winter 2002), 7–14.

Carafano, James J., and Paul Rosenzweig. *Winning the Long War: Lessons from the Cold War for Defeating Terrorism and Preserving Freedom.* Washington, DC: Heritage Books, 2005.

Clarke, Richard. *Against All Enemies: Inside America's War on Terror.* New York: Free Press, 2004.

Delpech, Therese. "The Imbalance of Terror." *Washington Quarterly* 25, 1 (Winter 2002), 31–41.

Doran, Michael Scott. "Somebody Else's Civil War." *Foreign Affairs* 81, 1 (January/February 2002), 22–42.

Fromkin, David. "The Strategy of Terrorism." *Foreign Affairs* 53, 3 (July 1975), 683–698.

Haass, Richard N. "Regime Change and Its Limits." *Foreign Affairs* 84, 1 (January/February 2005), 66–78.

Hoffman, Bruce. *Inside Terrorism,* 2nd ed. New York: Columbia University Press, 2006.

Hoffmann, Stanley. "Clash of Civilizations." *Foreign Affairs* 81, 4 (July/August 2002), 104–115.

Howard, Michael. "What's in a Name?" *Foreign Affairs* 81, 1 (January/February 2002), 8–13.

Kagan, Robert, and William Kristol (eds.). *Present Dangers: Crisis and Opportunities in American Foreign and Defense Policy.* San Francisco: Encounter Books, 2000.

Laqueur, Walter. *The Age of Terrorism.* Boston: Little Brown, 1987.

McFaul, Michael. "Democracy Promotion as a World Value." *Washington Quarterly* 28, 1 (Winter 2004/2005), 147–164.

Miller, Steven E. "The End of Unliateralism or Unilateralism Redux?" *Washington Quarterly* 25, 1 (Winter 2001/2002), 15–30.

Nacos, Brigette L. *Terrorism and Counterterrorism: Understanding Threats and Response in the Post-9/11 World.* New York: Penguin Classics, 2006.

Nye, Joseph S., Jr. "Transformational Leadership and U.S. Grand Strategy." *Foreign Affairs* 84, 4 (July/August 2006), 139–149.

O'Hanlon, Michael. "A Flawed Masterpiece." *Foreign Affairs* 81, 3 (May/June 2003), 47–63.

Pillar, Paul D. *Terrorism and U.S. Foreign Policy.* Washington, DC: Brookings Institution Press, 2003.

Shambaugh, David. "The New Strategic Triangle: U.S. and European Reaction to China's Rise." *Washington Quarterly* 28, 3 (Summer 2005), 7–26.

Snow, Donald M. *The Necessary Peace: Nuclear Weapons and Superpower Relations.* Lexington, MA: Lexington Press, 1987.

———. *What After Iraq? Getting In, Getting Out, and the Consequences.* New York: Pearson Longman, 2009.

Stern, Jessica. *Terrorism in the Name of God: Why Religious Militants Kill.* New York: HarperCollins, 2003.

The National Security Strategy of the United States. Washington, DC: The White House, September 2002.

Tucker, Robert W., and David C. Hendrickson. "The Sources of American Legitimacy." *Foreign Affairs* 83, 6 (November/December 2004), 18–32.

Wallerstein, Immanuel. "The Eagle Has Crash Landed." *Foreign Policy* (July/August 2002), 60–69.

Walt, Stephen M. "Taming American Power." *Foreign Affairs* 84, 5 (September/October 2005), 105–120.

Watanabe, Akio. "A Continuum of Change." *Washington Quarterly* 27, 4 (Autumn 2004), 137–146.

PART

I

THE CONTEXT

Part I consists of five chapters, each of which provides some perspective, or context, for understanding the national security situation. Chapter 2, looks at some basic dynamics of the system, including the idea of fault lines and their impact on change, the different perspectives people bring to the subject of national security, and the American role in the national security system. The discussion then turns to the operating rules of international politics since the peace of Westphalia, the so-called realist paradigm that defines the geopolitical approach, in Chapter 3. That paradigm was under fire during the 1990s as an adequate description of a globalizing world; it was revived with the campaign against terrorism and the U.S. war in Iraq as a way to evaluate those experiences. The United States has had a unique historical experience in matters of national security, and the evolution of that experience is the chief topic of Chapter 4. Among the elements of that experience has been a feeling of security based in the impregnability of the country—a feeling that has now been effectively deflated.

The Cold War was the major element in the environment in which much of current American national security policy was developed. Because of the holdover effect that Cold War thinking has on the present, Chapter 5 looks at the dynamics of how the Cold War worked and how it ended. The Cold War's end shares characteristics with September 11 in that both were almost entirely unanticipated and created the need for adjustment. The other thread in the ongoing debate about the nature of national security is globalization, the dominant theme of the 1990s. Because its relevance remains, Chapter 6 is devoted to the other important approach to the evolution of the post–World War II, contemporary international economic globalization.

CHAPTER 2

Fault Lines: World Politics in a New Millennium

PREVIEW

This chapter elaborates on themes laid out in Chapter 1. First, it examines the impact of two traumatic events, or fault lines, and the "aftershock" of Iraq on American security. These events have accentuated and defined deep divisions among Americans about politics in general and national security in particular. The text looks at factors that contribute to that debate, including the relative roles of geopolitics and globalization in the evolving nature of the world environment, the central roles of the United States in the evolving international system, and the factors that divide Americans on these matters. The chapter concludes with some initial speculation about the continuing role of force, leavened by Iraq, in the national security system of the early twenty-first century.

T he American public is deeply divided politically, as witnessed by the highly polarized presidential elections of 2000 and 2004 and the strongly partisan wrangling within Congress after the 2006 off-year elections and elsewhere over a broad range of issues. This disagreement has come to focus on the American role in the world and, more specifically, on American national security policy. The strong negative public reaction to the Iraq War has added to this polarization.

This chapter examines the debate from two angles. The first is the impact of the fundamental change events (the fault lines) on the operation of world politics. The second is through contrasting views of how the United States should deal with these changes based on differing political and philosophical orientations held by different individuals and groups.

As noted, interest in and concentration on matters of national security has varied across time, driven largely by the ebb and flow of events in the world and American reactions to them. In relatively tranquil times, when the United States feels unthreatened by forces that might do it harm, the level of interest and concern tends to be low. Most of American history between the end of the American Revolution and World War II was of this nature; only the self-infliction of the Civil War seriously interrupted national tranquility and made a concern about and commitment to the most obvious form of national security, military force, seem particularly important. Americans languidly reestablished the "normalcy" of nonconcern between the world wars and will almost certainly look back on the period between the end of the Cold War and the terrorist attacks of 2001 as a time of similar tranquility.

Times have not always been so tranquil, of course, and when they have not been, the level of concern with national security matters—with geopolitics—has been heightened. The Japanese surprise attack on Pearl Harbor—delivered an hour before the Japanese ambassador to Washington presented the American government with an ultimatum tantamount to a declaration of war (which was part of the plan)—rocked the American psyche, ended the appeal of isolationism, and propelled the country into a patriotic war to crush fascism. In the words of Japanese Admiral Isoroku Yamamato after learning of the failure to deliver the ultimatum before the attack began, "We have awakened a sleeping giant and filled him with a terrible resolve." That resolve carried over to the Cold War that followed World War II. The terrorist attacks of September 11, 2001, were similar in form and effect to Pearl Harbor; once again, attention is focused on matters of geopolitics and national security.

There have been two profound events in the past nearly decades. The distinguished Harvard political scientist Graham T. Allison Jr. analogized the first event, the end of the Cold War, to an earthquake, a "tectonic shift" in the structure of international relations and the American place in them; the effect of September 11 was similar. Put another way, 1989 and 2001 revealed major fault lines in the evolution of the international environment. Before the fault lines were revealed, the world looked one way; afterward, it looked very different. Before the end of the Cold War, geopolitics was the large concern in a hostile world environment, and that emphasis and perception returned after New York and Washington were victims of commercial airliners turned into lethal missiles. The period between the two major events witnessed a major ascendancy of the emphasis on economic globalization and interdependence.

These alternate emphases are not mutually exclusive, of course. The seeds of the globalization of the 1990s were sown in the last decades of the Cold War, and the contemporary system is struggling with how globalization is affected by and must adapt to an environment in which dealing with the geopolitical reality of international terrorism occupies center stage. Similarly, concern with geopolitics did not disappear in the geopolitical tranquility of the 1990s; it was just not as pronounced a concern as before and after the globalization decade.

The first fault line was revealed between 1989 and 1991 when the Cold War ended. Whether the beginning of that change is attributed to the rise of Gorbachev, to Poland's defiant election of a non-Communist president in 1989, to the breaching of the Berlin Wall on November 9, 1989, or to the official demise of the Soviet Union at the last tick of the clock in 1991 in Moscow's Red Square, the Cold War structure that dominated international politics for forty-plus years after the end of World War II has crumbled. The process of adjustment to those changes was still under way when the airplanes slammed into the World Trade Center and the Pentagon.

The end of the Cold War traumatized policy makers mostly because it was so unanticipated. Certainly, a few observers saw it coming: George F. Kennan prophesied in 1948 that vigilant containment could cause Communism's implosion, and New York Senator Daniel Patrick Moynihan consistently suggested its demise—but they were beacons whose message was largely ignored. The Soviet Union crumbled as Soviet republics declared their withdrawal from the union throughout 1991, but the policy of the American administration of George H. W. Bush tried to keep our mortal enemy of forty years intact nearly to the end, fearful and suspicious of the alternatives to a known enemy.

Had the United States anticipated what was going to happen, it might have been better prepared for it. World War II had hardly begun, for instance, when planning for the postwar world after the Axis defeat was instituted. As a result, the institution of a new structure for the international system could be implemented quickly after the guns were stilled. Unfortunately, so few believed in the end of the Cold War—and those who did were ridiculed for their "naïveté"—that no real planning was done to accommodate the possibility. The world was caught nearly entirely off guard.

The result was to leave the large contours of foreign policy adrift, and there is no place where that drift was more apparent than in thinking about and planning for national security. In some ways, the trauma is natural because of the nature and impact of change. The Cold War was, after all, a quintessentially geopolitical competition, and the centerpiece of that confrontation was the military might that both sides possessed and projected against one another. Two great land masses were locked into a deadly dance, and keeping the competition below the level of mutual inciner-ation was a time-consuming and energy-draining enterprise. With the stakes so great and the possibilities so grim, it is not surprising that those committed to the process would find the peaceful alternatives to Cold War the stuff of mere dreams.

But the Cold War ended, and observers and policy makers struggled for a decade conceptually and practically to describe and understand how the world was different. During the 1990s, the forces of economic globalization slowly overshad-owed the forces of geopolitics within the American administration and raised ques-tions about something like a paradigm shift from geopolitics to globalization. When George W. Bush entered the White House in 2001, he brought with him a foreign and national security team of Cold Warriors (people who had gained much of their knowledge and expertise in global affairs during the Cold War). Like the Clinton administration that preceded them, they struggled during their early months in of-fice for a basis upon which to reorient national security policy. That Bush was an avowed free trader (the heart of globalization) added to the indeterminacy about the appropriate paradigm. Response to the terrorist attacks provided that focus and largely defined the administration for the rest of its tenure.

The United States is still struggling to describe the new international system and appropriate policies and strategies with which to cope with it. This book examines the ensuing debate and its impact on national security policy. The two perspectives through which to view the question, as already suggested, are those of traditional geopolitics and more contemporary globalization, including permutations and combinations of the two, along with the theme of change. The first lens through which to conduct that examination is focused on the fault lines and their impacts.

THE FIRST FAULT LINE: THE WORLD AFTER THE COLD WAR

The new century began with a very different atmosphere and with very different perspectives and expectations than did the 1990s. In 1990 and 1991, breathtaking political change was virtually the norm; the central feature of that change, of course, was the death of Communism, as country after country peacefully (except in isolated cases like Romania) eschewed Marxism-Leninism, and the Soviet Union, the leader and enforcer of Communist orthodoxy worldwide, stood idly by. As noted, in 1991 constituent parts of the Soviet Union itself began the process of secession from the Union of Soviet Socialist Republics; ultimately, the Soviet empire (and it was, in many important respects, the last European empire, since much of the territory had been acquired by force by Russia) broke into fifteen independent states, all of which officially disavowed Communism. By the end of the decade, when the dust had settled on the Marxist experiment, only four states in the world remained nominally Communist. Two of those states, Cuba and North Korea, entered the twenty-first century professing a continued dedication to the principles of Communism, although most observers expect that façade to disappear when Fidel Castro leaves power in Cuba and North Korea reaches an accommodation with the South—both of which are events that could occur in the near future. The other Communist states, China and Vietnam, retain the dictatorship of the Communist Party politically but openly reject Marxist economics and are enthusiastic participants in the globalizing economy. As a competitive political ideology, the belief system articulated by Karl Marx and Friedrich Engels has essentially been consigned to the dust pile of history.

The implosion of Communism was the most obvious, dramatic, and important change of the last decade of the twentieth century and was arguably the most important international event since World War II. It was a unique series of events in the sense that a major global power source simply vacated the playing field without a shot being fired. The same Soviet Union that had, for the most part, brutally imposed Communist systems on most of what was known as the Second (or Socialist) World, simply watched those systems being toppled with scarcely a shrug of its national shoulders. The virtually peaceful implosion of the Soviet Union itself was an act of nonviolence without precedent; large states and empires had, of course, disappeared before, but virtually all the other dismemberments were the direct result of major hot wars. The Cold War ended with a whimper, not a bang, to borrow an old phrase.

The end of "operational Communism" (Communism as the official political organizing system for a country) has had major systemic impacts to which the world is still adjusting. The Cold War international system was what is called by political scientists a *bipolar system*, which means a system dominated by two opposing states (the United States and the Soviet Union) around which other states congregated and sought or imposed differing degrees of association. The nature of bipolarity had evolved during the Cold War period. In the first decade or so of the Cold War, the system was described as one of *tight* bipolarity, which meant the two dominant parties could influence or control the actions of their "client" states to a large degree. For a variety of reasons, this control was gradually relaxed, and the system evolved into one of *loose* bipolarity. The ultimate manifestation of loosening of control, of course, was the inability of the Soviet Union to keep the members of its bloc adherent to the political principle of Communism that was the source of their sameness.

The result has been a power vacuum. With one pole non-existent, the system can no longer be described as bipolar. There is only one pole left because Russia, the successor to the Soviet Union, has lacked the stature and resources to be a "superpower" in the Cold War sense beyond its continued possession of a large but, thanks to arms control agreements, shrinking arsenal of nuclear weapons (which was the major criterion for superpower status during the Cold War).

In recent years, there have, however, been some potential signs of a Russian revival, possibly as an adversary. This possibility, which some observers have suggested may have the potential to create a new Cold War–like environment, is examined in Amplification 2.1.

Amplification 2.1

RUSSIAN RESURGENCE?

Are events in contemporary Russia creating the prospect of a renewed competition between the United States and the major successor state of the Soviet Union? During the 1990s, Russia emerged from the rubble of the Communist state as an apparently democratizing but desperately poor country. Both these conditions have changed. Is the result a revived Russian superpower capable of and intent on reviving something like the Cold War?

Russia is indeed changing. The most visible aspect has been the erosion of political democracy (at least by American standards) by President Vladimir Putin, the successor of the late Boris Yeltsin. The most visible manifestation of the erosion has been the gradual accumulation of power by the president at the expense of the legislative branch. At the same time, Russia has emerged as the world's second largest exporter of petroleum, providing considerable wealth that allows the country to be, among other things, much more assertive in foreign affairs. A clear manifestation of the resulting independence of Russian policy was the broadly proclaimed testing of new Russian multiple warhead missiles in May 2007, designed to thwart the effects of a ballistic missile defense system in Europe planned by the United States—a program the Russians and the Soviets have opposed for decades.

Where will this lead? How much (or if) American-Russian relations will deteriorate is still an open question. The outcome of presidential elections in both countries in 2008 could, however, reveal a good deal about how each will approach the problem.

No one is willing to designate the resulting system *unipolar* because that would imply a level of American control that does not exist and that most other states would (and do) oppose. The United States remains the central power, but defining what that centrality means has been a critical part of defining the new system. It is probably of some symbolic importance that we never formed a consensus on what to call the new system and that the most common name describes what it is not—the post–Cold War world.

As it evolved over time, the Cold War had the major physical and intellectual advantage of developing a very orderly set of rules of interaction. The competition for global power and influence between the Communist and non-Communist worlds was well defined, as were the rules by which that competition was carried out. It was conceptually a *zero-sum game* in which the gains of one side were assumed to be the losses of the other and the possibility of *positive-sum* outcomes to situations (in which both sides gained) were infrequent and considered unlikely in any particular situation. The lingua franca of this competition ultimately was the enormous military machines each side maintained, capped by the possession of enormous arsenals of thermonuclear weapons that, if ever employed against one another, would probably have ended civilization as we know it.

Yet the system produced an orderliness around which the Cold Warriors could think about world problems and dynamics based in the competition and its management short of war. The end of the Cold War shattered that order. As Georgi Arbatov, director of the Soviet USA and Canada Institute and a member of the Central Committee of the Communist Party of the Soviet Union, put it to the Americans in mid-1991, "We have done a terrible thing. We have deprived you of an enemy." Conceptually, it was indeed a terrible thing in the sense that national security thinking clearly grounded in the Soviet threat and deflecting and managing that threat suddenly lost most, if not all, of its relevance. The result was both physical and intellectual disorder in how to think about the world. While the process was going on in 1990, University of Chicago political scientist John Mearsheimer even lamented in the title of an *Atlantic Monthly* article, "Why we shall soon miss the Cold War." What we would miss, he contended, was the order and predictability of events and the ability to act appropriately within the bounds of that order.

The debate over what should replace the bipolar international political system raged inconclusively until the debate was suspended by the events of 2001. The changes have produced clear benefits that hardly anyone could or would try to deny. At the same time, there are evolving systemic dynamics about which there is a considerable amount of disagreement within the academic and policy communities that continues to enliven debates within both of those communities.

Undeniable Benefits

The most obvious and most dangerous manifestation of the Cold War was the military confrontation between the competing blocs led by the United States and the Soviet Union. Managing that confrontation was a serious consequence of the nature of international politics and one that, given the possible consequences of a misstep, had to be taken very seriously. The prospect of general war employing nuclear weapons even produced a fatalistic political culture about the future and resulted in the expenditure of large amounts of resources in its name. Keeping the Cold War cold was the preeminent international responsibility beside which other priorities paled by comparison.

The post–Cold War world produced no equivalent of the East–West, Communist–anti-Communist military confrontation, and this fact had two obvious and overwhelming benefits for the citizenry of the 1990s. Both benefits condition how to think about the problem of national security in the contemporary world, even after the second fault line was revealed.

The first positive change, and the one most relieving for those who participated in the Cold War period, is the absence of any real concern about the possibility of a general systemic war that could threaten national and international survival. Within the context of the Cold War, the possibility—thought by some to be a probability—of a global World War III in which nuclear weapons would be used massively was an ever-present prospect, a problem that never went away. The two sides were certainly politically opposed enough to find adequate cause for war between them, and managing the competition in such a way to reduce the likelihood that such a war would begin was a major task.

Since then, the situation is both radically different and the same. Physically, Russia and the United States have reduced the size of their nuclear arsenals and conventional forces sizably, but they retain large enough nuclear forces to be able to do great damage to one another on a scale only slightly smaller than during the Cold War. The demise of Soviet Communism, however, has removed the political differences that could provide the rationale for war. Only a radical change in relations (see Amplification 2.1) could change that situation. The world is still deadly but less dangerous.

This changed dynamic enormously relaxed the security environment because it removed the "worst case" planning problem. All of the realistic contingencies for the present and foreseeable future are more limited in conduct and potential for expansion to general war. It is virtually impossible to conjure a realistic scenario that would lead the world to a general war that would cause the nuclear bombs to start being hurled in a general, systemic way, although the terrorist attacks reminded us the world could still be a dangerous place.

The result was to take some of the urgency and fervor out of the national security debate. To borrow a distinction from one of my other books (*When America Fights*), the United States faced very few potential situations in which it would *have* to fight and especially to use its total military might (employments of necessity); rather, Americans debated in which kinds of places the United States *might* use its forces, knowing the decision would not likely compromise American interests greatly one way or the other (employments of choice).

The second change flows from the first. During the Cold War confrontation, both potential adversaries and their major allies maintained large and expensive military machines that could be quickly inserted into the fray should war somehow break out. Given the destructiveness such a war could rapidly produce, it was assumed that it would be fought and completed with the forces on hand when it began—what was called the "force in being"—and both sides maintained large forces for that possibility.

It was a very expensive proposition. During the 1950s, the United States dedicated as much as half the federal budget to defense. After the spate of entitlement legislation was passed during the 1960s, that proportion fell to about 25 percent of the budget and into second place among categories of federal expenditures. Although reliable budget figures for the Soviet Union were always elusive, the estimates were that they spent between 15 and 25 percent of gross national product (GNP) on the military (with a much larger economic base, the spending equivalent for the United States never exceeded 6 percent of GNP).

The end of the Cold War was accompanied by a sizable demilitarization among the major players, and especially the leaders of the Cold War coalitions. Troop strength for the United States went from 2.15 million active duty troops in 1988 to 1.4 million in 1998. The Russians have cut their forces down even more, although the ten-year comparison is distorted in that 1988 figures reflect the entire Soviet Union, whereas 1998 figures (which show an active force of 1.16 million) are all Russian. In any case, force sizes and expenditure levels were down substantially for all the major powers.

Debatable Changes

While the danger of global war and the need to prepare for it undeniably were receding, the effects of other changes in the environment caused some level of disagreement. While making no pretense of inclusiveness or exhaustiveness, three interrelated changes with some impact on the security equation and the relevance of geopolitics and globalization are worth raising in this context.

One change, from which the others to an extent follow, was a greater emphasis on the developing world. In one sense, this emphasis did not represent much of a change at all in national security terms. While national security during the Cold War focused on the major power competition, virtually all the actual fighting involving American forces occurred in the developing world. The United States, for instance, *deployed* forces worldwide, including in the developed world (Europe, Japan); it *employed* force exclusively in the developing world (Korea, Vietnam, Grenada, for example). The reasons for this are complex, of course, but the fact that most of the violence and instability was in the developing world had something to do with this pattern of employment. More importantly, in most instances violent confrontations between clients of the two sides could be waged without a real danger of escalation to direct superpower confrontation. Since many of these conflicts had Communists battling anti-Communists, the use of force could be argued to have been necessary to avoid shifting the geopolitical balance between the East and the West.

The post–Cold War situation was both similar and different. Virtually all violent conflicts still take place in the developing states, and most of it is still internal in nature (the Balkans, Haiti, Afghanistan, for instance). This phenomenon has continued since 2001, because the developing world is also the seedbed for most international terrorism, the combating of which has become the fulcrum of national security concern. Thus, most of the opportunities to employ force are where they always were.

The result of tranquility among the major powers is that much more attention can be directed at the developing world than it could before. In a direct national security sense, this fact is reflected in debate over the nature and appropriate uses of force in the developing world that will be energized even more by the post-Iraq debate.

The point of contrast and continuity cannot be overstated, because it is so often erroneously suggested that potential involvement in things like peacekeeping operations in the developing world marks a radical departure for the United States and other major powers. To repeat, using military forces to influence internal wars and instabilities in the developing world is nothing unique to the post–Cold War world at all. What is different is the rationale for putting American or other troops potentially in harm's way and the ways in which they are employed.

During the Cold War, the developing world uses of American armed forces were conventional in terms of purpose and methods of employment: the reason to use American military might was to thwart Communist takeovers that might occur in the absence of American assistance, a direct extension of the central geopolitical competition. Whether that force was warranted or wise in particular places such as Vietnam was a matter of disagreement, but the central purpose was not. In those circumstances, the way forces were used—strategically if not always tactically—was conventional: the idea was military victory over a well-defined enemy. That enemy might fight unconventionally (asymmetrically) and thus create the need for tactical adjustment to bring about enemy defeat, as was the case in Vietnam, but the goal was traditional—fighting to support traditional governments.

Opportunities to employ force in the period between the fault lines were different on both counts. The disappearance of Communism meant that such involvement could no longer be justified in terms of the kinds of geopolitics that underlay Cold War actions. More typically, justifications became "softer," framed in terms of arresting and reversing humanitarian disasters in situations where clearly military conflict between defined military forces was not present. The purpose was more often framed in terms of reinstituting peace and protecting civilian populations from the return of atrocity. As a result, military victory in a traditional sense gave way to an open-ended commitment to imposing, enforcing, and keeping a fragile peace. That reorientation ran counter to traditional military ways of thinking about the use of force in the American experience.

When the new Bush administration entered office in 2001, it clearly demonstrated the ambivalence created by this debate over how and when to use force. During the 2000 campaign, Bush had come out strongly in opposition to future uses of American force for peacekeeping when American interests were not clearly engaged. Dr. Condoleezza Rice, who became national security advisor in the first Bush term and secretary of state in the second, was the point spokesperson for this position, arguing that the United States should not act as the "world's 911," that it was an improper role for elite American troops like the 82nd Airborne to be used to escort children to kindergarten in places like Kosovo, and that endless deployments were eroding troop morale. The Bush team even suggested the desirability of terminating American involvement in Kosovo and Bosnia.

These positions did not long survive the oath of office. American European allies quickly informed the new administration of the necessity of maintaining the missions in the Balkans and of the vitality of American presence in those missions. The rhetoric of noninvolvement was quietly cooled, and Secretary of Defense Donald Rumsfeld quickly announced a comprehensive review of American military strategy and missions, which presumably included involvement in peacekeeping operations. The new administration did, however, continue to harbor a disdain toward one of the obvious experiences of the 1990s—state building—which would be disastrously demonstrated in Iraq.

Globalization is the other trend with a significant developing world element, and disagreement exists about what it does and how or whether it should be promoted. Bursting upon the scene and coinciding with or stimulating (there is disagreement about which) the worldwide economic expansion and prosperity of the global economy in the most developed states, globalization spread to selected parts of the developing world during the 1990s as well. During the first half of the decade and beyond, the results appeared overwhelmingly positive and formed the core of the Clinton administration foreign policy of engagement and enlargement (engaging those countries most capable of joining the global economy and thereby enlarging what he called the circle of market democracies). In its purest form, the expansion of the globalizing economy would be accompanied by political democratization and contribute to a spreading *democratic peace* around the globe. In this scenario, as democracies increasingly came into power, peace would follow, since it is asserted that political democracies do not fight one another. Moreover, as the global economy reached out and encompassed more and more countries, the motivation to fight would give way to economic interdependence.

In this happy scenario, a geopolitical perspective that seeks to minimize violence and instability in the world appeared to coincide with and reinforce globalization, since they are both aimed at the same ends. Unfortunately, the rosy outlook of the 1990s began to fade as the twentieth century wound to an end. As the international system faced the new century, the desirability and contribution of globalization became more debatable.

At least three things contributed to the ambivalence about globalization. First, its proponents were too optimistic in their advocacies, and events proved their most expansive projections to be at least partially wrong. During the height of the "go-go" 1990s economy, some analysts predicted that globalization had fundamentally altered the nature of traditional economics; modern technology could make adjustments heretofore impossible in areas like product mix and inventory control, meaning the business cycle of boom and bust could effectively be surmounted, even eliminated.

These predictions proved overly optimistic, even wrong in some cases. Knowing they were producing too many automobiles did not keep the world's automakers from producing 80 million cars a year for a market that could absorb only 60 million in the late 1990s, and the result was large excess inventories as the century changed that resulted in layoffs, unprofitable discounting, and other phenomena familiar in the old economy. In 1997, a currency crisis broke out first in Thailand, spread rapidly to other East Asian states that were considered pillars of globalization, and even adversely affected the U.S. economy for a time. When the signs of economic weakness became evident even in Japan, the "economic miracle" that accompanied globalization seemed suspect.

The geopolitical consequences of globalization provided a second source of controversy. The argument to use economic globalization as a way to entangle and drag countries into the web of market democracies was no more vigorously pursued anywhere than it was in China. The prevailing idea was that by tying the Chinese to the global economy through mechanisms like most favored nation (MFN) status and membership in the World Trade Organization (WTO), pressure could be brought to bear that would force the Chinese to improve their human rights record and to allow for increased political democracy in the country. The Communist regime's obdurate resistance to loosening its political monopoly or allowing greater political (as opposed to individual) freedoms has made that strategy suspect and has kindled a renewed debate on how to treat China, which has continued as China proceeds through the transition to the fourth generation of Communist leaders beginning in late 2002.

The failure of globalization to produce all of its most optimistic (and probably unrealistic) outcomes has created a third problem, which is a backlash against the phenomenon of globalization—and especially its most prominent institutional manifestations. The first overt demonstration of strident, organized opposition to globalization came in late November 1999 at the Seattle annual meeting of the WTO, where an estimated twenty thousand demonstrators voiced their objections to the consequences of globalization (and engaged in considerable destructive vandalism in the "Emerald City"). Prominent participants included labor unions fearful of the movement of jobs to cheap labor markets and environmentalists fearful that multinational corporations and other private firms would ignore environmental protection. Other groups with parallel concerns, such as those fearful of U.S. global domination and groups seeing globalization as an assault on sovereignty, added their voices to the dissent.

This backlash became a regular and continuing part of the institutionalization of globalization in its various aspects and of the dialog on globalization. Attempts to disrupt organizations meeting to promote global values like free trade have become an apparently inevitable part of such meetings. The 2000 meeting of the International Bank for Reconstruction and Development (IBRD) in Washington, D.C., was interrupted by roughly the same coalition of rejectionists as those who had appeared in Seattle. In April 2001, this phenomenon was internationalized amid great worldwide television coverage as demonstrators at the third Summit of the Americas in Quebec City, Canada, battled tear gas-wielding police to oppose progress toward forming a Free Trade Area of the Americas (FTAA) among the thirty-four democratically elected governments of the Western Hemisphere (all countries except Cuba) by 2005, opposition that was repeated during demonstrations at the 2005 meeting in Argentina. The groups that have attracted demonstrators are diverse. The WTO has been in existence for over a decade with the purpose of promoting and monitoring the removal of trade barriers among its members (currently about 140 states); the World Bank is one of the original Bretton Woods institutions that came out of World War II to reorder the world economy principally by making loans to creditworthy countries; and the FTAA is an unratified proposal originally announced at the first Summit in Miami in 1994. The common thread among all three, however, is that they are a general part of the process of globalization.

THE SECOND FAULT LINE:
THE WORLD AFTER SEPTEMBER 11

It has proven difficult to specify the characteristics of the contemporary, post–September 11 international environment in terms as clear as those used to describe the Cold War. Like the post–Cold War world (1991–2001) it supersedes, it does not have a universally accepted name: the closest anyone has come in the immediate wake of the traumatic events is to proclaim it as the GWOT, but it is not clear that label is adequate. For one thing, the response to the terrorist acts is not a war in any traditional, recognizable way (a point argued at length in Chapter 12); and for another, it is not yet certain that the GWOT represents or accompanies a profound and *lasting* change has occurred in the way the system works. It is possible that international terrorism will be reduced to the status it had before the attacks (a peripheral place in the scheme of things) or eliminated, in which case history may view this period as an interlude in the post–Cold War world. Alternately, terrorism may be an enduring problem with which to contend concertedly for some time. It is simply too early to tell.

An accurate perspective is further clouded by subjective factors. Because the traumatic events were so recent, there is minimal perspective on the events or their long-term impacts. Powerful symbols of the United States were attacked, which makes the events of September 11 more personal and emotional than they might otherwise have been. The obvious equation of the attacks with the Japanese attack at Pearl Harbor creates a sense of "infamy" around the events, seeming to dictate a swift and decisive retribution that continues to remain elusive and adds to frustrations. The amorphous nature of a terrorist opponent that operates in the shadows makes it difficult to fashion effective ways to eradicate the "evil" that terrorism represents.

If it is difficult to agree on all aspects of the new environment in any detail, it is possible to discern differences on the post–September 11 side of the second fault line. Among other things, the balance between geopolitical and globalization concerns has clearly shifted from the latter to the former. Geopolitics has had a rebirth that is clear and undeniable if the search continues for adequate ways to describe the new geopolitical reality. One of the new forces that has clearly entered the public international calculus is the emergence of so-called nonstate actors in the form of international terrorists whose base and loyalties do not coincide with any country.

Iraq raises the question of how far the effort to suppress terrorism extends to other international conflict concerns. The debate between internationalism and unilateralism has also been affected, if in contradictory ways as events and reactions unfold. If globalization has receded, it is not clear exactly how far and in what direction.

The revealed vulnerability of American soil to attack has quickly revived an interest in the tool of geopolitics—military forces—in the American debate after a decade or more when they received much less attention. One of the most obvious beneficiaries has been military spending. In the patriotic outpouring following the terrorist attacks, this shift to an almost obsessive sense of national security emphasis went virtually unchallenged. In the area of defense spending, for instance, the expected tough debate over modernization—which new systems to buy—turned into a frenzy of trying to procure everything on the menu despite the tenuousness of the arguments of how different capabilities would contribute to the central thrust on combating terrorism. President Bush's suggestion during the 2000 campaign that the United States might simply leapfrog a generation of new weapons fell rapidly off the table in the process.

The ascendancy of geopolitics has been accompanied by the assertion that the United States is locked in a new and different kind of war, a theme raised shortly after September 11 by the Bush administration and dutifully adopted by the media. While it was never quite clear what was new about combating terrorism, it was widely advertised that the new and amorphous enemy engaged in *asymmetrical warfare*. Calling such approaches "new" strains credulity to the breaking point. The adoption of methods to negate the advantages of a larger and superior force is as old as the first time a weaker foe outdid a superior enemy, and the United States confronted—unsuccessfully—this kind of enemy in Vietnam a third of a century ago. There is certainly nothing new about the use of terrorism—only the instruments have changed. What *is* new in the contemporary context is the relative emphasis now being placed on combating unconventional opponents. During the Cold War, for instance, most emphasis was on strategic nuclear and large-scale conventional war with the Soviet Union in Europe—a sort of grand-scale reprise of World War II. Some emphasis on asymmetrical warfare—in forms such as antiterrorism and guerrilla warfare—was part of planning, but it was relegated to a lower order of priority. Special Operations Forces (SOFs) was the large repository of such concern, and because those missions were considered less important than the central conflict, the result was to help trivialize the importance of the SOFs and their missions. In a contemporary environment where there are few dangers of large-scale conventional warfare, priorities have been essentially inverted—witness the importance now attached to Special Forces as the United States confronts Bush's "axis of evil," in Afghanistan, for instance.

A more prominent characteristic of the new geopolitical order is its increased emphasis on nonstate actors, organizations that have neither a permanent territorial base nor loyalty to any particular country but that engage in activities that cross state borders. In a generic sense, such actors are also nothing new; the most prominent examples of nonstate actors are nongovernmental organizations (NGOs)—nonstate-based international organizations that perform a variety of useful functions within the system from provision of humanitarian assistance (CARE, Doctors without Borders) to monitoring of human rights violations (Amnesty International, Human Rights Watch), for example.

The terrorist attacks riveted attention to a subcategory of nonstate actors who are violent in their actions. Once again, violent transnational groups are not a novel feature of the post–Cold War world and beyond. In contemporary terms, the international drug cartels have been a prototype of sorts, and international terrorist organizations have operated for years. What is different is that organizations such as Al Qaeda occupy a central position in national security attention.

Dealing with nonstate actors in the form of international religious terrorist organizations poses some unique problems for national security policy makers (beyond the fact that they were not given high priority in the past). America's conventional and historical experience has been combating the agents of state-based governments who represented a conventional (or symmetrical) threat. Armed forces, doctrines for warfare, and the whole legal and ethical framework for warfare are geared to fighting such foes. International terrorism stands these concepts and rules on their heads in several ways.

One problem is how to depict efforts to combat international religious terrorists. The analogy of "war," which has its roots and designations in conventional interstate war and classic internal war over control of governments, does not clearly fit an opponent that has no territorial base or loyalty and is apparently uninterested in gaining and exercising authority over territory. Whom does one attack in this war? Historically, acts of war are committed against states and their agencies. In the case of international terrorists, such distinctions are at best indirect—for example, the designation of the Taliban regime as an opponent because of its shielding of Al Qaeda. It is relatively easy to assign blame when actions can clearly be identified with a particular state (and especially when that state acts overtly); it is more difficult when dealing with a nonstate-based opponent.

This difficulty became particularly clear in the case of Taliban and Al Qaeda prisoners sent to Guantanamo Bay (nicknamed "Gitmo") detainees in Cuba in 2002 and afterward after the campaign to overthrow the Taliban in Afghanistan succeeded. Were these individuals prisoners of war (POWs), in which case they were subject to treatment as such under the Geneva codes of war (see Amplification 2.2)? Or were they "detainees," as the administration maintained? Had there been a literal, legal state of war, there would have been no question about POW status. Since there was not, their status was debatable and controversial. The compromise solution of treating Taliban prisoners as POWs because they were soldiers of the Taliban regime and treating Al Qaeda prisoners as something else was not legally or politically pleasing. The situation at Gitmo remains uncomfortable and highly controversial.

Nonstate actors such as international terrorists are difficult to combat in conventional military terms, as the U.S. military has learned. These groups do indeed engage in asymmetrical forms of combat, in the process not honoring traditional rules of engagement or conventional laws of states. Terrorist acts invariably break laws and are considered criminal by the targets, just as they are considered acts of war by the terrorists.

THE RULES OF WAR: WHO IS A POW?

One of the fallouts of American participation in the campaign to overthrow the Taliban government of Afghanistan was the question of the status of hostile prisoners captured by American and Afghan forces. It was a complicated problem in two ways. The first complication revolved around whether a state of war existed, since war was never declared formally by the government, the coalition of forces seeking to overthrow the government, or the intervening United States. The other complication was that the prisoners included both soldiers supporting the Taliban regime and Al Qaeda terrorist members fighting alongside the Taliban. The first complication did not apply to international standards on treatment of prisoners; the second did.

The question of prisoner status was first raised when a number of captured Afghans were transported to detention at the U.S. naval base at Guantanamo Bay, Cuba. The explanation for the transfer was that the "detainees," as the Bush administration labeled them, were dangerous individuals who might escape if left in Afghanistan and cause havoc there. In addition, the United States wanted to isolate and interrogate suspected Al Qaeda members to aid in the campaign against terrorism.

The question became critical at this point. The Bush administration maintained that the detainees did not qualify for prisoner-of-war status under the Geneva Conventions of War (more specifically, Convention III: Relative to the Treatment of Prisoners of War, Geneva, August 1949), to which the United States is a signatory. After some discussion, it was conceded that the Taliban, as representatives of the government of Afghanistan, qualified under Article 4 of the convention, but that the Al Qaeda detainees did not. The administration, anxious to get as much information as possible from the detainees, initially resisted differentiating between members of the two groups. Article 5 of the convention, however, is quite clear on this matter: "Should any doubt arise as to whether persons, having committed a belligerent act and having fallen into the hands of the enemy, belong to any of the categories enumerated in Article 4, such persons *shall enjoy the protection of the present convention until such time as their status has been determined by a competent tribunal*" (emphasis added). Over five years after their arrival, no tribunals had been convened for that purpose.

Why was the administration so reluctant to afford prisoner-of-war status to the Afghans? The answer was straightforward: if the detainees were legal POWs, there were sharp limits on the American right to extract information from them. Part III, Section 1, Article 17, defines the problem: "Every prisoner of war, when questioned on the subject, is bound to give his surname, first names and rank, date of birth, and army, regimental, personal or serial number, or failing this, equivalent information." Since that is *all* the information a POW is required to provide, granting that status would clearly have hamstrung the antiterrorist effort. The question is whether the additional information was worth the price of the United States apparently violating a basic treaty obligation.

Source: Convention III: Relative to the Treatment of Prisoners of War. Geneva, Switzerland, August 1949. (Text available from the Society of Professional Journalists at http://www. thespa.com/genevaconventions/convention3.html).

A further characteristic of the changed environment is how the American role in the world is viewed. In particular, the question that has been raised particularly frequently is whether dealing with terrorism has predisposed the United States to act in concert with its allies and the international community (a position known as multilateralism), or on its own with little regard for others in what it believes to be its individual self-interest (unilateralism). This distinction is developed more fully later in the chapter.

In the immediate aftermath of September 11, 2001, there was great agreement on the perfidy of the attacks and on the need to combat them through concerted, broadly international action, and the Bush administration responded by calling for such action. The rationale was that since international terrorism represented a threat that did not honor borders, the response to it must be international as well in areas such as intelligence gathering and sharing, detention of suspected terrorists, and the like. The internationalist instinct seemed to prevail.

By the beginning of 2002, however, that consensus had begun to erode as the campaign to capture and destroy Usama bin Laden and his associates proved more difficult than imagined. In that atmosphere, the United States government began proposing more militarily oriented actions that met with cool receptions almost everywhere else. The first lightning rod of international concern was directed at the detainees at Guantanamo and the stern refusal of the United States to listen to international entreaties about their treatment. When President Bush announced the axis of evil designation of Iraq, Iran, and North Korea in his 2002 State of the Union address and threatened vaguely about the likelihood of military action to deal with their alleged transgressions without consulting American allies in advance, many in the international community saw a return to the unilateralism they had suspected before the attacks.

Finally, September 11 dampened discussions and emphases on globalization. Some of the optimism about spreading globalization had already been dampened by economic events of the end of the 1990s, as already noted. The shock of the terrorist events further removed the luster that had surrounded globalization, as the system reoriented its focus toward the problem of international terrorism. The more profound effects of the changed environment on globalization are examined throughout the book. For present purposes, it is sufficient simply to suggest the contours of short- and long-term prospects.

In the immediate wake of the attacks, negative impacts tended to be emphasized. For example, one of the reasons the Al Qaeda terrorists were able to enter the United States is the relative ease that people and products have in entering and leaving the country. That penetrability is a distinct asset for increasing international economic activity such as trade, but it also makes monitoring and interception of terrorists (as well as illegal immigrants and drug traffickers, as noted in Chapter 12) more difficult than would be the case with greater restrictions on movement. As discussions turned to the prospects of terrorists moving weapons of mass destruction into the country, there were quite understandable calls for increased security on America's borders. One question was how this could be accomplished without unduly strangling trade, effectively undoing globalization, and threatening freedoms integral to the American way of life.

In the longer term, it is possible to think of the emphases on geopolitics and globalization as being potentially reinforcing, part of a comprehensive policy toward the world. A reasonable consensus has emerged that a basic reason for terrorism is abysmal living conditions in parts of the world that are breeding grounds for the hopelessness that makes terrorism an attractive option. Economic development—draining the "swamps" in which terrorism thrives—thus becomes part of a longer term means of eliminating the terrorist threat. Since a major component of alleviating human misery is improving living conditions through economic prosperity, the spread of the globalizing economy to places that have hitherto been those swamps can become part of overall geopolitical strategy.

There are two "aftershocks" of the September 11 fault line that continue to affect U.S. national security policy. One, of course, is the continuing vitality of international religious terrorism. Despite some hard-fought efforts that have brought individual terrorists to justice and have disrupted or disabled their efforts, no one is arguing that "victory" in the GWOT is on the horizon. The long-war analogy is a tacit admission that not only is a decisive success not imminent, but also it is not even clear what strategic approaches will bring closure to the GWOT.

The other aftershock has been the Iraq War and the domestic and international reaction to it. The war is clearly tied to September 11: the clearest reasons for concern about Iraq (at least in public advocacies) were the formal and potential ties of the Saddam Hussein regime to terrorism (the alleged tie to Al Qaeda, the fear of WMD sharing with terrorists). Without the ability to allege these connections, the invasion would likely have remained the idle delusion of neoconservatives within the Bush administration. Internationally, very few countries accepted the alleged connections, and thus the world community overwhelmingly rejected the American actions that flowed from them.

The Iraq aftershock may have a seismic effect as profound as September 11, at least in the next decade or so for the United States. Once the American withdrawal of combat troops is complete, the United States will undergo a wrenching debate about what went wrong, why it went wrong, and how to avoid making the same mistakes again in the future. During the 1970s, "no more Vietnams" became the rallying cry across the political spectrum, although the phrase meant different things and had different implications for different groups. During the remainder of the 2000s and probably into the 2010s, "no more Iraqs" is likely to reverberate in similar ways. This debate will be particularly wrenching if residual American forces remain in Iraq or near its borders after combat troops leave, a contingency that seems likely.

DYNAMICS OF THE NEW INTERNATIONAL SYSTEM

The emergence of the fault lines has had major impacts on both the nature of the international system and how we think about our place in that system. This section introduces and briefly explores three aspects of these changes. First, it looks at the system's dynamics in terms of the relative ascendancy of geopolitics or globalization since the end of the Cold War and possible future relative emphases. Second, one of the obvious changes in the international system is the enhanced primacy of the United States in the international order, and that requires examining the nature and some of the implications of the United States' position as the sole remaining superpower. Third, this changing status has stimulated and coincided with a general political debate in the country about what the American approach and role *should* be, a debate that will be influenced by the Iraq experience.

Globalization and/or Geopolitics

As the discussion of the fault lines clearly suggests, the relationship between geopolitics and globalization is an intertwined, intimate, and evolving proposition, not an either/or matter. During the Cold War, geopolitical concerns were clearly and appropriately dominant given the nature of the international situation. Yet, while the geopolitics of East–West confrontation dominated the international agenda, the forces that would propel globalization were being set in place, ready to enter the calculus.

During the 1990s, two quite opposite forces were at play that changed the relative importance of globalization and geopolitics and ended up creating an exaggerated view of the post–Cold War world. One of these forces was the apparently receding importance of the most visible manifestation of geopolitics: military force. The demise of the superpower military confrontation clearly devalued standard, traditional military force within the major power conglomerate of important countries, and this devaluation led many states sharply to reduce their forces. Following the apparent last hurrah of twentieth-century-style warfare in the Persian Gulf War, military concerns shrunk to smaller tasks, such as peacekeeping.

At the same time, the impact of globalization was making enormous headway as the leading edge of the great and spreading prosperity of the 1990s. During the first seven or so years of the decade, economic growth and prosperity seemed inexorable at the very same time that major systemic instability and violence faded from the world stage. The result was a euphoria that would prove to be partially false with time. But to enthusiasts like *New York Times* correspondent Thomas L. Friedman, the world was entering the "age of globalization," a systematic transition from the old to the new.

At one level, the rise of globalization and other concerns is nothing more than the latest conceptual and physical reaction to the realism represented by the geopolitically dominated Cold War period. Because it is discussed in detail in Chapter 3, this is not the place either to describe or to critique realism. Suffice it to say that realism and geopolitics represent the conflictual side of international relations, the dark side or yin in politics. Globalization, on the other hand, emphasizes the cooperative side of the international equation, the idealist assault on the worst outcomes of a realist-dominated world—war. This assault has known many names, from interwar idealism and its attachment to international organization, to the functionalism of the early post–World War II emphasis on the U.N. system to make war functionally impossible. The more direct lineage attaches to the idea of complex interdependence popularized by Robert Keohane and Joseph S. Nye Jr. in the 1970s. Globalization emerges as the yang to the geopolitical yin.

The result is a fast-moving and changing international dynamic. The seemingly inexorable ascent of globalization was delivered a sobering blow by the East Asian crisis that swept through the global economy in 1997 and 1998 and reminded the world that the growing prosperity was neither automatic nor nonreversible. In turn, the ensuing turmoil brought geopolitical elements back to the fore in diverse places. In Indonesia, for example, the crash laid bare the last vestiges of corruption in the Suharto dictatorship, hastening his resignation from a presidency to which he had had himself appointed for life and setting in motion centrifugal forces in the archipelago that continue into the new century. In order to straighten out the economic mess revealed by the crisis, the old-fashioned economic instrument of power (although not called that) was invoked in the form of International Monetary Fund sanctions in offending countries. At the same time, the carrot and stick of WTO membership and MFN status was dangled in front of the Chinese in order to secure their adherence to other quite different standards such as human rights. The dark side of geopolitics reasserted itself decisively as the commercial airliners slammed into the icons of geopolitics (the Pentagon) and globalization (the World Trade Center).

What this reveals is that globalization and geopolitics have become intertwined in complicated ways, which will be explored in the pages that follow. In some ways, the economic aspects of globalization supplanted—at least part of the time and in some instances—the military aspects of geopolitics during the 1990s. Certainly this was true in relations within the developing world. At the same time, globalization may be the servant of geopolitics, as in the complex motivations and debates about the use of economic incentives toward China to entangle that country in a spider-like web that will draw them toward the economic and political values of the First World–dominated system.

Globalization and geopolitics may thus be the yin and yang of modern international relations, sometimes competing with one another and other times complementing one another. Before beginning the journey to try to decide the direction, nature, and velocity of that relationship, it is necessary to introduce one other major characteristic of the contemporary environment: the central role of the United States.

The American Role in the New World System

As already suggested, one of the ways the new international order is different from the Cold War era is in the distribution of power and influence among states. The language of bipolarity and multipolarity is clearly no longer descriptively accurate, and the use of the term *unipolarity* has connotations of a level of control, even hegemony, that the United States does not possess and that most Americans do not aspire to.

It has become fashionable, however, to describe the United States as the remaining superpower, but a new term has also entered the lexicon to describe how much more influential the United States is than other states in the system. That term is *hyperpower,* and it connotes the great qualitative advantage of the United States in addition to quantitative advantages such as having the world's largest economy and most lethal military. It is a term sometimes used out of awe and respect, but it is also attached to what the late Arkansas Senator J. William Fulbright called in a book title in 1966 "the arrogance of power."

What are the bases of American preeminence in the world? It is possible to use the traditional categories of measures of national power to compose that advantage: the political, economic, and military instruments of power. During the Cold War, the United States had the advantage in power employing each of these measures, but its advantage was challenged by different powers in each category. Marxism-Leninism posed a challenge (that turned out to be overestimated) to the political appeal of western democracy, the economies of Japan and the European Common Market (now Union) posed an economic challenge, and Soviet nuclear and massive conventional forces challenged American dominance on the military dimension as well.

During the 1990s, the United States clearly established its preeminence on all three measures of power. Part of the reason was that the United States outperformed its rivals, especially in the economic realm. At the same time, the demise of the Soviet Union meant the source of both the political and the military dimensions of opposition quit the field, leaving the United States alone as the sole possessor of significant amounts of all the instruments of power.

Politically, the United States emerged as "the indispensable nation," to use former Secretary of State Madeleine Albright's phrase. The basis of American political advantage was at least twofold. The power and appeal of the American system and political ideals (Nye's "soft power") made the United States the model that many states and peoples worldwide sought to emulate. At the same time, the United States is the only country that has truly global interests. This means that whenever situations arise almost anywhere, the United States is affected and has an interest in influencing the outcome, a situation highlighted when the United States became the direct victim of international terrorism. Because of American power on the other dimensions, American preferences are consequential and sought out regardless of the location.

The economic dimension is similar. After nearly two decades of economic doldrums during the 1970s and 1980s when it became popular in this country and abroad to talk about American decline, the American economy revived and led the expansion of the globalizing economy during the 1990s and into the 2000s. The United States had remained the world's largest economy even during the down years, but as expansion occurred and the globalization system became penultimately a trading system, the United States also blossomed as the world's great market, which everyone sought to enter. At the same time, America's primary economic rivals relatively declined. The German economic "miracle" was slowed by the greater than anticipated burden of absorbing the former German Democratic Republic (East Germany) into the Federal Republic in the early 1990s. By the end of the 1990s, the Japanese economy was faced with a serious downturn; joining the American-inspired and American-led "circle of market democracies" added to the luster of its soft power.

American military advantage increased the most. The most obvious reason for this was the decline of America's military rivals. Russian forces are far inferior in size and quality to the old Soviet military machine, and the burdensome retention of a nuclear arsenal comparable to that of the United States that the Russians cannot afford to maintain adequately is about the only way in which America's past rival poses any threat. As noted in Amplification 2.1, however, this Russian decline may not be permanent. Similarly, the People's Republic of China retains the world's largest army but has no way to project it far from its borders and spends about one-tenth the amount on defense that the United States does despite a major commitment to defense in recent years. As the adversaries have melted away, America's allies have also cut back their forces at a more rapid rate than has the United States, contributing to the substantial gap in military capability between the United States and everybody else.

The gap is qualitative as well as quantitative. As was first demonstrated convincingly in the Persian Gulf War, the results of the *revolution in military affairs* (RMA) in adapting technologies like electronics to the battlefield have given the United States (and its close allies) an enormous qualitative advantage militarily. The only other states that have undergone aspects of the RMA are First World allies like France and Great Britain. Third World states (like Iraq in 1991) simply stand no realistic chance when confronted by a military machine such as that which can be fielded by the United States and its North Atlantic Treaty Organization (NATO) allies.

The result of these military advantages is that the United States has the military reach to match its global interests, and it is the only country that can project military power globally. At the operational level, the United States is the only remaining power with a global blue water (major oceangoing) Navy, and it is the only country that has global air power projection capabilities. This means not only that the United States has great advantage in projecting its own forces into faraway places, but also that others must rely on American capabilities to get their own forces to distant battlefields or to deployments in the name of peacekeeping or emergency humanitarian relief, for instance.

This position of preeminence is not always or universally appreciated, and it is commonplace to hear objections to American global leadership on grounds such as American "arrogance" or some similar charge. At the same time, one of history's lessons would seem to be that nature abhors vacuums in all guises, including balances of power. Some argue that American singularity of power will create rivals to fill the vacuum left by the Soviets, and occasionally there is some mention of the possible formation of rival coalitions (such as Russia and China). These never seem to come to fruition, and American preeminence has remained unchallenged for well over a decade. In fact, following the Afghan campaign and American threats to bring down the government of Saddam Hussein unilaterally in the face of international opposition, there was speculation that American military prowess may have gotten too great—to the point the United States no longer needs its allies to accomplish military goals and thus can ignore their advice. Such concerns have been lessened to a degree in light of the quagmire of Iraq, where the American military "juggernaut" has been effectively tied down by a low-level insurgency in that country.

Acceptance of American leadership, in other words, remains controversial, and many other countries hope that the American reaction to Iraq will be to chasten American action in the future.

What *Should* the United States Do?

There is a major cleavage, accentuated by the reaction to Iraq, within the American populace about the proper and appropriate American role in the world. Much of this debate has been given simplistic, misleading labels to "describe" the positions people take—such as liberal, conservative, and neoconservative. These labels generally obscure rather than clarify the dynamics of the more subtle orientations toward national security concerns that people hold. These positions are generally nuanced combinations of a variety of views about the world. This section looks at views toward U.S. national security from five different perspectives that, individually and collectively, help clarify and elaborate the real positions people hold.

The review encompasses five aspects of the values people combine to produce their view of what the United States should do in the world. The categories are not mutually exclusive, but holding one view on a particular dimension does not automatically entail a particular position on other dimensions. The dimensions are arranged in roughly descending order, although readers may quibble with the ordering or even the composition of the list itself. The five dimensions are basic worldview, political orientation, approaches to involvement in the world, participation preferences, and judgments on the generalized efficacy of force in international dealings generally and in particular situations. Each is discussed individually but briefly, recognizing that the discussions cannot exhaust all facets of the distinction.

Basic Worldview. This dimension refers to the generalized view that a person has about the nature of the international system; the acceptability, desirability, and immutability of the way the system works; and how or whether one should act to change the arrangements that do exist. The basic orientations that dominate discussions in national security debates are *realism* and *idealism*.

Realism is the historically dominant philosophy and is the underlying belief system for the realist paradigm, which is the subject of the next chapter. Roughly speaking, realism (as the name implies) seeks to describe the world the way it is. Its central tenets are that world politics is a geopolitical struggle among sovereign states in an international system of anarchy (the absence of government), in which states are the central units that compete among themselves to maximize their most important values, known as national interests. Inherent in the description that realism portrays is the maintenance of and occasional resort to organized armed force as one way that states achieve their values.

The realist world is a quintessentially Hobbesian construct intended both to describe the world and to provide a set of methods to survive and succeed in the world. The code of behavior associated with realism is the realist paradigm. Realism does not purport to place a value on the "goodness" of the conditions it says order the world; rather, it suggests that the sensible approach of policy makers is to determine how to adapt to and make the best of the world as it is. Because part of the paradigm is the locus of power in the most prominent states of the world, realism is *state-centric* and generally opposes attempts to undercut the power and centrality of the state through efforts such as limitations on state sovereignty.

Idealism views the world differently. Most idealists accept the realist description of the world as basically accurate (if somewhat overdrawn). Where they differ is on the question of the immutability of the present condition and whether one should work to change the current arrangements. Idealists, in a general sense, believe that realism produces an imperfect world that is in need of reform and, in a more Lockean manner, that change is possible. For many idealists, the major imperfection of current international politics is its normalization of force as an acceptable method for bringing about change. The basic question idealists ask is, How can the world order be transformed to make the world a better (generally more peaceful) place?

Both realism and idealism are part of the American tradition. Realism tends to predominate among policy makers because it does offer a description of the structure and workings of the system and how to manipulate that system. For many people, attachment to realism also has a deceiving rhetorical quality—it is somehow more virile and worldly to be "realistic" about the world than to somehow be a dreamy idealist. As a result, many individuals describe themselves as realists without any particular philosophical underpinning behind the claim.

Idealism, however, also has its place, especially in the United States. As is argued in Chapter 4, Americans have always possessed a feeling of moral and other superiority (Ronald Reagan's depiction of the United States as the "shining house on the hill") that is accompanied by an evangelical desire to share that vision with the rest of the world. Thus, Woodrow Wilson sought to "make the world safe for democracy," and Wilsonian idealism, as it is known, had as its goal the restructuring of the international system along more democratic lines. Idealists often disagree on the method of achieving change. The Clinton and George W. Bush administrations, for instance, both had the idealistic goal of spreading democracy to places where it does not exist. They differed on how to go about the promotion: Clinton's goal was spreading American soft power through globalization, as opposed to the neoconservative credo of "regime change" (including the resort to force) of the Bush terms.

There is a political trick here as politicians align themselves on the realist–idealist axis. Politically, it is virtually suicidal to be viewed as an idealist because so many Americans view that orientation as "soft" or "unrealistic." As a result, an orientation that is indeed idealist must somehow be portrayed to the public as instead being realistic—that advocating basic change is the wisest geopolitical path. The prime current example of this attempted legerdemain is the neoconservative's open embrace of the Wilsonian ideal of advocating the spread of democracy (although through the use of force) as the realistic course for the country. (Thus, idealism becomes realism by calling idealism realism.)

Political Orientation. In the contemporary political debate, this is the most emotional and, in many cases, misleading dimension. It is most often manifested in the dichotomy between *liberalism* and *conservatism*, but these terms have become so emotionally laden that it is hard to determine their meaning out of some specific (e.g. issue) context. Both terms can be and often are used to convey either praise or condemnation.

It is helpful both to extend the categories and to define them. The basic liberal–conservative dichotomy omits too many other possibilities or requires placing people and their ideas into categories that do not truly fit them and whose inclusion unnecessarily broadens and distorts the meanings of the descriptive categories.

General political orientation can more usefully be divided into five orientations that form something of a continuum. Starting at the far "left" is *radicalism*. Radicals generally support substantial, even fundamental, change in political relationships, normally toward some currently nonexistent condition. Often, radicals display a willingness to resort to violence. Next comes *liberalism*. Classic liberalism has two major characteristics. First, it emphasizes tolerance of the views and opinions of others (indeed, one classic meaning of being liberal is that one is tolerant of others). Second, liberals are positively oriented toward political change and have a generally positive view of the role of government in promoting that change. Many liberals are also egalitarian and seek to level the conditions of citizens, although this is not a necessary part of being liberal (it *is*, however, the most controversial and criticized characteristic).

In the middle of the spectrum is *pragmatism*. Pragmatists do not espouse a predisposition one way or the other on the question of political change and the positive or negative role of government. Rather, they tend to be moderate on issues and to take positions on particular questions based on their assessment of the individual merits in particular situations. Pragmatism and moderation have historically been highly revered characteristics, but in an ideologically charged era, pragmatism has a bland image that seems to pale in the face of stronger positions across the board. At its most derisive, pragmatism is sometimes equated with a lack of principles or commitment to a set of principles.

To the right of center are *conservatism* and *reactionism*. Conservatism, in its literal sense, means support for the status quo: conservatives seek to "conserve" relationships as they exist. Thus, conservatives are generally opposed to or suspicious of political change, and since most change is associated with government activity, traditional conservatives generally favor a small and restricted role for the government in areas such as regulation and taxation (*social* conservatives, on the other hand, seek to enforce a particular social code and may or may not advocate governmental activism to achieve their goals). The major operational difference between liberals and conservatives indeed comes down to the question of how active government should be in promoting change or regulating behavior. Reactionism, on the other hand, is the advocacy of change to some past state of political affairs. Because such change generally includes a reduction of governmental activity and thus a reversion to some past set of relationships, reactionaries are more extreme than real conservatives.

Placing someone (including oneself) on this continuum is difficult. The boundaries between the categories, especially when presented as compactly as they are here, are not sharp and clear. At the same time, people do not always (even usually) consistently act from the premises of one position or another. An advocacy of tax cuts is, for instance, essentially a reactionary position, whereas setting up mandatory, federally regulated educational standards is a decidedly liberal act. Also, many people hold different philosophies when it comes to international and domestic issues. So-called Kennedy Democrats (supporters of the late President John F. Kennedy) were generally liberal on domestic issues but fairly sharply conservative on foreign policy matters. Similarly, contemporary traditional and social conservatives differ on a broad range of policies and approaches to government.

Approaches to Involvement. The third dimension refers to how active the United States should be in world affairs. In more tranquil times when the United States was not such a prominent international actor, this distinction was more important than it is now, but it still retains some salience.

The two major positions on American involvement are *internationalism* and *neo-isolationism*. Internationalists generally feel that the United States should take a prominent, activist position in the world and that acting as a world leader best serves the national interest. Neo-isolationists, on the other hand, are less inclined toward such activism. Instead, neo-isolationists believe that the United States should limit its participation in world affairs whenever and to the extent possible and concentrate instead on domestic American concerns.

This historically was a much livelier debate than it is now. Isolationism as a pure force seeking to insulate the United States as completely as possible from world affairs was a powerful force until World War II, when the Pearl Harbor attack rendered "splendid isolationism" anachronistic. Its more moderate form, neo-isolationism, resides at the fringes of the debate over security in the face of people like Ron Paul and tends to associate with opposition to globalization (arguing it hurts Americans more than it helps them). Most Americans consider themselves to be internationalists generally speaking, although the degree of international involvement that they advocate varies.

Participation Preferences. Regardless of how one feels about the extent to which the United States should involve itself in world affairs, a further question is the quality and nature of participation in those affairs. This concern centers around whether the United States should prefer to act in concert with as much of the international community as possible when it interacts with the world or instead should be willing to act on its own, even with the opposition of a substantial part of the international community, when it feels its interests are served by going it alone.

The two basic positions on this dimension are *multilateralism* and *unilateralism*. Multilateralism, which has been the dominant position for most of the period since World War II, asserts the belief that American policy and actions should generally be developed and coordinated with the policies of others in the international community, and especially American friends and allies. The underlying assumption is that American interests include keeping friends and that the wisest policies often reflect the development of international consensus on issues. Unilateralism, on the other hand, starts from the premise that U.S. interests should override international concerns and that the United States must be willing to go against international consensus when international views would harm American interests. This position has been most prominently associated with the neoconservatives within the George W. Bush administration.

Multilateralism and unilateralism are not entirely mutually exclusive. Multilateralists would, for instance, agree that there are occasions when the United States must ignore international views and act alone, and unilateralists would agree that developing an international consensus is preferable if possible. This latter position is the heart of President Bush's "distinctly American internationalism" imbedded in the 2002 *National Security Strategy of the United States*. Rather, the two positions can be thought of more accurately as predilections or strong preferences for ways to proceed in the world.

Efficacy of Force. The final distinction regards preference for *how* to attempt to promote American interests, and it hinges on the question of the broad range of situations in which the use of military force is appropriate and where in the hierarchy of "instruments of national power" one should place military power.

One way to state this distinction is between the *hawks* and the *doves*. The names, of course, are descriptive. Hawks are those individuals who have a generally positive view of the utility of force over a range of situations and thus believe that the possible recourse to "hard power" should be considered in a variety of cases. Doves, on the other hand, generally oppose the use of military force except in clear cases of employments of necessity and prefer to use "soft power" (economic and political instruments of power) to achieve national goals. One way to view the distinction is to ask whether military force should be used only as a last resort (doves) or whether it should be considered in less dire circumstances (hawks).

Historically, the hawk position has been associated with traditional realism. Traditional realism, however, has as one of its tenets the belief that military force should be used only in defense of vital American interests, or, in other words, in employments of necessity. This contrasts with the neoconservative version of the hawk preference, which is willing to employ force more broadly, including in pursuit of interests not unambiguously vital in their nature. This distinction helps explain, for instance, why a number of retired general officers opposed the neoconservative-inspired American invasion of Iraq. These retired officers were generally traditional realists who did not believe the outcome in Iraq affected truly vital American interests, and thus they opposed the deployment.

Compiling Profiles. The five dimensions can be combined to create profiles that are useful in distinguishing individuals and groups on grounds other than crude and generally ambiguous labels. Moreover, developing one's own personal inventory and comparing it to that of others (political candidates, for instance) can also provide a way to see if one agrees more with the position of one individual or side or another.

Applying the categories to political figures—presidential candidates, for instance—helps one to decide more precisely what different positions they occupy, how to categorize them within the range of conventional labels, and even how to compare the self-designation of candidates with their actual positions. Is, for instance, President Bush conservative, as he has consistently maintained himself to be? He is certainly not a traditional conservative, since he has neither exercised fiscal restraint nor limited the role of government. His most openly traditional conservative position has been on tax reductions, which, according to the definitions offered here, is actually reactionary. He has been a fairly consistent social conservative (at least in his rhetoric), but the advocacy of social codes (e.g., right to life) and governmental activism (e.g., restricted funding for abortion or stem-cell research) is hardly traditionally conservative. In international relations, his administration has consistently (like all other administrations) portrayed itself as realist, but advocating the imposition of democracy by force is a decidedly idealistic idea.

Building and applying the profiles has another, more personal potential. If one builds a personal profile (as the *Challenge!* box instructs) and compares that profile to similar constructs for political candidates, one can gain some idea about whether one agrees or disagrees with the positions of the candidate. Certainly, it is a more precise method than simply accepting a candidate's assertion that he or she is a conservative or a liberal and embracing or discarding the candidate on that basis.

Challenge!

YOUR OWN PERSONAL INVENTORY

To clarify how you feel about national security affairs, develop a personal inventory on the five dimensions. The central question about each dimension may help you categorize yourself.

Basic Worldview: Should the basic mission of policy makers be to adapt to and make the best of the world situation as it is (realist), or should they try to change world conditions (idealism)?

Political Orientation: Should government seek to induce change through any means available (radicalism); promote change through moderate, tolerant action (liberalism); view situations on their own merits alone (pragmatism); seek to preserve existing relationships within a limited view of government (conservatism); or seek to remove or roll back existing conditions (reactionism)?

Approaches to Involvement: Should the United States play a generally activist, leadership role in the world (internationalism) or avoid international involvement wherever possible (neo-isolationism)?

Participation Preference: Should the United States generally try to build international consensus before acting (multilateralism) or look at its own interests first without regard to international preferences (unilateralism)?

Efficacy of Force: Is force useful in a broad range of situations (hawk) or as a last resort (dove)?

CONCLUSION: THE CONTINUING ROLE OF FORCE

There are two broad interpretations about the extent to which the recourse to force has changed in the post–Cold War world. If one begins from an emphasis on the potential applications of force, then change has been dramatic, since the most notable potential use was the ultimate employment of necessity, a military confrontation with the Soviet Union. That contingency has obviously disappeared, and much of the potential use of force in conventional interstate warfare has faded in the general tranquility among those countries with conventional forces, notably the most developed countries. It is still possible to conjure interstate wars on the peripheries (the identification of the "axis of evil" states of Iraq, Iran, and North Korea as possible targets for American military wrath, for instance), but none of these has the immediacy and importance of the Cold War confrontation. Combating terrorism has replaced large-scale warfare at the pinnacle of national security priorities. This assessment, of course, has major implications for the kinds of forces the United States develops and the missions for which they are prepared.

The other way to look at the problem is how and where force was actually employed in the past and how it is employed in the present or future. From this vantage point, change is not very dramatic at all. As noted, the United States employed force exclusively in the old Third World during the Cold War, and the current pattern emphasizes deployments in the less developed countries of the world. In both periods, the conflicts were generally internal affairs, civil wars of one kind or another. The difference is in the motivation underlying involvement: during the Cold War, we were primarily motivated by ideological, Cold War reasons, whereas now the temptations to intervene are either to relieve human-induced chaos and suffering, in effect to save countries from themselves, or to root out sources of international terrorism. In addition, much terrorist violence is conducted by and against nonstate actors, a special problem addressed in Chapter 12.

This distinction regarding motivation for using force is not insignificant for at least three reasons. One is the relative importance attached to potential involvement. In the Cold War context, one could make the argument—admittedly sometimes a stretch—that the United States was impelled to act in the developing world because of the geopolitical implications of the outcome. Should our side lose, it would be yet one more instance of the "victory" of Communism in the global struggle. Thus, intervention could be arguably a matter of necessity. Such geopolitical motivations are generally missing in many contemporary situations, where the goal often is to restore order after some humanitarian disaster, promote democracy, eradicate terrorism, or some combination of those reasons. In any geopolitical sense, these are clearly employments of choice (efforts to combat terrorism are an obvious exception). The employments of necessity deal with terrorism; the elusive, secretive nature of the terrorist opponents, however, makes specification of where and how engagement might occur difficult.

The nature of involvement in internal wars has changed as well. During the Cold War, conflicts were usually clearly drawn competitions between a government and an insurgent group, each of which fielded an organized armed force and sought militarily to defeat the other. In these circumstances, the purpose of inserting American armed forces was to assist "our" side in defeating the enemy. American forces were sent "to fight and win" in familiar military terms. In the contemporary environment, this is not the case. Normally, the situation is one of more or less great chaos, where the contending parties are shadowy organizations with inarticulate political goals and supported by armed bands that are barely military in composition. The purpose for using force in these situations is to suspend the fighting and in effect to impose peace on the area. This is best done by simply intimidating the warring parties with a show of force and then keeping them physically apart. Ideally, the soldiers do no fighting at all because their simple presence accomplishes the goal. Force used in this manner is more difficult to understand than more traditional employment. The first phase of the Afghan campaign, where American force was used to help topple a regime, represents a return to a more traditional reason for fighting, at least for a limited period of time. The ongoing battle with terrorism is complicated by the fact that none of these descriptions clearly holds for dealing with terrorists.

Finally, the two different contexts require a rethinking of how to look at the international system. During the Cold War, thinking was dominated by geopolitics in the form of something called the *realist paradigm*, a construct that tied the use of force to the most important American interests and counseled that force not be used in less weighty circumstances. When the global balance between Communism and non-Communism was at stake, the paradigm provided guidance about when to use and when not to use force. Applying the same standards to the humanitarian disasters of the 1990s and 2000s could paralyze the use of force in ways that might be undesirable. Whether the realist paradigm is an adequate device for dealing with the contemporary use of force is one of the most fundamental questions facing contemporary thinking about national security. For that reason, Chapter 3 begins with a description and critique of the concept.

STUDY/DISCUSSION QUESTIONS

1. Describe the first fault line (the end of the Cold War) and the impact it had on the structure of the international system and the problems affecting American security policy. What were the major benefits and debatable impacts of that change?
2. Describe the second fault line (September 11) and its effects on the international system and the problems affecting American security policy. What does it mean to describe Iraq as an "aftershock" of this fault line?
3. Geopolitics and globalization have been described in the text as the yin and yang of the contemporary international system. What does that mean? Discuss.
4. What is the United States' role in the contemporary international system? What does it mean that the United States is the only remaining superpower?
5. Describe and discuss the five major dimensions presented in the text for defining views on security policy. What are the categories within each? Apply the categories to different figures— for instance, major presidential candidates or your instructor in this course.

SELECTED BIBLIOGRAPHY

Allison, Graham T., and Robert Blackwill. "America's Stake in the Soviet Future." *Foreign Affairs* 70, 3 (Summer 1991), 77–97.

Campbell, Kenneth J. *A Tale of Two Quagmires: Iraq, Vietnam, and the Hard Lessons of War.* New York: Paradigm, 2007.

Campbell, Kurt M., and Derek Chollet. "The New Tribalism: Cliques and the Making of U.S. Foreign Policy." *Washington Quarterly* 30, 1 (Winter 2006–2007), 193–203.

Friedman, Thomas L. *The Lexus and the Olive Tree: Understanding Globalization.* New York: Farrar, Straus, Giroux, 1999.

Fukuyama, Francis. *The End of History and the Last Man.* New York: Free Press, 1992.

Fulbright, J. William. *The Arrogance of Power.* New York: Random House, 1966.

Gaddis, John Lewis. "Setting Right in a Dangerous World." *Chronicle of Higher Education: The Chronicle Review* 48, 18 (January 11, 2002), B7–B10.

———. "Grand Strategy for the Second Term." *Foreign Affairs* 84, 1 (January/February 2005), 2–15.

Keohane, Robert O., and Joseph S. Nye Jr. *Power and Interdependence* (2nd ed.). Glenview, IL: Scott Foresman/Little Brown, 1989.

Lieven, Anatol. "The Essential Vladimir Putin." *Foreign Policy* 84, 1 (January/February 2005). 72–74.

Mearsheimer, John J. "Why We Shall Soon Miss the Cold War." *Atlantic Monthly* 266, 2 (August 1990), 35–50.

Nye, Joseph S., Jr. *Bound to Lead: The Changing Nature of American Power.* New York: Basic Books, 1990.

———. *The Paradox of American Power: Why the World's Superpower Can't Go It Alone.* New York: Oxford University Press, 2003.

Peters, Ralph. *New Glory: Expanding America's Global Supremacy.* New York: Sentinel, 2005.

Shevtsova, Lilia. "Russia's Ersatz Democracy." *Current History* 105, 693 (October 2006), 307–314.

Singer, Max, and the Estate of the Late Aaron Wildawsky. *The Real World Order: Zones of Peace, Zones of Turmoil* (rev. ed.). Chatham, NJ: Chatham House, 1996.

Snow, Donald M., and Eugene Brown. *International Relations: The Changing Contours of Power.* New York: Longman, 2000.

——— *Why America Fights: The Uses of U.S. Military Force.* Washington, DC: CQ Press, 2000.

Trenin, Dmitri. "Russia Leaves the West." *Foreign Affairs* 85, 4 (July/August 2006). 87–96.

Windsor, Jennifer. "Promoting Democratization Can Combat Terrorism." *Washington Quarterly* 26, 3 (Summer 2003), 43–59.

CHAPTER 3

Geopolitics: America and the Realist Paradigm

PREVIEW

Realism and the realist paradigm have been central to the operation of the international system and American attitudes toward the world. Moreover, geopolitics, one of the two competing themes around which this book is organized, finds its philosophical and operational basis in realism and the realist paradigm. Because of these factors, the chapter lays out the realist argument, its implications in a geopolitical world, and the controversy over its continuing relevance to help in understanding the contemporary national security environment. Many opponents of realism, including some advocates of globalization, question the validity of the paradigm and its consequences, and their objections are discussed. The chapter concludes with a discussion of the future applicability of the realist paradigm in light of the Iraq experience.

The United States has been a leading member of the international system at least since the end of World War II, meaning it has occupied a position as a major international force for the entire lifetime of most present Americans. Most Americans have never known a time when the United States was not a major player on the world scene. This fact has the potential to distort perceptions about global geopolitics and the American role within the national security arena in which geopolitics is acted out. As Americans look forward into the new millennium, it is necessary to place the national experience in perspective, which is the purpose of this chapter and Chapter 4.

This American preeminence has not always been the case. The simple fact is that geopolitical participation, and especially leadership, has been the exception rather than the rule for the United States. For most of its history, Americans sought to be above what was viewed as the corrupting influence of power politics, and the result has been a historical ambivalence about the American role in international politics, including its more openly geopolitical aspects. As a result, Americans wonder where they fit in the system and what role to take in structuring and participating in the geopolitical game. It also means that Americans are relative amateurs at geopolitics when their experience is compared with that of the traditional powers.

There are several reasons for this scenario, and while any list will be subject to criticism both for what it includes and for what it omits, at least three factors can be identified that form what might be called the American strategic culture and that capture the essence of typical American attitudes toward the world of geopolitics.

The first factor is what some analysts have called *American exceptionalism*. Rightly or wrongly, Americans have always thought of this country as a special place, one that is qualitatively better than other places. The United States was, after all, the first country in the world to adopt political democracy, and it has long provided a refuge from the tyranny of political ideologies (e.g., fascism, Communism) and practices (e.g., involuntary military service) elsewhere in the world: Europe in the eighteenth and nineteenth centuries and much of the rest of the world since. As a result, Americans think of themselves as a kind of chosen people and view intrusions from the outside as a potential source of taint. The fact of steady immigration into the country (contrasted by essentially no emigration) reinforces this preference captured in the Statue of Liberty's invitation to bring us "your huddled masses" seeking freedom and Ronald Reagan's image of the "shining house on the hill."

The perception of being exceptional leads to a second strain in America's historical view of itself: *isolationism*. Because contact with and participation in the international system is potentially tainting, there is a residual sentiment to limit the degree of American participation in an essentially corrupt and potentially corrupting enterprise. In its most extreme form between the world wars, this sentiment manifested itself in a virtual withdrawal from international politics (although not international economics) under the banner of "splendid isolation," as noted earlier. In a more contemporary sense, *neo*-isolationism argues for sharp limits on the degree of American interaction with and leadership in the world. This sentiment finds substantive voice in policy areas as disparate as American misgivings about participation in United Nations–sponsored peacekeeping missions and opposition to economic globalization. There is, quite simply, a strand in the American political experience that, like the late Swedish actress Greta Garbo, simply wants to be left alone. To many foreign and domestic critics of American policy, this tendency manifests itself as American *unilateralism*, the tendency to ignore the sentiments and advice of others and to act alone in international affairs.

There is another factor, which is what might be called American *ambivalence* about the effects of geopolitical participation. Very few Americans would describe themselves as isolationists or maintain that the United States has no leadership role in the world. Pure isolationism ended effectively with the Japanese attack on Pearl Harbor, and neo-isolationism was badly crippled by September 11, 2001. Nonetheless, ambivalence remains. The consequence of involvement often is to ensnare the country in a web of international rules and regulations (what are sometimes called regimes) that limit American independence in ways about which many have second thoughts, because such involvement can preclude some actions the country might prefer to take. Traditional European geopolitics is one of those traps that Americans in their idealism have sought to avoid.

American attitudes toward its sovereignty stand out as examples of national ambivalence. Sovereignty, which means supreme authority, is central to the realist paradigm and is discussed more fully in the next section of this chapter. For present purposes, suffice it to say that the United States is among the strongest defenders of state sovereignty (along with China) because strict sovereignty minimizes the extent to which the judgments or standards of outsiders can be imposed on the country or individual Americans. Thus, for instance, the United States is one of only a handful of states that has refused to ratify the statute of the International Criminal Court (ICC), which has the jurisdiction to try people accused of committing war crimes. The reason for the American government's refusal to accede to the statute is its reluctance to permit Americans to be tried by foreign judges if they are accused of committing war crimes. As an example, when an American soldier was accused of raping and killing a young girl in Kosovo shortly after the United States joined the Kosovo Force (KFOR) peacekeeping mission in 2000—an act deemed a crime against humanity and thus a war crime—he was whisked off to an American base in Germany and tried there by an American military tribunal rather than facing the ICC. (He was sentenced to life in prison, which is the most severe penalty he would have faced if he had been tried and convicted by the ICC.)

This reluctance to dilute authority puts the United States at odds with much of the international community on a number of matters, and American ambivalence toward participation results in anomalies and inconsistencies in the country's relations with the world. For instance, while American insistence on maintaining its sovereignty is not something to be challenged or violated, there are situations in which the United States has felt perfectly within its rights to violate other countries' sovereignty. The American invasion of Iraq was, among other things, a direct violation of Iraq's sovereignty. American relations with Cuba illustrate this ambivalence and occasional incongruity especially well.

Since 1960, the United States has imposed an economic boycott on dealings with the Communist government of Fidel Castro. This boycott is viewed by virtually the entire international community as anachronistic (a recent vote in the U.N. General Assembly condemned it by a tally of 143 to 3), and U.S. legislation to enforce it brings cries of violations of sovereignty from friends and allies alike. For instance, provisions of the Cuban Democracy Act of 1992 and the Helms-Burton Act of 1995 impose sanctions against foreign governments and corporations for doing business with Cuba, in effect making it illegal in the United States for a British company to sell its products in Cuba. This is accomplished by imposing sanctions on doing business with the United States if one violates the provisions of the acts. These are clear and obvious violations of the sovereignty of foreign governments and corporations that, if imposed on the United States, would be roundly condemned in this country, as pointed out by critics of U.S. policy toward Cuba and foreign companies and governments affected by its provisions.

These examples are simply illustrative of the tension, ambivalence, and complexity with which the United States fits itself into the geopolitics of the contemporary system, and these problems are likely to be accentuated as the United States adjusts its policies in light of the response to international terrorism. Moreover, these issues broadly define the differences between an internationalist emphasis on globalization and a narrower emphasis on geopolitics. To understand the geopolitical position more fully, the discussion first looks at the geopolitical system was inherited from the Cold War—the realist paradigm—and objections to it as the operating principle of international politics.

REALISM AND THE REALIST PARADIGM

Realism has been both a leading theoretical approach to the study of international relations and a useful way to organize an understanding of the world. In addition, realism has served as a practical guide for political leaders as they conduct foreign policy. Realism has thus served as an intellectual tool and a set of guidelines for policy makers. Whether it can continue to serve that purpose as well in the future as it has in the past is part of the contemporary critique of realism.

These dual functions are not coincidental. The academic basis of realism came from the study of international relations by scholars whose first interest was in physical observation of how world leaders, diplomats, soldiers, and the like actually carried on their relations. Developed and ordered into a coherent explanation of international relations during and after World War II, the content of theoretical realism roughly coincided with the actual conduct of international affairs at least through the Cold War. One of the reasons the approach is called realism is that it is said to reflect reality.

Realism is controversial, largely because many people—and especially a number of international relations scholars—dispute the reality the realists portray and seek more or less actively to reform or reverse some of the basic dynamics that the realists portray. Among the phenomena that realists describe and reformers wish to change is the "normalization" of the recourse to force—in other words, war. Additionally, some notoriety has been attached to realism because the name has been essentially "high-jacked" by actors who portray themselves as realist but who support policies that are decidedly nonrealist. Defenders of the decision to invade Iraq provide a good example.

As a basic approach, realism is as old as observation about the relations between independent political units. Many believe that Thucydides' *History of the Peloponnesian Wars*, written in the fifth century B.C., is the original statement of the philosophy of realism and would add the sixteenth-century Italian diplomat and advisor Niccolò Machiavelli's *The Prince* to the roster of realist classics.

Realism became a dominant approach to understanding international relations in the period surrounding World War II. At the end of World War I, a group of scholars known as "idealists" came to dominate the study of the international system. Given the enormous carnage of the Great War, there was considerable sentiment to reform a system whose rules—based in realism—had allowed the first great conflagration of the twentieth century to occur. They based their reform on the institutionalization of peace around the League of Nations and grounded their scholarship in ways to improve the peace system by improving the effectiveness of the League in reinforcing and preserving the peace.

Unfortunately, their advocacy (what they sought to accomplish) colored their observation of the actual international politics of the interwar period (what was actually occurring). The idealists either did not see World War II coming or felt it could be avoided, but the League-based institutional framework they had built to avoid war proved entirely inadequate to slow the rush to war in the 1930s. This failure was most dramatically stated by the English scholar E. H. Carr in his critique of idealism published in 1939, *The Twenty Years' Crisis, 1919–1939*.

Realism emerged from World War II as the dominant explanation of and approach to international politics. In 1947, Hans Morgenthau published the first edition of his landmark exposition, *Politics Among Nations*, in which he laid out in detail the realist position. Emphasizing the roles of things like power, conflict, and war, the resulting realist paradigm seemed particularly well suited for describing (in a scholarly sense) and organizing the policy response to the emerging Cold War competition between the Communist and non-Communist worlds.

Even at the height of the Cold War confrontation, realism never lacked for critics. Part of that criticism comes from the conjunction of the academic and practical aspects of realism: it is not only an academic "theory" for understanding the world, but also a set of rules of the road for conducting international affairs that includes at least a partial, implicit endorsement of its principles. The alternative to thinking about or acting outside the bounds of realism became thought of as unrealistic. Those who do not like the implications of a realist-run world generally do not like the academic approach either. In some cases, this intellectual objection is stated in terms of questioning the conceptual adequacy of the realist paradigm for describing and explaining international relations; in others, the objections are rooted in opposition to the effects of conceptualizing the world through the prism of the realist paradigm.

Resolving the theoretical debate about whether realism or some other theoretical framework produces better knowledge about international relations goes beyond present purposes. As it relates to questions about the actual conduct of foreign and national security affairs, the basic concepts of realism have formed the framework within which national security decisions have been made at least since the 1940s. As a result, the pattern of historic and contemporary national security concerns cannot adequately be understood without understanding (but not necessarily embracing) the realist paradigm. If the post–September 11 environment indeed represents a return to the ascendancy of geopolitics, then the contemporary world can only be fully appreciated by understanding realism. Similarly, criticisms of realism are important to us because their implementation would alter those rules within which we think about national security in ways the critics feel more fully reflect reality and the rationale for the globalizing 1990s.

BASIC CONCEPTS AND RELATIONSHIPS

Although it runs some risk of oversimplification, the realist paradigm can be reduced to a series of six propositions about the international system that can be arranged deductively in syllogistic order. Each individual statement contains one or more of the key concepts, and collectively they define the realist perspective. Numerous observers object to the implications of some of the observations that make up the paradigm and contest their implications. Because the paradigm has been such an important part of international reality, however, its content is important.

The six propositions composing the realist paradigm are as follows:

1. The international system is composed of sovereign states as the primary units in both a political and a legal sense.
2. Sovereign states possess vital interests and are the only units in the system entitled to vital interests.
3. Vital interests become matters of international concern when conditions of scarcity exist and are pressed by competing state actors.
4. When issues involving scarce resources are present in the relations between sovereign states, then power must be used to resolve the difference.
5. The exercise of power is the political means of conflict resolution in international relations.
6. One political instrument of power is military force, which is one option for resolving differences between states.

Following the syllogism from the first to the sixth proposition, the conclusion must be reached that in a system of sovereign states, states must possess, and from time to time use, military force to resolve problems that arise for them in the system. The realist paradigm therefore justifies a concern with national security defined, at least in part, in terms of military force. It is not surprising, then, that the realist paradigm finds considerably more intellectual favor among most students and practitioners of military affairs and varying levels of disregard and disdain among people opposed to the use of military force as a "legitimate" tool for resolving differences among states. (Some military thinkers, of course, share the critique of various parts of realism.)

As stated in terms of these propositions, the realist paradigm is only a skeleton of concepts and relationships. It gains meaning when the basic concepts that compose it are examined and put together in the logical sequence of their presentation as depicted in that set of propositions.

Sovereignty

The most basic and critical principle of international relations is that of *state sovereignty*. The idea was originally articulated by a sixteenth-century Frenchman named Jean Bodin as a way to justify concentrating the authority of the French monarch by asserting his supreme authority over lesser French nobles. Sovereignty was enshrined as the basic operating principle of international relations through the series of agreements ending the Thirty Years War (1618–1648) known as the *Peace of Westphalia*. The Thirty Years War had, in large measure, been about whether the church or the state would be the principal holder of political authority in the future. Those supporting the notion of state authority prevailed, and they seized upon state sovereignty as the institutional and legal basis for institutionalizing their secular triumph over sectarian authority.

Sovereignty means *supreme authority*. Within a system in which sovereignty is the basic value, no entity can have authority superior to that of the sovereign. When Bodin coined the term and it was adopted by others, such as the English philosopher Thomas Hobbes, sovereignty was thought to be a quality that primarily applied to the domestic relations among individuals and groups within states rather than the relations between states. In fact, Bodin never considered the effects on the relations between sovereign entities; the extension of the concept to the international level is usually associated with the seventeenth-century legal scholar Hugo Grotius. In the early days of the modern state system, that domestic sovereignty was considered to rest with the monarch. The extension of the principle to the international arena occurred over the next century and has been the principal operating rule underlying international politics ever since.

Both the domestic and the international ramifications of sovereignty remain largely in force, although with quite opposite effects. Domestic sovereignty remains the basis of the authority of the state over its territory, although sovereignty is now thought of as residing with the people (who confer part of their sovereignty on the government) rather than with a person—the monarch. The result of sovereignty applied domestically is to create the legal and philosophical basis for political *order*, since authority to act rests with the state.

The effect of sovereignty on international politics is to create *anarchy* (absence of government) as the basis of the relations between states. In the international arena, state sovereignty means no state can have any jurisdiction over what goes on within another state. Thus, all relations among states are among equals wherein no state has the authority to compel any other state to do anything, at least in a legal sense that does not always conform to actual practice. There is no authority above those with supreme authority, meaning there is no basis for governance in international relations. A formal state of anarchy therefore exists in the international realm. Jurisdiction over disputes resides with the parties to the dispute, who must figure out how to decide their differences on their own, usually without recourse to an outside authority. While the inviolability of state sovereignty has never been as absolute as the definition implies (states violate other states' sovereignty routinely), it remains the major organizational tool for defining relationships within the international system.

On the face of it, this seems like an odd way for the international system to conduct its business because the practical outcome is that there is no equivalent of the judicial branch of government to settle disputes, and the parties are left to fend for themselves when differences among them arise. The reason for this state of affairs, however, lies in the fact that states have matters of such importance to them that they are unwilling to have those matters left to the judgment of outsiders. As a consequence, states demand as total control over those matters as they can enforce. This leads us to the second major concept of the realist paradigm.

Vital Interests

The main reason states are generally unwilling to compromise on matters affecting their sovereignty is because states, unlike other entities in the Westphalian system, have what are called vital interests. Indeed, Morgenthau argued the centrality of "vital interests defined as power" to the entire realist theory. Defined as properties and conditions on which states will not willingly compromise, vital interests are matters the outcomes of which are too important to be submitted to any superior authority. Such interests are to be guarded to the fullest extent the state is capable of. Some analysts would add that a vital interest is any interest that is sufficiently important that the state will use force to ensure its realization.

Generally, states formally or informally rank their interests in a hierarchical fashion that denotes how important a particular interest is and hence what measures it will undertake to realize the condition or property in question. Donald Nuechterlein provides a useful way to categorize these interests in the form of the national interest matrix (Figure 3.1):

Figure 3.1: National Interest Matrix

Basic Interest at Stake	Intensity of Interest			
	Survival	Vital	Major	Peripheral
Homeland Defense				
Economic Well-Being				
Favorable World Order				
Values Promotion				

Both dimensions of the matrix are hierarchical. Clearly, the most intense interest a state has is its physical survival, followed by those interests on which the state will not willingly compromise (vital interests). Major interests are matters that would inconvenience or harm the state but that can be tolerated, and peripheral interests are, as the label implies, matters more of inconvenience than basic interest. Similarly, the most important basic interest a state has is in defending itself, followed by promoting its economic well-being, its view of the world order, and its own values.

The critical point as it relates to questions of national security is the boundary between vital and major interests, because it is generally agreed that vital interests are ones over which the state will use force to guarantee, and major interests fall below that threshold. The location of that boundary is a matter of disagreement within the national security debate when it is applied to individual situations.

The disagreement over whether the United States should have gone to war with Iraq in the first place can be thought of in these terms. For most traditional realists, the idea that vital interests are those important enough to use military force to achieve has the corollary that force should be used *only* when vital interests are involved. This latter assertion forms the basis for disagreement over Iraq. To critics who argue the United States should not have gone to war against Iraq, there were no factual outcomes of the Iraq–U.S. relationship that were sufficiently negative for the United States to justify using force to resolve them. For instance, there was agreement by virtually everyone that the removal of Saddam Hussein was desirable; critics of the war argue (often implicitly) that his removal was not sufficiently important *to the United States* (arguments that it was important to *Iraqis* were made later) to justify forcibly overthrowing his regime. Supporters of the war argued that the worst-case outcomes—Hussein's providing terrorists with WMDs—violated vital interests or were sufficiently intolerable to the United States to make the invasion necessary.

The boundary between vital and less-than-vital interests is and will always be an important point of contention within the domestic and international security debate, as illustrated in Amplification 3.1. Looking at the basic interests at stake, for instance, there is little disagreement that defending the homeland is vital to the state, and hence challenges to that interest will be met by force. Responding to the September 11 attacks clearly follows from this interest. As one goes down the list of basic interests, the question of vitality becomes more debatable. In the Persian Gulf War, for instance, the American interests involved were clearly economic (access to petroleum

Amplification 3.1

FINDING THE BOUNDARY BETWEEN VITAL AND LESS-THAN-VITAL INTERESTS

One of the major alternatives to the definition used here for vital interests is to say that vital interests are any interests worth fighting over. The danger of this definition is that, when reversed, it implies that any time a country is fighting, its vital interests must be engaged. This, of course, is a dubious proposition. But since people employ the distinction, it does mean the boundary between vital and less-than-vital interests is an important one in the study of national security.

Unfortunately, the boundary does not, in any literal sense, exist either in the abstract or regarding specific situations. The reason for this is psychological and subjective. What is an intolerable circumstance for some people may or may not be intolerable for others. One dictionary definition of security, for instance, is "safety or a feeling of safety." Beyond direct physical threats (e.g., a Russian missile or terrorist attack against the American homeland), most threats to security—or situations in which interests are at risk—fall within the psychological range of what makes people feel insecure and hence feel that interests are imperiled. Because people can and do honestly disagree on these matters, the location of the boundary between vital and less-than-vital interests becomes the benchmark in the national security debate over when to use force.

If one applies this abstract notion to the contemporary trouble spots in the world identified by the Bush administration as constituting the "axis of evil," the question to ask in each case is, How intolerable would the worst possible outcome be to American interests, and thus would one be willing to use force to ensure that worst outcome does not occur? If you compare your assessments with others, you will likely find there are instances of large-scale consensus: most would endorse the use of force if Iraq invaded Kuwait again; there would probably be less support for military action against North Korea or Iran. How important are these countries—specifically, their alleged programs to gain weapons of mass destruction—to the United States? What actions are warranted against them? Which interests are vital and which are less than vital?

energy that literally fuels the American economy). Interestingly, control of or guaranteed access to Iraqi oil (to which the United States had been denied access since 1972) may be an outcome in Iraq that would qualify as fulfilling a U.S. vital interest.

The activation of concern over vital interests occurs in situations of scarcity, where more than one claimant to a scarce resource asserts that claim as an interest. Scarcity, for present purposes is the situation in which all claimants to a resource cannot simultaneously have all that they want (or feel they need). The definition, of course, is drawn from economics, and economic resources such as wealth are indeed one obvious arena where scarcity may occur. Scarcity may also be political (political power or office when more than one individual wants the position), social (everyone cannot, by definition, be part of the elite), or physical (possession of a piece of disputed territory or access to a natural resource like water). Conflicts over vital interests are activated when competing parties put forward incompatible claims to a scarce resource and insist on a quantity of the resource that does not allow the other party to have as much of the resource as they deem necessary.

A historical example may illustrate the point. In the 1850s, as the United States expanded west toward the Pacific Ocean, it came into direct conflict with Great Britain over where the northern boundary of the United States and the southern border of Canada should lie. The Americans claimed parts of what is now Canada (Vancouver Island, for instance), and the British claimed parts of what is now Washington and Oregon. Clearly, both countries could not simultaneously possess the disputed territories, establishing their scarcity, and both sides deemed the outcome too important for compromise. At one point, there was even the threat of war by the American side under the slogan "Fifty-four Forty or Fight," the geographic latitude of the proposed American boundary. Ultimately, of course, the present boundary was negotiated without the recourse to violence.

Two final concepts about vital interests and sovereignty bear mention: because vital interests are so important, the state is unwilling to accept contrary judgments about its interests when it can avoid them. As a result, the state is unwilling to submit disputes to a higher authority (a sovereign above the state) for fear such an authority might rule against the state in an unacceptable manner that would have to be disobeyed or ignored in order to ensure an acceptable outcome. Vital interests, in other words, are matters that are too important to relinquish control over the outcomes. Having said that, the word "willingly" is part of the definition of vital interests, because when vital interests come into conflict, somebody wins and somebody loses. Usually, it is the weaker party who must unwillingly accept an unacceptable outcome, with the upshot that the interplay of vital interests in a realist world is an exercise in power politics.

Power Politics

International relations is an inherently political enterprise in which the principal political actors are states seeking to maximize their advantage in an environment where all cannot be equally successful. Who gets what is the essence of the political process in this arena. For this purpose, a variation of David Easton's definition of politics will be used: *politics is the ways in which conflicts of interest over scarce resources are resolved.*

This definition contains two related elements. The first is procedural: "the ways in which conflicts . . . are resolved." The second is substantive: what "scarce resources" have to be allocated and who gets those resources. The two dimensions are related both because the nature and importance of the resource may determine the procedures that are employed to decide the outcome, and because the procedures may influence or prejudice the substantive outcome. Generally, the less important the issue (in interest terms discussed earlier, major or peripheral interests), the more likely a state will be either to submit the matter to some outside authority to reach a judgment for an out- come or to accept a less than optimal outcome. When a matter is of the highest impor- tance to the state (a survival or vital interest), then the state is likely to invoke its own sovereign authority to maintain as much control over the outcome as it can.

The unique possession by states of vital interests produces a political structure in which state sovereignty is the central feature in determining political outcomes. As already noted, sovereignty has opposite effects: within states, it provides the basis for producing a political order; among states, sovereignty precludes the formation of polit- ical processes that can authoritatively allocate values in areas deemed vital by the contending parties. The result is international anarchy—at least in dealing with mat- ters of interests vital to the state. As long as states retain vital interests, this essential anarchy will remain the central procedural aspect of international politics.

In the situation of anarchical international relations, states achieve their interests to the extent they have the ability to do so—through a process sometimes known as *self-help*. Since the need to resolve important international political problems gener- ally occurs when vital interests are involved and scarcity exists, the outcome is by def- inition likely to be that one or all parties must accept less of a condition or property than they previously deemed vital. Determining outcomes is thus an exercise in the application of power.

Power is an elusive and highly controversial concept, but it is a central charac- teristic of the realist paradigm. Its elusiveness comes from trying to operationalize and measure power in order to predict who will prevail when states clash in the international arena. This difficulty is discussed in Amplification 3.2. If the exercise of power is central to an understanding of international relations, then it clearly would be desirable to be able to observe the basis of power so that one could predict in individual situations which party to a dispute could apply power to the other and thus prevail. This has led to a good deal of effort being expended on trying to de- velop ways to measure the power of states, none of which has proven entirely satis- factory in predicting political outcomes.

Power is also a controversial concept because one of the most obvious and prominent forms that power takes in the international arena (and within some states) is military force. Those who oppose the use of military force thus find them- selves in opposition to a system in which power, including military power, is a central, even normal, way to resolve differences. The key to a more tranquil, peaceful world lies in the abrogation of power as the basis of politics in this view.

Part of the controversy is definitional as well. Although some analysts would say the definition used here really describes influence rather than power, it is possible to adopt a common and straightforward definition of power: *the ability to get someone to*

Amplification 3.2

MEASURING POWER

Although the concept of power is pervasive as a means to describe international relations, efforts to measure it have remained largely elusive. As noted in the main text, finding ways adequately to measure and thus to be able to compare the power that different states possess would be highly desirable because it would make the outcomes of interactions between states much more predictable than they are in fact.

There are two difficulties involved. The first is finding physical measures that adequately describe the abilities of states to influence one another. A concerted effort has been to try to find concrete, physical measures, such as the size or sophistication of countries' armed forces or the productivity of states' industrial bases, that should indicate which is the more powerful country in any head-to-head confrontation. The problem is that such measures work only part of the time. There is, for instance, no physical measurement to compare national capabilities that would lead to the conclusion that North Vietnam had any chance of defeating the United States in a war, but they certainly did.

The second problem is that measures have difficulty getting at the psychological dimension of will and commitment that people may possess. How can an outside observer determine, for instance, when a clash of interests is clearly more important to one party to a dispute than it is to the other (at least before the fact)? Once again, the Vietnam War is illustrative. The outcome of that war—unification of the country—was clearly more important to the North Vietnamese and their southern allies than its avoidance was to the United States and the population of South Vietnam. This is clear in retrospect; it was not at all clear before and even during the conduct of hostilities. Being able to see clearly after the fact is of very little comfort to the policy maker. Having measures that accurately predict the future is a far greater value.

do something he or she would not otherwise do. The definition skirts the controversy over measurement of power by not specifying what power *is* so much as describing the *effects* of the application of power.

The definition highlights two major characteristics of a power situation. First, it says that power is not an attribute possessed by parties so much as it is a relationship between an entity seeking to exercise power and another entity seeking to resist the application of that power. A power relationship is commonly applied through the issuance of a threat (a promise to do something harmful unless what is demanded is complied with) by one party against the other. The outcome depends on the action of the threatened party. If the threatened party believes the threatening party both can (has the capability) and will (has the credibility) to carry out the threat in the face of noncompliance, the threatened party may comply. If, however, the threatened party doubts either the will or the ability of the threatening party to carry out the threat, it may conclude differently. At any rate, whether power is successfully applied is a mutual matter in the relationship between the parties, not something simple and concrete like a comparison of the sizes of military machines or industrial capacity (although these are clearly relevant when deciding if the threatening party has the wherewithal to carry out the threat).

The other characteristic of a power relationship is that it is situation-specific. What this means is that the application of power does not occur in an abstract sense but within very specific situations. It is important to recognize this fact because the vagaries and special circumstances surrounding any particular relationship may influence how a power relationship plays out, sometimes in unpredictable ways.

An example helps illustrate these characteristics. In the early 1970s, the African country of Uganda was ruled by a particularly harsh and objectionable ruler, Idi Amin Dada. Amin, a sergeant in the British colonial force who declared himself a general when Uganda achieved independence in 1962, had seized power from the postcolonial government in 1971. He had as many as three hundred thousand Ugandans of tribal origins other than his own killed, and in 1972, forty-five thousand Asian residents, who had formed the backbone of the country's commercial system were expelled. As the country drifted toward chaos, the United States withdrew its diplomatic personnel from Uganda in 1973. Despite this, Amin continued to provide gratuitous advice to President Richard M. Nixon in a series of letters advising Nixon about how he should handle his Watergate difficulties.

The United States—as well as a number of other countries—wanted Amin removed from the Ugandan presidency. Since Amin was not amenable to leaving, this meant that power would have to be applied to get Amin to do something he clearly would not otherwise do. The problem was, What kind of power did the United States have over the dictator? By any objective measure, the United States was overwhelmingly more powerful than Uganda, but was that power relevant to the specific situation of overthrowing him? Was there some form of leverage the United States could apply to remove Amin? Was American power relevant in this case?

The answer turned out to be that it was not. To try to achieve its goal, the United States threatened and implemented an embargo on the importation of Ugandan coffee into the United States (a prohibition ignored by the American firms that bought Ugandan coffee until they were caught violating the sanctions), but the volume was not enough to cause Amin to step down. In the end, Ugandan rebels, assisted by the neighboring Tanzanian armed forces, which possessed far less absolute but much more relevant and believable power than the Americans, finally managed to drive Amin out of power and into exile in April 1979.

It is the combination of capability and will that makes power effective in individual situations. In the Ugandan example, for instance, the United States clearly had the military capability to overthrow the Ugandan regime (or for that matter, obliterate it with nuclear weapons). What it lacked was the credible will to apply that force in a situation that was at most annoying but clearly did not rise to the level of vital interests.

In order to exercise power, however, the state must be capable of carrying out threats. Doing this requires possessing the *instruments of power*. In conventional, traditional terms, these instruments are divided into three categories: diplomatic (or political), economic, and military power. Diplomatic power encompasses qualities such as the persuasiveness of a country's diplomatic corps, the attractiveness of the country's political profile, and the ability to use the other implements to back up political rhetoric. Economic power is the use of economic rewards and deprivations for compliance with a country's demands. Military power is the threat or actual use of military threats or applications to achieve the country's goals. As noted in Chapter 2, one of the reasons for designating the United States as the sole remaining superpower is that it is the only country with significant assets in each of these categories, although the characteristics of power noted here do not mean its power is unchallengeable in individual situations.

Some authors, as suggested earlier, believe the list of instruments should be extended in the contemporary environment. A leading candidate is informational power, the ability to control and manipulate the amount and quality of information an adversary has in a power situation. Elements of this power include information-gathering ability (intelligence) and manipulation (interrupting information sources and transmission or distorting that flow). Information is so important that some analysts argue that intelligence should be considered an independent instrument of power. An exotic form, *cyberwar*, attempts to disrupt and control computer systems and their ability to collect, analyze, disseminate, or even retain information.

In an anarchical system, power and politics are intimately related. Politics, after all, is about who gets what in terms of scarce resources, and by definition, scarcity means that some parties will have to do what they otherwise prefer not to do. In the absence of authorities who can decide on allocations, the parties must help themselves through the application of power, including the use of military force on occasion.

PARADIGM SUMMARY

With these basic concepts and relationships established, the "rules of the road" that define the realist paradigm and how international relations are conducted in a system where its rules are paramount can be summarized. While a growing number of people decry the paradigm and its implications, it remains the basis on which a great deal of international relations are conducted today. Moreover, the paradigm is especially applicable to thinking about matters of national security and remains dominant as an operational road map for those charged with the development and conduct of national security policy in most parts of the world.

The realist paradigm begins with state sovereignty as its basic value, meaning there can ultimately be no higher authority than the state in determining what happens to the state. The absence of a higher authority is not coincidental but is the direct result of the possession of vital interests by states (but not other political entities). These vital interests are matters of such importance to the state that it will not willingly compromise on them and will use all means available, up to and including military force, to ensure that they are honored. The two concepts, sovereignty and vital interests, require and reinforce one another. The prosecution of vital interests in an anarchical system precludes the possibility that a superior authority could—possibly capriciously—compromise a vital interest of the state. Sovereignty provides the conceptual bedrock to deny that possibility, and it is not coincidental at all that the governments of countries are among the strongest and most consistent champions of sovereignty.

The government of the United States has been and continues to be among the world's staunchest defenders of state sovereignty, and at the bottom of almost all its defenses of the concept is the insistence that no outside power should be allowed to create conditions to which Americans do not want to and should not be subjected. Although this insistence often puts the United States in awkward, even embarrassing, international situations, it is the fear that a dilution of sovereignty will permit the violation of American vital interests that provides the politically inviolable base for U.S. policy in this area.

In a world of plenty, the state of international anarchy would not be a particular problem because states would rarely come into direct conflict with one another over who gets what. In the real world, of course, scarcity, not abundance, is often the case, meaning that political processes to determine outcomes of disagreemens are necessary. Sometimes those conflicts can be resolved peacefully and cooperatively, sometimes not. When these situations involve the vital interests of states, those states are generally unwilling to submit them to bodies that could exercise jurisdiction and instead rely on more informal means of conflict resolution to settle differences. Settlements in conditions of scarcity mean that some or all of the parties to a given dispute must accept less than they would have preferred—in other words, do something they would prefer not to do. Because of this, international politics inevitably is power politics.

In a world of sovereign states interacting through power politics, the state succeeds to the extent it can succeed—that is, through self-help. In order for one state to get others to do what it wants but the others do not, that state must possess the ability, in specific situations, to convince or compel other states to act in ways that serve its national interests. A state must, in other words, possess power to succeed.

Power comes in a variety of guises. The most common, but not only, forms are political or diplomatic power, economic power, and military power. While the applicability of any particular form of power will vary depending on the situation and both the ability the willingness of a state to use its power to gain compliance with its positions, generally speaking, the more power a state has, the more successful it will be in achieving its ends. In the anarchical situation of international politics, among the forms of power that must be available is military force. Thus, the international system ultimately is an environment in which the threat of or recourse to force is a "normal" activity some of the time and in which states that will succeed must possess armed forces "to prepare for and fight the country's wars," in military idiom.

CRITIQUES AND ANOMALIES
OF THE REALIST PARADIGM

Many analysts decry the sets of conditions produced by the realist paradigm and point both to anomalies that it produces in the interactions among states and to questions about its continuing empirical adequacy in describing international reality. To the critics, there is simply too much that occurs in the world that cannot be explained by realism, and thus the day-to-day debate about national security policy must be expanded beyond realism.

An exhaustive criticism of the realist paradigm goes beyond present intent. For present purposes, the criticisms can be viewed from two perspectives. One of these argues that the principles underlying the realist paradigm, and especially state sovereignty, have never been as strictly adhered to in fact as they are in principle—in other words, the paradigm is only partially accurate in describing the operation of the world system. The other perspective maintains that adherence to the paradigm produces a flawed international system—in other words, the paradigm's effects are pernicious. In both cases, the conclusion drawn by the critics is that the international system should be reformed on principles other than those on which the paradigm is based.

Critiques

Because state sovereignty lies at the heart of the Westphalian system, it is the realist concept that draws the greatest negative attention. The principle of state sovereignty creates an international institutional setting of purposive anarchy that necessitates a world of power politics and guarantees that international relations will emphasize conflict rather than cooperation. The critics maintain that state sovereignty has never been as absolute as its extreme representation would suggest. However, the more closely one hews to the practice of absolute sovereignty, the more pernicious the effects are within the international realm. The basic underlying theme of this critique is that realism is *empirically* inadequate to describe the world, a position increasingly held in academic and policy circles.

Early political theorists like Hobbes and Bodin favored something like the absolute sovereign powers of the state as a way to justify the power of monarchs. The suggestion that the principle of sovereignty results in an impenetrable state of authority that is unaffected or unlimited by outside forces is not, and never has been, more than a fiction. States interfere in the political lives of other states all the time, and the behavior of states is limited by international regulations (usually ones that they have explicitly agreed to be limited by) on a regular basis. Moreover, contemporary forces such as economic globalization and the impact of the telecommunications revolution are making state boundaries increasingly porous and state control over everything that happens within its jurisdiction increasingly difficult to maintain. Critics of sovereignty argue it is empirically false to maintain otherwise. Moreover, important trends in international relations suggest that sovereignty will continue to erode in fact, if not in principle. The staunch defense of absolute sovereignty is, in other words, a losing battle.

As sovereignty erodes, so does the salience of some of the operating principles of the paradigm, and this is nowhere truer than in areas related to national security and the use of force. It is, for instance, not at all clear that some uses of military force to achieve national interests are as acceptable today as they were a century or even a decade ago. Wars between states have virtually ceased. (The American invasion of Iraq was a notable exception.) All members of the United Nations renounced their right to declare war as part of their conditions for joining the world body, and although that does not mean that force has disappeared, no state has formally declared war on another state since World War II. As the international response to Iraq's 1990 invasion and conquest of Kuwait clearly demonstrated, the aggressive use of force across borders is no longer acceptable behavior. The issue of acceptability is, of course, not universal and is related to power. Iraq's action was deemed an unacceptable act of aggression against Kuwaiti sovereignty and was reversed. The failure of American efforts to influence the policies of Iraq after 1990 (see Amplification 3.3), which eventuated in the American invasion and conquest of Iraq in 2003, showed American power short of the application of the military instrument of power to be ineffective.

Amplification 3.3

THE LIMITS OF POWER: DEALING WITH SADDAM

With the possible exception of Fidel Castro, no leader in recent memory vexed American policy and policy makers more than Saddam Hussein of Iraq prior to his capture trial, and execution. He became a major irritant when he invaded and annexed Kuwait in 1990, forcing the United States to take the leadership in forming the coalition that evicted the Iraqis from Kuwait in 1991. After the Persian Gulf War fighting ended, a series of demands were placed upon Hussein that, by and large, he refused to comply with. A review of the difficulty the United States had influencing Saddam Hussein helps illustrate the limits of power.

In the years after the Persian Gulf War, U.S. policy toward Iraq and Saddam Hussein had at least three goals, all of which the Iraqi leader refused to accept. The first and most obvious goal was his physical removal from power. The second was the abandonment of Iraq's program of developing weapons of mass destruction (WMD), including comprehensive inspection of suspected WMD production facilities. The third was to leave the Kurdish and Shiite minorities, who rose to overthrow Hussein with American encouragement in 1991, alone.

The problem was how to force Hussein to comply with these conditions, which was a question of having the appropriate instruments of power in this particular situation. To try to bring Hussein down before the ultimate invasion of Iraq, the United States attempted to employ the diplomatic/political instrument of power, sponsoring international condemnation of the Iraqi regime in international forums like the United Nations and supporting political alternatives to Hussein in Iraq (the Bush administration, for instance, proposed $92 million in aid to political alternatives in 2001). Economically, the United States was the mainstay behind economic sanctions designed to gain compliance with the WMD ban. Militarily, the United States and Britain (France previously participated but has dropped out) enforced the so-called no-fly zones over the Kurdish and Shiite regions of the country under the banner of Operations Northern and Southern Watch.

The difficulty was that, with the partial exception of the application of the military instrument of power in defense of the Kurds and Shiites, none of the attempts to apply power worked. International condemnations were ineffective, and there was growing opposition to continuing them. Hussein had most of his opponents killed or chased into exile, making the identification and nurturing of "moderate" alternatives difficult. The economic sanctions, as is often the case, caused well-publicized hardship to innocent women and children rather than to the leadership (the so-called principle of punishing the innocent), did not force compliance, and were increasingly opposed by the international community, which wanted them lifted. Moreover, the sanctions made smuggling into Iraq rampant. Operations Northern and Southern Watch kept the Kurds and Shiites reasonably safe, but they were open-ended commitments that, if abandoned, would almost certainly have resulted in swift, savage suppression of those they were designed to protect. Moreover, wider bombing campaigns such as Operation Desert Fox in 1999 failed to change Hussein's behavior.

The relationship between Saddam Hussein and the most powerful country in the world during the 1990s and up to 2003 demonstrated clearly the limits of power. By any measure, the United States was more powerful than Iraq, yet American power proved inappropriate in forcing the defiant Iraqi leader to do things he did not want to do but that the United States would have had him do. Ultimately, only the invasion and conquest of Iraq provided adequate power for the United States to impose its will on Hussein.

The other major manifestation of the realist paradigm that is under question is the use of vital interests as the benchmark against which to measure when force should and should not be employed. This assault is largely the result of changes in the international threat environment since the end of the Cold War, and particularly the result of what I call the *interest–threat mismatch*—the situation in which important interests and threats do not coincide.

During the Cold War, when the realist paradigm was clearly the dominant worldview of policy makers on both sides of the conflict, there was no mismatch: vital interests (national survival, for instance) were threatened, and thus the idea that force would be threatened or used in East–West confrontations provided clear guidance for the development, deployment, and potential employment of force. Interests, and threats to those interests, were clearly aligned and coincided with one another.

The situation changed radically after the implosion of the Communist half of the Cold War. The important interests of the United States remain what they were before: American homeland security and a free and democratic Western Europe and Northeast Asia with which the United States can engage in commerce and political relations, for instance. What changed was that those vital interests were essentially no longer threatened. There is no Communist menace hanging over Western Europe; the West Europeans move steadily to incorporate more and more of formerly Communist Europe into institutions such as the European Union. Thus, where there were American vital interests, there was no meaningful threat that would justify the use of force—important interests and threats were misaligned.

There were and are, however, situations in the world that are threatening to the United States or the international system more generally. For instance, a whole series of internal wars rage in parts of the developing world, notably in Africa and parts of Asia. Indonesia, the world's fourth most populous country, has several ongoing conflicts the basic purpose of which is secession from the Indonesian republic, as well as terrorists who want to impose an Islamic fundamentalist state on the archipelago. In Africa, the HIV–AIDS pandemic has reached such enormous proportions that in 2000 then President Clinton declared it to be a national security concern, an emphasis that the Bush administration continued through the personal concern of former Secretary of State Colin Powell.

What these and other examples of world problems share is that essentially none of them reaches to the level of being vital interests that would activate the American security system within the realist framework. In terms of interests at stake, they are mostly favorable world order or value questions at the intensity level of major or, in most cases, peripheral interests to the United States. Threats do not measure up to important interests.

The interest–threat mismatch takes form from this assessment of the post–Cold War environment: *the most important American interests in the world are hardly threatened, and the threats that do exist are largely tangential (are hardly interesting).* International religious terrorism, of course, is the obvious exception to this observation. In these circumstances, if the realist paradigm is used as the sole (or main) criterion to determine when or if the United States will employ force in the world, the result will be paralytic because hardly any situations will meet the criterion of engaging vital interests and thus justifying force. During the Cold War, the realist paradigm was the hawk's standard because it counseled large and robust forces to deal with real threats to vital interests. In the post–Cold War world, that same paradigm turned the hawks into doves, since the paradigm directs non-involvement with military force when vital interests are not threatened. The post–September 11 response to international terrorism, of course, realigns interests and threats in that area of concern. The main problem is not the existence of the threat, but how to counter and remove it. For instance, it is not clear to what extent military power is the appropriate instrument to deal with this threat (see discussion in Chapter 12).

An example drawn from the 1990s may demonstrate how a part of the changing environment affects the relevance of the realist paradigm. One of the major sources of violence and instability in the world is the series of very bloody internal (civil) wars occurring in parts of the developing world. A number of these conflicts (e.g., Somalia, Bosnia, Sierra Leone, East Timor) went beyond the ability of the countries involved to resolve, resulting in great suffering to the affected civilian populations (casualty rates in these conflicts often approach 90 percent civilian). The gruesome nature of these conflicts led to international pleas for involvement with military forces designed to stop the fighting and suffering under the guise of something like *humanitarian intervention*. These conflicts generally occured in places where important American interests were absent, and the application of the realist paradigm would suggest that the United States remain aloof. The only way to justify the employment of force was either to ignore or expand the paradigm or to try to rationalize that heretofore less-than-vital interests were now more important (e.g., "Macedonia is important to the United States because it is important to American allies"). In these cases, application of the paradigm led to unacceptably inhumane results; only its modification allowed implementation of acceptable policies.

The salience of the realist paradigm in describing reality is not the only source of opposition by critics. To a large number of interested observers, the paradigm is objectionable both because of the activities it legitimizes and because of the kinds of viewpoints it deemphasizes. The most obvious objectionable activity is the acceptance, even promotion, of military force as a normal form of state action; the most obvious example of what it does not emphasize is cooperative behavior among states.

The realist paradigm legitimizes the recourse to armed violence as a means to achieve state interests by acknowledging military force as one of the normal instruments of power. In addition, the approach's emphasis on observation of "reality" (actual behavior of states) notes that states (and groups within states) do in fact occasionally resort to the use of force to achieve their ends and that in some cases they succeed in achieving their ends by doing so—the ends justify the means. Many realists would contend, for instance, that the attempt by the idealists to downplay and even ignore the role of military forces between the world wars contributed to the destabilization of the 1930s that ended with World War II. Moreover, given the predatory nature of some states (Bush's "axis of evil" is an example), the absence of force is a virtual invitation for states to take advantage of the militarily disadvantaged.

Opponents of realism contend that it is the very structure of an international system based in the realist paradigm that creates—even promotes—an emphasis on military force and the recourse to war. The villain, of course, is sovereignty-induced anarchy that leaves international politics a Hobbesian "war of all against all." In this view, the solution to the "problem" of war is institutional reform of the international system that creates orderliness through institutions that can enforce the peace and remove the vigilantism of a realist order. In order to accomplish this, the conceptual victim must be state sovereignty, replaced with ultimate authority either in the hands of a superior entity (e.g., a world government or the like) or returned to the people—popular sovereignty. At any rate, the object is the sovereign state, which the opponents of war argue must be fundamentally reformed before peace can be instituted and enforced.

In addition to its alleged warlike implications, other critics point out, the principle of state sovereignty also tends to emphasize noncooperative rather than cooperative behavior in the relations among states more generally by erecting barriers to interaction across state boundaries. For instance, the sovereign independence of states, it is argued, runs counter to the growing globalization of the world's economy by erecting physical barriers to the movement of people and goods across sovereign boundaries. This argument has particular salience in an age of terrorism when the protection of boundaries is an important part of protecting citizens from attack, a proposition that will be investigated in terms of its national security implications. Because examples of international cooperation are numerous and growing, the inability of strict realism to explain these exceptions to its anarchical, conflictual description of the world raises questions about its adequacy as an intellectual ordering device.

This line of objection can be put in a more general and theoretical form. Realism as an approach tends to emphasize the conflictual elements of international relations and to downplay evidence of international cooperation. While conflict is clearly an element of international relations, so too is international cooperation. There are certainly aspects of international interactions that are zero-sum (one party loses what the other party gains), but there are equally positive-sum situations (where both parties can gain). Those critical of realism argue that realists dismiss the cooperative aspects too often and that an approach placing great emphasis on cooperation not only results in a more accurate description of international relations, but also leads to the promotion of a greater level of cooperation and thus enhanced international tranquility.

In some ways, this difference goes back to the disagreement in the philosophies of Thomas Hobbes and John Locke (among others) about the nature of man and society. The realists portray a more Hobbesian world (indeed, some of the early realists explicitly included their assessment of man's base nature as flawed as part of the philosophical underpinning of their theorizing), whereas those who emphasize cooperation are manifesting a more Lockean philosophy (wherein people enter into society out of a positive desire for association with their fellows). In more contemporary terms, the debate can be couched in terms of which is the dominant international reality, globalization (cooperation) or geopolitics (conflict), or some combination—which, of course, is an underlying theme of this book.

Anomalies

There are also anomalies in an international system that is built on the philosophical basis of realism but that in practice does not precisely conform in its operation to the realist mold. Two examples, one American and one Russian, illustrate both the paradigm and its inconsistencies and difficulties.

As noted earlier, the United States joins the People's Republic of China as one of the staunchest defenders of the principle of state sovereignty in the world. The political and philosophical base of this strongly held position is the belief that Americans and the United States more generally should not be subject to imposition or control by foreigners and that, as a result, the United States should resist international attempts to place the United States under regimes that restrict the freedom of action of the country or its people.

Regardless of its merits, this position often forces the United States into a politically uncomfortable position in the world—often in opposition to the vast majority of other states and in the company of states with which it does not particularly like to be associated. Invariably, these situations involve American resistance or refusal to join international agreements that limit the right of signatories to engage in certain behavior (and are most ominous when the treaty includes provisions for international enforcement—a direct abrogation of sovereignty). Ironically, the agreements to which the United States objects are often proposed by the U.S. government itself (either the permanent bureaucracy or a previous administration), indicating substantial disagreement within the United States itself on the sovereignty issue.

The Bush administration's withdrawal of support for the Kyoto treaty on global warming in 2001 is an example of this situation. The treaty was negotiated and supported by the Clinton administration, which had announced its intention to join the international regime created by the accord. When he entered office, President Bush announced his administration's withdrawal from the agreement. Bush did not cite sovereignty directly but instead argued against what he called unequal and unfair obligations the United States would be forced to bear under treaty provisions and its preference for voluntary rather than mandatory compliance enforced internationally. The United States stands virtually alone among developed countries in its position and has earned a good deal of international criticism for its unilateralist stance.

The anomaly extends to a number of other issues. During the latter 1940s, the United States helped sponsor two important treaties establishing universal standards of human rights, the Universal Declaration on Human Rights and the Convention on Genocide. The Universal Declaration, in particular, was based largely on the American Bill of Rights, but the U.S. Senate refused to provide advice and consent on either document until the 1990s on the ground that they infringed on the rights of the American government to behave in ways prohibited by the agreements. In more contemporary, national security–related areas, the United States is one of the few countries that refuses to sign the international treaty banning land mines (which was originally proposed by a private American citizen) and the statute establishing a permanent war crimes tribunal, the International Criminal Court (ICC). In the latter case, the United States joins a handful of generally rogue states such as Myanmar and Iraq as the only states that refuse to accept the jurisdiction of the ICC.

The United States is not alone in being party to anomalies in the current system. Russia, which has acceded to the ICC, has for a decade been waging an arguably genocidal campaign in the renegade province of Chechnya, which has been actively attempting to secede from the Russian Federation since the middle 1990s. The Russians have brutally repressed this movement, and war crimes have clearly been committed under orders that possibly go all the way to the top of the Russian political leadership. Yet there have been no serious calls for an investigation of the situation by the international war crimes apparatus. Why? One reason is that Russia maintains the situation in Chechnya is purely an internal matter within the sovereign jurisdiction of the Russian government (and thus beyond the purview of any other authority). For another, Russia maintains its Muslim Chechen opponents are terrorists, since many of the "freedom fighters" waging the war allegedly are associated with the training regime in Afghanistan that produced Al Qaeda terrorists (thus giving the Russians status as participants in the war against terrorism). Finally,

Russia is also a large and powerful country that no one wishes to antagonize unnecessarily, so the position goes officially unchallenged.

The staunch American defense of sovereignty and the ambivalence Americans display when anomalous issues arise from its defense often confuse and mystify other countries, including both American friends and foes. Defying international norms in the name of defending American freedom of action is often equated with American unilateralism—a kind of disregard for the rest of the world. This was clearly the case in the early George W. Bush administration. Beyond reaction to the Kyoto convention, this was evident in 2001 regarding the administration's obdurately defended intention to field a national missile defense in the face of essentially universal opposition from abroad, in addition to opposition to the ICC and the land mines convention.

Defense of sovereign prerogative is also a politically partisan position in the United States, adding to international confusion. Although there are exceptions, the strongest advocates of protecting American sovereignty have tended to be conservative and Republican, whereas a willingness to subject the United States to sovereignty-restricting provisions of international agreements has tended to be more liberal and Democratic. On other than trade matters, the Democratic Party has been more internationalist than the Republicans, meaning there is a likelihood that the transition in control between the parties will continue to have a real impact on attitudes toward international issues with ramifications for American state sovereignty across time.

CONCLUSION: THE REALIST PARADIGM TODAY

Despite its limitations and the mounting criticism of it, realism remains the dominant organizational device by which the governments of sovereign states organize their approach to dealing with the world. The criticisms are, without doubt, growing. During the Cold War, these criticisms tended to be isolated within groups outside national governments—academics, liberal commentators, and members and advocates of NGOs, for example. Given the gravity of the task of managing international affairs in a world where the Soviet opponent was thoroughly committed to realist power politics, advocacies of ideas such as reducing the influence of sovereignty fell on mostly deaf ears, particularly among political decision makers responsible for protecting national interests in a dangerous world where the Soviet opponents were the ultimate realists. Communism could only be opposed in kind, according to the prevailing wisdom.

A less threatening, apparently more globalizing environment in the 1990s saw critical, less realist views become more acceptable in practice and in principle. At one level, the series of interventions in peacekeeping roles by U.N.-deputized forces represented an indirect assault on the notion of total sovereign control of territory. International agreements like the ban on land mines and the establishment of the permanent war crimes tribunal are more direct assaults, as they subjugate the rights of states to act unilaterally in the face of international norms. Some see this trend as a healthy maturing of international relations. Others see grave dangers in these erosions of state sovereignty and assaults on the structure of the Westphalian order.

The Clinton administration was more receptive to change; the Bush administration has proven less so, a predilection reinforced after the terrorist incident of 2001 and responses to it.

Does the realist paradigm fit the new, evolving international order? Any direct, categorical answer will, of course, oversimplify a more complicated world order in which yes-no answers exclude the middle ground between them and result in a distortion of ongoing reality. Cold War realism may not be the perfect paradigm for a post–Cold War and post–September 11 world, but its basic structure has not disappeared. The fault line that began to emerge in 1989 raised questions about the continuing relevance of the paradigm; such criticism has been much less evident since 2001. The *Challenge!* box "Justifying the U.S. Invasion of Iraq," offer one view of that relevance.

Challenge!

Justifying the U.S. Invasion of Iraq

Should the United States have invaded Iraq in 2003? What justifications were made in support of the decision? What does the realist paradigm tell us about whether or not the action was justified?

According to the arguments made by the U.S. government in 2003, the invasion was justified by the threat posed by the Saddam Hussein government to the United States and the rest of the world community. Stated that way, the criteria of the realist paradigm clearly can be applied to judging the decision. The assertion of a threat raises two questions by which the decision to invade can be judged. One is the truth of the threats asserted: Were the statements of threat accurate? Did the Iraqi government have the capability and intention to carry them out? The second is the adequacy of the threats to compel military action: Were the threats to vital or less-than-vital American interests?

At the time, the U.S. government made two interrelated claims about the Iraqi government of Saddam Hussein that it maintained constituted an adequate threat. The first was Iraq's possession of weapons of mass destruction (WMD): chemical and biological weapons and an alleged program to produce nuclear weapons. Given the instability of the Iraqi government and its hostility to the United States, these were asserted to pose a threat to American soil. The second was Iraq's purported ties to terrorism—and specifically to Al Qaeda—and thus an Iraqi link to the war on terrorism. The link between the two justifications was the possibility that the Iraqi government would supply its WMD to terrorist organizations like Al Qaeda.

When war was being contemplated, the truth of these assertions was publicly unknown, and evidence for both their truth and falsity was and continues to be debated. Although both lines of argumentation have since been essentially discredited, policy makers were generally given the benefit of the doubt, and most Americans at least *believed* the assertions to be true (an assumption that has come to be widely questioned as criticism of the war has mounted). In that case, did removing these threats rise to the level of a vital interest? Put another way, would Americans and their interests have been so compromised by the possession of WMD by Iraq and ties to terrorism to justify the recourse to force? What happens to the presumption of vitality of interest if one justification was true and the other false: Iraq had WMD but no ties to terrorism, or it had ties to terrorists but no WMD? What if both were false?

Was invading Iraq justified? What do you think?

A remarkable example may illustrate the evolution of the realist paradigm. On June 29, 2001, the late Slobadan Milosevic, the former president of Yugoslavia, was extradited from Belgrade to The Hague in the Netherlands, where he faced charges of crimes against humanity as specified in the statute of the ICC, which had issued the indictment under which his extradition was carried out (since the ICC statute had not been ratified by enough states to come into permanent being at the time, the indictment came from the tribunal established specifically for Yugoslavia).

The extradition was the remarkable aspect of the event. Milosevic had been indicted in 1999 for his alleged participation in crimes against humanity committed against Albanian Kosovars in Kosovo in 1999. Although Milosevic was defeated in 2000 in his bid for reelection, it was widely believed that the indictment was symbolic and that any trial of Milosevic would have to be carried out in his absence (*in absentia*) because the Yugoslav government, which was not a signatory of the ICC statute, would protect him on the grounds that any attempt to arrest and extradite him would be a violation of Yugoslav sovereignty. This obstinacy flew in the face of widespread world opinion, which regarded Milosevic as a war criminal—or at least believed he should face the charges against him. International economic sanctions against the country were put in place in 2000 to pressure the government into honoring the indictment.

So what changed the minds of members of the successor Yugoslav government of Vojislav Kostunica and caused them to turn over the former dictator to international authorities? The answer is that several factors, two of which bear mention, were involved and demonstrate the continuity and change of the new order.

The first was domestic and had the effect of eroding resistance to international demands for his surrender to international authorities. While many ethnic Serbs had denied the early charges of atrocities against the Kosovars ordered by the Milosevic government, evidence emerged in 2001 clearly showing that mass murders had been committed that could only be linked to the government in power at the time. Defense of Milosevic became much harder to sustain, and the defense of his freedom based in national sovereignty gradually eroded. In the end, fully 60 percent of the Serbian population of Yugoslavia favored extradition.

The other factor was international, the effect of the sanctions imposed by the international community because of the Yugoslav campaign in Kosovo. The people of Yugoslavia became more intolerant of the physical deprivation they were enduring as a result of the sanctions than they were committed to their sovereign control and protection of the former leader. The NATO allies promised the Kostunica government that economic penalties would be lifted as soon as Milosevic was turned over to authorities; it was hardly a day after he reached The Hague that economic assistance began to flow to Belgrade.

So which principle prevailed? Geopolitics or the new order of globalization? The answer is clearly both. The international norm was strengthened by the fact that Yugoslavia relented and allowed the dilution of some of its sovereign jurisdiction over a distinguished citizen, hardly a vindication of the realist paradigm. At the same time, what caused the international norm to succeed was the application of the economic instrument of power in a way that would make the most hardened realist proud. Regarding Milosevic personally, he died of natural causes a week before his trial was scheduled to be completed in 2006.

STUDY/DISCUSSION QUESTIONS

1. How do American exceptionalism, isolationism, and ambivalence toward the international system influence the American view of national security? Elaborate, using Kosovo and Cuba as examples.
2. What is realism? What is the realist paradigm, and how does it serve as both a theory of international relations and a guide to action for policy makers?
3. What are the key concepts in the realist paradigm? How do they form a syllogism that dictates that states must possess and occasionally use armed force?
4. Define and discuss the primary concepts of realism: sovereignty, vital interests, and power politics. Why is the boundary between vital and less-than-vital interests so critical in the area of national security?
5. What are the principal objections to the realist paradigm? Discuss each. What anomalies does strict defense of the realist paradigm create for U.S. policy?
6. Using the realist paradigm as your organizational tool, construct arguments for and against the Iraq War. Compare them. Which do you find most convincing? Why?

SELECTED BIBLIOGRAPHY

Art, Robert A., and Kenneth N. Waltz. *The Use of Force: Military Power and International Politics.* Lanham, MD: Rowman and Littlefield, 2004.

Bodin, Jean. *Six Books on the Commonwealth.* Oxford, UK: Basil Blackwell, 1955.

Brodie, Bernard. *War and Politics.* New York: Macmillan, 1973.

Carr, E. H. *The Twenty Years' Crisis, 1919–1939.* London: Macmillan, 1939.

Cusimano, Mary Ann (ed.). *Beyond Sovereignty.* New York: Bedford St. Martinís, 1999.

Fromkin, David. *The Independence of Nations.* New York: Praeger Special Studies, 1981.

Grotius, Hugo. *The Rights of War and Peace: Including the Law of Nature and Nations.* New York: M. W. Dunne, 1981.

Hashemi, Sohail H. (ed.). *State Sovereignty: Change and Persistence in International Relations.* University Park, PA: Pennsylvania State University Press, 1997.

Hobbes, Thomas. *Leviathan.* Oxford, UK: Clarendon, 1989.

Kegley, Charles W., Jr., and Gregory A. Raymond. *Exorcising the Ghost of Westphalia: Building World Order in the New Millennium.* Upper Saddle River, NJ: Prentice Hall, 2002.

Locke, John. *Two Treatises on Government.* New York: Cambridge University Press, 1988.

Lyons, Gene M., and Michael Mastanduno (eds.). *Beyond Westphalia: State Sovereignty and International Relations*. Baltimore, MD: Johns Hopkins University Press, 1995.

Machiavelli, Niccolo. *The Prince*. Irving, TX: University of Dallas Press, 1984.

Mills, Kurt. *Human Rights in the Emerging Global Order: A New Sovereignty*. New York: St. Martin's Press, 1998.

Morgenthau, Hans J. *Politics Among Nations* (6th ed., revised: Kenneth W. Thompson). New York: Alfred A. Knopf, 1985.

Nuechterlein, Donald E. *America Recommitted: United States National Interests in a Reconstructed World*. Lexington: University of Kentucky Press, 1991.

Schelling, Thomas. *Arms and Influence*. New Haven, CT: Yale University Press, 1966.

Snow, Donald M., and Eugene Brown. *International Relations: The Changing Contours of Power*. New York: Longman, 2000.

Snyder, Jack. "One World, Rival Theories." *Foreign Policy* (November/December 2004), 52–62.

Thucydides. *The History of the Peloponnesian Wars*. New York: Penguin Books, 1954.

Waltz, Kenneth. *Man, the State, and War: A Theoretical Analysis*. New York: Columbia University Press, 1959.

CHAPTER 4

The American Experience

PREVIEW

The extent to which a country embraces a purely geopolitical, realist, or some alternative orientation toward the world is influenced by the generalized historical experience the country has had. For most of American history, that experience has been primarily positive, with low levels and qualities of threat that make the current high-threat environment all the more distinct. This chapter begins by identifying general influences on the American experience and then looks at the question historically, designating and describing three parts of the national security experience. The chapter concludes with suggestions of how the past may influence the present and future.

As it is in all countries, the American attitude toward its security is conditioned by its historical experience and the "lessons" that experience appears to have taught. For some countries, the experience has been harsh. It is, for instance, impossible for the citizens of any country on the northern European plain not to have some historically based fear of a possible invasion against its territory from one direction or another and to view matters of national security very seriously as a result. At the other end of the spectrum, a country like Japan that successfully isolated itself physically from the rest of the world for hundreds of years has an equally distinctive worldview and perception of what constitutes security.

The United States is no exception to the effects of history. Although the American experience is shorter than that of the traditional European and Asian powers, it has been conditioned by a series of factors that are both historic and physical. The result of American history has been a generally positive view of the world and the security of the American place in it that did not require a great deal of emphasis or continuing effort on matters of national security until World War II and its aftermath. Americans have felt secure for most of their history as a country. This general sense of tranquility has certainly accentuated the sense of insecurity most Americans have experienced since September 11, 2001. Insecurity represents more of a discontinuity for the United States than it does for most other countries.

The American experience with national security concerns can be divided into three basic periods. Following a discussion of basic, underlying, conditioning factors that help shape the American worldview, the text begins with the formative period, from the beginning of the republic in the eighteenth century through World War II, a period of relatively low, episodic American involvement in international affairs, including concerns over national security. The second period encompasses the Cold War, when the United States was thrown literally into the middle of the geopolitical fray as one of the two major actors in the international system and had to learn to act in that environment. The chapter concludes with a discussion of the third period, the contemporary system, and the impact of the two major fault lines on the ongoing period. The discussion includes consideration of how the current situation resembles aspects of the formative or the Cold War system.

CONDITIONING FACTORS IN THE AMERICAN TRADITION

At least three factors stand out as important influences on the way Americans have come to view questions of defense and national security. Alternative lists could undoubtedly be constructed, but these influences are the essential American lack of a sense of history, particularly shared history; the unique American geographical endowment, which both isolated the United States from hostile others and provided the country with abundant resources that nurtured and permitted its isolation; and the country's Anglo-Saxon heritage, which affected Americans' earliest political attitudes.

American Ahistoricism

It is not unfair to typify the American people as basically ahistorical in their general attitude. This ahistoricism has several bases. One is that the American experience is fairly brief when compared to the historical experience of the major European and Asian counterparts. While the territory that occupies the United States was inhabited for thousands of years by Native Americans, most of those Indians did not keep a systematic history, and most Americans do not share a sense of ethnicity or history with these natives. Rather, American history, as most Americans perceive it, is about four hundred years old (dating to the English arrival in Virginia in 1607), and it is not even a history shared by most current Americans or their ancestors. The pattern of American population settlement has been in immigrant waves, and this means relatively few Americans can trace their own roots back to the beginnings of the American experience. It is, for instance, no coincidence that there are no Vietnamese Americans who are members of the Daughters of the American Revolution, and the same can be said for many other Americans whose ancestors had not immigrated to these shores when the "shot heard round the world" was fired in Massachusetts in April 1775.

This lack of historical experience has not been an altogether bad thing. Most Americans came to the United States either to escape some form of tyranny or calamity in their native lands or with the hope of becoming part of the greater prosperity that the United States appeared to offer, a trend that continues to this day. As Fareed Zakaria notes in a 2007 *Newsweek* analysis that more people immigrate annually to the United States than to all other countries in the world combined. As a result, there has been a greater sense of optimism in this country than is present in many more established cultures where the historical record offers a greater balance of positive and negative legacies. More pointedly, with the exception of some aspects of the Civil War, the United States has no national tragedy that mars the national consciousness and tempers our optimism in the way, for instance, that the Battle of Kosovo in 1389 has tainted Serbian history (after losing the battle to the Ottoman Turks, Serbia fell under foreign control until the early twentieth century).

American ahistoricism contributes to the American sense of exceptionalism and thus to American attitudes toward national security in a couple of ways. When combined with the fact and perception of American physical isolation from the world, the result has been a positive self-image about the United States and its military experience. On a general level, this perception of success extends to the American attitude toward war and matters of national security. Americans have historically viewed themselves as winners both at war and at peace. The contemporary revival of interest in America's most successful—and cherished—military experience, World War II (the "greatest generation"), is emblematic of this attitude. The general ahistoricism also allows Americans to ignore less glorious aspects of the military experience, such as our performance in the War of 1812 (in which the United States won decisively exactly one land battle, at New Orleans, fought two weeks after the peace treaty was signed). This general attitude of success has made acceptance of the outcome of the Vietnam and Iraq conflicts all the more difficult, just as the territorial attacks by the September 11 terrorists have assaulted our sense of isolation and invulnerability.

Americans have also liked to portray themselves as an essentially pacific people, slow to anger but capable of vanquishing any foe once aroused. The premise underlying this belief is the idea that peace is the normal and preferred condition and war is an abnormality that is thrust upon us and that we must dispatch. The Japanese sneak attack at Pearl Harbor that dragged a reluctant United States into World War II is symbolic of this conviction, as has been the introduction of terrorism to our shores. When we are victimized, we become Yamamoto's "sleeping giant," reference to which was made in Chapter 2.

Many outsiders, as well as native Americans, would, of course, contest both the notion of American passivity and the need to be provoked into violence. It is hard, for instance, to argue that most of the wars against the Indians of the plains and American West were "thrust" upon the United States, and the Spanish, who had already agreed to all of our terms when we declared war on them in 1898, would certainly question the reactive nature of the Americans in that situation, and so do most Iraqis. During the course of American history, the United States has fought six major wars (the Revolution, the Civil War, World Wars I and II, the Korean War, and the Vietnam War) and four minor wars (the War of 1812, the Mexican War, the Spanish-American War, and the Persian Gulf War). When one adds more minor engagements that do not qualify as wars (it is hard to know how to classify the war against Iraq since 2003 in these terms), the number of times Americans have taken up arms in anger rises to around 200, hardly the clearest evidence of peacefulness unless one is prepared to argue each instance was a response to an injustice. The persistence of this myth, however, partly explains why the Iraq war is not often portrayed in the United States as a naked aggression (which it was): Americans do not act that way.

Accident of Geography

Geography blessed the United States in at least two distinctly benign ways. First, the physical location of the United States between two of the world's great oceans made it virtually an island, at least as far as potential foreign incursions from Europe or Asia were concerned. When combined with comparatively weak or friendly countries on the northern or southern borders of the country, the result has been a condition of effective physical invulnerability for much of American history. With the exception of Pancho Villa's raids into the Southwest in the second decade of the twentieth century and a few submarine incursions during World War II along the West Coast, the forty-eight contiguous states (the continental United States, or CONUS) were safe from the danger of physical harm from 1814, when the British left at the end of the War of 1812, until 1957, when the successful testing of a Soviet intercontinental ballistic missile (ICBM) made the United States vulnerable to nuclear missile attacks. The only other sources of American physical vulnerability have come when the United States has expanded beyond the continental mass (e.g., Hawaii) or added foreign colonies (e.g., the Philippines).

The other part of the geographic legacy is resource abundance. The American continental land mass was blessed in two ways. First, the farmland in the central United States—some of the best in the world—allowed the United States to produce enough food for itself (and surpluses for export) without any necessary recourse to foreign sources. Second, the United States also possessed adequate supplies both of mineral wealth (e.g., iron ore, copper) and energy (e.g., coal, petroleum, natural gas) to allow it to proceed through most of the industrialization process without the need to rely on foreign sources of natural resources.

The result of both these geographic factors was to produce, as part of the American worldview, an essential independence and sense of invulnerability that set the country apart from most other countries of the world, most of which were physically vulnerable, foreign resource dependent, or both. The United States thus had to spend little time or effort framing its basic needs in national security terms. Absent the need to defend American territory from invading enemies, most uses of American force have been expeditionary, sending forces overseas either to defend some American interest (e.g., U.S. colonies) or to aid a besieged country somewhere in the world. At the same time, there was no need to prepare to protect access to natural resources or food supplies from vulnerable foreign sources. Effectively, the result was that the United States had, for most of its history, no compelling need to form a national security strategy to protect it from the vagaries of a world that it could largely ignore if it chose to do so.

These unique geographic advantages began to diminish by the middle of the twentieth century. The Pearl Harbor attack and the Japanese conquest of the Philippines demonstrated that an extended United States was no longer physically invulnerable. Soviet missile capability made that vulnerability more dramatic, and advances in telecommunications and transportation have produced arguable American vulnerabilities to things such as terrorist attacks or cyberwar, a vulnerability dramatically brought home in 2001 and a continuing source of concern.

American resource independence has also been eroded dramatically. Increased demand for energy resources such as petroleum at low prices has made the United States dependent on foreign supplies, with strong and controversial national security consequences in places such as the Persian Gulf, as discussed in Amplification 4.1 and in Chapter 5. At the same time, the development and use of more exotic materials that are unavailable in the United States, such as titanium for jet engines, has also reduced resource independence. The desire for exotic foodstuffs, such as year-round access to fresh fruits and vegetables, has made the United States an agricultural importer as well, and some foreign agricultural producers (notably the Chinese) can now beat the prices of U.S. foodstuffs in some categories. The reversal of American longtime isolation has made exposure to vulnerabilities more traumatic than it might otherwise have been.

The Anglo-Saxon Heritage

Although the country has greatly diversified ethnically and nationally and much of the original American culture has changed as a result, the United States was, of course, originally a British colony. Most of the original settlers in the United States were of British extraction, and they brought with them many of the customs and predilections of the mother country.

The Anglo-Saxon heritage affected the early American experience in a couple of obvious and enduring ways. First, it created an aversion to and suspicion of the military, and more specifically, the army, in peacetime. This aversion is largely the result of the British experience during the seventeenth century. During the Cromwellian period in the 1640s and beyond, the Commonwealth's armies were used to suppress political opposition to the regime. When the monarchy was restored in 1688, one of the provisions of the settlement of the Glorious Revolution was to forbid a standing army on British soil during peacetime to avoid a recurrence of military intrusion into civilian life. The British insistence on stationing elements of the British army in the American colonies after the French and Indian Wars became a serious issue that helped produce the American Revolution. (Americans resented being subjected to a condition that citizens of the mother country would have found intolerable.) This aversion manifested itself throughout the formative period of the American national security experience (see the next section) in the tendency to essentially disarm after major wars and to rely disproportionately on part-time citizen-soldiers for the country's defense. The prohibition on the use of American forces in a law enforcement role on American soil enacted in 1868 (known as *posse comitatus*) further reflects the fear of military abuse that has been

Amplification 4.1

DEALING WITH DEPENDENCE
ON PERSIAN GULF OIL

The Persian Gulf littoral, under which two-thirds of the world's known reserves of petroleum are located, has been a major concern and problem for the United States since 1979. Prior to 1979, American interests in the region—almost exclusively based in uninterrupted access to reasonably priced oil—were ensured by America's closest regionally, and the strongest power in the region, Shah Reza Pahlevi's Iran. In 1979, the Shah was overthrown by a violently anti-American revolution that catapulted Ayotollah Ruhollah Khomeini into effective power and resulted in the capture of the American embassy in Teheran and the holding captive of its personnel for the duration of the Iran hostage crisis. It also removed the enforcer of American policy in the region from power and thus called into question the continuing security of American access to the region's oil.

The Persian Gulf has been a source of major foreign and national security concern ever since. In 1980, President Jimmy Carter issued the Carter Doctrine declaring access to Gulf oil to be a vital American interest. In 1990 and 1991, the United States led the coalition that evicted Iraq from Kuwait, followed by American leadership in trying to keep Iraq's Saddam Hussein from obtaining weapons of mass destruction. Usama bin Laden's ordered terrorist attack on the United States in 2001 was, by his own profession, carried out to help convince the United States to leave Saudi soil. The result is a continuing presence in Afghanistan. Some argue that guaranteed access to Iraqi oil was an important factor leading to war.

American policy in the Persian Gulf derives directly from U.S. dependence on petroleum from the region. There are alternative sources of oil, but they are inadequate, inaccessible, or more expensive than Persian Gulf oil. In the case of Russian reserves, there is the ongoing question of political stability and geopolitical effects raised in Chapter 5. Assuming the United States would prefer to be less dependent on oil from the region—and thus more independent in its policy options—what are the alternatives?

As framed in the partisan American debates on the subject, there are two alternatives. One, largely associated with Democrats, calls for an emphasis on conservation, thereby reducing the amount of Persian Gulf and other foreign oil needed by actions such as better fuel economy in transportation, movement to other sources of energy, and the like. The other alternative, favored by the Bush administration, features the development of alternate sources of petroleum and other energy sources plus some conservation, such as opening the Caspian Sea reserves or sources in places such as Alaska. Until one or both of these approaches are adopted, it seems inevitable that the United States will be inextricably bound to the politics of the region, including its violence.

invoked when some officials proposed an expanded military role in waging the GWOT and for patrolling the Mexican border, for instance.

The other Anglo-Saxon legacy is a strong commitment to constitutional rule, especially to the guarantee of individual rights and liberties. Since military service, especially when it is the result of conscription, is a clear intrusion on individual liberty, there has always been a political reluctance to compel Americans into service. The only exceptions to this have been American involvement in major conflicts requiring the raising of large forces, such as in the world wars, and during the Cold War, when it was accepted that a large "force in being" (standing active-duty armed force) was necessary to deter the menace of expansionist Communism. This aversion reappeared when American opinion turned decisively against the war in Vietnam, which, in its latter stages, was fought mostly by draftees. The fact that no American has been involuntarily inducted into service since the end of 1972 partially reflects attitudes that go back to the formation of the republic; the involuntary extension of voluntary enlistments under the "stop loss" provision of service in Iraq is a partial exception to this trend, arguably necessitated by the need for larger forces than could be recruited voluntarily.

The fear of incursion on individual liberties has had a more complicated history and has arisen with particular clarity regarding actions by the Bush administration (notably the USA PATRIOT Act, discussed in Chapter 8) in support of the GWOT (see Chapter 11) and the war in Iraq (see Chapters 7 and 10). In essence, there has been an ongoing debate about the extent (if any) to which strict adherence to individual rights can or must be relaxed in wartime in the name of national security. As a general rule, the court system has allowed some relaxation of these rights during times of war, as in President Lincoln's suspension of habeas corpus during the Civil War and the government's forcible internment of Japanese Americans in camps in World War II. These actions have been controversial in the past and have been particularly questioned in the contemporary context, as demonstrated by citations in the "Selected Bibliography" at the end of this chapter.

EVOLUTION OF THE AMERICAN EXPERIENCE

The American military tradition has evolved over time and with different experiences the country has endured. As noted earlier, that experience can be divided into three historical periods: a formative period from the beginning of the republic to the end of World War II, the Cold War experience, and the contemporary, ongoing period. The two earlier historical periods were distinct from one another in two clear ways. In terms of the levels of threats posed to the United States and the American role in the world, the longer, formative period was one of low threats and commitments, and the Cold War featured high threats and commitments. As we look at the contemporary environment, however, neither historic combination perfectly fits. On one hand, the level of American involvement in the world since 1989 has never been higher. At the same time, the degree of threat to the United States was greatly reduced during the period between the fault lines (1989–2001), but threats appeared to intensify greatly after September 11, 2001. A question that will be addressed in the conclusion of the chapter is which of the historical parts of the past may best inform the process of understanding and dealing with the present and future.

THE FORMATIVE PERIOD, 1789–1945

The period following the birth of the American republic was obviously critical in developing what would become the American military tradition and how Americans would look at military force. The period was heavily influenced by the events surrounding the Revolution itself and why it had come about. In retrospect (and certainly in comparison to the nature of modern revolutions), the American Revolution was a rather low-key affair in terms of both its motivations and its conduct. As Dennis Drew and I have argued in *From Lexington to Desert Storm and Beyond*, it might not have occurred at all had the British government acceded to the American demands to be treated not as colonial subjects but as British citizens, including not stationing British forces on American territory. When the fighting began more or less accidentally at Lexington and Concord in April 1775, it took the colonials almost 15 months to declare they were in fact revolting by issuing the Declaration of Independence on July 4, 1776. The war itself was, by current standards, a fairly low-intensity conflict fought between relatively small armed forces mostly when the weather was good. Although the style of linear warfare fought at the time could produce sizable casualties in pitched, "set piece" battles, bloodshed was also modest by contemporary standards.

A series of "lessons" about military force arose from the revolutionary experience and were, by and large, reinforced during the next century and a half before the United States was thrust into World War II and could no longer remain aloof from the power politics of the world. Five elements of the American military tradition were born during this formative period. The first four—an antimilitary bias, the belief in the efficacy of the citizen-soldier, the myth of invincibility, and the preference for rapid mobilization and demobilization—can be directly attributed to the revolutionary experience. The fifth, a preference for total war, was more a product of the Civil War and the events that followed that conflict in the international system generally. All of these elements collectively reinforce a general sort of disdain for things military that manifested itself, until the Korean War, in an American military establishment that was, except during wartime, small, physically isolated, and generally held in low regard.

At first glance, one may wonder about the application of these influences in the contemporary world, and more specifically within the context of the post-Iraq debate. Clearly, the antimilitary bias has faded (largely the result of the greater status accorded the military due to their role in the Cold War), and the near-disaster of Korea (where demobilization after World War II had left the ranks so depleted that only the remobilization of World War II veterans in the Reserves prevented the

complete conquest of the Korean peninsula by North Korea) deflated the demobilization effect. At the same time, the role of Reservist citizen-soldiers has clearly
been raised by Iraq and will need to be reexamined, the myth of U.S. military invincibility has once again been questioned in ways not seen since Vietnam, and appropriate post-Iraq force levels (an aspect of mobilization) are part of the debate as
well. Sorting out the meanings of victory and defeat raises familiar refrains from the
historical conceptual simplicity of total war.

Antimilitary Bias

It may sound strange to assert today, when public opinion polls regularly rate military service as one of the more prestigious professions, but prior to the Cold War,
military service was not universally held in high regard in the United States. The
peacetime military was generally a small, skeletal body whose purpose was to be
ready to train a civilian force for military duty when the need arose. For the most
part, the professional military (especially the army) was consigned to military posts
in remote areas of the country, where the general population's day-to-day exposure
to it was fairly limited. Moreover, outside the ranks of the professional military itself, soldiering was not thought of as a particularly prestigious occupation. Bar signs
can still occasionally be found in New England antique stores declaring "No dogs or
soldiers allowed," capturing the sentiment held by many Americans. As is the case
today, there were regional differences in the extent of this bias, with Southerners
more generally supportive of the military than their Northern counterparts.

Much of this sentiment has its origins in the Anglo-Saxon tradition and the issue of British military presence in the colonies prior to the American Revolution.
After the French and Indian Wars that coincided with the Seven Years' War in
Europe between 1756 and 1763, the Redcoats were stationed on colonial soil to
provide protection against frontier Indians. The colonists thought they could contain the Indians themselves. The presence of the Redcoats would not have been tolerated in England itself; moreover, the colonists were expected to subsidize this
unwanted element by paying taxes, the levy of which was enacted without their
permission. The soldiers were a potential menace politically, and when they were
used to aid in tax collection, they became overtly political actors as well. This revul-
sion and suspicion were most highly developed in New England, where most of the
soldiers were assigned and their negative consequences suffered.

In addition to creating a predilection toward keeping the military as small—
and thus nonthreatening—as possible, this antimilitary bias also favored keeping
the military apolitical, and hence politically nonthreatening, as well. The United
States Military Academy at West Point, for instance, was designed essentially as an
engineering school to teach the science of war but not the reasons for war (a precedent primarily followed in the other service academies). The leading work detailing
the relationship between war and its political purposes, Carl von Clausewitz's On
War, was originally published in 1832 but was not translated into English and entered into the West Point curriculum until 1876. Moreover, professional members of
the military were effectively disenfranchised until 1944, when legislation permitting

absentee balloting was enacted. Prior to that, military personnel could vote only if they happened to be physically in their hometowns on election day, which rarely happened. Keeping the military apolitical was thought to be important enough that disenfranchisement was not abrogated until the heat of World War II.

The Citizen-Soldier

How could a disdain and distrust for the military be reconciled with the occasional need for military forces to prosecute the wars foisted on the United States? Part of the answer, of course, was to keep the military as small and unthreatening as possible during peacetime. Because much of the distrust was based on the fear of military intrusion into politics, another part was to make the military as apolitical as possible. In addition, the other element was to develop a part-time military whose members were also integral parts of the civilian society from which they came. The result was to reinforce and glorify the militia tradition that was part of the colonial experience.

Militia members were part-time soldiers. As the lineal forefathers of the National Guard and Reserves, they served in the militia for fixed terms and with limited commitments as members. Just as contemporary Guard and Reserve units have historically served for limited periods each year (e.g., a weekend a month, two weeks in summer camp), militia units would drill periodically, often for short periods (some as little as a few days per year). The idea was that such limited commitment would not "infect" these citizen-soldiers with military values to the point they would lose their primary attachment to the civilian community. The citizen-soldiers would, in other words, remain more citizens than soldiers. The activation of Guard and Reserve units for extended (including involuntary extended) deployments in Iraq is a direct violation of this tradition that has effectively made members more soldiers than citizens, at least temporarily. This alteration of roles also helps explain the hemorrhage in reenlistment rates in the Guard and Reserves that became evident in 2005. Whether and how the Guard and Reserves can be returned to their historical status and the implication of changes in their status will be one of the most fundamental aspects of the post-Iraq debate.

This arrangement was satisfactory if one could assume the militias were competent to carry out the country's military needs. From the revolutionary period, the myth was developed that this was indeed the case. To some measure, this belief was little more than wishful thinking, but militia units were involved in enough successful operations (Lexington and Concord, Breed's Hill, Saratoga, Cowpens) that their performance could be embellished and instances when militia units dissolved and ran when confronted with regular British Army opponents (Camden) could be ignored. When the country was not at war, the question was largely moot because militias were rarely called upon to demonstrate their strictly military competence.

The argument over the efficacy of the militia has never disappeared and remains an active part of the debate over current and future forces. Reserve and Guard units remain an integral part of the U.S. armed forces, although they are assigned generally noncombatant roles; however, Reserve units have been increasingly placed in combat roles in Iraq due to shortages of full-time, active-duty personnel. Their virtues are that they are less expensive than active-duty soldiers, and their attachment to their communities makes them popular politically, especially with members of Congress in the districts where they are located. The regular armed forces have a generally lower opinion of these successors of the militia men, emphasizing that the citizen component makes them less effective soldiers and thus of lesser value in military operations than full-time, active-duty forces. One of the controversies surrounding Iraq is certainly the expansion of the roles of citizen-soldiers beyond the historical expectations for them.

Myth of Invincibility

The myth of invincibility asserts the indomitable nature of the American military and is the product of a selective reading of American military history. Its core is the idea that regardless of the circumstances, when the United States is forced to fight, it prevails. The general truth value of this belief is, of course, questionable. While it is true that the United States has generally been successful in war, American triumphs are liberally interspersed with episodes in which the country was less than successful. A more precise statement of the myth would probably be that when the United States becomes involved in long, total wars in which superior American physical resources can be brought to bear to wear out an opponent, fighting according to prevailing rules and American preferences (in other words, symmetrically), it generally prevails. But even that generalization must be tempered; in Vietnam, the opponent refused to wear out or to fight according to established norms (it fought asymmetrically), and the result was certainly not victory. The same has arguably proven true in Iraq.

This generally positive assessment of the American military experience has two corollaries. The first is the "can do" syndrome, the idea that no military task is too difficult to overcome if Americans truly apply themselves to surmounting it. Conjuring the image of a John Wayne World War II movie, the syndrome can be a major impediment to objective assessment of potential missions for which American military forces might be employed. There is, for instance, little on the public record to suggest that any appropriate military officials considered in advance the prospects that the United States might not be able to prevail in Vietnam; no one in the appropriate position to do so effectively said "*can't* do," a more accurate assessment and one held by many mid-level professional military and civilian analysts at the time. This failure is described with regard to Vietnam in McMaster's *Dereliction of Duty* and with regard to Iraq in Yingling's "A Failure in Generalship."

The other corollary is that Americans prevail because of the brilliance and skill with which they fight. The facts fly largely in the face of such an assertion. The United States has, for instance, produced no major strategist of land warfare, although it has produced exceptional battlefield generals like George S. Patton and strategists who have contributed in other media (sea and air). Moreover, although American fighting forces have acquitted themselves well, the United States entered all its wars prior to Vietnam almost absolutely unprepared to fight them, meaning that in the early stages of those wars, American forces did not excel.

Mobilization and Demobilization

Through most of American history, the pattern of mobilization and demobilization has dominated the American military experience: when war seemed imminent or was thrust upon the country, it would raise and train a force to fight it, but as soon as the fighting ended, it would decommission that force and return it to the normalcy of civilian life. This preference reflected numerous elements of the American culture, from a belief in the abnormality of war to the fear of a standing military in peacetime. It also meant that after every major war until Korea, the United States returned its armed forces to the skeletal form that had existed before the war.

The tradition was sustainable throughout the formative period because the United States was never confronted with an enemy that could pose a direct and imminent threat to American territory—the accident of American geography prevented that occurrence. The luxury of forming a force only when necessary was always available as a policy option. The experience in World War II and the Cold War that followed changed that conclusion. Following the attack on Pearl Harbor (see Amplification 4.2), American forces in the Pacific were nearly overrun and defeated to the extent that it would have been difficult to regain the initiative, and only the heroic efforts of Americans at places like the Battle of Midway and Guadalcanal allowed the United States to recover while it rapidly mobilized an adequate force to meet the emergency. The absence of preparedness was the problem then, and when a similar circumstance nearly prevailed in Korea, as already noted, the luxury of not having forces in existence was revealed as unacceptable.

Total War Preference

While the impact of the first four elements of the American tradition are largely negative in their influence on thinking about the use of military force, there developed during the formative period a preference for involvement in total wars that at first glance appears paradoxical in light of the rest of the tradition. At one level, this development reflected changes in the international environment between the eighteenth and the middle of the twentieth centuries regarding the purposes of war. At the same time, it also was the result of an American perception that if it were to go to war, it should be for grand, righteous purposes that made it worthwhile.

The period of time between the mid-nineteenth and mid-twentieth centuries witnessed an expansion in both the means by and the purposes for which war was conducted. The expansion of means was largely the result of the progressive application of the innovations of the Industrial Revolution to warfare. Gradually, it became possible to expand the extent of warfare by increasing the deadly effects of weapons and by increasing the media in which war could be fought. In 1789, warfare was largely limited to ground combat wherever armies could march and organize their linear formations (essentially large, open fields) and the surface of the ocean; by 1945, the only place war could not be conducted was in space (a deficiency since overcome). War became larger in terms of where and to what effect it could be fought, and thus why it could be fought.

Amplification 4.2

READINESS AND PEARL HARBOR

The Japanese air attack on American naval and other military facilities at Pearl Harbor was one of the most traumatic events in American military history. Despite a variety of warning signs (e.g., intercepted intelligence reports, suspicious ship movements, growing strains in relations between the two countries), the United States was totally unprepared for the attack when it came early in the morning on Sunday, December 7, 1941. None of the bases on Oahu were on alert status—in fact, most of the personnel at Pearl Harbor had been out at social events the night before and had not yet reported for duty when the Japanese arrived. Virtually no one was even looking for evidence of an imminent attack, which added to the tragedy and destruction when it occurred.

It was partly the fault of the American military tradition that the attack came as such a complete surprise. To most Americans, nearly a century and a third of virtual invincibility had left them complacent, not mindful that such an attack could occur. Despite a war that had been raging for over two years in Europe and the growing expansion of the Japanese Empire into the South Pacific and East Asia, where it would inevitably collide with American interests, there had not yet been anything resembling a mobilization of the military by the United States. Prominent Americans like Charles Lindbergh and his fellow members of America First argued that the war was none of America's business and should be avoided at all costs. American isolationism, prominently a part of the tradition in the formative stage, was still in full bloom before Pearl Harbor.

The elements of the American tradition that allowed the country to be so unready at Pearl Harbor suffered a humiliating discrediting when the Japanese attacked and destroyed much of the American Pacific fleet that, ironically, had been moved from San Diego to the much more militarily vulnerable base at Pearl Harbor to be closer to the theater should war occur. But the lesson was partially lost in the war itself. When the Japanese surrendered aboard the USS *Missouri* (which is moored permanently at Pearl Harbor) to end hostilities, the United States promptly demobilized again, only to be shocked back to reality five years later by the North Korean invasion of South Korea.

This expansion in means coincided with and reinforced an expansion in the reasons for fighting. The triggering events in the expansion of purposes were the American and (especially) French revolutions, which reintroduced political ideology into the causes of war. In the period after the end of the Thirty Years War in 1648, the system had been dominated by more or less absolutist monarchies who did not disagree on political matters and generally limited their fighting to small purposes. The French Revolution's evangelical period, when it spread its ideas across Europe, changed that, and as the means to conduct war expanded, so too did the reasons for fighting.

The purpose of war became the overthrow of enemy governments, which is the definition of total war. Although it was scarcely realized as such at the time, the prototype was probably the latter stages of the American Civil War, when the destruction of the Confederate Army and the overthrow of the government of the Confederacy were accepted as the necessary preconditions for reunion. The overthrow of the German government became the ultimate goal in World War I, and the epitome of total war was reached in the commitment to the unconditional surrender of Germany and Japan in World War II.

Total war fit the American worldview. American exceptionalism has always had an evangelical component that suggests the virtue of sharing the American ideal with others, and that evangelism could be extended to provide an adequate moral justification to breach the normalcy of peace and go to war. The epitome of this zeal is captured in Woodrow Wilson's address to Congress proposing an American declaration of war in 1917: "The day has come when America is privileged to spend her blood and her might for the principles that gave her birth and happiness. God helping her, she can do no other."

Total wars are much simpler to understand than the limited wars since 1945. In total war, the enemy is considered to be totally reprehensible to the point that only the overthrow of its government is acceptable, and military force is raised and employed with the unified purpose of crushing resistance to the overthrow of that government. By definition, wars are between countries whose governments are the objects of contention, and once the enemy is defeated and its government replaced, the war is over and normalcy (peace) is restored. Because the enemy was depicted as evil, its toppling is morally satisfying as well.

Modern war is not so simple. Because the ultimate contemporary total war is an all-out nuclear exchange (the horror scenario of the Cold War), wars are now limited. The object is not to overthrow the opponent's government (Iraq is an exception) but rather to force the government to stop doing something (supporting terrorists, for instance). The opposition often consists of so-called nonstate actors lacking territory or a population to attack, and there is no sharp and definitive point at which war ends and peace is restored (a particularly painful lesson in Iraq). Some critics of the U.S. military effort in Iraq argue that the American military in particular remains conceptually wedded to traditional concepts of war and that the failure to adapt is, in Yingling's words, "a crisis in an entire institution."

THE COLD WAR, 1945–1989

The end of World War II radically changed America's place in the world and the way in which the United States had to consider matters of national security. As the wartime collaboration with the Soviet Union gradually deteriorated into the confrontation that would be the key reality in the Cold War, the question of national security moved from the peripheries to center stage in the political constellation. When North Korea invaded South Korea on June 25, 1950, and the United States responded (through the United Nations) by coming to the aid of the southerners, any doubt about the changed nature of international politics and the American role in it disappeared.

The Cold War made military affairs—national security defined in largely military terms—a central reality of American peacetime life. Geopolitics was clearly dominant for the first time in U.S. history. Realizing from the Korean experience that a demobilized United States could not compete with a heavily armed Soviet opponent, the traditional practices of the formative period could no longer be afforded.

The Cold War presented the United States an apparently permanent military enemy for the first time since the rivalry with Great Britain was resolved after the War of 1812. Since the Soviets posed primarily a military threat through the challenge of expansionist Communism, American policy had to respond militarily. The result was the emergence of a *national security state* in which matters of national defense took on a coequal footing with other foreign policy considerations, and a large, permanent military establishment became an equally permanent part of the landscape.

The military culture changed because of several new conditioning factors in the environment, especially after the Korean conflict. Each factor represented a direct change and even, in some cases, contradiction with the previous American experience, yet the nature of the Cold War caused these changes to be accepted without fundamental challenges from most Americans.

First, the Korean War created the recognition that the Cold War would require the United States to maintain a large active-duty force all of the time. Part of the reason for this was the nearly disastrous Korean experience. At the same time, the Soviets did not demobilize after World War II, and they and their allies maintained large, offensive forces. Should the Soviets decide to invade Western Europe, as was widely feared, there would be no time to mobilize, train, and transport a force to the war zone. Instead, what became known as the "force in being" would have to be available on the scene at all times.

Second, this prospect of large standing forces meant that the United States would be in a permanent state of mobilization. During peacetime, a force of this size could be sustained only by the existence of a national conscription system, the first time an involuntary draft system had actually been used in peacetime in American history. As well, this state of perpetual mobilization meant that defense budgets had to be greatly expanded to support the defense effort. During the middle 1950s (before the entitlement programs of Lyndon Johnson's Great Society inflated the overall government budget), the defense budget was fully half the overall federal budget; between the end of the Vietnam conflict and the end of the Cold War, defense spending hovered between 20 and 25 percent of government outlays, about where it stands today.

Third, this expanded role and prominence of the military resulted in much greater prestige being bestowed on members of the military profession than before. With a constant threat against which to protect, the work of the military now seemed more vital than it had previously. The respect that Americans had bestowed on the World War II military was transferred to the Cold Warriors as well. Military service, and even a military career, now became attractive to growing numbers of Americans who would probably not have considered such a career before, a fortuitous phenomenon given the need for more military members.

Fourth, the growing lethality of the military balance created an urgency and vitality toward national security that had heretofore never been bestowed upon it. The major agent of this change was the advent and expansion of thermonuclear weapons and the development and deployment of intercontinental range missiles by both sides. At the height of the Cold War competition, the two sides faced one another with arsenals of between ten thousand and twelve thousand thermonuclear warheads capable of attacking targets in the other country and against which there were no defenses. An all-out nuclear war between the two would clearly destroy both as functioning societies and would have unknown but possibly catastrophic consequences for the rest of the world. In those circumstances, the successful management of the nuclear balance in such a way that nuclear war was avoided—nuclear deterrence—was the country's most crucial business (a literal survival interest). This life-and-death struggle added to the prestige and importance of the national security establishment that designed, developed, and deployed strategies for deterrence. The Cold War world was a potentially very deadly place.

Fifth, there was also general acceptance that the Cold War confrontation was a protracted competition from which no one could project a peaceful ending. In the minds of almost all analysts, the only alternatives were Cold War and hot war, and since the latter would probably be nuclear, it had to be avoided at virtually all costs. This added a sense of grim vigilance to the entire national security enterprise. It also contributed to the absolute surprise of nearly all observers when the Communist world began to disintegrate in 1989. The possibility that one side or the other would simply collapse and that the competition would end with a whimper rather than a bang had not even been considered by most students of the Cold War, nearly all of whom would have dismissed the possibility as fuzzy-headed idealism.

Two things are notable about all these factors. The first and most obvious is that they represent circumstances that directly contradicted the American experience to that point. The idea of permanent mobilization of large standing forces, for instance, would have absolutely appalled the Founding Fathers, many of whom equated standing armed forces with the potential for Cromwellian style tyranny. A world of perpetual and potentially disastrous military conflict requiring constant vigilance and extensive preparation and spending was entirely foreign to a country whose broad oceans had provided a barrier that permitted the leisure and luxury of a general mobilization. The idea that a military career would bring great prestige would never have occurred to most of the champions of the militia tradition.

The second remarkable thing about these changed conditions is how readily they were accepted. Americans who had never been willing to (or had the need to) allow themselves to be taxed to support a large standing military and who would previously have been fundamentally opposed to the existence of a draft during peacetime accepted both with virtually no complaint. The main reason for this changed acceptance, of course, was a threat that was real and ominous enough to justify greater sacrifices than during the formative period of the American experience.

During the Cold War period, two additional elements of the American military tradition rose in prominence to become permanent parts of the military environment. Both the news media and democratic institutions had, of course, been present throughout American history. In the period surrounding the Vietnam conflict, however, their roles became more defined and influential.

The Role of the Media

The relationship between the media and the military has changed over time. At times, the media have championed acts of war (e.g., the Spanish-American War); at other times, they have opposed it (e.g., Vietnam). It has always been a complex and contentious relationship, with the two institutions eyeing one another with some distrust and occasionally disdain that was worsened by the very sour experience of the Vietnam conflict and coverage of it. The relationship has arguably become even worse since the end of the Cold War.

There have always been two major concerns about the relationship of the media to national security matters. The first has to do with what is reported, a concern that centers especially but not exclusively on combat operations. The positions are diametrically opposed. From the vantage point of the press, coverage should be as complete and unfettered as possible. The press should have access to combat operations (whether they have a right to protection in combat zones is another controversial matter) and should be allowed to report what they observe. The media's underlying value is the public's right to know what its government's representatives (in this case its military) are doing.

This viewpoint creates two problems for the military. The first is whether unfettered coverage will provide too much information, including material that, in the hands of the enemy, could compromise the integrity of military operations and even put soldiers at additional risk. Reporting the locations and outcomes of battles and the directions of troop or other movements are examples of how reportage could aid the enemy and jeopardize forces. The other concern is that reportage, particularly of less-than-successful military actions, can have a negative impact on public morale and give solace to an enemy. As an example, pictures of American Marines raising the flag on Mount Surabachi at Iwo Jima during World War II were a morale booster that became an important symbol for the Marines. Photographs of the bodies of Americans floating in the surf where they were killed assaulting the beaches at Iwo Jima (which were not published at the time) would have had quite a different impact.

The solution to this dilemma historically has been military censorship. Reporters at the front could get their stories to their media outlets only by using military means of communications, thereby allowing the military to inspect outgoing material and remove anything it viewed as objectionable. The workability of this arrangement depended on two underlying dynamics. The first was a relative degree of trust between the soldier-censor and the reporter. The reporter had to believe the censor was acting out of legitimate security concerns and not trying to hide evidence of military ineptitude; the censor basically had to believe the reporter was acting out of good faith in the stories he or she filed. While that relationship always had some adversarial content, it worked adequately until the Vietnam conflict. The other dynamic was the dependence of the media on government means of transmission of their stories from the battleground to home. That dependence has been broken by the invention of the video camcorder and the telecommunications satellite. In combination, these two technologies allow the reporter to witness, record, and transmit material without any assistance (or interference) from military censors.

The interaction between the media and the military in Vietnam transformed the relationship to one of nearly total animosity. Early in the war, the relationship was tranquil because reportage was passive: the military would tell the press its version of what happened in the fighting, and the press would dutifully report that information. The picture portrayed was uniformly positive and suggested not only that progress toward winning the war was occurring, but also that victory was imminent.

That tranquility was destroyed by the Tet offensive by the North Vietnamese and Viet Cong in January 1968. The enemy launched a general attack throughout the country, and especially against the cities, including the South Vietnamese capital of Saigon. The press was outraged and dismayed as they watched Viet Cong racing around the grounds of the American embassy. When the first footage of Tet reached New York, Walter Cronkite, the most revered and trusted figure in American journalism at the time, replied, "What the hell is going on here?" The basis of his question was that the adversary could not possibly have mounted such an extensive action if the numbers of enemy killed that had been reported to the media in the months and years before Tet were true. The conclusion was that the military had systematically lied about enemy casualties and that the media had been duped into accepting inflated figures that, if true, would have left the North Vietnamese Army and the Viet Cong with too few remaining effective forces for such an attack. Tet showed that the media had been lied to about progress and had been duped into reporting those distortions as facts. As a result, the media lost trust in the military and refused to report successes—even when they were quite genuine. The military, in turn, blamed the media for undermining morale by refusing to report success after Tet. The relationship had become more adversarial than ever before.

It was in that atmosphere that the ability of the media to bypass military censorship electronically became a major factor. The military's response to the inability to edit coverage before its release has been to restrict media access to military operations. The intended effect is to restrict what the media can report (or misreport). This approach, predictably condemned by the media, was demonstrated in the Persian Gulf War, when only a few press members were allowed to accompany military forays, and then only carefully selected actions. Although media criticism of the military was muted by patriotic concerns in the Afghan campaign, reporters rarely witnessed military operations in that theater either or in Iraq (see Amplification 4.3).

The other concern, especially since Vietnam, has been the supposed role of the media as agenda setters. Vietnam was the stimulus because many veterans who were in the military during Vietnam were convinced that adverse coverage of the war effort after the Tet offensive was decisive in forcing an unsuccessful termination of the American participation in the conflict. It is, of course, a matter of major disagreement whether the United States could have prevailed in the Vietnam conflict under any circumstances, and the argument that the media helped force the American withdrawal—thus preventing victory—has obscured that argument for many critics.

Amplification 4.3

THE MEDIA AND THE IRAQ WAR

Coverage of the Iraq War illustrates vividly the ever-changing relationship between the media and the U.S. military. That relationship had become highly adversarial during the Vietnam conflict. After Vietnam, the media remained suspicious of anything the military told them that they had not witnessed themselves, and many in the military continued to believe the "liberal" media were out to get them.

The military's position combines legitimate concern over compromising security, which leads it to want to restrict media access, with a great—arguably exaggerated—sensitivity toward criticism over how it does its job, which reporters want to observe and report. Finding the proper balance between these concerns is contentious and is manifested in the pull-and-tug over how much access the media should have to combat zones. It is an ongoing debate to which Iraq has contributed.

The military's solution to this problem in Iraq was to "imbed" reporters with individual units. Under this arrangement, a few selected reporters were allowed to accompany military operations in Iraq, but they were highly restricted in what they were allowed to observe and report. The military argued the restrictions were necessary to avoid reporting things that might compromise military operations and to ensure the physical safety of the reporters. The media generally accepted this arrangement because it allowed them to be part of the "action" more than had been the case in Desert Storm a long decade earlier, and many more reporters were allowed some access than were allowed twelve years earlier. The major criticism of the arrangement was that it fostered narrow, myopic reporting because it restricted reporters to observation only of narrow aspects of the war.

That the media accepted the restrictions placed upon it in Iraq has itself been the cause of additional controversy. Many have argued that the imposed myopia created by narrow access to isolated aspects of the war has produced bland, unanalytical coverage that has been generally uncritical as well. Moreover, many conservatives inside and outside the military have come to equate critical coverage with a lack of patriotism and have in some cases impugned the motives of critical reporters. The debate that centers on but ultimately transcends Iraq is whether timid, even cowed, reporting serves the national interest.

Two additional factors have influenced coverage. One is the existence of foreign media forms like Al Jazeera, whose coverage cannot be censored. The other is amateur recordings of events, such as videotapes of abuses at Abu Ghraib prison. Both limit the ability of the U.S. government to restrict information flow.

The perception was also affected by electronic technology that broadened both cable television and worldwide television. One of the outgrowths of the telecommunications revolution has been the development of 24-hour-a-day news networks, the prototypes of which are the Cable News Network (CNN) and the British Independent Television Network (ITN). These outlets, and others that followed the 1980 birth of CNN, have voracious news needs, and they have greatly internationalized news coverage, especially in combat zones.

The result is something known as the "CNN effect" that is the core of the concern for those who argue that the media serve as agenda settes. Critics allege (and the media generally deny) that policy makers tend to emphasize those international events that CNN and the others publicize, and that the news items they bring to light are often those involving war and other forms of human suffering for which military force may be viewed as an appropriate response. Thus, the argument goes that emphasis of policy becomes the handmaiden of the media and the media's attention or inattention on different matters. General John Shalikashvili, chairman of the Joint Chiefs of Staff under Clinton, somewhat cynically captured the CNN effect on military operations: "We don't win until CNN says we win."

The role of the media will undoubtedly be revisited as part of the post-Iraq examination of national security policy. In some ways, the media role in Iraq has paralleled the Vietnam pattern. In the early part of the war (e.g., 2003 and most of 2004), media coverage was basically positive and remarkably uncritical, as Isikoff and Corn have pointed out in *Hubris* and Boehlert has argued in *Lapdogs*. Media coverage has gradually become more critical, not so much of the state of affairs on the "battlefield" as of the trends and apparent lack of progress both militarily and in the state-building process. There has been no incident of the dramatic equivalent of the Tet offensive in Iraq, but reports of apparent incompetence (the outpatient facilities at Walter Reed Hospital in Washington) and malfeasance (the Abu Ghraib scandal) have combined to create much more critical coverage as the war has proceeded. Whether the media were sufficiently vigilant early in the war and whether their later criticism has helped undermine the war effort will be among the questions raised in assessing Iraq's legacy.

The Impact of Democratic Institutions

Within a political democracy, popular will is, of course, always a matter of concern in the making of policy and especially in an area such as national security, where the ultimate expression of that policy can be war and the placing of citizens at physical risk. Having said that, the "democratization" of national security affairs is largely a post–World War II phenomenon that, like so many other influences on contemporary affairs, was accentuated by American participation in Vietnam. During most of the formative period of the American republic, national security affairs were either of lesser importance or were more consensual in nature. During peacetime, there was little concern with military affairs, and most wars either were highly popular (the world wars, the Spanish-American War) or affected relatively few Americans directly by compelling them into service for unpopular causes (the Indian Wars). A partial exception to this depiction was selective Northern resistance to the Union cause in the American Civil War, particularly by immigrant groups such as the Irish who could not avoid forced service.

The Cold War placed national security concerns into the spotlight. Suddenly, matters of national security quite literally became matters of potential life and death, and how well those matters were conducted became very serious and very personal business for the entire population, especially for those young Americans who might be involuntarily conscripted into military service. This first became a concern in 1950 when thousands of World War II veterans had to be recalled to active duty and an army of draftees was assembled to defend a Korea that many of them were unaware of before they were called into the service. It became particularly a concern as the Vietnam conflict dragged on and the American conscript force fought a war the public, including many of those inducted, opposed.

The sour taste of the Vietnam experience for many Americans helped elevate the role of popular control over the democratic institutions making decisions about war and peace. In the wake of Vietnam, the military itself engaged in a good deal of self-examination of what went wrong, and a large part of its conclusion was that the war effort was undermined by public support and opinion that evaporated around them as the war dragged on (Vietnam was the longest war in American history). To the military, the war violated the Clausewitzian trinity, which posited that war can only be successfully waged when there is a bond between the people, the military, and the government. Reasoning that the political authority had never explicitly solicited popular support for the Vietnam conflict (for a discussion, see Snow and Drew, Chapter 7), the armed forces (especially the Army) vowed that this would not happen again.

Ironically, one of the primary Army responses to the lack (or erosion) of support for Vietnam instituted by General Creighton Abrams, Army Chief of Staff, after the war was to expand the role of the Guard and Reserves. During Vietnam, these elements were scarcely tapped, largely out of fear that pulling Reservists out of their communities might produce a negative reaction toward the war effort. Abrams reasoned that the possibility of a negative reaction could serve as a kind of referendum on future wars that Vietnam lacked. To ensure a "vote of confidence" in the future, Army functions were rearranged to place Guard and Reserve units in critical roles such that their activation would be necessary early in any conflict. Thus, if the people opposed a particular deployment, they could voice that displeasure over the prospect of Reserve activation.

The irony of this decision occurred in Iraq. The Abrams reforms ensured that large numbers of Reservists were activated and forced into extended, repeated tours of duty well beyond what most of them expected when they enlisted. The problem that the Abrams reformers apparently failed to anticipate is that the popular "vote" on the deployment—which has become negative—did not occur until the Reserves were mired inextricably in a conflict that could not have been sustained had they voted "no" at the beginning, as Abrams hoped they would have a chance to do. Clearly, this will be part of the Iraq postmortem as well.

CONCLUSION: THE CONTEMPORARY PERIOD, 1989 TO PRESENT

The end of the Cold War represented a major change in the environment and thus in the ways Americans think about matters of national security. This change was not immediately recognized, nor was there a great initial effort to test the nature and implications of the collapse of the Soviet empire. The response to September 11, 2001, has further stimulated changed thinking.

The reasons for a slow intellectual adjustment during the 1990s are numerous, and they are discussed in some detail elsewhere (see Snow, *When America Fights*, Chapter 1). One reason was that the national security and foreign policy community was caught off guard by the sea change represented by the collapse of Communism. Planners had four years of combat to plan for the post–World War II international order and devoted considerable effort to the task. There was no equivalent adjustment period when Communism imploded.

Thinking about and adjusting to change was also retarded by the fact that the national security bureaucracy was dominated by veteran observers of the Cold War who were both very conservative and suspicious of the changes they were observing. The tendency was either to disbelieve how fundamental the change was or to hedge against the possibility that the confrontation might soon reappear. Moreover, the Cold War mindset was a comfortable intellectual construct that, once mastered, made people reluctant to shed it for the greater uncertainty apparent in the unfolding post–Cold War environment. At the same time, this new environment was clearly less threatening than the Cold War had been, and even if it contained new and annoying problems such as terrorism, the urgency of adaptation was clearly not as great.

With over a decade and a half of the new environment behind us and the second fault line of terrorism revealed, how will the American tradition adapt to and be shaped by the contemporary situation? Key elements in the past two situations have included the role of the United States in the international system and the level of threat the environment provided, as noted earlier. The American past experience reveals a contrast on these two variables, as shown in Figure 4.1. As the figure reveals, the two historic periods show the United States has experienced both the "pure" combinations: high threat and a large international role during the Cold War and low threat and a small role during most of the formative period.

The contemporary period represents a hybrid of these circumstances. Clearly, the American role in the world is large, and with the collapse of the Cold War opposition, it is arguably relatively larger than it has ever been before. The question becomes, Which part of the American tradition will dominate the contemporary view of the world? In some manner, the neo-isolationists, who would reduce America's aggressive presence and role, represented the legacy of the formative period's preference basically to be left alone. The cutback in active-duty troop strength and the disappearance of

Figure 4.1: American Roles and Threats

Role	Threats	
	High	Low
Large	Cold War	?
Small	?	Formative

conscription as part of the potential political agenda suggested that all the elements from the formative period have not disappeared and may reassert themselves as the United States returns from the "abnormality" of the Cold War to a more comfortable past.

The role of the United States, however, did not recede to where it was in the formative period, but has remained at least as prominent as it was during the Cold War. Does this mean that the internationalism that dominated the Cold War approach of the United States toward the world has become such a permanent part of the landscape as to be inescapable? The Bush administration entered office in 2001 with the stated intention of trimming back America's commitments in areas such as peacekeeping, but it was mere months before the terrorist attack caused it to quietly jettison that rhetoric and adopt an aggressive military posture favored by the neoconservatives to

Challenge!

HOW MUCH HAS CHANGED?

Did the terrorist attacks on New York and Washington and the subsequent worldwide campaign against international terrorism fundamentally change the threat and role of the United States in a security sense? Prior to the attacks, the United States was in the new situation of having a large role in an international milieu that posed few meaningful threats—a kind of hybrid of the formative and Cold War experiences. But what is the situation now?

The question requires an assessment of how fundamental the threat posed by international terrorism really is. In the immediate wake of the 2001 incidents, the initial response of both the administration and the public was to portray the problem as global, pervasive, and extremely highly threatening. The Bush administration's pronouncements and actions seemed to reinforce, even to inflame, this perception. Troops were sent to Afghanistan in 2001 and the Philippines in early 2002 to fight the "war" on terrorism, and deployments were contemplated in numerous other places. The president's labeling of Iran, Iraq, and North Korea as the "axis of evil" extended the problem beyond a contest with nonstate actors to an interstate basis. Domestically, the Office of Homeland Security was created and began periodically issuing terrorist alerts, while an alternative government went underground to ensure governmental continuity in the event of a massive, crippling terrorist attack. The creation of the Cabinet-level Department of Homeland Security (see Chapter 8) capped this effort.

Is all this activity warranted by the actual scale of the threat? Al Qaeda certainly does not have the capabilities to wreak havoc that a nuclear-armed Soviet Union could, but it also has shown the ability to launch an operation that killed three thousand Americans. Where does that place us in the matrix presented in Figure 4.1? In a high-threat environment, a low-threat environment, or somewhere in between? What one concludes has, or should have, major implications for future national security considerations.

the international environment. In 2003, it reactivated the Middle East peace process between Palestine and Israel and invaded Iraq. The continuing struggle in Iraq and the ongoing GWOT suggest a commitment to a major role in the world for the United States, if a more military approach than in the 1990s.

The past is never, of course, a perfect road map for the present or future, but the past is the context within which the future comes to be. As suggested in the preceding pages, there have been two distinct historical influences on how the American military tradition has evolved and shaped the way Americans view the role of force in the world. Whether one of those influences will dominate the future or whether that future orientation will be a polyglot of those influences is an interesting question to ponder and to observe. As the *Challenge!* box asks, "How much has changed?"

STUDY/DISCUSSION QUESTIONS

1. What are the three conditioning factors affecting the American view of national security? Discuss each, including how each has changed.
2. What is the formative period of American national security experience? What principles did it produce? Which have been the most enduring and which have changed the most? Why?
3. How did the Cold War represent a major change in how the United States views national security? Discuss.
4. What are the two major influences on national security that came out of the Cold War? Discuss each, and how each influence has evolved.
5. The ways in which the American experience has influenced how the United States has viewed Iraq and how Iraq has affected how the United States may view national security in the future have been major themes throughout the chapter. Discuss these influences in both directions.

SELECTED BIBLIOGRAPHY

Ackerman, Bruce. *Before the Next Attack: Preserving Civil Liberties in an Age of Terrorism*. New Haven, CT: Yale University Press, 2006.

Applebaum, Anne. "In Search of Pro-Americanism." *Foreign Policy* (July/August 2005), 32–41.

Boehlert, Eric. *Lapdogs: How the Press Rolled Over for Bush*. New York: Free Press, 2006.

Brodie, Bernard. *War and Politics*. New York: Macmillan, 1973.

Chandrasekaran, Rajiv. *Imperial Life in the Emerald City: Inside Iraq's Green Zone*. New York: Alfred A. Knopf, 2007.

Clausewitz, Carl von. *On War* (rev. ed.). Translated and edited by Michael Howard and Peter Paret. Princeton, NJ: Princeton University Press, 1984.

Cole, David, and James X. Dempsey. *Terrorism and the Constitution: Sacrificing Civil Liberties in the Name of National Security*. New York: New Press, 2002.

Dupuy, D. Ernest, and Trevor N. Dupuy. *The Encyclopedia of Military History*. New York: Harper and Row, 1972.

Gaddis, John Lewis. *Strategies of Containment: A Critical Appraisal of Postwar American National Security Policy*. Oxford, UK: Oxford University Press, 1982.

Hassler, Warren W., Jr. *With Shield and Sword: American Military Affairs, Colonial Times to the Present.* Ames: Iowa State University Press, 1984.

Heymann, Philip B., and Juliette Kayyem. *Protecting Liberty in an Age of Terror.* Cambridge, MA: MIT Press, 2005.

Isikoff, Michael, and David Corn. *Hubris: The Inside Story of Spin.* New York: Crown Publishers, 2005.

Leckie, Robert. *The Wars of America* (revised and updated ed.). New York: Harper and Row, 1981.

McMaster, H. R. *Dereliction of Duty.* New York: HarperPerennial, 1997.

Millett, Allan R., and Peter Maslowski. *For the Common Defense: A Military History of the United States of America.* New York: Free Press, 1984.

Snow, Donald M., and Dennis M. Drew. *From Lexington to Desert Storm and Beyond: War and Politics in the American Experience* (2nd ed.). Armonk, NY: M. E. Sharpe, 2000.

————. *When America Fights: The Uses of U.S. Military Force.* Washington, DC: CQ Press, 2000.

Tucker, Robert W., and Donald C. Hendrickson. "The Sources of American Legitimacy." *Foreign Affairs* 83, 6 (November/December 2004), 18–32.

Weigley, Russell F. *The American Way of War.* New York: Macmillan, 1973.

Williams, T. Harry. *A History of American Wars: From Colonial Times to World War II.* New York: Alfred A. Knopf, 1981.

Yingling, Paul. "A Failure of Generalship." *Armed Forces Journal (online)*, May 2007.

Zakaria, Fareed. "Beyond Bush." *Newsweek,* June 11, 2007, 22–29.

CHAPTER 5

The Nature, End, and Consequences of the Cold War

PREVIEW

Although the Cold War has been over for more than a decade and a half, the international and domestic structures and attitudes it produced continue to have an impact on the contemporary world. A distinctly American form of geopolitics was one product of the forty-year confrontation, many of the national security leaders today had their intellectual grounding during the Cold War, and the American military structure still predominantly reflects preparation to fight World War III against a Soviet-style opponent. The Cold War is the dominating influence of the American experience as we face a changed environment. Understanding how the Cold War occurred and evolved—especially in a military but also in a political sense—and what residues remain is therefore crucial to understanding how we are predisposed to respond to the future.

The contemporary international environment can only fully be understood in the context of the Cold War international system from which it evolved and which helped form the contemporary world. These impacts of the Cold War on the present and future include the enormous influence the Cold War had on reforming the American attitude toward the world and the United States' role in it; the influence the Cold War had on the worldview of the generations who presided over it, including much of the present leadership; and the traumatic effect of the Cold War collapse on the international system and American attitudes toward it.

The Cold War was a national baptism for the United States into the world arena. In the formative period, the country had not been a consistent major player in international relations for reasons already discussed: the accident of geography, disdain for a corrupt international system, and a general preference to be left alone to realize American manifest destiny. These factors combined to keep the United States on the periphery of a European-centered international system. That system, in turn, had little need most of the time for American involvement in its affairs except during systemic traumas like the world wars.

The end of World War II left a return to isolation from the world impossible and thrust a reluctant, inexperienced United States onto the center stage of world events. When the last guns of the war were stilled, only two states, the United States and the Soviet Union, retained enough power to influence international events and to reorganize an international system laid prostrate by the war. The implications of this bipolar balance of power—and especially its adversarial content—were not clear immediately but took shape in the five-year period that was climaxed by the Korean conflict. As a result, the United States was propelled into the *realpolitik* of international relations for the first time.

The changed nature of the international system was especially dramatic. Through most of American history, its configuration was *multipolar*, a condition in which there were several countries of importance in the system that competed for positions of power but in which no single state predominated (although Germany arguably came close twice in the twentieth century). In this system, the United States gradually rose from being a weak, peripheral power to a more central role.

The post–World War II world was different. Except for the United States and the Soviet Union, all the traditional powers were so weakened by the war effort that they were unable or unwilling to remain major powers. In this situation, the system became *bipolar* with the United States and the Soviet Union as the major powers (or poles) around which other states more or less willingly congregated, and the system became competitive between the resulting blocs of states. With the end of the Cold War, the Soviet pole disappeared, and the system has been undergoing a process of reconfiguration ever since.

Understanding and managing the Cold War became the central task for the next generations of American policy makers, strategists, and scholars who had to manage and explain change as the world slid toward the Cold War between 1945 and 1950 and then had to adapt to the Cold War system for another forty years. Lurking constantly over their shoulders was the shadow cast by the possibility the Cold War could go very hot in a totally ruinous nuclear war.

The major organizing construct they built and managed was, of course, the realist paradigm discussed in Chapter 3. It was a harsh, confrontational relationship for most of its existence, and it became a very *conservative* construct in the pure sense of that term: it sought to conserve the system below the level of general war that both sides quite rightly feared. In the end, that construct and fear helped contribute to the end of the Cold War. But while the Cold War lasted, it provided a virtually uncontested worldview, and those who challenged it were dismissed as dreamers and visionaries whose suggestions were too risky or foolhardy to be considered seriously.

It is important to emphasize the pervasive nature of the Cold War because it affects the way many people look at the world. The military people who have flag rank (generals or admirals) in the services today were by and large educated in the late 1960s and 1970s and had their first personal experiences in the world in the 1970s and 1980s, and the same is true of the majority of civilians in the foreign and national security community. Many have, with varying degrees of success, sought to shed some of the inapplicable aspects of the Cold War mentality, but they remain at least partly Cold Warriors nonetheless. The equation of the U.S. response to terrorism as a war between good and evil, for instance, has antecedents in the Cold War against "godless Communism." President Bush's "axis of evil" and President Reagan's "evil empire" come from the same intellectual cloth.

The way the Cold War ended influences the present as well. It was neither a planned nor an anticipated event. With the considerable benefit of hindsight, there were a whole series of signs of the impending doom for the Soviet Union that were nowhere nearly so obvious at the time. The key player in the drama was clearly Mikhail S. Gorbachev, who became the Soviet leader in 1985 at the end of a succession crisis following the death of longtime strongman Leonid Brezhnev.

The Cold War and its demise are history, but it is important history that is relevant to us now. As a result, this chapter is devoted to the Cold War. It begins by looking briefly at the essence of the Cold War relationship as a distinct international system. The text then turns to the distinctly military competition that was at the center of U.S.–Soviet conflict. That military confrontation, in the end, helped contribute to the end of the Cold War. Finally, some residues of the Cold War remain part of the current reality. For instance, as the United States aligns itself with former Soviet states in the name of fighting terrorism, some of these concerns affect the content and effects of policy on the future.

THE COLD WAR SYSTEM

At the end of World War II, the international system was confronted with two fundamental questions, the consequences of which would evolve and dominate international relations for most of the rest of the twentieth century. One question centered on nuclear weapons. The use of atomic bombs against Hiroshima and Nagasaki, Japan, by the United States helped to break Japan's will to continue the war and meant these novel and enormously deadly weapons would be part of the calculation of future military affairs. Hence, a fundamental question facing planners was what difference these weapons would make.

The other question was about the wartime collaboration between the United States and the Soviet Union. Would friendship continue in the postwar world, or would the deep ideological differences between them result in a future of conflict and confrontation? In retrospect, the answer seems stunningly obvious, and most observers at the time suspected that the collaboration could not be sustained. But if continued cooperation could be maintained, the result could be a much more tranquil international environment, and this hopeful possibility could not be dismissed out of hand.

Planning for dealing with these postwar contingencies had gone on throughout the war in the United States and especially in collaboration between the Americans and the British. Unlike the end of the Cold War, which caught everyone off guard, there was ample time to think about and plan for the postwar world. Uncertainty about what kind of relationship would exist among what became the superpowers of the Cold War system dominated the policy process. In the face of this uncertainty, the planners devised a structure to accommodate both outcomes—collaboration or confrontation.

The principal instrument for organizing the postwar world was the United Nations Charter. The primary purpose of the organization was to create a viable mechanism to organize the peace that would avoid a repetition of the slide to World War II. Critical to crafting a viable, working system was whether the major powers, the United States and the Soviet Union, could agree upon a form of the peace they were willing to enforce.

Since the two powers had very opposing worldviews, the task of finding a mutually acceptable peace to defend was not going to be easy. Clearly, the United States preferred a world of western-style political democracies and capitalist-based economies like its own, and the Soviets equally fervently wanted to promote the expansion of Communism in the world. Both sides were evangelical, and the secular "religions" they were promoting were incompatible. Thus, the prospects of peace and cooperation were prejudiced from the beginning.

What the U.N. Charter drafters sought to do was create a mechanism that would allow enforcement of the peace if the major powers could cooperate on a common vision but that would be disengaged if they could not. Cooperation would be accomplished institutionally through the U.N. Security Council, which the Charter empowers (through Chapters VI and VII) to take effective actions to squelch threats to or breaches of the peace. Each of the permanent members of the Council (the major victorious allies in the war—the United States, the Soviet Union, Great Britain, France, and China) was given a veto over any action, thereby providing the disabling mechanism when the major powers disagreed in any given situation. In the event that disagreement became pervasive, the Charter, through Article 51, allowed the members the right to engage in "individual and collective self-defense," providing the basis for the opposing military alliances that institutionalized confrontation.

Collaboration was not sustainable, of course, because the two sides could not agree on the world they preferred. Thus, the mechanisms for organizing the peace through cooperation remained disabled and disengaged for the duration of the Cold War. The United Nations was able to act on Korea in 1950 because the Soviets were boycotting the organization in protest of the refusal to seat the new Communist government of China rather than the Nationalist government of Chiang kai-Shek in Taiwan and thus did not veto the action. After Korea, the mechanisms for enforcing the peace in essence went into a veto-induced hibernation for forty years. Then a Russia that was no longer Communist did not have ideological grounds to veto U.N. potential actions, and the world body returned to life as promoter of the peace.

The North Korean invasion of 1950 removed any lingering doubt that confrontation rather than collaboration would be the central feature of the Soviet–American relationship. After the Soviets exploded their first atomic bomb in 1949, the question of the role of nuclear weapons was added to the calculus of what became the Cold War international system. This system had several prominent characteristics that are worth considering. It also had within it the sources of future change.

Characteristics

First, the Cold War *political and military competition dominated international politics.* Among the world's powers, only the United States and the Soviet Union emerged from World War II with enough residual power to organize and influence international events. The bases of American power were economic and military. The American industrial system was strengthened by the war and towered above everyone else (for a period in the 1940s, the American economy accounted for nearly 40 percent of world productivity, as opposed to about half that today). Military power was guaranteed through the sole possession of nuclear weapons. The much weaker Soviet economy had been virtually destroyed by the war, but the Soviets kept armed forces of close to 12 million under arms (the United States was demobilizing to around 1 million in 1946).

This distribution of power defined the international system as *bipolar* in nature: the United States and the Soviet Union stood as the two remaining powers (or poles) around which other states congregated and could be controlled or influenced. The American lever of power was economic; everyone in the West needed American money and goods for recovery. The Red Army occupation in Eastern Europe was able to impose friendly regimes in the occupied countries that became reluctant parts of its orbit; it could not then and was truly never able to compete economically.

The Cold War's pervasive nature took root first in a Europe divided by what British statesman Winston Churchill first called the Iron Curtain in a speech in Fulton, Missouri, in 1947. The relationship became formally militarized through the formation of the North Atlantic Treaty Organization (NATO) in 1949 and later its Communist counterpart, the Warsaw Treaty Organization (WTO or the Warsaw Pact) in 1955. The ideological struggle spread to the developing world as countries emerged from colonial rule principally in Asia and Africa during the 1950s and 1960s.

Nothing symbolized the fervor of the Cold War more dramatically than the superpower nuclear competition. At one level, the competition was incongruous as both sides built arsenals for potential use against one another so large and excessive that a war between them would almost certainly destroy both. It became popular to depict the relationship as two scorpions in a bottle: each scorpion was ready to kill the other and itself in a conflict both feared the other might be tempted to initiate if they showed weakness or vulnerability. Each came gradually to dread the prospect of that conflict enough that nuclear weapons contributed to defusing the Cold War. The ultimate lunacy of the relationship, however, did not prevent either side from spending lavishly to ensure that the other did not gain what was sometimes described as an "exploitable advantage" in some measure of the weaponry.

Second, the conflict was viewed as *protracted*, a long-term competition for which only great patience would suffice and the management of which required great vigilance. The Cold War was a battle between two diametrically opposed systems of political belief that was enduring and that had an uncertain outcome. There was very little consideration of a peaceful end of the relationship. It was broadly assumed that the only means by which closure could come was through a massive military clash, World War III, that would likely become nuclear and could destroy both sides.

The protracted nature of the competition became both a prediction of the future and a prime value, given its extremely destructive alternative. There was always something curious in this assessment, however. It was a matter of firm belief in the West that the Communist philosophy was inherently inferior to its capitalist economic and democratic political ideals. Somehow this belief was hardly ever translated into the idea that Communism might collapse on its own as those flaws became manifest (which, of course, is exactly what happened). Indeed, for a time it was even argued in some circles that Communism had a competitive edge in the developing world where much of the competition played out, because Communist ideology laid out a concrete blueprint for development, whereas democracy offered only choices but little guidance. That the concrete blueprint was itself flawed and the choices it offered ultimately unpalatable never really entered the discussion. One particularly fatalistic expression is captured in Amplification 5.1.

The perceived basis of Communist strength was the totalitarian nature of Soviet rule. Soviet Communism, the argument went, could not fail because its coercive strength was so great that any opposition would be crushed mercilessly. Thus, even if the regime lacked broad popular support, as it did, its power could not be challenged effectively.

In retrospect, this was also a curious proposition. In the western tradition, democratic theory argues that the basis of political stability is popular support for the government, or legitimacy. Legitimacy was the source of strength in democracies. Arguments about the endurance of Communism implicitly maintained that legitimacy simply did not apply if a regime had enough guns and other forms of coercion to control the population. Coercion effectively trumped legitimacy. What this line of reasoning failed to consider was that the reason Communist governments needed to be totalitarian was because they were illegitimate. The monopoly on power was really an indirect indication of the weakness, not the strength, of regimes. When populations throughout the Communist world shucked the system with no remorse or regret starting in 1989, it demonstrated that coercion only artificially and temporarily substitutes for legitimacy.

These intellectual blinders meant that there was much less consideration about ending the Cold War than if participants began with the proposition that the competition was intellectually tilted in favor of the democracies. Over the years, a few observers had seen this, but their prophecies were largely ignored. George F. Kennan, the American diplomat who was the intellectual father of the American foreign policy of containment, argued that a policy of diligence could contain Communism within the boundaries it had achieved. If containment was applied consistently, the

Amplification 5.1

BETTER DEAD THAN RED?
BETTER RED THAN DEAD?

The 1950s was the decade when the Cold War was at its most intense and assessment of the future was most pessimistic. The Korean War, which had become intensely unpopular after it stalemated in 1951 but dragged on until 1953, was a recent memory of apparent failure. The liberation of North Korea had not been accomplished, and the Communist Viet Minh of Ho Chi Minh had prevailed in French Indochina, another victory for expanding Communism. When the Soviet Union beat the United States into space by launching *Sputnik* into the heavens first and Americans peered into the nighttime sky and saw it blink by overhead, there seemed reason to be suspicious of who was prevailing in the competition. Nuclear war drills in schools and public buildings only added to the growing hysteria. The flaws of operational Communism had not become obvious to anyone.

In this atmosphere, a kind of despair emerged about how the Cold War might end. One possibility was that the Soviet Union might actually prevail, in which case the debate was whether it would be preferable to accept Soviet domination or to go down fighting in a cataclysmic nuclear war: better Red than dead? The second possibility was that war between the two systems was inevitable. It was not a question of whether there would be war, but *when*. The debate was turned around to ask if perishing in such a conflict was preferable to Communist overlordship: better dead than Red? In that atmosphere, hardly anyone could imagine the outcome that eventually prevailed: *neither dead nor Red.*

inherent inferiority of the Communist system would eventually cause it to implode. He was, of course, proven correct.

A third characteristic of the Cold War system was that it became *global*. Originally, it was geographically limited to the boundary between Western and Eastern Europe and, after 1949, the area surrounding China. As independence movements produced new states in Asia and Africa during the 1950s, 1960s, and early 1970s (decolonization was effectively over in 1975 when Portugal granted independence to the last members of its empire), both sides scrambled to gain favor, even allegiance, from newly installed governments in new states.

Because the new countries gained their independence from European states, and most adopted nominally democratic systems based upon the colonialist's form of government, the West initially was thought to have the advantage in this competition. Most of these new states, however, were desperately poor and in need of developmental assistance that was generally not available in adequate supply. Their new governments often proved to be inept or corrupt (or both), leading to a spiral of instability and violence. Those circumstances presented the Soviets with an opportunity to attempt to spread their influence by arguing they advocated a superior alternative to the West.

This global spread of the competition universalized the Cold War, meaning Cold War concerns permeated even the most remote parts of the globe. The American policy of containment was extended all along the Sino–Soviet periphery (over the objections of Kennan) and was manifested in a whole series of bilateral and multi-lateral collective defense arrangements (alliances) that globalized U.S. commitments and both justified and demanded robust forces capable of global projection. While the competition generally remained below the level of direct military confrontation, American- and Soviet-supported forces did fight in areas where American interests consisted mainly of denying Soviet interests, and vice versa.

The Cold War competition changed over time. The presumption of an in-tractable, negative relationship in the 1950s softened with experience to the point that, at the time the Cold War ended, Soviet political leader Gorbachev was one of the most popular politicians in the West and adorned the cover of *Time* magazine as its Man of the Year.

Sources of Change

The Cold War dynamics led to change in two ways. The first occurred in the 1950s but was not widely recognized at the time—the two superpowers began to lose some control over their individual blocs. The early postwar system had been known as one of *tight* bipolarity, meaning the major powers could control events within their blocs fairly closely. The system evolved, however, to one of *loose* bipolarity, wherein the ability to order events slipped for both.

Two events in 1956 started the change from tight to loose bipolarity. First, Great Britain joined France and Israel in an attack on Egypt, the purpose of which was to occupy the Suez Canal Zone (which Egyptian President Gamal Abdul Nasser had nationalized the previous year). The action was taken without prior consulta-tion with the U.S. government (which almost certainly would have opposed it). When the United States joined the Soviet Union in sponsoring a Security Council resolution condemning the invasion, the French concluded the United States could no longer be trusted and began the process of moving away from the United States to a more independent position in international affairs. The American ability to control its bloc suffered a major setback.

The second event that started this change in control was the brutal suppression of the Hungarian Rebellion by Soviet forces later in that same year. Initially seen as proof of Soviet ruthless control over its bloc, there was a longer-term and quite oppo-site effect. The United States took the lead in an anti-Soviet publicity campaign that included widely disseminating pictures throughout the developing world of Soviet tanks rumbling through Budapest. The Soviets suffered an enormous propaganda black eye, because they had portrayed themselves as the peace-loving champions of freedom and self-determination, and they were clearly lying. The result was that the Soviets—and their client states—realized they needed to avoid another similar embarrassment. East European countries learned that as long as they did not threaten Soviet security, they could act more independently than before, a sign of decay in the Soviet control of its bloc.

The second great change was in the nature of the competition, and the symbolic event was the Cuban Missile Crisis of 1962. In that confrontation over the Soviet attempt to deploy nuclear-tipped missiles aimed at the United States from Cuba, there was a military standoff that almost all observers believed was the closest the two sides had come to nuclear war. That realization convinced both powers that their prior assessment—that they had nothing in common—was at least partly wrong. At a minimum, both sides realized a joint interest in avoiding destroying one another and possibly the world.

The Cuban crisis was the watershed in the confrontational nature of the Cold War. Prior to the crisis, the relationship was regularly marked by direct confrontations with at least some potential to spiral out of control—the Berlin blockade, Korea, and the Berlin Wall incident, to mention three. These crises shared an escalatory potential to direct confrontation. After the Cuban missile crisis, that changed, and direct Cold War confrontations with obvious escalatory potential essentially disappeared.

The Cuban watershed changed the nature of the relationship in two ways, both of which reduced the likelihood they would once again meet at the precipice of nuclear war. First, they began a process of nuclear arms control, signing a whole series of treaties aimed first at limiting where nuclear testing could occur and later at limiting the size and characteristics of the arsenals they aimed at one another (a process that has continued to the present). This process became a prominent forum for Soviet-American dialog for the rest of the Cold War. Although avoiding the proliferation of nuclear weapons to states that did not already have them was part of the motivation, the shared realization of an interest in avoiding mutual incineration provided the compelling rationale for the efforts. After the missile crisis, direct confrontations with escalatory possibilities simply vanished from the international scene, although some argue that the Yom Kippur crisis of 1973 is an exception to that statement.

From a twenty-first-century perspective, much of this flavor of the Cold War may seem odd, even anachronistic and unreal. It was, however, very serious business to those who made and implemented policy, many of whom, to repeat, are still active in national security policy today. Nowhere is the furtiveness of the competition more evident than in the way the two sides prepared themselves for potential armed conflict.

FORMS OF MILITARY COMPETITION

The Cold War was both a military and a political competition, with emphasis on one aspect or another across time and in different places. Originally, it was both. The communization of the occupied Eastern European countries was accomplished almost exclusively by the Red Army rather than the political interplay of Communist and non-Communist elements. At the same time, Communist parties competed politically in several Western European countries and even enjoyed some electoral success in France and Italy. By the end of the decade, however, the totalitarian nature of

Communist regimes had been clearly demonstrated in countries like Czechoslovakia (where a democratically elected government was overthrown by the Soviets and their Czech surrogates). From 1950 until 1991, the Cold War in Europe was almost exclusively a military competition between NATO and the Warsaw Pact (after the WTO became operational in 1956).

The political dimension of the Cold War was limited to the peripheries—Africa, Asia, and to a lesser extent, Latin America. The process of decolonization and the subsequent emergence of inexperienced postindependence governments created considerable political ferment into which both sides plunged hoping either to gain influence or, more modestly, to deny influence to the other side. One of the means of currying favor was providing military aid to various governments (or factions within countries). Occasionally, involvement would devolve into military intervention, as it did for the United States in 1965 in the Dominican Republic and Vietnam and for the Soviets in Afghanistan a decade and a half later. Nonetheless, the competition in the developing world had both a political and a military dimension.

The heart of the Cold War, however, was played out in Europe along the Central Front in Germany, the presumed focus of a Soviet invasion of Western Europe. That possibility formed the worst-case scenario against which NATO planners prepared. The rarely questioned presumption within NATO was that the Soviet Union had serious designs on controlling Western Europe and might unleash the vast Red Army into NATO territory unless NATO demonstrated sufficient military strength and resolve to convince them of the futility of such an attack.

How serious a threat the Soviets indeed posed to Western Europe is not the point here. Certainly, the Soviets maintained military forces far in excess of those needed for a purely defensive stance in Europe (as did NATO), and there was ample ideological antagonism between the two sides to place the worst possible interpretations on the intentions of the adversaries. Thus, it was not at all difficult for members of the alliance to project a real and lively threat against which vigilant defensive preparation was the only prudent recourse. The underlying point is thus that planners *believed* in the existence of the military threat and acted militarily on those beliefs.

The perceived nature of the military threat was colored by the time and place in which it occurred. The fact that the competition emerged in Europe on the heels of history's largest conventional war affected the shape and purposes of military forces to this day, when the military situation is quite different. Militarily, the Cold War began as an extension of the global conflict featuring conventional armed forces preparing to fight symmetrically. The military dimension of the Cold War mirrored this inherited reality in terms of both how it would be fought and with what kinds of forces. Even though the weapons became more sophisticated and deadly across time and would have produced a much bloodier result, a war in Europe where the United States and the Soviet Union were the principal adversaries would have been very much like World War II. Since the military and political leaders on both sides were, by and large, veterans of World War II, this was not an uncomfortable projection and basis for preparation for them. Hidden within the assumptions about preparing for World War III was the notion that the forces and doctrines would also be effective against smaller, unconventional (asymmetrical) foes. That assumption has proven dubious.

The wild card, of course, was nuclear weapons. The Cold War provided the first occasion when a war could be fought by two opponents both armed with these remarkably destructive weapons. Whether a war in Europe could be fought without releasing the nuclear genie was a hotly debated issue in military, political, and academic circles around which no real consensus ever emerged. A second lively question was whether their employment could be restricted to the immediate theater of operations (a possibility about which the Europeans who would experience a nuclear defense understandably had little enthusiasm) or whether their use would somehow inexorably spread more widely beyond the battlefield. Whether conventional war in Europe would escalate into a general nuclear exchange engulfing the homelands of the superpowers was the ultimate concern for American, and presumably Soviet, planners.

These concerns have not entirely disappeared. The nuclear balance remains intact, if at reduced levels, even if Russia and the United States lack the realistic motivation to attack one another. American conventional armed forces are still largely structured basically the same way they were during the Cold War. Despite the efforts of Secretary of Defense Donald Rumsfeld and others before him to reshape that force, such efforts continue to be resisted by military and civilian leaderships at least implicitly clinging to Cold War roles and missions. Understanding those forces and why they are constructed the way they are is a necessary preface to dealing with contemporary forces for contemporary problems.

Conventional Forces

The heart of the Cold War was a confrontation between conventional (nonnuclear) forces facing one another across the no-man's-land that comprised the Iron Curtain, and most especially the so-called inter-German border that divided East and West Germany and was widely expected to be the initial battleground in a NATO–Warsaw Pact war. For NATO planning purposes, a heavily armored Soviet breakout at the Fulda Gap in Germany seemed the most likely way that war would begin.

World War II and the military predilections of the leaders of the two coalitions heavily colored the way they conceptualized the problem. Everyone envisioned the battlefield would be somewhere on the northern European plain, relatively flat terrain that gave the advantage to mobile yet heavily armed forces, such as the tank armies that leaders like General George S. Patton had popularized in World War II.

Both the Americans and the Soviets were oriented to this style of warfare in which huge forces slugged it out in an orgy of incredible violence until one side collapsed. For the Americans, this had historically meant committing the superior American productive system to building so much sophisticated equipment that the enemy eventually was beaten down by the sheer weight of arms. The Soviet experience on the Eastern Front had taught them that overwhelming numbers of troops could eventually carry the day, if at terrible human costs. The prospect of these two behemoths colliding on the battlefield created a nightmare scenario of unprecedented carnage and destruction that, among other things, would leave the European landscape on which it was fought largely devastated. It was a plan for the ultimate expression of European-style symmetrical warfare.

The way the war would likely be fought affected the politics of war preparation. The focus of NATO preparation was to provide a sufficiently daunting prospect to the Soviets that they would be deterred from starting a war. But politics got in the way. Since the Soviets always had a quantitatively much larger force than NATO and would have the advantage of choosing when and where to attack, how was NATO to provide such an inhibiting presence? The domestic politics of the NATO democracies made it politically suicidal to suggest conscripting a force that could match the Soviets soldier for soldier. Moreover, the longer that war was avoided, the less belief in the need for the sacrifice of military service existed.

The major concern was with what NATO fought, and this concern was colored by perceptions of the conventional military balance that heavily favored the Communists. In 1985, for instance, the Red Army was nearly two-and-a-half times the size of its American counterpart and had four times the number of tanks and armored vehicles and half again the number of combat aircraft. The United States had the advantage in helicopters and naval vessels, but their direct applicability to the central front in Germany was questionable. Numbers favored the Soviets.

Regardless of how the relative quality of the two forces was rated, these comparisons left the very real prospect that a Soviet-led assault in Germany might succeed *if the war remained strictly conventional*. What the NATO allies needed was so-called force multipliers, ways in which to enhance the comparative capability of those NATO forces (multiply their effectiveness). The most obvious candidates for this enhancement were battlefield and theater nuclear weapons, and analysts wondered out loud whether it would be better to accept conventional defeat on the battlefield or to escalate to nuclear exchange, with all the uncertainties that such a change would create for possible escalation to a general homeland exchange between the two superpowers, raising grim prospects such as those raised in Amplification 5.1.

How did the United States respond to these challenges? The question is germane because the blueprint for defending Europe is still largely in place as the rationale for current forces (despite efforts at change by Rumsfeld and others) and was the basis for the plan that defeated Saddam Hussein in 1991.

These strategies were never implemented in Europe, of course, but they did produce a distinctive force structure and mindset for fighting that continues to this day. To many military planners, the plans were vindicated in the Persian Gulf War, where the basic blueprint for engaging and defeating the Iraqis was the highly mobile air-land battle concept (a plan made easier to implement because there were no natural or man-made obstacles to rapid mobility in the Kuwaiti desert). That very success reinforced the continuing adherence in the Army to a heavily armored concept and in the Navy to forces based on aircraft carriers (which carried out a large part of the air mission in Desert Storm), despite arguments that both tanks and carriers are vulnerable and obsolete in an era dominated by missiles. Overwhelming force, a core element of the strategy, appeared to work in 2003 in Iraq, but unaccompanied by conventional mass (large members of forces), it proved inadequate for the ensuing occupation.

Nuclear Forces

Everyone should, of course, be grateful that the concepts adopted by the United States to fight the Soviet Union were never tested, because, as already noted, there was considerable question about what their larger consequences might have been. Indeed, in some circles it was privately maintained that NATO's conventional role was simply to slow a Soviet invasion down enough so that one of two things could occur: either the diplomats could arrange a truce wherein the Soviets could be convinced to settle for less than their total goals, or there would be time to make a rational decision between escalation to nuclear weapons use or capitulation.

Nuclear weapons were the other legacy of World War II. A number of countries were studying nuclear physics on the eve of the war, and Albert Einstein convinced President Franklin D. Roosevelt of the need to engage in research on the weapons potential of nuclear power to hedge against the success of the German research program (which never reached fruition in large part because a number of the critical German scientists were Jewish and fled the country). The American Manhattan Project succeeded in producing a bomb in early 1945, and the United States emerged from the war as the only nuclear power.

The U.S. nuclear monopoly did not last long. The Soviet Union exploded its first atomic (fission) device in 1949, and both countries successfully developed far deadlier nuclear explosives in the early 1950s. These thermonuclear (fission-fusion) devices replicate the energy production methods of the sun and produce explosions measurable in the equivalents of *millions of tons (megatons) of TNT*; by contrast, the atomic bombs of the 1940s produced explosions the equivalent of thousands of tons, or kilotons, of TNT. For some real-world comparison, the explosion of Mount St. Helens in Oregon in the 1980s was estimated at 40 megatons.

Parallel research was going on in the area of delivering nuclear and other weapons to their targets. Advances in rocketry produced the first successful Soviet intercontinental ballistic missile (ICBM) in 1957, a feat rapidly duplicated by the United States. Combined with similar work on shorter range missiles, both sides had missile-borne nuclear bombs aimed at one another by the time of the Cuban crisis, and the weapons could be delivered against their targets with no reasonable expectation they could be intercepted or neutralized. During the 1960s and 1970s, the arsenals grew enormously on both sides, with strategic inventories (those aimed at one another's homelands) numbering over ten thousand apiece and shorter range missiles dedicated to support of military forces in the European or other theaters numbering in the tens of thousands. Nuclear weapons thus served two distinct functions. The most dramatic and best publicized function was that assigned to the strategic nuclear forces (SNF), developed for potential use against the adversary's territory. The other was to support conventional operations.

As the arsenal sizes grew and became impossible to defend against, the thrust in nuclear weapons thinking and planning shifted to *deterrence*, the development and maintenance of weaponry to convince the opponent not to use its weapons against you. Since neither side could defend itself against an attack that was launched against it by nuclear-tipped missiles, the threat had to be based in retaliation and punishment of a nuclear transgressor. The idea was that a potential aggressor would realize that the victim of the attack would retain such a large surviving force as to be able to launch a devastating retaliatory strike, making the initial attack in effect suicidal. One concept used to describe this dynamic and the strategy to implement it in the 1960s was *assured destruction*, to which a detractor added the prefix "mutual," thereby creating an acronym reflecting his assessment of the idea: MAD.

It required the mindset of the Cold War for this nuclear balance to make sense, especially as the arsenals grew to the point that an all-out attack possessed enough destructive capacity to effectively immolate the enemy several times over—"make the rubble bounce," in Winston Churchill's phrase. Both sides continued aggressively to research and deploy yet more deadly weapons out of the fear that failing to do so would create some advantage the other might feel it could exploit in a nuclear attack. Lamenting this aspect of the nuclear arms race, President Jimmy Carter's Secretary of Defense Harold Brown summarized it: "We build, they build; we stop, they build." That the result was a policy and effective strategy of genocide and countergenocide (the effect if the arsenals were used) bothered mostly the nuclear disarmers.

The other role for nuclear weapons was in support of conventional operations, primarily in Europe. The purpose of these "battlefield" or "theater" nuclear weapons (TNWs) was as a force multiplier. In American planning, for instance, a major mission for TNWs was to help blunt the massive Soviet tank offensive that was presumed would be the opening foray of World War III. When masses of Soviet tanks approached the border, they would be attacked with nuclear warheads, thereby breaking up the assault. A special form of nuclear explosive, the enhanced radiation warhead, or neutron bomb, was applied specifically to this purpose (see Amplification 5.2).

Theater nuclear weapons were always more controversial than their strategic counterparts, especially among the European allies who would be "defended" by them. There was deep suspicion in Europe that their use could not be controlled: once the first nuclear weapons were used on the battlefield, the result would be escalation to broader use. Whether expansion would be limited to the theater or would expand to homeland exchanges between the superpowers could not be demonstrated. Since nuclear weapons had never been used in anger when both sides possessed them, there was absolutely no evidence to support or refute claims about whether or how escalation might occur.

Regardless of escalatory potential, most Europeans agreed that anyplace nuclear weapons were used would be a loser, an irradiated wasteland that would be uninhabitable until the radiation dissipated. Some Europeans even suspected that after decimating parts of Europe, the superpowers would pause, conclude that any further escalation placed their own territory at risk, and stop, arguing that they had done their duty to defend their allies.

Amplification 5.2

THE CAPITALIST BOMB

A major objection to the contemplated use of nuclear weapons in Europe was the enormous devastation their use would create for the very territory they were designed to defend. Europe—and especially Germany, where the bulk of the initial fighting would take place—would be a scarred and cratered radioactive moonscape unlikely to sustain life for years to come. On the other hand, nuclear weapons seemed militarily an effective way to destroy the concentrated armored tank assault that would spearhead the Soviet attack and against which there were inadequate alternatives.

These two diametrically opposed priorities were partially reconciled by a new form of nuclear explosive first tested in the early 1970s and proposed for deployment by the Carter administration during the latter 1970s. The new technology was something called the enhanced radiation warhead (ERW), which quickly earned the popular name the neutron bomb. Its innovation was to rearrange the relative effects of nuclear explosives. Any nuclear explosive produces four effects: a fireball of heat, extremely high winds known as blast overpressure, initial or prompt (beta and gamma ray) radiation, and residual radiation, also known as fallout. The chief culprits in a conventional nuclear explosion were blast overpressure, which knocks down structures and craters the landscape; the fireball, which causes fires; and fallout, which lingers in the physical environment for years to come. The fourth effect, prompt radiation, sends out deadly rays during the explosion itself, but once the explosion ends, it becomes relatively benign.

The neutron bomb rearranged nuclear effects so that 75 to 80 percent of the nuclear explosion involved the release of prompt radiation. This had two advantages given the problem it sought to overcome. First, the other effects of the weapon were reduced greatly, thereby doing less environmental damage—the concern of the local citizenry. Second, it seemed ideal against the Soviet tank threat. If the weapons were detonated over advancing Soviet tank columns, the deadly gamma and beta rays would penetrate Soviet armor and incapacitate and eventually kill the crews without destroying the tanks. The attacks would thus be halted, and one grisly plan was to have NATO troops remove the bodies and turn the tanks on the aggressors with NATO crews.

The Soviets howled at the proposal. They labeled it "the capitalist bomb," a weapon that killed people in a grotesquely cruel manner but did not destroy the productive system it sought to protect. They threatened to produce their own neutron bombs, and the Europeans could never quite bring themselves to support any nuclear defense of Europe. Deployment was delayed, and eventually the plan to deploy the capitalist bomb in Europe was scrapped with the signing of the Intermediate Nuclear Forces (INF) Treaty in 1988, which removed most nuclear weapons from Europe.

DEADLOCK OF THE COMPETITION

Even when the Cold War competition was proceeding in its most vigorous manner, the seeds of its demise were being sown. By the 1970s, two trends, unrecognized at the time, were beginning to congeal that would militate toward the end of the Cold War. One trend was the weakening of the Soviet economy both absolutely and in comparison to that of the United States. The other was a growing recognition of a deadlock in the military competition between the superpower blocs. By the 1980s, they coalesced to create the conditions that led to the end of the Cold War.

The Economic Dimension

The economic implosion that eventually engulfed the Soviet state had its roots in the 1970s or even before. By the 1970s, economic growth began to slow, and by the end of the decade, the Soviet economy had stopped growing altogether, what Soviet economists would later call the "era of stagnation." By the early 1980s, the only economic growth in the Soviet Union was apparently in the production of vodka, and if vodka production was removed from measures of productivity, the Soviet economy was in absolute decline. Indeed, when Gorbachev mandated limits in vodka production in the mid-1980s, the economy was adversely affected.

This problem was known to some Soviet academic economists, but they lacked access to the leadership cadre associated with Soviet leader Leonid Brezhnev (known as the *nomenklatua*), who benefited from the system and were uninterested in seeing change that might adversely affect their privilege. Instead, the academic economists allied themselves with a rising star within the Communist Party, Mikhail S. Gorbachev, whose wife, Raisa, was their colleague at Moscow State University. When Gorbachev achieved power in 1985, this cadre was ready to roll out the mechanisms of reform. Unfortunately for them, their efforts were too little and too late.

A good bit of the Soviet decline was due to lagging behind in science and technology. The Soviets were largely excluded from the high-technology revolution in the West that underlay the economic expansion of the 1980s and 1990s and the process of globalization of the world economy. Part of this exclusion was purposive—to shield a shaky economy from outside competition. Two additional dynamics exacerbated this technological gap. First, the problem was progressive. The motor of technological growth was the development of more sophisticated generations of computers. This is a progressive process, because the major tool for designing the next generation of computers is the current generation. Thus, the computer industry's future health depends on its current competitiveness. Moreover, the developmental time between generations has grown shorter because of the greater power of newer machines. Translated, that means the farther a country is behind (the more generations removed from the cutting edge), the farther it gets behind in the future. By the early 1980s, the Soviet Union was approximately three generations behind the United States, and the gap was widening.

The Soviets could not close the gap. The decision to concentrate on military development had been at the expense of the computer research section of the Soviet Academy of Scientists in the 1960s, and its personnel were distributed to military research. The Soviets even stole computers, tore them down, and put them back together again so they could replicate the system (a process known as reverse engineering). It did not help. The systems they stole represented current technology becoming obsolete, and reverse engineering took longer than the development of new generations.

The second dynamic was that the Soviets were not allowed to collaborate with the West in technology. Almost all the technologies in which the Soviets were behind were *dual use*, meaning they had both military and civilian applications. For instance, a computer designed for research in theoretical physics could be converted to applying physical principles to weapons design. As long as the Soviet Union was the avowed enemy, the United States and the rest of the West were not going to provide the Soviets with capabilities that might produce weapons with which to menace them.

Most of these dynamics went largely unnoticed in the West at the time. Soviet economists were rarely allowed to communicate with their western counterparts, the Soviet government doctored economic statistics that were notoriously inaccurate anyway (and thus disbelieved), and the military production system, on which attention was concentrated, seemed to be working well. In fact, when the Central Intelligence Agency produced an analysis of the Soviet economy in the middle 1970s suggesting the possibility of its decline, the report was condemned and an alternate panel was assembled to reassess the material. That group produced a more ominous analysis, which was largely wrong. Since its conclusions reinforced what officials believed to be the case, it was widely accepted.

The Military Dimension

The military competition was, by the end of the 1970s, also undergoing change to the ultimate disadvantage of the Soviet Union. The competition had essentially deadlocked into a very deadly but ritual confrontation in which neither side seemed to be able to obtain meaningful advantage. This competition was enormously burdensome to a Soviet economy that was much smaller than that of the United States and that needed to divert the resources devoted to the military for economic purposes if the Soviets hoped to compete economically. The military competition, in a word, had become a millstone around the neck of the Soviet future. The weight became unbearable in the late 1980s, when their ill-fated, expensive, and unpopular intervention in Afghanistan contributed to the demise of the Soviet state.

The seeds for military deadlock can be traced back to the Cuban crisis, when both sides confronted the potential reality of nuclear war and did not like what they saw. Despite the recognition of a mutual interest in avoiding nuclear war that was the major outgrowth of that crisis, the military competition, if anything, expanded and intensified in the following years. Many in the American national security community remained deeply suspicious of anything the Soviets did (and vice versa) and continued to build up stocks of arms, especially in the area of strategic nuclear forces, as if the Cuban experience had not changed anything.

While the potential deadliness of the nuclear balance expanded, the danger of nuclear war was actually declining, even if this decline was mostly unrealized. The prospect of nuclear war with the levels of arms available in 1962 was sobering, but the prospect of such a war fought with the arsenals of 1980 was positively catastrophic. Leaders on both sides going back as far as President Dwight D. Eisenhower in the 1950s and Soviet Premier Nikita Khrushchev in the early 1960s had publicly proclaimed the unacceptability of nuclear war as a means to resolve East–West differences. These original pronouncements were made when arsenal sizes numbered in the hundreds; when both sides recognized what could happen if the ten thousand or more weapons both possessed were unleashed, avoiding such a war became imperative.

The necessary step to reduce the danger—or likelihood—of war between the two sides was to add the unacceptability of conventional war to the relationship. The key element in accomplishing this was the uncertainty of the escalatory process. A conventional war would become a nuclear war if escalation occurred, and there was no empirical basis on which to predict confidently whether that escalation would occur. In that circumstance, the only certain way to avoid nuclear war between the superpowers was to avoid *any* war between them.

This "necessary peace," as I described it in a 1987 book with that title, reduced the Cold War military competition to ritual status. Both sides developed and deployed weapons and conducted war games with them for the precise reason of avoiding their use in war. The old military axiom of "preparing for and fighting the country's wars" became twisted to "preparing to avoid fighting the country's wars."

The recognition of military deadlock came at a time when the burden of the arms race was clearly contributing to the crisis of the Soviet economy. The Soviets were plowing upward of one-quarter of a gross national product (GNP) into defense spending from an economy probably only about one-third the size of the American economy. When support for foreign adventures in places like Cuba and Mozambique and the direct expense of their war in Afghanistan were added to the Cold War "bill" for the Soviets, the burden was becoming overwhelming. In 1981, the administration of Ronald W. Reagan announced the largest arms buildup in peacetime American history, and one of the explicit purposes of the increase in arms was to force the Soviets into an economically ruinous arms race by trying to keep up with the American expansion.

Convergence

These two dimensions had converged as Gorbachev succeeded Konstantin Chernenko as the Soviet leader in 1985. Gorbachev seemed a new kind of Soviet leader. He was the first leader of the Soviet Union with a college degree, was a lawyer by training, and was clearly more urbane and sophisticated than his predecessors, preferring well-tailored Italian silk suits to the baggy gray gabardine associated with older Soviet leaders. His professor wife Raisa was also a handsome, urbane, and very public figure—in contrast to the dowager images of Gorbachev's predecessors' wives (some of whom were never seen in public). When Gorbachev went to London as one of his first acts and clearly charmed British Prime Minister Margaret Thatcher, it was clear that he was a different character than those he succeeded.

Gorbachev faced a daunting set of problems. He knew about the economic problems from the Soviet professors, and he sought to reform the economic system. As a believing Marxist, his approach was to fine-tune the existing system, but the system itself was beyond repair, and he was slow in recognizing that the system and the assumptions on which it rested were the problem.

He also realized that much of the economic problem was the result of the isolation of the Soviet economy. Gorbachev ultimately recognized that the only chance for economic redemption was to open the country to the West. Western technology was absolutely critical to any attempts at economic modernization and hence competitiveness, and an influx of Western capital was clearly necessary to fund improved economic performance. But how could the Soviets convince a suspicious West to engage itself with the Soviet economic system? How could they convince an even more suspicious American national security establishment that shared technology would not be turned into hostile tools of war?

The military problem was much the same. When Gorbachev entered office, the Soviets were engaged in their fifth year of a frustrating, unsuccessful war in Afghanistan that was draining the treasury and corroding the society in ways not dissimilar to the effects of the Vietnam War on the United States. Eventually, Soviet forces would have to withdraw from Afghanistan in disgrace, which became a factor in the ultimate demise of the Soviet Union. The effects of trying to match the Reagan buildup were adding to the strains, and pitiful client states like Cuba looked increasingly like unaffordable luxuries.

What was Gorbachev to do? The choices were not attractive. The status quo certainly could not be sustained, and trying to tinker with the system through the economic and political reforms known as *perestroika* was not working. The Soviet Union was sinking fast as a state and as a power. A radical solution was needed.

The answer was to sacrifice the Cold War competition. The logic of the Soviet situation dictated the decision. Economic stagnation was eroding the standing of the Soviet Union in the world and was progressively reducing the standard of living of Soviet citizens. The Soviet Union was becoming, as many critics described it, "a third-world country with nuclear weapons." To change that situation, they needed access to western technology and capital, and their only hope was to cease being the enemy and to join the community of states as a normal rather than a rogue member. The same logic held for the military dimension. Competing with the Reagan buildup, continuing the frustrating burden of the Afghanistan war, and supporting losers like Castro were becoming unbearable and unsustainable. Canceling the losing game the Cold War had become was an increasingly attractive option.

The world stood by in stunned silence as the Soviet leader began to unravel the forty-year-long confrontation. Gorbachev published a blueprint of the changes he proposed in a 1987 book, *Perestroika: New Thinking for Our Country and the World.* In it, he proposed a detailed internal reform plan. In the international realm, he detailed the transformation of the Soviet Union into a "normal" state by policy changes such as noninterference in the affairs of other states and renunciation of the so-called Brezhnev Doctrine that had justified Soviet intervention in Socialist states and had been used as the rationale for Soviet invasions of Hungary, Czechoslovakia, and Afghanistan.

Perestroika was initially greeted with skepticism in the West. Many analysts presumed that the book was nothing more than an elaborate web of lies to lower the West's guard. But then Gorbachev began to act in accordance with the book's proposals. In 1989, the Soviet Union completed its military withdrawal from Afghanistan, despite having accomplished none of its goals. Also in 1989, it stood idly by when the Polish parliament seated a non-Communist government, an act that opened the floodgates for the rapid decommunization of Eastern Europe and, in 1991, the formal dissolution of the Warsaw Pact. These inactions seemed to implement renunciation of the Brezhnev Doctrine and the principle of noninterference in the affairs of other states.

Domestic reform was not dramatic or attractive enough to avoid the breakup of the Soviet Union itself. Led by the Baltic states (Lithuania, Latvia, and Estonia), the constituent republics of the Soviet Union announced their intention to withdraw from the union and establish themselves as independent states. On the last tick of the clock of 1991, the red Soviet flag came down from the Kremlin for the last time, replaced the next day by the Russian tricolor of red, white, and blue.

The peaceful implosion of the Soviet state was—and is—an unprecedented political act in world history. States, including major powers, have from time to time ceased to exist through Carthaginian peaces or partition at the ends of wars, but for one of the world's two most powerful countries simply to vote itself out of existence was something that had not happened before and that was entirely unanticipated both within and outside Russia. Ultimately, the reason hardly anyone considered adequately, the excluded possibility of a peaceful end of the Cold War, was because nothing like what happened ever had occurred before.

So why did Gorbachev end the Cold War? The short answer is that he had no choice. The old system was broken, if not exactly the way he and his advisors thought at the time. Knowing the system could not be revived without considerable outside assistance, Gorbachev also understood that the *sine qua non* for assistance was to end the Cold War and to remove its most obviously annoying symbols: the Iron Curtain, the Berlin Wall, and most important, the structure of military confrontation. They did not foresee that the cost would be the destruction of the edifice they had sought to strengthen.

Fascinating questions remain. Could the Cold War have been ended without the destruction of the Soviet Union? If so, what would world politics look like today? If Gorbachev had anticipated the real price of ending the Cold War, would he have gone through with it? In another vein, was the outcome foreordained regardless of who was in the Kremlin in the middle 1980s, or was it the unique contribution of

Gorbachev to stimulate the destruction of the internal barriers to change and the Soviet state itself? What problems did the end of the Cold War leave behind? More recently, the question "Could it return?" has been added to the mix.

COLD WAR RESIDUES

The end of the Cold War left a geopolitical void in the international system. Most of the gaping hole was in Europe and centered around two axes. The first, and potentially most traumatic, was what succeeded a former Soviet Union now divided into fifteen independent states, of which the Russian Federation is the pivot, and the second was the collapse of the Communist order in Eastern Europe. There still remains some process of adjustment among the states of the former Soviet Union itself, and most of the East European transitions from Communism to Western forms have occurred or are well under way. More recently, however, the possible resurgence of Russia as a world power (introduced earlier) has become a cause for concern.

Russia and the Successor States

When the Soviet Union dissolved, Russia was the largest single state that emerged from the breakup, containing roughly half the population and three-quarters of the land mass of the old Soviet Union. Russia also has maintained most of the military power of the old Soviet Union, notably the thermonuclear arsenal. Although beset by enormous and debilitating political and economic problems that unquestionably diminished its place in the world in the 1990s, Russia's growing oil wealth has reversed that fate, and Russia and its future remain an important international concern.

The Russian situation can be divided into political, economic, and military questions. The political and economic aspects focus on the transformation of the Russian system away from its totalitarian, socialist past under Communism to some more western democratic and capitalist future. Its progress in these areas has been mixed. Militarily, Russia has been in a process of decline that began before the fall of Communism, but it remains a nuclear superpower.

The political and economic transformation of Russia has moved forward in interrelated fits and starts. The political system has had to develop democratic support in a system where economic chaos and even free fall have become virtually institutional features. Economically, an attempt to institute market practices is being grafted onto an inherited institutional framework woefully inappropriate and inadequate for the market to take hold and prosper. When the Soviet Union became Russia, for instance, the country had essentially no banking or other financial laws or institutions, making it virtually impossible to regulate financial dealings. It lacked mechanisms to collect taxes to run the government. The breakdown of the Communist levers of state coercion left the country with inadequate policing capacity that has resulted in the violent actions of the *Mafioso* and other forms of lawlessness. Pensioners who believed the Communist state would support their old age found themselves holding the bag, as the "social net" promised by the Communist state was withdrawn from them.

Politically, the record is also mixed. Russia has held four relatively free elections for president, and in the third one in 2000, power was peacefully passed from Boris Yeltsin to Vladimir Putin, a momentous occasion in Russian history. Since the re-election of Putin in 2004, some international concern has been raised (especially by the United States) about the Russian president's commitment to Western democracy as a result of actions that have had the effect of greatly centralizing power in his hands. Putin dismisses these criticisms as manifestations of a distinctly Russian form and evolution of democracy, a stance that continues to raise concerns. The 2008 presidential elections in Russia in which Putin would not be a candidate will be an important benchmark.

Russia also has serious military and security problems. One of the major themes of Russian history has been a concern—some argue paranoia—with military security that has been reinforced by invaders as diverse as the Mongol hordes, Napoleon Bonaparte, and Adolf Hitler. A major reason for constructing the Communist empire in Eastern Europe after World War II, after all, was to provide a *cordon sanitaire* (buffer zone) between Russia and future invaders. That buffer zone is gone.

The relative assurance of Russian physical security was a victim of both the end of the Cold War and the breakup of the Soviet Union. The demise of the Cold War meant Russia lost its Warsaw Pact allies; the breakup of the Soviet Union meant Ukrainians, Moldavians, and others were no longer part of the Russian security scheme and might even become part of the new security problem.

Russia has other military problems. Partly because of budgetary problems, the military itself has deteriorated markedly. Because they are unable to subsist on wages that often are not paid, it has not been unusual to see Russian soldiers in uniform working second jobs or panhandling on the streets of Moscow. The backbone of the Russian army is first-term conscripts, many of whom desert at the first possible opportunity with the implicit approval of the society. Even the prestigious Strategic Rocket Forces that control the Russian nuclear forces are leading advocates of arms control–dictated deep cuts in arsenal size, since they cannot maintain the current arsenal at any acceptable level of readiness and security. The army's efficiency has been reduced to the point that it was unable to put down a ragtag Muslim rebellion in Chechnya and resorted to atrocities and the virtual leveling of the province to maintain control. The importance of Chechnya to Russia is explored in Amplification 5.3.

The solution to the Russian security problem centers on its evolving relationship with NATO. Originally, of course, NATO was formed largely to deter Soviet aggression; today, security is served by courting and embracing Russia. The problem is, How? Full NATO membership for Russia is one possibility, but it faces opposition that has to this point proven insurmountable. The chief obstacle is the status of Russia if it is a member—would it be a regular member like France or Germany or a "special" member like the United States? Currently, the solution is Russian participation through the NATO-Russian Council, a consultative relationship and arrangement that allows Russian access to NATO short of being a member.

Amplification 5.3

CHECHNYA AND THE PIPELINE

Russian security concerns and adaptation to a post–Cold War world have, in important ways, coalesced over the issue of Chechnya, a renegade republic in the Caucasus region of Russia that declared its independence from the Russian Federation in 1994 and has been fighting the Russians ever since to become an independent Muslim state. Like many other areas of the southern part of Russia, the citizens are not ethnic Russians and live in areas forcefully annexed to Russia.

Chechnya represents the Soviet dilemma of dealing with the post–Cold War period in at least three ways. One is clearly the precedent that would be set if Chechnya were allowed to secede from a Russia already diminished by the dissolution of the Soviet Union. Second, the ferocity—even barbarism—of the fighting created a public relations nightmare for the Russian government. The once proud Russian army has largely been ineffective in putting down the rebellion and has been reduced to leveling Chechen cities like Grozny to the ground, with pictorial documentation widely available worldwide. In the process, widespread accusations by human rights groups of atrocities committed by the Russians have caused embarrassment to the Russians and slowed the flow of developmental assistance to Russia. Since September 11, 2001, the Russians have sought to portray the Chechens as part of the web of international terrorism operating out of Afghanistan and Pakistan. Some of the Chechen "freedom fighters" have been shown to have common roots with Al Qaeda and other terrorist groups, and this depiction by the Russians has stilled much of the criticism of their brutality toward Chechnya.

The real heart of the Russian problem in Chechnya, however, revolves around getting Caspian Sea oil from Azerbaijan to markets in the West. Because the pipelines that will carry the oil can be taxed, there is great potential wealth that can be accrued to whatever country wins the competition to have the pipeline built across its territory. The possible routes are across Iran (not much of an alternative, since much of the reason for exploiting Caspian oil is to reduce dependence on the Persian Gulf), Turkey, and Russia. The Russians argue the revenue is absolutely vital to Russian economic development because it would greatly augment the central government's tax revenues. The problem, however, is that by far the most direct and economically viable way to build a pipeline across Russia is to build it through Chechnya. As long as there is an embarrassing armed rebellion in that republic, Russia's chances are visibly diminished (the pipeline problem is discussed in some detail in Snow, *Cases in International Relations*, Chapter 14).

The ideal outcome to the Russian situation is the gradual emergence of Russia as a fully westernized political democracy with a growing and prosperous market-based economy that is a full participant in the international system. The alternative, explored in the next section, is the possible resurgence of an authoritarian and possibly antagonistic Russia.

The direction and future of the poorer and more remote successor states, and especially those in central Asia, have also become a source of concern. Most of these new countries are very poor, have few prospects for economic development or the emergence of democracy (generally lacking any democratic traditions), and have Muslim majorities or minorities that threaten to drag them into the instability of Muslim fundamentalism. In 2002, a number of these states were drawn into the campaign against international terrorism by the United States, with uncertain effects (discussed in the *Challenge!* box).

Challenge!

THE FORMER SOVIET UNION AND THE WAR ON TERRORISM

War, it is sometimes said, makes strange bedfellows, and the attempt by the U.S. government to internationalize its warlike campaign against terrorism seems to provide some evidence for the truth of that proposition. Nowhere is that relationship more clearly demonstrated than in the extension of partnership in the "war on terrorism" to central Asian states and Russia itself.

One of chief problems the Bush administration encountered early in trying to mount military, and especially ground, operations to clear out Al Qaeda and Taliban residues in Afghanistan was staging grounds for such efforts. For a variety of reasons, the territory of some American associates was either unavailable politically for such actions (Saudi Arabia, Pakistan, for instance) or was too remote for efficient use (Turkey). In those circumstances, the United States turned to contiguous states, former Soviet central Asian republics that had gained their independence with the breakup of the Soviet Union. To facilitate the military campaign, the United States signed basing agreements with states including Tajikistan, Kyrgyzstan, and Uzbekistan and opened discussions with others.

These arrangements immediately brought the American government into policy disagreement with itself, a problem that extended to Russian assistance to the effort as well (after eight years of war in Afghanistan, the Russians are a major source of intelligence on that country). The policy incompatibility pitted counterterrorism policy against human rights policy, because many of the new allies in the campaign against terrorism, including Russia, were also on the Department of State's list (as well as those of independent sources such as Amnesty International and Human Rights Watch) of states that violated the civil rights of their citizens and thus were to be sanctioned until those practices ceased.

How is the dilemma to be resolved? Is the war on terrorism such an important priority that it overrides other concerns, in this case human rights? Is there a parallel to the Cold War here? During the Cold War, the United States supported many corrupt right-wing regimes that regularly abused their citizens because their leaders professed staunch anti-Communism. Anti-Communism overrode other concerns. Is the profession of opposition to terrorism and willingness to aid in the campaign against terrorism the new anti-Communism of the contemporary age? Is it worth the price in the long run to be associated with regimes that abuse their citizens? Decide for yourself.

Russian Resurgence

The balance of the 1990s after the dissolution of the Soviet Union was problematical for Russia. The Soviet superpower that Russia had dominated (indeed, some analysts referred to the Soviet Union as a twentieth-century Russian empire) shrunk physically and geopolitically. A mixture of often antagonistic regimes arose in the successor states, which the Russians referred to as the "near abroad" (indicating a special relationship with the Russians generally not felt in those countries but reflecting the sizable remaining Russian minorities that had been planted there as part of Soviet policy), and these regimes viewed Russia with defiant distrust. Despite its maintenance of Soviet nuclear weapons, Russia's conventional power receded to the point that many who had feared the Soviets ceased fearing Russia. As the 1990s progressed, the Russian economy continued to decline into a state of chaos that left many wondering if the non-authoritarian regime could maintain power. Russian political democracy hung in the balance. As the change of millennia took place, the prognosis for the Russian state was clearly in question.

By the middle of the 2000s, that prognosis had changed radically. The cause of change has been a resurgent Russian economy, and the engine of that resurgence has been Russia's emergence as the second-leading exporter of petroleum in the world, as noted earlier. The economic results have been striking. As Ukrainian political leader Yuliya Tymoshenko pointed out in a 2007 *Foreign Affairs* article, Russia is now sustaining a 6.5 percent annual economic growth rate and is in the process of paying off most of the external debt accumulated during the 1990s. Economic prosperity has come—albeit selectively—to Russia and Russians.

The political dynamics associated with this resurgence have been more potentially troublesome both domestically and internationally. Domestically, there has been a gradual accumulation of power to the presidency at the expense of the Russian parliament (the Duma) under Putin, and that trend has been particularly pronounced during the second Putin term, which has coincided with Russia's emergence as a major petroleum exporter. The concentration of power in the presidency has caused concern among observers (Tymoshenko and Azar Gat, for instance) and President Bush that Russia may be returning to aspects of its authoritarian past.

Much of this turn in Russian internal politics has gone on virtually unnoticed by many in the West. One aspect of authoritarian change has been repression of the Soviet media, meaning there has been less public venting of opposition than in the pre-Putin era. There has also not been a great deal of dissent to Putin's consolidation of power except among democratic reformers who have been the victims of the process. Why?

There are two basic answers, one largely domestic and the other international and at the heart of international concerns. Thomas L. Friedman describes the domestic side in terms of Russia's emergence as a *petrolist* state. In states that have great petroleum wealth but lack firm democratic traditions, governments can sometimes strike a kind of Faustian bargain with their populations wherein petroleum wealth is distributed to the citizenry to improve their material conditions, and in return the citizens cede some political rights to the government. The dynamic is what Friedman calls the first law of petropolitics: "the price of oil and the pace of freedom always move in opposite directions in oil-rich petrolist states." Putin and Venezuela's Hugo Chavez are specifically cited as practitioners of petrolist politics.

This movement toward authoritarian politics has impeded Russia's full entrance into the circle of democratic states, but it also has potentially troubling international repercussions. During the 1990s, Russia was a non-assertive, compliant member of the international order, at least in part because its increasingly desperate economic condition left it in no position to pursue the assertive, expansionist foreign policy of its predecessor. This change has been humiliating to many Russians, who seek a return to Russian status as a major world power. The decline of Russian military power has been especially vexing, as witnessed by the inability of the military to crush Chechen resistance and anti-Russian actions in "near abroad" states like Georgia.

Russian oil wealth at least partly mitigates this condition. The possession of a scarce resource provides Russia with a new source of leverage unavailable to its Soviet predecessor, and European dependence on Russian oil and natural gas provides the Russians with significance in Europe. Oil wealth also provides the possibility of significantly rebuilding Russia's shattered armed forces should it choose to do so.

Hardly anyone is confidently projecting the international impact of Russian resurgence. The worst-case scenario is that Russia will be transformed into a new authoritarian—if capitalist—state that could become as antagonistic as the fascist states of the 1930s and reinstate something like a new Cold War. Most observers find this extreme outcome unlikely or at least premature to project at this time. Nonetheless, the retreat of Russia from the democratizing trajectory of the 1990s and very early 2000s represents a troubling phenomenon. The outcome of scheduled elections in 2008 will help shed light on whether Russia will evolve as a petrolist or democratic state and what that evolution means for Russia's role in the world. Which outcome emerges, of course, has tremendous implications for American national security.

CONCLUSION: THE END OF THE COLD WAR IN PERSPECTIVE

Viewed strictly from the vantage point of the twenty-first century, the Cold War years must seem an anomalous period, one that probably should be consigned to the history books. Although many of the problems and tensions associated with the second half of the twentieth century have proven to be less enduring than those who witnessed them thought they would be, such a view would be shortsighted and would miss the point of how the Cold War continues to influence the present and possibly the future.

The Cold War remains the context from which the contemporary system is emerging. Among the overarching concerns of the new millennium are the integration of the formerly Marxist-Leninist states into the globalization system, a problem that clearly could not have existed had there not been a furtive competition between ideologically defined contenders in the first place. This process of integration is being stimulated by the enlistment of former enemies as allies in the campaign against terrorism. The consequences of this initiative are uncertain but probably extend beyond the terrorism campaign itself. For better or worse, many of the contemporary difficulties with which the world grapples have their origins in the Cold War and can only be fully understood in that light.

There is a more fundamental reason to understand the Cold War and its ending. Most of the people in important decision-making positions in the 1990s and 2000s—and especially senior people in senior positions—have the Cold War as their formative experience, and their thinking was and continues to be influenced by the very grim, determined worldview that "working" the Cold War produced. In the Bush administration, the list of foreign and national security policy insiders with Cold War credentials includes former Secretary of Defense Rumsfeld and his successor Robert Gates (who is by training a Russian historian), Secretary of State Rice, and Vice President Richard Cheney, to name the most prominent.

Russia's evolution is not yet complete. Russia may be neither Communist nor the Soviet Union, but it is still the largest country in the world physically, it is the largest unexploited source of many mineral and energy resources, it still has nuclear weapons, and petroleum is fueling its resurgence among the world's powers. The decline of Russia so dramatically witnessed in the 1990s is giving way to a new, possibly more traditional power role in the 2000s, the contours and dimensions of which are not entirely clear.

STUDY/DISCUSSION QUESTIONS

1. How and why did the dissolution of the Soviet Union and the end of the Cold War represent a traumatic event for the international system? Discuss.
2. Discuss the Cold War system. What were its major characteristics, and how did they help define how the system operated? What were the sources of change that occurred over time?
3. The heart of the Cold War system was the military competition between the United States and the Soviet Union. Discuss the dimensions of that competition.
4. How did the East–West competition deadlock? Discuss the economic and military dimensions of that deadlock and how they led Soviet leader Mikhail S. Gorbachev to conclude the competition had to be ended.
5. What are the two major residues of the end of the Cold War? In particular, analyze the problem of Russian resurgence.
6. Based on your reading, what kind of Russia do you think is likely to evolve in the future? Why?

SELECTED BIBLIOGRAPHY

Aslund, Anders. "The Hunt for Russia's Riches." *Foreign Policy* (January/February 2006), 42–49.

Bialer, Seweryn, and Michael Mandelbaum (eds.). *Gorbachev's Russia and American Foreign Policy.* Boulder, CO: Westview Press, 1988.

Bremmer, Jan, and Samuel Charap. "The Sikoriki in Putin's Russia: Who They Are and What They Want." *Washington Quarterly* 30, 1 (Winter 2006–2007), 83–92.

Brzezinski, Zbigniew. "The Cold War and Its Aftermath." *Foreign Affairs* 71, 4 (Fall 1992), 31–49.

Clark, Ronald W. *The Greatest Power on Earth: The International Race for Nuclear Supremacy, Earliest Theory to Three Mile Island.* New York: Harper and Row, 1980.

Claude, Inis L. *The Changing United Nations.* New York: Random House, 1967.

Friedman, Thomas L. "The First Law of Petropolitics." *Foreign Policy* (May/June 2006), 28–36.

Fukuyama, Francis. *The End of History and the Last Man.* New York: Free Press, 1992.

Gaddis, John Lewis. *The United States and the End of the Cold War: Implications, Reconsiderations, Provocations.* New York: Oxford University Press, 1992.

Gat, Azar. "The Return of Authoritarian Great Powers." *Foreign Affairs* 86, 4 (July/August 2007), 59–69.

Gorbachev, Mikhail S. *Perestroika: New Thinking for Our Country and the World.* New York: Harper and Row, 1987.

Lieven, Anatol. "The Essential Vladimir Putin." *Foreign Policy* (January/February 2005), 72–74.

Mearsheimer, John J. "Why We Shall Soon Miss the Cold War." *Atlantic Monthly* 262, 2 (August 1990), 35–50.

Mendelson, Sarah, and Theodore P. Gerber. "Failing the Stalin Test." *Foreign Affairs* 85, 1 (January/February 2006), 2–8.

———. "Soviet Nostalgia: An Impediment to Russian Democratization." *Washington Quarterly* 29, 1 (Winter 2005–2006), 81–96.

Orlov, Vladimir A., and Miriam Fugfugosh. "The G-8 Strelna Summit and Russia's National Power." *Washington Quarterly* 29, 3 (Summer 2006), 35–49.

Rose, Richard, William Mishler, and Neil Munro. *Russia Transformed: Developing Popular Support for a New Regime.* New York: Cambridge University Press, 2006.

Shevtsova, Lilia. "Russia's Ersatz Democracy." *Current History* 105, 693 (October 2006), 307–314.

Simes, Dmitri. "The Return of Russian History." *Foreign Affairs* 73, 1 (January/February 1992), 67–82.

Snow, Donald M. *The Necessary Peace: Nuclear Weapons and Superpower Relations.* Lexington, MA: Lexington Books, 1987.

———. *The Shape of the Future: The Post–Cold War World* (3rd ed.). Armonk, NY: M. E. Sharpe, 1999.

———. *Cases in International Relations: Portraits of the Future* (3rd ed.). New York: Pearson Longman 2008.

Stephenova, Ekaterina. "War and Peace Building." *Washington Quarterly* 27, 4 (Autumn 2004), 127–136.

Tymoshenko, Yuliya. "Containing Russia." *Foreign Affairs* 86, 3 (May/June 2007), 69–82.

Wallander, Celeste A. "Suspended Animation: The US and Russia After the G-8." *Current History* 105, 693 (October 2006), 315–320.

CHAPTER 6

Globalization and Beyond: New Influences on National Security

PREVIEW

The geopolitical perspective that casts national security in terms of power with a heavy military tone is not the only way to think about security. Other ways of thinking about what makes the United States safe have historically competed with the military conceptualization; in the 1990s, economic considerations in the guise of globalization arguably challenged geopolitics as the dominant security paradigm. Globalization and other security concerns will continue to be important influences on national security in a post-Iraq world. This chapter looks at the post–World War II emergence and evolution of the economic factors culminating in globalization in the 1990s. It then examines the lower-profile influence of globalization in the 2000s, including domestic and international reactions to globalization and the emergence of alternate sources of security concern—notably, energy, the environment, and the U.S. border. The chapter concludes by speculating on possible effects globalization and these other concerns may have on the post-Iraq conceptualization of security.

Americans have historically not been entirely comfortable thinking of the world and their place in it entirely in geopolitical terms, in which war and the use of military force play a prominent part in the national existence. In the 150-plus years of the formative period, military affairs—and especially the use of military force—were considered aberrations, unwelcome interruptions in the normalcy of peace. As the

United States emerged on the world stage after the American Civil War, it was American economic prowess, not military power, that distinguished the country as a world power. The economic instrument of power, of which globalization is the newest manifestation, has a long-held place in American life.

Since the end of World War II, geopolitics has been boosted to the forefront first by the Cold War and more recently by September 11 and the Iraq War. The end of the Cold War provided a reprise during the 1990s in which globalization served as the instrument of economic challenge to geopolitics. Will the reaction to Iraq, along with other concerns, create a similar reaction? In order to assess that possibility (which is attempted in the conclusion of this chapter), it is first necessary to examine the nature and evolution of globalization and other challenges such as energy, the environment, and more recently, the U.S. border.

Globalization and the impact of the globalizing economy were the centerpiece of the 1990s, just as terrorism has become the lightning rod of the early 2000s. During the 1990s, the international system moved away from its Cold War emphasis on geopolitically based national security concerns. After the global economic recession of 1991 faded in 1992 and 1993, a period of growing economic prosperity and expansion blossomed as a trade-driven global phenomenon, and the economies of participating countries expanded in a near decade of unprecedented economic growth. This phenomenon was felt in most of the developed and parts of the developing world, but nowhere was it more evident than in the U.S. economy and for individual Americans. The U.S. economy emerged from a decade or more of relative economic listlessness to reclaim its position as the dominant economic force in the world.

This period of economic expansion induced an overreaction about the degree and depth of transformation that had occurred. Until the system endured a major shakeup in the form of the East Asian crisis of 1997, there was a near-euphoria about the benefits and endurance of globalization's seemingly inexorable benefits. Analysts suggested that this new phenomenon of globalization was fundamentally altering the world system. Globalization simultaneously accelerated and changed the product cycle and production system at a dizzying pace and allowed for unprecedented levels and speed of communication between governments, citizens, and firms worldwide. To its most vocal adherents, realism-based geopolitics was giving way to globalization as the dominant force in international relations.

The relative roles of geopolitics and globalization fit into the broader debate about America's place in the world after Iraq developed throughout the book. The internationalist strain in America's view of the world has always been strongly represented in the economic debate, and the United States has been a leader in the promotion of increased world trade since it emerged as an industrial power after the American Civil War. Even when the country withdrew *politically* from international affairs between the world wars into "splendid isolationism," it remained a very active member of the international economic system. The same internationalism that manifests itself in a politically activist role and an expansive view of the country's military obligations is also a part of the economic debate, the current focus of which is globalization.

The strains of geopolitics and globalization represent different places in thinking about national security as well. Clearly, the two perspectives are not mutually exclusive but exist more along a continuum of relative emphasis on one element or the other. Geopolitics, for instance, may emphasize power and military force as chief elements of national security, but those elements have little meaning if not applied to the furtherance of American interests in areas such as economics, environmental degradation, or other substantive conditions that define security. At the same time, the pursuit of economic or other security conditions is likely to be incomplete, even impossible, without traditional military force somewhere in the background.

The purpose of this chapter is to create a foundation for thinking about the role and impact of economic and other concerns on foreign and national security policy. It proceeds historically from the end of World War II, dividing the American international economic experience into three distinct periods. The discussion begins with the American-dominated economic system that emerged from World War II, the Bretton Woods system. It then moves to the transitional period between the American denunciation of the gold standard in 1971 and the emergence of globalism somewhere around the end of the 1980s. It concludes with the contemporary period of globalization and where it may be leading, particularly in light of the resurgence of terrorism-led geopolitics in 2001. This contemporary period has also witnessed the addition of other national security agenda items, which are noted and briefly described.

THE BRETTON WOODS SYSTEM, 1945–1971

What became known as the Bretton Woods system had its roots in World War II. It reflected perceptions about how the interwar international economic system had helped precipitate the war and about the nature of the postwar international economic situation. The result was a series of international negotiations dominated by the Americans and the British that produced an institutional framework that organized the revised and rejuvenated economic order.

The Setting

Two overarching international economic facts dominated the international scene in 1945 and were the major concerns of postwar planners seeking to recreate an international system that would not slide back to instability and yet another devastating war. How, in other words, could the international economic system contribute to the geopolitical goal of war avoidance? First, the United States emerged from the war with the overwhelmingly largest and most robust economy in the world. It was thus the only country capable of leading a postwar reconstruction of the global economy. Second, most economic observers believed that economic policies pursued between the world wars had contributed significantly to the slide toward war. Each fact had major implications for the restructuring of the global economy.

The American economy had been rescued and strengthened absolutely and relatively by World War II. The U.S. economy had been hard hit by the Great Depression (as had Germany's, and that impact was partially blamed for the rise of Hitler and thus the war). When the United States entered the war, its unused industrial capacity was activated to transform the country's industrial base into the "arsenal of democracy," producing the war materiel that would bring down the Axis powers. The unemployment that had been the most visible symbol of the depression evaporated in the economic and military mobilization. The American economy was thus revived by the war, and when it was over, it was ready to turn its full strength to fulfilling consumer demand that had been frustrated by the war effort.

American economic preeminence meant the United States was the only candidate to lead any global economic recovery. Because the United States possessed an enormous amount of leverage to structure that system, it was very difficult for the other World War II participants to resist American preferences. The question was whether and how the Americans would lead the world economy to a stable new prosperity, or whether the United States might revert to prewar isolationism.

Answers about the direction of the global economy were worked out as part of the wartime allied collaboration that also produced the United Nations. The security problem during the interwar years had been a League of Nations that was not strong enough to enforce policies that would maintain the peace. The economic realm was even worse: an international institutional void in the area of economics allowed states to pursue policies that created an economic crisis in the 1930s that many believed led to the war.

A major culprit in interwar economics had been the punitive nature of the Versailles peace treaty that ended World War I. In 1919, Germany was forced to accept total responsibility for starting the war through the War Guilt Clause, Article 231. This provision justified sizable reparations from Germany to pay for the destruction in France (where most of the physical fighting on the western front occurred) and also to Great Britain. The reparations payments virtually ensured that Germany could not recover from the war economically. The effect was that the Great Depression hit Germany harder than any other country on the continent. Amid enormous depression-induced economic suffering in the early 1930s, the same Adolf Hitler who was laughed at and jailed when he first appeared on the political scene in the more prosperous 1920s was elected chancellor of Germany in 1932. Part of his appeal was the promise of restoring economic prosperity.

The Great Depression also set off a wave of economic nationalism that worsened matters worldwide. As the effects of the depression spread throughout Europe and threatened the integrity of industries and businesses, governments responded with protective barriers in the form of very high tariffs and other devices designed to protect indigenous industries from foreign competition by making outside goods and services artificially more expensive than domestic counterparts. These barriers reduced trade to a trickle of its pre-depression levels and added to the general animosity between countries that was greasing the slide to world war.

These perceptions helped predispose those who would take the lead in fashioning the postwar economic system. The isolationism that had been a firm part of the economic nationalism—some called it economic warfare—of the 1930s was firmly rejected. So was the notion of a punitive peace that had crippled the defeated Central Powers of WW I, ensured they could not fully embrace the peace settlement, and ultimately encouraged another global war.

The Bretton Woods Institutions

Formal planning for the revised economic order was a wartime enterprise dominated by the Americans and the British. Each had somewhat different perspectives on what should be done after the war ended, and each produced different blueprints for the future.

The initial international conference to craft a new set of structures was held in July 1944 in the New Hampshire resort town of Bretton Woods at the picturesque Hotel Washington nestled at the foot of Mount Washington in the White Mountains. Representing forty-four countries, the planners at Bretton Woods began by agreeing that the economic protectionism of the interwar years had contributed to the war and that protectionism had to be attacked if economic stability was to be reinstated. Specifically, they were concerned about international financial and economic practices: large fluctuations in exchange rates of currencies, chronic balance of payments problems experienced by some countries, and the high tariffs that had dominated the 1930s. All of these problems restricted the flow of international commerce, and there was a clear underlying preference for moving toward a system of considerably freer trade than had existed before the war. This free trade, internationalist position dominated the American delegation to Bretton Woods, although there remained significant protectionist sentiment within Congress and some conservative American organizations like the U.S. Chamber of Commerce.

The conferees produced agreements that created two institutions forming the core of the Bretton Woods system. At the same time, they deferred consideration of the more politically divisive issue of institutionalizing free trade until after the war was over. The institutions created were the *International Monetary Fund (IMF)* and the *International Bank for Reconstruction and Development (IBRD or World Bank)*. Both had the initial purpose of dealing with the specific problems identified as economic problems during the war. The IMF would deal with currency stabilization and balance of payments difficulties by authorizing what amounted to lines of credit to countries suffering difficulties in these areas. The World Bank was authorized to grant loans, as its formal name implied, for assisting in reconstructing war-torn economies and later developing less developed countries. Both organizations were funded by subscriptions from the members, with weighted voting privileges depending on the amount of initial subscription. Because the United States had the most money to subscribe, it received the largest bloc of votes (about one-third at the time) in both organizations.

The fate of institutionalized free trade was not so smooth, reflecting historic American debates about America's role and American economic and political independence in the world. Aside from questions of internationalism and protectionism, the desirability of the United States being institutionally entwined in free trade regimes also raised questions about impingement on state sovereignty among critics and opponents. These opposing viewpoints were as present in 1945 as they are today.

The attempt to institutionalize international free trade began when the war ended but faced a perilous political course. Within the American administration of Harry S. Truman, there was great support for an institutional commitment through an organization parallel to the IMF and IBRD, thus completing the Bretton Woods institutions as a troika of international economic organizations. This idea, however, had both domestic and international opponents who effectively blocked the movement.

The Truman administration's strategy for lowering trade barriers consisted of two parts, both of which have their parallels in the contemporary debate over trade. One of these was to pursue bilateral and multilateral reductions in tariffs and quotas under the provisions of the Reciprocal Trade Agreements Act (RTAA) of 1934. The RTAA, which was passed in reaction to the extreme protectionism of the Smoot-Hawley Tariff Act of 1930, authorized the administration to reduce tariffs on specific items by up to 50 percent with other countries, but only if the reductions were reciprocal. It did not authorize the elimination of any trade barriers and thus was only a modest first step toward the administration's goal of freeing trade. It was the precursor to so-called fast-track (or what the Bush administration has called trade promotion) authority.

The heart of the free trade initiative was to be an international organization, the *International Trade Organization (ITO)*. The purposes of this organization were to promote free trade among its members and to create an enforcement mechanism to investigate and punish those who violated trade agreements into which they had entered. In order to draft a statute for the ITO similar to those of the Bretton Woods institutions, a preliminary meeting was held in 1947 in Geneva, Switzerland, to lay out trading principles under the name of the *General Agreement on Tariffs and Trade (GATT)*. The GATT was intended as a temporary umbrella, an expedient device wherein general principles could be drafted to govern the permanent ITO.

The meeting at which the ITO was proposed was held in Havana in November 1947. By the time it was convened, domestic and foreign opponents to the principle of universal free trade had organized themselves well enough to dilute the outcome. These early "rejectionists" argued against domestic and international impacts of loosening trading restrictions and for the protection of special arrangements, such as the British Imperial Preference System (which created special tariff status between Great Britain and members of the empire and Commonwealth). In addition, other national delegations refused to grant the United States the deference accorded it through weighted voting in the IMF and IBRD. Instead, they insisted that the United States would be given a single vote like any other country.

Geopolitics and globalization clashed, and the ITO never came into being. President Truman refused to submit the ITO treaty to the Senate in 1948. He feared that in an election year, free trade, with considerable opposition in Congress and the public (see Amplification 6.1), might become a campaign issue. In 1949, the administration's effort to gain ratification of the North Atlantic Treaty (the first peacetime military alliance in American history) pushed the ITO off the agenda. By the time the president submitted the treaty to the Senate in April 1950, enthusiasm for international organizational solutions to problems had cooled, and the outbreak of the Korean War in June 1950

Amplification 6.1

THE ITO AND THE ANTI–FREE TRADERS

The noteworthy failure of the Bretton Woods process was the inability to bring the International Trade Organization (ITO) into existence. The result stymied the maximum promotion of free trade, which was one of the major objectives of the architects of the Bretton Woods system. Reflecting the long-standing American ambivalence about the proper role for the United States in the international economic order, the United States both proposed the ITO to the international community and brought about its defeat by failing to ratify the ITO treaty.

As a domestic political event, the scenario was familiar. The principal backers of the ITO were in the executive branch: the original impetus for the body came from State Department planners during World War II, and when Harry S. Truman succeeded the late Franklin D. Roosevelt, his administration took the lead in proposing a United Nations Conference on Trade and Development in 1946 to draft the statute for the ITO.

Major opposition congealed in the Congress. The major elements in the protectionist coalition were Republicans who were influenced by major business and commercial interest groups that believed in protecting American products from foreign competition. Both manufacturing and farm elements were represented in this effort. At the other extreme, a number of liberal Democrats who believed the ITO statute was too timid a document in promoting free trade joined the opposition, as did conservatives who opposed the ITO on the grounds that it represented a dangerous assault on American sovereignty. The opposition successfully blocked Senate advice and consent on the matter and provided a precedent for the kind of odd-bedfellows coalition that would emerge as rejectionists at the turn of the twenty-first century.

reinforced that sentiment. In November 1950, Truman withdrew the ITO proposal from Senate consideration, and the ITO idea was a dead horse until it was revived in 1993 as the World Trade Organization (WTO).

The GATT, however, survived. Although protectionists did not like it much more than the ITO, it was less threatening to their cause. The GATT was not an organization at all, but a series of periodically convened negotiating sessions between sovereign states. This lack of structure meant that it would have no permanent investigating or enforcing staff that could enforce objectionable rules on countries and thereby infringe on their sovereignty. Also, as a series of negotiations (that became known as "rounds"), the individual states retained maximum control over what they were willing or unwilling to be bound to accept by signing or not signing individual proposals.

The GATT thus became the banner around which the free traders could congregate until the time was right for them to assert their case for a permanent international organization. In the process, the GATT developed a set of four principles that defined its operation and remain important points of reference to this day (summarized in Rothgeb, p. 75). These include *nondiscrimination* (the promotion of most-favored nation—MFN—status to all subscribing countries), *transparency* (the unacceptability of secret trade restrictions and barriers), *consultation and dispute settlement* (resolution of disputes through direct negotiations), and *reciprocity* (the idea all members should incur balanced obligations).

The free trade issues raised in the 1940s are instructive because they are parallel to and even anticipate the same kinds of debates and problems that enliven the 2000s. The debate over the extent to which free trade should be an active part of American international economic policy stands at the vortex of the issue. Generally speaking, there has been a domestic political debate with strong interbranch implications: the White House in the 1940s was the epicenter of free trade advocacy under Roosevelt and Truman, and has been for the last decade under Clinton and Bush. On the other side of the coin, organized political opposition has largely come from elements in Congress with constituencies harmed by and thus opposed to free trade. What is different is that in the 1940s, most of the organized congressional opposition was Republican, whereas much of the current opposition is Democratic.

This disagreement manifests itself in two distinct ways. One is the amount of discretion the Congress is willing to grant the executive to negotiate trade arrangements. The general outcome has been to give the president some tethered leeway. Congress granted the president limited authority to negotiate tariff reductions through the RTAA of 1934, but it restricted what he could negotiate and under what circumstances. Moreover, the RTAA was time-limited legislation that automatically expired in 1948. The Congress continued to renew the RTAA annually until 1962, but the threat of nonrenewal—presumably if the president exceeded his authority—provided the congressional tether. A parallel exists over the so-called fast-track legislation that authorized the president to negotiate trade agreements the Congress can only approve or disapprove but cannot amend. That legislation was also renewable and expired in 1993. The efforts first by President Clinton and later by Bush to get it reinstated have been an ongoing interbranch struggle with strong free trade bases that was resolved for now by extending the authority to Bush in 2002.

The other form of disagreement was over the international institutionalization of free trade. Congressional opposition effectively killed the ITO when Truman determined he did not have the votes in the Senate for ratification, and the issue remained dormant for over four decades. The call for an international organization, the WTO, emerged from the 1993 Uruguay Round of the GATT, and in a changed economic atmosphere where cutting-edge American industries in areas such as telecommunications and financial services would clearly benefit from institutionalization, the Senate passed the treaty forming the WTO (which took effect on January 1, 1995). The ITO was thus reborn as the WTO.

The Breakdown of Bretton Woods

For the first two decades following World War II, the Bretton Woods system dominated in international economics. During this time, the United States held sway over the international economic system basically because the U.S. economy was the dominant economic force in the world. Because countries needed U.S. economic resources and goods, the dollar became the only "hard" currency in the world (the only currency universally accepted in international trade). Regulating the supply of dollars in the international system provided a considerable source of leverage for the United States in international financial circles.

The attractiveness of the dollar was also enhanced because it was tied to the gold standard. As a matter of U.S. policy, every dollar in circulation was backed by gold in the amount that one ounce of gold was worth $35. The gold standard meant that, at least theoretically, anyone with $35 in cash could trade it in for one ounce of gold from Fort Knox, Kentucky, or some other federal gold depository. The gold standard was always a fiction (the United States never possessed enough gold to redeem all the dollars in circulation), but the promise of the gold standard created an aura of confidence around the value of the dollar that stabilized the entire financial system.

The strength of the Bretton Woods system was predicated on the preeminence of the American economic system and currency, and the system was bound to founder as the relative position of the United States in the world economic order faltered, which began to happen in the 1960s. Some of these changes were the direct consequence of American actions in the world; others were the result of domestically based political decisions.

Part of the change was the postwar recovery in Europe and Japan. In the late 1940s, the American economy was producing about 40 percent of all the goods and services produced worldwide. Although a remarkable testimony to American productivity, this also reflected the absence of productivity in the other traditional industrial countries, all of which were struggling to recover and rebuild from the ravages of the war.

Faced with the geopolitical Soviet menace, it had been explicit U.S. policy starting in the 1940s to assist in the recovery of the European and Japanese economies through programs such as the Marshall Plan. The motivation for this was largely geopolitical—to increase the status of these countries as anti-Communist bastions and to ensure that Communism did not appeal to their citizens. Pumped up by American dollars, the European and Japanese economies did recover—as intended—and became economic competitors to the United States. In the process, the American relative share of global GNP began to shrink, moving downward to the low 20 percents in the 1970s, where it has essentially remained since. The United States did not cease to be the preeminent economic power in the world, but it no longer enjoyed the same overwhelming level of superiority it once occupied.

Since purchases of goods and services in international trade are by and large made in the currency of the country from which those purchases are made, there suddenly was a demand for currencies other than the dollar to pay for goods and services from other countries. In addition, political and economic events during the 1960s were making continuing adherence to the gold standard an increasingly impossible fiction.

Several domestic events and trends in the 1960s contributed to this problem. In the mid-1960s, President Lyndon Johnson made the fateful decision to simultaneously finance the Vietnam War and the complex of entitlement programs known collectively as the Great Society without raising taxes. The result was the first sizable budget deficits and consequent accumulation of national debt in the United States since World War II. One consequence was a decline in confidence in the American economy, which, coupled with rising inflation and competition from foreign goods and services, created a new atmosphere in which American economic predominance was actually called into question for the first time since the end of the war.

The ultimate event occurred in 1971, when adherence to the gold standard became such a millstone on the American economy that it could no longer be sustained. The inflationary spiral of the 1960s had resulted in such a flood of dollars into circulation that the fiction of redemption of dollars for gold was increasingly obviously hollow. Moreover, pegging the value of the dollar to gold resulted in overvaluation of the dollar against other currencies. That, in turn, made it difficult for American producers to compete with their overseas counterparts (it took too many units of a foreign currency to buy enough American dollars to purchase American goods compared to goods from other countries).

These factors combined to force the U.S. government to renounce the gold standard in 1971. Dollars would no longer be redeemable in gold. More important, the value of the dollar would no longer be determined against a set quantity of the precious metal. Instead, the dollar would be allowed to "float" against other currencies, with its value set at whatever price others were willing to pay for it in other currencies. The dollar thus essentially became a commodity like other commodities and would have to compete with other currencies in the marketplace. Almost instantly, other currencies (especially those from places such as Germany and Japan, which produced goods and services desired in world markets) became hard currencies. The global economic competition was on, and American preeminence was no longer to be taken for granted.

THE TRANSITIONAL PERIOD, 1971–1990

The renunciation of the gold standard ushered in a period of change in the structure of the international economic system. The broad theme of the period was apparent American decline in military and political power (largely the result of the Vietnam experience), but especially in the economic realm during the 1970s, followed by resurgence by the end of the 1980s.

The 1970s was a difficult period of transition in the United States. Economic turbulence was assured by the oil shocks of 1973 and 1977. Led by its Middle East members, the Organization of Petroleum Exporting Countries (OPEC) took a series of joint actions that greatly raised the price of oil to all consuming countries. In 1973, these actions were accompanied by a boycott of countries that did not denounce Israel after the Yom Kippur War. The consequent shortages in the United States and the Netherlands (the only major states that refused to condemn Israel) resulted in long gas lines and higher prices at the pump in both countries.

The rise in the price of oil had structural effects on the global economy. Europe and Japan were rebuilt after World War II using petroleum as the basic energy source. The reason was that Middle Eastern oil was plentiful and was largely controlled by the major western oil companies (known as the Seven Sisters), thereby guaranteeing availability at a low cost ($3 to $5 a barrel). Most of Europe and Japan became heavily dependent on imported oil, since neither had domestic sources (the North Sea oil fields had not been exploited at this point). As the price of oil rose to $20 a barrel and more, the First Tier states became debtors to the oil-producing states, and successful competition in global markets to sell goods and services to buy petroleum became a serious business. Economic competitiveness in global markets became increasingly important for overall prosperity. It would not be the last time petroleum would become a national security concern for the United States.

American Decline

Economic bad news accompanied the United States' political and military mishaps. One of the apparent legacies of deficits created by financing the war in Vietnam was a high rate of inflation. By the end of the 1970s, it had become "double digit" (over 10 percent annually). Inflation eroded consumer buying power and created a sense of economic malaise. Worse yet, there was growing evidence that American industry was losing its competitive edge against other countries (especially Germany and Japan) and that the United States was in apparent economic decline. The question in the minds of many Americans was not whether this was happening but how pervasive the losses were and how permanent the phenomenon was.

The evidence of economic decline seemed to cut across the board. American industries appeared to have become soft, no longer innovating as were competitors in Europe and Japan. American industries were losing market share in a wide variety of products from consumer electronics to heavy machinery, from hospital equipment to automobiles. Some dark predictions hinted this condition might even worsen to the point that the United States would fade into second-class status. One widely discussed prediction, put forward by Yale historian Paul Kennedy went so far as to prophesy that the United States would fade as a world power due to imperial overreach.

The potential national security consequences of the Vietnam "hangover" and economic decline seemed to go hand in hand. If the American economy might no longer dominate the international economic system and there was a decline in American military strength and will as well, it was not unreasonable to agree with Kennedy's pessimistic conclusions about a future in which America's power and its place in the world might be in permanent decline. Fortunately, the dire predictions proved premature and false.

Driven by advances in high technology and changing policies and attitudes within the business and policy communities, things began to change in the 1980s. It was a quiet, virtually subterranean revolution. Much of the perception of malaise from the 1970s continued to dominate the public debate, and until the latter part of the decade, the Cold War continued to be the focal point of international concerns. One was much more likely to hear about the lack of competitiveness of American electronics or the seemingly endless military competition with the Soviets than about the crumbling of the Soviet empire or the resurgence of the American economy.

American Revival

Beginning in the 1970s and accelerating in the 1980s, policy and science coalesced to promote positive change. The policy arena of the 1980s was heavily influenced by the efforts of the Republican administration of Ronald W. Reagan in the United States and the Conservative British Prime Minister Margaret Thatcher, both of whom preached for and advocated a reduced role for government in the economic sector and a much more pure form of capitalism. Reagan's economic legacy was based on two predilections. His domestic economic program is remembered most distinctively for the huge tax reduction he pushed through Congress in 1981 that resulted in runaway government deficits and a skyrocketing debt the reduction of which became the centerpiece of Clinton fiscal policy in the 1990s. The recurring theme of the Reagan policy was "getting government off the people's backs."

Reagan and those around him also believed that the less government interference in and control over the economy, the better. Reagan's general belief, supported by Thatcher, was that in economic matters, the private sector almost always made better decisions than did government officials and thus should be as unfettered from government intrusion as possible (a classic traditional conservative position as discussed in Chapter 2).

These predilections resulted in two policy thrusts. *Privatization* involved getting government out of operating businesses and turning formerly government-operated functions over to private entrepreneurs and corporations. The idea was that privatization would result in increased efficiency and thus greater value for consumers. This thrust was particularly important to Thatcher because the British economy had considerably more public intrusion into economic affairs than was true in the United States. In the United States, the breakup of government monopolies such as long-distance telephone service illustrated this philosophy.

Deregulation was the other shibboleth. A major perceived cause of the supposed economic decline, the Reaganites believed, was too much regulation of the private sector by the government, thereby stultifying the ability of the private sector to be flexible and to compete both domestically and internationally. By removing strictures on how business could be done, the result was to be greater efficiency in operation and hence competitiveness. Airline deregulation is a primary example of this philosophy in action.

Other forces were coming together to reinforce this set of policy predilections. A major source of change was emerging in the area of high technology, where the fruits of advances in computing and telecommunications (and the merger of these two industries to create the information age) were together changing the content and nature of what composed the cutting edge of economic and scientific activity. If the early post–World War II period had been dominated by the manufacture of goods, services and the monopoly on the most desired information came to represent the "commodity" of greatest value in the evolving economy. Figuratively speaking, software replaced steel-belted tires as the symbol of productivity. American preeminence in these areas became the basis for the American resurgence.

The attractiveness of the American political and social system contributed to this growing American strength that became the basis for American resurgence in the 1990s.

Fired by technological developments in computing, the birth of the Internet, and the like, the centers of American attraction emerged in the 1980s as magnets for the best young minds and most ambitious entrepreneurs in the world. They tended to congregate in places where there were clusters of great universities and pleasant living conditions and lifestyles. The Silicon Valley in California, nestled between and nurtured by great universities like Stanford and California–Berkeley, became the model for the further development of emerging technology, followed by places such as the Route 128 corridor outside Boston (in the shadow of Harvard and the Massachusetts Institute of Technology, among other schools), the Research Triangle in North Carolina, and others. These enclaves became the collective seedbed of America's return to preeminence.

The private sector contributed as well. During the period of American decline, a major criticism was that the American manufacturing industry in particular had gone soft and complacent and that industries in hungrier and more ambitious countries had gained advantages, especially in the area of overseas trade. A primary example is the invidious comparison between the American and Japanese automobile industries.

This situation began to change in the 1980s, as the American manufacturing community began to reform itself by imitating the practices of countries such as Japan and restructuring the "sunset industries" (those declining in importance) through actions such as the now-familiar practice of "downsizing." As traditional American industries began to narrow the gap with their ambitious foreign rivals combined with new economic emphases in which the United States had a built-in advantage and as the impact of foreign investment such as manufacturing plants on American soil came to the fore, the United States became poised for the resumption of economic leadership in the world.

Both the American decline and its resurgence in the economic realm were gradual and, for the most part, not very dramatic. For those whose experience is limited to the bountiful expansion of the 1990s, it may seem difficult to think of a time when there was a more fearful, less confident United States sitting astride the world of geopolitics and globalization, but this was indeed the case during the 1970s and most of the 1980s.

The events that ushered in the age of globalization were political and not economic, although many of the most noticeable effects have been economic in the long run. The most obvious manifestations of change came from the end of the Cold War and the demise of Soviet and world Communism as the 1980s made the transition to the twentieth century's final decade. The end of the Cold War effectively ended the competition between economic ideologies and military machines. Socialist economics was so thoroughly discredited by the collapse of the politico-economic system that had enshrined Marx's and Engel's ideas that it has effectively disappeared.

THE GLOBALIZING ECONOMY, 1990–PRESENT

The system of globalization resulted from a series of individually unspectacular but cumulatively significant trends that came together in the 1990s, unlike a traumatic economic event like American renunciation of the gold standard in 1971. The collapse of Communism provides a political benchmark of that emergence with some economic ramifications in the rise of globalism. The fall of Communism concluded the economic competition between socialism and capitalism, but the globalizing economy would probably have emerged anyway. Indeed, the economic disparities created by globalization might have been the economic force that toppled the Communist world in the 1990s, although many analysts argue that the inability of the Soviets to compete militarily was an equally or even more important factor in the collapse. Imagine the pressure on the socialist societies of Eastern Europe to join the general prosperity had they remained on the wrong side of a still-existing Iron Curtain but still could see how the West lived. Even more dramatically, imagine the trauma for China being a geopolitical enemy of the United States while simultaneously trying actively to participate in trade with this country.

Globalization began with a distinctive set of values forged during the transition and to which the value of trade has been added as the 1990s' most important contribution to its evolution. Acceptance of the rules and values of globalization is the *sine qua non* for membership in the global economy and thus, for most purposes, participation in the prosperity that became a part of the globalizing economy in the 1990s. Those countries that rejected participation had to suffer the economic consequences in terms of prosperity. The pressure to become part of the globalizing economy may seem less obvious in a mid-2000s environment more closely focused on terrorism, but the pressures were strong in the 1990s and remain a potent force for many countries.

The emergence of the globalizing economy coincided with and helped contribute to the general global prosperity of most of the 1990s. At its height, the pressures toward globalization seemed ineluctable, and criticisms were weak and overwhelmed by advocates—even cheerleaders—such as the *New York Times*' Thomas L. Friedman. The euphoria has proven at least partially overly inflated. As chinks appeared in the armor of globalization enthusiasm, the domestic and international critics have come forward in increasingly public ways.

Although there has been great shock at the apparently radical nature of the objections raised by the rejectionists and their political allies, the basic arguments go back to fundamental arguments in the American political debate about the American place in the world (internationalism versus isolationism) and participation in the global economy (free trade versus protectionism), to say nothing of the parallel debate about national security (realism versus idealism). The result is a debate about the attractiveness of globalization as an alternative paradigm to geopolitics that requires looking at its characteristics and objections to it.

Characteristics and Values

The building blocks of the evolving "system of globalization" (to borrow Friedman's phrase) are central economic phenomena from the 1980s and the 1990s. The major contribution of the 1980s, as already mentioned, was the reassertion of the capitalist ethic of market-based economics. This philosophical underpinning proposed to free national economies from the government meddling and interference that it was argued had been a barrier to entrepreneurial growth and innovation. Privatization and deregulation were major tools in this policy change.

The major contributions of the 1990s represented a continuation but also a reversal of some policies with their roots in the 1980s. The continuity came in the form of the election of free trader Bill Clinton to succeed free trader George H. W. Bush as president. The result was that free trade advocacy has dominated in the executive branch of the U.S. government during most of the 1990s and beyond. The reversal in policy came through Clinton's successful commitment to wiping out budget deficits and reducing government debt as a way to improve the atmosphere in which economic entities did business in the 1990s, an emphasis largely abandoned after September 11. The combined effect was to create the so-called American model as the basis for the globalizing system.

A caveat to the legacy of the 1980s—market capitalism *within* national economies—must be added. The market capitalists rejected governmental management of economic activity, but they did *not* reject all governmental participation in providing a nurturing business environment. The specific area of policy in which government participation is welcome is in governmental regulation, especially in overseeing the activities of financial institutions and in adopting macroeconomic policies that facilitate how business operates.

The willingness to accept some regulation of fiscal activity—especially the actions of banks and other financial institutions—has its American roots in the so-called S&L (savings and loan) scandal of the 1980s. The scandal is important because almost the same problems and solutions were encountered during the East Asian crisis of 1997 and its aftermath, when international institutions sought to enforce the same solutions on East Asian economies as the United States had adopted for itself.

Prior to the S&L scandal, there had been very little regulation, and especially public accounting, of this part of the banking industry. The "thrifts," as they were known, were limited-purpose financial institutions specializing in activities such as home mortgages and business lending. Their attractiveness to investors was that they generally paid higher interest rates than regular banks and were thus desirable depositories for small investors to put their savings. They were not, however, subject to the same standards of reporting of activities as were regular banks, a matter that was not of great concern because savings accounts were insured by the government, and none had ever failed.

The scandal emerged when a number of S&Ls went bankrupt and threatened to dishonor investor accounts. The most famous bankruptcies were associated with the S&L empire of Arizona entrepreneur Charles Keating Jr. The investigation of a number of his institutions revealed a pattern of investor fund misuse through bad loans that could not be repaid (called nonperforming loans) and even bribes to public officials (five U.S. senators, known as the Keating Five, received favors from the banker) that had been concealed because of lax accounting rules. As the modest savings of many Americans were threatened, the U.S. Congress passed legislation aimed at guaranteeing investor confidence by ensuring honesty and "transparency" (having records of transactions, the financial conditions of financial institutions, and the like publicly available for inspection) within these institutions. The reforms enacted in response to the S&L crisis restored public confidence and willingness to invest in institutions that loan funds to entrepreneurs. Over the objections of a Clinton administration that wanted them strengthened, these rules regarding accounting standards were relaxed after 1994, leading to the corporate scandals of 2002, which stimulated yet another round of reform legislation once again to create transparency.

The same rationale—bolstering public trust—applies to other forms of macroeconomic policy. Proponents of the American model believe the government has a limited useful role in the economy beyond making sure that bankers and others are honest. More specifically, the government can provide a useful service in creating a favorable fiscal climate for business and in providing services that are otherwise burdensome for the private sector.

The major beneficial macroeconomic policy of the 1990s was deficit reduction and elimination, a direct reversal of the practices of the Reagan years championed by Clinton and his closest economic advisors. A major impact of the Reagan deficits was to force large-scale government borrowing to cover obligations for which there were inadequate tax receipts. Much of this borrowing came from the American private sector, to which the government had primary access before private enterprises. Some of the money borrowed came from foreign sources (a controversial matter in its own right), but a sizable amount came from American sources. With the government in effect skimming funds available for borrowing before private firms got a chance, the result was a smaller pool of financial resources available for private firm innovation and investment. This problem has recurred and contributed to slower economic growth rates in the mid-2000s; it is made more problematical because most of it now comes from foreign lenders to whom the U.S. is indebted.

Reducing and ultimately eliminating deficits and beginning the process of reducing the overall debt reduction were largely the result of policies fashioned by Clinton Secretary of the Treasury Robert Rubin and enacted during the eight years of Bill Clinton's tenure in the White House. Even some of Clinton's critics have been forced to admit that it is no coincidence these policies and the prosperity of the 1990s coincided. Massive deficits have returned with the George W. Bush emphases on tax reductions and increased spending on the GWOT and Iraq.

The government also encourages entrepreneurial activity by providing the social net in the form of social security and related benefits for the general population. Doing so frees private concerns from having to develop such systems themselves, thus becoming the social net for their employees, and provides considerable flexibility for firms in their operations. Employees, for instance, are no longer tied closely to individual companies upon which they rely for things like health care and social security upon retirement. Instead, devices such as portable health insurance and government-provided pensions theoretically free companies to tailor and downsize their workforce without undue regard for the social consequences of laying off workers whose functions have been bypassed by change. The default on private pension obligations by United Airlines in 2005, followed by other companies that had also not contributed resources to pension funds in promised amounts, demonstrated that the relationship is less than foolproof.

The other policy triumph of the 1990s was the victory of free trade, a primary emphasis and legacy of Clinton. In concept, free trade represents the extension of David Ricardo's theory of comparative advantage to international economics. Politically, it represented the triumph, at least for the balance of the 1990s, of the free traders over the protectionists.

The ascendancy of free trade represented more of a practical than an ideological victory, as the negative reaction to free trade at the end of the decade and beyond showed. When Clinton came to office, one of his first priorities was the successful passage of the North American Free Trade Agreement (NAFTA) negotiated by George H. W. Bush through the Congress. The traditional coalitions had lined up in support and opposition based upon general preferences about American participation in international economics and the like. The authorizing legislation for NAFTA passed by a narrow margin in both houses of Congress (as an economic agreement rather than a treaty, it required House as well as Senate approval). NAFTA was followed by a flood of other activity supported by the free traders that, by the end of the decade, had locked the United States into a web of free trade associations in addition to NAFTA, such as the Asia-Pacific Economic Cooperation (APEC) at the regional level and the WTO at the global level. During much of Clinton's tenure, this process proceeded with virtually no organized or coordinated objections, with the major exception of the Congress's refusal to grant the administration fast-track authority (trade promotion authority) on two occasions.

Advocacy of globalization has become more subdued in the contemporary environment for both economic and geopolitical reasons. Why? Economically, the broad answer is that economic circumstances have changed. When Clinton came to office, the recession of 1991 that had helped defeat the incumbent Bush in the 1992 election was lifting, replaced by an eight-year period of sustained growth in the local and global economy. One can debate the degree to which Clinton was responsible for or simply the beneficiary of this expansion, but it was a period of unprecedented growth from which the vast majority benefited economically. The trade that Clinton promoted was clearly a major element in the prosperity, as cheaper foreign goods poured into the country to benefit consumers. While some American industries such as textiles suffered, in most cases there was enough prosperity to absorb most of those displaced. The argument that freeing trade was at least partially responsible for the prosperity was difficult to refute in that atmosphere, a situation that free trader Clinton nurtured and exploited.

The slowing of the economy at the end of the 1990s and the revival of opposition to free trade coincided. The results have been to reduce support for the globalization process internally within the United States and to revive political opposition that was latent during the booming 1990s. As has always been the case, free trade and protectionism have varied bases and varying arguments. Politically, the divide in the United States tends to be between the Congress and the executive branch rather than along party lines.

In geopolitical terms, of course, the emphasis has moved away from globalization to a virtually total interest in the aftermath of September 11—notably, the GWOT and extensions of it, such as the Iraq War. Globalization has not disappeared from the scene—trade levels continue to grow, and efforts to expand free trade (such as the Central American Free Trade Area or CAFTA) also go on. What has changed is the relative emphasis given to globalization. Large, spectacular efforts such as the Free Trade Area of the Americas (a proposal to make a free trade area of all the Western Hemisphere other than Cuba) have been deemphasized or quietly shelved in favor of bilateral or more limited international agreements like CAFTA that require less energy to consummate. The lowering of the profile of globalization has also coincided with growing domestic and international criticism of globalization and the continuing intrusion of other concerns on the national security agenda.

Objections to Globalization

The glow that surrounded globalization in the 1990s (at least before the East Asian financial crisis of 1997 began to reduce that glow) was probably too bright to sustain. In the early and mid-1990s, the globalization-driven expansion in the world economy seemed to be a "rising tide that lifts all boats," promising a growing prosperity to all that joined it and a seemingly brighter alternative to the dreary, bellicose ambience of the Cold War. Globalization seemed to provide a brighter future to everyone.

That bright future, as it turns out, was overblown. Internationally, the first blow came with the East Asian financial crisis of 1997. In that case, the Thai currency (the *baht*) collapsed following superheating of the economy triggered by what turned out to be excessive foreign investment (amounts that could not be productively absorbed), and the ensuing panic spread regionally. As the millennium changed, the global economy cooled and other national economies suffered setbacks as well that led to modifications of the rising tide analogy. It became apparent that the tide of globalization lifted some boats much higher than others and that it even swamped some of the smaller, less seaworthy boats. Domestically, the Ricardian consequence of comparative advantage was being felt as uncompetitive industries were being undercut, costing Americans and other nationals jobs. This, in turn, helped fan the flames tended by those who had objected to globalization all along.

International Objections. Globalization has become controversial in ways that would have seemed inconceivable except among its most diehard opponents in the 1990s. The January/February 2007 issues of *Foreign Policy* and *Foreign Affairs* featured articles titled "How Globalization Went Bad" and "Has Globalization Reached Its Peak?" Both assertions would have generally been considered heretical a decade ago, but they captured the tone of global criticisms, which can be grouped around four objections.

The first objection centers on the western, and especially American, domination that accompanies subscription to globalization and participation in the global economy. In order to become an active, participating partner in the globalization system, countries are required to accept the rules of conduct of the so-called Washington consensus. These rules are based heavily on the American conceptualization of capitalism and require governments to do a series of things to become "eligible" to participate in the system (which effectively means to gain the kind of international rating that encourages investment and trade with other members). These restrictions include things like balancing governmental budgets, instituting strict banking and other procedures that make the financial sector more "transparent" (open to outside inspection), and removing subsidies for noncompetitive industrial and other sectors of the economy.

These restrictions become sources of objection in several ways. One is they tend to be uniform for all countries (what *New York Times* correspondent and globalization advocate Thomas L. Friedman calls "one size fits all"), thereby ignoring what may be special and idiosyncratic factors in different countries. Forcing countries into a uniform mold may have particularly painful economic and political repercussions, as is seen particularly in South America (these issues are considered in Snow, *Cases in International Relations*, third edition, especially Chapter 8). These objections are often phrased in terms of assaults on the cultures of target countries to which the Washington consensus is insensitive (views on social welfare, for instance). Rather, the consensus reflects American economic (and political) values, and imposing the consensus on other countries has the residual effects of making them more like the United States—an outcome that some find objectionable.

The imposition of the Washington consensus also may distort the economies of target countries, especially during the transition from whatever form the economy of a given country possessed to the "golden straitjacket" (Friedman's term) of conformance with the Washington consensus. Almost all countries undergoing globalization are required to undergo economic belt tightening, which has negative economic and political effects on the population and the regime. During the good times of the 1990s, when all boats were being lifted enough that differentials could be ignored, these strictures seemed acceptable, if painful. In the less economically expansive 2000s, the sacrifices have seemed more painful and less acceptable, triggering negative reactions that have resulted in the election of antiglobalization governments in a number of countries that sought to enter the globalization system in the 1990s. Many of these countries are in Latin America. In addition (and particularly relevant in the Latin American context), one of the domestic consequences of globalization tends to be a greater income inequality within affected societies; in highly economically stratified societies like those found in Latin America, globalization just makes a bad situation worse in the eyes of those who do not benefit. One reaction has been the election of populist, antiglobalization administrations in countries like Argentina, Bolivia, and Venezuela, to cite three examples.

A third objection involves the difference between the broad systemic (or macro) and the individual or group (or micro) effects of globalization—a factor with both international and domestic impacts. Generally speaking, most of the arguments favoring globalization are made at the macro level: globalization—and its handmaiden, free trade—expands the global economy and the economies of various countries that are part of the globalization system. That is true, and in some countries, it has resulted in a broad enthusiasm and embrace of globalization (India is a notable example). While the macroeconomic argument is generally not assailed, its impacts at the microeconomic level are. The micro level reflects the impact of globalization on individuals and groups within societies, and the impacts can be quite negative.

In macroeconomic theory based in the principle of comparative advantage, those in uncompetitive industries are displaced from their unproductive endeavors and go to work in areas where the country has comparative advantage. Doing so theoretically strengthens all economies, because it means greater specialization in production by those industries that are producing the best goods (or services) at the lowest prices. The problem is that theory and practice do not always coincide.

Two examples of the microeconomic malaise that fuels opposition to globalization stand out. The first, which is basically domestic in the countries where it occurs, is that forcing uncompetitive industries out of business does not always lead to retraining displaced workforces for productive careers. Instead, those displaced simply become unemployed (or underemployed in lower paying, less skilled jobs), where they become a source of political dissent. The second is the process of so-called outsourcing: maintaining competitive advantage by moving production away from its current base to somewhere else where the function can be performed at lower costs. Those industries employing electronic media have been particularly notable in this regard; shipping telemarketing jobs from the United States to India, is one example. In any case, the result is unhappy former workers who now find foreigners doing the jobs they had performed. The result may be a stronger economy at the macro level but opposition at the micro level.

Finally, there is the question of the inevitability of globalization. Proponents argue that globalization is essentially inexorable, and that all those who resist inclusion in the globalization system risk consignment to what amounts to the economic dustbin. To many countries, the question is whether there are other, non-self-destructive choices that can be exercised as to whether to participate in globalization or the extent of participation. To countries (India, for instance) that have wholeheartedly embraced globalization, the problem is academic, because these countries have accepted the virtue of globalization. Even in these societies, there are doubtless individuals and groups who benefit less or not at all and probably do not share that enthusiasm, but if they are politically inconsequential (as in India), it is not a problem.

Resistance to the inexorable nature of globalization comes from two basic sources. For some countries (mostly the poorest), there is essentially nothing that they produce at comparative advantage, meaning they do not benefit from participation. In fact, adopting free trade means undercutting their domestic production, which is, by definition, uncompetitive. It is notable that the largest group of countries that are not members of the World Trade Organization comprises extremely poor countries. The other countries that respond negatively to the notion of inevitability are those that have politically consequential groups that are adversely affected by globalization. One of the consequences of making the transition to the globalization system is accepting economic austerity measures, and these measures tend to create privation that is absorbed primarily by the lower classes in developing countries. Where there is a tradition of populism (as is the case in many countries in South America), these disaffected groups can wield (or be mobilized to wield) significant opposition to globalization. The rise of populists like Venezuela's Hugo Chavez is at least partly the result of this phenomenon.

Advocates of globalization argue both that globalization is inevitable and that it must be accepted and implemented *in toto*. This raises political hackles among those who will be adversely affected, but it also raises difficulties in places that are culturally or otherwise resistant to the incursions of a globalized society. Acceptance of globalization's economic values tends to entail acceptance of the western political and social system as well, and it can be argued that countries in the globalization system tend to become increasingly similar. They generally, for instance, become secularized, and this is a problem in areas where religious values and the intertwining of church and state are accepted parts of life. The fear of being westernized helps explain the reluctance of most of the Middle East to seek participation in the globalization system.

None of these objections seemed of great consequence during the 1990s, when it appeared that globalization was not only inevitable, but also universally beneficial. When it began to become evident that those benefits were neither so automatic nor as munificent as first argued, then opposition began to surface. That opposition, in turn, weakens the power of globalization as an instrument around which to organize the system, because it means the lever that grants or denies participation is not so universal. It would, for instance, be helpful to the U.S. government to be able to threaten Chavez with the prospect of nonparticipation in globalization if he does not moderate his anti-American policies; since Venezuela has basically opted out of the globalization system and rejected its values, such a threat lacks force. On a smaller scale, the same is true elsewhere.

Domestic Objections. Some of the sources of resistance to globalization being manifested in other countries are also present in the United States. During the heyday of globalization during the 1990s, opposition was mostly limited to traditional anti–free trade groups that were the successors of opponents of the ITO during the 1940s. Their composition is described in Amplification 6.2.

The domestic opposition to globalization tends to focus on the adverse economic impacts of globalization on different groups within American society. One strong strain of this opposition comes from the perceived bias of globalization toward big business. William Greider, writing in *The Nation*, for instance, complains of "corporate-led globalization" and its alleged pernicious effects. These include "all the benefits of being American—government services and subsidies, the protection of the US military—while discarding reciprocal obligations to the country: jobs, economic investment and paying a fair share of the tax burden." In this view, globalization provides a vehicle for American corporations to maximize their profits at the expense of the country at large.

The second, and loudest complaint, is one already mentioned: the impact on jobs. Even Ben Bernanke, chairman of the Federal Reserve Board, admitted this problem in August 2006 (quoted in Abdedal and Segal). "Changes in the pattern of production are likely to threaten the livelihoods of some workers and the profits of some firms, even when these changes lead to greater productivity and output overall," he said. "The natural reaction of those affected is to resist change, for example, by seeking the passage of protectionist measures." This statement encapsulates the

Amplification 6.2

THE REJECTIONISTS

The series of protests and protesters first seen in Seattle, and a grim part of nearly every international economic event since, represents a coalition of very different groups and individuals. Unless placed in the context of the historic debate about free trade and protectionism, their grouping makes little sense. But the same coalition that has taken to the streets of Quebec City, Washington, D.C., Genoa, and elsewhere represents a long-standing tradition of opposition that was clearly present in the 1940s (see Amplification 6.1). The tactics and actors may have changed, but the underlying positions remain very similar.

Who are the rejectionists? They are a single-issue coalition bound together in their opposition to various aspects or implications of globalization that have very few, if any, other common interests. The interests they represent, however, have been present for a long time. First, there are the protectionists, who feel personally threatened by lowering trade barriers. In the 1940s, the protectionists were mostly conservative Republicans representing big business and commerce; today, they are predominantly Democrats representing the interests of trade unionists in industries that cannot compete successfully without trade protection. Second are those who feel that efforts to institutionalize globalization are too timid. Environmentalists, for instance, believe that institutions like the WTO will not adequately regulate environmental degradation by international corporations and governments (they believe that globalization is dominated by private interests with little environmental sensitivity). At the same time, others believe that the interests of Second Tier countries left out of the globalization policy are underrepresented as well. Finally, there are objections from groups that feel globalization undercuts national sovereignty.

The coalition is conceptually quite similar to the group that successfully fought the ITO over a half-century ago. The major difference is the violent, confrontational tactics that are now employed in opposition to globalization. While those tactics have not yet led to the successful blocking or slowing of the globalization process, they have succeeded in creating an atmosphere of intimidation that, among other things, caused the World Bank and IMF to shorten their annual meeting for 2001 at their Washington, D.C., headquarters to two days to minimize demonstrations.

micro-macro level of disagreement; while Bernanke is attempting to make the macro point, he is also acknowledging the micro perspective.

A final objection, which tends to receive less public attention, relates to trade deficits being experienced by the United States. These deficits have steadily increased as globalization has taken hold, although they are selectively of more or less consequence. The largest American trade deficits (which essentially reflect areas of production where the United States lacks comparative advantage in items imported and not enough advantage in products exported to compensate) are with East Asian countries, notably Japan and China. These deficits are controversial: no one argues that deficits are a good thing, but they disagree on how bad they are—or may become. Because China is a potential adversary, the consequences of owing a large amount to the Chinese seems ominous to some. Those who downplay the importance of this factor tend to emphasize the fact that most of the deficit figures represent balances of trade in products rather than goods and services. In the service area (consulting, for instance), the United States has a sizable surplus that largely compensates for the deficit in goods.

Domestic objections to globalization have helped stunt the advocacy of globalization as a part of foreign and national security policy. Two recent examples help show these new strictures. When the CAFTA proposal was presented to the Congress, it barely passed, despite the knowledge that it would have minimal effects in the United States (most of the impact will be on citrus fruit growers). A basically innocuous agreement, in other words, was almost blocked. Also in 2006, the Congress refused to extend fast-track/trade promotion authority to the president, a major tool in promoting trade agreements that has to be renewed every four years by law. The refusal was both a rebuke for the president and a statement about the congressional mood toward globalization.

New Additions to the National Security Agenda

The more relaxed geopolitical environment of the 1990s and the more changed atmosphere of the 2000s also saw the addition of several other concerns to the list of items that affect national security. These new items represent an expansion of the basic concept of what constitutes security beyond its roots in protecting American soil from hostile military threats. Security has become more than military and economic security, and any discussion that seeks to represent the surveys of influences that contribute to the American sense of safety must include additional items, for three reasons.

First, most of the elevations come from the same atmosphere of reduced military threat as the dynamic that allowed globalization to claim marquee status. With less need to concentrate energies on military matters, there was time to focus on other matters that affect the national sense of well-being, such as environmental degradation. Second, a number of the new items are themselves the result of the same dynamics that produced globalization. The very differentials in quality of life created by NAFTA helped contribute to the dynamic that has resulted in a border security issue. Third, since globalization and these new factors do extend the range of what we think of as constituting national security, there is not universal agreement that they are important—vital—enough to be considered alongside and parallel to conventional national security concerns.

No list of these new agenda items will be inclusive enough to satisfy everyone, and so no claim of inclusiveness is made here. Rather, several new factors that represent the additional kinds of concerns that have been added to the national security agenda are presented. For this purpose, there are three candidates for national security concern: energy security, environmental security, and border security. All three have some relationship to globalization: energy consumption is the motor of economic productivity; the environment is clearly one of the concerns surrounding globalization; and border security has become an issue because globalization has had more beneficial impacts in some places than in others. Each topic is examined by raising three questions: How important is the issue (does it represent a threat to vital interests, the traditional criterion for military-based national security concerns)? Does its outcome affect the country's basic security, and if so, how? And what means, military or nonmilitary, are most appropriate for dealing with it?

Energy Security. As suggested in Chapter 4, the problem of having secure access to energy supplies is relatively new for the United States. Historically, the United States had within its boundaries adequate supplies of necessary sources of energy (coal, petroleum, later uranium) to meet the country's needs as it developed as a major power. That situation changed during the period after World War II and has evolved to a situation where the United States is now dependent on energy—principally petroleum—from foreign sources. The reasons for this change are numerous but include the exhaustion of cheap domestic sources of petroleum (oil that could be extracted at low prices because of dilution of readily available supplies) and increases in demand for petroleum-based energy.

This transition has created vulnerability for the United States that is shared by most of the world that does not possess large, easily accessible petroleum resources. The United States, for instance, consumes nearly 22 million barrels of oil daily (out of a global supply of 85 million barrels a day). Half of that petroleum is imported from the volatile Persian Gulf region, and other parts of its come from places like Venezuela and Nigeria, neither of which is the most reliable supplier to the United States (Nigeria because of unstable politics, Venezuela potentially because of its political difficulties with the United States). Worldwide demand for petroleum is increasing: the decisions by China and India to mass-produce automobiles for its population will add a major source of demand for petroleum beyond current available supplies (worldwide demand is about 83 million barrels a day). If demand continues at current levels, the results will include a much more furtive competition among oil consumers to curry friendship and favor with current and projected producers and a resultant increase in the political leverage of those producers.

The energy problem will not reduce itself. It is linked vitally to two contradictory international imperatives. One is the prosperity attached to the globalization system: energy consumption is the single strongest correlate of economic productivity. To join the economic prosperity or to keep (or increase) one's place in the globalizing economy, secure access to energy, which means petroleum-based energy for the foreseeable future, is absolutely necessary. The contradictory influence is the effect of fossil-fuel burning for the atmosphere (greenhouse gas emission) and hence global warming (see below). Environmentalism seems to militate for reduced (or alternate) energy use, whereas prosperity—and an alternative to a geopolitical basis of security—calls for greater consumption and thus greater geopolitical competition.

The continued addiction of the United States (currently the world's leading importer of foreign petroleum) to foreign energy creates distinctive national security dilemmas that would, at a minimum, be different in the absence of that need. The most obvious is in the Middle East. Two-thirds of the world's established reserves of petroleum are in the Persian Gulf littoral area, and secure access to it has been deemed so important to the United States that President Carter declared that access to be a vital interest to the United States in his 1980 State of the Union address (the so-called Carter Doctrine). That declaration has formed the basis for American policy in the region ever since Carter declared it. The consequences are, of course, debatable but include American leadership in the Persian Gulf War of 1990–1991, continued military interaction with Iraq throughout the 1990s (Operations Northern and Southern Watch), and the Iraq War. Whether these involvements would have occurred or been the same without America's need for petroleum from the area is debatable. That need has, however, created the perceived dictate for a continuous American military presence in the region since 1990, which Usama bin Laden has repeatedly stated is one of the major bases of his animus toward the United States (see Chapter 12).

Another consequence, raised in Chapter 5, surrounds the emerging role of Russia given its newfound prominence as a petroleum and natural gas exporter. As noted, Russia is now the world's second-largest exporter of petroleum and controls very large reserves of petroleum and natural gas in the Caspian Sea area and in Siberia. America's closest political allies in Europe are highly dependent on Russian energy, and the potential to interrupt that supply gives the Russians enormous potential leverage in Europe (a point of some relevance, for instance, regarding the American proposed and Russian opposed missile defense scheme in Eastern Europe discussed in Chapter 9). While the United States is not itself dependent on Russian energy, that energy is underpinning the Russian revival as a world power.

Energy accessibility will remain a major direct American security issue as long as the United States depends critically on foreign supplies for its vitality. Lessening that dependency has become recognized as a major priority for American security, although exactly how to achieve it is controversial because all the solutions entail painful political decisions. The chief proposed alternatives are making the transition to alternate energy sources and conservation (independently or in combination), but both have drawbacks. Alternate sources are either questionably adequate (wind and solar energy, for instance), questionably responsive to other problems (coal and the environment, as an example), or opposed on other grounds (nuclear energy, for instance). There is also the question of whether these sources are individually or collectively adequate as a substitute for imported petroleum. The other alternative is conservation, but implementing meaningful (enough to reduce imports noticeably) conservation measures either requires lifestyle changes Americans are reluctant to undergo (e.g., driving less in lighter, smaller, and more fuel-efficient vehicles) or is potentially disastrous (the effects of energy reductions on economic productivity). The failure to come to grips with the current energy problem, of course, means that measures—including military deployments and employment—to keep access to necessary foreign energy sources will remain high on the national security agenda.

Environmental Security. The direct ties between efforts to sustain the environment and national security are less direct than with energy, with which it is associated. The idea that the maintenance, protection, and promotion of a healthy, sustainable environment should be a security concern is of reasonably recent vintage, and the equation of the two concerns tends to galvanize two politically opposing forces, environmentalists and those with a primarily traditional national security orientation toward military affairs. Thus, the process of identifying whether and how the two concepts are conjoined has been a not entirely easy one.

The major environmental issue with national security implications is global warming. Part of that conjunction has already been suggested: the fact that much of the carbon dioxide problem at the root of the global warming phenomenon is the result of producing energy from the very fossil fuels discussed directly above. Reductions in petroleum consumption would clearly assist the efforts to reduce or reverse greenhouse gas emission and would thus aid the global environmental condition. Efforts to do so, however, have geopolitical implications, since reductions by some countries but not others could hurt the productivity of the compliers while promoting the productivity of the abusers and thus affect the global power formula. It is this fear, for instance, that fuels at least part of the Bush administration insistence on including China in the formula for carbon dioxide reductions mandated by the Kyoto Protocols (China and India, potentially two of the largest polluters, are excluded from Kyoto provisions as developing countries).

A major difficulty of treating environmental issues within a national security framework is the problem of immediacy. Most national security analyses focus on immediate, here-and-now threats to the country, of which military and even economic examples are plentiful. Environmental threats, however, lack such urgency. No one, for instance, argues that the worst possible outcomes of global warming (or even some of the less than worst consequences) would not affect the security of many Americans (and citizens elsewhere). A modest rise in sea levels, for instance, would have very strong impacts on the millions of Americans living in the coastal southeastern United States (the Carolinas, Georgia, and most of Florida), where homes and businesses are only a few feet above current sea levels. Should these be endangered immediately (as was the case in New Orleans because of Hurricane Katrina), it would be considered a national security emergency. Because these projections are both conjectural (not everyone agrees they are likely to occur) and generally distant (over the next fifty to one hundred years), they do not evince the same immediacy of concern as, for instance, the dangers of an international religious terrorist attack.

There are two generally underemphasized national security concerns that are environmentally based. One regards environmental pollution by the military. Many military bases (Ft. Ord in California is a prime example) were so polluted by military activities (firing artillery shells, burying waste, etc.) that their future use has been endangered pending expensive cleanup that the military has been reluctant to undertake as an unnecessary diversion of scarce resources. The other concern is that the United States has been at the forefront of opposition to environmental activities during most of the 2000s to date, and this has soured its relations with various countries in other areas. While there is, for instance, no direct link between what foreign governments feel about American opposition to participation in the Kyoto process (which most deride) and support or opposition to other American security concerns (Iraq, for instance), at a minimum the United States standing at odds with much of the world community on environmental issues does not enhance support for the United States on other issues. The announced agreement of the United States to participate in follow-on talks beyond Kyoto at the global warming summit in december 2007 in Bali, Indonesia may reflect a new sensitivity to global opinion.

Border Security. The problem of lack of immediacy does not extend to the current national security issue of border security for the United States. Making the borders safe from unwanted incursion is one of the major responsibilities of any government; without that ability, there is little operational meaning to sovereign control of territory. Thus, the frontiers between countries and between countries and the bodies of water that may form their boundaries are a natural and basic national security concern for all countries.

As in other matters, border security has not occupied a high priority historically for the United States. Especially through the long formative period of the republic, ocean boundaries provided a buffer for the United States from potential hostile others who would have to sail either the Atlantic or the Pacific Ocean to exact harm against the country. The land borders with Canada and Mexico were likewise innocuous from a security vantage point, since neither country posed any particular threat to the United States. The result was that both boundaries, and especially the long U.S.–Canada border, were essentially unfortified and unguarded.

That pristine condition has, of course, disappeared, and the sanctity of America's borders has become a major political issue. The catalyst for this concern has been the issue of illegal immigration by Mexicans and Central Americans across the southern border into the United States, but that is not the only reason the U.S. government worries about the status of the border. In addition, the flow of illegal drugs across the Mexican-American border (where estimates are that up to 90 percent of illicit drugs entering the country transit) and onto the American shoreline became an issue as part of the "war on drugs" during the administration of George H. W. Bush between 1989 and 1993, and the GWOT has added a concern with terrorist penetration of the United States to the mix. Illegal immigration (by other than terrorists) and drugs are not a particular problem regarding the Canadian border, and most of the emphasis on securing the coastline has centered on the smuggling of drugs into the country by sea and by air. The three aspects of the border problem—immigration, drugs, and terrorism—come together on the currently volatile issue of the U.S.–Mexico border.

Each of these aspects is a separate problem. Illegal immigration has become a major problem since the middle 1990s, when the number of Mexicans and other illegal residents of the United States began to soar from about 1.5 million to current estimates of 12 million or more. This focus has become the political epicenter of concern, although it is not a national security problem in any conventional threat (the immigrants pose no military threat to the United States, for instance). Their numbers do, however, contribute to other domestic problems, such as health care, education, and jobs. The drug problem has a more conventional national security aspect, since the trafficking in drugs contributes to criminality, including violence, against American citizens and has a major corrupting and destabilizing effect politically in countries through which the drugs pass on their way to the United States, notably Mexico. The problem of terrorists sneaking across the border, of course, has direct national security impact, since people entering in this manner successfully clearly evade identification and detection by appropriate authority, making it more difficult to interfere with any terrorist act in which they may seek to engage.

The current focus of the border problem has been how to seal the border from unwanted intrusion of all three of these problems—with the emphasis on illegal aliens. Currently, the major proposal for doing so has centered on a fence that would put a physical barrier along about 700 of the 1,933 miles of the U.S.–Mexico border. Building such a fence was authorized by legislation passed by Congress and signed by President Bush in 2006 (the Border Protection, Antiterrorism, and Illegal Immigration Control Act), but construction has not yet been begun in earnest because of controversies surrounding the proposal. These include whether a fence that leaves almost two-thirds of the border not barricaded will work (most of Texas, for instance, will not have a fence), whether any fence can stop the immigration (some argue that building a fence will simply make it more expensive for immigrants to get across the border by hiring criminal guides), and how to build the fence. According to the Department of Homeland Security, which would have jurisdiction over the project, a "state of the art" fence would cost between $4 and $8 billion (for the 700 miles), whereas a ten-foot prison-style fence (chain link topped with concertina wire) would cost about $850 million (plus an extra $360 million to electrify it), and a twelve-foot high, two-foot thick concrete wall would cost about $2 billion. Past experience (notably the fence built along the border adjacent to San Diego) suggests the probability of significant cost overruns. Moreover, it is not entirely clear how this fence would protect against people simply walking across the border at unprotected locations (often at considerable personal danger) or burrowing under the fence (a favorite method among drug dealers).

The other question raised by a multipurpose fence is that of jurisdiction. Different agencies, after all, have jurisdiction over the various objects with which the fence is supposed to deal, and it is apparently not unusual to find representatives of the Drug Enforcement Agency (drugs), Immigration and Customs Enforcement (terrorists), and Border Patrol (immigrants) at odds in particular cases. The most notorious case to date has involved the arrest and conviction of two Border Patrol agents for shooting and killing a drug trafficker with connections to the DEA crossing the border. Other aspects of the border issue—notably port security—are discussed in Chapter 12.

Conclusion: Globalization and Other Factors in American Security

Globalization in some evolving form is simply a fact of international life in the 2000s, and the only way it or other concerns raised in this chapter could be reversed altogether would likely be as the result of some catastrophic international event such as a global war. That outcome may seem unlikely in the current context, but it is at least a theoretical possibility that could be made more plausible if nuclear proliferation continues to occur (see Chapter 9).

Is globalization, the major concern, a good thing for the United States? The question, of course, is too simply put to be answered: it assumes there is *a* globalism, when in fact globalization is an evolving condition whereby economic interconnectedness is gradually increasing. It is also too simple because the process is so multifaceted that it will almost certainly have some beneficial and some harmful effects on any country and will spread unevenly (if at all) to different countries and parts of the world.

The real question is, on balance, Does globalization add to or detract from the American place in the world and thus American security? And what can be done to improve problematical aspects to make the process better serve those interests, including enhancing security? In the prosperous 1990s when globalization was given credit—rightly or wrongly—for helping to create and sustain prosperity, the answer was likely to be automatically positive. In the more cautious economic condition of a postmillennial era more focused on terrorist and other assaults on physical security, the assessment is likely to be more guarded and critical.

One aspect of the question, which also provides an intellectual bridge to the next chapter, may illustrate the difficulty of reaching expansive conclusions. It is the connection between globalization and sovereignty. As noted in Chapter 3, the retention of state sovereignty is a core realist value that has always been particularly important to the United States. Guarding American sovereignty has sometimes forced the United States out of step with the rest of the world.

By definition, the retention of effective state sovereignty is a major element of the country's national security, making the relationship between sovereignty and globalization an important matter. At the same time, if globalization contributes to the greater economic well-being of Americans, is any dilution of sovereignty that results from globalization a good bargain? Moreover, a virtue of globalization has been to impose American economic values on others, bringing them into conformance with our ideals. Should the question therefore be, Whose sovereignty is compromised?

An example may help us think about this. One part of the statute creating the WTO gives it the power to investigate allegations of trade violations by member states and, where it finds violations, to prosecute and impose mandatory sanctions against violating governments. In the ratification debate over WTO, this provision was widely condemned by defenders of American sovereignty, as had been the case over a similar provision in the proposed ITO in the 1940s. The counterargument was that most of the rules of the WTO would enforce were American values, making vulnerability minimal and assuring that others would be forced to conform as well. Conformance to the WTO charter thus cuts both ways: it dilutes the sovereign control of both the country and those other countries it seeks to influence.

The statute has indeed had both effects. A major argument for sponsoring Chinese membership in the WTO was that it would force China to reform its economic practices in ways that would lessen the ability of the Chinese government to maintain authoritarian control over the economy and ultimately, it was hoped, over the political system. While this is a difficult step for a Chinese government that is also a prime defender of state sovereignty, it is the price China has had to pay for full membership in the global economy. In this case, the U.S. government has used the international dilution of sovereignty to tie China more firmly into the global system and to increase American security.

But the statute does cut both ways. Shortly after the WTO came into force in 1995, the Clinton administration sought to improve its balance of payments situation with Japan by forcing the Japanese to buy more American automotive components to put into Japanese cars. To this end, Clinton announced his intention to place a high excise tax on Japanese luxury cars entering the United States that would have made them uncompetitive with domestic models. The hope was that the Japanese would cave in and agree to import more American car batteries and tires to avoid these penalties. Instead, the Japanese cried unfair trade practices and threatened to drag the United States before the WTO, where the United States would certainly have lost any judgment rendered. Faced with that likelihood, the Clinton administration withdrew the threat to exercise its state sovereignty through the excise tax.

The example suggests that the answers to apparently simple questions are rarely themselves simple. For the most part, globalization has helped the United States reassert its position in a global economic system in which it had slipped in preeminence after 1971. Whether the United States will continue to benefit depends on how it defines international interests, the degree to which it can influence the system in ways that benefit the most Americans, and how it reacts to unforeseen and sometimes unforeseeable changes.

STUDY/DISCUSSION QUESTIONS

1. Compare and contrast the concepts of globalization and geopolitics. Are they compatible and mutually reinforcing or antithetical, or both? Discuss.
2. What was the Bretton Woods system? What institutions did it create for what purposes? How has it evolved? How do the concepts of globalization and free trade fit into its evolution? Discuss in terms of the ITO–WTO process. How and why did the Bretton Woods system break down?
3. What distinguished the transitional period between 1971 and 1990? How did its evolution form the base for the globalization system?
4. What is the globalization system? What are its major characteristics and values?
5. What have been the major international and domestic objections to globalization? How are they related to one another?
6. Discuss energy as a national security problem. How would the use of military power by the United States have been different over the past twenty-five years without a U.S. dependency on Middle Eastern oil?
7. How and why can environmentalism be thought of as a national security problem? Discuss.
8. Discuss the various aspects and locations of the U.S. border problem. Regarding the current emphasis on the Mexican-American border, what are the most important aspects of the problem? How are they national security problems (or are they)? Will building a fence along roughly one-third of the border solve the problem?

Selected Bibliography

Abdedal, Rawi, and Adam Segal. "Has Globalization Reached Its Peak?" *Foreign Affairs* 86, 1 (January/February 2007), 103–114.

Antholes, William. "Pragmatic Engagement or Photo Opportunity: What Will the G-8 Become?" *Washington Quarterly* 24, 3 (Summer 2001), 213–226.

Baker, Gerald. "The Budget Debacle." *Foreign Policy* (March/April 2005), 42–47.

Barshefky, Charlene. "Trade Policy in a Networked World." *Foreign Affairs* 80, 2 (March/April 2001), 134–146.

Blinder, Alan S. "Offshoring: The Next Industrial Revolution." *Foreign Affairs* 85, 2 (March/April 2006), 113–128.

Diehl, Paul R., and Niles Peter Gleditsch (eds.). *Environmental Conflict*. Boulder, CO: Westview Press, 2001.

Dregner, Daniel W. *U.S. Free Trade Policy: Free versus Fair*. New York: Council on Foreign Relations Press, 2006.

Dunn, Robert. "Has the United States Really Been Globalized?" *Washington Quarterly* 24, 1 (Winter 2001), 53–64.

Feldstein, Martin. "A Self-Help Guide to Emerging Markets." *Foreign Affairs* 78, 2 (March/April 1999), 93–109.

Friedman, Thomas L. *The Lexus and the Olive Tree: Understanding Globalization*. New York: Farrar, Straus, and Giroux, 1999.

———. *The World Is Flat: A Brief History of the Twenty-First Century*. New York: Farrar, Straus, and Giroux, 2005.

Fukuyama, Francis. *The End of History and the Last Man*. New York: Free Press, 1992.

Greider, William. "Comment: A Globalization Offensive." *The Nation* 284, 4 (January 27, 2007), 5–6.

Kennedy, Paul. *The Rise and Fall of the Great Powers: Economic Change and Military Change from 1500 to 2000*. New York: Random House, 1987.

Keohane, Robert O., and Joseph S. Nye Jr. *Power and Interdependence* (2nd ed.). Glenview, IL: Scott Foresman/Little Brown, 1989.

Levey, David H., and Stuart S. Brown. "The Overstretch Myth." *Foreign Affairs* 84, 2 (March/April 2005), 2–7.

Luttwak, Edward. "From Geopolitics to Geo-economics: Logic of Conflict, Grammar of Commerce." *National Interest* 20 (Summer 1990), 17–24.

Lynn-Jones, Sean, and Stephen Miller (eds.). *Global Dangers: Changing Dimensions of International Security*. Cambridge, MA: MIT Press, 1995.

McBride, Stephen, and John Wiseman (eds.). *Globalization and Its Discontents*. New York: St. Martin's Press, 2000.

Nye, Joseph S., Jr. *Bound to Lead: The Changing Nature of American Power*. New York: Basic Books, 1990.

Payan, Terry. *Three U.S.-Mexican Border Wars: Drugs, Immigration, and Homeland Security*. Westport, CT: Greenwood, 2006.

Pirages, Dennis C., and Theresa Manley Degeest. *Ecological Security: An Evolutionary Perspective on Globalization*. New York: Rowman and Littlefield, 2004.

Podesta, John, and Peter Ogden. "The Security Implications of Climate Change." *Washington Quarterly* 31, 1 (Winter 2007–2008), 115–138.

Rockenbach, Leslie J. *The Mexican-American Border: NAFTA and Global Linkages*. Oxford, UK: Routledge, 2001.

Rothgeb, John M. J. *U.S. Trade Policy: Balancing Economic Dreams and Political Realities*. Washington, DC: CQ Press, 2001.

Sachs, Jeffrey. "International Economics: Unlocking the Mysteries of Globalization." *Foreign Policy* 10 (Spring 1998), 97–111.

Snow, Donald M. *Cases in International Relations: Portraits of the Future* (3rd ed.). New York: Pearson Longman, 2008.

Spero, Joan Edelman. *The Politics of International Economic Relations* (4th ed.). New York: St. Martin's Press, 1990.

Weber, Steven, Naazneen Barma, Matthew Kroenig, and Ely Ratner. "How Globalization Went Bad." *Foreign Policy* (January/February 2007), 48–54.

Yergin, Daniel. "Ensuring Energy Security." *Foreign Affairs* 85, 2 (March/April 2006), 69–82.

PART
II

THE CHANGING WORLD

The international environment is the setting in which national security policy is crafted to secure the country's interests in the world. Part I examined some of the historical factors that shaped how the United States looks at security matters, culminating in the rise and fall of the Cold War and the emergence of globalization after the first fault line was breached.

The second fault line of September 11, 2001, created another tectonic shift in the security environment. Part II explores various aspects of how the world is different and how those differences affect the American role in the world. Chapter 7 emphasizes the basic concepts around which security concerns revolve—security, risk, interests, and power—and how these have changed. The basic message is that interests remain largely the same as they were before, but there is a new configuration of threats to those interests, and those interests must be pursued in different ways. Chapter 8 attempts to assess the contemporary environment from the domestic perspective, how the U.S. government is organized to deal with changing circumstances, emphasizing the National Security Council (NSC) system and homeland security. Chapter 9 looks at the traditional military means and roles that American force has taken and how they are relevant to today's world. It examines the changing roles of both nuclear weapons and conventional or traditional armed forces, including military reform and manpower. Chapter 10 examines the possible influences of the end of American military participation in Iraq, particularly on American predilections to use force, the kinds of opportunities that will be available for employing that force, and possible restructuring of those forces for future contingencies.

CHAPTER 7

Security, Interests, and Power

PREVIEW

The shock of events, such as those revealed by the opening of the fault lines, tend to focus our concern on the trauma and extent of change rather than on how those events fit into the broader context of national concerns that transcend time and more strongly balance continuity with change. This chapter seeks to place recent traumas into the kind of analytical context with which national security policy grapples. It analyzes the impact of change on four basic categories of ongoing importance. First, what is the nature of security? Second, how has the nature and extent of risk been affected? Third, what impact has change had on basic interests? Fourth, what is the changing nature of effective power in the present and the future?

The contemporary national security environment contains elements of both continuity and change. From the vantage point of any particular point in time, including now, the unique set of forces and events of the moment may seem to predominate and emphasize change and the uniqueness of the evolving system. Thus, attention is drawn to the two major fault lines and aftershocks and their consequent effects on highlighting globalization or geopolitics as the principal system dynamic.

At the same time, some forces that seem unique in a narrow perspective appear less so within the general evolution of the international system and America's place in it. The twentieth century began with the belief that there was little likelihood of future violence. A general optimism prevailed, based on the perception of a growing economic interdependence driven by trade that was supposed to simultaneously assure future prosperity and make the recourse to war progressively less thinkable. The shock of the terrorist attacks makes it easy to forget that on January 1, 2000, most people felt basically the same about the future as their ancestors did on January 1, 1900.

National security analysis tries to determine what it is in the environment that may provide concern for the security and well-being of Americans and citizens of the world generally and to determine what, if anything, can be done to attenuate or eliminate the sources of disturbance. The same questions are asked today that were asked fifty or a hundred years ago; it is the answers that change to a greater or lesser extent, based upon the flow of events.

The United States is clearly still in the process of reassessing the national security problem for a new century, particularly in light of its personal and intimate introduction to international terrorism, a force not previously confronted and certainly not resolved by the Iraq War. Before that introduction, the environment seemed less negative than it did during the Cold War. People questioned the amount of effort that should be devoted to the national security enterprise and, at a more personal level, the amount of personal effort or sacrifice that should be expected. Those commercial airliners slamming into their targets removed the complacency about security that had developed in the tranquil 1990s. "Everything has changed" became the mantra after September 11, 2001; "nothing will ever be the same again." Dormant security concerns have been revived and now seem permanent parts of an environment that is unalterably changed. Or is it?

As noted earlier, the period leading to September 11 has been called the "long peace." If the first half of the twentieth century was arguably the bloodiest period in human history, the second half was relatively benign in terms of the toll of war. The hypothetical consequences of general war may have been great during the Cold War, but the reality was that bloodshed was basically confined to the peripheries—the developing world—where the major powers only became involved when they chose to become involved, as the Americans did in Vietnam and the Soviets in Afghanistan. After 1991, breaches of the peace were basically isolated to internal war in parts of the world outside the normal range of important American interests. The terrorist attacks that killed 3,000 Americans and other nationals darkened that sunny horizon and presented a new national security imperative, the beginning of the "long war." But is it a temporary interruption of the long peace or something more permanent and ominous?

The discussion proceeds through four sequential steps. Keeping the United States and Americans safe from harm—or secure—is the basic value of national security policy, so the discussion begins by exploring what makes people secure. Because safety is potentially imperiled from a variety of sources that may exceed resources, it looks at the question of how to decide what to protect and what to accept as risk. Deciding where to nullify and where to accept risk is a matter of what the country's most important interests are, and so the discussion returns to the matter of determining levels of interest. This assessment leads to a concern about how the United States can use its powers to the service of its security in the future.

THINKING ABOUT SECURITY

Security is a variable. What makes people safe or *feel* safe (the physical and psychological dimensions of security) depends upon two basic phenomena, each of which can assume different values, or can vary. The most obvious source of challenge to our security is factors that threaten the things that people value. As noted earlier, the most objective of these are physical threats, such as the ability of Russia to destroy the United States with nuclear weapons. Psychological threats—what makes people feel secure or insecure—are often less tangible and are subject to individual interpretation: different people feel secure or insecure in the same situation. The degree to which individuals are personally threatened by the prospect of terrorist activity reflects that dimension.

This leads to the second variable about security, which is the interpretation of the environment. Does the environment make one feel secure or insecure? Thus, what actions might be contemplated to change the environment and make it less threatening (increase our sense of security)? Clearly, the two variable aspects are related to one another: a hostile physical environment will diminish the psychological feeling of security more than a benign environment where there are few adversaries posing few threats to our interests and our security.

The environmental aspect of security has apparently changed considerably since the end of the Cold War. With the demise of the Soviet adversary, the physical sense of insecurity diminished considerably for the United States. Russia still maintains a large stock of nuclear weapons but lacks any compelling rationale to use them. The Cold War threat to American and allied security posed by the forces of Soviet Communism has disappeared and not been replaced by any worthy successor, what the initial (1997) Quadrennial Defense Review (QDR) first called the lack of a "peer competitor" (true, worthy enemy).

The discussion about these aspects of security can be divided into two related steps. The first is the changing balance between military and nonmilitary sources of security concern. This leads to and is conditioned by the second step: the various levels of security that affect different actors in international politics and an assessment of how concepts of security may be changing.

Military and Nonmilitary Elements of Security

Historically, as noted, national security and military security have been largely synonymous. Although other matters might threaten the well-being of the country, those threats with which policy makers and analysts were principally worried and which fell most obviously into the category of national security dealt with military threats. Military elements were certainly the predominant form of threats during the Cold War.

The inclusion of nonmilitary elements into what was considered national security began to occur during the Cold War, particularly in the area of economic security, raised in Chapter 6. There have been previous occasions when economic and other concerns entered the national security arena—trade matters with Great Britain, for instance, had been an important part of the conduct of the American Civil War, and a major threat to the United States of a German victory in World War I was the possible exclusion of American manufactures from the European continent. Likewise, suppression of the Barbary Pirates in the early 1800s may have been the first time that responding to what are now called nonstate actors became a national security concern.

Nonmilitary and semimilitary elements have been added to concepts of security. Among the nonmilitary aspects (threats with no military component), "economic security" has been broadened to encompass environmental security, for instance. Other added security concerns are partly military and partly nonmilitary. A primary example of these *semimilitary* aspects of security and responses to them is the problem of international terrorism. As the campaign against the Taliban and Al Qaeda in Afghanistan has demonstrated, these problems can have a clearly military component, but significant aspects of terrorism and its suppression are also political and law enforcement concerns, and the "long war" is arguably a less intense, if more persistent, phenomenon.

Military, semimilitary, and nonmilitary elements have melded in the post–Cold War period, in part because the purely traditional military elements of security are clearly less extensive and less intense than they were before. The virtually total absence of the danger of a major, system-threatening military conflict like the world wars or the breakdown of the Cold War into a hot war is a major characteristic of the contemporary system, even after September 11. In some sense, the long peace continues to get longer.

The nonmilitary and semimilitary elements of security have risen in relative importance as military threats have receded. For the most part, these are a series of smaller military threats, some of which existed during the Cold War but received less attention then, and some of which have emerged since. What they have in common is that none provides a direct, general threat to the United States physically in the way a potential Soviet nuclear attack did. The 2001 terrorist threat against the United States demonstrated that the American homeland has become vulnerable to harm that can kill many Americans, but these attacks do not currently place the integrity of the United States at direct risk. (see *Challenge!* box).

Other than terrorism, the remaining security threats are at a lower level of urgency and importance, placing them squarely within the psychological dimension of security, where people can and do disagree about the importance of the threat. Some threats existed during the Cold War but paled by comparison to the larger problem. The danger and threat of the proliferation of weapons of mass destruction (WMD) to countries in the Second Tier was a problem then and now, for instance (see Chapter 9).

As purely military elements of security have declined, nonmilitary and semimilitary elements have been on the rise. Because of globalization, some of the most important nonmilitary elements are now in the area of international economics, where concerns like conditions of trade have risen to levels of concern comparable to military matters. The semimilitary threat of terrorism has occupied a special place since 2001, but it is a concern that has been long held at a lower level of intensity.

The military and nonmilitary elements of security come together in concrete ways. The situation between the United States and China is an example. China was, of course, a Cold War military adversary of the United States, even if the threat it posed was somewhat ambiguous after the split between China and the Soviet Union and the opening of Sino-American relations in 1972. Still, national security planners during the 1960s planned for two simultaneous major wars, one with the Soviets and one with the Chinese (the two-war strategy). The focus of Sino-American military rivalry was and is over the Nationalist Chinese government of Taiwan, which China periodically threatens.

After Deng Xiao-peng's announcement of the "Four Modernizations" in 1979 and their implementation during the 1980s and 1990s, an economic relationship

DEFINING TERRORISM AS A SECURITY THREAT

What kind of a threat does international terrorism pose to the United States? Much of the discussion of post–September 11, 2001, efforts by the United States to quell this problem has been described as constituting a "war," which suggests the problem is a military one with a military solution. The "global war on terrorism" (GWOT) is what the Bush administration initially labeled the effort, and that designation has been picked up and repeated to the point that it is now the common designation for the effort.

Much of the initial effort seemed to justify this designation. The insertion of American forces into Afghanistan first to help topple the Taliban government and then to try to round up and destroy remaining pockets of Al Qaeda and Taliban resistance was clearly military in content. When American forces were sent to places like the Philippines and Yemen to train local forces better to resist terrorists, this also represented a military response, albeit at the lower end of the spectrum of military responses.

This text disagrees with the assertion that countering terrorism falls within the category of military dimensions of security. Clearly, suppressing terrorism has a military element, as demonstrated by initial actions, and terrorism experts like Stephen Sloan specifically include military responses as part of dealing with terrorism. Thus, the response to terrorism clearly does not fall within the nonmilitary dimension either.

The text has placed terrorism in the category of semimilitary responses. The basic argument is that suppressing terrorism has some elements that involve various uses of military force but that the effort also clearly includes elements that are either nonmilitary or quasi-military. Gathering intelligence information on terrorist plans and activities to frustrate the terrorists and arresting and prosecuting those who engage in or plot to commit terrorist acts are also important parts of dealing with the problem, and they are not military actions.

Is the distinction of dealing with terrorism within the semimilitary dimension of security important or just a matter of splitting hairs? If the problem is only partially military in origin and solution, put another way, does the analogy with "war" hold? If it does, that helps frame the public debate—for instance, the justification for greater defense expenditures. If the effort is only partly military, on the other hand, then the rhetoric of war—questioning the loyalty of those who question the effort as unpatriotic because we are "at war"—may be excessive and run counter to democratic rule. What do you think?

emerged that began to lessen the intensity of the military rivalry. A major pillar of the modernizations was to allow the development of private enterprises in the Special Economic Zones (SEZs) of the southeastern part of the China. When the Cold War ended and the age of globalization came into full bloom, a burgeoning trade between the two countries developed and largely replaced the military rivalry.

Is China currently a national security threat to the United States? From a purely military viewpoint, one can make a small case for a "Chinese threat" in the form of a small, primitive nuclear capability and large conventional armed forces that cannot be projected far from China's shore. Taiwanese rumblings about declaring its independence regularly bring Chinese saber rattling, and incidents like the spy plane episode of April 2001 (when an American reconnaissance plane collided with a Chinese jet fighter off the coast of China) caused some concern. Balanced against those problems, Beijing will host the 2008 Olympics (a major achievement that will likely have China on its best behavior), and the Chinese Communist Party announced in August 2001 that capitalists will be permitted to join the Communist Party (a seeming oxymoron). China continues to be a major provider of consumer goods for Americans and has been further integrated into the world economy as a member of the WTO. Thus, calculating Sino-American military threats is no longer an easy or clear-cut matter as the relationship evolves to one of so-called complex interdependence. Whether there is also a potential threat imbedded in the relationship remains a matter of debate (see Snow, "China Rising," in *Cases in International Relations*).

The Chinese example is not the only one in which the intersection of military and nonmilitary aspects of security become blurred. Not all are directly American. One source of insecurity is and always has been over access to important resources. Among these issues, access to water could provide a similar dynamic in the relatively near future, as Amplification 7.1 suggests.

Amplification 7.1

ISRAEL, SYRIA, THE GOLAN HEIGHTS, AND WATER

One of the ways in which concerns over security have been changing in the contemporary environment is the expansion of situations and conditions about which states may feel insecure and thus feel the need to take action to ensure their security. Military security has, in other words, been augmented by economic security, environmental security, energy security, and a variety of other concerns (discussed extensively in Chapter 14).

One scarce resource that will assuredly climb to the top of the agenda of security concerns in some places is access to adequate supplies of potable water. Nowhere in the world is this concern more evident than in the arid Middle East, where very few states have adequate supplies, particularly to service populations expected to grow in the future and place additional demands on dwindling supplies (Turkey is the exception to this rule). Although it receives little publicity outside the region itself, the problem of water remains a major barrier to the ability of Israel to reach an accord with the last of the countries that has opposed it in war, Syria.

The major remaining issue between the Israelis and the Syrians is the return of the Golan Heights to Syria. Before the 1967 Six Days' War, Syria had used the Heights, a series of low mountains that border on northern Israel, to launch mortar and artillery attacks on the Israeli settlements in the valley below. As a result, when Israel was occupying territories of its neighbors because of the war (the West Bank from Jordan, the Sinai Peninsula and Gaza Strip from Egypt), it also occupied the Golan Heights to assure that Syria could not physically resume its attacks.

The Golan Heights are also important because of water. Much of the water that Israel (and Jordan) uses comes from the Jordan River, the source of which is the Sea of Galilee. As the map shows, the eastern shore of the Sea forms the border between Israel and Syria when Syria possesses the Golan Heights, thereby affording the Syrians the physical ability to interfere with that source of Israeli water. The problem is moot with Israel occupying the Heights, since the Syrians are physically kept away from the seashore. Return of the Golan Heights to Syria is the *sine qua non* for a peace settlement between the two countries. Before Israel agrees to transfer the territory back, however, it must have an iron-clad agreement covering military attacks from the Golan Heights and, perhaps more important, assuring that Syria will not interfere with Israel's water supply.

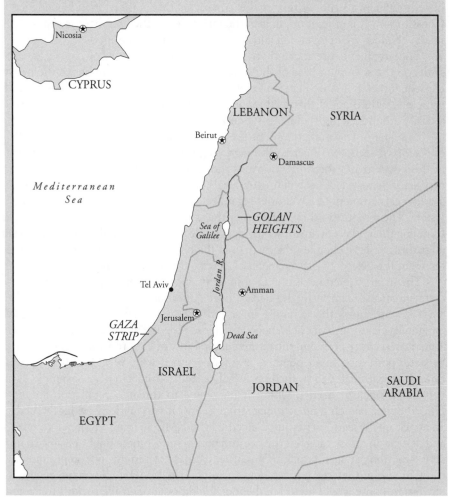

Levels of Security

The previous discussion centered on the idea of state security, which is the primary focus of concern in a system where the realist paradigm predominates. This focus is one of the more controversial consequences of a realist paradigm world and has caused many reformers to suggest that there should be a more balanced approach to legitimate security concerns both below and above the level of the state.

Competing levels of security arguments run closely parallel to the debate about sovereignty. The idea that there could be a source of superior authority to the state was, of course, a major issue in the Thirty Years War in the clash between sectarian and secular authority and dynastic and territorial claims. There are parallels within the contemporary assertion that the security of subnational groups and individuals should be primary considerations. This assertion reflects the notion of popular sovereignty first put forward by political thinkers such as Locke and Rousseau that also heavily influenced the writers of the American Declaration of Independence and Constitution. It is at least implicit in the rationale of other democratic systems (minimally, the idea that power and authority flow from the people).

The arguments are more than academic. Some of them, of course, reflect assaults on the sovereign base of the state system and tend to emphasize the negative consequences of a state-centered system with state security as its underlying first principle. Others assert the need for and positive consequences of a reorientation of security around the individual or supranational concerns.

One line of reasoning questions the consequences of states acting principally out of their own security concerns while ignoring other levels. A most basic formulation of this concern is something known as the *security dilemma*. In this construct, states may act in ways—such as building up levels of armaments—to increase their security against real or potential adversaries regardless of the effect on the larger international system. The response of those targeted by the original action may be to respond in kind (building their levels of arms), which may result in an arms spiral wherein, in the end, all parties are left feeling less secure than in the beginning. Security dilemma situations represent the perspective of *international security*, the security of the overall system.

The security dilemma is not an abstract problem but can be seen in ongoing, concrete situations. Currently, the debate over American construction of a missile defense system shows the dynamic in action. The national missile defense (NMD) program is clearly an American *national* defense proposal aimed at solving a perceived American security problem, the future vulnerability of U.S. territory to missile attacks by states possessing small numbers of missiles armed with WMD. Other states may, however, feel threatened by the U.S. WMD system. China is a prime example. It has a very small nuclear arsenal, which it maintains to threaten retaliation should the United States launch a nuclear first strike against it (no matter how far-fetched such an attack might seem). They are concerned the NMD system is designed to intercept and destroy an attack of about the size and nature the Chinese might be able to mount after absorbing a first attack. Thus, the Chinese deterrent is compromised, and the Chinese are left to ponder how to respond if NMD deployment occurs. One obvious response would be to build enough additional offensive rockets to guarantee overcoming the NMD with surviving missiles after an American first strike with offensive weapons. The result could be to make the United States more vulnerable to China armed with more missiles than before NMD deployment—the security dilemma in action. India, the state that feels most threatened by Chinese weapons, might then feel the need to respond to a Chinese buildup, a ripple effect that could then extend to Pakistan, further destabilizing the system. A similar dynamic underlies Russian objections to building a missile defense system in Eastern Europe.

The American terrorism campaign also raises levels of security concerns. The American military response in Afghanistan was clearly framed in terms of American state security—removing the source of a threat to the American homeland. Very few in the world argued with this campaign. When the United States threatened to widen the campaign to other sources of potential threat—notably Iraq's suspected WMD program and the incumbency of Saddam Hussein—leaders from France's Jacques Chirac to Jordan's King Abdullah in effect raised the security dilemma in objection. American actions to strengthen what some leaders saw as its own security could so destabilize the Middle East as to leave everyone worse off, thereby creating a security dilemma situation.

The other level of concern is that of *individual security*, a primary orientation of security around individuals and groups. This emphasis is most often associated with the protection of the safety of people within states. The problem arises from traditional interpretations of the absolute power state sovereignty provides for the state over its population. The consequences of this power become an international concern in the post–Cold War environment of internal wars that involve atrocities against victim populations and groups within populations.

Traditional definitions of sovereignty give the state total control over its territorial base, including the treatment of individual citizens and groups, and makes illegitimate any outside efforts to affect that treatment. In the cases of particularly tyrannical regimes, the result has often been state-sponsored or state-conducted campaigns against their own citizens, which the international community technically cannot prevent or alleviate; it is none of anybody else's business how a state treats its citizens.

An assertion of the validity of individual security challenges that assumption. It is related to the assertion of popular sovereignty, since presumably no one would delegate to the state the right to abuse them. The history of individual security, however, is relatively recent and based in two post–World War II phenomena: reaction to the Holocaust and the emergence of notions of individual, enforceable human rights.

The Holocaust was a terribly traumatic event for the international community and gave a black eye to advocates of the notion of total sovereign control. Among other things, it revealed the lengths to which unrestrained governments might go in mistreating their citizens—state sovereignty had run amok. Yet, in the early war crimes trials at Nuremberg, a prominent participating American jurist opined that Nazis could be tried for killing non-German Jews and Gypsies (among others), but not German Jews or Gypsies, since they had sovereign authority over their own populations.

Reaction to the Holocaust boosted advocacies of universal human rights after the war and helped result in a number of international treaties asserting that individuals everywhere had certain rights that could not be denied by governments. Since nondemocratic governments existed and routinely denied and repressed these rights, individual rights and a concept such as individual security reinforced one another.

Once again, the importance of this distinction is not abstract in the post–Cold War world. Although mass atrocities occurred during the Cold War (e.g., the Khmer Rouge slaughter in Cambodia during the 1970s), brutal civil wars have been a major part of post–Cold War violence. Ethnic cleansing—the displacement or extermination of ethnic, religious, and other groups—and the violent suppression of human rights have been a focus of violence within the international system.

The question of security—what makes people secure—is not as simple as thinking about military force and military threats. Security does take on different forms—military, semimilitary, and nonmilitary. And different entities—individuals, states, even the international system—have security concerns. When these are combined, objects of security are both complex and numerous. It is a long list of entities that can be threatened in different ways, and all the resources necessary to remove all kinds of threats to security are not always available. In that circumstance, choices must be made, raising the problem of risk and its management.

RISK AND RISK MANAGEMENT

In an ideal world, the means would be available to remove all our sources of insecurity. In the real world, however, the threats that we face—or potentially face—always outnumber the resources available to negate those threats to safety. The gap between the threats and the resources to nullify those threats is *risk*, and it can be depicted in the suggestive formula: risk equals threat minus capability (risk = threat – capability).

Since risk is calculated on the basis of threats to security, it is also a variable quantity. How much threat must be endured is, according to the formula, the result of two factors, each of which can vary. The first and most elastic of these quantities is threat. As already explained, the degree of threat experienced is the result of physical and psychological aspects of security. Primarily, this means that the amount of potential risk people face is the result of what makes them *feel* secure or insecure, and people differ on what frightens them and must thus be countered to reduce insecurity. For instance, almost all agree that international terrorism threatens the United States but may disagree on what potential aspects of the terrorism problem are most dangerous and immediate and thus threatening.

Threat can also vary depending on the amount of exposure one has to potentially threatening forces, and this element of threat is partially controllable either by exposing oneself to the security problem or by avoiding it. A global power like the United States will have more threats to its security than a smaller state with more parochial interests, for instance, meaning the threat to the United States will exceed that of most others. On the other hand, the way potentially threatening opponents are treated can increase or decrease the amount of threat that must be nullified. For instance, American policy toward the Democratic People's Republic of Korea (DPRK, or North Korea) during the 1990s had largely convinced the North Koreans not to pursue their nuclear weapons program, partly because of U.S. policy toward the DPRK in the 2000s. The North Korean threat in 2008 is considerably larger than it was in 1995; more conciliatory changes in U.S. policy could conceivably reduce that threat to its previous level. This problem is explored in Amplification 7.2.

Amplification 7.2

What Should the United States Do About North Korea?

For the past several years, the United States has been involved in a direct confrontation with the government of the Democratic People's Republic of Korea (DPRK, or North Korea). It is, of course, not the first time the two countries have been at odds: America's first major military conflict of the Cold War occurred in 1950 when the North Koreans invaded the Republic of Korea (South Korea), and the United States intervened to restore South Korean sovereignty in a war that lasted over three years and cost over 37,000 American lives.

The DPRK is one of the most destitute, remote countries in the world. It shares with Cuba the distinction of being one of the two remaining countries practicing Communist ideology both politically and economically (the other Communist states, China and Vietnam, have effectively renounced socialist economics). Politically, the country has had only two leaders, the late Kim Il Sung and, since the self-designated "Great Leader" died in 1994, his son Kim Jung Il. The country is among the poorest in the world and suffers periodically from harsh famines because it does not produce enough farm products to feed itself.

The long-standing source of controversy between the United States and the DPRK surrounds the North Korean nuclear program. Although the North Koreans have been members of the Nuclear Non-Proliferation Treaty (NPT)—whose members vow not to develop nuclear weapons—Pyongyang has maintained an active nuclear research program and has the material to build nuclear weapons. Additionally, it has an active missile program, which could become a delivery capability should they produce nuclear weapons.

During the 1990s, relations between the two countries had reduced tensions. In 1993, the DPRK became the first country to announce its intentions to withdraw from the NPT, which produced a flurry of activity. In 1994, the North Koreans suspended their withdrawal in an interim agreement with the United States that called for American assistance to the regime, and in 1999, a further agreement reduced, among other things, travel restrictions between North Korea and the world. This was followed by the first open relations between North and South Korea and with Japan. North Korea was viewed as a relatively minor risk.

(continued)

That changed with the election of George W. Bush. In addition to designating North Korea a member of the "axis of evil" (along with Iran and Iraq), the administration suspended bilateral contacts with the Kim Jung Il regime. Slighted by these actions, North Korea angrily announced its resumption of efforts to produce nuclear weapons. At American initiative, six-power talks (North and South Korea, China, Japan, Russia, and the United States) have attempted to quell this development but with only limited success. In 2007, the DPRK agreed to dismantle its nuclear program in return for assistance from outside powers very similar to those negotiated in 1994.

What should the United States do about North Korea? One answer is to go back to bilateral diplomacy, which proponents of current policy say was demeaning and ineffective. Another is to continue the six-party talks, which the North Koreans do not like because they prefer bilateral negotiations. A third alternative is for the United States to use military force to deprive North Korea of the ability to make nuclear weapons, an action that could provoke another war on the peninsula that no one wants. The final option is for the United States to ignore the situation and leave it to regional solution. None is an overwhelmingly obvious solution. What do you think?

Capability, defined as the capacity to take actions that nullify threats, is also a variable, although not an infinitely elastic or expansible one. Capability is generally defined in terms of various kinds of power available to ensure that threats cannot be successfully carried out against us. In the simplest terms, for instance, the existence and structure of the United States armed forces is designed to ensure that any foreign military invader would be repulsed, thereby nullifying the threat of invasion and conquest of the United States. The semimilitary threat of harm posed by terrorists, on the other hand, is so diverse and diffuse that it is not clear what resources are needed to nullify entirely the risks posed by terrorist threats to do harm to the country.

In general terms, it is almost always true that threats will exceed the capability to nullify them, and this observation is particularly true in the current context of international terrorism. There are so many potential targets for terrorist attacks on American soil and overseas (see Chapter 12 for a discussion) that removing all of them from harm's way is, as a practical matter, impossible. This means that choices must be made about which threats to nullify and which targets to leave at risk. Since the potential list of what makes people feel safe or unsafe is subjective, it is always more expansible than the capabilities one might marshal to protect everything.

Those threats that cannot be nullified (although one does not admit that there is such a list or what is on it, for obvious reasons) constitute risk. Determining what risks will and will not be nullified is the job of policy makers, who regularly engage in what amounts to the triage of risk reduction and risk management. Risk reduction, as the name implies, consists of those actions that maximize the threats that are nullified. Which threats will be nullified and which will remain risks lie in the realm of risk management.

Risk can be modulated by manipulating either element of the formula. One way to reduce risk is to redefine those things that are considered threatening. Illegal immigration poses a threat that needs to be addressed only if one defines such immigration as a problem. If immigration were declared no longer to be a problem, then the threat is reduced and so is the risk (see the discussion in Chapter 14). This particularly controversial example is cited purposely, since any attempt to define away risks will almost always be highly controversial.

The other way to reduce risk is to increase the capability to address and attack threats. In political terms, this means increasing the resources allocated to the particular problem. To continue the illegal immigrant example, if continued illegal immigration is defined as a threat to the United States, the obvious risk-reducing response would be to make the borders more impermeable—for instance, by hiring additional border guards or immigration and Border Patrol employees. That solution would cost money, opening political debates on taxes, deficits, and the reallocation of resources from some other functions—for instance, guarding national parks or monuments from potential terrorist attacks.

THINKING ABOUT INTERESTS

Where risk is accepted and where it is not depends on the hierarchy of things that are valued, or interests. Questions about the role and implications of interests mirror differences over what constitutes security in the contemporary order. The interplay of interests—whose are realized and whose are not—are central to the dynamics of international relations organized around the realist paradigm. The interests at the base of these calculations are invariably state interests. Constructed in this manner, the military aspects of security are prominent because force is one of the options available to achieve the state's most important (or vital) interests.

For better or worse, interest-driven calculations remain the criteria by which states operate in the anarchical international system. When the interests of states come into conflict, the question of which states' interests will prevail also arises, and this leads to trying to determine how important interests are, where and how they are threatened (one at risk), and thus what means will be employed to attempt to achieve them. Thus, the question of levels of interest must be addressed, although within a somewhat different context than the question of security. These levels, in turn, suggest different national security and military and nonmilitary implications, including economic implications connected to the theme of globalization. Finally, the challenge to traditional concepts of national interest in the form of broader variants of what constitute vital interests is addressed.

Levels of Interests

The various levels and intensities of interest introduced in Chapter 3 need not be repeated here. The heart of that discussion, however, dealt with the critical traditional national security question of the boundary between *vital* interests and those that are deemed less than vital. The salience of that boundary is that it is theoretically the demarcation point of when the state will contemplate the use of military

Figure 7.1: Interest Levels and Security Means Dimensions

		Interest Level	
		Vital	Less-Than-Vital
Security	Military	Cell 1	Cell 2
Means	Semimilitary	Cell 3	Cell 4
Dimension	Nonmilitary	Cell 5	Cell 6

force to realize its goals. Interests failing the test of vitality (major or peripheral interests) imply the use of means of lesser intensity than those that are vital. Most of the economic methods of achieving goals that are compatible with globalization presumably are useful for less-than-vital interest realization. There are instances when economic weapons may be applied to vital interests, such as the boycott and economic isolation of Saddam Hussein to gain his compliance with international norms of WMD inspection, but such actions have a very limited success rate and are relatively infrequent. In the case of semimilitary threats, the invocation of vital interests may suggest both military and nonmilitary responses.

This conjunction between interests and security can be depicted in matrix form, as is done in Figure 7.1. Cells 1 and 6 are the easiest to describe. It is the heart of the realist formulation that when vital interests are threatened, force may become an option if the situation is solvable by using force (military security, as depicted in cell 1). At the same time, when less-than-vital interests come into conflict, they are normally solved nonmilitarily because military force is either inappropriate or more drastic than the situation dictates (cell 6). An imminent attack on one's territory would be a clear cell 1 situation; a dispute over tariff schedules would clearly fall in cell 6. When vital interests are involved, the first inclination is to try to use nonmilitary means to resolve the differences—maintaining force as a "last resort" if all else fails (cell 5). Applying economic sanctions would be an example.

The real debate is over the situation in which vital interests are not engaged but military aspects of security may be contemplated because they are the only means that may bring about a satisfactory resolution (cell 2). A strict interpretation of the realist paradigm is very restrictive in this regard: if American vital interests are not threatened, for instance, then American use of force should not be contemplated. This was the basic stance taken by the Bush campaign in 2000 when it argued that the United States should not be the "world's 911"; that stance was arguably relaxed when the United States invaded Iraq in 2003.

The continued controversy over applying realist criteria for using force rages in cell 2 with strong national security and military implications. Because the United States possesses such an overwhelming amount of force, there is some temptation to apply it to a variety of situations. As Clinton Secretary of State Madeleine Albright once said, "What is the point of having armed forces if you never use them?" The retort from the realist paradigm is that you only use them when the situation is really important (vital interests) and when force is appropriate. Whether the removal of Saddam Hussein was important enough to justify invading Iraq is a cell 1–cell 2 dispute.

The role of force is more complicated in cells 3 and 4 (semimilitary dimensions). Where vital interests are at stake, force is justified to the extent it can be effective. The military aspects of the war on terrorism are a clear cell 3 application. The questions revolve around how much of a role force plays when it may be a necessary, but not sufficient, condition for success. The war on drugs arguably represents cell 4, since drug use is an important but probably not system-threatening (vital interest) problem. In this case, questions can be raised about whether the problem is severe enough to invoke force and whether the use of force is appropriate for dealing with the problem.

Remember that the boundary between military and nonmilitary dimensions (vital and major interests) is not a fixed line. It is more like a movable confidence interval of changing widths and locations. Where the line should be and just how wide the interval around it ought to be is the heart of the national security debate about using force. It is a highly political debate about which reasonable people can disagree over specific situations and that changes location as time passes and circumstance change. While there will always be high levels of consensus on some vital items, there will equally always be disagreement about the exact location of the intellectual barrier separating those situations that do and do not justify the employment of American armed forces. The existence of semimilitary situations only further blurs the distinction.

The debate within cell 2 and in cells 3 and 4 can thus be seen as a question about how much the change in the international environment of the post–Cold War world has moved the width of the band surrounding what is and is not vital and the extent and role of force in semimilitary situations. During the Cold War period, the location was relatively clear. The United States could and would use force when Soviet-inspired or Soviet-directed Communist movements threatened to come to power at the expense of American friends and allies. The clearest cases were those in which the United States had clearly important interests—Western Europe and northeast Asia (Japan and Korea)—and, of course, in which the Soviets could threaten the United States directly with nuclear weapons. In cases that put the physical survival or independence of the American homeland or the territory of its closest friends at stake (the physical dimension of security), it was clear that military security was at stake and that force would be used (cell 1).

Even during the Cold War, the demarcation was an interval, not a line, and this was most clearly seen in places that might be of interest to the United States in Communist–non-Communist terms but where otherwise the United States had few other interests. Those situations occurred most often in developing world areas such as Africa and much of Asia, and the American assessment became more debatable, falling within the psychological dimension of what makes us feel secure and about which reasonable people can disagree. These are the instances that fall into cell 2.

Two potentially similar situations on which opposite conclusions were reached illustrate this relationship between interests and security. The first is the American involvement in Vietnam. When the United States replaced France as the principal barrier to Communist victory there after the Geneva Conference of 1954, there was relatively little debate about American direct interests in the outcome of that conflict. Rather, the prevailing criterion for some level of involvement was opposition to Communist expansion globally, of which Southeast Asia happened to be the then most current example. Opposition to Communism as a general proposition was viewed as important enough to ask the question, How will American interests be affected by the worst possible outcome (the unification of the country under Communist control)?

In retrospect, it is probably unfortunate that the specific question was not raised in the public debate and fully considered at the time, because quite likely the assessment would have been negative. In the end, the worst possible outcome did occur, but except for the self-inflicted angst the country experienced because we "lost" the war, American interests otherwise were hardly affected at all—the answer to how interests were affected was "not very much." What looked at the time like a cell 1 situation looks much more like a cell 2 or even cell 6 situation in retrospect. This same analysis can be applied to Iraq as is done in Amplification 7.3.

The other example is Nicaragua in the 1980s. How important Sandinista rule was to the interests of the United States was argued both as a matter of the competition between the Communist and non-Communist rule and on the basis of geography. At one level, a Marxist Nicaragua provided a foothold for Communism on the mainland of the Americas through which Soviet assistance could be funneled

Amplification 7.3

VITAL AND LESS-THAN-VITAL INTERESTS AND IRAQ

One of the critiques of the American decision to invade Iraq was that the situation there did not constitute a threat to American vital interests and that, by applying the realist paradigm, the use of force was unjustified. Put in terms presented here, critics essentially argued the situation did not fall into cell 1 of Figure 7.1, but more probably was a cell 4 situation wherein semimilitary responses would have been more appropriate.

Assessing this argument requires making two judgments, each of which is at least partially subjective. One is the nature of the situation and hinges on two assertions made to justify the action: whether Iraq possessed WMD and whether the regime was linked to international religious terrorists (to whom the Iraqis might provide WMD). An assessment of the nature and tolerability of the situation could be made based on this judgment about the situation.

The second question was on which side of the vital/less-than-vital line the assessment fell. The nature of this determination is discussed in Amplification 3.1, and the essence boils down to how tolerable the worse-case assessment (Iraq with WMD and linked to terrorists) was to the United States and thus whether Iraq was a cell 1 or a cell 4 situation.

through Cuba into Nicaragua and on to destinations such as El Salvador, where the pro-American government was facing a Marxist insurgency. At another level, an activist Nicaragua might stir up trouble generally in the region, possibly eventually threatening control of the Panama Canal and even destabilizing the southern part of Mexico, where there was an incipient antigovernment insurgent movement active.

Did the Nicaraguan situation rise to a threat to a vital interest, justifying a military response (cell 1), or were the interests less than vital, in which case a military response might or might not be appropriate? There was disagreement between the White House and the Congress on this question, and the ultimate decision was to treat it as either a cell 2 or a cell 6 situation, one not requiring the employment of American military forces—a determination vindicated when the Nicaraguans voted the Sandinistas out of office in 1990.

Why engage in such a lengthy discussion of the relationship between security dimensions and interest levels? For one thing, it illustrates that in the real world, such determinations are difficult and ambiguous. Were the world made up exclusively of clearly cell 1 or cell 6 situations, making and implementing national security policy would be simple. In fact, one of the sources of nostalgia about the Cold War is that the central confrontation between the United States and the Soviet Union was such a precisely cell 1 instance. Because of that, building security policy from that central construct was intellectually straightforward and relatively noncontroversial. Having said that, the United States never used military force during the Cold War in an unambiguously cell 1 situation (the closest possible exception may have been Korea); Americans *deployed* forces to deal with cell 1 contingencies (NATO forces in Europe), but they were *employed* in situations more closely associated with cell 2.

The post–Cold War world is composed almost exclusively of situations that cause debate about where the boundary between vital and less-than-vital interests should be placed and what kinds of responses—military, semimilitary, or nonmilitary—are most appropriate. Because of the interest–threat mismatch, there are hardly any clear cell 1 situations for which to prepare and around which to ground planning. If international religious terrorism truly threatened the physical integrity of the United States and was a force appropriate for military eradication, it might rise to cell 1. American military preponderance makes it difficult even to think of potential cell 1 situations in the near future because no state or coalition of states poses a threatening symmetrical threat.

The ongoing environment exists outside the realm of vital interests—in cells 2, 3, 4, and 6. Part of the problem involves determining which of those cells is appropriate to describe any given concrete situation and to suggest appropriate ways to deal with them. At the same time, arguably vital interests are engaged in areas outside of national survival and where semimilitary solutions may be appropriate. Also, economic well-being such as terms of trade with Japan demonstrates situations in which nonmilitary aspects of security are clearly more appropriate (cell 5). There are, in other words, more ambiguous decisions to be made than there are clear-cut determinations such as whether the country should be prepared to defend a Soviet invasion through the Fulda Gap in Germany.

Security and Interests in the Contemporary Environment

It is an old saw that national interests rarely change but that threats to those interests change. A stable, free Western Europe, for instance, is just as important to the United States today as it was a half-century ago; what is different today is that there are no realistic threats to the security of the countries of Western Europe. At the same time, new (or apparently new) threats to long-term interests may emerge, as the terrorist threat to American territory exhibits. In the terrorist case, interests and threats converge, and the only question is how to deal with them.

This situation creates an intellectual bind for those who think about and plan for national security, especially the military dimension of national security. While there may be a variety of situations that potentially engage American vital interests in the contemporary world, the only one that has activated American interest has been the alleged vital interest in Iraq. When Saddam Hussein invaded and conquered Kuwait in 1990, he threatened American guaranteed access to Middle Eastern oil, a clear American vital interest. When he was alleged to have been stockpiling WMD and consorting with terrorists in 2002, the red flag of vital interests was raised again, a more debatable proposition discussed in Amplification 7.3. Similarly, it is still possible that North Korea might try to cross the 38th Parallel into South Korea or that China might venture across the Straits of Taiwan to annex the island into the Chinese polity; neither of these contingencies is especially likely, but both clearly violate American vital interests.

Potential conventional military threats to vital American interests are unlikely in the short or medium term. Countries may and do have major disagreements with the United States on a variety of issues, but because of the enormous advantage the United States has in symmetrical capabilities, it is implausible that any state or group of states would or could challenge the United States in conventional arms. Iraq's de facto nondefense against the American invasion of 2003 is testimony to this calculation. This situation is explored in more detail in Chapter 10.

The terrorist attacks of 2001 and the continuing campaign to deal with terrorism—the second fault line—add a new element to the mix. Protecting the homeland is clearly a vital interest, but the threat is asymmetrical in size and only semimilitary in response. At one level, interests and threats converge, but at another level, they remain mismatched. Although overthrowing the Taliban and disrupting the bin Laden network's sanctuary in Afghanistan was a fairly traditional military mission, the post-Afghanistan campaign against terrorism is not being waged on any battlefield with a climactic confrontation. Rather, it must be conducted against an opponent using unconventional methods, including acts of terror (asymmetrical warfare). Beyond the direct attacks on American soil on September 1, 2001, the earlier pattern of actions carried out by bin Laden probably represent the nature and scale of response that the United States faces. Bin Laden's intent is to harm as many Americans as he can. His means of doing so has been to commission acts of terror against select American targets, such as the U.S. embassies in Dar es Salaam, Tanzania, and Nairobi, Kenya, and the suicide attack against the USS *Cole* in a Yemeni port. He was also involved in the attack against the World Trade Center towers in New York in 1993.

What defines these acts is their size and responses to them. The African embassy attacks killed around two dozen Americans (as well as hundreds of Kenyans and Tanzanians), and seventeen sailors died on the *Cole*. While these losses were tragic, they were not on a scale that threatens the basic integrity of the United States. It is also not clear how to respond to these kinds of acts. The United States retaliated for the embassy bombings by launching cruise missiles against suspected terrorist training camps in Afghanistan run by bin Laden, but they failed either to kill the Saudi expatriate (which officials later said was their intent) or to slow down his activities. A major conceptual problem arises from the Al Qaeda lack of a territorial base that can be attacked, which is a main use of conventional force in symmetrical war situations. That the only semblance of a territorial base for Al Qaeda is in Waziristan, a province of U.S. ally Pakistan, further complicates the problem.

How to use armed forces when the kinds of situations for which they have traditionally been employed (securing vital interests) are basically absent or partially appropriate is a major agenda item in the current debate about national security. Clearly, many of the actual threats to American national interests arguably fall on the less-than-vital side of the demarcation line. The clear implication is that there is not clear guidance about what military forces, and especially conventional forces, should do in these situations. What, then, are the implications for the constellation of American instruments of power, including military force?

How does one deal with such circumstances? One way is to enforce the realist paradigm and accept the decreased saliency of regular military force in the current milieu. If American forces are to be used only when vital interests are at stake, then they will be used relatively infrequently in the near future, or they will only be a variable part of responses to worthy threats. The other solution is to broaden the criteria under which force employment is allowable. This amounts to moving the line between vital and less-than-vital interests more into the less-than-vital category of actions. The primary "beneficiary" of such a movement comes currently in the form of deployments of American forces into peacekeeping missions in places such as Bosnia and Kosovo (and conceivably in places like Sudan) under the justification of so-called *humanitarian vital interests*, to which allusion was made in chapter 1 of this book.

APPLYING INSTRUMENTS OF POWER

The anarchical nature of international relations requires that states engage in self-help in order to realize their interests. A recourse to some superior source of authority before which they could adjudicate conflicts of their interests with those of others does not exist. There is no such authority, of course, because states have vital interests that might not prevail if some outside authority decided the outcomes of conflicts of interests. Since, by definition, a state will not willingly accept denial of its most important interests, the solution is to avoid having any body that can make adverse rulings that would probably have to be disobeyed.

This depiction is at the heart of the operation of the realist paradigm in the international system. In such a system, states achieve their goals to the extent of their ability to coerce or convince others to comply with their goals or interests. One can applaud or decry that situation, but it is the dynamic that energizes the system in the absence of some fundamental reform that has yet to occur.

Instruments of power (introduced in Chapter 3) generically refer to the array of methods a state possesses to gain conformance with its interests. Power situations (in which one state seeks to get another to do what it does not want to do) involve situation-specific relationships. That means that what will work to gain compliance in one situation will not necessarily have the same result in another, because power interplays involve discrete relationships between the players. Therefore, the more varied and robust the instruments a state has, the more likely it is to prevail more of the time. Operationally, a state's rank among the powers refers to both the variety and the depth of its power across the spectrum of instruments.

Using the Instruments

The instruments of power do not exist in a vacuum but gain their meaning in terms of whether their application accomplishes the purposes for which they are used. For an instrument to be potentially effective, it must possess two traditionally defined characteristics, to which an implied third can be added. First, a state must possess the physical wherewithal to take the actions it proposes, what is known as *capability*. The absence of capability renders a threat ineffectual if the threatened party recognizes the deficiency. A Chinese threat to close the strategic Straits of Malacca by interdicting shipping transiting the straits would be ignored because China lacks the long-range aircraft (and refueling capability) or navy to sustain such action. Second, objects of threats must believe the threatening state would actually employ those capabilities in the ways it says it would in order to accomplish its ends, what is known as *credibility*. Based upon his perceptions of post-Vietnam unwillingness to use force, Saddam Hussein wrongly believed the United States would not use force to reverse his conquest of Kuwait. Beyond capability and credibility is the ability to apply the instrument in a manner that achieves the sought-after goal, or what we can call *efficacy*. During the Cold War, the United States could always have leveled the Soviet Union with nuclear weapons in the events of some transgression, but such an action would have resulted in a Soviet response that would have destroyed the United States and thus would have served no useful purpose.

These characteristics are clearly interrelated. Capability and credibility are linked. At the most obvious level, no state is going to believe a threat based on a capability the threatening state does not possess. Nicaragua, for instance, cannot threaten to invade Mexico because it lacks the military capability to do so. Conversely, however, the ability to carry out a threat does not imply the willingness to use that power. The United States becomes annoyed with France frequently over France's attempts to keep symbols of American culture, such as American popular music and films, out of the country (or to limit the amount of penetration of French culture). While it is physically possible for the United States to threaten a nuclear attack against France to force it to lift these restrictions, no one would believe such a threat, meaning it lacks credibility. At the same time, a country may possess—and employ—a variety of instruments that will not achieve the goal for which they are intended. The American economic boycott against Cuba for the past forty years has not accomplished its principal goal of removing Fidel Castro from power or of lifting Communist rule from the island state.

Orchestrating the uses of the instruments of power is a delicate activity, one that involves considerable uncertainties arising from the fact that whether power is effectively applied is largely a complex psychological exercise. At one level, it is a duel between the state threatening to employ an instrument and the state receiving the threat. Assuming the threatened party knows whether the threatener has the capability to do what is proposed (which the threatening party may seek to obscure), it then has to assess whether the threat is credible, which is an exercise in mind reading. There may be some evidence based upon how the threatening state has acted in similar circumstances in the past to provide an indication of the threatener's will, but since no two situations are identical, that evidence may or may not be conclusive: Will he or will he not?

The threatening partner must also make a psychological assessment of the party against whom it is seeking to apply power in a situation of less-than-perfect knowledge of the other party's mental state. Will the other party believe the threatener would carry out the threat or call his/her bluff? At the same time, will the threat gain compliance without having to be carried out (the best possible outcome, since carrying out threats normally involves some harm for all parties)? If not, will carrying out the threat convince the other party to do what the threatening party wanted done in the first place, or will it fail?

The answers to these questions are generally not cut-and-dried in real-world situations. The calculations sound like the reasoning in a poker game, where capabilities are defined by the hands the players hold but where part of the hand is obscured (capability), where betting is a form of indicating credibility, and the success of maneuvers such as bluffing measure the efficacy of the threats that raising bets represent. Employing power in the real world, however, has added complications, such as the emotions of the interplay of national pride, different and largely nonmeasurable (at least in advance) factors such as national resolve, and the importance of outcomes to all the players.

During the Cold War, much of this calculation had been worked out, and the dynamics were reasonably clearly defined. Among the instruments of power, the military instrument was conceded to be of the greatest importance, at least in the relations among the contending superpowers. The economic instrument was clearly more important in the relations within the developed countries headed by the United States, but economic sanctions and rewards had virtually no impact on East–West relations. The greatest ambiguities about which instruments had efficacy were in the developing world, both in the extension of the East–West confrontation and in relations over matters like political and economic development.

The Contemporary Balance of Instruments of Power

Whether there is a real change in how international relations occur today is largely a matter of the state of the third criterion identified for applying instruments: efficacy. The question of change can be rephrased to ask whether other, nonmilitary forces induce change in the post–Cold War world more than did those (normally military) in the Cold War era. Assertions of dramatic change will almost inevitably overshoot the truth, but there may be some discernible differences.

The efficacy of the traditional military instrument has clearly become more restricted. Military threats or actions among the major powers of the developed world absolutely lack credibility. This is really not a change, however, because it was equally unlikely that the western allies (including the market democracies of Asia) would have fought one another during the Cold War. If there is a difference, it is that what President Clinton liked to call the "circle of market democracies" has been gradually enlarging, including the addition of former authoritarian foes from the old Communist world. In these cases, positive military inducements may have supplanted threats as the instrument to advance American interests in spreading market democracy. Actions such as military arms sales, training programs, and membership and participation in military alliances like NATO are means to induce formerly nondemocratic countries into the general peace.

The use of military force in the developing world has similarly undergone only modest, peripheral change. Most of the violence in the world occurs within (as opposed to between) developing world states, as was generally the case during the Cold War. What has changed are the incentives for outside involvement in these conflicts. During the Cold War, the American motivation was to prevent the victory of Communist elements, and the calculus included the likelihood and intolerability of Communist success. In the contemporary environment prior to 2001, the incentives tended to cluster around humanitarian concerns. The calculus involved whether any lasting good could be achieved by physical involvement and what levels of sacrifice are tolerable to accomplish various levels of good. These were less compelling interests than fighting Communism. Blunting and suppressing terrorism has provided a firmer basis for applying the military instrument; as a semimilitary concern, striking a balance between the use of military and nonmilitary instruments is the problem.

The major contraction in the efficacy of military force surrounds the avoidance of major war with potent and threatening adversaries. Only the utter failure of market democracy in a major state such as China or Russia (both possibilities) could produce the underlying animosities necessary to produce a new peer competitor for the United States. Such a transformation would, of course, be carefully monitored from the beginning, and actions would certainly be taken to reduce or contain such developments. Moreover, the reversion could occur only by the failure of the very economic modernization on which a potent military is built. Russia, for instance, until recently could not afford the military forces it needs to be a competitive power. Will that change?

What this suggests about the military instrument is that its efficacy has shrunk in the most important and costly area it occupied formerly. If that is the case and the likelihood of a returned equivalent threat is unlikely, then those facts should have major implications for the capability component of the capability/credibility/efficacy equation that energizes the instruments of power.

It is easy to overstate how much the economic instrument has undergone change. Globalization has clearly expanded the arsenal of economic instruments of power. The emphasis on trade and the removal of trade barriers create opportunities for countries with large markets such as the United States to obtain leverage among those who wish to compete in the American domestic market. Membership in the various universal and regional trading associations can provide the ability to influence economic decisions in various countries, and the ability of the International Monetary Fund (IMF) and other international monitors to guide the development of developing economies has clearly been enhanced as well. The desire to share in the general prosperity creates opportunities to shape the behavior of states outside but wanting into the global prosperity.

New forms of power may blossom in the future. The telecommunications revolution has been a particularly potent force in economic expansion, information explosion, and a variety of other areas. The positive expansion of the information age to nonparticipants is an enormous positive inducement to influence behavior. This positive aspect, however, has a darker side in the form of threats to disrupt the very fragile systems on which the telecommunications revolution rests. Cyber terror may become an all-too-familiar instrument of power given the increasingly electronic dependency of the international system. The possibilities are only bound by human imagination.

CONCLUSION: THE CHANGING NATURE OF INFLUENCE

This chapter has raised and examined four related concerns about contemporary international politics and the transition from the Cold War environment to the present. The first concern was with security and asked how a changed environment affects American national security in both a physical and a psychological sense. Is American security enhanced or detracted from due to changes that have occurred? The second concern was how the changed security environment affects the kind and amount of risk the country must endure and the problem of risk reduction and risk management. Is the world a riskier place? The third concern was with national interests, phrased in terms of whether the most important interests were more imperiled or reinforced today. Can the United States better realize its interests today than previously? The fourth concern was with how those interests are realized in the form of changes in the effectiveness of the various instruments of power. Are different instruments more efficacious than they were before for realizing interests in the changed environment?

Overall, the major conclusion one must reach is that the post–Cold War world, despite the intrusion of international religious terrorism, is a more secure, less threatening place than before for the United States, and one in which the country is basically better able to realize its interests. One can easily overstate both the pervasiveness of change and the improvement of the situation, but at least in a marginal sense, the generalizations seem to hold, even if the one major source of insecurity that terrorism represents is factored in.

The chief cause of improvement is, of course, the end of the Cold War and thus the removal of the largest challenge to security, the possibility of a general systemic war in which the nuclear-armed superpowers confront one another on the battlefield with the fate of civilization in the balance. The vulnerability of American territory to terrorist attacks remains a significant threat, but not on the scale of a potential World War III during the Cold War.

As large-scale military power has depreciated in value, economic leverage arising from globalization has expanded in the quiver of elements of national power. The reassertion of a robust American economy that remains the world's premier market provides the United States with considerable leverage to promote an international economy and national economies and policies based on the American value of market democracy. Although the terrorist threat and the emergence of other security concerns have eclipsed the 1990s preeminence of globalization, it remains a global force.

What could cause a deterioration of the current situation and the American place in it? A cataclysmic turn of the global economy like the Great Depression of the 1930s would certainly represent the worst possible case. One of the fears surrounding the emergence of international terrorism was the prospect that it might trigger a general economic downturn, for instance. Hardly anyone expects that to occur, but there are still potential dangers on a lesser scale.

Reaction to American supremacy probably represents the greatest potential for negative change. Many commentators have pointed out that the current epoch is remarkable because, unlike other historic periods when a single political entity dominated the world scene, no competitor or coalition of competitors has arisen to oppose and counterbalance American power. Initially, this seemed to be the case because, unlike other states, the United States was rarely viewed as a threatening power in the system. As time has passed, however, erosive influences have emerged in the form of reactions to what are perceived as American inconstancy and even arrogance in its dealings with the rest of the world. Iraq has provided the irritant fueling much of this reaction.

The United States faces a period of introspection when the Iraq War winds down that will affect all four of the concerns raised in this chapter. Will the United States have to redefine what makes it feel secure in light of the trauma of an arguable misrepresentation and misapplication of security concerns in Iraq? Will the post-Iraq environment be a more or less secure place, and how will the United States respond to that judgment? On the second question of risk, will the United Sates pull back from an aggressive pursuit of risk reduction that eliminating the Iraqi regime and its alleged WMD and ties to terror symbolized? Or will risk be redefined to accept these kinds of situations as less threatening? The third concern surrounds what constitutes vital interests and how they are protected. The aggressive actions taken by the Bush administration represented the expansive view of what constitutes vital interests. Will that vision be sustained, or will the country return to a more restrictive vision of what is worth pursuing with armed forces?

Finally, there is the question of applying instruments of power. If there is indeed an Iraq "hangover" as posited in these pages, how will the United States change the mix of instruments it employs in a mood where military force is, at last temporarily, depreciated?

STUDY/DISCUSSION QUESTIONS

1. What are the major elements that compose security? At what levels does security exist? How are conceptions changing relative to one another? Discuss.
2. What is risk? How does one deal with the problem of risk? What are the chief means by which risk can be managed? Elaborate.
3. Relate levels of interest—focusing on the vital and less-than-vital levels—and means to realize them. In what combinations of interest and means do the most controversial situations arise? Which combinations are most frequent in the contemporary environment?
4. Define the idea and content of instruments of power. Discuss how the uses of different instruments have changed and are likely to change in the future.
5. Is the international environment more dangerous (less secure) for the United States now or during the Cold War? How does the text answer this question? Do you agree or disagree? Why?

SELECTED BIBLIOGRAPHY

Art, Robert J., and Kenneth N. Waltz. *The Use of Force: Military Power and International Politics* (5th ed.). London: Rowman and Littlefield, 2003.

Bauman, Zygmut. *Globalization: The Human Consequences*. New York: Columbia University Press, 1998.

Berkowitz, Bruce. *The New Face of War: How War Will Be Fought in the 21st Century*. New York: Free Press, 2003.

Burton, Daniel F., Victor Gotbaum, and Felix Rohatyn (eds.). *Visions of the 1990s: U.S. Strategy and the Global Economy*. Cambridge, MA: Ballinger, 1989.

Cusimano, Maryann (ed.). *Beyond Sovereignty*. Boston: Bedford St. Martin's Press, 1999.

Djerejian, Edward P. "From Conflict Management to Conflict Resolution." *Foreign Affairs* 85, 6 (November/December 2006), 41–48.

Drew, Dennis M., and Donald M. Snow. *Making Twenty-First Century Strategy: An Introduction to Modern Nation Security Processes and Problems*. Montgomery, AL: Air University Press, 2006.

Etzioni, Amitai. *Security First: For a Muscular, Moral Foreign Policy*. New Haven, CT: Yale University Press, 2007.

Flanagan, Stephen J., Ellen L. Frost, and Richard Kugler. *Challenges of the Global Century: Report of the Project on Globalization and National Security*. Washington, DC: Institute for National Strategic Studies (National Defense University), 2001.

Friedman, Thomas L. "The First Law of Petropolitics." *Foreign Policy* (May/June 2006), 36–42.

Kaplan, Robert D. *The Coming Anarchy: Shattering the Dreams of the Post–Cold War*. New York: Random House, 2000.

Luttwak, Edward N. *Strategy: The Logic of War and Peace*. Cambridge, MA: Belknap, 1987.

Nuechterlein, Donald. *America Recommitted: United States National Interests in a Reconstructed World*. Lexington: University of Kentucky Press, 1991.

Pfaff, William. "Invitation to War." *Foreign Affairs* 72, 3 (Summer 1993), 97–109.

Pilat, Joseph F. "Reassessing Security Assurances in a Unipolar World." *Washington Quarterly* 28, 2 (Spring 2005), 159–167.

Rogov, Sergei. "International Security and the Collapse of the Soviet Union." *Washington Quarterly* 15, 2 (Spring 1992), 16–28.

Sloan, Stephen. *Beating International Terrorism: An Action Strategy for Preemption and Punishment* (rev. ed.). Montgomery, AL: Air University Press, 2000.

Smith, W. Y. "U.S. National Security After the Cold War." *Washington Quarterly* 15, 4 (Winter 1992), 21–35.

Snow, Donald M. *When America Fights: The Uses of U.S. Military Power.* Washington, DC: CQ Press, 2000.

———. "China Rising" and "'Let Them Drink Oil," in *Cases in International Relations: Portraits of the Future* (3rd ed.). New York: Pearson Longman, 2008.

Wolf, Martin. *Why Globalization Works.* New Haven, CT: Yale University Press, 2004.

CHAPTER 8

The Domestic Environment

PREVIEW

How environmental changes affect policy and our approach and response to national security challenges is more than just an abstract matter. This chapter examines how the influences of the domestic political environment have an impact on political processes and outcomes. Because there is some difference in generalized view of how the environment operates in the area of national security, the chapter begins by looking at the domestic context. It then turns to the question of how internal political processes affect and are affected by national security changes. In particular, it examines the chief institutional response to international terrorism, the Department of Homeland Security, and its enigmatic evolution, as well as related policy areas.

Just as the threat environment is largely defined by international political forces that oppose American interest and even reflect harmful desires toward the United States, so too is the domestic political system an important factor in defining the national security environment. Domestic politics interacts with the world in both directions. In one direction, forces in the international environment define the threats with which the country must cope, and domestic actions can make those threats more or less dangerous and poignant. International religious terrorism, for instance, emanates from the international environment, but actions taken by the United States (for instance, successfully pursuing and disabling terrorists, increasing or lowering their appeal as the result of U.S. policies in the Middle East) can make the environment more or less troubling and hostile.

National security policy is largely about how the country responds to threats, suggesting the other direction. To some large degree, what threatens the United States and the extent to which those threats require different levels of response are subjective determinations arising from the psychological dimension of security. At this level, people can and do disagree, particularly when decisions require the expenditure of scarce resources (which they inevitably do) that reduce or eliminate risk in one area while potentially leaving threats uncountered in some other area. The politics involved in such situations can often be quite intense, sometimes in ways not always directly connected to national security. The debate over border security (highlighted later in this chapter and in Chapter 14) is an example where there is disagreement over the nature and seriousness of the problem and what to do about it with national security implications. Building the 700-mile fence along the U.S.–Mexico border authorized in 2006 by Congress would require expending resources to reduce whatever risk illegal immigration creates at the expense of other risks, such as those associated with port security.

Confusion over the environment is reflected in domestic politics. Partly, the debate is a philosophical discussion about the extent of American activism in the world that reflects an assessment of what the world out there is really like and the degree to which the United States has some role, obligation, or ability to affect the environment. The 1990s was a period largely of American internationalism and activism under the Clintonian foreign policy sobriquet "engagement and enlargement."

The domestic equation changed after the 2000 election, and even more dramatically after September 11, 2001. The new Bush administration initially professed a more limited approach to the American role in the world than its predecessor, arguing the United States neither could nor should attempt to involve itself everywhere and that it was willing to act unilaterally when it felt it needed to do so. The inclination to limit activism was doused by the actions of Al Qaeda. Unilateralism temporarily gave way to an international effort to combat the problem, but it returned when the international community disagreed with aspects of the American approach, as much of it did over the forceful removal of Saddam Hussein and the general war effort in Iraq.

National security problems and their resolution can only be fully analyzed and understood in their political setting. Defending the country is one of the most important functions for which government exists, even arguably the penultimate purpose of the state and its government. No one questions the importance of security among state purposes, and for this reason, there is a tendency to elevate the processes by which national security policy is made above the normal political dialog as too vital to be subjected to the rough-and-tumble of "politics as usual." At its best, this instinct can provide a sense of purpose in times of crisis that is unmistakable to enemies as a sign of national resolve. At its most controversial, this same exercise can be used to justify actions by government that cannot otherwise be justified.

Politicians seize upon this importance to try to create the belief that their particular solutions to problem are the only "reasonable" means to achieve national security ends and that alternative analyses are not only incorrect, but also even insidious or seditious. National security, in other words, is (or certainly should be) above politics.

The problem that arises from following this line of reasoning is that it denies that national security is part of the normal process by which scarce resources are allocated to deal with national problems and priorities that always exceed those resources. Within the realm of national security, there are always multiple candidates for attention, and there are also inevitably disagreements on which situations do and do not constitute threats to security, the relative importance of threats, and what solutions in what order of priority should be undertaken. In some rare cases—September 11 stands out—the situation is crystalline, as is what must be done about it. Most of the time, however, national security policy areas are matters of disagreement that can only be solved through a process in which "conflicts of interest over scarce resources are resolved"—politics.

If national security policy is part of the broader political process, it occupies a distinct place in that process, for two reasons. The first is the unique subject matter of national security. At the bottom line, national security policy is about national survival, a distinction not shared by other policy areas. The second is the amount of national resources devoted to national security. Although the country spends more on entitlement programs than on national security, the defense budget is the largest discretionary part of the budget (a distinction discussed later in the chapter).

Too much can be—and often is—made about the life-and-death nature of national security policy. Decisions made in the health and medical areas—whether to fund stem-cell research, for instance—also affect who lives and dies and the quality of life and conditions surrounding death, but the connection is neither as immediate nor as causally consequential as if a national security decision emboldens a national enemy to launch a massive attack against the United States that would not have occurred in the absence of that decision. This worst-case possibility always lurks in the background of national security decisions as a rejoinder against precipitous change—and especially reductions in defense efforts. The logic behind being "better safe than sorry" is particularly powerful when the potential outcome is catastrophic. The result is a process that is weighted toward maximum risk reduction, where the response to additional threats is to expand the resources available to reduce risk (i.e., to spend more), and where efforts directed at risk management are perpetuated even if their causal relationship to risk abatement is not demonstrable or is questionable (since change could lead to the worst case). These dynamics guarantee a very expensive, highly conservative national security process.

How these influences come together provides the domestic context for national security concerns. To understand how this process operates, the discussion begins by looking at the historical context, including the attitudes of the founding fathers and the framework created for the Cold War through the National Security Act of 1947. This context leads to the institutional framework for the national security process within and between the executive and legislative branches of government. The chapter then moves to applications of the process in action, institutionally through the homeland security reaction to September 11 and more politically through the controversy over border security.

THE HISTORICAL DOMESTIC CONTEXT

When the founding fathers were designing the American political system, matters that are now considered national security concerns were not a major part of their agenda. The American Revolution had expelled foreign forces from American soil, and the major priorities of the country concentrated on devising and developing a new polity in a largely virgin, undeveloped setting. Most of the "security" problems facing Americans were peripheral and marginally threatening (e.g., subduing and replacing American Indians on the frontier) or aberrational (the self-infliction of the Civil War). Because the founding fathers neither envisioned nor sought extensive international interactions that could become conflictual, they were particularly spare in creating a constitutional framework in this area. That framework is summarized in Amplifications 8.1 and 8.2 and is discussed in the next section.

A skeletal political and legal framework served the country adequately before World War II, but in the wake of the world's bloodiest conflict and the Cold War, it was clear that the traditional, more informal system would be inadequate for the "national security state" that would manage the Cold War. The major political response was the National Security Act of 1947. A related theme was the attempt to reform the military to make it more functional for the threat environment. Both elements continue to influence the contemporary environment.

The National Security Act of 1947 created the institutional framework that has defined the national security policy process to this day. A remarkably comprehensive and foresighted document that was signed into law on July 26, 1947, the act transformed a highly fragmented and inefficient governmental structure that had shown great strains during World War II into a highly durable structure that managed the Cold War successfully and that remains the basic framework throughout the post–Cold War and post–September 11 worlds. Efforts to reform the national security apparatus start from the structure created in 1947.

The National Security Act created five institutions, each of which remains a vital part of the domestic national security effort. The first was the *Department of Defense (DOD)*. Prior to 1947, each of the independent services (the Army and the Navy) was an independent Cabinet-level agency, a condition that had proven an impediment to the most efficient conduct of World War II, and there was great pressure to create a unified military department to supersede the old prewar structure. The basic idea was to force greater cooperation and coordination among the military services in the areas of planning, war fighting, and budgets, as well as to establish the principle of civilian control of the military. The new structure was originally called the National Military Establishment under the law and was changed to the current DOD by the amending National Security Act of 1949. At the time, this merger of military assets into one department was generally favored by the Army and what would become the Air Force (which was then the Army Air Corps, a part of the Army) and opposed by the Navy (which felt it could lobby for its budget more effectively as an independent Department of the Navy). As partial compensation for the Navy, Admiral James Forrestal was named the first secretary of defense. This structure remains essentially intact and has been durable. Among the areas of some continuing controversy is the relationship between civilian and military elements within the department. The original intent was to subordinate military influence on policy making through the establishment of an Office of the Secretary of Defense (OSD) at the top of the organizational pyramid of the department. After the Vietnam War and surrounding decision making for Iraq, there have been questions raised about whether the result is a military leadership that is *too* subservient to its civilian leaders, failing to advise the civilian leadership of the operational impossibility of implementing some of the policies civilians may favor. McMaster wrote the definitive statement of this position on Vietnam; Yingling recently produced a similar statement about Iraq.

As part of the DOD structure, the act created a second institution, the *Joint Chiefs of Staff (JCS)*. The purpose of the JCS was to create a staff of senior officers from the various services who would work together to coordinate and cooperate on military problems facing the country and provide military advice directly to the president. Opposition to this idea arose from individuals fearful that the new JCS might become a super-elite group like the Prussian General Staff in Germany. Under provisions of the act, the chief of staff of each service serves as a member, with the chairmanship of the body (the chairman of the JCS, or CJCS) chosen from the services on a rotating basis. By statute, the CJCS is the chief *military* advisor to the president (as opposed to the secretary of defense, who is the chief *defense* advisor to the president). Because the retrospective on the Vietnam War suggested that this structure had not produced a maximally integrated effort to fight that conflict (air missions against North Vietnam by the Air Force and Navy, for instance, were often uncoordinated), the Congress passed the *Goldwater-Nichols Act of 1986* mandating much higher and more meaningful cooperation and coordination (known as *jointness*), a policy that resulted in much greater interservice cooperation in both the Persian Gulf and the Iraq Wars.

The third institution created by the act was the *Central Intelligence Agency (CIA)*. Prior to World War II, the United States had possessed no peacetime civilian intelligence-gathering and -analyzing organization. To remedy that situation, President Franklin D. Roosevelt had created the Office of Strategic Services (OSS) under the leadership of Colonel (retired) William Donovan to provide intelligence to the government, but the OSS mandate ended with the conclusion of hostilities. Recognizing the emerging threat posed by an increasingly hostile Communist bloc led by the Soviet Union, this condition was deemed intolerable for the Cold War, and the result was the creation of the CIA as the country's first permanent peacetime intelligence agency.

Even at the time of its inception, the new CIA was plagued with two problems that continue to be part of the contemporary debate about the agency. The first was its place within the community of intelligence assets of the country. In addition to the CIA, there are major intelligence capabilities in several other areas of government. The most notable of these are within the DOD—the National Security Agency, the Defense Intelligence Agency, and the intelligence assets of the various services (which cumulatively comprise about four-fifths of the country's intelligence assets). The CIA was designated as the lead agency for intelligence (including the responsibility of providing intelligence information and advice to the president), and its head, the director of central intelligence (DCI), is also designated as the chair of the intelligence community, the common forum of the various intelligence agencies in the government where intelligence assignments are made. This has always been an awkward arrangement, and it was the subject of reform as recommended by the 9/11 Commission discussed later in the chapter.

At the same time, there has always been some controversy about what the CIA does or should do. The gathering, compilation, and reporting of information (intelligence) is its basic and least assailable mission, but there has always been debate about what the CIA should be able to do in addition to intelligence collection. The controversy has centered on the area known as "operations," which refers to active efforts the CIA may clandestinely undertake to influence international events (known as covert actions). Within the original legislation creating the CIA is a provision for the agency to carry out "other functions and duties related to intelligence." This somewhat vague formulation has led to a variety of actions that have been deemed offensive by some within the political realm and have surfaced with regard to some actions taken in the prosecution of the Iraq War such as, extreme renditions (the practice of sending prisoners to countries that practice torture as a means to extract information from them) and the Guantanamo detention facilities.

The fourth institution created by the act was an independent U.S. Air Force. During World War II, the air assets of the United States were divided among the Navy (including the Marines) and the Army (the Army Air Corps). The proponents of airpower had long lobbied for an independent air force to consolidate the various roles and missions assigned to airpower. They were successful to the extent of extricating themselves from the Army and being established as an independent U.S. Air Force (USAF). They were not successful in that the Navy and Marines maintained control of their own air forces, and the Army managed to get back into the air business through the application of helicopters for military purposes. Rationalizing the military uses of the atmosphere (and beyond) has been a recurring theme in attempts at military reform, which are discussed below.

The fifth, and in many ways most important, accomplishment of the National Security Act was the creation of the *National Security Council (NSC)*. The NSC was of enormous symbolic importance in depicting the American role in the postwar world. At its most basic level, it recognized the new and growing importance of the United States and the consequent need for some formal mechanism to assist in how the United States would react in the world. It also implied and boosted the centrality of defense matters within the hierarchy of foreign policy concerns. The statutory members of the NSC were the president, the vice president, the secretary of state, and the new secretary of defense (the president can add other members as he chooses, and subsequent legislation and practice have increased the normal membership to include the DCI, CJCS, and others). The symbolism of the composition was the placement of the Secretary of Defense (SECDEF) as the lineal equivalent of the secretary of state, indicating that the line between foreign policy (with diplomacy as its heart) and national security policy (with the military at its core) would be less clear than in the past and that much of foreign policy would indeed be virtually indistinguishable from national security policy. The fact that the Cold War emerged as a political competition largely framed in military terms reinforced this placement of the SECDEF within the structure. The NSC has proven an exceptionally durable institution that continues to the present and has been further elaborated through a system of executive branch mechanisms known collectively as the interagency process (discussed in the next section).

A recurring subtheme was also part of the crucible of concerns that surrounded the National Security Act. That theme is military reform, and it is as lively today as it was in 1947. It is worth raising in passing here because the call to reform how the services define what they do (internally and in relationship to one another) and how they carry out those missions remains a point of contention in the emerging post-Iraq debate.

Interservice rivalry had been evident in World War II. The American role in the war even enhanced that rivalry, as the war was, at the operational level, two separate wars in which the two major services had contrasting roles. The war in Europe was essentially a ground war and, as such, was dominated by the U.S. Army, which had primary responsibility for its successful conduct, with a subordinate role for the Navy (essentially ferrying personnel and supplies to the theater of operation). In the Pacific, the Navy was the dominant service, as the Navy first eliminated the Japanese Navy and then employed the Marines (an institutional part of the Navy) in the campaign of island hopping closer and closer to Japan. The Army was assigned the basic task of consolidating (or "mopping up" resistance on) the islands the Navy/Marines captured. This structure discouraged cooperation between the services, which would be dysfunctional against a comprehensive Communist opponent after the war.

Admiral Forrestal foresaw this difficulty and commissioned the first roles and missions conference among the services at Key West, Florida, in 1948. Without going into details, the services basically agreed to concentrate on what they had done previously and to split the new defense budget in rough terms into thirds for each service: the Army, the Navy (including the Marines), and the new Air Force. The division left some anomalies that have continued across time. The most famous of these is duplication of effort. It is said, for instance, that the United States possesses four air forces (the USAF, the Navy's land- and sea-based air forces, the Marines' air forces for close air support, and the Army's helicopter-based forces) and three armies (the U.S. Army, the Navy's army—the Marines—and the Air Force's smaller army to guard air bases). The same is true in the area of special forces, as each service has its own special operations forces, although they are coordinated through the U.S. Special Operation Command (USSOCOM). Periodic efforts are made to rationalize this structure, with varying success. As the armed forces face restructuring and altered missions in the aftermath of the Iraq War, these questions are likely to reappear.

THE STRUCTURE OF DOMESTIC POLITICS

National security policy is, as it has evolved, among the most contentious political areas within the American federal system. As already noted, the content of national security policy is potentially very important, ultimately including decisions that can affect the very physical survival of the country and, less dramatically, decisions about when Americans may be compelled to put themselves in harm's way to defend American interests.

National security policy is also highly political because it involves the expenditure of very large amounts of money. Currently, defense spending is the second-largest category in the federal budget, behind spending on entitlements (social security, Medicare, and the like) and just ahead of service on the interest on the national debt. Historically, defense was also the second-largest category of expenditures during the Cold War, involving roughly a quarter of the federal budget and 5 to 6 percent of gross national product (GNP). In the mid-1950s, before many of the entitlement programs were enacted, it accounted for nearly one-half of federal spending.

Defense spending is highly political for other reasons as well. One of the important characteristics of the defense budget is that it is the largest discretionary element within the federal budget. One way to distinguish items in the federal budget is to divide them into discretionary or controllable and nondiscretionary or uncontrollable elements. A discretionary element is one that must be appropriated annually; thus, the Congress exercises its discretion over whether that element will be funded. A nondiscretionary element is one that is automatically appropriated unless there is specific legislation altering or rescinding the appropriation (social security is the best example). Nearly two-thirds of the discretionary money in the federal budget comes from defense, meaning that attempts to increase, decrease, or alter the pattern of federal spending often begin with the defense budget.

The political nature also reflects the impact of national security spending on Americans. Not only is a lot of money spent on defense, but also those expenditures are made in a large number of physical locales, wherever concentrations of military installations and defense industries are found. The competition for defense contracts or the locations of bases or posts is a highly competitive process wherein the financial health and prosperity of communities can be vitally affected by the effectiveness of congressional delegations able to win federal contracts for their states and districts.

National security spending is also contentious because much of the money is spent on highly durable procurements. The decision, for instance, to build an aircraft carrier not only involves appropriating several billion dollars for its construction (money that is fed into the local community wherever the ship is built, of course), but also involves investment in a weapons "platform" that is expected to be in the arsenal for 30 years or longer. Procurement decisions affect not only the arsenal characteristics of whatever administration commissions them, but also the military capability available to a commander-in-chief a quarter-century or more in the future. The same is true of procuring new fighter or bomber aircraft, a new model of main battle tank, and the like.

There is an old saw that "policy is what gets funded," and that truism holds for the national security area generally and is particularly true in the current milieu. Two things are coming together to create a sharp poignancy for the political, and especially budgetary, elements of the national security decision process. One is the nature of the current military arsenal. The military characteristics of the current force include the fact that it was largely shaped to confront a Soviet military threat that no longer exists and is not being replicated by any emerging potential adversary. Moreover, the force is getting old, and much of it needs replacement. A major question is how to modernize the force. One group, led by former Secretary of Defense Donald Rumsfeld, argues for the application of the *revolution in military affairs (RMA)*, applying very sophisticated technologies to warfare to produce such a qualitatively superior force as to be unassailable. Others argue against such a heavy investment on the grounds that it would be excessive to any actual or likely threat facing the United States, and that the United States could decrease military spending and enjoy a "peace dividend" (savings) such as was promised but never really delivered in the 1990s. Allies worry that the American force has already become so comparatively sophisticated as to render their own forces obsolete and expendable. The crucible of Iraq has affected this debate, as discussed in Chapter 10.

The other side of this debate is over spending priorities more generally within the federal government. As the budget surpluses generated during the 1990s have been transformed into record-setting deficits in the early 2000s because of tax reductions and increased defense spending (including paying for the Iraq War), all areas of federal spending have come under close scrutiny. While the Bush administration has argued for enhanced spending on national security, the amount and direction of that spending has become intensely controversial. Because of the inherent vulnerability of the defense budget (its controllable nature), it will remain the subject of considerable political concern. The GWOT and the Iraq War muted this debate for a time, but it will clearly be revived as part of the post-Iraq debate.

The politics of national security is played out at various levels that come together in the budget process. One level is within the executive branch of government, where the representatives of various government agencies and functions compete for priority within federal policy, including the budget. This competition extends to the legislative branch, where the same kind of competition occurs within the various layers of the committee system in hammering out what budget the executive will ultimately have to spend. Ultimately, decisions involve the interaction of the two principal legislating branches of the government (a process in which the judiciary is rarely involved).

The Executive Branch

National security policy within the executive branch of the government operates on two separate tracks that are, in some ways, paralleled conceptually within the Congress. The day-to-day conduct of national security (as part of overall foreign policy) occurs within the federal agencies with authority in the field, such as the State Department, Department of Defense (DOD), and Central Intelligence Agency (CIA), at the direction of the president. Policy decisions are coordinated and implemented

THE PRESIDENT, THE CONSTITUTION, AND NATIONAL SECURITY

Because the founding fathers did not anticipate a level of involvement in international affairs that even mildly resembles the extent to which the country interacts with the rest of the world today, the U.S. Constitution does not lay out an elaborate list of powers for the president in the area of national security or foreign policy, as noted. Such specific powers as are provided are found in Article II of the Constitution, and as shown in Amplification 8.2, essentially all are counterbalanced by contrary powers given to the Congress as part of the "checks and balances" system that characterizes the entire document. The result is an "invitation to struggle" (see Crabb and Holt) intended to make the two branches coequal in this area.

The Constitution lists six powers for the president that directly apply to national security and defense policy. They are the positions of chief executive, chief of state, commander in chief of the armed forces, treaty negotiator, nominator of key personnel, and recognizer of foreign government.

Chief Executive. In this capacity, the president is designated as the major presider over the executive agencies of the government, all of which report directly to the president. In the area of foreign and national security policy, these agencies include the Departments of State and Defense, the Central Intelligence Agency, and the various economic agencies, including the Departments of the Treasury and Commerce and the U.S. Trade Representative. These agencies collectively are the chief repositories of the expertise of the federal government on foreign matters, and the president's access to them provides an important advantage in dealing with foreign and national security matters.

Chief of State. In this largely symbolic role, the president is designated as the chief representative of the U.S. government to all foreign governments. This means, for instance, that officials of foreign governments (ambassadors, for example) are accredited to the president, and when the heads of other states interact with the U.S. government, it is with the president or a representative of the president.

Commander in Chief. The president is designated as the commander in chief of the armed forces of the United States. This means, among other things, that he is the highest military official of the government to whom all members of the armed forces are subsidiary and that it is the president's authority to employ the armed forces in support of various public policies, including the commitment of force in combat (although this power is circumscribed by congressional limitation).

Treaty Negotiator. Only the president of the United States or his or her specified representative (known as plenipotentiary) is authorized to enter into negotiations with foreign governments leading to formal relationships and obligations on behalf of the U.S. government. Although only a small percentage of agreements between the United States and foreign governments come in the form of formal treaties, this nonetheless sets the precedent for presidential leadership in all arrangements with foreign governments.

Nominator of Key Personnel. The president alone has the power to name key officials of his or her administration. Most of the important appointments are at the Cabinet levels (the various secretaries of executive agencies), the National Security Council, and the deputy and assistant secretaries, such as those who serve on the various committees of the National Security Council system.

Recognizer of Foreign Governments. Only the president has the authority to extend or remove formal recognition of foreign governments by the U.S. government. This is one of the few powers of the president that does not require some form of formal supporting action by the Congress.

through the *interagency process*, the chief vehicle of which has been the National Security Council (NSC) and its subordinate bodies. New institutional actors, such as the Department of Homeland Security (DHS) and the director of national intelligence (DNI), are being integated into this system. This process of policy development and implementation is conceptually similar to the role of the authorizing committees of the Congress. The other track is the competition for funding, which is the heart of the budgetary process, and it pits parts of the national security community against one another and against competing functions of the government. The framework for this interaction, of course, is the constitutionally mandated roles for the various branches of government laid out by the founding fathers, as discussed in Amplification 8.1.

The Interagency Process. As noted, the foundation of what has evolved since the Eisenhower administration in the 1950s as the interagency process was the National Security Act of 1947. The act was not specific about how the NSC would function at the operational level, and both its structure and its operations have evolved over time. During its early evolution, its importance varied. Dwight Eisenhower used it extensively as a kind of military advisory board, and John Kennedy used it much less often. Lyndon Johnson expanded its use during the Vietnam War, and it began to take on its present form during the Nixon and Ford years. This has largely been a matter of presidential preference rather than legislative mandate. There is, for instance, no provision for a national security advisor (NSA) in the legislation, and that position has evolved from being a coordinator and officer manager to being a major presidential advisor on foreign affairs. Similarly, there is no provision for a system of committees and subcommittees within the NSC structure, but that is what has evolved.

The NSC system began to congeal during the Eisenhower administration of the 1950s and evolved after that. In its present form as the interagency process, it came into being during the 1980s, and it is a fairly elaborate system. The NSC itself consists of the four permanent members and whomever else the president may designate to attend and participate for any particular purpose. The White House chief of staff is normally always included, and on military matters, so is the CJCS and the NSA. The purpose of the Council is purely advisory. The members offer advice to the president that he is free to accept or reject. No votes are ever taken, ensuring that the president will not be swayed by what the majority may favor.

Directly below the NSC itself is the *Principals Committee (PC)*. This group is composed of the same membership as the NSC itself, except the president does not attend. There are two basic occasions when the NSC meets as the Principals Committee. If there are matters that do not require direct presidential involvement and thus intrusion on his busy agenda, the others may meet without him. At the same time, the president will occasionally absent himself in order to facilitate a more frank exchange of views than might occur when he is present, and he feels the other members might be unwilling to champion views they think he might oppose. This latter reason was used by John F. Kennedy during portions of the Cuban Missile Crisis when the Principals Committee was known as the ExComm (Executive Committee).

The next layer in the system is the *Deputies Committee (DC)*. As the name suggests, this group is composed of the principal deputies of the members of the NSC. The meetings are traditionally chaired by the president's principal deputy for national security, the NSA, although in the early days of the Bush administration there was an unsuccessful attempt by Vice President Richard Cheney to usurp that role from then NSA Condoleeza Rice. The Deputies Committee is more of a working-level body, and its roles include formulating policy proposals for action by the NSC or Principals Committee and figuring out how to implement decisions made in those bodies. Other members of the Deputies Committee include the undersecretary of state for political affairs, the undersecretary of defense for policy, the deputy director of central intelligence, and the vice chairman of the JCS. Full implementation of the 9/11 Commission reforms could alter this structure somewhat, especially in the intelligence area.

These levels of the process normally labor outside the public eye. When *Time* magazine revealed that plans for countering Al Qaeda had been developed in the Clinton administration but had become bogged down in the pre–September 11 Bush regime, the Deputies Committee and Principals Committee were specifically singled out as institutional loci where the plans languished, a rare public exposure of the workings of the interagency process.

At the bottom of the process are the *Policy Coordinating Committees (PCCs)*. This is a series of committees formed along both functional and geographic lines. The functional committees are chaired by the assistant secretary (or equivalent) from the Cabinet department with the most direct and obvious responsibility. There are, for instance, functional PCCs for defense, intelligence, arms control, and international economics. The geographic PCCs are all chaired by the assistant secretaries of state for the particular regions. It is the role of the PCCs to monitor their areas of responsibility (the PCC for the Near East and East Asia keeps tabs on the activities of Iraq, for instance), to provide options to the Deputies Committee and above on assigned problems, and to carry out the detailed policies adopted elsewhere in the process.

Reflecting his own interests and perceptions about change in the international environment, President Clinton created a parallel body, the *National Economic*

Council (NEC), by executive order in January 1993. It differed from the NSC in that it was not created by legislation and thus could be dismantled without congressional action. Clinton gave it four charges that parallel the duties of the older body: (1) to coordinate the economic policy-making process with respect to domestic and international economic issues; (2) to coordinate economic policy advice to the president; (3) to ensure that economic policy decisions and programs are consistent with the president's goals; and (4) to monitor implementation of the president's economic agenda.

The NEC was a prominent and important part of national security policy during the Clinton years between the fault lines and reflected the paramount importance of economic policy during the 1990s. The NEC was chaired personally by Clinton, and in addition, it had its own Deputies Committee and staff capability through the Trade Policy Review Group and the Trade Policy Staff Committee. The first task assigned to the first director of the NEC, Robert Rubin (later secretary of the treasury), was Clinton's comprehensive budget reduction plan, which succeeded in balancing the budget in 1998, and the NEC was prominent in trade policy and multilateral negotiations on trade promotion. When he came to office in 2001, President George W. Bush threatened to do away with the NEC as an unnecessary relic from his predecessor but has retained it at a much lower level of visibility and with much less personal involvement.

How the interagency process works is largely a matter of how the president wants it to operate. The NSC is assisted by the NSC staff, all of whom are members of the president's personal staff and thus not subject to congressional confirmation, review, or scrutiny. Because they serve at the president's pleasure, they are highly loyal to the chief executive and generally closely reflect the president's views. The degree to which the president utilizes this asset depends on presidential prerogative. Richard Nixon, for instance, had a long and deep-seated distrust of the State Department. State Department officials have civil service protection and cannot be fired (except in extreme circumstances), and most generally opposed Nixon's policies. As a result, he enlarged the NSC staff and used it in effect as an alternate State Department to ensure his policy preferences would be implemented. Presidents who are highly activist in foreign affairs, such as George H. W. Bush and Bill Clinton in his second term, rely heavily upon the NSC to carry out their desires, whereas those with less interest (such as Gerald Ford) use the NSC less and rely more on the executive agencies to conduct policy on their own.

Funding Security. The other dimension of policy making within the executive branch focuses on the competition for resources to fund various government functions and programs. The principal manifestation of this political battle is the formation of the presidential budget request to the Congress and how that is translated into the working budget of the federal govenment of the United States. The budget process is one of the most complicated, arcane, yet fundamental political activities of the government. If one accepts the notion that policy is what gets funded, it is also the heart of the political process.

The complexity of the process of allocating public monies for the various things government does goes well beyond the purposes of this volume to unravel in detail.

Instead, two aspects of the politics of national security budget making—the competition among the services for resources and the competition between defense and other government functions in the formation of the executive branch's request to the Congress (some of the politics of the congressional response to the president's budget request is found in the next section of this chapter)—will be examined.

Budgeting is an ongoing, continuous process within the United States government. At any point in time, the DOD, for instance, is working on at least three different budgets: the budget for the current fiscal year, which has been appropriated and is being expended; the budget proposal for the next fiscal year, which has been proposed to Congress and to which the Congress is responding; and the next year's budget proposal, which is being formulated for presentation to the Congress in the following fiscal year. In addition, some long-range programs are funded over several years, meaning funds appropriated in earlier budget cycles are also being spent at any given time (known as "out years").

The competition between the services and between defense and nondefense spending is closely related to this process. Under the provisions of the planning, programming, budgeting, and spending (PPBS) system first introduced by the McNamara Pentagon in the early 1960s, initial planning for a budget begins approximately two and a half years before the first money is spent (assuming the Congress and the executive branch agree on a budget before the beginning of the fiscal year in which spending is to occur). Thus, planning for spending in fiscal year 2008 (which began on October 1, 2007) began in January 2006, when initial planning requests were sent to operational units within the DOD and elsewhere in the government. In spring 2006, the requests from defense units such as the military services were compared with other equivalent requests and reconciled with one another and then processed through the programming and budgeting phases during the late summer and fall of 2006. In turn, the DOD's proposal was compared with requests from other executive agencies and reconciled into a budget request that would accompany the president's State of the Union address to the Congress in January 2007. Legislative enactment would occur between January and September 2007, and if all went well, there would be a budget agreed to by both branches of the government that would go into effect on October 1, 2007. While legislative action was going on in 2007, the planning process for the fiscal year 2009 budget was set in motion, and the Defense Department was spending resources from the fiscal year 2007 budget.

Much of the politics within the executive branch occurs during the initial phases, when the president's budget request is being formulated. At the beginning, the military services are asked to formulate their individual requests. All units know that the aggregated requests (what are sometimes known as the "wish list") of the services will exceed by some large order of magnitude the resources that will actually be available to the services. Nonetheless, each makes the request for everything it wants regardless of funding expectations, for two reasons. First, doing so creates a record of what, say, the Army feels it really should have to carry out its mission most effectively. Second, since all the services know their requests will be cut—and, based on experience, approximately by what percentage they are likely to be cut—submitting a request that combines what the services think they will actually receive plus what they assume will be cut reasonably ensures that after cuts are made, the services will get roughly what they expected. Submitting a more modest and realistic request and having it cut probably means getting less than expected and needed.

The politics of interservice competition is particularly important over military procurement of new equipment, and especially for major weapons systems. During the process of proposal and negotiations, it is fair to say the services provide a valuable public service to the budgeting process by offering detailed critiques of the requests of the *other* services in order to find weaknesses in the other services' requests that might be turned to their own advantage. The motivation combines self-interest and civic-mindedness, and it serves the useful purpose of providing a kind of informal check and balance within the process through expert monitoring of rival service requests.

Once the defense request has been formulated, the national security budget comes into direct competition with other spending priorities within the federal budget. As in the internal defense process, the requests from agencies representing the range of government activity invariably exceed the total amount of money the Congress is likely to be willing to appropriate in any given year, meaning budget compromises must be negotiated to get the total budget request within realistic parameters.

The defense budget is especially vulnerable during this phase of the process. The first and most obvious source of vulnerability has already been mentioned: the defense budget contains the largest discretionary elements within the total federal budget and is thus a tempting target for budget cutters with other priorities. Increases in social security benefits are mandated and automatically appropriated in the absence of specific legislation changing those benefits; the funding for new fighter aircraft for the Air Force must be expressly appropriated each year. At the same time, despite colorful political campaign rhetoric to the contrary, there is relatively little "fat" in other budgets that can easily be used to compensate for other priorities.

The politics of budgeting in the executive branch was dramatically demonstrated in the first year of the Bush administration in 2001. The new president inherited a budget request formulated in 2000, when Bill Clinton was president, and which reflected Clinton's priorities (as well as Al Gore's, who would have inherited the request had he been declared winner of the election). This formulation contained modest but real increases in defense funding, much of which the military planned to invest in force modernization. As is always the case, the new administration had a short period to alter budget priorities before sending its request to Capitol Hill as part of the State of the Union. Usually, these alterations are relatively minor, and it is normally assumed that the second year's budget (in this case, the budget request for January 2002) would be the first "true" budget of a new administration.

President Bush had different ideas. Inheriting a budget request that emphasized federal debt reduction (through maximizing government surpluses to retiring the debt) and bolstering social security, he introduced new priorities. The most dramatic of these, of course, was a massive tax cut that the critics said would reduce the surplus dramatically and mean curtailing other budgetary priorities. Bush, however, proposed budget increases in funding for education and for national missile defense and insisted he would not compromise on either goal.

These changes had a direct impact on budgeting within the DOD. Secretary of Defense Rumsfeld, intent on implementing the president's NMD proposal, combed the defense budget as part of the QDR process in order to force the services to find ways to save money that could be diverted to the NMD. This change of emphasis meant potentially unraveling earlier budget agreements and modernization commitments that had been hammered out the preceding year for a missile defense program that had very little support within the uniformed services anyway. The result was a major, if temporary, confrontation between a new administration that had campaigned partially on increased support for the military and a military establishment that felt it had been rudely jilted by its former suitor.

The confrontation was defused by the terrorist attacks, which directed attention away from both the budget battle and the QDR to the new threat. Defense budget increases became part of the homeland security effort in the fiscal year 2003 budget presented to Congress in 2002 that included a $46 billion increase above projected levels in previous budgeting cycles. The result was that the services received most of the modernization requests from previous wish lists.

The Congress

The Constitution establishes the executive, legislative, and judicial branches as co-equals in governing the country. As a matter of practice, the judicial branch does not insert itself into the national security policy process except in limited areas such as the parameters of executive authority during times of war. In this area of policy, the "invitation to struggle" is largely between the president and the Congress, as it always has been and as was envisioned by the founding fathers. The basic principle involved is checks and balances: for every executive power, there is a countervailing congressional power. The formal provisions are summarized in Amplification 8.2.

In the first six years of the George W. Bush administration, the clash between the branches was not as obvious as it often has been and as it has become. There are two basic reasons for this aberration between 2001 and 2007. On one hand, the reaction to September 11 created a "rally round the flag" effect of support for the GWOT that centered (as it normally does during national emergencies) around the presidency and was reflected in support for Bush. Normal partisan and interbranch disagreements were muted because critics were afraid of being depicted as unpatriotic and wanted to lend support for a united response to the tragedy. Also, between January 2001 and January 2007, both the presidency and the Congress were controlled by the Republican Party, and the congressional leaders were less critical of a president of their own party than they might have been had the president been a Democrat.

In 2007, both conditions changed. After four increasingly unpopular years of fighting, the public turned by a two-thirds majority against the administration's major symbol of the GWOT, the war in Iraq. Because of this change of heart about Iraq, the Democratic Party was returned to a majority status in both houses of Congress with a broad mandate to end the war. These Democrats confronted a

Amplification 8.2

THE CONGRESS, THE CONSTITUTION, AND NATIONAL SECURITY

The U.S. Constitution is similarly as compact in its enumeration of congressional responsibility over foreign and national security affairs as it is with the executive branch. The powers of the Congress are enumerated in Article I of the Constitution. Some of these are direct responses to and limitations upon presidential powers, and others derive from the application of more general congressional authority to the national security arena. These powers include lawmaking power, the power of the purse, war-making power, confirmation, ratification, and general oversight of the executive branch.

Lawmaking Power. Nearly all of the actions taken by the government are the result of the passage of legislation by the Congress or the application of previous legislation. As noted in the text, all legislation must begin in one house of the Congress or the other and must have the concurrence of both houses. The president may, of course, veto any legislation he or she deems unacceptable.

Power of the Purse. The Constitution specifies that all authorization of the expenditure of public funds must be initiated in the House of Representatives and have the specific concurrence of both houses of the Congress. Particularly in the area of national security, this is a significant power because large amounts of money are spent on national security and because most of those funds are controllable and must therefore be appropriated each year.

War Powers. Although the president is the commander in chief of the armed forces, the Congress has important countervailing powers. The Congress sets the size and composition of the armed forces (promotions for officers, for instance, must formally be approved by Congress before they can take effect). The president can have no larger armed forces than the Congress authorizes. Moreover, the Congress is the only agency of government that can declare war. While this provision has only been used five times in the country's history, it remains a strong limitation on the president's practical ability to place American armed forces into harm's way.

Confirmation of Officials. Presidential appointees to high offices in the administration (with the exception of the National Security Council staff, who are considered part of the president's personal staff and thus are exempt) are subject to confirmation by the U.S. Senate. The purpose of this provision is to ensure that the president does not appoint personnel who are personally obnoxious or politically objectionable in a policy sense.

Ratification of Treaties. Although the president is the only official who can negotiate agreements with foreign governments, none of these can take force until they have the positive advice and consent of two-thirds of the U.S. Senate. This limitation is necessary because a ratified treaty is coequal to laws passed by the Congress. Because of the sheer volume of the relations between the United States and other governments, only a small portion of the dealings with other governments are in the form of treaties (most are executive agreements that do not require senatorial ratification), but most of the more important relationships are in the form of treaties.

Oversight. Although it is not specifically enumerated in the Constitution, the power to review how laws are implemented by the executive branch and to examine how well executive agencies operate has long been an accepted form of congressional limitation on executive actions. The chief mechanism for this oversight is through the various congressional authorizing committees that mirror major executive branch functions (the Armed Services Committees and the Department of Defense, for instance).

president in the last two years of his tenure (and thus a so-called lame duck) in increasingly partisan ways. Among other things, the change gave the Democrats control of the committee chairs in both houses, a powerful tool.

The formal political process within the U.S. Congress is theoretically simpler and more compact than within the executive branch. The structure for considering the budget request of the administration is more direct, for instance, consisting of three prescribed steps rather than the multiple steps in the formulation process within the executive branch. Compactness is facilitated because the Congress does not have to develop a budget on its own. It only has to respond to a presidential request, which it can accept, reject, or modify.

Other factors also influence this process. For instance, the two houses of Congress are in fact two large and often unruly committees, consisting of 100 highly independent senators and 435 equally independent members of the House of Representatives. Unlike the politically appointed officials of the executive branch, they are divided politically by party and by political philosophy. Moreover, the disposition of the defense budget is particularly important to individual members because defense dollars are spent in individual congressional districts and states. Members of Congress thus have an acute built-in self-interest in the outcomes. The result is quintessential politics.

The heart of congressional action in the area of national security occurs largely through two mechanisms: the committee system and the budget process. The process is important because it produces the resources that fund efforts to ensure the national security and thus provides much of the shape and nature of the national security effort. The budget process is also of particular importance to the Congress because it is the power imbedded in the American Constitution that gives it the most leverage over the executive branch in matters pertaining to national security.

The Committee System. Because of its size and consequent unwieldiness, the Congress does relatively little of its most important business acting as overall houses of Congress. The real, detailed business of the Congress is performed by the committee system, wherein smaller groups of senators and representatives, all of whom have volunteered for the committees on which they serve (although by no means do all members get membership on all the committees they desire), hammer out congressional positions, oversee the activities of the executive agencies they parallel, and respond to presidential budgetary and policy initiatives. When the Congress is working properly (which it does not always do), the agreements that are reached in committee are ratified by the overall bodies.

One might reasonably ask why committees are so important and powerful within the Congress. For one thing, the various committees (including their staffs) are the major repositories of congressional expertise on the area of their focus. Congressional members typically volunteer for committee assignments in which they or their constituents are interested or in which they have particular expertise. Thus, a congressional district with a large concentration of military facilities or defense contractors will produce congressional members who will develop an interest in and knowledge of defense matters because the outcomes of defense issues may affect their constituents. The longer members of Congress stay in the Senate or House and remain on the Armed Services Committees, for instance, the more expertise and seniority they acquire and the more influence they develop. The most prominent and knowledgeable members attain the status of congressional leaders in their area of expertise. Former Georgia Senator Sam Nunn, who served as chair of the Senate Armed Services Committee during the 1980s and early 1990s, developed a particular reputation as a defense intellectual both within and outside Congress.

These experts—especially the chairs and the ranking members of the minority party (who become chairs if their party attains majority)—become chief congressional spokespeople in their area of expertise. Members with less expertise than the experts tend to defer to the judgments of these leaders (especially members of the same party) and generally vote the way the chairs recommend. The same is true of the major subcommittees of the major committees, where the chairs develop great expertise in their narrower subject area (military manpower, for instance). The rise in partisanship and especially ideological division within both houses of Congress during the 1990s has made members more independent of their leaderships and thus decreased some of the deference paid to the chairs, but their impact on legislation remains formidable. It has also hardened along party lines on important matters.

Another reason the committee system is so powerful is because of the smaller and more manageable size of committees compared to the full houses of Congress. It has often been said of the houses of Congress themselves that their size and organization make them great debating forums for the discussion of public policy, but that they are so large and unwieldy as to be terrible places to enact and especially to frame legislation. The major committees of Congress, normally with memberships of twenty or fewer members, are more compact and can give more thorough and knowledgeable consideration to matters of legislative review, including such things as calling for and considering the views of expert witnesses. The recommendations of the appropriate committees thus have a considerable impact on how the Congress as a whole acts on matters that come before it. If one wants to get a sense of what the Congress thinks about a particular matter, the person to listen to is the chair of the appropriate committee.

Being the majority or minority party in Congress has particular importance in establishing control of the Congress. At the beginning of each congressional session, members of each house are assigned to committees in numbers reflecting their majority or minority status. In turn, the committees elect their chairs, almost invariably from the majority party or its allies (Senator Joseph Liebermann, an independent from Connecticut, received a chair in the Congress seated in 2007). Chairs, in turn, have control of committee agendas, including the calling of hearings and investigations of the executive branch activities the various committees oversee. This power is critical to understanding the surge in critical oversight of the Bush administration by a Democratic majority in both houses since the 2006 election and the relative absence of such scrutiny during the previous six years of Republican control of the Congress.

The Budget. The budgetary process is the essence of the congressional committee system in operation. It consists of three steps. The first comes reasonably early in the legislative session that convenes in January and consists of actions leading to a *budget resolution*. When the president's proposed budget is submitted to the Congress, the budget committees of the two houses receive and analyze the request, both overall and by budget category (one of which is national defense). The review establishes likely budgetary ceilings for the overall budget and for each category. When the committees of the two houses reach agreements on these general goals and their acceptability is acknowledged by the executive, the result is the joint budget resolution.

This resolution is a nonbinding agreement about the general shape of the budget that is supposed to guide other congressional committees in legislating the details of the budget package. Sometimes the final budget conforms fairly closely to the guidelines, but often it does not. The resolution provides the basic parameters about what can and cannot be spent within the budget, but the increasing use of supplemental appropriations (see below) has become an often used method for ignoring the resolution.

After the budget resolution is in place, the serious work of budgeting begins in the Congress. This process is depicted in Figure 8.1. This process is, in a sense, both simpler and more complicated than it may seem. The second and third steps in the congressional budgeting process occur through the actions of the authorizing committees of each house, the Senate and House Armed Services Committees (SASC and HASC) and the appropriations subcommittee on defense of each house. The role of the authorizing committees in budgetary action is programmatic: they review the programs requested in the budget and decide which of these to authorize and at what level of support. They do not, however, make specific recommendations about how much should be spent on individual programs and the overall budget, although there are clearly budgetary implications in areas such as procurement—approving a program for a given quantity of a particular weapons system costs has predictable budgetary consequences.

Actual recommendations on the size of the budget and on what can be spent are made by the appropriations committee of each house and, in the case of defense, the

Figure 8.1: The Budget Process

House	Senate
President's Budget Request	
Budget Resolution	Budget Resolution
Joint Budget Resolution	
Authorizing Committee (HASC)	Authorizing Committee (SASC)
Appropriations Subcommittee	Appropriations Subcommittee
Conference Committee	
House	Senate
President	

appropriations subcommittee for defense. The role of the overall appropriations committee is to develop the total congressional version of the federal budget, and that of the subcommittees, one of which parallels each functional authorizing committee (including defense), is to make recommendations for that function that are aggregated in the overall budget.

The process becomes political and controversial when there is disagreement among the various initiating and reviewing bodies, as there normally is. These disagreements can come about in three basic ways. First, the authorizing and appropriating committees in either or both of the houses can disagree on both programmatic priorities and budgetary size. The result is a mismatch between approved programs and resources to fund them. Second, the committees in the two houses, when each reaches accord on its vision of the budget, can disagree. The results can be different programs or appropriations between houses. Third, the president can disagree with the overall outcome. The more these possible points of disagreement come into conflict, the more contentious the overall process becomes and the more problematic is the outcome. These disagreements are particularly vivid when the executive and legislative branches (or the two houses of Congress) are controlled by different political parties.

The authorizing and appropriations functions theoretically should be sequential. In a totally rational world, the authorizing committee would review the budget request programmatically and decide which programs are meritorious and worthy of funding. They would then pass their recommendations along to the appropriations subcommittees, which would allocate appropriate funding. In fact, the two forms of committee actions occur more or less simultaneously and independently within each house and with little formal coordination either within or between the houses. The result is often four more or less conflicting recommendations that require reconciliation before a budget bill can be passed along to either house for enactment.

If this seems a disorganized approach to enacting a budget, the reasons derive from the consequences of the outcomes. Members of appropriations subcommittees, like their counterparts on authorizing committees, commonly represent constituencies with interests in the outcomes and hence want to be certain their interests are thoroughly represented. This not only is true regarding the defense budget, but also has parallels in every other area of budgetary and policy concern—the agricultural committees and subcommittees in both houses, for instance, overwhelmingly have members from farm states who want to protect the interests of their constituents.

When differences exist between the authorizing and appropriations subcommittees within the two houses, they are resolved by joint meetings whose purpose is to produce accommodations and compromises acceptable to all. Normally, there is informal contact with the parallel committee leaderships in the other house. In some cases, the president may well invite the leaderships of the committees to the White House to "jawbone" them into reaching agreements as close as possible to his position.

The ultimate outcome unfolds from this interaction. Each house passes a defense budget allocation based on the interaction of the authorization and appropriations committees. If these are identical (which they rarely are), they go directly to the president. If they are different, they are sent to a conference committee composed of members of the appropriate committees of the two houses to reach agreement on identical bills, which are then sent back to the individual houses to be voted upon. When each house has approved the bill, it is then sent to the president for his signature. The president may accede and sign the budget, veto it, or ask for revisions.

The budgetary process is further complicated by the increasing reliance on *supplemental appropriations* as a means to finance important governmental operations, particularly in the area of national defense and security. What are these supplemental appropriations? A study by OMB Watch, a watchdog group that studies and critiques government spending, offers a useful definition. According to that study, supplemental appropriations involve "spending legislation, generally but not exclusively requested by the President, intended to address a need not known or foreseen when the annual budget for a given fiscal year was drawn up." The use of this form of funding dates back to the first Congress in 1790 and has been used, to a greater or lesser degree, ever since. The key notion historically has been tying such appropriations to dealing with emergency situations; increasingly, they are used for a variety of other purposes.

The use, and some would argue abuse, of this process has been a prominent part of the budgeting process during the Bush administration—and more specifically, for funding the war in Iraq—to the point that over 6 percent of government-proposed spending for fiscal year 2007 was proposed through supplemental requests. As the OMB Watch study asserts, "The use of supplemental appropriations has mushroomed during the Bush administration, and the emergency requirement has faded. The Iraq and Afghanistan wars have been almost entirely financed by emergency supplementals." The administration has continued to designate its requests for funding of these military adventures using the emergency language, because doing so avoids the restrictions on spending imposed by the annual budget resolution that sets the parameters for regular governmental spending. Since the ongoing war in Iraq hardly qualifies as an unforeseen emergency, some argue that the use of this device for this purpose distorts the historical tradition in this area.

The amount of funds involved is not inconsequential. For fiscal year 2006, a supplemental appropriation of $91 billion was passed by Congress on March 8, 2006. Approximately $68 billion of that amount were earmarked for Iraq, Afghanistan, and the GWOT; about $19.5 billion were allocated to Hurricane Katrina relief (an expenditure more in line with original intent), and slightly over $4 billion were allocated for international activities such as relief for Darfur and the catastrophic 2005 earthquake in Pakistan. The request for fiscal year 2007 was $99.7 billion.

Why has this device become such a popular way to fund government activities? Clearly, some of the reasons are legitimate and unimpeachable. Supplemental appropriations to deal with the original intent of spending on truly unanticipated events such as Katrina relief are certainly a case in point. One can make a case for using this process for dealing with one-time expenses so that they do not get built into the permanent budgets of agencies and result in the difficult task of rescinding a budget element. Aid for Darfur probably qualifies. Also, the process allows the administration to adjust funds to pressing needs when emergencies apply.

The use of supplemental appropriations has a more controversial side, however, that has become particularly prominent in the current context. One source of controversy is that these appropriations are "off budget," meaning they do not figure into accounting at the end of the year for the government. Thus, since almost all of the expenses associated with Iraq come from supplemental funding, a review of the DOD regular budget reveals virtually no expenditures for that purpose. It has, moreover, been the practice of the Bush administration to make such requests without "offsets": proposals to decrease spending in other areas to compensate for funds allocated to the supplemental purposes. The result is that these expenses do *not* appear in calculations of the federal deficit or debt, since those calculations are based on the regular budget. If the funds expended on Iraq and Afghanistan were part of regular debt accounting, the staggering debts incurred by the Bush administration would be much greater than they are reported to be. In addition, supplemental requests avoid the regular budgetary process and often receive far less scrutiny than does the regular budget. That fact explains why a Republican-controlled Congress did not highlight funding for Iraq for six years, whereas a Democrat-controlled Congress has seized upon the supplemental requests of the administration since it obtained the majority.

APPLICATIONS: THE HOMELAND SECURITY RESPONSE TO THE ENVIRONMENT

The interaction between the changing international environment and the vagaries of domestic politics can best be demonstrated by looking at actual policy arenas where the two come into play. In the post–September 11 context, the major change in emphasis has been in dealing with terrorism. The GWOT has been concentrated on military efforts to track down and suppress foreign terrorists. The greatest domestic change has been in the creation of the DHS as the institutional response to organizing and coordinating efforts aimed at reducing the risks posed by terrorists. It has been a mixed success.

The Department of Homeland Security

One of the most important questions raised after September 11, 2001, was the institutional adequacy of the U.S. government in the face of terrorism. In the days and months following the attacks, information became available that there had been intimations of the impending attacks circulating at lower levels of the government in the months before the actual attacks and even a planning document and monitoring held over from the Clinton administration specifically aimed at Al Qaeda. And yet efforts the attacks appeared to come as an awful surprise. Why? In order to answer the question and to make some sense of the process, three aspects of homeland security are examined: the historical evolution of concern with homeland security, its institutionalization as DHS through the Homeland Security Act of 2002, and problems of the homeland security effort.

Background and Evolution

Although the term *homeland security* appeared abruptly after September 11 and thus seemed to be a very new kind of phenomenon, it is not. If homeland security is defined as that part of the national security effort focusing primarily on the protection of the physical territory and citizens of the United States, then homeland security has been a major, if largely implicit, cornerstone of American national security policy since the formation of the republic.

As suggested in Chapter 4, however, what is now called homeland security has not been a major operational problem for the United States throughout American national history. The reason, of course, has been the accident of geography that provided the United States with nonthreatening neighbors and broad oceans that protected it from harm. The vulnerability of the American homeland to attack was not a problem until the latter 1950s, when Soviet nuclear-tipped missiles became capable of attacking and destroying the American homeland. That danger, of course, remained theoretical and abstract throughout the Cold War; the terrorist attacks of September 11 made the problem concrete and immediate. The impact of the attacks was to create an equation between homeland security and a concrete threat, that of terrorism. The vulnerability of the homeland to harm, a familiar reality to many other countries, had been abstract to Americans. September 11 made it concrete and immediate.

The modern evolution of homeland security has proceeded along two policy thrusts. The first of these is emergency management. Largely associated at the federal level with the actions of agencies such as the Federal Emergency Management Agency (FEMA) and at the state and local levels with first responders like police and fire agencies, this effort had two major emphases: protection against and reaction to natural disasters (hurricanes, tornados, earthquakes, etc.) and man-made disasters. Problems with the former were vividly illustrated by continuing responses to Hurricanes Katrina and Rita; the latter was associated primarily with civil defense efforts in the event of a nuclear attack against the American homeland.

The suppression of terrorism was added to the homeland security portfolio during the 1980s, although at a much more muted level of publicity than the current effort. During the 1980s, a number of actions were taken within the federal government to create federal capabilities in the areas of antiterrorism and counterterrorism and to elevate and attempt to coordinate the efforts of the principal federal agencies with responsibility for terrorism: the CIA, FBI, and Immigration and Naturalization Service (INS). INS functions are now assigned to Immigration and Customs Enforcement (ICE) and DHS. Operational responsibility for dealing with on-site efforts when terrorists might strike remained at the state and local levels.

The two efforts have remained parallel, although with some tensions that were apparent from the beginning but that lacked enough urgency before September 11 to compel rationalization. Terrorism suppression is primarily a federal function, for instance, whereas emergency management is mostly state and local in execution. Operationally, the federal government is more interested in preventing disasters like terrorist attacks and is secondarily concerned with dealing with the consequences of disasters; the order of emphasis is reversed for the emergency managers. These differences are manifested in allegations of poor communications between the federal and the state and local levels and in the competition for funding for homeland security. FEMA, with responsibilities in both areas, has become something of a whipping boy for problems of coordination, particularly in light of the poor coordination of efforts in New Orleans that was one of the most visible deficiencies in federal responses to Katrina.

The process of trying to organize the government to deal with these matters dates back to the Reagan administration. In 1986, President Reagan issued National Security Directive (NSD) 207, which did three things. First, it created the Interagency Working Group (IWG) under the National Security Council. Second, it designated the IWG as the mechanism to coordinate responses to terrorism. Third, it established the lead agency designation (the federal agency with primary responsibility) of the State Department in regard to international terrorism and the FBI over domestic terrorism.

The Clinton administration was also active during the 1990s. In 1995, Clinton issued Presidential Decision Directive (PDD) 39, with three emphases: preventing terrorist acts, responding to terrorist acts and provocations, and managing the consequences of terrorist attacks. The FBI was given broader responsibility domestically, including the formation of domestic emergency support teams (DESTs)to act in the event of significant problems. Clinton also authorized the suspension of *posse comitatus* (an 1869 law that prevents the use of the military for domestic police functions) during emergencies and designated FEMA to lead "consequence management" efforts. Clinton issued two other relevant documents in 1998. PDD 62 created the Office of the Coordinator for Security, Infrastructure Protection, and Counterterrorism, and PDD 63 added the problem of cyber terrorism specifically to the agenda under the designation of "information infrastructure." (Much of this evolution is detailed in Richard Clarke's *Against All Enemies*.)

The point of this discussion is not its details but that there was governmental activity in the area that has become homeland security for at least a decade and a half before September 11, 2001. The potential for terrorism was known within specialized parts of the federal government, but the efforts were low-key and generally low priority, as terrorism remained, for the most part, a peripheral concern for most Americans despite overseas instances of terrorist attacks against Americans and American facilities (the African Embassy bombings of 1998, the attack on the USS *Cole* in Yemen in 2000) and despite even the 1993 attack on the World Trade Center towers (later linked to Al Qaeda)in New York. During this time period, the dual emphases on terrorism suppression and emergency management were established, and homeland security was largely equated with terrorism as a military and law enforcement problem. These efforts, however, remained at the peripheries of the public agenda until a compelling event caused them to be thrust on center stage.

The Homeland Security Response to September 11

The Al Qaeda attacks against New York and Washington instantly elevated the concept of homeland security to the heart of the national political process. The initial institutional reactions included the creation of a Homeland Security Council parallel in structure to the National Security Council, the establishment of an Office of Homeland Security, and the appointment of a director for the effort. Militarily, the DOD established a Northern Command (from the old Force Command) to coordinate military responses to threats against the American homeland. This process ultimately resulted in the passage of the Homeland Security Act of 2002, which President Bush lauded as the single most important and sweeping reorganization of government in fifty years (a comparison with the National Security Act of 1947). The DHS came into existence in 2003 as a result of that legislation. Its role and structure are still evolving.

The initial response to the September 11 problem was the creation of the Office of Homeland Security within the White House and the appointment of former Pennsylvania Governor Tom Ridge as its director. Ridge was given a position conceptually similar to that of the national security advisor (at least in terms of purported access to the president) and was charged with rationalizing and coordinating improved government capabilities for dealing with terrorism. Critics at the time maintained that Ridge's position left him as little more than a figurehead who could not compel agencies to do anything, especially to cooperate with one another in activities in which they had not previously done so.

In June 2002, the administration proposed a stronger way to institutionalize the effort—the creation of the DHS. The new department, with full Cabinet status, was legislated into being in November 2002 and mandated to perform four functions: border and transportation security; emergency preparedness and response; chemical, biological, radiological, and nuclear countermeasures; and information analysis and infrastructure protection. To accomplish its tasks, the president proposed pulling resources from a number of existing agencies under the control of the new department.

Virtually no one opposed either the general proposition of this effort or its implementation in principle. As is often the case, however, the devil has proven to be in the details of implementation. The kinds of reorganization authorized by the act moved over 170,000 employees from twenty-two major federal agencies under the umbrella of DHS. Such a movement in and of itself is daunting, as many agencies, individuals, and organizations with contrasting work cultures and methods of operation and little or no tradition of interaction and coordination were suddenly thrust in positions in which they are expected to work as a team acting in a common effort. At the same time, there have been significant "turf wars" over which agencies (and their budgets) will find their way into DHS and which should remain within their traditional homes. These political problems have spilled significantly over into the oversight relationship between DHS and the Congress.

The first and most difficult problem was which agencies would be drawn into the new department and which would not. As already suggested, there are three federal agencies with primary responsibility operationally in the terrorism field that form a kind of golden triangle of federal efforts. Ideally, the CIA (which, until legislation establishing the DNI passed in 2004, was an independent agency) has primary responsibility for discovering and monitoring the existence and activities of overseas terrorists; the INS (part of the Department of Justice) has responsibility for monitoring and intercepting aliens entering the country; and the FBI (also part of Justice) monitors and arrests terrorists committing acts within the country. Within this relationship, the CIA should tell the INS who is attempting to enter the country, and when suspicious aliens do come into the United States, the INS should then inform the FBI so it can begin its role of monitoring. In order to maximize the likelihood that this relationship is seamless and effective against terrorism, it follows that all three agencies should have been included in DHS.

They are not. The INS and Customs Service are part of Homeland Security (mostly because INS has had so many political problems that Justice was glad to get rid of it) with the INS redesignated as Immigration and Customs Enforcement (ICE). The CIA and FBI remain independent of DHS, with only directions to coordinate with the DHS. Why? Both the CIA and the FBI argued, apparently effectively, that terrorism is only one part of their responsibilities. Virtually all the agencies that might be included in the new department could make the same argument that they had terrorism as only part of their portfolios, but the FBI and CIA were sufficiently powerful that their arguments succeeded while other failed. In the process, of course, the traditional budgets of the FBI and CIA were protected as well. FEMA, also an independent agency created in 1979, was included in DHS, mostly because it lacked enough powerful supporters to block its inclusion .

The amalgamation of agencies into DHS has been analogized to a similar process that created the Department of Energy (DOE) in 1977. Both agencies share three major commonalities. First, they were both created as responses to national emergencies: the oil shocks of the 1970s led to demands for a DOE, just as the terrorist attacks of 2001 created the momentum for the DHS. Second, both departments represent attempts to reorganize the federal government by rearranging the federal organization chart, pulling agencies and responsibilities out of existing structures and putting them under the umbrella of the new agency. With regard to DHS, this is a daunting task internally. The analogy with DOE, however, provides another invidious political comparison that has plagued both agencies—the problem of congressional oversight.

Third, both were done "on the cheap." The Bush administration initially argued that the DHS would require no added funding because resources would be made available by agencies contributing people and other resources to the DHS (which proved largely false). Underfunding remains a problem: the DHS budget for 2004, for instance, was under $30 billion. In fiscal year 2007, it was around $50 billion.

Each function of the executive branch of government is overseen for programmatic and budgetary purposes by committees and subcommittees of the two houses of Congress. The oversight function is a significant part of the power base of the members of Congress because it provides real clout in determining who receives and does not receive funding under whatever function they may control. As a result, members of Congress are quite jealous of their prerogatives with regard to oversight and are particularly resistant to the idea that a function over which they have some control might move from the department their particular committee oversees to a committee created to oversee a new department like DOE or DHS, on whose committee they do not serve. Reform at the executive level, in other words, threatens the power of members of Congress. The result is resistance to change of the effective structure that can make the work of the new agencies all the more difficult.

DOE is a miniature version of the congressional problem faced by DHS. The DOE solution in Congress was largely to leave budget and programmatic aspects of agencies included in DOE under their previous committee purviews. The result is that the DOE secretary must report to seventeen committees and subcommittees of the Congress, a daunting and time-consuming way to get policy advice and funds. Moreover, since most of these bodies do not have energy per se as their sole or even primary focus, the advice and funding recommendations are likely to be at odds with one another. No one recommends the DOE precedent as the right way to organize a new department.

The DOE's problem with Congress is child's play compared to that faced by DHS. In aggregating the various agencies into the DHS organization chart, the responsibilities of no fewer than eighty-eight committees and subcommittees in the two houses were affected by the transfers. When the DHS came into being in 2003, a survey showed that *all one hundred* senators and all but twenty members of the House were on committees whose jurisdictions were potentially affected by the reorganization. While everyone could agree in abstract principle that the new DHS would face the smoothest possible sailing in admittedly troubled waters if there was a single authorizing committee and single appropriating committee in each house (which is the case for traditional departments), the potential consequence of moving toward that ideal end was to erode the power of virtually every member of the Congress by removing some power from a committee or subcommittee he or she sits on. This potential erosion of power has caused sufficient opposition to reforming the congressional part of the relationship that there is no permanent Homeland Security Committee in the Senate and a committee with largely symbolic value in the House of Representatives.

Two other important problems attended the creation of DHS. One was with regard to funding. The Homeland Security Act was passed at the same time that President George W. Bush was pushing for additional tax cuts beyond those he had achieved during his first year in office, and one consequence of this emphasis was that he did not want to appear to be increasing funding in other areas of the federal budget at a time when he was arguably reducing revenues. As a result, the decision was made that the new effort would require no additional funding, since the funding of agencies and functions moving out of their old agencies into DHS would simply follow them into the new agency and provide the budgetary base for DHS. This assertion was, of course, a fiction: as noted, agencies would fight tooth and nail to maintain their budgets, and the new mandates given DHS clearly required new funds. The precedent, however, was set, and DHS attempts to gain additional resources have suffered from the albatross created by the original fiction.

There has been the additional problem of mandate. At one level, protecting the American homeland from foreign enemies—notably terrorists—would seem to be a fairly straightforward task, but in operation, it has proven to be complicated. Securing American territory encompasses a wide range of duties, from monitoring who comes into the country through customs to border security to the protection of specific potential terrorist targets to port security. Each of these duties requires different skills and puts demands on the system for additional resources, not all of which have been available, particularly if one aggregates all of these sources of threat and tries to eliminate them. Put in a way raised in Chapter 7, achieving an acceptable level of risk reduction and risk management has been a difficult task for the planners at DHS. Funding and other resource deficiencies associated with the DHS response to Hurricane Katrina (largely through FEMA) illustrate the consequences of assuming this risk.

Nowhere have these anomalies been more evident than in the current controversy over illegal immigrants coming across the U.S.–Mexico border. The flow is not strictly a national security problem, because the immigrants are overwhelmingly peaceful, law-abiding job seekers fleeing poverty and pose no military or other security risk (that they may pose other political problems is a separate matter). Their status has politically been raised to threat status by advocates of stricter control of access to the United States across the border. The DHS is caught in the middle of this conflict because the Border Patrol and ICE, both parts of DHS, have roles in regulating entrance into the country, including the possible penetration of the borders by terrorists. Becoming enmeshed in this controversy inevitably means diverting energies and resources to border control that could be used for other priorities to prevent terrorism, such as port security. The illegal immigrant problem is not a duty DHS needs or wants, but it is one it cannot avoid altogether. This problem is discussed more fully in Chapter 14.

Despite all its problems, the DHS has, of course, come into being and functioned for five years. The process of building a new agency to deal with a complex set of tasks that were poorly handled in the past has proven to be a daunting task, the eventual success of which has yet to be determined. As long as international terrorism remains a top priority in Washington, the DHS will remain an important work in progress.

Ongoing Problems and Controversies

Some of the difficulties associated with the evolution of the new DHS can be attributed to growing pains. Whether one accepts the claim of the monumental stature of the Homeland Security Act as accurate or as political hype, it has created the basis for a very large governmental overhaul in a large, high-priority area of concern. As suggested, the effort has become politicized, and this has made accomplishment of the ambitious goals set forward for the new agency even more difficult. Only a few months into his tenure as the replacement for Tom Ridge as secretary of DHS, Michael Chertoff announced his firm intention to engage in a massive reform of the agency, notably its intelligence capabilities, in June 2005. No one thought this task would be easy to accomplish; some thought it was essentially impossible.

Several ongoing questions and controversies surround the DHS and its mission. For present purposes, four of them can be mentioned and briefly examined: the emphasis of the agency between the federal and the state and local levels, with special attention to budgetary and political concerns; the evolution of the critical intelligence function both within DHS and in its dealings with other agencies; the division of responsibilities between DHS and other agencies, a subject on which the 9/11 Commission has weighed in; and the extent to which the DHS effort collides with the rights of citizens.

Mission and Political Emphasis. Although it was the stated intention of the homeland security legislation to elevate this important governmental function above the political fray, that effort has not been altogether successful. The reason, simply enough, is that setting priorities and emphases has budgetary implications, and that means politics inevitably intrudes.

Beyond the question of moving funding among federal agencies, this question of emphasis has come to center on the debate over relative emphasis on combating and preventing attacks against the United States (the federal emphasis) and emergency management by first responders (the state and local emphasis). Originally, the pattern was for the federal government to mandate actions by the states and localities, for which they were to find funds (unfunded mandates)—a way to maintain the fiction that homeland security required no new funds. As concern with avoiding new spending has ebbed, however, funding has become available for the first responders, mostly in the form of equipment grants and funding for emergency plans and the like. The availability of these kinds of funds, in turn, provides opportunities for members of Congress to endear themselves to their constituencies by gaining funding for new ambulances, fire trucks with hazardous materials (hazmat) capabilities, police communications capabilities, and the like. To some observers, provisions like this are evidence of a commitment to first response; to others, they are pure "pork" (needless expenditures). Benjamin Friedman, writing in *Foreign Policy*, cites 2003 allocations of $725,000 for port security in Tulsa, Oklahoma, and $1.5 million in federal funds to Fargo, North Dakota, to purchase trailers equipped to respond to nuclear attacks and "more biochemical suits than it has police officers." Secretary Chertoff has responded with a plan to base future allocations on the basis of risk (the higher the threat to a potential target, the greater its priority for funding), to which first responders (and their congressional supporters) respond that this is a disguised way of promoting federal programs. The effort remains inextricably enmeshed in the political controversy over pork barrel politics that roils attempts at governmental reform.

Amplification 8.3

RECOMMENDATIONS OF THE 9/11 COMMISSION

In assessing why the September 11 tragedy occurred, part of the view of the 9/11 Commission was that structural deficiencies had contributed to the government's inability to predict and prevent the disaster. To deal with that problem, the commission made a number of structural recommendations, three of which stand out.

First, the commission called for the creation of the National Counterterrorism Center (NCTC). The NCTC is to be the central focus for joint planning and operations in dealing with terrorism. It is to be headed by a director who is appointed directly by the president and whose position is equivalent to that of deputy secretary (second in command) in a Cabinet-level agency. The director is to be confirmed by the Senate and required to testify before the Congress (subject to subpoena). This provision has not been implemented by the Bush administration on the grounds that having such a position answerable to Congress presents a dangerous precedent that could be applied to other presidential aides.

Second, the commission recommended creation of the DNI. The DNI is to oversee the operation of all other intelligence agencies and is to have power over all intelligence budgets. The DNI is to have three principal assistants: the director of central intelligence for foreign intelligence, the undersecretary of defense for intelligence for defense-related intelligence, and the undersecretary of homeland security for domestic matters. Control over budgets, especially those in the Defense Department (which controls 80 to 85 percent of all intelligence funds), has been a sticking point in the total implementation of this provision. This job description of the DNI closely parallels the original role envisioned for the DCI in 1947. The DNI position has been in place since 2005 but has largely been symbolic, since the incumbent has no operational or budgetary controls over the various agencies under his titular control.

Third, the commission calls for congressional reform, notably the creation of a single Homeland Security Committee and a single Appropriations Subcommittee for Homeland Security in each house to reduce reporting and budgeting problems. As noted in the text, this recommendation has been fiercely resisted within the Congress.

Improving Intelligence. There has been universal agreement since September 11 that a major component in the disaster was a failure of the intelligence community to penetrate the conspiracy and allow it to be prevented. The 9/11 Commission was particularly critical of the intelligence breakdowns that permitted the attacks to occur, recommending major reforms to the overall process. In addition to the creation of a National Counterterrorism Center (NCTC), the commission recommended a consolidation of the fifteen federal agencies engaged in intelligence activities and the creation of the position and office of the director of national intelligence. The structural reforms recommended by the commission are summarized in Amplification 8.3, Recommendations of the 9/11 Commission.

The DHS was also given responsibilities for intelligence analysis, and personnel were assigned within the agency to develop the capability to analyze raw intelligence and analysis generated from other agencies in terms of the DHS mandate. Secretary Chertoff maintains that the department has not done a good job of "collecting, piecing together, and sharing" the intelligence it receives and analyzes, and he promises reform of the intelligence function as a major part of his reforms of DHS. One possibility that he has raised is the creation of the position of a deputy director for intelligence within the agency, which subsequently was done.

Homeland Security and Terrorism Mandates. While the idea of DHS was to consolidate governmental efforts in the homeland security area within a single governmental location, the 9/11 Commission also argued that this has not truly been the case. As noted earlier, of the three core agencies in identifying and dealing with terrorist threats to homeland security (CIA, INS, and FBI), only one (INS, now ICE) is part of the DHS structure. The CIA and FBI remain in their customary positions within government. In addition, the DOD has independent intelligence responsibilities and control of special operations and the Central and Northern Commands.

Challenge!

THE "ANGRY LIBRARIANS" AND CIVIL LIBERTIES

While a number of provisions of the USA PATRIOT Act have been the subject of opposition and even derision, one provision, Section 215, has come to symbolize what critics believe is most egregious about it. Because it deals partly with governmental access to library records of individuals, it has been given the nickname "the attack of the angry librarians."

The section contains three provisions its detractors find obnoxious. First, it permits government investigators access to a wide range of information about suspects, including what library books they have checked out (which critics view as invasion of privacy). Second, secret subpoenas that cannot be contested in court (should someone find out about them) can be issued to gain access (thus denying the right to contest the subpoenas). Third, there is no requirement that the government disclose its investigations to those under scrutiny (thereby denying rights of due process). All the provisions are justified as necessary national security actions in the "war" on terrorism.

Are such actions justified by the homeland security threat? In the absence of the assertion of a national security basis for them, they would unambiguously be declared unconstitutional, violations of fundamental rights guaranteed to all Americans. The government's counterargument is that in the state of war between the United States and terrorism, they are necessary and appropriate actions. Do you agree? How much individual freedom can and should be sacrificed in the name of security? What do you think?

The State Department maintains primary responsibility for international policy co-ordination and cooperation, and the NSC and Homeland Security Council stand outside the control of DHS. Among other things, this diffusion of responsibility puts a strain on the fairly narrow talent pool available in the homeland security area.

Homeland Security and Civil Rights. A fairly muted but significant level of concern has been raised about the impact of homeland security efforts on the civil rights of American and other citizens. The problem of potential infringements on people's rights has not been specific to DHS but has tinged the entire problem. Much of the concern centers domestically on provisions of the USA PATRIOT (Uniting and Strengthening America by Providing Appropriate Tools Required to Intercept and Obstruct Terrorists) Act of 2001, most of which were renewed in 2005. Critics argue the act's provisions represent an unreasonable infringement on civil liberties, and supporters contend the provisions are necessary for the successful pursuit of terrorists (see the *Challenge!* box, The "Angry Librarians" and Civil Liberties). Internationally, the open-ended detention of suspected terrorists and their sympathizers at Guantanamo Bay, Cuba, has added to the global concern about the problem.

CONCLUSION: THE ENVIRONMENT SINCE SEPTEMBER 11, 2001

Thinking about and dealing with the national security environment was set on its head by the events of September 11, 2001. Suddenly, a mostly benign and tranquil environment was revealed to have a very dark and hostile side that had heretofore been the subject of adventure motion pictures and novels. Before the attacks on major symbols of American military and financial power, the only instances of foreign-inspired and foreign-committed acts had been small and relatively primitive—the most notable example was the 1993 attack on the World Trade Center towers by a single truck laden with explosives that killed six people. The scale of the 2001 attacks and the enormous loss of life revealed a level and quality of vulnerability that few Americans had imagined in their worst of nightmares. The body politic was thrown into convulsion about how it could have happened, how it could be avoided in the future, and how to punish those behind the atrocity.

The shock of the attacks and the ambiguity about appropriate responses confused the debate, raising doubts but few obvious solutions. The conventional debate was particularly muddied. National security planning has concentrated on dealing with the concrete, conventional military threats posed by other sovereign states or groups within states. Although the importance of those threats, and hence how to counter them, was tinged by a certain level of implausibility, at least the discussions could proceed within a common frame of reference that all parties understood. Suddenly, the area of homeland security moved to the center of our attention; as the preceding discussion has suggested, fashioning an organizational and policy response is still a work in progress.

The massive attacks by nonstate actors engaging in the most unimaginable forms of "warfare" did not fit within standard categories. Shadowy, private terrorist organizations that do not represent states and that have small, elusive units (or cells) do not lend themselves to conventional military responses. The idea of using commercial aircraft heavily laden with jet fuel essentially as cruise missiles to attack urban, civilian targets had no precedent within military doctrine or practice and could only be found in escapist fiction (Tom Clancy's *Badge of Honor* revolves around using an airliner to attack the national capitol). How does the country define such a threat? Moreover, how can forces and capabilities be developed that can counter and negate this kind of problem? The answers were and are not clear, but it was evident that one had to move beyond conventional thinking to formulate responses.

STUDY/DISCUSSION QUESTIONS

1. What is the National Security Act of 1947? Why was it necessary? What are its principal provisions? Why are they important today?
2. What are the constitutional powers provided to the executive branch in the area of national security? What are the congressional powers? Compare and contrast them.
3. What is the interagency process? Discuss its structure and its role in the national security decision process.
4. Discuss the budget process within the executive branch. Compare it to the process in Congress. How do they fit together? Why is the defense budget so important and so controversial?
5. Why has the relationship between Congress and the executive changed since the 2006 election? Do you think divided government (different parties controlling the legislative and executive branches) or unified government (one party controlling both branches) better serves the national security of the country? Why?
6. What is a supplemental appropriation? Why do they exist? Why are they important in understanding contemporary defense spending, especially on the Iraq War?
7. The major political response to September 11 domestically has been the creation of the Department of Homeland Security (DHS). Discuss the process leading to forming the DHS, its structures (including those agencies included and excluded), and the difficulties associated with the new agency.
8. What are the major ongoing controversies surrounding homeland security? Discuss each.

SELECTED BIBLIOGRAPHY

9/11 Commission. *The 9/11 Commission Report: Final Report of the National Commission on Terrorist Attacks upon the United States* (authorized ed.). New York: W.W. Norton, 2004.

9/11 Public Discourse Project. *Report on 9/11 Commission Recommendations*. Washington, DC: Public Discourse Project, December 5, 2005.

Ackerman, Bruce. *Before the Next Attack: Preserving Civil Liberties in an Age of Terrorism*. New Haven, CT: Yale University Press, 2006.

Ball, Howard. *The USA PATRIOT Act: Balancing Civil Liberties and National Security: A Reference Book*. Santa Barbara, CA: ABC–CLIO, 2004.

Berkowitz, Peter (ed.). *The Future of American Intelligence*. Palo Alto, CA: Stanford University Press, 2006.

Clarke, Richard. *Against All Enemies: Inside America's War on Terror*. New York: Free Press, 2004.

Crabb, Cecil V., Jr., and Pat Holt. *Invitation to Struggle: Congress, the President, and Foreign Policy* (2nd. ed.). Washington, DC: CQ Press, 1984.

Flynn, Stephen. "The Neglected Home Front." *Foreign Affairs* 83, 5 (September/October 2004), 20–33.

———. *America the Vulnerable: How Our Government Is Failing to Protect Us from Terrorism.* New York: Harper Perennials, 2005.

Friedman, Benjamin. "Think Again: Homeland Security." *Foreign Policy*, (July/August 2005), 22–29.

Fullilove, Michael. "All the President's Men." *Foreign Affairs* 94, 2 (March/April 2005), 13–18.

Harty, Maura. "U.S. Visa Policy: Securing Borders and Opening Doors." *Washington Quarterly* 28, 2 (Spring 2005), 23–34.

Heymann, Philip B., and Juliette Kayyem. *Protecting Liberty in an Age of Terror.* Cambridge, MA: MIT Press, 2005.

Hillyard, Michael J. "Organizing for Homeland Security." *Parameters* 32, 1 (Spring 2002), 75–85.

Hilsman, Roger. *The Politics of Policy Making in Defense and Foreign Affairs: Conceptual Models and Bureaucratic Politics* (3rd. ed.). Englewood Cliffs, NJ: Prentice-Hall, 1993.

Irwin, Paul M., and Larry Nowels. *FY 2006 Supplemental Appropriations: Iraq and Other International Activities, Additional Katrina Hurricane Relief.* Washington, DC: Congressional Research Service, March 10, 2006.

Johnson, Loch. *Bombs, Bugs, Drugs, and Thugs: Intelligence and America's Quest for Security.* New York: New York University Press, 2000.

Kettl, Donald L. *System Under Stress: Homeland Security and American Politics.* Washington, DC: CQ Press, 2004.

Lehrer, Eli. "The Homeland Security Bureaucracy." *Public Interest* 256 (Summer 2004), 71–85.

Maxwell, Bruce (ed.). *Homeland Security: A Documentary History.* Washington, DC: CQ Press, 2004.

McMaster, H. R. *Dereliction of Duty: Lyndon Johnson, Robert McNamara, the Joint Chiefs of Staff, and the Lies That Led to Vietnam.* New York: Harper Perennials, 1997.

Nakayama, Andrea C. (ed.). *Homeland Security.* Detroit, MI: Greenhaven Press, 2005.

OMB Watch. *Background Brief: Supplemental Appropriations.* Washington, DC: OMB Watch, March 2007. (http://www.ombwatch.org/budget/supplementalbackgrounder.pdf)

Rothkopf, David J. "Inside the Committee That Rules the World." *Foreign Policy* (March/April 2005), 30–41.

Snow, Donald M. *United States Foreign Policy: Politics Beyond the Water's Edge* (3rd ed.). Belmont, CA: Wadsworth, 2005.

Yingling, Paul (Lt. Col.). "A Failure in Generalship." *Armed Forces Journal* (online) May 2007.

CHAPTER 9

Traditional Military Problems

PREVIEW

Thinking about and planning for large-scale war between armed forces as they were developed for and fought in World War II—conventional forces for symmetrical warfare and strategic nuclear war—predate and postdate September 11, 2001. The traditional purposes for which these forces were developed largely disappeared with the end of the Cold War, and only the United States retains a robust traditional capability that it proposes to augment through force modernization. At the same time, critics say these large, European-style forces are anachronisms in a world of shadowy asymmetrical threats. Before assessing these criticisms, it is necessary to describe traditional forces and missions, first nuclear forces and then conventional forces and the residual problems associated with each that have a continuing impact, notably weapons of mass destruction (WMD) and the problems their spread to other states and nonstate entities (proliferation) creates. The chapter concludes with some assessment of the relevance of these forces in the future.

The past, it is sometimes said, is the prologue of the future, and nowhere is that observation more applicable than in the area of military forces. War is an ancient institution, and it has evolved and changed over time, but it retains significant continuities in how and why it is fought. Doctrine—beliefs about the best ways to accomplish military ends—has a long past, and much of the doctrine employed today is rooted in the cumulative worldview that existed before September 11. The past is thus relevant to the future.

What does it mean to refer to traditional problems and conventional forces and solutions? Basically, such allusions describe the structure of the American armed forces in the European style that evolved through the formative period of the American military experience and congealed in World War II. The structures of armies, navies, and air forces armed with nuclear and nonnuclear (conventional) weapons are designed to confront and defeat similarly armed and organized opponents in symmetrical warfare. These forces remain the backbone of American capabilities. A major question against which they must be measured is their relevance in a world of asymmetrical threats. This chapter describes those forces; Chapters 10 and 11 assess their relevance in a world of asymmetrical threats.

Why is this description important? There are four reasons. First, these forces and uses have been important in the past. Second, they are still major components of the package of forces with which the United States confronts the world—the components military planners best understand and are most comfortable with. The ways in which forces have been designated and employed in Iraq is testimony to this endurance. Third, modernizing and enhancing the capabilities they represent is a major part of the added defense expenditures proposed by the current administration and will be a major concern in the post-Iraq debate. Finally, it may be necessary to use these forces again in the future against some currently unforeseen or foreseen foe. Their continuing relevance and applicability to the evolving structure of threat is a relevant concern. Any of these reasons is sufficient to warrant a review and analysis of the traditional security components of national security; collectively these reasons are compelling.

This chapter examines the inheritance of two major functions of armed forces during the Cold War competition: thermonuclear forces and the strategies governing their potential use, and so-called conventional armed forces. Both capabilities were developed explicitly for a Cold War confrontation and environment that no longer exists, but the capabilities and plans for their use remain essentially intact today and influence the current national security debate. Moreover, these forces frame what the United States can and cannot do militarily in the world and especially in the most militarily stressful situations it may face. Their continued relevance in a world where hardly anyone else has a counterpart force is a major question.

The relevance of these traditional uses of armed force was a matter of debate before September 11, 2001. The series of events set in motion by those tragedies quickly added the semimilitary nature of terrorism to the menu and made Americans aware of an entirely different kind of war that a few analysts had been predicting for a decade or more but that had by and large been downplayed within the national security community.

This chapter approaches the traditional problems of national security sequentially. It begins with nuclear forces and deterrence, the historically unique military problem of the Cold War. The possibilities of nuclear Armageddon, however remote, were of such enormous potential consequence as to receive the highest priority in defense planning and thinking. While a nuclear World War III has faded as a major concern, the continuing existence of nuclear weapons and their possible spread to potential opponents remains a central concern.

The other side of the traditional balance is the continuing utility of conventional (or nonnuclear) forces. The Cold War's military competition featured very robust nonnuclear forces—large, heavily equipped armies; highly capable surface, subsurface, and aerial navies; and sophisticated bomber- and fighter-based air forces—developed to deter and, if necessary, fight the "central battle" in Europe. The preparations undertaken came from a vision of an even larger and bloodier reprise of World War II. Of the two massive forces that conducted that competition, only American forces remain as large and configured with the kinds of capabilities the Cold War dictated.

These two types of forces continue to exist, although their traditional roles have largely been overcome by events. There are, however, residual issues arising for each type. For nuclear forces, these include the problems of nuclear proliferation and missile defenses. For conventional forces, military manpower and military force reform are important residues.

NUCLEAR FORCES AND DETERRENCE

The nuclear age was formally born in the predawn hours of July 16, 1945, when the first atomic explosion lighted the skies around ground zero at the Trinity Site at White Sands, New Mexico. The light from the explosion could be seen as far away as Albuquerque, New Mexico, a hundred miles or so away. Robert Oppenheimer, the physicist considered the "father" of the atomic bomb, was so overwhelmed by the event that he said later, "There floated through my mind a line from Bhagavad-Gita, 'I am become death, the shatterer of worlds.'" General Lesley Grove, the military commander of the Manhattan Project that produced the bomb, intoned, "This is the end of traditional warfare," as he viewed the explosion. His view was, of course, overstated, and traditional warfare continued despite this monumental change in destructive capability. The clear difference, however, is that wars are now conducted with nuclear escalation as a possibility, especially when nuclear-capable states are involved.

The thought surrounding nuclear weapons has its rich, distinct history, much of which has faded from public view and policy concern. The "shadow of the mushroom-shaped cloud" is, however, a remaining artifact of the second half of the twentieth century, and thus it is worthwhile briefly sketching its dynamics, highlighting those with continuing relevance.

Seminal Events of the Nuclear Age

The nuclear age did not burst upon us suddenly at White Sands. Scientific research into nuclear physics went back nearly a century through more-or-less independent investigations in Europe and North America. (Clark's *The Greatest Power on Earth* is a particularly good history of this evolution.) The impending clouds of World War II and intelligence reports that Nazi Germany was attempting to harness and weaponize nuclear physics alarmed Albert Einstein to the extent that he wrote a letter at the behest of more politically active colleagues like Enrico Fermi to President Franklin D. Roosevelt warning of the potential problem such weapons could pose in the hands of the Nazis. Roosevelt's response was to commission the Manhattan Project, which began the crash program that produced nuclear bombs shortly before the end of the war.

The first operational atomic bombs were, of course, used against Hiroshima and Nagasaki, Japan, on August 6 and 9, 1945, to shorten the war in the Pacific by forcing Japanese capitulation short of an anticipated bloody invasion of the Japanese home islands. (This vision was made especially vivid by the spirited Japanese defense of Okinawa, which, interestingly, included Japanese soldiers wrapping themselves with explosives and committing suicide by blowing themselves up.) When the second bomb exploded, the American arsenal was temporarily exhausted; for the last time, the world had no nuclear weapons. In the next quarter-century, the nuclear world evolved from those primitive days through the cumulative impact of a series of nuclear events.

The Atomic (Fission) Bomb. The successful conclusion of the Manhattan Project was, of course, *the* seminal event of the nuclear age, since none of the other sophistications would have been possible without having taken the first step. The original atomic bomb was what is known as a fission device—the basic physical reaction that makes the bomb explode and produce its deadly effects occurs through the breaking apart (or fission) of atoms of unstable isotopes of uranium. The atomic bomb represented a quantitative change in the deadliness of war. The delivery of an atomic bomb over a target could produce deadly effects that otherwise could only have been produced by literally hundreds or thousands of attacks by conventional bombardment. The campaigns against Dresden, Germany, and Tokyo with incendiary bombs (both of which were more destructive than the atomic attacks) had required attacks by many hundreds of aircraft, because the characteristics of those bombs were insufficient to create an undeniably qualitative change in warfare. Atomic bombs made bombardment incredibly more "efficient" than it was in the prenuclear age.

The Hydrogen (Fission-Fusion) Bomb. The second major event was the successful development of a qualitatively larger form of nuclear explosive, the fission-fusion or hydrogen bomb. Known as the "Super" at the time because of the orders of magnitude increase in deadly effect that it had, a prototype of the hydrogen bomb was successfully tested by the United States in 1952. The Soviet Union followed suit a year later. As the name implies, the physical reaction behind this new form of nuclear explosion involves two steps—the explosion of a small fission "trigger" to induce the second step, which is fusion. This reaction involves the fusion of atoms of heavy hydrogen (deuterium or tritium), which produces the release of an enormous amount of energy far in excess of that possible with a fission reaction.

The effects of a thermonuclear explosion are awesome. Fission bombs produced yields that were the equivalent of thousands of tons (*kilotons*) of TNT; fission-fusion devices produced explosions with destructive effects measured in *megatons* (*MT*), or the equivalents of *millions* of tons of TNT. During the Cold War, the Soviet Union was reported to have tested a fission-fusion device that produced an 85 MT blast.

The entry of thermonuclear bombs into the arsenals of the two sides altered the calculus of nuclear weapons and their use in two ways. First, it altered the calculation of survivability in a nuclear war. A society might endure grievous damage as the result of an attack with atomic bombs, but it could reasonably anticipate surviving such an attack. The same attack with thermonuclear bombs—a quantum leap in destructive capability—made survivability questionable and meant the new weapons represented a *qualitative*, rather than a quantitative, increase in the deadliness of war.

Second, during the early 1950s, scientists achieved considerable success in designing bombs that were more compact and much lighter than the Hiroshima and Nagasaki prototypes. This made possible the delivery of these deadly weapons by missiles, a further qualitative change.

The Intercontinental Ballistic Missile (ICBM). The effort to weaponize rocketry began in the period between the world wars, when the first rockets were developed and tested in Germany and the United States, among other places. In World War II, the first prototypes, the V-1 "buzz bombs" and the V-Rockets, were used against Great Britain in a desperate act by the Germans to break British will. These early designs were so grossly inaccurate as to have little impact on the war, and rockets were considered little more than terrorist weapons. By the 1950s, advances in rocketry allowed nuclear weapons to be transported over intercontinental ranges and land close enough to their targets to destroy them.

The result of these advances fundamentally altered the impact of nuclear weapons on war more than any of the other seminal events. The reasons were (and are) profound and cumulative. The thermonuclear bomb had removed the ability to calculate surviving a nuclear war if a large number of these devices were used. The ICBM produced the perfect delivery device for such weapons, since there was (and arguably still is) *no known defense capable of defending against a nuclear rocket attack*. The result is total societal vulnerability to nuclear devastation, and when both sides have this offensive capability, the condition is known as *mutual societal vulnerability*. In this situation, the only way to avoid being killed in a nuclear war was to avoid having such a war at all. Nuclear war avoidance (or nuclear deterrence) became and remains the prime value and concern.

The Multiple Independently Targetable Reentry Vehicle (MIRV). The fourth development was a major increase in the deadliness and extensiveness of nuclear arsenals—the perfection of a means to dispense more than one nuclear bomb (or warhead) from the tip of a single rocket. The military capability was achieved by the United States in 1970, when it began to add MIRV capability to its arsenal; the same feat was achieved by the Soviet Union in 1975.

The MIRV had two major effects on the nuclear equation. The first was to multiply the size of nuclear arsenals without increasing the number of nuclear missiles within those arsenals, a phenomenon known as "fractionalization," which meant that a single rocket's capacity could be increased by the number of additional warheads that the MIRV permitted to be added (or fractionated). The MIRVing of superpower arsenals had a second, anomalous effect. During the 1970s, arms control negotiations with the purpose of reducing the likelihood of nuclear war between the superpowers were particularly active, and one of their purposes was to place limits on the size and capabilities of the two offensive arsenals. MIRVs, however, had been excluded from those discussions by the Soviets (who lagged in the technology and did not want to negotiate away their chance to catch up), and the process of converting arsenals to MIRV status meant that the number of warheads actually increased greatly during the decade. The MIRV was the reason.

Ballistic Missile Defense (BMD). The fifth seminal event—defenses against missile attacks—has not yet definitively occurred but is instead a residue of the Cold War. It has been a high priority of the Bush administration and could, in certain circumstances, alter the nuclear calculus as much as the others. The current round of debate about missile defenses is nothing new. In fact, investigation of how to try to destroy incoming ballistic missiles proceeded parallel to the development of offensive applications of rocketry, and all the theoretical problems of missile defense had been solved before the first ICBM was launched in 1957. The problem has not been the concept; the difficulty has been, and continues to be, execution of the proposed mission, as discussed later in the chapter.

Why would the development of effective defenses represent a seminal event in the nuclear age? The answer is that an effective system should be capable of intercepting and destroying all of an incoming nuclear missile attack (it is not clear it would function against attacks by other than missile delivery). A truly effective, reliable defense would thus remove dependence on deterrence as the only basis on which to prevent the ravages of a missile-launched nuclear war. Rather than relying on the threat of robust retaliation after absorbing an attack (the basic threat under theories of deterrence as they have been practiced), a defensive system that worked could render such an attack ineffective and futile and make nuclear weapons "impotent and obsolete," in Ronald Reagan's depiction of the purpose of his Strategic Defense Initiative. A truly effective defense would rank with the ICBM in importance in nuclear evolution and change the way we thought and think about nuclear weapons.

Theories of Deterrence

As the nuclear balance evolved, two broad conceptualizations of deterrence emerged to dominate theorizing and defense planning in the United States, including the development and deployment of nuclear arsenals. Both positions were first articulated in two works published in 1946, one very famous (Bernard Brodie's *The Absolute Weapon*) and one not so well known (William Liscum Borden's *There Will Be No Time*).

These formulations sound strange, even macabre or bizarre, when taken out of the context of the times. Brodie's formulation evolved to the strategy of assured destruction, which a detractor modified by putting the word "mutual" in front of it to produce the acronym MAD. Borden's position evolved by the 1980s to a strategy known as limited nuclear options (LNOs) or countervailance; a detractor gave its adherents the title Nuclear Utilization Theorists, or NUTS. The intellectual debate about what best deterred a nuclear attack thus became a dialog between those who were MAD and those who were NUTS.

Assured Destruction. The title of Brodie's book gives its thesis away. According to Brodie and his associates at Yale University who collaborated on *The Absolute Weapon*, nuclear weapons fundamentally changed the nature and calculation of war. The destructiveness of those weapons was so great that, in Brodie's opinion, conventional war—which could escalate to nuclear war—was now obsolete. Thus, the only reason states could have for maintaining military forces (including nuclear weapons) was to avoid their use against them—in other words, deterrence. Borden disagreed, arguing that nuclear weapons were weapons, after all, and that weapons are eventually used.

Much of the debate lay fallow for over a decade. The event that enlivened the question of deterrence, of course, was the successful testing and deployment of ICBMs in the latter 1950s. Since the only way to guarantee not being killed in a nuclear war when ICBMs were present was to make certain that a nuclear war did not occur, the question became, What kind of nuclear strategy best assured the avoidance of nuclear hostilities?

The Brodie position was the first answer to dominate the debate and was articulated in the early 1960s as assured destruction. The first premise of the strategy, which came directly from Brodie himself, was that all sides would lose in any nuclear war, meaning that only war avoidance was acceptable. The question was how best to assure that no one could ever miscalculate the possibility of succeeding in a nuclear war and thus decide to start one. The answer was the assured destruction threat.

The basic assured destruction threat was that any Soviet nuclear attack would be met by a fierce and destructive American retaliation that would destroy the Soviet Union and rob it of any possible calculation that it had "won" anything. ICBMs guaranteed the condition of mutual societal vulnerability under which such a retaliation would occur against an initial attacker; and the upshot was that launching a nuclear strike became the equivalent of committing national suicide.

The implementation and implications of assured destruction are ghoulish and created a lively opposition. In order to reinforce to Soviets the suicidal nature of an attack, the strategy features *countervalue targeting* by American retaliatory forces against Soviet targets. This antiseptic term means aiming weapons at the things people value most, notably their lives and the conditions that make life commodious. The prototypical countervalue target is an urban complex, the larger the better, since the purpose is to convince the adversary's leadership and population they will die if they attack the United States. This logic, of course, has its contemporary counterpart in the fear that terrorists in possession of nulcear weapons would threaten to—or actually—use them against urban targets.

Limited Nuclear Options. The murderous implications of assured destruction did not go unnoticed or uncriticized. Arguing that such a threat was both gruesome beyond belief and incredible because of the ghoulish consequences, a second strand of thought emerged within nuclear strategy circles suggesting a different role for nuclear forces. In the curious world of nuclear weapons and deterrence, the argument began with the belief that the assured destruction threat was unbelievable because of the moral abyss that implementation of the strategy promised and then posed a supposedly more humane alternative. Thus, nuclear planning must contain ways to use nuclear weapons that do not necessarily entail Armageddon.

This basic idea, extrapolating from Borden, became known as limited options in the 1970s and 1980s and posited proportionality as the basis of deterrence. The defenders began by arguing that the assured destruction threat was believable only in the event of an all-out Soviet first-strike attack against the United States. Since the Soviets knew the consequences of such an attack, it was the least likely form of attack for them to undertake. Thus, any nuclear attack they might actually contemplate would be less than all-out, leaving the president with only the options of doing nothing or launching the entire arsenal. As a result, the assured destruction threat emerges from this analysis as a credible threat against the least likely form of nuclear aggression and an ineffective threat against other and, by definition, more likely forms of provocation.

Limited nuclear options remedies this deficiency by creating within the Single Integrated Operational Plan (SIOP, the actual plan for implementing nuclear attacks) a series of options short of all-out response (hence the name limited options). The idea is to provide the president with a whole array of possible responses proportional to the original attack by the Soviet Union. Thus, for instance, if the Soviets were to launch twenty to thirty missiles against U.S. ICBM fields in North Dakota, the United States should have the capability and plan to respond by taking out a similar target in the Soviet Union. Presumably, the threat and ability to do so would have two salutary effects. First, a proportional response would be more believable than an all-out counterattack. Second, knowing the United States could effectively play tit-for-tat in the event of any provocation, they would realize that any action they might initiate would be countered effectively; their attack would be trumped and provide no advantage.

The debate between advocates of assured destruction and limited options continued inconclusively for decades, because there was no hard evidence to conclude which construction produced deterrence better. The central contention always boiled down to the question of whether nuclear war could be limited. Happily, the debate between those who were MAD and those who were NUTS did end indecisively with the end of the Cold War and thus the end of the reason for the competition. In the end, deterrence prevailed in the sense that nuclear war was in fact avoided. Whether this success was an act of enormous insight and persistence or the mere avoidance of what would have been the stupidest (and possibly last) decision in human history is a judgment to be left to the reader and to history.

Nuclear Residues

Nuclear weapons may have lost the prominent role they played during the Cold War, but that does not mean nuclear considerations have simply disappeared from national security concerns. Indeed, there are at least two related concerns about nuclear weapons that remain on the agenda: problems of nuclear proliferation and the alleged need for BMD. Each is a concern of long standing. The spread of nuclear weapons to states that do not currently have them was one of the earliest worries of nuclear thinkers in the 1960s, and the prospects of and debates about missile defenses predate the actual deployment of the missiles that the defenses seek to stymie.

Nuclear Proliferation. The problems associated with the prospect or reality of states attaining nuclear weapons capability that previously lacked those weapons are by no means something new. Indeed, these problems were born, as a practical matter, when the United States reached nuclear capacity at White Sands and began to worry about the prospect that a potentially antagonistic Soviet Union would follow suit, and they are problems that have created agony among politicians and analysts as the nuclear "club" (the states with nuclear weapons) has increased across time.

The traditional nuclear proliferation concern centered on the additional problems produced if additional sovereign states gained nuclear weapons. In the contemporary context, that concern remains but with a twist that did not concern nuclear planners during the Cold War but does today. In the contemporary context, additional states that might gain nuclear weapons capability (Iran and North Korea being the most publicized examples) remain problematical, but there are two other matters of concern. The first is that the proliferation concern has broadened beyond nuclear weapons, which are difficult to acquire, to other forms of weapons of mass destruction (WMD) such as biological and chemical weapons that are less deadly but more accessible. The second concern is that the WMD, but especially nuclear weapons, might fall into the hands of nonstate actors and, more specifically, terrorist organizations. These two additional concerns are conjoined because of the fear raised most dramatically (if falsely) about the possibility that a WMD-armed Iraq might share these weapons with terrorists in their efforts against the United States.

Nuclear proliferation can take on two guises. The first is so-called *horizontal proliferation*, which refers to the spread of nuclear weapons to states that do not currently possess them. This is the proliferation problem that is most commonly the basis of contemporary concerns. The second form, however, is *vertical proliferation*, which refers to growth in the arsenals of current nuclear weapons states. As particularly the superpower nuclear arsenals mushroomed after the advent of MIRV, this phenomenon became entangled with horizontal proliferation, as potential new nuclear members (notably India) argued that their continuing abstention from joining the nuclear club was tied (as specified in the Non-Proliferation Treaty or NPT) to a reduction in the arsenals of the superpowers. The failure of the United States and the Soviet Union to engage in arsenal cutbacks was used to justify the Indian decision to join the nuclear club in 1998.

The dynamics of horizontal proliferation are captured in a construct called the $N+1$ *problem*. This artifact of the Cold War is as valid today as it was forty years ago when it was articulated. In this formulation, N stands for the number of states that currently possess nuclear weapons, and $+1$ refers to the additional problems created if additional states gain these weapons. The problems are conventionally described in terms of how new members destabilize the system by adding additional "fingers to the nuclear button" (increasing the number of states that, by virtue of having the weapons, can start a nuclear war). Implicit in this formulation is the assumption that new members are *more likely* to start a war than current members; if they were not, the concern would be less well grounded.

The heart of the $N+1$ problem is the differential perceptions of the two groups. The N states implicitly (sometimes explicitly) argue that the possession of the weapons by states that already have them is acceptable, and their evidence is that the current possessors have avoided nuclear war. Additional states, however, pose unpredictable new dangers and dynamics that it is safer to avoid, thus forming the basis for opposition. At least implicit in this assessment is the underlying premise that new possessing states would act more irresponsibly with the weapons than current possessors. Since the same charges were made against current members before they joined N (China in particular), it is difficult publicly to defend this position without being openly condescending to the potential proliferators.

Potential new members (+1 states) discount that *their* possession would make things more unstable and argue that, if anything, their membership in the club would increase their own security (this seems to be a prime argument made by Iran and North Korea, who state that they need nuclear weapons to deter the *United States* from attacking them). Once +1 states get the weapons, however, they tend to accept the argument that N (of which they are now a part) produces an acceptable balance but that additional accretions to the club would be unacceptable.

The divide between possessing and nonpossessing nuclear states over *whether* an N+1 problem exists cannot be overstated, because it reflects basic cleavages about how states view one another. Put bluntly, the supposition that it is all right for currently possessing states to perpetuate their nuclear arsenals and destabilizing for other states to join them is discriminatory at a minimum and condescendingly racist at worst. The loudest detractors of nuclear weapons spread have been the United States, Russia, Great Britain, and France, all of which are European by tradition. Obviously, some possessors (China, India, and Pakistan, for instance) are not European, but they are also the most worrisome members of N (somewhat interestingly, the possession of these weapons by Israel rarely evokes this concern).

The +1 states, on the other hand, come mostly from the developing world. Moreover, claiming that some countries are more responsible than others possessing these weapons in effect accuses the pretenders of being more reckless and irresponsible, which, at a minimum, is condescending. Why, for instance, does the United States so vociferously oppose the spread of nuclear weapons to Iran and the Democratic People's Republic of Korea (DPRK or North Korea)? The answer is that such spread would be destabilizing, which effectively means that those countries would likely be less responsible possessors. Operationally, this means they would be more likely to use nuclear weapons against their enemies (including the United States) or might provide access to them to terrorists. Why? Because the Kim Il Jung regime of the DPRK and the Ahmadinejad regime of Iran (how much power he actually would wield over these weapons is questionable) are less responsible than the current possessors. That logic may make sense to Americans; it cannot possibly be viewed by North Koreans or Iranians as anything other than insulting.

This logical dilemma infects the major international effort to discourage nuclear weapons acquisition, the Non-Proliferation Treaty that was negotiated in 1968 and entered into force in 1970. The treaty in essence creates a caste system. On the one hand are the states that already possess nuclear weapons, who are required not to encourage or assist nonpossessors to gain these weapons and who are committed to reducing their own possession to zero (reverse vertical proliferation). These states have been much better at meeting the former than the latter requirement. Nonpossessing states are required to renounce their intention ever to build these weapons. Those states unwilling to make that pledge (Israel and India are the most prominent examples) simply refuse to become members of the treaty (North Korea and Iran *are* members).

The concern over horizontal proliferation extends beyond nuclear weapons, although these are the core worry. The other forms of WMD include biological (agents of biological origin) and chemical weapons. Both forms are prohibited by international treaties to which most counties are members. Biological and chemical weapons are of a lesser order of concern mostly because their effects are more limited. An attack with a chemical or biological aerosol may kill or debilitate those on whom it falls, but generally the radius of destruction is limited. Moreover, the use of either is problematical, because particularly airborne agents are subject to vagaries such as the shifting direction and velocity of wind. Most of these weapons lack the potential for massive devastation of a target population that nuclear weapons possess. On the other hand, they are easier to construct using materials that are much more readily available internationally than the fissile materials necessary to build nuclear weapons, and their development and stockpiling are relatively easier to accomplish clandestinely than nuclear programs. The fear that Iraq had manufactured and was secretly stockpiling such weapons was, after all, a primary justification for invading that country.

How does one deter horizontal proliferation? There are two basic approaches. One is *acquisition deterrence*, which consists of attempts to dissuade countries from acquiring the weapons. The techniques for accomplishing this form of deterrence include positive incentives not to engage in provocative actions, such as providing safeguarded nuclear fuels (fuel sources that cannot be transformed into weapons-grade materials) and monetary incentives for demurring from weapons development, and negative actions, such as sanctions. Both techniques are currently being used against the DPRK (sanctions when the North Koreans engage in nuclear developments, assistance such as nonnuclear fuels and foodstuffs when they comply) and Iran (mostly from countries other than the United States). If countries (India, for instance) cannot be dissuaded from developing these weapons, then one must revert to *employment deterrence*, which consists of efforts to avoid the use of nuclear weapons by states who gain them. The techniques for doing so tend to be those associated with traditional bilateral U.S.–USSR deterrence during the Cold War, such as threatening devastating retaliation against some state that attacks one with these weapons or building missile defenses (see below) to make such attacks ineffective.

Two more points should be made about nuclear proliferation. First, the key to avoiding new states getting such weapons is avoiding the transfer of weapons-grade (particular isotopes of uranium and plutonium) materials to acquiring states. The physics of making nuclear bombs is generally well known, and most potential proliferators can assemble the scientific and engineering teams to create nuclear weapons (it is not, it should be added, clear that most terrorist groups can meet this criterion). The secret is the control of weapons-grade materials, and that has been the heart of most attempts to limit the spread of nuclear weapons.

The second point concerns the addition of nonstate actors (most prominently terrorist groups) to the list of nuclear pretenders. Arguments about the irresponsibility of this category of potential nuclear club members are much more convincing than the same arguments made against states. Notably, the allegation is made that a terrorist group such as Al Qaeda would be more likely to use such weapons if it had them because its members lack the fear of the consequences—retaliation—that impedes state possessors, for two reasons. On the one hand, the principle of martyrdom is built into the ethos of many of these groups, who would thus not fear a retaliation the way most states would. On the other hand, nonstate actors lack identified, claimed territorial bases against which to retaliate. Should Al Qaeda launch a nuclear attack somewhere (blow up a bomb in an American city, for instance), what would the United States annihilate in retaliation? If the attacker is Russia, the answer is obvious. But if it is Al Qaeda, does that mean leveling Waziristan, which is a province of an American ally, Pakistan? This problem recurs when dealing with terrorists across the board, as will be discussed in Chapter 12.

There are currently seven admitted members of the nuclear club (in order of "admission," the United States, the Soviet Union/Russia, Great Britain, France, China, India, and Pakistan), one state that neither confirms nor denies its possession but is universally considered a member (Israel), one state that developed these weapons but subsequently dismantled its weapons and renounced their possession (South Africa), and one state that entered the club but backed out in 2006 (the DPRK). Predictions made several decades ago suggested that twenty to thirty states might by now have gained the capability, but they have not. Moreover, proliferation has not been accompanied by its most dire possible consequence, nuclear war. The potential that other states and, more ominously, nonstate actors might join the club keeps the concern over the proliferation problem lively, because the potential consequences of a rogue +1 entity gaining possession of the capability are so dire.

The proliferation question remains controversial. No one—with the exception of countries attempting to obtain the weapons—thinks that proliferation is a good idea or that the world would be a better place with more nuclear weapons–possessing states. At the same time, there is disagreement about *how much* of a problem it is. At least four different points are made regarding the nature and seriousness of the proliferation threat. The points largely mirror points already made.

One argument is that the problem is essentially overblown. While the undesirability of proliferation has been bemoaned for forty years or more amid dire predictions of the number of states that might attain these weapons, in fact very few have. Of the members listed above, only the last three have joined the nuclear "club" in the past forty years. Lists of potential proliferators have routinely suggested the prospects of a much larger number of new nuclear states, and these predictions have simply been incorrect.

A second argument is that much of the gist of the proliferation argument is insulting, even racist (as noted). Implicit in arguments to prevent nuclear weapons spread is that it is all right for current possessors to keep their weapons, while it is destabilizing if other states obtain them. Despite pompous rhetoric to the contrary, this conceit is also included in the Nuclear Non-Proliferation Treaty's provisions, which state that nonpossessors should abjure trying to get the weapons while possessors should move toward nuclear disarmament (which none of them have). At the bottom line, however, is the implicit statement that current possessors are more responsible with the weapons than the states that might gain them. Such an assertion is arguably true but is both condescending and insulting.

Third, the rationale for stifling the spread of nuclear weapons is that proliferation will make the world a more unsafe place because it increases the number of "fingers on the nuclear button" and thus the likelihood of nuclear war. This concern, of course, is greatest if "rogue states" or, even worse, nonstate terrorists obtain nuclear capability. But is that rationale justified by experience? The world has, after all, witnessed seven instances of proliferation, but there has not been a single instance of nuclear weapons usage. In fact, a contrary case can be made that gaining nuclear weapons actually stabilizes situations, either because that possession makes countries feel less vulnerable (China, for instance) or because mutual possession by historical enemies sobers them about the consequences of future conflict (India and Pakistan).

There is a fourth and very ironic argument about proliferation in the current context. It is that countries seek nuclear weapons in order to guard against being attacked by their enemies—a deterrence argument. Nuclear weapons possession, it is argued, provides status and respect from potential predators: no state in possession of nuclear weapons has ever been attacked. The irony is that this argument is currently voiced most prominently as a reason for gaining nuclear weapons in Iran and North Korea, and the country they seek to deter with those weapons is the United States.

From this perspective, Saddam Hussein's greatest mistake was *not* pursuing nuclear weapons, because if he had possessed them, the United States might not have attacked him for fear of a nuclear retaliation by Iraq.

Missile Defenses. The long-standing Bush administration proposal to build a missile defense is also not a new idea. In fact, the *national missile defense (NMD)* is the third generation of advocacy for developing and deploying a defense against ballistic missile attack. The first proposal was put forward in the latter 1960s and early 1970s as the Sentinel and later as the Safeguard system. Its purported purpose was to guard against a Chinese nuclear capability that was projected for the future, and as such, it was similar to the current NMD plan in intent (see Amplification 9.1, The Chinese Nuclear Threat).

In 1983, President Ronald Reagan proposed a much more ambitious system, the *Strategic Defense Initiative (SDI)*. The Reagan SDI had the grand purpose of providing a comprehensive, totally effective shield against a massive launch of nuclear weapons (essentially an assured destruction attack) by the Soviet Union. The impenetrability of the SDI screen would render nuclear weapons "impotent and obsolete," in Reagan's own words. Reagan's longer view was that such a shield would make nuclear weapons themselves irrelevant and thus lead to nuclear disarmament, his real goal. The SDI program lost focus during the first Bush administration and was formally scuttled by President Clinton. What remained after the demise of SDI was research on a more limited form of defense. The current NMD proposal came from this ongoing program.

The Clinton White House never showed great enthusiasm for missile defense, and the program was kept alive largely because of congressional interest. President George W. Bush took up the cause of missile defense in his 2000 campaign and continued that advocacy once elected. The events of September 11, 2001, temporarily sidetracked what had been active attempts both to gain support for the program and to overcome foreign (notably Russian, but also Chinese) objections to deploying

Amplification 9.1

THE CHINESE NUCLEAR THREAT

Current proposals to deploy a national missile defense (NMD) bear an eerie resemblance to similar arguments made nearly forty years ago when the People's Republic of China's fledgling nuclear capability was the major objective of the United States' proposed Sentinel and later Safeguard antimissile systems. What critics of NMD argue was particularly instructive about the comparison was that the "threat" posed by China was, at the time, potential rather than actual. At the time, China had nuclear warheads but no ballistic missiles capable of delivering them against the United States. The projected problem was the assertion that China would soon acquire such a capability and that missile defenses were needed to deter a Chinese launch against the United States when they indeed acquired the capability.

In retrospect, the arguments appear nearly hysterical, although the state of U.S.–China animosity in the late 1960s made them appear more plausible than they do today. In 1967, after all, the United Sates had no formal relations with the Chinese (and had not since the Communists assumed power in 1949), and this country had fought Chinese "volunteers" in the Korean War (Chinese forces sent to Korea were officially designated as volunteers to avoid a direct legal and political confrontation between the two countries). Moreover, Chinese leader Mao Zedung had publicly proclaimed after China joined the nuclear weapons club that China's huge population meant it was the only country that could physically survive a nuclear war.

The irony of the rationale was not only that the projections of Chinese acquisition of delivery capacity against United States targets were premature, but also that the capability has never been meaningfully achieved. As of 2007, the Chinese arsenal, although undergoing modernization, remains minuscule, consisting of a handful of unreliable liquid-fuel land-based and sea-based missiles that cannot be kept at a high state of readiness because their means of propulsion cannot be stored in the rockets and they would have to be "gassed up" before a launch. These missiles arguably pose a potential threat to neighboring Taiwan but not the United States. The question is whether potential acquisition of delivery capability by "axis of evil" states such as Iran and North Korea may be as fanciful as the Chinese "threat" against which the first missile shield was proposed.

such a system, objections that continue to the present and are reflected in Putin's opposition to a missile shield in Eastern Europe. The antiterrorist campaign has since been used to argue both the greater necessity of a missile screen and its relevance as a tool to frustrate terrorist organizations from attempting to use a nuclear weapon against the United States.

The idea of missile defense is inherently appealing. That appeal arises from the realization that deterrence can in fact fail (i.e., a nuclear terrorist attack can be launched). In that event, the absence of some form of defense leaves the population absolutely vulnerable to being killed, a decidedly unappealing prospect and one against which it is appealing to try to hedge. In some advocacies, it is further suggested that it is immoral not to try to mount a defense against a missile attack.

There are several objections to developing and deploying the NMD, almost all of which have been raised against its predecessor proposals as well. The first and most fundamental objection is *workability*. Although the theoretical principles for missile defenses had been worked out before the first ICBM was fired successfully, developing a system that actually could shoot down missiles with any proven reliability has been and remains illusive. Nevertheless, the deployment of elements of the NMD shield in Alaska that began in 2004 proceeded without any operational demonstration of the system's effectiveness.

A second critique deals with the *need* for a defense. As Amplification 9.1 points out, the original Sentinel/Safeguard system was designed to thwart a projected Chinese nuclear threat to the United States that has yet to emerge more than forty years later. While no one questioned that the Soviets posed a threat for which an effective SDI might provide a remedy, the NMD proposal is more similar to Sentinel/Safeguard than to SDI. The NMD is not designed as a counter to an existing threat but rather as a hedge against the emergence of a threat by rogue states or, in the wake of the September 11 terrorist attacks, by nonstate actors. Critics argue that, as in the 1960s, this threat may never emerge, and if it does, it is far enough in the future to wait until a truly effective system can be designed.

The third objection is *cost*. A major characteristic of all three missile defense proposals has been widely diverging speculation about how much a system designed to fulfill its mission would cost. The numbers are always high. The most extreme case was the comprehensive SDI, the most ambitious of the proposals. The cost of deploying SDI was estimated at anywhere between $500 billion and $2 trillion over a ten-year deployment period. Estimates for the NMD have run upwards of $60 billion.

Controversies over cost vary with estimates of effectiveness and need and are conditioned by assessments of the state of the economy and thus the ability to bear the costs. Clearly, a costly defense the effectiveness of which is unknown is harder to sell than a system of known high-quality performance, and the costs are easier to justify against a real and menacing threat than in a more uncertain environment. The increased defense spending deployment would entail (unless those costs are absorbed by cutbacks elsewhere in defense) is easier to justify in a vibrant economy such as that of the 1990s than it is in the softer economic conditions of the middle 2000s. Moreover, most estimates conclude that BMD schemes can be thwarted by building additional offensive forces to overwhelm the defenses, and that such offensive increments are cheaper to field than additional defenses.

Two other problems have affected NMD. The first comes from the international political environment. Virtually all countries (Israel being a notable exception) oppose deployment of the system as destabilizing and cite Bush administration insistence on building it as evidence of American unilateralism. The Bush administration mounted a massive diplomatic initiative in 2001 to overcome those objections with some limited success, such as gaining a limited agreement with Putin to allow the United States to test and develop the system while holding Anti-Ballistic Missile

(ABM) Treaty prohibitions on testing in abeyance. Much of the international objection was based in the fact that deploying the system would force the United States to abrogate the ABM Treaty, which is viewed as the symbolic apex of Cold War arms control success. American announcement of its intention to withdraw from the treaty in 2001, however, created little fanfare in the international community.

The other problem is the impact of the terrorist campaign against the United States begun on September 11, 2001, and the need for missile defenses. Advocates of NMD argue that the willingness of terrorists to attack American soil directly demonstrates the need for comprehensive defense of the homeland, including protection against possible future missile attacks. This kind of reasoning underlies much of the rationale for the "axis of evil" designation of Iran, Iraq, and North Korea, as already noted. Critics counter that the NMD would have had no effect on preventing the attacks that occurred against New York and Washington, so the attacks actually prove the irrelevance of NMD in light of real threats. Terrorists, in other words, are unlikely to have missiles against which the NMD might be a response, but they would likely smuggle into the country on a ship or truck a device against which the NMD would have no effect. Moreover, critics argue, coping with terrorism will require a broad range of national efforts that will put large demands on government resources, and NMD should not occupy a high place on any list of priorities.

More recently, the Russians have revived their historical objections to American intentions to build a missile defense in Eastern Europe, the stated purpose of which is to defend against a small missile launch by a so-called rogue state like Iran. Russia, which has opposed missile defenses for decades, opposes the deployment on three grounds. First, it argues that the threat is bogus and that Iran neither does nor will pose such a threat in the foreseeable future (similar to the Chinese nuclear threat). Second, Russia opposes operational missile defenses close to its borders as provocative and aimed implicitly at Russia. Third, it has never accepted that defensive systems can work (at least *Russia* has never been able to build one) but fears that an American deployment might provide the kind of operational experience that could lead to perfection of such a system, thereby leaving Russia at a disadvantage. Pique over the controversy became so great that in July 2007, despite Bush's assurances to Putin at a mini-summit earlier that month at the president's father's retreat in Maine, the Russians announced they were suspending their participation in the Treaty on Conventional Armed Forces in Europe signed in 1990 and the basis of constrained conventional force levels in Europe since. The July 13, 2007, announcement in Moscow suggested the Russian move was necessitated by "extraordinary circumstances . . . which affect the security of the Russian federation and require immediate measures" (quoted in Kramer).

CONVENTIONAL FORCES AND THE FUTURE

Both of the fault lines highlight the question of the future of conventional forces. As already noted in the introduction to this chapter and in Chapter 5, the bulk of American conventional military forces and the expenses associated with them were

devoted to maintaining and modernizing a force that was largely designed and configured to fight World War III in Europe. The end of the Cold War made this kind of a
conflict extremely unlikely, and no realistic substitute has emerged to confront the
United States in traditional symmetrical warfare (both sides fighting stand-up western-
style war), nor is one likely to emerge in the near future. Saddam Hussein challenged
the United States on its own military terms in the Persian Gulf War in 1990–1991, and
he failed miserably. His experience was instructive for all who might challenge the
West, and especially the United States, on its own terms in the future. The end of the
Cold War started the process by which the United States' conventional power has become so great that it has made itself virtually obsolete, a kind of self-fulfilling prophecy
in which American prowess has eliminated the problem for which it was devised.

The campaign against terrorism has simply accentuated this situation. Following
the fairly conventional first phase (overthrowing the Taliban), the campaign in
Afghanistan has witnessed a very different way of waging hostilities and raises some further questions about the continuing relevancy of traditional military forces to deal with
these kinds of problems. Where do conventional forces fit in this environment? In the
remaining pages of this chapter, we look at the traditional roles such forces have played
and the fate of attempts to reform those forces, the question of force modernization in
light of environmental changes and revised missions for the military caused by dynamics associated with fault lines, and the impact of recent events on the equation.

Traditional Roles

World War II was the major formative period for American conventional military
forces as they now exist and are configured today. The purpose of that conflict was the
defeat of Nazi aggression by large, heavily armed, mechanized forces fighting European
style, and the United States and its allies responded with symmetrical forces. Although the structure of active-duty forces was largely dismantled in the years immediately after that war, it served as the model for the Korean conflict, with some
peripheral modifications to reflect technological innovations (such as jet aircraft and
helicopters). Since this force remained in being after Korea rather than following the
American tradition of mobilization for war and then rapid demobilization at war's
conclusion, the conventional force for the Cold War was one with which veterans of
World War II were comfortable and familiar. Only the adversary changed, and since
the Soviets were similarly organized and were likely to fight symmetrically, the model
seemed vindicated. This force structure has largely survived reductions in size since
the end of the Cold War but is under more intense scrutiny in a new century. Sidetracked by the Iraq War, the debate will return in the post-Iraq assessment. Anticipating the discussion in the next chapter, two models are available for future structure.

The Heavy Force Model. The bulk of the American nonnuclear armed forces can
be reasonably accurately described using two adjectives, *heavy* and *conventional*, that
define what the military likes to refer to as *legacy forces*. The term *heavy* refers to the
way the force is configured and how it is equipped to perform its mission. More
specifically, it describes a force designed to fight large-unit, concentrated-firepower

combat by mobile mechanized units against a similarly configured opponent in brutal, positional land, air, and naval warfare. The symbols of heavy warfare are tanks and mobile artillery on land, bombers with large payloads in the air, and large capital ships (battleships, aircraft carriers) on the sea. By contrast, *light* forces feature more lightly armed and mobile forces capable of engaging in a variety of forms of warfare and generally not preferring the kinds of direct confrontations between armies, navies, and air forces typical of heavy forces.

Heavy forces are designed to fight *conventional* warfare, which is the style that was perfected during World War II and that has been called European. Sometimes referred to as the "Western way of war," its military purpose is to overcome adversary "hostile ability" (the capacity to resist the other side's armed forces physically) through the direct confrontation of armed forces. The military purpose is to destroy "in detail" or to break the cohesion of enemy armies, sink enemy navies, and shoot down enemy air assets. Collectively, the objective is to gain military superiority over an adversary in order to impose political objectives on that enemy by overcoming its physical ability to resist that imposition. Warfare employing heavy forces is most closely attached to wars of total political purpose (in which the objective is the overthrow of the enemy government) such as World War II, although in some circumstances these forces are effective in lesser contingencies. Heavy forces are designed and best suited for confronting similar forces possessed by the opponent. They are the tools of symmetrical warfare.

A heavy force was appropriate for the Cold War confrontation with the Soviet Union and its allies. United States and Soviet armed forces were virtual mirror images of one another physically, and both shared similar plans in the event of war. The doctrines of both sides emphasized mass (having more force at the point of engagement). A war between them, it was assumed, would resemble World War II except that it would be much bloodier and more violent, and one side or another would exhaust its weaponry and its ability to continue first. Moreover, such a war would likely be total in purpose, with one side or the other having its government overthrown (unless, of course, the war escalated to system-destroying nuclear war, in which case both sides would lose). The heavy model proved durable for fighting and winning World War II and confronting the Soviet Union short of war during the Cold War.

The prospects of this kind of war have not survived the end of the Cold War. With the collapse of the Soviet Union, the United States and to a lesser extent its NATO allies stand alone in possessing heavy forces, and no country or conceivable coalition could mount a force that could challenge the American heavy force combination or is likely to try. In a very real sense, the United States has perfected conventional warfare to the point that no one can (or will) fight one with it, a point previously made but worth reiterating. At the same time, the sheer size and mass of a heavy force may be useful in other situations, such as an extended occupation where hostile elements are present and must be controlled (Iraq), if such a force is available in sufficient (e.g., large) quantity.

The Light Force Model. The alternative approach to building heavy military forces is the light force model. Light forces generally refer to military structures that deemphasize large military equipment and that, at the extreme, are largely limited to equipment (e.g., rifles, small-caliber mortars) that can be carried physically by soldiers on foot or transported by helicopter or similar conveyance. The emphasis of light forces is on speed, maneuverability, and surprise. They are not designed to confront and "slug it out" with heavy forces, against which they stand little chance in symmetrical warfare. Rather, they are forces best adapted to rapid movement, to special assignments for which speed and deception are critical, and to missions that heavy forces cannot accomplish because of their relative lack of speed and flexibility—capturing fugitives or rescuing hostages, for instance.

In the developing world, light forces have been associated with guerrilla warfare, particularly in the jungles of the mountainous "green belt" surrounding the Equator, where it is easier for such forces to maneuver, and especially to engage in hit-and-run tactics in the face of more firepower-intensive heavy forces. The Viet Cong during the Vietnam conflict were classic practitioners of this style of warfare, and it consistently frustrated the efforts of much more heavily armed American regular forces until they adopted similar approaches.

The light model has always been a part of the western tradition, although its relative importance has varied. Some might suggest that the cavalry tradition is the prototype for light forces in the American system, comparing the cavalry on horseback with helicopter-borne "air cavalry." Special Forces and Rangers are also examples of the light force model.

A major criticism of light forces is their inability to match up with heavy forces in direct combat; a soldier with a rifle stands little chance against a tank. This criticism is valid and carries considerable weight when the opponent is heavy, in which case heavy forces are the necessary counterweight. A light force facing a heavy force can only deal with it successfully by avoiding the kind of direct confrontations in which the superior firepower of heavy force can be brought to bear to "frame" and destroy the lighter force. This was the lesson painfully learned by Taliban light forces that remained massed in the face of American air forces in 2001. Heavy forces, however, have not always prevailed over light forces in unconventional asymmetrical warfare, as Vietnam provides ample evidence. If the future is likely to hold more asymmetrical than symmetrical foes, then the primacy of heavy forces is not to be taken for granted.

Light or Heavy Futures? If the heavy model served the United States well in the twentieth century, is it equally durable and serviceable for confronting the environment of the twenty-first century? Clearly, the environment within which the use of armed forces is contemplated has changed. The prospect of fighting a symmetrical war against heavy forces using conventional means has all but disappeared. In the words of the original 1997 version of the QDR, the United States lacks a "peer competitor," or foreseeable adversary that poses the kind of military threat for which those forces would be historically appropriate. The question becomes whether this type of force and style of warfare is appropriate for the challenges ahead. The experience of the United States in Afghanistan, where both heavy and light forces were employed in both symmetrical and asymmetrical settings and ways, does little to clarify this debate, as Amplification 9.2 explains. However, there is nothing really new in the debate, nor is it likely to be resolved definitively anytime soon.

Amplification 9.2

LIGHT *AND* HEAVY FORCES?

For a country with considerable resources available to it, the debate over heavy or light forces is not an either/or proposition. Very poor countries may have no affordable alternative to lightly armed forces. The United States, on the other hand, can afford both kinds of forces, and although there will always be a debate over which kind to emphasize at different times and in differing situations, one form or the other is extremely unlikely to disappear.

There are several good reasons why the debate is over emphasis, not the exclusive existence of one kind of force or the other. First, keeping both kinds of forces is politically the easiest solution, especially in the relations between civil authorities and the military itself. An emphasis on light forces has considerably more support within the civilian community than it does within the career military, most of whose leaders have emerged from backgrounds in "heavy" military specialties. Considerable political capital is preserved by arguing the need for both kinds of forces.

Second, it is difficult to argue for the elimination of either emphasis in an uncertain environment. As military apologists are quick to point out, for instance, no one foresaw as little as a few months before the fact that Iraq would invade and conquer Kuwait in 1990. In order to oust the Iraqis, heavy forces were clearly necessary to confront and defeat a heavy Iraqi opponent. Had the choice been made in advance to draw down American heavy assets, the effort would have been considerably more difficult and expensive. A wide variety of forces, in other words, is a hedge against unforeseen contingencies.

Third, eliminating or drastically cutting back heavy armed forces would eliminate the principal military advantage the United States possesses in the world. Confronting the United States frontally in symmetrical combat may be unthinkable under current circumstances, but if the United States self-abnegated its advantage, then such warfare might once again emerge as a real and lively problem.

The arguments over what kinds of forces are preferable in any given environment are endless, and they are almost certainly going to be inconclusive. Heavy forces may arguably be anachronistic today, but that does not mean they always will be. Both light and heavy forces have long traditions in the American and other militaries. Neither is likely to disappear.

The experience in Iraq offers another, different "lesson" about heavy and light forces. The force used to invade and conquer that country was basically light, a highly maneuverable, rapidly mobile force that darted around and through bewildered Iraqi defenders, a very effective application of "shock and awe." These forces were not, however, obviously well configured for the hostile occupation that followed. Highly mobile force vehicles like Hummers had very little (if any) armor. Stripped of armor, they could move rapidly on the attack, but patrolling at low speeds as occupiers, they were vulnerable to enemy snipers and improvised explosive devices (IEDs). The lesson may be that light forces are effective for capturing territory, but heavy forces are necessary for keeping it. Whether the future will hold conquest and occupation is a cornerstone of the post-Iraq debate.

TRADITIONAL RESIDUES

The proper types of traditional military forces and their applications in today's environment remain in question, and the experience of the United States in Iraq and Afghanistan further clouds the outcome. In fact, this evolving experience has called into strong relief two related residual questions about these forces that must be answered for the future application of traditional forces. One question centers on military manpower: how many forces will be needed for what purposes, and how will we acquire them? The other question surrounds military reform and centers on what kind of forces the United States will need or be able to develop to confront the environment in the future.

Military Manpower

In the middle of 2005, and especially since, the United States has faced a mounting manpower problem that threatens to become more acute, to the point of jeopardizing the American military ability to meet current and future military obligations. The major symptom of this crisis was the inability of the armed forces to meet recruiting goals (numbers of recruits necessary to replace retiring members) for several months in a row, necessitating increasingly long, involuntary, and unpopular deployments of existing forces. The major questions this crisis raised were why and how the problem emerged, and what might be done to remedy it, especially in the post-Iraq environment.

The crisis was, in its most general sense, the result of the reversal of two trends from the 1990s. The first is greater utilization of the force, increased operational tempo (or op tempo in military jargon), than in the 1990s. Some increase in force deployment and employment is a natural outgrowth of the attacks of September 11 and the increased need for military force in places like Afghanistan. The principal cause of increased deployment, of course, is the war in Iraq, which is also the cause of much of the manpower crisis.

The Iraq commitment has brought the manpower problem to a head. As of 2007, over 140,000 American troops remained in Iraq, despite congressional and public demands for their withdrawal, and these numbers represented a much larger physical commitment than the administration apparently anticipated in its prewar assessment of the situation (although purely military estimates called for an occupation force of 250,000 to 300,000). In order to have a rotation schedule that is not destructive of troop morale, there has been a heavy reliance on Guard and Reserve units, some of which were experiencing second and third deployments in Iraq that they had not expected when they enlisted.

The result, of course, is the manpower crisis that has emerged. It has two major components and one major implication for the United States. One component is recruiting shortfalls—all of the services have, at one time or another, failed to meet their recruitment goals, and in some cases, the deficits have been substantial. The problem is most acute for ground forces—the so-called combat arms—as is normally the case. The most commonly cited reason that eligible young Americans are not enlisting is their reluctance to serve in Iraq. The combat arms problem is especially acute in the Guard and Reserves. The other component is lower-than-normal reenlistment rates for current military members. Once again, the greatest part of the problem is in the Guard and Reserves, where non-reenlistment rates have approached 50 percent in some cases and might be higher except for "stop loss" orders that keep soldiers involuntarily in uniform and deployed beyond the periods of their enlistment. As long as this situation continues (and the United States maintains a significant force in Iraq), the implication is clear: American armed forces are effectively tied up in that Middle Eastern country, and it would be difficult to organize and mount major military operations elsewhere in any timely fashion.

What can the United States do about this problem? The answer is parallel to the discussion of risk. One way to reduce risk is to increase capability to deflect risk; the parallel for the military would be to increase the size of the armed force. The question is, How? One way is to increase recruitment, by creating greater incentives to join (e.g., more money for college tuition, signing bonuses) or offering better terms of service (e.g., shorter enlistment periods, fewer overseas deployments). The problem in the current context is the opposition of parents to their children's enlistments—opposition that incentives are unlikely to change. The other way to increase the force, of course, is through involuntary service—conscription or the draft—a prospect that is politically suicidal.

Another way to reduce risk is to reduce the threat. In military manpower terms, the parallel would be a decrease in op tempo for the force. With fewer overseas deployments, for instance, major objections to enlistment would be eased, and more current members would likely reenlist (especially Guard and Reserve elements). Clearly, the way to decrease op tempo most dramatically would be a major reduction of the force in Iraq, a move that would have enormous policy implications. The accompanying *Challenge!* box explores this future, which is further examined in the next chapter.

Military Reform

Changes in how and what the military does—military reform—come in several forms, not all of which are relevant for present purposes. Reform may, for instance, refer to changing rules about who can join the military (females, gays) and for what purposes (women in combat roles). It can refer to proper military conduct or the relationship between civilian and military authorities, and a broad variety of other areas of military concern.

For present purposes, consideration will be limited to the questions of military missions and the appropriate and most efficiently configured forces to carry out

Challenge!

MILITARY SERVICE AFTER IRAQ

No American who was not at least eighteen years old on January 1, 1972, has ever been subjected to the possibility of involuntary conscription into the U.S. armed forces. One of the consequences of that condition—the result of negative reactions to the Vietnam War—is that few young Americans have had to give serious thought to the prospect of military service. Since exemption from involuntary service now spans two generations, this means that relatively few Americans in what used to be the "draft eligible" age pool of eighteen- to twenty-six-year-olds even have fathers who served voluntarily or involuntarily.

The attacks on the World Trade Center and the Pentagon produced a spike in interest in enlistment in the armed forces from young men and women across the board, including college students, who were heretofore among the least likely to enlist. This proved to be a temporary reaction—enlistments by college students did not rise appreciably after September 11. The problem of enlistment is more acute regarding Iraq.

What will the post-Iraq situation be like? Prior to our invasion, had military service occurred to you? If it had, what did you conclude about joining one of the services? Has your attitude changed because of the Iraq War? More specifically, has your view changed enough that you give more consideration or less to the services than before?

those missions, questions that will be prominent in the post-Iraq debate. The questions, generally speaking, are logical and sequential. The first concern is what kinds of situations the military will be forced to confront and what outcomes are likely. The second is whether current forces are appropriate for achieving current and future assigned missions, and if they are not, what changes should be made to better align missions and forces. (One could, of course, reverse the sequence of these concerns and determine what to do based on what can be done, but that would be a self-limiting approach more appropriate for a smaller and weaker state with more limited goals in the world than for the United States.)

Military reform in this context is a dynamic and ongoing process, since situations are always changing, as is the ability to deal with the changes that occur. Military reform, however, is an especially wrenching task for military professionals to undertake. The nature of the problem for which military forces are developed is profoundly serious, ultimately the protection of the population from harm, even their survival. That mission tends to make the military conservative in approach, more prone to "tried and true" methods than to untested innovations that might fail at critical points, as suggested in the last chapter. Institutionally, most military professionals get into positions where they may be charged with assessing reform proposals only after they have served long careers in specific warfare specialties to which they have great allegiance and loyalty and which they believe are necessary to the successful prosecution of war. Moreover, the "American way of war" emphasizes the western tradition in warfare and has been relatively successful in prosecuting warfare fought by forces with similar values and rules of war (what are sometimes called conventions of war). Military traditions and values are simply resistant, if not impervious, to reform efforts unless truly traumatic experiences force change upon the military establishment of the day. This observation is not intended to be demeaning or insulting to those charged with reform but only to reflect sources of and reasons for resistance.

The history of military reform efforts since the end of World War II reflects this resistance. As previously noted, the first systematic effort was convened by new Secretary of Defense James Forrestal in 1948 at Key West, Florida, to rationalize military roles and missions. In the early 1990s, President Clinton's first defense secretary, Les Aspin (a former chair of the House Armed Services Committee) commissioned the "Bottom Up Review" (BUR) to conduct an exhaustive review of how the military should operate with the collapse of the Soviet threat. When that effort failed to produce meaningful reform, a frustrated Congress pushed through legislation requiring the QDR. The initial report was produced in 1997. When the George W. Bush administration entered office in January 2001, one of the first assignments facing Secretary of Defense Rumsfeld was to complete the 2001 QDR by September 30 of that year. Overwhelmed by the terrorist attacks of September 11, the new QDR was issued without fanfare on October 1, 2001. A subsequent QDR was produced in 2006, but many of its calls for change were sidetracked when Rumsfeld resigned as secretary shortly after the 2006 election.

Those formulating the 2001 QDR were faced with two major challenges. The first was to describe a national security environment that had changed markedly since the Soviet Union collapsed but that remained murky, shapeless, and difficult to describe adequately. The events of September 11, which occurred after the document was in final draft, seemed to add a new dynamic to that environment. The operational implications of this "new kind of war" were not immediately obvious but were clearly unconventional, adding to rather than clarifying the essential amorphousness of a threat environment that was suddenly more compelling but no less confusing than before.

At the same time, the American military stood at a junction point in terms of force modernization. Critics of the Clinton administration had argued for several years that the numerous deployments of American forces in places like Somalia, Haiti, Bosnia, and Kosovo had come at the expense of modernizing and reequipping a force in desperate need of replenishment and updating. Each of the services had impressive arrays of new and potent weapons systems they were anxious to field to increase their effectiveness. Much of this process was derailed by the operational costs of prosecuting the Iraq War.

The political reactions to terrorism radically changed the fiscal situation for defense. Concerns about the contributions of increased defense spending to returning the country to deficit spending (which had originally been raised over the Bush tax cuts earlier in the year) simply evaporated in the patriotic fervor the attacks created among Americans. Suddenly, resources for the war on terrorism were not in short supply. But what to spend the newly available resources on? And for what purposes should the military receive these rewards? The QDR was intended to provide major guidance in answering both of those questions; as the Iraq War winds down, they will undoubtedly be reenergized.

One of the characteristics of the post-Iraq situation will be, in conventional terms, the lack of a concrete opponent. There is thus no measurable threat against which to develop capabilities. Instead, in the 2001 QDR's words, "the United States is likely to be challenged by adversaries who possess a wide range of capabilities, including asymmetric approaches to warfare, particularly weapons of mass destruction." With uncertainty as the backdrop, force planning will thus be based on capabilities rather than threats in the face of a potentially diverse set of requirements.

A capability-based approach to force development works in two ways. First, it attempts to identify the range of likely problems the country may confront and to develop forces to nullify that range of threats. An example is the projected problem of possession of weapons of mass destruction by rogue states or nonstate actors like Usama bin Laden. The national missile defense system is advertised by its champions as an example of a capability-based response to this potential threat. At the same time, the approach is also designed to exploit American technological superiority in weapons development through the revolution in military affairs. The environment, the 2001 report argues, "requires the transformation of U.S. forces, capabilities, and institutions to extend America's asymmetric advantages well into the future." As an example of exploiting advantage, the Bush administration's first announced modernization (other than its stated commitment to NMD) involved buying three thousand units of the Joint Strike Fighter, a versatile fighter-bomber that will be used in various modified versions by the U.S. Air Force, Navy, and Marines to guarantee American air superiority well into the century.

One of the more interesting questions not fully discussed in the 2001 QDR regards military manpower. The numbers of Americans either on active duty or in the Reserves and National Guard have shrunk from Cold War numbers by about one-third. Partly in response to these reduced overall numbers, the armed forces have turned to the Reserves for a variety of tasks formerly assigned to active forces. Reserves were prominent in the Persian Gulf War (the first major Reserve activation since Korea), and they have played an increasingly major and controversial role in Iraq, as noted. As Amplification 9.3 explains, this increased role was also a conscious Army response to Vietnam, but one that has gone awry.

The new QDR produced in early 2006 largely failed to change this calculus by offering an alternative view of the environment. A radically different assessment was unlikely, however, because the same people who drafted the 2001 document are basically in office now and because, evidence from Iraq notwithstanding, the Bush administration continues to contend the world has not changed much since 2001.

Amplification 9.3

CREIGHTON ABRAMS AND THE ROLE
OF THE RESERVES

In its postmortem of the military experience in Vietnam, one of the questions the U.S. military, and especially the Army, asked was why the military lost the support of the American public for the war effort. Putting the argument in Clausewitzian terms, the trinity of unity among the people, the government, and the army—which the Prussian had argued was essential for successful prosecution of war—had been severed as public support for the war eroded to the point that American withdrawal from the war became inevitable. The question was both why this had happened in Vietnam and how the Army could avoid a recurrence in the future.

The answers were sequential. After carefully reviewing the record, the Army concluded that what allowed the tie between the Army and the public to fray and eventually break was that the public had never been asked to commit to the struggle when the war was contemplated, and that lack of commitment eventually turned into outright opposition. The only overt display of political support for military action in Vietnam was the Gulf of Tonkin Resolution of 1964, when the Congress (acting as the people's representatives) overwhelmingly provided President Lyndon B. Johnson with the authority to take appropriate military action in retaliation for alleged attacks against American warships in the Gulf of Tonkin—a dubious mandate for an eight-year military excursion. The Army, under the leadership of Army Chief of Staff General Creighton B. Abrams, further concluded that the reason public support was not solicited was the fear that the public would voice opposition that would effectively veto the military action before it could be mounted. There was no World War II–style call to war to which the population could reply "yea" or "nay," and Abrams and his colleagues concluded that parallel situations might arise in the future, potentially creating the same problem as occurred in Vietnam.

The Army had a solution: the Reserves. They reasoned that one effective way to ensure that the public had a chance to voice its opinion about potential military deployments was through the prospect of Reserve activation in future conflicts. The prospect that Reserves would be among the first forces called to action meant the people, through their elected representatives, would in effect be asked to voice their approval or disapproval through their willingness to see their friends, neighbors, and loved ones activated and sent off to war. To ensure that Reserve activation would have to occur, the Abrams-led Army took the lead in transferring critical tasks exclusively to the Reserves so that future deployments would be impossible without Reserve participation. Thus, mostly noncombat functions such as medical care, transportation, civic affairs, and aerial refueling are now Reserve responsibilities, and when deployments occur, the Reserves are among the first to be called upon in the defense of their country.

The Abrams strategy backfired in the Iraq War. When the war began, the Guard and Reserves were among the first called to duty. There was little dissent over their activation at the time, both because the action was successfully portrayed as part of the

GWOT (thereby reinforcing the "rally round the flag" effect) and because the war was advertised as a quick and decisive campaign of limited duration (Rumsfeld predicted American troop presence would be down to 6,000 by summer's end of 2003). The Abrams strategy was premised on reasonably short activations (e.g., the Persian Gulf War) or situations where the public did not later turn on the war. In Iraq, the Army got the worst of both worlds: an unpopular war and strain on the Reserves.

Conclusion: The Continuing Relevance of Traditional Forces

By and large, the traditional military problems discussed in this chapter are artifacts of the Cold War and thinking about that period, conditioned by the experience of the first half of the twentieth century (notably the world wars). The end of the Cold War provided a reprieve from the worst possible consequences of the Cold War going "hot" and produced a decade of relative relaxation of military concerns effectively suspended by September 11. The decade of the 1990s was inconclusive in assessing change, and September 11 preempted the conversation. Many of the concerns have been revived by the Iraq War, and its ebb will almost certainly reenergize the debate of the 1990s.

There is clearly much more agreement that change is occurring in the role of military force than there is about its actual direction. In a speech in early November 2001, Secretary of State Colin S. Powell went so far as to declare not only that the Cold War was over, but also that the post–Cold War period had been surmounted as well. He did not, however, describe the new era into which the United States is entering.

What seems clear is that the military requirements of the post–September 11 defense environment are considerably different than those of the Cold War. The large end of the scale of threat with huge arsenals of nuclear weapons and massive conventional forces facing one another in what could have been mankind's most destructive, and possibly last, war has largely disappeared from operations consideration. Russia, the successor to the menacing Soviet Union, is now virtually an American ally, even if there remain sources of strain such as those over missile defenses. The titanic clash that once seemed inevitable now seems a more fanciful possibility. The military artifacts of that confrontation seem oddly archaic as well.

The small end of the scale with no "peer competitor" directly in front or on the horizon is now the most likely source of scenarios. The threats to American security come from more remote places where American interests are less engaged and where the scale and nature of American involvement are less well defined but generally more limited. The terrorism of bin Laden against the American homeland is the apparent exception to that rule, but it is not yet entirely clear whether his, or some other, form of terrorism will fill the center stage of concern or prove to have been a historical aberration.

How relevant are the military concerns and forces of the Cold War for the present and the future? Certainly, the conventional forces and structures inherited from that era proved to be highly useful during the Persian Gulf War of 1990–1991, which helps explain why a more thorough critique of future roles has not been undertaken. The defenders of tradition received a reprieve in the Kuwaiti desert. As the United States began to conduct military operations in Afghanistan in the fall of 2001, those forces seemed adequate to the task as well. Whether either experience was reminiscent of the past or a harbinger of the future is less certain. Iraq fielded a symmetrical Russian-organized and -equipped force in 1990 and apparently learned its lesson and did not stand to fight in 2003. Will future opponents be cooperative and fight by American rules? The inability of America's conventional forces to pacify Iraq raises further questions about the future.

The huge nuclear arsenals and the elaborate constructs for their deterrent roles seem particularly anachronistic, which is partly why Putin and Bush are moving forward on largely dismantling them. Nuclear weapons are not completely irrelevant, of course, because several states possess them and others, including terrorists, may attempt to get them. Both the United States and Russia will clearly maintain arsenals adequately large to promise that an aggressor contemplating attacking either one with weapons of mass destruction will be given pause to face the suicidal consequences of such actions. In the meantime, the emphasis will be on arsenal reductions, the security of remaining forces from undesirable hands, and whether the threat from those undesirable others is sufficient to undertake highly expensive defenses against ballistic missile delivery of WMD.

The structure of conventional forces is also questionable. As noted, the heavy composition of American (and most other western) forces was designed for a massive, western-style World War III clash with like forces from the Soviet world. Now, the only countries that possess those kinds of forces are American allies or friends, and it is not clear how adaptable those forces are for other contingencies, especially the kinds of asymmetrical wars that may be the future. If one needs any preview of how well conventional forces perform in the contemporary environment, one has only to look at Russian performance in Chechnya, where it has pummeled a rag-tag guerrilla force with everything in its conventional arsenal for nearly a decade but has been unable to bring the Chechens, reinforced with *mujahadeen* from other Islamic countries in the region, to their knees. American conventional forces are undoubtedly more capable than their Russian counterparts, but the question remains. Iraq is the current testing ground; the results are not encouraging.

Conventional forces are buffeted from both ends of the spectrum. On one hand, their relevance in the face of unconventional forces bent on devising ways to negate their advantages has not been proven. If technological proficiency and mass always prevail, the United States must have won in Vietnam. At the same time, the United States may well produce capabilities that make current capabilities obsolete or vulnerable. Although not reflected in the 2001 or 2006 QDR, candidate Bush talked about simply leapfrogging a generation of weapons procurement for this reason—for instance, not building a new generation of manned fighter aircraft, but waiting for the technology to provide unmanned drone aircraft to do the same things fighters do without endangering human pilots. In the same vein, some naval critics see aircraft carriers becoming as obsolete as battleships did in World War II. Just as aircraft flying off carriers reduced battleships from dreadnaughts to targets, so too may advanced cruise missiles reduce current carriers to vulnerable targets.

Traditional thinking, planning, and force structure and uses were not discredited by Iraq, but neither have they been vindicated. If the military purpose in Iraq was to create the conditions where a pro-western democracy could take root and prosper (the stated objective), it has not been achieved. The question is, Why? The answer is complex and murky. Whatever the answer may be, it will undoubtedly have profound implications for the reformulation of traditional problems—and their solutions.

STUDY/DISCUSSION QUESTIONS

1. How are current American conceptions of traditional military problems tied to the Cold War? Discuss.
2. Discuss the evolution of strategic nuclear forces and plans for their use in terms of the seminal events of the nuclear age, the concept of deterrence, and U.S. nuclear strategies of deterrence.
3. What is nuclear proliferation? Discuss its aspects and evolution, its dynamics (the $N+1$ problem), and the current state of the concern, including the problems associated with attempts to limit proliferation.
4. What is missile defense? What are the arguments for and against it? What is the current controversy over American plans to deploy such defenses?
5. Discuss the traditional role of conventional forces, including the debate over heavy and light forces.
6. What is the contemporary debate over military manpower? How has this debate been made more lively by the Iraq War?
7. Why is the debate over military reform so contentious? What is the current state of that debate?

SELECTED BIBLIOGRAPHY

Borden, William Liscum. *There Will Be No Time: The Revolution in Strategy*. New York: Macmillan, 1946.

Brodie, Bernard. *The Absolute Weapon: Atomic Power and World Order*. New York: Harcourt Brace, 1946.

———. *Strategy in the Missile Age*. Princeton, NJ: Princeton University Press, 1959.

Carter, Ashton B. "How to Counter WMD." *Foreign Affairs* 83, 5 (September/October 2004), 72–85.

Clark, Ronald W. *The Greatest Power on Earth: The International Race for Nuclear Supremacy from Earliest Theory to Three-Mile Island*. New York: Harper and Row, 1980.

Clausewitz, Carl von. *On War*. Princeton, NJ: Princeton University Press, 1976.

Collins, John M. *Grand Strategy: Principles and Practices*. Annapolis, MD: Naval Institute Press, 1973.

Deutch, John. "A Nuclear Posture for Today." *Foreign Affairs* 84, 1 (January/February 2005), 49–60.

Drew, Dennis M., and Donald M. Snow. *Making Strategy for the Twenty-First Century: An Introduction to National Security Processes and Problems*. Montgomery, AL: Air University Press, 2006.

Gabel, Josiane. "The Role of Nuclear Weapons After September 11." *Washington Quarterly* 28, 1 (Winter 2004–2005), 181–195.

Gormley, Dennis M. "Missile Defence Myopia: Lessons from the Iraq War." *Survival* 45 (Winter 2003–2004), 61–86.

Guertner, Gary L., and Donald M. Snow. *The Last Frontier: An Analysis of the Strategic Defense Initiative*. Lexington, MA: Lexington Books, 1986.

Harrison, Selig. "Did North Korea Cheat?" *Foreign Affairs* 84, 1 (January/February 2005), 99–110.

Ivanov, Igor. "The Missile Defense Mistake: Undermining Strategic Stability and the ABM Treaty." *Foreign Affairs* 79, 5 (September/October 2000), 15–20.

Kramer, Andrew E. "Russia Steps Back from Key Arms Treaty." *New York Times* (online) July 14, 2007.

Lieber, Kier A., and Daryl G. Press. "The Rise of U.S. Nuclear Superiority." *Foreign Affairs* 85, 2 (March/April 2006), 42–54.

McCaffrey, Barry R. "Looking Beyond Iraqi Freedom: Future Enemies Won't Roll Over So Easily." *Armed Forces Journal* 140 (July 2003), 8–9.

McNamara, Robert S. "Apocalypse Soon." *Foreign Policy* (May/June 2005), 28–35.

Nuechterlein, Donald E. *A Cold War Odyssey*. Lexington: University of Kentucky Press, 1997.

Payne, Keith B. "The Nuclear Posture Review: Setting the Record Straight." *Washington Quarterly* 28, 3 (Summer 2005), 135–152.

Perkowich, George. "How to Be a Nuclear Watchdog." *Foreign Policy* (January/February 2005), 28–35.

Pilat, Joseph F. "Reassessing Assurances in a Unipolar World." *Washington Quarterly* 28, 2 (Spring 2005), 59–70.

Quadrennial Defense Review. Washington, DC: U.S. Department of Defense, 2001 and 2006.

Rhodes, Richard. *The Making of the Atomic Bomb*. New York: Touchstone Books, 1998.

Snow, Donald M. *Nuclear Strategy in a Dynamic World: Policy for the 1980s*. Tuscaloosa: University of Alabama Press, 1981.

———. *The Necessary Peace: Nuclear Weapons and Superpower Relations*. Lexington, MA: Lexington Books, 1987.

Specter, Arlen, with Christopher Walsh. "Dialogue with Adversaries." *Washington Quarterly* 30, 1 (Winter 2006–2007), 9–26.

Winner, Andrew C. "The Proliferation Security Initiative: The New Face of Interdiction." *Washington Quarterly* 28, 2 (Spring 2005), 129–143.

CHAPTER 10

The Legacies of Iraq

PREVIEW

It has been maintained throughout the text that the outcome of the Iraq War will affect the way the United States acts in national security matters for some time after the war is over. This chapter examines why and how that outcome will have an effect. It begins by looking at the evolution of the American relationship with Iraq leading to and including the invasion, asking whether the invasion was worthwhile and whether its goals were attainable, with a focus on the five-year-long American occupation. It then raises the question of what went wrong in Iraq, beginning with a comparison between the American experiences in Vietnam and Iraq and including an assessment of how the American exit is likely to occur and with what consequences. The chapter concludes by looking at how the entire Iraq experience will influence the post-Iraq attitudes of the United States, with conscious comparisons between the post-Vietnam and post-Iraq eras.

At this juncture, it is difficult, and some would argue impossible, to discuss the legacies of the Iraq War for the United States. What are the lessons of the American war effort in Iraq for Iraq and the Iraqi people? And what do those lessons mean for the future of American national security policy? Will the outcome embolden the United States to engage in future actions in places where an analogy with Iraq can be made, or will it discourage such future actions? Clearly, these are pivotal questions the answers to which will help shape the American defense posture and attitude toward the world in the years immediately ahead. But how can Americans know, or even speculate reasonably, about what those lessons and their meanings are?

At mid-year 2008, when this edition of this text first appeared, U.S. forces remained engaged in Iraq and seemed destined to stay there in some numbers at least until the end of the Bush administration and almost certainly for some period of time into the term of Bush's successor. Describing and analyzing the aftermath of an ongoing event inevitably involves extrapolating beyond facts (events that have happened) into a projection of likely facts that may or may not occur—predicting the future. Predictions, of course, can prove to be either right or wrong, and since the human (social and behavioral) sciences lack the established theories of the natural sciences that allow reliable predictions, one cannot know for sure whether those predictions are true or false until after the fact. That is simply a consequence of the nature and extent of human knowledge about human behavior.

That having been said, certain predictions seem sufficiently rooted in actual experience to appear reasonably safe, and it is on the basis of those projections that a tentative list of legacies of the Iraq experience can be hypothesized (recognizing that hypotheses can prove right or wrong). One reasonably safe projection is that American participation in a war it started will wind down toward an end in the not-so-distant future, and that the end of that engagement will not likely be because of some dramatic turn of events that supporters and critics can agree constitutes "victory" for the United States or for the Iraqis (or at least certainly not all Iraqis). Rather, the ultimate resolution of the Iraq situation will be determined by Iraqis (probably influenced by their regional neighbors) after the Americans leave. When the Americans depart, the situation will almost certainly be fluid and uncertain, and almost certainly accompanied by some increase in violence and suffering among the Iraqi people until a settlement is reached and some form of order returns to the country.

Supporters of the war in the United States will likely contest the desirability of this outcome, but a bloody form of conflict resolution in Iraq will likely occur regardless of when the United States decides to end its involvement, and the violence that ensues after that departure will increase American angst over the outcome because of the unavoidable knowledge that most of it probably would not have occurred (if any of it would have) had the United States not intruded itself into Iraq in the first place. As part of this process, supporters of the war will continue to assert that the United States should continue its involvement until the Iraqis are able to fend peacefully for themselves, and opponents will maintain equally forcefully that such an outcome is impossible regardless of how long the United States stays. What is clear is that American patience with the war in Iraq is at least as frayed as it was in Vietnam thirty-five years ago and that those who argue for disengagement will prevail, just as they did in Southeast Asia.

The process by which disengagement will occur was generally evident by early 2007, and the parallels with Vietnam were stunning. The 2006 off-year elections that returned Democratic Party majorities to both houses of Congress were a direct mandate by the American people in repudiation of the Iraq War. The Bush administration did not acknowledge this mandate directly but instead began a process eerily similar to the process of Vietnamization in that conflict. In Vietnam, the American objective shifted from assuring the independence of South Vietnam (the Republic of Vietnam) to giving the regime a *reasonable chance* to maintain its sovereignty by arming it and attempting to remove the ability of the North Vietnamese to penetrate the country. These efforts, of course, ultimately failed when American combat forces withdrew in 1973.

Although supporters of the war deny it, a similar policy of *Iraqification* was set in place in 2007 (the term appeared briefly in 2004 but was dismissed as defeatist by the administration). The tool for instituting the policy was the so-called surge of additional American forces into Iraq. Their purposes were to reduce the pressure on the regime from various insurgent groups (Sunnis, Shiites, and Al Qaeda in Iraq) while preparing (arming and training) military and constabulary forces loyal to the regime to replace those American forces, at which point the United States can safely leave. Because the Iraqi government continued to balk at the kinds of reforms the United States felt necessary throughout 2007, the withdrawal could not be justified as *guaranteeing* the outcome of Iraqi democracy but rather as offering a maximum possibility of this outcome. In Vietnam, the South Vietnamese were declared ready to protect themselves in 1973, more because that declaration was politically necessary in the United States than because of the objective state of those forces. The same will almost certainly prove true in Iraq.

A second safe assumption is that Americans will be divided about the outcome in Iraq regardless of what it is. If one rules out the likelihood of a clear-cut American "victory" (depending on how that is defined) around which almost all Americans could unite, the American people will likely be divided into three groups regarding the outcome. Some Americans, most of whom have opposed the war all along or who have come to oppose it, will support the outcome, because they feel either it was inevitable or it produces what they view as the greater good of removing Americans from Iraqi harm's way. Some Americans, most of whom have been generally supportive of the war, will decry the outcome, because it does not achieve the American political objectives for going into Iraq and because the result will entail additional suffering for Iraqis whose suffering at the hands of Saddam Hussein was one of their reasons for supporting the invasion in the first place. Yet others, who may have been supporters or opponents or even neutral for some time, will simply be relieved the war is over and will not care a great deal about what happens in Iraq afterward, a sentiment widely felt in the United States after the fall of Saigon in 1975. How Americans feel about leaving Iraq will, in turn, influence what they feel is to be learned from it.

A third reasonably safe prediction is that the post-Iraq assessment of the war—the debate over "lessons learned," in military parlance—will be contentious, and in some cases acrimonious and vindictive. Because the Iraq War became intensely unpopular and divisive in a way and to an extent not seen in the United States since the Vietnam War, there will be a "blame game" of recriminations about how and why the United States stumbled into what a growing consensus agrees was a mistaken adventure. In some ways, the public acrimony has been lessened because President Bush's intransigence in the face of demands for disengagement has almost certainly increased and solidified opposition to the war in the same way that Americans rallied against the war policies of Lyndon Johnson a generation ago.

Whether one accepts that there is a valid analogy between Vietnam and Iraq or not or the extent to which the analogy holds, there will be parallels drawn between these two conflicts as military and civilian institutions and analysts dissect and argue about what went wrong. Rightly or wrongly, the focus of these discussions will be on the mistakes that were made, whether in deciding if the United States should have become involved in the first place, how that mission has been carried out, or ultimately, how and under what circumstances to leave.

A fourth safe prediction is that the Iraq War will produce a revived debate about the circumstances and means of using American forces in the future. In some ways, this debate will be a revival of discussions begun in the 1990s and suspended by September 11 and the subsequent GWOT—of which, after all, Iraq has been described as an application or "theater." This debate will likely be reminiscent in tone and thoroughness to a similar retrospective after the American disengagement from Vietnam. Whether the analogy will hold regarding conclusions is, to some extent, unknowable, but Iraq has the significant potential to have as profound an impact on American national security as did Vietnam. There *will be* an Iraq hangover, just as there was a Vietnam hangover. What the "cure" for this current hangover will or may be is the subject of this chapter.

There is a further note of comparison between the Vietnam and Iraq conflicts that should be mentioned at the outset by means of helping to create the framework within which the current analysis will proceed. Vietnam produced an absolute flood of literature, almost all of it critical of why and how the United States became so involved in that country's travails and failed to resolve them to American satisfaction. The same is true of the Iraq War, which has produced particularly impressive analyses both of why the United States became involved—with an emphasis on the mistaken nature of that involvement—and why it has failed to achieve its objectives in the war (largely critiques of the way the Bush administration sought to rebuild the country after the initial conquest). This literature is already extensive, is growing, and covers much of the critical ground about the war. A hopefully helpful sample of this literature is included in the "Selected Bibliography" for the chapter. The point is that it is both impossible and unnecessary to cover all the matters in all the details that this literature includes in this chapter, since others have done so, mostly in more articulate fashion than here.

With that said, the chapter will proceed as follows. First, it will look at the decision process leading to the American decision and implementation of that decision to engage in an act of international aggression and invade, conquer, and occupy the sovereign state of Iraq. Some may question the tone (or even the relevance) of that typecasting of the act, but it is internationally legally sound. The theme of this examination will be whether the United States *should* have invaded Iraq (and by extension, what it should do in similar situations in the future). Second, the analysis will turn to the actual conduct of the war and, more specifically, what went wrong and whether the problems were foreseeable and remediable. This examination will include a comparison between the Vietnam and Iraq experiences, since common points may influence the depth of lessons and changes derived from the retrospective. Third, there will be an examination of the lessons of Iraq, which emphasizes what the United States did correctly and incorrectly and thus what from the experience should be retained and replicated and what should be changed. Finally, the chapter will conclude with the legacies of the Iraq War in the sense of how that experience will help shape the American national security environment, American perceptions of that environment, and how the United States will organize to interact with and influence that environment in the coming years.

MARCHING OR STUMBLING INTO IRAQ?

Prior to 1990, most Americans had barely heard of the Middle Eastern country of Iraq, at alone know who its leader was or what relationship the United States had with that distant part of the world. Then, in August 1990, Iraq invaded neighboring Kuwait at the direction of its dictatorial leader, Saddam Hussein, thereby imperiling American and other access to the region's primary commodity, petroleum. Suddenly, the United States took the global leadership in evicting the Iraqi dictator from Kuwait under the banner of Operation Desert Shield/Storm, leading to the brief and highly successful Persian Gulf War of 1990–1991. Equally suddenly, all Americans knew about Iraq and Saddam Hussein.

The Persian Gulf War did not end to the satisfaction of all observers. The coalition formed to react to Saddam Hussein's aggression fulfilled its United Nations mandate to restore the *status quo ante*, which meant evicting Iraq from Kuwait and restoring Kuwaiti sovereignty. The Hussein government, however, remained intact and unrepentant, and this fact troubled some observers, including a group who became known as the *neoconservatives* (or neocons, for short) who had advocated his overthrow for years before his action in Kuwait. In the eyes of some (but not all) observers, the Iraq War of 2003 was born of the decision not to overthrow Hussein in 1991.

The Iraqi situation remained contentious but less than critical between 1991 and the terrorist attacks of 2001. The neoconservatives (e.g., Richard Perle, Paul Wolfowitz, and Douglas Feith) who had argued volubly for going ahead and marching into Baghdad in 1991 and toppling the Iraqi regime left power with the election of Democrat William J. Clinton in 1992. Iraq never left the public agenda altogether, as the United States, Great Britain, and (for a time) France maintained a "no-fly zone" over much of northern and southern Iraq to keep the Hussein regime from wreaking revenge on Kurdish and Shiite groups that had engaged in a 1991 plot (encouraged informally by the United States) to overthrow the regime. Operation Provide Comfort (renamed Northern Watch) and Southern Watch put the United States at odds with the Iraqi regime, resulting in numerous incidents of the Iraqis attempting to shoot down allied reconnaissance aircraft. In addition, President Clinton authorized a limited bombing campaign against Iraq in 1998 (Operation Desert Fox). Policy toward Iraq was part of the broader regional policy of "dual containment," aimed at containing the ambitions of both Iraq and Iran. When George W. Bush was elected the forty-third president of the United States in 2000, Iraq policy was once again on the table, leading to the Iraq War.

The Road to War: Was the United States Justified?

The election of George W. Bush was critical to the road to war in three ways. First, Bush himself had become convinced that Saddam Hussein needed to be overthrown. In December 1997, he had given an interview to a San Antonio newspaper in which he argued that his father had been correct in not taking the Iraqi regime down, because the result would have been a "civil war." By 1999, he had changed his mind, hinting broadly in a December speech at the Ronald Reagan library that he favored "regime change" (the early euphemism for overthrowing Saddam Hussein). As he prepared for the 2000 election campaign, Paul D. Wolfowitz, who would later be christened the "father" of the Iraq War, was one of his closest foreign policy advisors (one of the "Vulcans" organized by Condoleezza Rice and described by Mann). Even before September 11, war against Iraq was not far from the center of the foreign policy agenda.

Second, the election of Bush brought the neoconservatives into key policy positions for the first time. Supported by figures like Vice President Cheney and Secretary of Defense Rumsfeld, a number of advisors like Wolfowitz found their way back into government in more powerful and influential positions than they had previously held. Among their major agenda items were overthrowing Saddam Hussein and replacing his regime with a "model" democracy in Iraq and guaranteeing the security of Israel. The two policies were linked by the belief that the flowering of democracy in Iraq would result in demands in other Middle Eastern countries for democratization, which, in turn, would produce more peaceful regimes in the region less hostile to Israel.

The third event, of course, was the terrorist attacks of September 11. Their direct ties to activating plans for attacking Iraq are disputed, but observers such as Clarke and Woodward maintain that one of the first post–September 11 queries by President Bush was for evidence of Iraqi complicity. The Bush administration denies this assertion, but as Chandrasekaran (among others) maintains, Bush "gave the order to begin planning for the invasion of Iraq just a few months after the September 11, 2001, attacks." This claim is widely accepted by others (see Gordon and Trainor, Packer, Record, Ricks, and Woodward, for instance) and is obliquely admitted by the commander of the operation, General Tommy Franks, in his autobiography. At a minimum, the September 11 tragedy brought to the fore the possible ties of Iraq to terrorists, which became part of the official rationale for overthrowing the regime, as energized by alleged Iraqi possession of WMD that the Iraqi regime might provide to terrorists. Thus, a bridge was built to the emerging GWOT.

The rising justification for an invasion of Iraq was thus the result of a pastiche of motivations that were gradually tied together. Bush himself had virtually no experience in foreign affairs and no known expertise on the Middle East, but he disliked Saddam Hussein, because of his alleged authorization of an assassination attempt in 1993 against Bush's father (on a visit to Kuwait) and because Bush had apparently been influenced by advisors who favored the overthrow. As a result, Iraq was included in the "axis of evil" designation (along with the DPRK and Iran) in Bush's January 2002 State of the Union address. Saddam Hussein's regime had been less than totally forthcoming during the 1990s regarding whether it maintained or was producing WMD (a possession they denied), and the regime had become increasingly notorious for its ruthless suppression of its Kurdish and Shiite populations, including allegations of crimes against humanity by the regime (which were the basis for trying and executing Hussein). The resulting demonization of the regime was completed by the allegations of ties between the Iraqis and Al Qaeda (although not Al Qaeda in Iraq, which did not come into existence until 2004). This confluence provided the fuel needed by the neoconservatives to press the case successfully for what they had wanted to do all along—overthrow Saddam Hussein.

Was the invasion, conquest, and occupation of Iraq justified? In other words, should the United States have done what it did? In the debate that has surrounded the prosecution of the war (and especially the various forms of insurgency that have been ongoing since at least 2004), this question has largely been submerged on the basis that the *real* problem is what to do now. The imputation is that whether the effort was justifiable in the first place is academic, since the United States is engaged and must figure out how to make the best of the situation.

Whether the United States should have gone into Iraq in the first place is, however, critical in determining what can be learned from the experience. The comparison with Vietnam again looms. In retrospect, most observers would agree that American participation in that war was unwarranted and that the country would have been better off had it abstained. The basic retrospective argument is that American vital interests were never engaged in Vietnam, and the evidence is that the worst-case outcome, the North Vietnamese uniting of the country, occurred and the United States was not especially affected fundamentally by that outcome. If anything, all the involvement did was to prolong the war and cause enormous suffering for the Vietnamese and for the Americans that simply delayed an outcome that would have occurred much more rapidly and with much less bloodshed had the United States not intervened. Moreover, the erosive effects on the United States that participation in the eight-year-long war caused would have been avoided. It is hard to argue that the United States would not have been better off if the country had never intervened in Vietnam.

The situation in Iraq, of course, was not the same as in Vietnam. In Vietnam, there was an ongoing conflict (whether it was an internal civil war or a war between sovereign countries—North and South Vietnam—was disputed) that the United States sought to influence. In Iraq, there was undoubtedly great privation and injustice, but there was no war until the United States started it by invading. That said, the question remains whether the United States should have taken the action it did. Like Vietnam, that is a two-part question that is a matter of perspective. The parts include whether the case was adequate at the time for invasion and whether it appears to have been justifiable in retrospect. People can reasonably disagree depending on the perspectives from which they come and based on the determination of facts not so clear at the time as they became later.

Vietnam was justified largely in terms of the spread of Communism and specifically the so-called domino effect that argued if Vietnam fell to Communism, other neighbors would follow like rows of dominos being toppled. This assessment proved correct but largely irrelevant, since the companion assumption that U.S. interests would be vitally affected by the dominos falling proved false—something not entirely knowable at the time initial decisions were made. The decision to invade Iraq was based officially on arguments already mentioned: Saddam Hussein's purported possession of WMD and his intransigence in the face of international inspectors of the country; his alleged ties to terrorism, thus ties of the Iraqi regime to the GWOT; and, more nebulously, the desirability of instituting a model democracy in Iraq that would serve as a regional beacon.

Two questions must be raised about these justifications. First, were they it accurate (and should those who made the allegations have known if they were not)? In the acrimony over Iraq, it has been generally established that the Iraqis did not have WMD (none has ever been found) and that there were no ties to Al Qaeda (in fact, the secular Hussein regime opposed the religious terrorism associated with Al Qaeda). One can debate the desirability of democratizing Iraq, although the question of whether this was ever feasible (discussed below) remains contentious. The question of whether those who made the decision did or should have known the truth of their justifications remains contentious; there were, however, numerous critics in and out of government who denied both the principal reasons were true. Whether there were other, hidden reasons also remains a matter of disagreement, discussed in Amplification 10.1.

The second question is whether these justifications, even if true, constituted sufficient grounds to undertake the actions that were carried out. This question largely pits the traditional realists against the neoconservatives and centers on the question of vital interests. Put in ways raised in Chapter 7, would the worst possible outcome of the situation in Iraq (possession of WMD, ties to terrorists, possible collaboration with terrorists on WMD) create a situation so intolerable that force was necessary to bring about a tolerable outcome? The answer varied, depending on the perspective from which the analyst comes.

From the neoconservative position, the question was irrelevant: the goal of creating a new Middle East reality was so compelling that traditional concerns based in vital interests did not apply. Indeed, one administration aide, in response to a question on the subject of the relevance of realism to the situation, allegedly replied, "We make our own realities." From the other side of the ledger, traditional realists answered the vital interest question negatively, arguing that the policy of dual containment had effectively managed relations with Iraq and that the prospect that Iraq would supply terrorists with WMD that might ultimately be used against the United States was theoretically possible but too remote to justify the strong measures taken. The subsequent revelations that both the WMD and the terrorism arguments were based on false assertions only added to this criticism.

Was the Mission Feasible?

The other major prewar question was whether the objectives the United States laid out for itself in Iraq were attainable. That question is also critical to a post-Iraq assessment: if the Iraq mission was in fact impossible to achieve, then it was arguably a fool's errand to undertake it in the first place. That is a harsh accusation, and it requires examination from both a political and a military standpoint, with implicit comparisons to the parallel process in Vietnam.

The Political Objective. Whether the political objective in Iraq was feasible depends on what that objective was (for a discussion of this concept, see Snow and Drew). If it was the overthrow and removal from power of Saddam Hussein—which was certainly at least an instrumental goal necessary before others could be attained—or the

Amplification 10.1

HIDDEN AGENDAS IN IRAQ?

Like Vietnam, the war in Iraq has fueled speculation about whether the stated objectives of the United States were the *actual* reasons for the war or whether there were other, more subterranean motivations. In both cases, such speculation was stimulated by judgments that the stated objectives did not justify the options chosen, so that there *must* have been deeper, but not publicly stated, reasons. In Vietnam, these alternate explanations tended to be conspiratorial: the need of the military-industrial complex to have a war to create profits or the desire to control natural resources in Southeast Asia, for example. In Iraq, two alternate objectives have been put forward (and denied by those in decision-making positions): petroleum and Israeli security.

The argument about petroleum is straightforward and is believed by many Iraqis. In this argument, the real underlying motivation of the United States is control of the considerable Iraqi oil reserves through the overthrow of the Saddam Hussein regime and its replacement with a compliant Iraqi regime that would guarantee the United States secure access to Persian Gulf petroleum at a reasonable price, much as the Shah of Iran did before the Iranian Revolution of 1979, and free the United States of its dependence on a fickle ally, Saudi Arabia. As Record puts it, "The creation of an American client state in Iraq would, it was believed, provide a substitute for a U.S.-Saudi security relationship compromised by Saudi promotion of Islamic extremism," a reference to Saudi Arabia's reluctance to suppress known anti-American, pro–Al Qaeda supporters. Indeed, a rumor circulated in the Pentagon before Operation Iraqi Freedom (OIF, the code name for the invasion) began that planners had initially favored calling the mission Operation Iraqi Liberation before someone pointed out the potentially embarrassing acronym (OIL) the name would create.

The other argument is that the real underlying reason for the invasion was to secure Israeli security in the region. This argument is consistent with the general neoconservative belief that American and Israeli interests and security in the region are closely intertwined—if not synonymous—and that the requisite for Israeli security is a reduction of animosity toward Israel among the Islamic states of the region. Extrapolating from this premise and adding the *democratic peace hypothesis* (that democratic states do not attack one another), it then follows that the installation of a model democratic regime in Iraq (which would be envied and emulated by its neighbors) is a necessary and important first step toward securing Israeli security and thus a more tranquil Middle East (which, incidentally, would be more amenable to guaranteeing American access to the region's petroleum). In addition, Record argues, "a benign Iraq . . . would redound to the immense strategic benefit of Israel, America's chief client state in the Middle East and a major focus of neoconservative security strategy."

removal of Iraqi WMD (which apparently did not exist), then it was clearly attainable. Likewise, the connection between Iraq and terrorism proved false and, like the American objective of ending impressments in the War of 1812 (a British policy it had renounced before the war began), had been achieved before the war. If anything, the invasion *created* the terrorist problem, since Al Qaeda in Iraq came into existence in 2004, at least partially as a response to the American occupation.

If one accepts that the real political objective in Iraq was to transform that country into a model democratic, free-enterprise country, then the question of feasibility arises. As virtually anyone who has ever studied Iraq knows, it is an almost totally artificial state—a country with no historical, linguistic, religious, or other reason for being in its present configuration—with enormously deep rifts within the population that virtually guarantee its instability. The by-now-familiar divisions within the population (Arabs versus Kurds, Sunnis versus Shiites, for instance) were widely known in the expert community, which almost universally regarded Iraq as one of the worst places on Earth in which to try to create a political democracy—or, for that matter, to become involved in at almost any significant level. Moreover, most of the economy was state-owned, and transforming it into a kind of American-model free-enterprise status was a daunting physical and legal proposition.

Was this perspective known and available to the Bush administration when it reached the decision to invade Iraq (regardless of exactly when that determination was made)? The answer is yes. More specifically, *all of the problems associated with Iraq that have become obvious since the occupation began were known in advance of the invasion, and they were ignored.* That is a harsh indictment, but it is one supported overwhelmingly by the evidence. On the eve of the war, Deputy Secretary of Defense Paul D. Wolfowitz was so bold as to tell a congressional committee that invading Iraq would be much easier than dealing with Afghanistan, because there were *no ethnic divisions* in Iraq. As plans for the occupation were being made and implemented, so-called Arabists (people with knowledge and experience in the area) were consciously excluded from the process because their experience allegedly prejudiced them against the goal of democratization (this allegation is confirmed by virtually all the sources listed in the "Selected Bibliography"). To cite an example of this ignorance, Chandrasekaran raises the case of one U.S. official sent to Baghdad as part of the occupation, Thomas Foley, an investment banker and classmate of President Bush at Harvard Business School. Foley's mission was to privatize the Iraqi economy, which meant expropriating state-owned enterprises and selling them to private investors. Under the Geneva Conventions of War (1899), such expropriations by an occupying power are illegal under international law. When informed of this fact, Foley allegedly replied, "I don't give a s– about international law. I made a commitment to the president that I'd privatize Iraq's businesses."

There was thus considerable sentiment, primarily within the expert (academic and policy-examining) community, that an attempt to democratize Iraq faced, at a minimum, an uphill fight. Larry Diamond, who was a pro-democracy scholar and former colleague of Condoleezza Rice at Stanford University and who became a part of the administration's attempt to institute democracy, provides a particularly detailed account of the problems encountered. Moreover, the president himself had, as noted, correctly predicted that overthrowing Hussein would result in a civil war, an assessment also made by the State Department and concurred in by the CIA, both of which produced detailed assessments of the problems that would be encountered in an occupation (among other things, that the occupation would not long be viewed as a liberation). Indeed, a prewar study in early 2003 by Crane and Terrill of the U.S. Army's Strategic Studies Institute (an arm of the Army War College) conclusively made the argument in some prescient detail about the problems war on Iraq would create. Yet there was relatively little vocal objection in advance, and there is hardly any evidence that negative assessments were considered within the administration. Why not?

The answer bears another eerie parallel to Vietnam. Within the Johnson administration, there was also counsel that the situation was a civil war that the United States could not "win" (in the sense of assuring the success of interests it favored) by a variety of sources, and most notably Southeast Asia experts in and outside the government (see, for instance, Kattenburg). These voices were ignored in the rush to contain Communism on the Southeast Asian peninsula, just as skeptics of the prospects for Iraqi democracy were likewise ignored by proponents of the war. In both cases, most of the critics came from outside an administration that placed particular value on loyalty and conformance to established positions. Opposition was not only not to be heard or tolerated, but also to be punished whenever possible.

If the stated mission in Iraq was indeed quixotic, then one can argue that it should not have been undertaken in the first place. As the prospects of a democratic outcome have faded, the fallback position is that the United States did remove a hated and ruthless dictator and give the Iraqi people the ability to engage in self-determination. Three questions, however, remain, that must be part of the post-Iraq assessment, just as they were after Vietnam.

The first and most obvious is whether the stated goal of the mission—democratization of Iraq—was a reasonable goal or a neoconservative pipe dream. Was it possible to attain the objective? If not (and those involved did or should have known it was not), should it have been attempted? Second, was attaining the goal worthy of the use of the military instrument of power? Were American vital interests involved in instituting democracy in Iraq? How is the international environment more or less tolerable for the United States with a democratic or nondemocratic Iraq? Third, was the current result (Iraq in the midst of a multisided insurgency that neither the Iraqis nor American arms can quell) predictable in advance? Did, in other words, the invasion do more harm than good? And was that outcome knowable in advance?

The postwar assessment about Vietnam would seem to be that the mission was not feasible, that subsequent events have demonstrated that the desired (and failed) American outcome has not indelibly harmed American interests, and that the net effect of the eight-year involvement was mostly to increase the number of Vietnamese (and Americans) killed to achieve the same outcome that would have occurred without that involvement. Will the assessment about Iraq be the same? And what does that tell Americans about similar future situations?

The Military Objective. Militarily, Iraq is a tale of two wars, one highly successful and one arguably quite unsuccessful. The successful phase was the *invasion and conquest* of Iraq. With a few minor problems that are predictable in war (see Franks and Gordon and Trainor), this phase of the war went smoothly. Whether the ease of attaining the necessary (but clearly not sufficient) goal of toppling the regime was the result of exquisite planning and execution (the official view) or the lack of an organized resistance by the Iraqis is a question that eventually will have to be answered, but the military has, by and large, been highly self-congratulatory about the operation with little dissent.

The other part of the war, the *occupation*, is another matter. This aspect, known as Phase IV by war planners, has been the subject of withering criticism, on two basic grounds. First, critics (including the preponderance of military professionals) have argued that the size and composition of the occupation force was and continues to be grossly inadequate for the task of occupying, pacifying, and rebuilding the country. The OIF force that invaded the country was around 150,000 strong, despite admonitions from, among others, Army Chief of Staff Eric Shinseki that a force of 250,000–300,000 was needed to conquer *and* pacify the country. When the invasion's initial phase was successful with lower numbers, Shinseki (and others like him) were dismissed as alarmists by overly optimistic supporters of Secretary Rumsfeld, who had demanded the smaller-sized force that carried out the mission. It will be recalled that Rumsfeld (and Cheney) believed before the war that the Americans would be treated as liberators and that only a small residual American force would remain in Iraq after summer 2003. The need to augment the remaining 130,000 Americans in Iraq in 2007 with a "surge" of additional combat troops to put down the insurgency (and help create the conditions for Iraqification) provides further evidence that, over four years after the invade and conquer phase, the numbers were still not adequate for Phase IV occupation and rebuilding. It might be added that calls for the surge in American combat troops begun in late spring 2007, and especially its possible augmentation with more additional troops in July 2007, bore an eerie resemblance to General William Westmoreland's plea in late 1967 for additional troops to finish off the North Vietnamese and Viet Cong, because he could see "a light at the end of the tunnel" reachable with those extra troops.

The second criticism of Phase IV has been about the inadequacy of planning and execution for what followed the conquest. The available literature suggests that planning was flawed in at least two ways. One is that it was not considered very important by wartime planners, who simply assumed that things would work out on their own. Rumsfeld's famous "freedom's untidy" response to reports of looting in Baghdad is exemplary of this lack of concern. Such planning as occurred went on in Douglas Feith's Office of Special Plans within the Pentagon, a mid-level part of the Department of Defense bureaucracy, and was heavily influenced by exiles like neoconservative favorite Ahmed Chalabi. The expert community was studiously ignored: the State Department because of its negativity toward the prospects of success in Iraq and United Nations experts in postconflict reconstruction and state building because they were deemed to be "too liberal." In retrospect, those ignored experts very accurately predicted the problems that would be encountered and that were predictable.

The most obvious likely problems were so stunningly obvious that it is amazing they were, even could be, overlooked. It is, for instance, a first principle in occupation doctrine that the first thing one must do when occupying another country's territory is to provide for the physical security of the population, through bringing in your own or the local police forces and/or military forces. Moreover, it is universally agreed that physical safety, followed closely by the provision of necessities of life and amenities (e.g., electric power, garbage pickup, sanitation), is absolutely necessary to making postconflict progress. *And yet these areas were almost totally ignored in Phase IV planning.* The official explanation was that the police and other security officers of the newly conquered country (especially Baghdad) *would simply report to duty as they normally did*, despite the physical impact of the invasion.

Possibly the most egregious error made in the planning, and a particular chestnut of Vice President Cheney, was the expectation that the Iraqis would treat the Americans as liberators, and that they would continue to hold the Americans in that regard even as the occupation lasted. This assumption might not have been entirely specious if, as the planners apparently assumed, the occupation was very short. Indeed, there was apparently an initial positive reaction among many Iraqis at being liberated from the Hussein regime; that perception faded as the Americans continued to stay and did not improve living conditions in the country. This point was made by Sir Robert Thompson in describing the 1948 Malay insurgency in his book *Make for the Hills:* "There is no hope for democracy if nothing works. Reliance on a military solution will always fail, particularly when sought by foreign troops." There is considerable evidence that the seemingly open-ended American occupation was responsible for creating the conditions that allowed for the formation and support for Al Qaeda in Iraq (see Chandrasekaran, among others). The present author discussed this dynamic in *Distant Thunder:* "The level of involvement (by outsiders) and the ability to influence the outcome are often inversely related. The more public the intervention and the more obvious the degree to which the regime depends on the assistance, the more resentment is likely to be created in the population. The insurgents' propaganda will be fueled by that dependence." If true, this observation is devastating for arguments made in defense of the occupation that the longer the United States stays, the more likely success is.

The other flaw was the execution of the plans—Phase IV was a poor plan poorly executed. This criticism has run through the critical literature on Iraq and has centered not only on the conceptual paucity and lack of preparedness of American officials to oversee Phase IV, but also on the incredible ineptitude and, in some cases, arrogance of those given the jobs of carrying out the occupation and rebuilding of the country.

This criticism has two distinct aspects. One is the sheer paucity of preinvasion planning, which meant occupation administrators (carefully not designated as such) arrived in Iraq with no programs to administer, since details of what happened after the fall of Hussein were simply supposed to work themselves out. Diamond, who went to the country with a missionary zeal about democratizing the country, records starkly the reality he found: "from the moment the war ended, Iraq fell into a deepening quagmire of chaos, criminality, insurgency, and terrorism. . . . Iraq became a black hole of instability." This "black hole" covered the range of public services from basic security and public services to the reform of the economy and the rebuilding of Iraq's schools and other parts of the infrastructure. While many of the things that needed doing (for instance, many aspects of the infrastructure) had suffered under Saddam Hussein, Iraqis presumed the Americans would fix them and improve their conditions of life; when this did not occur (or did so with remarkable slowness), the Iraqis became increasingly disillusioned with the Americans, who came to look increasingly like occupiers rather than liberators. This change of perspective, in turn, helped spark and fuel the armed resistance to the Americans by various factions.

The situation was made worse by the kinds of personnel who were sent to administer the rebuilding of Iraq. It seems highly controversial and partisan to say, but those who have written about Iraq overwhelmingly agree that the personnel sent, and particularly those associated with the Coalition Provisional Authority (CPA) headed by Ambassador L. Paul ("Jerry") Bremer III, were almost uniformly inept, incompetent, and inexpert for the positions they assumed. Once again, Chandrasekaran depicts their qualities most thoroughly. He (along with others) observes that the major criterion for appointment was not competence of expertise but political loyalty to the Republican Party and, more specifically, President Bush. A large percentage of the administrators brought in were in their twenties and, when they arrived in Baghdad, had left American soil for the first time. Moreover, their commitment was to create an American-style political democracy and capitalist-based, privatized economy, quite regardless of the political realities and traditions of Iraq. Most were unaware of the realities of Iraq anyway, since, as already noted, people with substantial expertise on Iraq and the Middle East in general (especially if they were affiliated with the State Department) were excluded because their expertise tended to make them unacceptably skeptical of the enterprise.

The role of the military itself must inevitably be part of any assessment. The professional military had been chastened greatly by the Vietnam experience, in which it had been remarkably compliant in accepting the mistaken political leadership that had impelled the military into a war that many of its leaders knew at the time could not be won. As in Iraq, dissent was not rewarded in Vietnam. One of the Kennedy and Johnson administrations' top experts on guerrilla warfare, Roger Hilsman (who had served as an organizer of guerrilla opponents to the Japanese in World War II), served as assistant secretary of state for Far Eastern affairs as the decision to intervene in Vietnam was being made. As he put it at the time, "those of us against escalating the struggle in Vietnam reached exactly the opposite conclusion: that the mistake would not be letting Vietnam go down the drain but for the United States to intervene." His views did not prevail, and he left the government on March 15, 1964, removing an obstacle to implementing what proved to be a disastrous military and political decision.

The military itself was not blameless in Vietnam (see McMaster's scathing indictment of the military's acquiescent role in that conflict). It was even less blameless in Iraq, because most of the senior leaders who agreed to the decision to invade Iraq were products of the professional military education system that had dissected the Vietnam experience and concluded such a mistake should not be made again. At the middle ranks of the officer corps (majors through colonels), there was opposition based on the application of those lessons to Iraq. At the top of the ranks, however, there was, by and large, silence. Some of that undoubtedly was the result of the experience of General Shinseki, who was publicly ridiculed and quietly forced into retirement after his opposition to the war plans. In Vietnam, the generals said "can do" to a mission they could not successfully complete, and they did not, at a minimum, say "can't do" in Iraq. Lieutenant Colonel Paul Yingling, a serving U.S. Army officer, summarizes the "failure of generalship" in Iraq most vividly: "America's generals have repeated the mistakes of Vietnam in Iraq. First, throughout the 1990s our generals failed to envision the conditions of future conflict and prepare their forces accordingly. Second, America's generals failed to estimate correctly both the means and the ways necessary to achieve the aims of policy prior to beginning the war in Iraq. Finally, the generals did not provide Congress and the public with an accurate assessment of the conflict in Iraq."

To answer the question raised in the section heading, the United States marched briskly into Iraq. It stumbled, however, in both its assessment of why to go into that country and its organization and execution of the mission. An argument can be made, and is made by critics, that the fundamental premise of the Iraq War—that a Saddam Hussein-led Iraq posed a threat to the United States sufficient to justify invading the country and overthrowing Hussein—was false and should never have been reached. Had such a judgment, held by many but expressed adequately loudly by few, held sway in 2003, there would have been no Iraq War.

But that argument did not prevail, and one major avenue of assessment is why it did not and how to avoid that same mistake in the future (essentially the same question that was asked about Vietnam). The decision to invade Iraq was made not only on the basis of questionable premises about whether it was necessary and desirable, but also on the basis of questionable views of the objective (a free and democratic Iraq) and how easily that objective could be attained. If, for instance, the administration had told the American public on the eve of the invasion the result would be a long (over five years and counting) and expensive (in treasure and blood) quagmire, would the American people have accepted the idea of the invasion? They did not offer a negative judgment because the basis for one was not forcefully presented to them by figures whose judgment they would have recognized and respected. As in Vietnam, there were dissenters, but they were too few and isolated, and they were pilloried by war supporters for their dissent. Did that process serve the American interest well? If not, what lessons (reinforced by similar lessons learned and forgotten about Vietnam) can be taken to assure that the same mistakes are not made again? There would not, after all, have been an inept administration of the occupation of Iraq had there been no war.

WHAT WENT WRONG AND WHY?

Hardly anyone, even in an administration that continues to assert that progress is somehow possible and occurring, would argue that the Iraq effort represents any kind of exemplary experience that should be repeated. The administration's early assertions of a quick, bloodless, and highly successful experience that would cost the American taxpayers essentially nothing (Iraqi oil revenues were supposed to cover most of the costs) seem almost comical in retrospect, but they are not. The projections that led the United States into Iraq were almost systematically wrong, as were the projections of what would happen afterward. Why? One answer is that the United States failed to understand at critical junctures the nature of the conflict, and especially the analogy between Iraq and the American failed experiment in Vietnam. The result has been a situation where the final outcomes of the American involvement are most decidedly Vietnam-like.

Iraq and Vietnam

Supporters of the Iraq War have gone to great lengths to deny and to try to refute any comparisons between what happened to the United States in Vietnam and what has happened in Iraq. The protestations are understandable, because Vietnam was a failure, and the more Iraq resembles Vietnam, the more observers are drawn to the conclusion that the United States will fail in Iraq as well, which, of course, is an unacceptable conclusion. Nonetheless, there are some marked similarities between the two that will help reinforce arguments in the post-Iraq debate, as well as some dissimilarities that will leaven the comparisons. Both need to be examined briefly.

Dissimilarities. The major basis on which arguments about the dissimilarities between Iraq and Vietnam arise is the largely physical differences between the two conflicts. Three of these stand out. The first and most obvious is the nature of the war itself. The Vietnam War was an internal civil war (although not recognized as such at the time and still denied by some apologists of the war), the purpose of which was either to unite the two provisional (from the Geneva Accords) Vietnams (North and South) or to prevent that reuniting. It was an ongoing war when the United States entered it and reversed what appeared to be an imminent North Vietnamese/National Liberation Front victory over a South Vietnamese government supported by the United States, at least for a time. This dynamic stands in stark contrast to Iraq, where there was no war until the United States initiated one and where the insurgency was not an existing reality that the United States confronted but rather a movement that it largely created. Moreover, the purposes of the wars were different as well: internal Vietnamese nationalism and self-determination versus the outsider creation of Iraqi democracy or, as the situation has devolved, at least a stable Iraq.

The second point of dissimilarity is physical and demographic. On a strictly physical level, of course, Vietnam is a green belt equatorial country marked by dense jungle and mountains (other than the coastal plain), whereas most of Iraq is a desert punctuated by some arid mountains in the north and east and swamplands in the south. As a result, the style of fighting in the two places is different. Vietnam, for instance, is perfect topography for the kind of guerrilla warfare fought by North Vietnamese regulars (whom Moore and Galloway described as the "finest light infantry in the world" in *We Were Soldiers Once . . . and Young*) and the Viet Cong and totally inappropriate for the kinds of maneuver warfare conducted by heavy units favored by the United States. By contrast, the comparatively open landscape of Iraq provided favorable terrain for the maneuver warfare supported by overwhelming firepower that formed the basis of American "shock and awe" tactics in Iraq. The lack of jungle cover also meant that once the insurgency began, it had to use urban settings as an equivalent of the Vietnamese mountainous jungles. Iraq, in other words, did not look physically like Vietnam.

Finally, the scales of the two wars are dissimilar. Vietnam became a war of attrition, where the goal was to deplete the enemy of his ability to fight (the American objective) or to inflict enough casualties to break the opponent's will to resist (the North Vietnamese objective against the Americans). The result was, during the active American combat phase of the war between 1965 and 1973, a high level of carnage: over 58,000 American dead and Vietnamese losses well over a million—by some accounts topping two million. By contrast, the Iraq War has produced much lower casualty rates: American combat losses moved seemingly inexorably toward 4,000 during 2007 and Iraqi civilian and military casualties were estimated to be in the general (and disputed in both directions) area of 100,000. Because global television was so much more advanced in 2007 than it was in 1967, the scale of suffering is more visible in Iraq than it was in Vietnam. If military action is reflected in casualties, however, Iraq is by no means comparable to Vietnam.

Similarities. Those who argue that Vietnam and Iraq are indeed similar maintain that the dissimilarities focus largely on cosmetic aspects of the war, so-called atmospherics, and that below those apparent differences, the real, underlying dynamics are in fact quite similar. These similarities can be combined into five categories: the nature of the situation in both countries and their relationship to the United States; the intractability of the political and military situations in each country, making American success problematical at best in each situation; the fact this intractability was known, with predicted negative outcomes, and ignored by the American administration; the perverse dynamic that continued involvement may actually make settlement less likely; and the predictable, unpalatable consequences of both involvements, including disengagement (Iraqification) and resistance to it and the long-term problem of refugees.

The first similarity is between the situations, and it has three aspects. Both Iraq and Vietnam were unstable, Third World countries, although for different reasons. Vietnamese instability had been foisted upon it by the artificial division of the country (which had no historical precedent other than the artificial division of the country by the French during the colonial period), and the war, at least from the North Vietnamese side, was about rectifying that situation; the fact that the unifying nationalists were also Communists overwhelmed American perceptions of the situation and resulted in it being depicted in Communist–anti-Communist terms. Iraq, on the other hand, is a totally artificial state created by the British and French in 1919. Its centripetal potential was latent because of the harsh Sunni dictatorship of Saddam Hussein, which suppressed the differences among factions cruelly but effectively. When his rule was removed, the centripetal tendencies percolated to the top. The

United States, of course, had a role in both instabilities, by serving as the major author of the Geneva Accords on Vietnam in 1954 and by toppling Saddam Hussein.

At the same time, there was—particularly in retrospect—the absence of compelling American interests, especially unambiguously *vital* interests, in both cases. This point has already been made about Vietnam: all the worst predictions about what might happen in the absence of American intervention occurred, and the United States is hardly worse for it. One of the great ironies is that there is now a thriving tourist trade of American veterans revisiting Vietnamese battlefields, where Vietnamese Communists provide host conditions that rival those for tourists in the most capitalist resort areas. The case has been presented that a similar assessment can be made about Iraq and is discussed in the *Challenge!* What If It Were All True in Iraq?

Challenge!

WHAT IF IT WERE ALL TRUE IN IRAQ?

Assume for a minute that all the charges made by the administration in defense of invading Iraq were true: that Iraq possessed WMD; that there were links between the Iraqi regime and Al Qaeda; and that the Iraqis might collaborate with terrorists and supply them with WMD. Each poses a threat to the United States, but how great a threat? If Iraq possessed WMD, it did not possess the ability to deliver them far from their borders. How much of a threat was this to the United States or Americans (except those Americans residing in Middle Eastern locations that the Iraqis might have been capable of hitting)? If Iraq had ties with terrorists, how much would that have changed the threat those terrorists pose to the United States or the ability of the United States to monitor and frustrate the terrorists (who have an alternate safe haven in Pakistan)? How much more dangerous would Al Qaeda be to the United States if it possessed Iraqi-manufactured WMD? Does it make a difference what kinds of WMD (chemical, biological, or nuclear) the Iraqis might have supplied them with? How intolerable were any of these worst cases to American security—vital or less than vital?

And then there is the positive side of the equation: the establishment of a model democracy in Iraq. Were this possible, how would it change the geopolitics of the region? Would it affect Israeli security and thus the stability of the region? Would it have made American access to Persian Gulf petroleum more secure (remember that Saudi Arabia, America's largest supplier, is hardly a democracy or advocate of democratization in the region)? How important was achieving this goal to *American* security? Given the difficulties involved and the improbability of success, was it worth the risk? None of these questions has a clear-cut answer, and all will continue to be debated. Interestingly, however, the answers are much different—and especially clearer—if one asks the same questions about the effects of various actions and outcomes on *Israeli* security.

The comparative question is how the worst-case analysis in Iraq will affect American vital interests. The worst-case scenario suggests a chaotic Iraq internally with outside interference in favor of both the Sunnis (probably from Syria and Saudi Arabia) and the Shiites (from Iran) that, in the very worst event, could lead to a regionwide war (although this extreme possibility is generally discounted). Meanwhile, the Kurds would be left basically on their own, with possible negative pressure from Turkey should Iraqi Kurds begin to actively advocate the uniting of Iraqi and Turkish Kurdish regions. During this period, large-scale violence could be expected in Iraq, including increased sectarian violence, more massive emigration of those Iraqis most negatively impacted (especially professional and wealthy Sunnis), and suppression of those Iraqis who had collaborated with the retreating American occupiers. In fact, the U.S. government admitted this problem in a July 22, 2007, cable from Ambassador Ryan Crocker, the U.S. envoy in Baghdad, seeking immigration visas for Iraqis working for the occupation effort (as reported by Hsu in the *Washington Post*). There was also great internal unrest and suffering in Vietnam when the United States left in 1975, but did that greatly affect American interests? Will the exit from Iraq be different?

One can also argue a third aspect of this first similarity: that the United States found itself on the wrong side in each of these conflicts. The case is clearer in Vietnam, where American support for a South Vietnamese government that never had great public support put the United States firmly in opposition to Vietnamese nationalism, represented by the North Vietnamese. In Iraq, American opposition to Saddam Hussein effectively put the country in alignment with a political void, where there was no obvious alternative to the hated dictator and where American support of any political movement was an effective kiss of death because such movement would be perceived as collaborating with the occupier and thus assigned the status of quisling.

The second broad similarity between the situations is their intractability. In both cases, this intractability was explained in advance and the advice was ignored. In Vietnam, officials like Kattenburg warned of the political impossibility of the situation, and others like Hilsman warned of the military problems of counterinsurgency. As McMaster and others have pointed out, both the political and the military leadership ignored this advice and ended up bogged down in a conflict they neither understood nor could win.

The situation is remarkably similar in Iraq. Although authors like Pollack argued the case for invading Iraq, there was a wealth of negative opinion, some of which is included in the "Selected Bibliography" (see, for instance, Glantz and Hersh). Moreover, there was military advice that suggested the military situation was far more complicated than the successful conquest of the country. Bush himself, it will be remembered, at one point agreed with the assessment that the conquest of Iraq would lead to an insurgency. He was, ironically, quite correct.

The third broad similarity, suggested by the second, is that what happened in Iraq and Vietnam was knowable and predictable in advance. This point has, of course, already been made but is certainly worth reiterating because it represents a systemic problem that arguably should be addressed more fully so that the

United States will not repeat ignoring the lessons of Vietnam in some future place where it ignores the lessons of *both* Vietnam and Iraq.

The major point of commonality here appears to be the institutional ability to ignore or block out dissident voices that provided what proved to be prescient assessments of both situations. In both cases, military intervention in the name of laudable political goals was advocated by elites within the government, and support of those interventions was elevated to patriotic necessity. Likewise, there was opposition in the expert communities (both political and military) to involvement, but it was either shunted aside or ignored, often as unpatriotic (negative political judgments) or even cowardly (negative military judgments). Both Lyndon Johnson and George W. Bush used their "bloody pulpits" to trumpet the necessity of action, and opposition was swamped in the process. Only later, when the bankruptcy of the wars became evident to all but the most committed supporters, were the voices of dissent heard.

The obvious answer to this problem is a more thorough dissection of these situations before commitments are made. The result of such an assessment in either Vietnam or Iraq might have led to the same result that occurred, but it also might have resulted in a negative response or a much more measured and limited affirmation that might have lessened the American action. Ironically, the nature of these kinds of situations militates against such a thorough vetting of ideas, because advocates will (and did) argue that dissent in effect aided and abetted the (potential) enemy by demonstrating the American public was not united behind the cause.

The fourth general similarity is less often mentioned but is both powerful and perverse. In Vietnam, the more the United States became involved in the war, the more the American stake in the war increased, and the more difficult or impossible withdrawal seemed to appear—because of the accumulating stake in the outcome. The South Vietnamese government of Ngo Dinh Diem came to understand this dilemma the Americans faced and concluded that he could resist or ignore American demands, because the Americans could not meaningfully threaten him with leaving if he did not comply. As the present author put it in *Distant Thunder*, "the amount of assistance and the degree of influence over the government may be inverse, as the government realizes the extent to which outsider investment makes it harder to cut the government off even if it ignores good advice." Thomas L. Friedman offers an analogy for Iraq in a July 2007 column: "Staying in means simply containing the Iraqi civil war, but at a price of Americans and Iraqis continuing to die, and *at a price of the United States having no real leverage on the parties inside or outside of Iraq to negotiate a settlement, because everyone knows we're staying so they can dither*" (emphasis added).

The fifth similarity is the negative outcomes of both situations. This is more difficult to discuss because, although the outcome has occurred in Vietnam, it still remains in process in Iraq and will remain in process for at least several years (which is why the next section is devoted to that outcome). Having said that, three commonalities, in some form, seem likely.

The first outcome is that the war will end in what most Americans (and at least many Iraqis) consider an unsatisfactory, unsatisfying manner. When the United States withdraws, it will almost certainly be without having achieved its goal of a model Iraqi democracy. Rather, Iraq will be in some state of flux and transition to some end state that cannot be confidently predicted at this point. It is also predictable that supporters of the war will blame opponents for not "staying the course" to allow a favorable outcome and that opponents will reply that the outcome was likely regardless of how long the United States stays. Whether the outcome will be as totally negative in Iraq as in Vietnam (the uniting of the country under Communist rule) remains to be seen.

The second outcome is that there will be residual instability and suffering in Iraq, and one of its most poignant symbols will be a continuing refugee stream out of the country. In Vietnam, Vietnamese who had supported the United States were suppressed, jailed, and even killed after the United States left the country, and much of the ethnic Chinese minority was thrown out of the country (the "boat people"). Many Iraqis have already fled Iraq, and depending on how the political winds blow after the Americans leave, more likely will. Up to now, the majority of Iraqis who have fled have been Sunnis, meaning a drain of both professional expertise and money (since the Sunnis dominated prewar Iraq). If the Sunnis are treated poorly in post-American Iraq, this drain will be accentuated, with negative consequences for the Iraqi future.

This concern with refugees conjures powerful remembered images of the U.S. exit from the embassy in Saigon in 1975—most prominently the scene of American helicopters evacuating personnel from the embassy roof as Vietnamese civilian employees clambered for space aboard and even clung to the struts of the helicopters as they took off. The Bush administration has at least partially anticipated this wrenching scene and proposed an expansion of immigration visas for Iraqis working for the Americans in Baghdad in July 2007. As of June 30 of that year, however, only sixty-nine such visas had been granted for the year, with ninety-three pending, according to the State Department, a mere trickle.

The third outcome will be an "Iraq hangover" in the United States that may resemble the Vietnam hangover of a past generation. After Vietnam, the prestige of the military plummeted, resulting in an underfunded force that had difficulty filling its ranks with qualified people and that the American people turned their back on. Through the remainder of the 1970s, this hangover meant no president (Nixon, Ford, or Carter) could expect support for military adventure from a public that had been "burned" and "burned out" by Vietnam. In Vietnam, this hangover was amplified by the obvious and unambiguous failure of the United States to achieve any of its goals in the war (hence, the misleading charge that Vietnam was the first war the United States ever "lost"). Iraq may avoid being remembered as quite the abject failure as Vietnam, but it will certainly be impossible to depict it as a triumph. How much of a hangover there will be, in turn, depends on the outcome of the war, which is to say, the conditions under which the United States ends its involvement.

How Will the Iraq War End?

The answer to this question has two distinct, if interrelated, parts that lead to the conclusion, which is what Iraq will be like after the war. One part is the causation and timing of American withdrawal, and the other is the physical situation on the ground in Iraq when that withdrawal occurs. The Vietnam comparison may help sharpen the possibilities.

The possible outcomes form a continuum, the extremities of which can be safely eliminated as highly improbable. One extreme is a total and unambiguous U.S. "victory," which means the creation of a stable, model democracy in Iraq that can defeat an insurgency that lacks popular support (which has been transferred to the government) and which unites Iraqis into a pro-American post-war polity. This outcome is easily as much a victory for the United States as it is for the Iraqis, since it is unclear what conditions would be acceptable to the Iraqis as a whole to allow this outcome. It is highly improbable because of the deep divisions within Iraq— arguably exacerbated by the Americans—that were present before the war but suppressed by the Hussein regime and that form the heart of critical judgments about intervening in the first place. Just as there was insufficient support for the American-favored independence of South Vietnam in 1973, there is also almost certainly not sufficient support for the American-favored outcome in Iraq either.

The second extreme is an abject American loss in Iraq. Proponents of the war argue this is the outcome most likely if the United States withdraws "prematurely" (it is never quite clear when the situation is "mature" enough for withdrawal other than when the president insists the United States has prevailed). Such a scenario would mean the American withdrawal would result in a new dictatorship (the apotheosis of a democracy) that would turn Iraq into a full-blown terrorist-supporting state. This outcome is also unlikely. The imposition of a new autocracy (almost certainly Shiite if it occurs) would be widely opposed regionally and would further ignite Kurdish separatism. A multicommunal authoritarian state that can gradually democratize over time may be the more realistic possibility. At the same time, relatively few Iraqis support the foreign-dominated Al Qaeda in Iraq organization, and what little support it does have is based in opposition to the American occupation. Without that occupation, Al Qaeda in Iraq is hardly likely to prosper. In the sense of total, undeniable defeat, Iraq will almost certainly not be Vietnam redux.

This leaves an outcome somewhere in between, some form of Iraqification, as the remaining candidate. Some form of this strategy is clearly being implemented along lines parallel to the Vietnamization policy. Vietnamization had as its major purpose preparing the South Vietnamese to defend themselves against attempts to reunify all of Vietnam by force. The operational tools for attempting to accomplish this goal included maximum training and equipping of the South Vietnamese, the provision of military assistance to their operations (the use of U.S. close air support when the North Vietnamese attempted to invade in 1972—the Easter Offensive), and the insulation of South Vietnam from outside intervention by sealing infiltration routes through Cambodia and Laos (efforts that ultimately failed).

The same dynamics have been applied in Iraq since about 2005. They have centered on building Iraqi armed forces and police to defend the country against the various forms of the insurgency, a direct parallel to similar efforts in Vietnam. As in Vietnam, the effort has been partially hamstrung by the inability to recruit and train a force sufficient for the job, if for different reasons (the need to conscript the South Vietnamese force, coercion and violence and ethnic loyalties in Iraq). The result, at some point, will be the same: the declaration that the Iraqis are as prepared as the Americans can make them, and that it will be up to them to defend the country, at which point the Americans will withdraw. At the same time, the United States will try to make Iraq as impervious to outside influence as possible, as was attempted in Vietnam. In the Iraqi case, this will be attempted by using diplomacy to try to ensure the absence of outside confessional intervention and by posting American forces "over the horizon" in places from which they could conceivably redeploy into Iraq, such as Kuwait and Kurdish Iraq. This latter, of course, was an option unavailable to the United States in Vietnam, since the American public was so revulsed by the entire experience that it simply wanted Americans out of Southeast Asia altogether.

The remaining debate over the terms of American withdrawal from Iraq falls within this middle range of possibilities. If unambiguous victory is unattainable (and always was) and equally unambiguous defeat is too politically unacceptable in the United States to be allowed, then some form of ambiguous withdrawal that leaves the final outcome to the Iraqis themselves and allows Americans to rationalize that "we have done all we could" is the best that can be expected. It is essentially a face-saving device, which is what Vietnamization was. The reluctance to call it Iraqification arises both from the reluctance of Iraq War supporters to admit the parallels with Vietnam and from the recognition that Vietnamization ultimately failed. Iraqification by whatever name may also fail, in which case Americans will be left to bicker about whether it would have succeeded if some other disengagement point (e.g., level of preparedness of the Iraqis) had been chosen. When Vietnamization ultimately failed with the fall of Saigon in 1975, Americans by and large did not care; they were exhausted by the long trauma and simply wanted to put it behind them. Will Americans feel the same way about Iraq? The answer will help shape the legacy of Iraq.

THE LEGACIES OF THE IRAQ WAR

How the Iraq War is remembered by the American people will, of course, be influenced by how it ends. If the analysis to this point is at all cogent, that memory is almost certain to be negative, or at least to have significant negative aspects that will color how the entire episode is placed in public consciousness. Those perceptions will, in turn, play a large role in determining what the legacies of the war are for the future.

Certain broad lessons seem inevitable. One is that Iraq cannot possibly be considered a military success if the military aspect is viewed in its totality. The war from invasion to conquest will likely be remembered positively, although some of the sheen of that memory will likely be eroded by closer "after tour" examination. Phase IV operations surrounding the occupation, rehabilitation, and preparation of Iraq for a return to fully sovereign status (despite the so-called return of sovereignty in late 2004) will almost certainly be viewed as a failure. It is the major outcome at which fingers will be pointed and attempts at blame alleged. The major questions in this regard will likely revolve around whose fault it was that the preparations for and execution of Phase IV were so poorly conceived and so wretchedly implemented and why it was not done better.

The initial blame on these matters has already been laid in the numerous accounts cited above and included in the chapter's "Selected Bibliography." The assignment of all aspects of the war to a Pentagon that was not truly interested in Phase IV and that then handed implementation to an almost totally unprepared and inept set of administrators seems to be the common theme. The most shocking indictment of all was the conscious exclusion of experts on Iraq and Phase IV–type operations from the occupation team, from Ambassador Bremer down to middle-level administrators. Whether the assignment of the true "best and brightest" would have resulted in a noticeably more positive outcome is arguable; that the failure of the effort as mounted was virtually inevitable is not.

Who will be tarnished by this assessment? Certainly, the political leadership that did not insist on adequate Phase IV planning (on the apparent assumption it was unneeded because the occupation would be short and painless) and left the implementation to amateurs will bear much of the blame, with the obvious lesson that better planning is dictated in the future. The military, however, also bears part of the responsibility. After Vietnam, the military, principally through its professional military education (PME) system, sought to educate its members on modern warfare as a multifaceted affair that includes Phase IV–type operations, and it had the chance to "practice" these lessons in the 1990s in places like Haiti, Bosnia, and Kosovo. Those in the military may not have liked this addition to their duties, but they understood it. Yet when it came to a similar situation in Iraq, they did not forcefully object to orders to ignore the realities they knew were there. Retired Marine General Anthony Zinni, the commander of Central Command whom General Franks succeeded, states the indictment (in Clancy) dramatically: "In the lead-up to the war and its later conduct, I saw, at a minimum, true dereliction, negligence, and irresponsibility; at worst, lying, incompetence, and corruption. False rationales presented as a justification; a flawed strategy; lack of planning; the unnecessary alienation of our allies; the underestimation of the task; the unnecessary distraction from real threats; and the unbearable strain dumped on our overstretched military."

The broad political lesson of Iraq, shared to a lesser extent with Vietnam, is the failure to achieve the political objectives of the enterprise. In Vietnam, that judgment was black and white: the North Vietnamese succeeded in achieving their political goal of reuniting Vietnam by force, and the United States failed to prevent that reunification (keep South Vietnam independent). In Iraq, the United States will not have succeeded in instituting a western-style democracy; whether the final outcome is as abjectly opposite of that outcome as was the case in Vietnam remains to be seen. The advantage this time is that there is unlikely to be an event as dramatic as the fall of Saigon to provide the final punctuation mark on American failure; Iraq after the United States leaves may well slide into further, deeper civil war, but it is likely to be a matter of degree, not of kind.

There are two lines of argument for the failure to achieve the political objective in Iraq. Both were known (or knowable) in advance but were ignored. The first is that the objective was unattainable under any circumstances. Certainly, there were multiple voices suggesting that the institution of a model democracy in Iraq was a neoconservative pipe dream, but such warnings were ignored as, to borrow Albert Gore's depiction of global warming, "inconvenient truths." The second is that there was no meaningful way to translate this objective into a workable strategy (plan of action) that could be implemented by the military or political authorities. The chief barriers to implementing the plan were a long-standing history of intergroup animosities in Iraq and an absolute absence of anything resembling a democratic tradition in the country. Iraq was one of the most unlikely places in the world for a democratic experiment, a point on which most of the expert community was in agreement. The idea that a physical occupation would somehow lead to a transformation toward the desired goal was ludicrous.

For better or worse, Iraq is the foundation on which the military and political leaderships must prepare for the future. Iraq in 1990, and to an extent in 2003, is the last of the traditional wars, in which the United States is likely to encounter a traditional military opponent. In Zinni's colorful terms, "we managed to go up against the only jerk on the planet who was stupid enough to challenge us to refight World War Two." Future situations will be much more like what Iraq has become (the insurgency), and what America takes away as the legacies of Iraq will influence the way the country responds in the future. Using the Vietnam War as a base, the present author published a book, *When America Fights*, in 2000 that discussed these same matters; in essence, the lessons and legacies are not that much different. Iraq simply provides another example of what happens when one ignores the legacies of the past. In the Iraq case, three are worth mentioning.

The Political Legacy: Be Careful Where You Intervene

At the turn of the millennium, the United States was afflicted with the belief that it had unprecedented and ineluctable power in the world, and one heard frequent analogies between the United States and the Roman Empire at its apex. The terrorist attacks of September 11 sent the country reeling temporarily, but it rebounded with a fierce determination to right that wrong. The might of the United States could be applied to "make reality," in the neoconservative sense. After an early apparent success (tempered by time) in Afghanistan, Iraq became the next great political battleground. In Iraq, the United States would take its first step toward transforming the Middle East and the world.

American power was, of course, exaggerated in these descriptions, and the failure to bring democracy to Iraq should cause the United States to reassess what it can and cannot do, especially unilaterally, in the world. The decision to go into Iraq reflected the triumph of the idealistic neoconservatives and the temporary defeat of the traditional realists. With Iraq heading toward an ending far removed from the neoconservative vision, that group of analysts is in disorderly retreat. In their place, a new generation of people with views closer to the traditional realists will almost certainly arise, and they will ask different questions about involving the United States in different situations, all with the theme of greater care in applying force in the future.

Although the questions can be arranged in various ways, one possible ordering suggests three basic questions. The first surrounds the feasibility of adopting any particular political objective: Is success possible? Is it likely or unlikely? How can you assess likelihood in advance? The second surrounds the desirability or necessity of involvement: Is a proposed involvement one of necessity (where the failure to act will result in intolerable disadvantage—affect vital interests) or one of choice (where vital outcomes are not engaged)? If vital interests are not involved, should force be considered, or should alternative means be explored and the use of force eliminated or at least shelved? The third, and related, question has to do with the endurance of support for an action if taken: will the United States remain diligent even if achieving the objective is long and costly?

These three questions are, of course, related to one another. Following an unattainable objective is quixotic, and a negative answer to the question of attainability should counsel a negative reaction unless the objective is so overwhelmingly important that it must be pursued as a matter of principle. An easily achievable goal will not test the vitality or endurance question, since such goals (for instance, rescuing Americans from the besieged U.S. embassy in Monrovia, Liberia, in the 1990s) can be achieved with minimum effort and expense. Likewise, the American people are more likely to provide enduring support for an effort that is clearly vital to its interests than one that is not.

These kinds of questions will be asked in the future about American military involvement in unstable situations in the world. Most of the situations will be ambiguous and the answers difficult to determine easily. The Iraq War experience will, however, create skepticism about optimistic assessments that sound anything like the ramp-up to the invasion in 2003. Because these situations will be in places that are foreign and alien to many Americans, expert opinion should have a greater impact on the debate than it did for Iraq. The more of the basic questions that are answered negatively—or that cannot be convincingly argued positively—the less likelihood that a positive decision for involvement will be sustainable.

The Military Legacy: What Kind of Foe to Prepare For

It was a virtual mantra before the Iraq War that asymmetrical warfare was the wave of the future, and that warfare fought by unconventional means represented the kind of military exigency with which the United States would most likely have to deal. Although the American military leaders accepted this vision publicly, it was not a style of warfare that they liked or one with which they could identify. The Persian Gulf War, fought under the leadership of Zinni's last "jerk" to take on the United States conventionally, provided a respite from the new reality, and by and large, the invasion and conquest phase of the Iraq War of 2003 was fought in a modified version of World War II–style maneuver warfare, adding further vindication to not abandoning the "old" ways of war. Operation Iraqi Freedom was used to vindicate two continuing illusions about the application of military force. Military traditionalists saw it as vindication of the conventional application of force, even if many of them chafed at the size of the force, especially for the postmilitary phase

(Phase IV) of the action. Supporters of Donald Rumsfeld's concept of a smaller, more technologically oriented force that could move more quickly and lethally than the old force believed the rapid movement of forces through Iraq vindicated his vision of the future as well.

The various forms of the Iraq insurgency brought that illusion to an end. Even as American forces moved through Iraq, they encountered—much to their surprise—isolated pockets of resistance, such as individual fighters or groups engaged in ambushes and harassing actions against them. The disbanding of the Iraqi Army and police provided a virtual trove of potential recruits for the various insurgent groups—armed, angry, unemployed men who could blame their conditions on the occupiers. That all major sides—the Kurds and their *pesh merga* ("those who face death") and the Sunni and Shiite militias, augmented by Al Qaeda in Iraq foreigners after 2004—emerged to form a multisided resistance that the Bush administration refused to designate a civil war should not have come as a surprise. Despite thirty years of studying the dynamics of insurgency and counterinsurgency (culminating in the publication of Field Manual 3-24 on counterinsurgency in 2006, among whose lead authors was General David Petraeus), the United States has not found a successful way to quell the violence after over five years of trying. Whether it is possible for outsiders to end such insurgencies is problematical, a topic discussed in *Distant Thunder*.

Iraq may have begun as a conventional military operation, but it has been transformed into an asymmetrical war. Dissecting that style of warfare is the topic of Chapter 11 and need not be described here. Two points of note should be mentioned in the present context of Iraqi legacies. The first is that asymmetrical warfare against the American occupation has been sufficiently successful that it will almost certainly be adopted by future opponents of the United States. The various parts of the insurgency have not defeated the Americans on the battlefield, but they have held at bay the American military goliath. Depending on the final nature of American withdrawal, some of its proponents will almost certainly claim they have prevailed over the Americans. At any rate, the experience will almost certainly be that asymmetrical warfare is the way to combat the United States, and as a result, that is the kind of opponent the United States should anticipate and attempt to overcome in the future.

The other point is how the various Iraqi insurgents have learned to adapt their method to maximize its effectiveness. Earlier forms of asymmetrical warfare, such as Vietnam, were fought in rural settings, generally in the tropical green belt that surrounds the earth's Equator. In Iraq, most of the fighting has been in the setting of urban guerrilla warfare, and the asymmetrical opponents have adapted classical insurgent techniques like ambush to the new setting. In Iraq, two innovations have stood out. The most prominent, of course, has been the use of improvised explosive devices (IEDs), essentially booby traps to destroy Americans riding in what have turned out to be inadequately armored vehicles, and this tactic has been enhanced by lying in wait with antiaircraft missiles to shoot down helicopters trying to reach the scene of IED attacks to ferry out survivors. The other has been the use of suicide bombers against urban targets. Neither technique is entirely novel, but both have confounded the American occupiers. Their legacy is twofold: these kinds of tactics will almost certainly be used the next time the United States faces an asymmetrical opponent, and just as these were novel tactics in the Iraq War, the next opponent will almost certainly have equally ingenious adaptations to present as problems for the Americans.

Iraq and the American Military: What Kind of Force

A consequence of the backlash that will compose the Iraq hangover is that the U.S. military will have to regroup before it faces a future foe. From this vantage point, a useful aspect of the hangover is that the political system in the United States has been chastened by the Iraq experience and will be very wary of similar adventures. While this reluctance to see Americans put in harm's way will provide a breathing space for this regrouping, it is not clear what happens if, during the period of skepticism about military employments, a real crisis—a war of necessity—is thrust upon the country. But just as the Vietnam hangover left the military the balance of the 1970s to regroup and reorder itself, so the Iraq hangover will probably provide a period when the military is not likely to be called back into large-scale action. At the same time, part of the hangover will quite possibly be a reorientation of national priorities in which the military must compete for reinvigorating resources and will not always prevail in that competition.

At least two elements will play into the equation as the military looks forward. The first has to do with how it physically regenerates itself in the face of the almost certain hemorrhage of many from its ranks and a likely lack of enthusiasm among potential new recruits. The other is conceptual and has to do with how (or whether) the military can make the transition from an almost exclusively heavy, symmetrical structure with some asymmetrical add-ons to a force that balances more enthusiastically and physically a future where asymmetrical threats at least equal symmetrical ones.

Manpower. The manpower problem is the more immediate and pressing concern. In Iraq, the government has essentially "robbed Peter to pay Paul" in the sense of overextending, overusing, and even arguably abusing the force it has to the breaking point. The litany is familiar: multiple deployments of active-duty and reserve units to Iraq arguably without adequate breaks, "stop loss" measures to prevent those whose terms of enlistment have expired from leaving the service, and mistreatment of wounded and other veterans when they return to the United States, for example. These conditions have already made potential recruits wary of joining; the U.S. Army, for instance, failed to meet its recruitment goals in both May and June 2007, a problem that will not abate soon. Moreover, when the American withdrawal finally occurs (or there is a new administration in Washington) and there is inadequate reason to keep military members involuntarily in service, there will almost certainly be a large number of resignations and failures to reenlist.

The military faced this same problem after Vietnam, and the short-term results are not encouraging for current military planners. The problem was probably worse in Vietnam, because the military itself (rightly or wrongly) was largely blamed for the outcome, a verdict that it resented and that helped fuel the Abrams reforms, which, as argued, backfired in Iraq. In Iraq, the military bears part of the blame but has not been discredited institutionally as much as in the 1970s (unless, of course, the public verdict is that the military "lost" the war, but that seems unlikely). Nonetheless, the experience that American soldiers and sailors have had in Iraq will make the task of military recruiters more difficult than it was before the war.

The size and nature of the future military and its future missions are intimately related. If the United States projects more involvements of the size and nature of Iraq, then it will require a substantially larger force than would be the case if it envisages smaller deployments and missions. Conversely, the size of the military makes possible and impossible different kinds of missions. A clear lesson of Iraq, for instance, is that the current U.S. armed forces are not large enough comfortably to accommodate the military occupation of a middle-sized or larger opponent. If the greatest flexibility of potential uses (a logical outgrowth of worst-case planning) is desired, the force must be large enough to accommodate all contingencies.

The military, of course, does not determine its own size, which is a prerogative of the Congress. What size force the United States needs after Iraq will be the decision of the political system, which will pass judgments both on the desired size and missions of the military and on the physical and political difficulties of attaining different sizes and qualities of force. In looking at the question, there are five possible ways for the armed forces of the post-Iraq era to "man" themselves.

The first is the *status quo*: the continuation of the ongoing all-volunteer force recruited in the current manner. This will almost certainly be the approach attempted initially after the Iraq involvement ends. The rationale for continuing the present system will be that it worked before Iraq in producing the kind of force the country desired and that it represents a structure and approach with which the military is familiar and comfortable. Moreover, removing the shadow of Iraq should reduce the reluctance of new recruits to come forward and existing troops to reenlist. The negative side of this argument is that the shadow of Iraq will linger and that potential new members (as well as reenlisting present members) will be reluctant to commit until they see tangible evidence that there will not be another Iraq in their futures.

If the status quo is inadequate, as it arguably will be, the second option is *enhanced recruitment*. This can take on several guises. It can mean increased incentives for enlistment/reenlistment, such as larger bonuses, college tuition vouchers, and the like. It can also mean reaching out to new constituencies, such as recruiting more females or members from minority groups into the service. Shorter terms of enlistment and guaranteed leave time can also be part of the package, as can amenities like better living conditions for military members (greater access to the Internet and e-mail for deployed troops, for instance). These approaches seek to widen the recruitment/retention base of the armed forces and to keep members satisfied while not diluting their quality. The problems include the expense of bonuses and incentives and the danger of turning the force into one of more disproportionate minority composition than it already is.

A variant of enhanced recruitment offers a third possibility—*lowering standards for recruits*. To some extent, this has already been incorporated into attempts to maintain force levels in Iraq, and it can consist of two actions, both of which enlarge the potential pool of military accessions. The first is to lower educational/ intellectual standards. By statute, the military can only recruit a very small percentage of troops who lack high school diplomas (the standard measuring stick), and increasing the percentage of nongraduates increases the pool. The problem is that high school dropouts, as a group, are probably less capable than those who graduate, resulting in a less capable force. The other, and controversial, method is to allow recruitment of people convicted of some categories of crime who are now precluded from service.

If the first three methods are inadequate or unacceptable, a fourth is a return to *conscription (the draft)*. Although it has not been activated or used since the end of 1972, the United States still retains a selective service system that registers eighteen-year-olds and that could be reactivated without specific legislation. The draft system, by which the military obtained most of the force that fought in Vietnam, was a victim of the backlash against that conflict. Since Vietnam, even raising the possibility of a return to involuntary military service creates a political firestorm of opposition that no political actor will seriously advocate (Representative Charles Rangel (D–NY) regularly presents an advocacy of the draft but for the symbolic purpose of pointing to inequities and flaws in the current system). Much of the opposition to the draft arises from the inequities of the old system, but many of these have been overcome. Nonetheless, the idea of a draft continues to be problematical, as investigated in Amplification 10.2.

The fifth alternative is largely an artifact of Iraq: the *privatization of parts of the force*. In Iraq, for instance, Avant reports that Rumsfeld estimated there were 20,000 "private security personnel" in Iraq in 2004, making them "the second largest member of the 'coalition of the willing.'" The use of these forces provided by so-called private security contractors (PSCs) has certain advantages, as catalogued by Avant: they can be mobilized quickly to provide flexibility and surge capacity; they often possess special skills, since they are recruited from the open market; they can be recruited internationally; and they are politically less costly than regular soldiers. The disadvantages include cost, especially when they are used in high-risk situations; reliability, since they do not report through normal military chains of command; integration into regular forces; and legal ambiguity (status under the laws of war).

In one sense, privatization of the military is simply an extension of the principle of privatizing government functions generally and has been extended to a number of other military tasks already—food service is an example. On the other hand, the use of these kinds of forces strikes many as a resort to mercenary forces (defenders argue they are not mercenaries, because they only sign up to fight for the United States and are not generally available to the highest bidder, as mercenaries are); moreover, they raise the same kinds of problems of control and responsibility as does an organization like the French Foreign Legion, with which private forces like Blackwater have been analogized. Moreover, scandals surrounded Blackwater in 2007

Amplification 10.2

THE DRAFT OPTION

A major reason for opposition to the old selective service system was that it was riddled with inequities that allowed those with money, privilege, or power to evade service but ensnared those lacking such advantages. To some extent, the issue of equity will always plague any conscription system, although those inequities can be minimized.

Inequity has two sources. The first is at the front end of the process and involves who is "eligible" to be drafted. Under the Vietnam-era system, there was an extensive set of exemptions from service, including educational participation (attending college), family concerns (married status), and even employment in occupations deemed to be vital to national security (which included college professors and graduate students preparing to become professors). Moreover, all women were exempt. This created an economic and educational gap between those who might be chosen to serve and those who would not. This form of inequity can be lessened by removing all sources of exemption (except strictly defined physical or mental disability), thereby also increasing the eligibility pool beyond what used to exist. The problem is that this would mean the children of those with power and wealth would be part of the eligible pool rather than being exempt, making implementation even more difficult to achieve.

The other source of inequity, which cannot be erased, is inequity in terms of who serves. A *selective* service system is premised on the idea that the military (or any alternative forms of service) does not need or want all of the members of the eligible pool and thus selects some and bypasses others. The result is inequity: some endure the sacrifice of service, and others do not. A major approach to reducing this inequity is to provide rewards (e.g., college expenses) for those who serve but not for those who do not. Because selection and induction into the armed forces potentially involves being placed in harm's way, the gap cannot be removed altogether.

(see Snow, *What After Iraq?*). One intriguing question is whether one is more willing to risk these kinds of forces in situations where one would not place citizen-soldiers whose "expenditure" would have greater political consequences.

Manpower and Missions. The impact of the Iraq hangover on military manpower will be to make it more difficult, at least for a time, to recruit a force that replaces the current force or especially to create a larger force more adequate for Iraq-sized or larger future missions. For some, this limitation will be viewed as a virtue, because it means the United States cannot contemplate another episode like Iraq until the hangover has passed (this was clearly the case after Vietnam).

The relationship between military mission and manpower requirements will be one of the most important elements of the post-Iraq debate. Barring unforeseen changes of fortune, the exit from Iraq will tend to reinforce rather than negate the tendency of Americans to eschew military solutions to problems for a time, during which the military services (and especially the Army and Marines) will physically and psychologically attempt to assess the experience and try to recuperate from the harm the war has done to their ranks and their images in the world. If there are no calls for large-scale deployments over the next half-decade or so, the combat arms will not complain.

There are likely to be two major lightning rods in the postmortem in the wake of Iraq. One is how to reassess, and probably scale back, the military's activism and still remain committed to the GWOT (or whatever name supersedes it). The new administration in 2009 will inherit the problem of international religious terrorism, and especially the virtual certainty that it will leave behind some remnant of Al Qaeda in Iraq on the ground there. Al Qaeda itself will likely remain solidly, if unofficially, domiciled in the mountainous outreaches of the Pakistan–Afghanistan border region (Waziristan). In the short run, the response may well be restricted to aerial raids. The advantage is that such raids do not directly tax the overused Army and Marines, and their violation of Afghan and Pak sovereignty is not as great as if ground troops were used. The disadvantage is that such forms of attack are rarely conclusive and have not successfully targeted bin Laden and his cohorts in the past. A new administration may well partially demilitarize the effort against terrorism (see Chapter 12), but it cannot ignore it or the contention by many that the military is an, or *the*, appropriate instrument for this war.

The manpower problem will be ubiquitous. Will the United States rebuild the Army and Marines back to their pre–Iraq War levels? Or will they be made larger or smaller? The Iraq War so tied down American ground forces that it has been virtually impossible (and fortunately not necessary) to conduct a major deployment elsewhere simultaneously. Is that what Americans want? Conversely, a smaller force—even if technologically augmented to create force multipliers—can presumably be used less than a larger force, which some see as an advantage. A larger force, on the other hand, can be used for purposes that may allow it to guarantee a greater level of security or to get into more mischief, depending on one's perspective.

The question is whether the vision of future needs or the reality of recruitment and retention prospects will drive strategy. Rebuilding the force, and especially the Reserves, is not going to be an easy task after the way the force was exploited in Iraq, and the bigger the force one projects, the more difficult the problem is, at least if manpower procurement and retention are thought of in conventional terms. If the prospect of mission necessities is greater than what the manpower system can produce, what does one do then? As just discussed, there are two answers, neither without its particular baggage. One can involuntarily "recruit" force members through conscription, but conventional wisdom suggests this is political suicide. Privatizing the force is already under way but was generally unnoticed before the Blackwater controversy of 2007. Contracting out the country's defense, if that is the way the prospect is framed, could be an enormously complicated and controversial proposition.

CONCLUSION: SECURITY AFTER IRAQ

Like Vietnam, the Iraq War makes planning for and executing policy aimed at furthering national security more difficult than it was before the war. Although the military itself is likely to avoid the tarnish of blame for the lack of success in Iraq more than was the case for the post-Vietnam military, there will indeed be an Iraq hangover that will, at a minimum, make the necessary reconstitution of the armed forces more difficult than it otherwise would be. At the same time, the notion that military force is a multifunctional instrument that can solve a wide range of problems has also been brought into question by the war. The prime promoters of this multifaceted dimension of military force, the neoconservatives, have largely been discredited by the effort, and their influence is almost certain to decline, if not to disappear altogether.

The successor administration will almost certainly view the use of force more cautiously than has the Bush administration. Military activism will lie fallow for a time while the military rebuilds itself, both physically and in terms of what it does and how it does it. One can only hope it takes advantage of its enforced introspection to provide an outlook more forward-looking than the post-Vietnam assessment did.

Although one hates to do so, it is necessary to end the chapter on a somber note. The lesson of Vietnam was "no more Vietnams," which roughly meant no more involvement in quixotic causes where the realistic prospects of success were minimal. Iraq, unfortunately, met the definition of what was to be avoided, and the United States immersed itself in yet another Vietnam-like lost cause. One of the lessons of Iraq will also be "no more Iraqs." But will the United States actually learn the lesson this time? Or will there just be another interval before it forgets and repeats the same errors again?

STUDY/DISCUSSION QUESTIONS

1. The text predicts certain characteristics about the post-Iraq environment. What are they? Will they prove true or false? How do any discrepancies between the predictions and the reality affect the text's assessment of that environment and its predictions about the post-Iraq world?
2. Discuss the road to the Iraq War, starting with the legacy of the Persian Gulf War and moving forward to 2003. Include a discussion of the role of the neoconservatives in your answer.
3. Why did the United States decide to invade Iraq? Assess both the stated and the unstated possibilities.
4. Was the U.S. action in Iraq politically or militarily feasible? Assess the feasibility on both measures.
5. Compare the arguments that Iraq and Vietnam are dissimilar and similar. Which do you find more compelling? Why?
6. How will the Iraq War end? Assess the possible outcomes and the effects of those outcomes on both Iraq and the United States.
7. What are the broad lessons of the Iraq War? Discuss and assess each lesson.
8. What legacies derive from the Iraq War experience? Discuss and assess each critically.
9. How should the United States decide to man the post-Iraq military? At what levels and for what purposes should it be sized? How should the requisite numbers be obtained?

10. What do you think of the idea of privatizing parts of the American military? Discuss pros and cons and reach some personal conclusion that you can defend.

SELECTED BIBLIOGRAPHY

Avant, Deborah D. *The Market for Force: The Consequences of Privatizing Security*. New York: Cambridge University Press, 2005.

——. "Contracting for Services in U.S. Military Operations." *PS: Political Science and Politics* 40, 3 (July 2007), 457–460.

Bacevich, Andrew J. "Who's Bearing the Burden? Iraq and the Demise of the All-Volunteer Army." *Commonweal* 132 (July 15, 2005), 13–15.

Baker, James A., III, and Lee H. Hamilton (co-chairs). *The Iraq Study Group Report: The Way Forward—A New Approach* (authorized ed.). New York: Vintage Books, 2006.

Chandrasekaran, Rajiv. *Imperial Life in the Emerald City: Inside Iraq's Green Zone*. New York: Alfred A. Knopf, 2007.

Clancy, Tom, with General Tony Zinni and Tony Koltz. *Battle Ready*. New York: G. P. Putnam's Sons, 2004.

Clarke, Richard. *Against All Enemies: Inside America's War on Terror*. New York: Free Press, 2004.

Crane, Conrad C., and W. Andrew Terrill. *Reconstructing Iraq: Insights, Challenges, and Missions for Military Forces in a Post-conflict Scenario*. Carlisle Barracks, PA: Strategic Studies Institute, February 2003.

De Young, Karen, and Thomas E. Ricks. "Exit Strategies." *Washington Post*, July 17, 2007, A01.

Diamond, Larry. *Squandering Victory: The American Occupation and the Bungled Effort to Bring Democracy to Iraq*. New York: Times Books (Henry Holt and Company), 2005.

Franks, General Tommy, with Malcolm McConnell. *American Soldier*. New York: Regan Books, 2004.

Friedman, Thomas L. "Neither Democrats nor Republicans Offer Realistic Strategies for Leaving Iraq." *New York Times*, July 14, 2007 (reproduced in *Island Packet* (SC), July 15, 2007, AA04).

Frum, David, and Richard Perle. *An End to Evil: How to Win the War on Terror*. New York: Random House, 2003.

Glantz, Aaron. *How America Lost Iraq*. New York: Jeremy P. Tarcher/Penguin, 2005.

Gordon, Michael R., and General Bernard E. Trainor. *Cobra II: The Inside Story of the Invasion and Occupation of Iraq*. New York: Pantheon, 2006.

Hersh, Seymour M. *Chain of Command: The Road from September 11 to Abu Ghraib*. New York: HarperCollins, 2004.

Hilsman, Roger. *American Guerrilla: My War Behind Japanese Lines*. Washington, DC: Brassey's (U.S.), 1990.

Hsu, Spencer S. "Envoy Urges Visas for Iraqis Aiding U.S." *Washington Post*, July 22, 2007, A01.

Kagan, Robert, and William Kristol (eds.). *Present Dangers: Crisis and Opportunity in American Foreign and Defense Policy*. San Francisco: Encounter Books, 2000.

Kattenburg, Paul M. *The Vietnam Trauma in American Foreign Policy, 1945–1973*. New Brunswick, NJ: Transaction Books, 1980.

Mann, James. *Rise of the Vulcans: The History of Bush's War Cabinet*. New York: Viking, 2004.

McMaster. H. R. *Dereliction of Duty: Lyndon Johnson, Robert McNamara, the Joint Chiefs of Staff, and the Lies That Led to Vietnam*. New York: HarperPerennial, 1997.

Moore, Lt. General Harold G., and Joseph L. Galloway. *We Were Soldiers Once . . . and Young: Ia Drang: The Battle That Changed the War in Vietnam.* New York: HarperPerennial, 1992.

Packer, George. *The Assassin's Gate: America in Iraq.* New York: Farrar, Straus, Giroux, 2005.

Peters, Ralph. *Beyond Baghdad: Postmodern War and Peace.* Mechanicsburg, PA: Stackpole Books, 2003.

Pollack, Kenneth M. *The Threatening Storm: The Case for Invading Iraq.* A Council on Foreign Relations Book. New York: Random House, 2002.

Record, Jeffrey. *Dark Victory: America's Second War Against Iraq.* Annapolis, MD: Naval Institute Press, 2004.

Ricks, Thomas E. *Fiasco: The American Military Adventure in Iraq.* New York: Penguin Press, 2006.

Snow, Donald M. *Distant Thunder: Patterns of Conflict in the Developing World* (2nd ed.). Armonk, NY: M. E. Sharpe, 1997.

———. *What After Iraq? Getting In, Getting Out, and the Consequences.* New York: Pearson Longman, 2009.

———. *When America Fights: The Uses of U.S. Military Force.* Washington, DC: CQ Press, 2000.

———, and Dennis M. Drew. *From Lexington to Desert Storm and Beyond: War and Politics in the American Experience.* (2nd ed.). Armonk, NY: M. E. Sharpe, 2000.

Thompson, Sir Robert. *Make for the Hills: Memories of Far Eastern Wars.* London: Lee Cooper, 1989.

Woodward, Bob. *State of Denial: Bush at War, Part III.* New York: Simon and Schuster, 2006.

Yingling, Paul (Lt. Col.). "A Failure of Generalship." *Armed Forces Journal* (online). May 2007.

PART

III

NEW CHALLENGES

The contemporary environment, highlighted by the Iraq War, has created a new set of security problems with which the United States must wrestle in order to secure itself in the world. The purpose of Part III is to examine these problems, why they are important to the United States, and how they individually and collectively produce opportunities and challenges for the United States.

In the wake of the terrorist attack of September 11, 2001, Chapter 11 explores systematically what is sometimes called the "new kind of war." While fighting against nontraditional opponents may appear to provide some unique problems, the basic argument is that nontraditional, asymmetrical warfare is not something new but the repackaging of ideas and approaches that have given the United States and other countries problems in the past and will continue to do so in the future. The Iraqi insurgency is simply the latest instance of this problem. Chapter 12 looks at what has been identified as the most dangerous military and semimilitary problem the United States faces—terrorism—and what the country can do to reduce the risks caused by terrorists. One of the consequences of conflicts that are dominant in the world today is the need to rebuild and rehabilitate countries after the fighting stops, a problem dramatically illustrated by Iraq. Because of this, Chapter 13 looks specifically at the problems of peacekeeping and state building in war-ravaged countries. Chapter 14 explores less traditional sources of national security concern, so-called transnational issues with direct national security implications—resource scarcity, the environment, disease, and national borders.

CHAPTER 11

Asymmetrical Warfare: The "New Kind of War"

PREVIEW

The events of September 11, 2001, reintroduced the United States to a form of warfare it had experienced in the past, previously in Vietnam nearly forty years ago and more recently in Iraq. Because the United States prefers to engage in traditional, conventional (symmetrical) warfare and has had an undistinguished history against unconventional foes, the attacks were all the more difficult to comprehend. Had the United States indeed discovered a new kind of war that represents the future? Or had the emergence of the United States as the world's premier symmetrical warrior forced others to adopt asymmetrical warfare as the only way to confront American might? To answer these questions, this chapter first defines and describes asymmetrical and symmetrical warfare, with an emphasis on the more unfamiliar former. Following that examination, it looks at asymmetrical futures in the forms of fourth-generation warfare, the new internal wars (NIWs), and Iraq. The chapter concludes by looking at how "new" this kind of war really is.

The horrendous events of September 11, 2001 and the Iraq War have revived the public debate over the uses of American military force for the future. In the decade following the end of the Cold War, important American interests at which armed force might be employed were largely unchallenged, and as a result, the debate over how and when to use force had been largely muted. The principal international dynamic in a national security sense was the interest–threat mismatch in which American vital interests were hardly threatened anywhere and the threats that did exist were so peripheral as to be hardly interesting. No country on Earth appeared to pose a meaningful threat to basic American security. The only remaining super-power reigned supreme, and the only apparent needs for American armed forces were in "deployments of choice" (situations in which the United States elected but was not compelled to employ armed forces) in remote and obscure locales such as Haiti, Bosnia, and Kosovo to quell humanitarian disasters.

This seeming tranquility did not mean that questions were not being asked about the future of American military activity. Within the professional defense intellectual community, the future was a lively concern that centered on two related questions. The first question was the kind of circumstance in which Americans might have to bear arms, and the answers tended to suggest that the most likely scenarios were nontraditional conflicts occurring in the developing world. A few writers were even predicting the kinds of concerns that have been raised since September 11, 2001, although their exhortations were clearly not prevalent during the 1990s. The other question was how the United States should prepare for future contingencies, and it was focused on issues of force modernization and possible restructuring, introduced in Chapter 9.

The future came home with a literal crash with the terrorist attacks against New York and Washington, D.C. The events themselves were galvanizing and shocking enough to raise basic concerns about national security. As the reaction to the airplane attacks settled in our collective consciousnesses, an immediate victim of the exposure of the second fault line was American complacency about a supposedly tranquil and nonthreatening environment. At the bottom line, the attacks revealed that the United States was indeed vulnerable to attack. Even if the country lacked a major foe that could imperil its survival, its previously assumed invulnerability to harm was shown to be false and could not easily or quickly be restored, and leaders lacked any clear consensus on the larger meaning of what had happened and what could be done about it.

In the immediate, shocked response, the analogy that dominated descriptions of the new situation was that of "war." President Bush rapidly described the attacks as acts of war equivalent in their infamy to the Japanese attack on Pearl Harbor sixty years earlier. The media, and especially the electronic news networks, promptly seized the analogy, with Cable News Network (CNN), for instance, proclaiming the "new kind of war" as the masthead of its news coverage for months after the fact.

Shock masked an important dynamic of the new environment. In the decade or so since the Cold War, the United States had developed the most powerful conventional (symmetrical) armed forces in the world, forces that were compared to the Roman legions. These forces were so potent at symmetrical warfare, as demonstrated against Iraq in 1991 and 2003, that no other country could face the Americans on their own terms and hope to succeed. The United States had become a military juggernaut that could not be defied.

The result was that the United States failed to see the inevitable reaction to its prowess. Realizing that a symmetrical response to the Americans was suicidal, opponents did what groups have always done: they adopted approaches to fighting—what is now called asymmetrical warfare—that negate the American advantage. The unrecognized consequence of American strength was to negate its application: the United States became so good at symmetrical warfare that, in a classic self-fulfilling prophecy, it made such warfare obsolete. No one will (or should) play the game the way Americans want to play it.

The law of unintended consequences was at work here. The United States developed its prowess to advance its interests in the world, but the world responded by changing the nature of the competition to give itself a chance against the American behemoth. The unintended consequence of American power is that the country is now confronted by a new problem, asymmetrical warfare, that it has not historically been very good at confronting.

It is not a problem likely to disappear anytime soon. The simple fact is that asymmetrical warfare does succeed in leveling the playing field and gives what appears to be a hopelessly outmanned force a chance to compete, even to succeed. The Iraqi insurgency is only the most recent instance of this dynamic.

The extension of the antiterrorist campaign to Afghanistan and the effort to remove the Taliban government shielding Al Qaeda from capture added to the conceptual confusion. In Afghanistan itself, forces loyal to the Taliban were waging a very traditional civil war against a series of opponents led by the Northern Alliance. It was traditional, or *symmetrical*, warfare in the sense that both sides were fighting in similar manners and for the traditional goal of maintaining or gaining control of the government. When the United States entered that situation, it was indeed involved in what quite properly could be described as a war, where American airpower and special forces were employed in absolutely traditional ways to help overthrow the Taliban government. When the Taliban were overthrown and the objective returned to rooting out Al Qaeda from its hideouts in the caves of the Tora Bora Mountains, the enterprise moved away somewhat from traditional warfare. The Afghan campaign thus mixed symmetrical and asymmetrical elements and helped obscure the emergence of the distinctive asymmetrical problem.

The attacks of September 11 set a tone for listening and thinking about asymmetrical war. Terrorism (the subject of Chapter 12) is an extreme form of asymmetrical warfare, although it is not exactly "war" even in the unconventional manner so much as a semimilitary problem. The attacks were obviously successful, however, and led the United States to seek retribution against a real and concrete opponent, the Taliban government of Afghanistan, which was physically providing sanctuary for the Al Qaeda terrorists.

These are not merely academic concerns, and they must be taken in the context of the debate that was ongoing before the terrorists violated American soil. The future face of war has, for instance, very strong implications for the future evolution of American forces and missions, as argued in Chapter 10. As the war in Afghanistan began to take shape, American Special Operations Forces (SOFs) became very prominent in the early going, serving as advisors to the anti-Taliban forces and as spotters directing American air strikes to their targets. Later they helped organize and conduct operations against remnants of the Taliban and Al Qaeda hiding in caves in the Afghan mountains. Is the future one in which SOFs occupy a much more central place in the Army than they did in the past? Because the Taliban forces chose not to abandon conventional war when the American bombers arrived, they were left in concentrated, vulnerable positions. American airpower had its most successful showing since the Persian Gulf War, killing and helping to destroy the cohesion of those Taliban who maintained their positions along traditional military lines and ended up serving as fodder for the bombers. Does this mean the future lies in the greater decisiveness of airpower, as its proponents have long argued? Is this how the military will go after Al Qaeda in Waziristan?

The aftermath of September 11 raises more questions than it answers, but it has provided a new emphasis for the debate about war in the future. What is clear is that the menu of violence has changed in at least two ways. First, the likelihood of American involvement in classic conventional war has been reduced dramatically (there is no one who will fight us this way), meaning any involvements experienced will in some way be asymmetrical. Second, the asymmetrical pattern will—by definition—change. Asymmetrical warfare is an approach to war, not a set of instructions for making war. The asymmetrical warrior fights in whatever way works at any place and point in time, and that is an evolving process of experience and adaptation.

SYMMETRICAL AND ASYMMETRICAL WARFARE

A basic consideration in thinking about the nature of warfare is through the conceptualizations of war that the different participants have. For most of the American experience, wars have been fought by traditional, conventional military forces, where both sides were organized in pretty much the same way, had largely the same (if opposing) purposes, served as representatives of sovereign states (or of groups seeking to gain or maintain control of states), and accepted the same general conventions (or laws) surrounding proper and improper ways to conduct war. The term used to describe warfare among similar opponents is *symmetrical warfare*, in the sense that the contending sides resemble or mirror one another along the axes of organization, purpose, affiliation, and intent. The world wars represent the epitome of symmetrical wars.

Symmetrical warfare suggests the existence of its opposite. One of the newer terms to enter the public debate is *asymmetrical warfare*, and it has been used throughout the text. In its broadest connotations, asymmetrical warfare represents the opposite of symmetrical warfare. In this form of combat, one side fights conventionally while the other side organizes itself differently, may or may not share the same objectives as its opponent, may or may not represent a government or a movement aspiring to become a government, and rejects the conventions or laws of warfare propounded by the conventional side.

In the current context, symmetrical warfare is associated with the western military tradition practiced in modern Europe and, more recently, North America and other parts of the world that have adopted its norms. The salient characteristics of countries operating in this tradition include the fielding of mass armies, navies, and air forces that are similarly organized and configured (e.g., wearing regular uniforms, organized in traditional rank orderings), follow Clausewitzian principles regarding the subordination of war to its political purposes, fight as representatives of state governments seeking to realize the interests of states, and accept common rules about what is permissible and impermissible in war (e.g., treatment of prisoners, acceptability of purposely targeting civilians). While not all wars fought in this tradition completely mirror all of these characterizations, it is the general and expected means of war. Those who hold these values view adherence to them as honorable and deviation from them as somehow less than honorable.

In the current debate, asymmetrical approaches are more closely related to what is described as the Asiatic (including Middle Eastern) approach to war. This tradition goes back to the beginning of recorded theories of war and is currently manifested in military conduct in which at least one of the opponents is organized in a manner different from a standard armed force (guerrilla fighters, for instance), may or may not have gaining or maintaining government control as its central purpose, may not represent governments or insurgents, and does not accept or practice warfare (especially limits on permissible actions) in accord with western conventions.

There is nothing new about asymmetrical warfare other than the name. Its underlying motivations are clear and have deep roots. As already argued, asymmetrical approaches to warfare are attractive to those who cannot compete successfully using conventional methods and whose only chance for success requires changing the playing field so that they do have a chance. As Vincent Goulding Jr. put it, it is the approach by which "weaker opponents have sought to neutralize their enemy's technological or numerical superiority by fighting in ways or on battlefields that nullify it." If you cannot win fighting one way, it makes sense to find another way at which you can at least hope to succeed. The principle is as old as the first armed group that faced a superior enemy it could not possibly defeat if it fought according to the accepted rules of the day.

Put a slightly different way, asymmetrical warfare is unconventional warfare. Symmetrical warfare is the preference of those entities that are advantaged under accepted forms of war, whereas asymmetrical approaches are appealing to those who cannot compete successfully within the constraints of those rules. In the current environment, the world's most vociferous champion of symmetrical warfare is quite understandably the United States, whereas its opponents are inexorably drawn to asymmetrical approaches.

Evolution of Asymmetrical Warfare

As already stated, the term *asymmetrical warfare* is much newer than the general phenomenon it describes. Methods of warfare displaying some or all of this style of warfare have a long history, have been described with a variety of names, and have long been at least a small part of the American military tradition.

The idea of trying to negate the advantages of opponents fighting the conventional warfare of the day is as old as organized warfare. Although styles and tactics have changed, conventional warfare has almost always been conducted by massed, uniformed armies divided into ranks who used their weight and firepower to confront and overwhelm opponents. It is how the Roman Legion generally fought, although Belfigio (see "Selected Bibliography") points out that they also occasionally engaged in what is now called asymmetrical methods as well, and it is how the various combatants in World War I and II conducted war. Normally, this style of warfare is conducted in conformance to some broad set of rules of engagement that specify acceptable and unacceptable conduct in battle. Through history, there have been, of course, notable exceptions to this depiction—the Mongol Hordes substituted maneuver for mass and ignored conventions on the treatment of prisoners, for instance. The tradition of this style of warfare, now called symmetrical warfare, is highly western in content and values. More to the point, it is key to the "American way of war."

Normally, an opposing force that lacks the mass of a conventional armed force in either quantitative or qualitative terms cannot successfully confront a conventional force on its own terms and prevail. In that circumstance, the options available to the inferior force are to quit the contest and surrender, to stand before and be destroyed by the superior force, or to adopt a style of warfare that negates the advantages of the superior force and provides an opportunity for success. In other words, the only possible avenue for victory is to fight asymmetrically.

The asymmetrical tradition is most associated with Asian styles of fighting. The original Chinese military manual, Sun Tzu's *Art of War*, is a virtual primer on how to shift the advantage from a superior to an inferior force (see Amplification 11.1). Many of the principles originally laid out by Sun Tzu were adapted and operationalized by Mao Zedung in his campaigns against the Guomintang led by Chiang kai-Shek in the twenty-plus years of the Chinese Civil War and were, in turn, adapted by the Vietnamese historian-turned-general Vo Nguyen Giap in his campaigns first

Amplification 11.1

SUN TZU ON ASYMMETRICAL WARFARE

Little is known about Sun Tzu, a Chinese military thinker who advised several warlords in China approximately three thousand years ago. Some argue that he did not exist at all, but that the work attributed to him was the collection of experiences of others. His classic military manual *The Art of War* (similar in intent to Machiavelli's political manual *The Prince* for Italian leaders in the sixteenth century) was little studied in the West until it became known that it was one of the sources of inspiration for Mao Zedung in his campaign to seize control of China over a twenty-year period ending in 1949.

The heart of Sun Tzu's military advice, which would be familiar to practitioners of what is now called asymmetrical warfare, was knowing when and how to fight. His philosophy of indirection and asymmetry is best stated in his advice to military leaders of his time: "When the enemy advances, we retreat; when the enemy halts, we harass; when the enemy seeks to avoid battle, we attack; when the enemy retreats, we pursue." In addition, he adds that the victor on the battlefield has a superior understanding of his opponent that allows him to deceive and thus alter favorably the battle: "All warfare is based on deception. . . . To subdue the enemy without fighting is the acme of skill. Thus, what is of supreme importance is to attack the enemy's strategy." Echoing that sentiment three thousand years later, Goulding adds, "War might usually favor the side with the heaviest battalions, but it *always* favors the smartest." Does war really change?

against the French and later against the Americans between 1945 and 1975. Hundreds of years earlier, the Vietnamese successfully evicted Kublai Khan and the Mongols from Vietnam during the thirteenth century using similar techniques.

The style of warfare represented by the asymmetrical tradition has known different names across time. A parallel term is guerrilla warfare, used to describe a particular style of warfare involving highly unconventional tactics employed for the traditional end of gaining control of government. Unconventional warfare is to conventional what asymmetrical is to symmetrical. Terms like *partisan* or *people's war* have also been used as synonyms. The purpose of saying this is not to confuse the reader but to point out that asymmetrical warfare has known many names and that the names change more than the underlying principles on which they are based.

It is also part of the American military tradition, beginning in the earliest days of white settlement of North America. Most of the Indians whom the settlers encountered fought unconventionally at the tactical level, engaging in ambushes, hiding behind trees and rocks, and otherwise behaving in ways that did not conform to the tactics of linear warfare practiced in Europe. When the American Revolution began, it quite quickly became apparent that the fledgling Continental Army could not successfully contest the British Army in linear battles, and some of its tactics moved from the symmetrical to the asymmetrical. America's first great victory in the Revolutionary War, at Saratoga in 1777, was a classic linear clash, but its success was largely the result of attrition of the British expeditionary force coming down from Lake Champlain by American militiamen fighting Indian style. By the time General Burgoyne's army finally reached Saratoga, attrition had reduced it to about half the size of its American counterpart. Francis ("the Swamp Fox") Marion in South Carolina and George Rogers Clark in the Northwest Territories were notable practitioners of this form of warfare during the Revolution. The United States faced asymmetrical opponents in the Seminole Wars in the 1820s in Florida, in the campaigns against the Western Indians after the Civil War, in the Filipino Insurgency at the turn of the twentieth century, and against Pancho Villa in New Mexico and Arizona in the 1910s.

The United States' most extensive and traumatic encounter with an opponent practicing a form of asymmetrical warfare was, of course, in Vietnam. The basic situation conforms neatly to the distinctions already made and, as argued in the last chapter, has some parallels in the ongoing campaign against the remnants of the Taliban in Afghanistan and against insurgents in Iraq.

Consider the basic structure of the military situation in Vietnam. The Vietnamese insurgents (the North Vietnamese and Viet Cong) faced an American-organized and hence thoroughly conventional South Vietnamese opponent. Following the basic outlines of the Maoist mobile-guerrilla warfare strategy (see Snow, *Distant Thunder*, Chapter 3, for a description), the North Vietnamese Army (NVA) and the Viet Cong (VC) had worn down the Army of the Republic of Vietnam (ARVN) through a guerrilla war of attrition and, by 1964, had gained such a military advantage that it converted to conventional warfare, confronting the ARVN in a symmetrical fashion for the purpose of destroying the ARVN and seizing political power.

The United States entered the fray with combat forces in 1965. The South Vietnamese were in desperate straits when intervention occurred, but American conventional military power quickly reversed the military situation. This change was first demonstrated in the two-day Battle of the Ia Drang Valley in November 1965, an encounter vividly captured in Moore and Galloway's *We Were Soldiers Once . . . and Young* (which was the basis of the motion picture *We Were Soldiers*). On the first day of the battle, an NVA conventional force encountered and engaged an American force in a conventional battle. The overwhelming American advantage in firepower (mass) turned the confrontation into a deadly shooting gallery in which the NVA was severely bloodied. On the second day, however, the Americans began a march to the staging area from which they were to be evacuated that stretched the troops single file over three miles, and the NVA responded by reverting to guerrilla tactics of ambush and hit-and-run attacks by small units that could avoid American concentrated firepower. The result was a defeat for the Americans.

Although largely unrecognized at the time, the Ia Drang experience was a parable of sorts for understanding the dynamics both of Vietnam and of symmetrical and asymmetrical warfare. Prior to the American intervention, the NVA and VC were fighting symmetrical (conventional) war against the ARVN, and they were succeeding (the ARVN continued to fight that way because although it was losing, this was the only way the ARVN knew how to fight). When the United States entered the contest, however, the much more modestly equipped NVA and VC realized they could not compete with American firepower in symmetrical combat, leaving them the choices of surrender, loss, or a change of the rules to provide them with a chance of success.

The asymmetrical style they selected was the guerrilla phase of mobile-guerrilla warfare. Instead of standing toe-to-toe with the Americans, they reverted to guerrilla tactics such as ambush and avoidance of concentrations of American forces. Capturing and holding territory ceased to be a central concern; instead, they sought to wear down the American forces, to drag out the war until the Americans wearied of the contest and public opinion demanded they leave. It was the classic Vietnamese approach that they had used seven hundred years earlier to rid themselves of the Mongols, and it ultimately worked equally well against the Americans. And, of course, when the Americans left in 1973, the NVA abandoned asymmetrical methods and returned to conventional, symmetrical warfare to finish off the job the Americans had interrupted during their stay.

The Contemporary Setting

If the American military experience in Vietnam was a harbinger of our encounter with asymmetrical warfare, and post–Cold War and post–September 11 environments have reinforced that precedent. As already noted, the 1990s witnessed the emergence of the United States as the military hyperpower: although U.S. troop strength declined during this period, the forces of other countries declined even more. At the same time, the application of electronic technology to warfare, the revolution in military affairs (RMA), was added to the American arsenal. The result was the overwhelming and growing military disparity between the most advanced countries—and especially the United States—and the rest, including the developing countries in which violence most often occurs. This trend was made evident to all serious observers originally in the Persian Gulf War, and it was reinforced in the campaign against the Taliban and Al Qaeda. The major implication of the trend has been an increase in the adoption of asymmetrical methods when confronting western—and especially American—forces.

The Impact of the RMA. The growing gap in qualitative military capabilities is largely the result of the RMA. Without going into diverting detail, the idea of an RMA (there have been several of them historically) is the impact of a particular technology or series of technologies on the battlefield when those scientific discoveries are applied to warfare. The classic study of how new weaponry changes the nature and outcome of war was the Brodies' *From Crossbow to H-Bomb*. A good twentieth-century example of the effects of applying new technology to warfare was the impact of the internal combustion engine, which allowed the development of weapons such as the tank and the armored personnel carrier and made possible the *blitzkrieg* tactics introduced by the Germans in World War II and widely employed by all combatants in that war.

The current RMA features the application of advances in computing and telecommunications to modern warfare. The "computer revolution" was first applied by the United States in the Vietnam conflict in ways such as using electronic sensing of VC and NVA troop movements. At the time, the applications were fairly primitive (for example, the VC stymied the sensors by hanging sacks of human waste above the sensors, which emitted heat and chemical signatures that caused the sensors constantly to record troops going by when none were), and there was an inadequate appreciation of the strategic implications of the application of technology to the war. The early attempts in Vietnam, however, were no more than the tip of the iceberg of contemporary applications.

The "weaponization" of high technology began to mature in the years following Vietnam. Although technology has had a pervasive influence, it has been most dramatic in two related areas that have most widened capability disparities: reconnaissance and weapons accuracy. Reconnaissance has been enhanced dramatically by satellite imagery, which, when wedded with the most modern telecommunications equipment, allows the location of both friendly and adversary forces over a wide area and in considerable detail. To aid in visualization of the battlefield, for instance, high definition television (HDTV) was subsidized by the U.S. Department of Defense to produce the most vivid, detailed pictures of combat areas possible. Particularly when this kind of information is available to one side but not the other, the result is a considerable advantage for the possessor and an almost insurmountable disadvantage for the side lacking the capacity. In its most extreme manifestation, the possessor knows where the opponent is and can target him all of the time, whereas the nonpossessor never knows where the enemy is or when and how that enemy is likely to strike.

The second advance has been in guidance capabilities that allow the precision delivery of munitions—usually airborne from cruise missiles or bomber aircraft—over long distances with astonishing accuracy. This capability makes it possible for the possessor, once the enemy is found, to attack promptly and with a very high degree of success. Because the munitions normally can be fired from distances outside visual range and at speeds such that they cannot be seen, the victim is helpless to protect himself. Reconnaissance and precision delivery are just two of the more important aspects of the current RMA. All these applications have the effect of being *force multipliers*, or enhancers of the effectiveness (lethality) of the force that possesses them. In addition, they all reduce dramatically the vulnerability of the warriors who possess them, thereby dramatically reducing casualty rates for the possessing state while increasing the rate for the victims.

The resulting technology gap becomes an illustrative problem that the asymmetrical warrior must negate. Electronic surveillance works only when the target can be found, and thus the asymmetrical warrior will likely take countermeasures (like hiding) to avoid detection. It does not matter how accurate a weapon is if it cannot find its target, so denying "target acquisition" is a major asymmetrical objective. The feckless campaign to locate and capture or kill Usama bin Laden demonstrates that the asymmetrical warrior can sometimes succeed in foiling the fruits of the RMA.

The Persian Gulf War Example. The first application of this growing disparity occurred in the Persian Gulf War of 1990–1991. After the Iraqi invasion, conquest, and threatened annexation of tiny Kuwait in August 1990, a military coalition was organized to reverse that outcome. The United States took the lead in organizing the effort under United Nations auspices and eventually brought together a coalition of twenty-five states, including some Islamic countries from the region, to oppose Saddam Hussein.

At the time, there was great concern about how difficult the military task of dislodging the Iraqis from Kuwait would be. Iraq possessed the fourth largest army in the world, it was pointed out, and it was a battle-tested force, having fought for eight years in the Iran–Iraq war that ended in 1988. In those circumstances, many predicted a stout defense by the Iraqis, and speculations abounded about, among other things, the level of casualties the United States would incur.

Those who predicted large numbers of casualties, of course, were proven wrong, as the war turned out to be a walkover in military terms. The applications of the RMA to the forces of the major western powers had created such a technological disparity between the two opponents that the Iraqis stood no practical chance against the coalition troops. Saddam Hussein also misperceived American will (he believed the United States was still so traumatized by Vietnam that it would not react decisively) and the relative strength of his forces arrayed against the Americans and their allies. As a result, he engaged his Soviet-trained and Soviet-styled armed forces in conventional, symmetrical warfare fought on the terms of the coalition, against which he could not prevail.

The major difference was the RMA. When the air war commenced, the Americans attacked and destroyed the Iraqi radar and communications infrastructure on the first day. For the rest of the campaign, the United States had uncontested control of the skies while the Iraqis were limited in their ability to monitor activities of the coalition literally to what they could see standing on the ground. Meanwhile, satellites provided detailed images of Iraqi locations and movements that Iraq absolutely lacked. As an example, the global positioning system—or GPS—meant Americans always knew where they were in the featureless Arabian Desert, whereas the Iraqis were never certain of their own, much less the enemy's, location. At the same time, the Americans were able to locate Iraqi targets and to direct precision munitions to them well out of range of Iraqi retaliatory capabilities. Although subsequent assessments have indicated that some of the more dramatic claims of superiority were inflated, nevertheless, the results were an overwhelming coalition victory with very few coalition—and specifically American—war deaths (less than 150, not all of which were the result of hostile action). The implication for future developing countries taking on the United States symmetrically using American rules was clear to all concerned.

The Afghanistan Reprise. The same dynamic occurred again in 2001 when the United States broadened its response to the terrorist attacks of September 11, 2001, to include deposing the Taliban government of Afghanistan. In order to achieve its underlying purpose—the destruction of the bin Laden organization, Al Qaeda, which was being shielded by the Taliban regime—it was determined that a prefatory step had to be the overthrow of the Afghan regime that refused to turn over bin Laden and his followers to the United States for prosecution. The result was to involve the United States in what had been a reasonably conventional civil war between the Taliban and opposing factions, notably the Northern Coalition.

Prior to the United States' entry into the conflict with SOFs and airpower, the Taliban had been engaged in a conventional civil conflict with their opponents. Success and failure in that conflict was measured by territory controlled, and the clear purpose was for one side to maintain or the other to gain political power territorially defined—clearly traditional purposes. The fighting itself was reasonably conventional, with thrusts and parries in one direction or the other and fortified lines facing one another across the harsh Afghan vista. It was war the way it had been fought for centuries among Afghan factions, and it was a war in which the Taliban were holding their own or winning.

Enter the Americans. After the Taliban leadership refused to capture and relinquish bin Laden and his followers into international custody, the United States began to mount a military campaign the purpose of which was to force the Taliban to comply and turn over the terrorist or, failing in obtaining that goal, physically to assist in the overthrow of the regime, thereby removing that barrier to bringing the terrorist to justice.

The military campaign involved the use of both conventional and unconventional forces. SOFs were among the first dispatched to Afghanistan, coordinating efforts with anti-Taliban rebel forces, securing crucial staging grounds such as airfields (a task for which Marines were also used), and acting as spotters directing the bombers to their targets. The real hammer of the operation, of course, was airpower, both from fixed-wing aircraft relentlessly bombing Taliban and later Al Qaeda positions and from helicopter gunships strafing suspected concentrations of enemy forces.

The Taliban apparently did not anticipate either the fury or the deadly effect of the American action. It is arguable that the Taliban failed to anticipate American actions because they believed bin Laden's assessment of prior American responses to terrorist attacks. In those cases, bin Laden had publicly argued that the United States had either done nothing in retaliation, as occurred after the Khobar apartments attack in 1996 in Saudi Arabia and the attack on the USS *Cole* in 2000 in Yemen, or carried out a symbolic but ineffective response, as in the cruise missile attacks on supposed terrorist training camps in Afghanistan in 1998 after the bombings of the American embassies in Dar es Salaam and Nairobi (Operation Desert Fox). Bin Laden had also suggested in various of his pronouncements that he believed the Americans were obsessed with avoiding casualties under any circumstances and clearly would not put American forces in harm's way.

Whatever the basis of their assessment, the Taliban were clearly wrong and did not respond appropriately to the American aerial assault. Past experience has suggested (at least to some) that airpower can be devastating to concentrations of exposed forces (in other words, forces fighting western-style symmetrical warfare), but that it loses some of its effect if its targets take evasive action, such as dispersing and retreating into more impregnable positions, like the Afghan mountains (in other words, adopt asymmetrical methods). To do this, of course, the Taliban forces would have had to abandon the lines they used to protect the physical areas under their control to the advancing Northern Alliance and other opponents.

The Taliban options were devil's choices. Beyond the option of surrender, they could either continue the war as they had been fighting it, which meant symmetrically, or they could stage a Maoist reversion to asymmetrical warfare. In either case, they were likely to lose, either by being pounded into submission by their airpower-aided opponents in a continuation of the conventional war or by retreating into the mountains, where they would become the hunted opposition that had abandoned the territory they controlled. They initially chose to stand and fight, leaving themselves ready targets for American bombs. The effect was predictable: in addition to killing a large number of Taliban fighters, the sheer shock effect of the bombing apparently destroyed the cohesion of the Taliban forces, sapping their morale and will to continue fighting. With the Taliban bombed into disarray, they and the remaining Al Qaeda fighters retreated to the mountains, where they have managed to regroup and mount a resistance to the Afghan government by adopting long-held asymmetrical tactics such as evasion.

The Iraq War. The impact of the RMA, combined with *blitzkrieg*-style maneuver techniques, was also felt dramatically in Iraq. The Americans and the British were able to sweep through the country virtually unopposed except in a few cities like Basra. In addition to the "shock and awe" effects of massive precision bombing, the heart of the success was the extreme speed with which the coalition forces moved, demoralizing and dispiriting their Iraqi foes.

The RMA has had at least one perverse impact on military planning. To Secretary Rumsfeld and his supporters, the technological prowess of RMA-equipped forces meant the effectiveness of individual soldiers was magnified (the force multiplier effect), and the implication was that numerically smaller forces could accomplish the same—or even broader—objectives that historically larger forces carried out. This principle underlay the numbers and tactics employed in Operation Iraqi Freedom, and their "shock and awe" effects were apparently quite effective in the invasion and conquest phases of the war, but they were proved inadequate for Phase IV operations.

There was a resulting apparently unanticipated development—the Iraqi resistance. While the regular Iraqi forces did not mount a spirited defense and eventually capitulated, some of their colleagues instead went underground to prepare for the asymmetrical campaign that has been going on ever since. According to our analysis, this was probably the logical—and only—way the American occupation could be opposed with any hope of success.

The Strategic Effects. The dual lessons of the Persian Gulf War and the Afghanistan campaign should be clear, and so should their implications be clear for likely uses of American force in the future. The assessment is not without irony, as already noted. At the bottom line, the United States and its closest allies have become so proficient at conventional warfare that they are likely to be able to engage in such methods only against extremely foolish or masochistic opponents. At the same time, the maintenance of such force will continue to be necessary to remind potential future opponents of the folly of challenging the United States symmetrically and to perform the kinds of tasks for which such forces are adept, such as military occupation.

The two experiences clearly reinforce the gap in conventional capabilities that has been widened to a chasm between RMA-proficient forces and conventional forces that do not share those capabilities. In Kuwait, Afghanistan, and Iraq, the opponents of the United States both stood and to some extent fought symmetrically in circumstances where they realistically had no chance of prevailing, and in all cases, their conventional forces were thoroughly and efficiently routed. This gap in capability between the military "haves" and "have nots" will only widen further in the future, meaning the consequences will remain in the future as well.

Much has been said since Vietnam about the failure of American will, especially the American aversion to accepting casualties. Two factors from the Kuwait, Afghanistan, and Iraq experiences should mitigate this perception and thus temper future assessments of how or if the United States will respond when provoked. One of the consequences of American conventional dominance that was first demonstrated in Kuwait and reinforced in Afghanistan has been the ability to greatly reduce American casualties through the application of technology. The mass of American firepower and the distance from which it can be employed not only devastate its opponents if they try to confront it directly, but also save American lives. The old perception (foretold by American actions in Lebanon and Somalia) that an opponent can force an American withdrawal by killing a few American soldiers is very difficult to achieve fighting symmetrically with the Americans. The current testing ground of American willingness to incur losses is the ongoing Iraqi resistance.

The Afghanistan experience provides another rejoinder about American willingness to accept battle losses. The reaction to the terrorist attacks reminded the United States of another factor, that Americans have always been willing to put lives at risk *if the cause was sufficient*. The question of the unacceptability of casualties has arisen when people thought the cause was insufficient to justify the sacrifice, as in places such as Somalia. In that sense, the analogy between the terrorist attacks on September 11, 2001, and Pearl Harbor is apt: the United States may be reluctant to respond when the situation does not clearly dictate a response, but it will when the reasons are obvious and compelling. When American support for the cause wavers, as it has in Iraq, then the aversion to casualties returns.

The lessons of these combined experiences for future potential American (or more broadly western) opponents should be fairly obvious. The most obvious lesson, of course, is that it is fool's work to challenge the western powers at their own game; symmetrical warfare with the West is suicidal. It has been suggested that one way for weaker states to level the playing field would be to introduce WMD such as chemical or biological weapons on the battlefield. Such a suggestion misses the essential point and actually reinforces the disparity. Should Saddam Hussein have introduced chemical or biological agents into the Gulf War (as it has been suggested he contemplated doing), the overwhelming western advantage in WMD would have simply made his defeat all the more decisive, with the United States, for instance, responding to a chemical attack against its forces with a more or less controlled nuclear response. Fortunately for most potential opponents of the West, they lack the military resources for a symmetrical challenge anyway.

The other obvious lesson is how to fight the West if a clash becomes inevitable. The overwhelming weight of American and other western might means a challenger cannot confront that power directly and only has some chance of success by changing the rules. Vietnam again provides a model of sorts. The North Vietnamese government understood shortly after the American intervention that it could not defeat the United States symmetrically, so its forces reverted to an asymmetrical style (guerrilla warfare) that negated the American advantages in technology and firepower. Instead, they attacked the American will to continue the contest by inflicting a large enough number of casualties on the Americans (although the numbers were trifles compared to the casualties they incurred themselves) to convince the American public and its leaders that persevering was not worthwhile. What ultimately undermined the American campaign was not, as Saddam Hussein and Usama bin Laden apparently concluded, American unwillingness to incur losses; it was our unwillingness to do so in what we concluded was a *less than worthy cause.* The fate of the Iraq campaign will likely ultimately be decided in those terms: Americans have concluded that Iraq was not worth the amount of sacrifice that it entailed, and the result has been a demand to terminate the involvement.

This assessment leaves some ironic implications for American preparation for the future. On the one hand, the only countries that could possibly confront the United States in conventional, symmetrical warfare are our closest allies (NATO) and other countries with which we have developed such close relations that war is unthinkable (Russia, China). All realistic potential foes either lack an armed force that could challenge us directly or realize such a force would lose. Thus, the very kind of application of force at which we most excel is the least likely kind of force we will have occasion to use in the near future. The clear lesson of the Iraq occupation, however, is that mass and numbers, the data of symmetrical warfare, still matter in these situations.

Thus, conventional force cannot be abandoned, dismantled, or substantially diminished. While one can argue about whether current American forces deter *all* kinds of attacks on the United States (future terrorist assaults, for instance), they certainly do deter conventional attacks that might be contemplated in their absence. At the same time, both Kuwait and Afghanistan demonstrate that periodically situations can arise in which such forces can be brought to bear with decisive effect.

What this analysis suggests is that, in the future, most of the situations in which the United States will have the opportunity to use force will be against an opponent adopting asymmetrical methods to try to obviate the American dominance in conventional warfare. This would suggest an emphasis on light forces (see Chapter 9) and on special purpose forces, such as SOFs, as well as precision airpower. At the same time, it is equally clear that asymmetrical opponents will continue to make adaptations to the means they employ against us, thus requiring flexibility in countering new methods they devise. On the other hand, if the United States wants to engage in conventional missions, like military occupations, it will need the mass of symmetrical forces to be successful.

ASYMMETRICAL FUTURES?

The asymmetrical approach to warfare—changing the rules to negate disadvantages—is ancient, even if some of the tactical means of applying asymmetrical warfare principles are new and evolving. In order to get a better idea of what the dynamics of asymmetrical warfare are and how they may affect the future, it is helpful to look at two models. One of them is a more or less theoretical construct predicting what some analysts during the 1990s thought about the likely future of warfare and providing a generic description of that future—what has been called *fourth-generation warfare*. The other, about which I have written in *Uncivil Wars* and other works, is a description of the empirical nature of a series of chaotic civil wars of the 1990s and beyond that I have called the *new internal wars* (NIWs). They are basically similar depictions, with NIWs essentially serving as concrete examples of how the fourth generation of warfare may look in parts of the world. These constructs are important to examine in terms of the context of whether they will become the dominant form of future conflict or just an additional element of the pattern of war, as well as to consider in assessing the impact of Iraq.

Fourth-Generation Warfare

A body of thought among military historians and other analysts has for some time argued that conventional, western-style warfare, especially warfare conducted along Clausewitzian lines, represents an aberration rather than a universal phenomenon. In particular, these analysts maintain the kind of warfare described here as symmetrical is a temporal oddity. Among the champions of this position has been the British historian John Keegan, who argues there has been a kind of Clausewitzian interlude beginning with the Napoleonic era and ending with World War II when Clausewitz's trinitarian relationship between the people, government, and armed forces was dominant and western norms of warfare prevailed. Keegan argues that era has passed and the dominant pattern of warfare in the future, as it was in the past before the

Napoleonic period, will be what has been identified here as asymmetrical warfare. A persistent band of contemporary analysts agrees; for some of them, the dominant analogy is fourth-generation warfare.

Fourth-generation warfare represents a conceptual and physical departure from the dominance of western-style warfare. One of the earlier depictions of this change, described by a group headed by a former aide to Senator Gary Hart, William Lind, examines the evolution of warfare from the Napoleonic period forward in an article published in the October 1989 *Marine Corps Gazette*. The authors maintain that the first generation of warfare was dominated by linear formations of armies clashing in open fields where the dominant weaponry was the smooth-bore musket. This form of fighting favored the offensive actions of the conventional armies in combat. The second generation was the result of the introduction of much more accurate rifles and muskets that made the charges of tightly configured formations suicidal. The trench warfare of World War I is the epitome of this kind of defensively dominated war. With the weaponization of technologies like the truck and tank and the storage battery (for propelling submarines), the pendulum swung back to the offensive advantage, as maneuver was reintroduced onto the battlefield. The epitome of this style of warfare was the *blitzkrieg* style of fighting mastered by Germany in World War II.

What is notable about these three generations is how geopolitically and militarily traditional they are. In all three cases, they describe warfare fought by western national armies organized conventionally and with clear and identifiable political purposes for their actions. The changes from generation to generation are not radical but largely the result of changes in weapons technologies and adaptation of strategies and tactics that reflect those changes. At the same time, this western-style warfare features the clash of armies frontally when the major purpose of conflict is for one side or the other to defeat the enemy on the field of battle as a necessary preface to imposing its political will on the vanquished. It is fundamentally a Clausewitzian vision of war.

Those who suggest a new kind of war, whether or not they use the fourth-generation analogy, maintain that the world is entering a period of radical change in warfare. One of the apostles of this change is the Israeli analyst Martin van Creveld, who described the magnitude of the change he foresees in 1991 in his *The Transformation of War*. His basic argument is that the western paradigm of war is being broken. The Clausewitzian base, for instance, is shattered because, "should present trends continue, the kind of war that is based on the division between government, army, and people seems to be on its way out." The result will be the crumbling of conventional nationally based military forces. As he puts it, "Much present-day military power is simply irrelevant as an instrument for extending or defending political interests over much of the globe."

What replaces conventional, trinitarian warfare in the van Creveld scheme? He argues the change is fundamental in terms of the units that wage war, the methods of combat they use, and the purposes for which they fight. In his words, "In the future, wars will not be waged by armies but by groups whom we today call terrorists, guerrillas, bandits and robbers. Their organizations are likely to be constructed on charismatic lines rather than institutional ones, and to be motivated less by 'professionalism' than by fanatical, ideologically based loyalties." The new kind of war, in other words, turns the traditional warfare of the first three generations on its head both organizationally and in terms of its underlying purposes. It also describes Al Qaeda and the Iraqi resistance well before they existed.

The arguments surrounding this alleged transformation are, of course, controversial. While they have been made for a decade or more, most of the discussions have been confined to places like the war colleges, where they have been extensively debated and dissected. The events of September 11, 2001, have brought these arguments out of the shadows and onto center stage. The actions by bin Laden and his cohorts clearly meet parts of the description of future war described by van Creveld, and the popularization of the term *new kind of war* has sent many scrambling to find out what this newness is. There is no consensus at this point.

All the controversy cannot be settled here. What can be done is to describe what the champions of the new form of war claim about it. Because the terrorist attacks and the subsequent campaigns against the Taliban, Al Qaeda, and the Iraqi resistance proved the stimulus for consideration of the fourth generation, one can also ask how an assessment of that experience reinforces or undercuts the claims of those arguing fundamental change.

Characteristics of Fourth-Generation Warfare. Although there are other depictions available that differ in detail, the framework of Lind and his colleagues is useful for describing what people mean when they talk about fourth-generation warfare. What is interesting about their analysis is that it not only argues the change that marks the fourth generation, but also points out how important elements of the new environment have their roots in the past and evolving kinds of war.

Lind and his colleagues argue that there is a series of characteristics of fourth-generation warfare that can be traced to the past. In terms of the conduct of hostilities, for instance, they maintain in the future there will be no distinctions between civilians and military forces in terms of targeting: society is the battlefield in the new environment. There will be an absence of definable battlefields or fronts, and the places where fighting occurs will be dispersed and undefined: everywhere and nowhere is the front lines. The result is a much more fluid military situation in which traditional concerns like logistics and measures such as land gained or lost will largely lose meaning as measures of military success.

The purposes of fighting will also change, at least for those who adopt the methodologies of the fourth generation. The goal will not be traditional military defeat but instead the internal political collapse of the opponent and its will to continue. The manipulation of the media will be a skill that is highly sought by practitioners of the fourth generation, and the targets of much of this activity will be popular support for the government or whatever force against which the campaign is waged.

To this point, the description of fourth-generation warfare is still not terribly innovative. While one can see elements of it in the terrorist attacks (not distinguishing between military and civilian targets, for instance), almost all of these characteristics could easily be ascribed to the NVA and VC asymmetrical campaign against the United States a third of a century ago. In fact, this part of the description is largely attributable to the postmortem of the American experience in Vietnam.

Lind and his colleagues extend these characteristics in trying to describe the basic nature of the fourth generation. First, they argue explicitly the nonwestern, Asiatic (including Middle Eastern) basis of this form of warfare. In an article published in October 2001, Keegan embellished this connection:

> The Oriental tradition, however, has not been eliminated. It reappeared . . . particularly in the tactics of evasion and retreat practiced by the Vietcong against the United States in the Vietnam war. On September 11, 2001, it returned in an absolutely traditional form. Arabs, appearing suddenly out of empty space like their desert raider ancestors, assaulted the heartlands of Western power in a terrifying surprise raid and did appalling damage.

Second, they argue that terrorism is a standard tactic of practitioners of the fourth generation. Because they are militarily weaker in the traditional (symmetrical) sense, their terrorist tactics provide an asymmetrical way to bypass the conventional strength of western militaries and to strike at the homeland. They are aided in accomplishing these acts by the very openness of free societies that makes them more easily penetrable. Third, a major objective of fourth-generation practitioners is the disruption of target societies, what Lind and his colleagues call the "culture of order," which is the direct objective of the attacks. Finally, they argue that movements adopting fourth-generation warfare will often not be nationally based governments but will have a transnational and, on some occasions, even a religious base.

These descriptions, published twelve years before the September 11 attacks, have an eerily prescient ring in terms of what happened in New York and Washington. Van Creveld adds (once again, in 1991) another evidence of similarity: "There will be a tendency to treat leaders as criminals who richly deserve the worst fate that can be inflicted on them. Hence, many leaders will probably decide to remain unattached and lead a semi-nomadic life."

The Fourth Generation and September 11, 2001. The descriptions of the nature and implications of fourth-generation warfare seemed virtually to predict the terrible events of September 11, 2001, a decade or more ago, which is, in large measure, why they are reproduced and quoted in some detail. Imbedded in these discussions, however, is the further assertion that nonstate-based warfare fought using asymmetrical methods and for nonconventional purposes will become the dominant form of warfare in the future. Implied in that prediction is the further assertion that traditional, western national military forces will become obsolete relics because of the new form of warfare.

Does the experience of the terrorist attacks and responses to them bear out these implications? In some ways, they clearly do. The attacks against the Pentagon and the World Trade Center towers clearly fit the descriptions and motivations of the purveyors of this new "model" of warfare. Not all the attributes were new, of course—terrorism is a decidedly old tactic, and terrorist acts committed by nonstate actors are hardly novel in the American or international experience. What sets the attacks apart in the contemporary context is their audacity and scale. Terrorist attacks by individuals and groups with no formal state affiliation that kill a relatively small number of people are, if not common, not entirely uncommon. When thousands of innocent people are killed in such attacks, then the problem achieves another order of magnitude.

Did the attacks and the subsequent campaign to overthrow the Taliban, destroy the Al Qaeda, and capture bin Laden vindicate the apostles of the fourth generation of warfare? In other words, were the attributes of how America's asymmetrical foes fought sufficiently frustrating to the United States that we felt the need to reformulate how the military goes about its business in the face of future repetitions that may become the norm for future violence?

The short-term answer would seem to be overwhelmingly in the negative. Admittedly, the Taliban did not engage in a campaign of asymmetrical warfare after the Americans entered the civil war to bring about their ouster, which was a major mistake caused by the irony of their situation. At the same time, part of the reason for their defeat may also have been a seething, if repressed, hatred for their rule, which meant most of their countrymen offered them neither aid nor comfort when they came under the relentless fury of the American bombers. Some of the ease with which the Taliban were dispatched, in other words, stemmed from their lack of popular support at home.

Al Qaeda, on the other hand, did attempt to fight asymmetrically, and it did them more good. While the Taliban remained in their conventional lines providing target practice for the bombers and the Northern Alliance, the Al Qaeda fighters headed for the cave-pocked mountains, where they went into deep hiding, emulating their earlier Viet Cong predecessors.

Ultimately, Al Qaeda ended up in the Tora Bora Mountains and beyond, where they were pounded by the combined conventional might of the Americans and the various Afghan factions, but not entirely broken. All the adherence to apparently novel forms of warfare did not keep them from being forced to go deep underground, and bin Laden and his closest cohorts evaded the dragnet out to snare them. Conventional force and counterterrorist actions were able to reduce Al Qaeda to a shadow of its prewar status but have not been able to destroy it completely. The resilience that Al Qaeda has demonstrated will, in all likelihood, be part of the model for future asymmetrical warriors, as well as a characteristic of its continuing existence.

New Internal Wars

Before the events of September 11, 2001, caught the world's attention, another form of warfare had been raging over the last decade or more in parts of the developing world in the form of often grotesque and hideous conflicts that I have identified as the new internal wars (NIWs).

These kinds of wars broke onto the public scene during the 1990s, although there were a few internal conflicts during the Cold War that met all or most of the criteria for classification as NIWs. What sets these conflicts apart is their disorderliness and the extreme violence and apparent senselessness of the suffering being exacted mainly against civilian populations by their countrymen. Moreover, although they have occurred most often in places far from the geopolitical spotlight, the unrelenting eye of global electronic mediation has focused upon them as the "warts" in what, until September 11, 2001, had appeared a very benign international environment, at least in terms of threats and violence. The genocide in the Sudan has brought NIW-style conflicts back into public attention.

The end of the Cold War contributed to the emergence of the NIWs as a major phenomenon in the pattern of world violence. Internal conflicts were, of course, the dominant form of war during the Cold War, and in that sense, the NIWs represent a continuation of the pattern that occurred during the period of superpower competition. At the same time, civil conflict during the Cold War generally had the character of traditional insurgency, where the structure of the violence featured a government seeking to maintain itself in power and supported by one of the superpowers (usually the United States) and an insurgency employing some form of mobile-guerrilla war model that sought power and was supported by the other superpower (usually the Soviet Union). Superpower presence layered an often irrelevant Communist–anti-Communist aspect to contests more properly understood in other terms (ethnic or tribal dominance, for instance), but it also brought restraint to the fighting, since neither superpower wanted its client (and by extension, itself) charged with atrocities.

The war in Cambodia in the 1970s between the Khmer Rouge and its opponents was the major exception to this rule (the contending sides were sponsored by the Soviet Union and China), and in many ways, it was the prototype for the NIWs. The brutal, genocidal campaign by the Khmer Rouge government to transform Cambodian society into a pastoral, docile condition produced a litany of horrors that war crimes investigators are still unraveling. They also provided a frightening portent of the future of internal war that was largely ignored at the time.

The list of the most prominent instances of these new internal wars is familiar. The post–Cold War prototype occurred (and in limited form is still going on) in Somalia, where a combination of a long drought and the use of international food supplies as weapons in the clan-based conflict for power threatened to result in massive starvation until an international peacekeeping force intervened to interrupt the suffering. "Ethnic cleansing" was added to the language of international politics as Serbs, Croats, and Bosnian Muslims struggled to partition the Bosnian successor state to Yugoslavia, and that phenomenon was reprised a half decade later in Kosovo. Between those Balkan conflicts, the United States intervened in Haiti, and the Rwandan nightmare was added to the list in 1994. Simmering NIWs dot the map of Africa, notably in places like Sierra Leone (noted in Amplification 11.2).

Characteristics of New Internal Wars. The characteristics ascribed to NIWs are derived differently than those for fourth-generation wars, making any precise form of comparison difficult. As noted, the *Marine Corps Gazette* article from which the list of fourth-generation characteristics was derived combined historical observation of trends with extrapolations into the future. While some of the characteristics of NIWs also come from past experiences, the characterizations of NIWs are limited to experience to date.

The characteristics can be divided into political and military categories. At the political level, the most striking feature of these wars is their nearly total reversal of

Amplification 11.2

THE "BATTLE" FOR SIERRA LEONE

The civil conflict that wracked the small West African country of Sierra Leone for a decade and that has been terminated by the insertion of a United Nations–sponsored peacekeeping force UNAMSIL (United Nations Mission in Sierra Leone) is, in some ways, the epitome of the phenomenon of new internal war.

First, it was not a war in the common sense of the reasons for which war is fought. At various times, three different groups have been involved in shifting coalitions with one another: a weak and unsupported government, an equally weak Sierra Leone army, and the Revolutionary United Front (RUF). The objective of the war was only indirectly control of the Sierra Leone political system, especially for the RUF. The real objective was political destabilization of the country so that there is no legitimate authority that could interfere in the criminal exploitation and smuggling of the country's primary resource, diamonds.

Second, the war was not military in any recognizable sense. The RUF did not even pretend to be soldiers, rather preferring the designation of "fighters," and there were no battles between the sides worthy of the name. The principal distinguishing mark of the RUF, before the peace was imposed, consisted of more or less random acts of terror against members of the population. The preferred form of terror has been amputation of hands and feet, leaving Sierra Leone with an enormous prosthetics need that nongovernmental organizations (NGOs) such as *Medicins sans Frontieres* (MSF, translated into English as Doctors Without Borders) have only recently tried to deal with. The result of the "battle" over Sierra Leone has been a helpless, prostrate country that it will take years of concerted effort to rebuild.

the kinds of goals found in traditional insurgencies. Unlike traditional civil wars, the control of government is often not the clear objective of both sides. In a number of cases of NIWs, the "rebel" force articulates no political objectives or statements of ideological principles about how it would organize itself to rule. The Revolutionary United Front (RUF) of Sierra Leone, for instance, never issued a manifesto of any kind, and this is not unusual. The apparent reason for this is that the RUF movement has had neither the intention nor the desire to gain control of and govern the country, and this is not unusual in NIWs. Rather, in a number of cases, the highly nontraditional political purpose is anarchical, in the sense of seeking to destabilize the country from governmental control by anyone. Creating anarchy is, of course, a political goal but not one that is accorded legitimacy in a state-centered, Westphalian world. In these cases, most notably the narco-insurgencies of South America and some parts of Asia and the criminal insurgencies of parts of Africa, the real goal is to create a sense of total lawlessness that maximizes the group's ability to enrich itself either through thievery and worse or by controlling or protecting narcotics trafficking. Such groups often adopt splendid political ("revolutionary front") or otherwise high-sounding (the "Lord's Army" of Uganda) names to mask the basic criminality that forms their purpose.

There is another political characteristic that also helps differentiate NIWs from traditional internal wars and explain the savagery that often dominates these conflicts. Traditional civil wars are fought for control of the government of a country, and a central factor in which side prevails is the loyalty of the country's population—the "hearts and minds" of the people. This "center of gravity" is a point of competition for both sides, and neither wants to drive the people into the other side's arms by committing hideous and unacceptable acts of violence against the population. The need to appeal to the people thus moderates the violence, especially against noncombatant civilians.

Since the goal in NIWs is not to govern but to intimidate or kill those members of the population who might be in opposition, there is no such motivation toward moderation. In Bosnia during the first half of the 1990s, Bosnian Serbs did not seek to appeal to Bosnian Muslims or vice versa; rather, their aim was to drive people from their homes, move in, and claim the land by virtue of possession. Similarly, the Rwandan Hutus were clearly not appealing politically for the support of the Tutsi as the rampage proceeded; they simply wanted to kill as many people as possible. The religious purification of the Sudan by murdering non-Muslims is similar. This absence of a shared center of gravity that needs to be nurtured makes NIWs effectively like wars between states (interstate wars) rather than internal wars (intrastate wars) politically. Like interstate wars, the purpose is to subdue, not to win over, the opponent. Unlike traditional intrastate wars, there is no battle for the "hearts and minds of men" to moderate the slaughter. The internal fighting in Iraq certainly bears this characteristic as well.

The military characteristics of NIWs follow from these nontraditional political characteristics and provide a close parallel with the military characteristics of fourth-generation warfare. Since there are no clear political objectives for these affairs, they do not translate into strategic guidance to form conventional military objectives and operations. The military units that conduct these forms of hostilities are typically highly irregular, not uniformed or organized into coherent rank orderings of officers and enlisted soldiers. They are poorly trained, if they have received any military training at all, and are unaware or contemptuous of normal conventions of war. Similarly, they normally lack a sense of military order or discipline. In a number of instances, these fighters have been little more than children, with members of the ranks reportedly no more than ten- to twelve-year-olds, often kidnapped and forced into service by the fear of personal or family consequences if they refuse (the Lord's Army of Uganda, for instance, kidnaps children from orphanages and threatens to kill them if they resist becoming "soldiers").

Given these characteristics of the forces, the savagery and atrocity associated with these wars should come as little surprise. Echoing the fourth-generation lack of distinction between civilians and military targets, they are marked by high incidences of attacks by fighters against unarmed civilians, notably women and children, the elderly, and other similarly helpless beings (atrocities in the Sudan are a particularly gruesome example). In most NIWs, there are rarely any encounters between the organized armed forces of the two (or more) contending sides. The large reason for this pattern is that the sides are not organized into military forces that can contend against other organized forces; attacking, mutilating, or killing helpless, innocent civilians is their form of asymmetrical warfare.

The Prospects for NIWs. One of the notable aspects of NIWs is where they occur. For the most part, internal violence, of which the NIWs are a prominent part, happen in the poorest parts of the world where the lives of average citizens are among the most miserable and where there is little sense that things can get much worse. This is also the description of the places that have been the breeding grounds of some terrorists—notably, the recruitment grounds for a number of the fighters associated with Al Qaeda and other terrorist organizations. While the practitioners of asymmetrical warfare may be motivated by different end states and aspirations, they do share a fairly common breeding ground (this is discussed in the terrorist context in Chapter 12).

Before September 11, 2001, refocused attention, there was a policy debate about whether it was wise for the United States to involve itself in these situations. A major observation about NIWs is that they generally cannot be ended internally, because neither the government nor its opposition possesses the physical capability for toppling the other (which the "insurgents" may not want to do, preferring to have an ineffectual government to the prospects of an effective successor). It then becomes a question of whether there is sufficient outside interest in trying to do something to end whatever atrocity is occurring. This is an ongoing problem that is examined in its operational and philosophical aspects in Chapter 13. The point is that the prospects for future NIWs, not unlike terrorism, are as good as is the amount of suffering in the world.

The Iraq Hybrid

The so-called insurgency (or insurgencies) in Iraq is a hybrid of fourth-generation and new internal wars. The violence is clearly asymmetrical and bears many of the physical characteristics of the fourth generation (the use of terrorist tactics, for instance). It also bears some of the politically and militarily chaotic nature of NIWs. Although the various elements implicitly have shared the common goal of evicting the American occupiers, their actions have also sought to prevent the emergence of *any* strong central Iraqi government that might suppress their particular group's desire for domination. In that sense, they very much resemble the anarchical movements in places like Sierra Leone.

What distinguishes this Iraqi hybrid has been its scale and the consequent difficulty of suppressing it. Most NIWs, for instance, have been in relatively small countries, and the groups fomenting them have been relatively small and relatively weak—except compared to their domestic opponents. In these cases, outside intervening forces have been able to quell the violence and restore order. In Iraq, the various insurgents operate over a large amount of territory, are better organized, and apparently are more numerous and more adept at asymmetrical, fourth-generation warfare. As a result, they have successfully avoided suppression by a large American (and coalition) force for nearly five years.

CONCLUSION: NEW FORM OR NEW FACE OF WAR?

The chapter concludes by going back and asking the question raised at the beginning of the chapter: Is the kind of warfare that America faces literally something new? Or is asymmetrical warfare a "back to the future" proposition, borrowing from the title of Goulding's article in the U.S. Army's journal, *Parameters*? As the analysis has sought to demonstrate, in a purely military sense, what is now called asymmetrical warfare does not represent a great change in war but is instead the approach that has been taken throughout history by weaker protagonists when facing superior forces. The American reintroduction to this kind of warfare in Vietnam did not, however, prepare it for an opponent who would change the rules of engagement so radically as to attack and destroy the kinds of civilian targets that were attacked on September 11, 2001. The innovation was not the dynamics of war; it was the physical object of attack.

If asymmetrical warfare as a generic concept is nothing really new, its manifestations in fourth-generation warfare, NIWs, and Iraq do pose some differences from past experience. Clearly, the high level of irregularity of the forces faced—in terms of composition, style, methods, and objectives of fighting—is a factor not encountered before. At the same time, fighting not directed at political goals of gaining or maintaining governance is a novelty in the American experience that creates wartime difficulties of sorting out the sides and postwar difficulties in reconstructing a peace.

The U.S. had better anticipate, however, that it will face more asymmetrical foes in the future. One of the other clear characteristics of the contemporary environment is the huge and growing chasm of conventional military capabilities between the countries of the West and the rest of the world. The RMA means, to repeat, that no developing world country or movement has any military chance against the United States or its friends and allies if they fight on western terms (symmetrically). The Iraqis did not understand that in 1991 and paid a price they were unwilling to pay again in 2003. The Taliban either did not understand it or could not adapt quickly enough when confronted with western airpower in 2001. Not many others are going to make the same mistake.

That leads to the conclusion that, at a minimum, future opponents are likely to confront the United Sates with highly unorthodox, unconventional, and unanticipated problems. If what is learned from September 11, 2001, is how to combat terrorism (see Chapter 12) and no more, the United States will have missed the real novelty of the "new kind of war," which is the need to change and adapt and to be ready for the unexpected. The alternatives are unattractive. As Goulding puts it, "Military forces like those of the United States and its allies who constitute the bulk of 'well organized and well paid regular forces' and generally play by the rules may, in their next battles, wish fervently that it was against soldiers of their own ilk they were fighting."

If the concepts underlying asymmetrical war are hardly new, the ways in which it is conducted are constantly evolving and adapting to changed physical and political circumstances. The tactics that worked in the Vietnamese mountains and jungles are not directly applicable to arid Iraq, and so the Iraqi resistance to the American occupation fights differently to rid themselves of the Americans than

Challenge!

IS THERE A NEW KIND OF WAR?

The initial, highly emotional reaction to the terrorist attacks of September 11, 2001, in the United States suggested that these were somehow an unprecedented phenomenon, and the rage and smoldering desire for revenge could most easily be translated into the analogy of militarily crushing those who had committed these atrocious acts. The idea that Americans were faced with a new kind of war was born of this conjunction of the apparent uniqueness of the act and the desire for a military reaction.

Is the analogy accurate? The burden of much of the analysis in this chapter has been that it is not. The central point has been that terrorism has long been a central manner in which weak groups attempt to assert their will over stronger groups. A major thrust of these efforts involves changing the rules of engagement between contending forces to remove some of the advantage the stronger party has and to, in effect, level the playing field or tilt it in the weaker party's favor. Since part of that leveling entails rejecting the rules and conventions under which the dominant player operates, the result is likely to be outrage when the weaker party attacks. This dynamic of fourth-generation or asymmetrical warfare dates back to antiquity. The uniqueness of the current application is its scale and the fact it has been visited directly against the American population. Would Americans have the same sense of rage and the same depth of reaction if airliners had attacked the 1,381-foot Jin Mao building of Shanghai in China? Or the world's tallest buildings, the 1,483-foot Petronas towers in Kuala Lumpur, Malaysia?

The question asked in the title of this *Challenge!* is really two related questions. Is the form of activity in which the United States is engaged properly described as a form of war? And is that activity something new? The answer to the second question is fairly clearly no, but the answer to whether this is a form of war is not so clear. Is it more useful to think about this kind of campaign in warlike terms, or is some other framework more useful? What do you think? If you believe war is not the best way to think about countering terrorism, what do you think is a better way?

Clearly, the Iraqi resistance is a form of asymmetrical war and urban guerrilla warfare using ambushes and random bombings with, improvised explosive devices (IEDs) and suicide bombers as the primary tools of combat, and leading the United States to conclude that it is not worth the pain being caused is the method chosen to force the Americans to abandon their quest. Is it worth it for the United States to persevere? Should the United States have anticipated this problem? What do you think?

did the Vietnamese. Future asymmetrical opponents will also seek to present us with novel problems for which we are unprepared. The secret to confounding asymmetrical warriors is anticipating and preparing for what they will do before they can do it. But, as the *Challenge!* box asks, is there *really* a new kind of war?

STUDY/DISCUSSION QUESTIONS

1. What are symmetrical and asymmetrical forms of warfare? Describe each. Under what circumstances does a country or group prefer one approach to the other?
2. Is asymmetrical warfare a new idea? Describe its history and evolution, with some emphasis on Vietnam.
3. Describe the contemporary military setting facing the United States. What is the RMA? How has it affected the American approach to force and the international environment? Apply this impact to the Persian Gulf War, Afghanistan, and Iraq.
4. What is fourth-generation warfare? Where does the term come from? What are the characteristics of fourth-generation warfare? Cite examples, including September 11.
5. What are the new internal wars (NIWs)? Discuss how and when they emerge, what their political and military characteristics are, and what makes them different than other kinds of warfare.
6. What does it mean to call the Iraqi insurgency a hybrid of fourth-generation and new internal wars?
7. Is asymmetrical warfare the military challenge of the future? Is it something new to the United States? What should the United States do about it?

SELECTED BIBLIOGRAPHY

Barnett, Thomas P. M. *The Pentagon's New Map: War and Peace in the Twenty-First Century.* New York: Berkley Books, 2004.

Belfigio, Valentine J. *A Study of Ancient Roman Amphibious and Offensive Sea-Ground Tasks for Operations.* Lewiston, NY: Edwin Mellen Press, 2001.

Boot, Max. "The Struggle to Transform the Military." *Foreign Affairs* 84, 2 (March/April 2005), 103–118.

Brodie, Bernard, and Fawn M. Brodie. *From Crossbow to H-Bomb: The Evolution of Weapons and Tactics of Warfare.* Bloomington: Indiana University Press, 1973.

Cothran, Helen (ed.). *National Security: Opposing Viewpoints.* San Diego, CA: Greenhaven Press, 2004.

Dobbins, James. "Iraq: Winning the Unwinnable War." *Foreign Affairs* 84, 1 (January/February 2005), 6–25.

Duncan, Stephen M. *A War of a Different Kind: Military Forces and America's Search for Homeland Security.* Annapolis, MD: Naval Institute Press, 2004.

Gallagher, James J. *Low-Intensity Conflict: A Guide for Tactics, Techniques, and Procedures.* Mechanicsburg, PA: Stackpole Books, 1992.

Gerstein, Daniel M. *Securing America's Future: National Security in the Information Age.* Westport, CT: Praeger Security International, 2005.

Goulding, Vincent J., Jr. "Back to the Future with Asymmetrical Warfare." *Parameters* 30, 4 (Winter 2000–2001), 21–30.

Haass, Richard N. "Regime Change and Its Limits." *Foreign Affairs* 84, 1 (January/February 2005), 66–78.

Hentz, James J. (ed.). *The Obligation of Empire: United States' Grand Strategy for a New Century.* Lexington: University Press of Kentucky, 2004.

Keegan, John. *A History of Warfare.* London: Hutchison, 1991.

Lacquement, Richard A. *Shaping American Military Capabilities After the Cold War.* Westport, CT: Praeger, 2003.

Lewis, Bernard. "Freedom and Justice in the Modern Middle East." *Foreign Affairs* 84, 3 (May/June 2005), 36–51.

Lind, William S., Keith Nightengale, John F. Schmitt, Joseph W. Sutton, and Gary J. Wilson. "The Changing Face of War: Into the Fourth Generation." *Marine Corps Gazette*, October 1989, 21–26.

Luttwak, Edward N. "Iraq: The Logic of Disengagement." *Foreign Affairs* 84, 1 (January/February 2005), 26–36.

Mao tse-Tung. *Mao tse-Tung on Guerrilla Warfare* (translatd by Samuel B. Griffith). New York: Praeger, 1961.

Moore, Lt. General Harold G., and James L. Galloway. *We Were Soldiers Once . . . and Young: Ia Drang: The Battle That Changed the War in Vietnam*. New York: Harper and Row, 1993.

O'Hanlon, Michael E. *Defense Strategy for the Post-Saddam Era*. Washington, DC: Brookings Institution Press, 2005.

Peters, Ralph. *Fighting for the Future: Will America Triumph?* Mechanicsburg, PA: Stackpole Books, 2001.

Snow, Donald M. *Uncivil Wars: International Security and the New Internal Conflicts*. Boulder, CO: Lynne Rienner Publishers, 1996.

———. *Distant Thunder: Patterns of Conflict in the Developing World* (2nd ed.). Armonk, NY: M. E. Sharpe, 1997.

———. *When America Fights: The Uses of U.S. Military Force*. Washington, DC: CQ Press, 2000.

Sun Tzu. *The Art of War* (translated by Samuel B. Griffith). Oxford, UK: Oxford University Press, 1963.

van Creveld, Martin. *The Transformation of War*. New York: Free Press, 1991.

CHAPTER 12

Terrorism

PREVIEW

The most dramatic form that asymmetrical warfare presents to the United States is terrorism, and more specifically, the international religious terrorism represented by organizations like Al Qaeda. The terrorist attacks of September 11 galvanized public attention on this problem, and American national security policy has had the global war on terrorism (GWOT) as its central focus ever since. This chapter investigates the nature of the terrorist problem, how it is changing, and what can be done about it. It begins by examining the dynamics of terrorism: what is it, what do terrorists seek to do, who are they, and what causes people to become terrorists? It then moves to how terrorism has evolved as a problem since September 11 and what kinds of efforts we can mount against it. Based on this information and perspectives raised throughout, the chapter concludes by suggesting some elements of a comprehensive terrorism suppression strategy.

Terrorism and the well-publicized GWOT have dominated the national security agenda in the United States since the September 11 attacks by Al Qaeda against New York and Washington, D.C., targets. The problem of terrorism was not unknown within the government and expert communities before September 11, and it has been revealed after the fact that there had been premonitions and even fairly specific warnings that Al Qaeda would attempt something like what they did. Because terrorism had heretofore been an apparently minor problem that had captured the central attention of neither the public nor top political leaders, the warnings went unheeded and American vulnerability was revealed in shocking, bloody relief.

The problem of terrorism is unique and enigmatic. It is an ancient practice that most historians date back at least to biblical times, and it has recurred episodically and persistently ever since to the point that it is not unfair to characterize the phenomenon of terrorism as a permanent feature of the international environment. Individual terrorists and their causes come and go, but terrorism remains. At the same time, terrorism is one, arguably the most extreme, form of asymmetrical warfare and thus an important part of the overall national security environment. Finding a way to deal effectively with terrorism is thus a central factor in modern, post–September 11 defense policy.

The GWOT, as the central organizing device for dealing with this problem, is now over five years old. It has had some successes, notably in capturing or otherwise suppressing elements of the old Al Qaeda network, but the problem of terrorism and Al Qaeda has not abated. The apparently monolithic threat posed by Al Qaeda itself is arguably smaller than it was in 2001, but the problem of terrorism itself is not: new permutations have arisen that are, if anything, more provocative and dangerous. Al Qaeda in Iraq is an example. Most share radical Islam as a foundation, but from Chechnya to Indonesia, new and different organizations have emerged as new challenges: international terrorism has become a hydra-headed beast.

Before turning to the examination of the phenomenon, four related observations are necessary to condition the comments that follow. First, although people speak of a GWOT, the use of the term *war* is unfortunate, deceiving, and distorting. As the term is normally used, war refers to armed combat between combatants organized as states or states versus organized oppositions within states. War, in other words, is an action that pits people against other people and the groups attack one another to impose their will on those other people. Terrorism, on the other hand, is a more intangible idea, a method by which people seek to accomplish goals. One cannot attack and subdue an idea as if it were an enemy army. What one can do is to oppose and subdue people who act from ideas—to make war on terrorist organizations like Al Qaeda (although their lack of a territorial base makes subduing them difficult); the best one can do with an idea is to discredit it.

The second observation flows from the first: the war analogy is further flawed because it implies that the opposition can be defeated—that the purpose of the war is to suppress and eliminate the opposition. Terrorism is indeed an ancient practice that transcends efforts to suppress and defeat individual manifestations—defeating Al Qaeda or any other terrorist organization will not eliminate the phenomenon, just particular practitioners. There will always be terrorists somewhere, and the realistic purpose of those opposed to terrorism is to *contain* the problem, not eliminate it.

Third, because terrorism cannot ever be eliminated altogether, efforts in opposition to it are exercises in *risk reduction*, not risk elimination. Risk, as already noted in Chapter 7, is the difference between threats to interests and capabilities (or resources) to counter, contain, or eliminate those threats. Although the level of terrorist threat ebbs and flows across time, it is essentially always potentially greater than the resources available to effectively thwart all manifestations of the threat. Terrorism, to paraphrase ex-German Chancellor Helmut Schmidt, is a problem to be worked, not solved for once and for all. Any strategy or policy that is aimed at "smashing" or "defeating" terrorism is bound to come up short.

Fourth, terrorism is not only an international, and thus a national security, problem. Domestic terrorists also pose a threat to the safety of Americans, as evidenced by Timothy McVeigh and Theodore Kaczynski (the Unabomber). Up to now, however, most domestic terrorism has been carried out on a comparatively narrow basis that constitutes more of a criminal than a national security problem. The long terrorist campaign by the Ku Klux Klan against selected Americans is the major exception to this rule. Thus, the discussion largely centers on the international terrorism level, although it also incorporates domestic terrorism examples in the discussion.

DEFINING TERRORISM

The first step in coming to grips with terrorism is defining the term. It is an important consideration because so many phenomena in the contemporary international arena are labeled terrorist. For some (including many in government), terrorism has become the sobriquet for anything or anybody to be opposed. This makes a definition particularly important as a means to measure whether a particular movement or act is terrorist or not. Without a set of criteria to define what does and does not constitute terrorism, one is left disabled in trying to make a determination.

This is not merely a semantic exercise. Take, for instance, the recent emphasis on Chechen separatists and their campaign that the Russian government has called terrorist. Certainly, actions such as enlisting suicide terrorists to blow up two Russian airliners and the brutal siege of the school in Beslan in the Caucasus were hideous, brutal acts that comport with an understanding of terrorism, but is it correct to label the movement that commissioned and carried out the acts terrorist as a result? In context, when the Russian government of then President Boris Yeltsin used the Russian army to attack Chechnya in 1995 to wipe out the secessionist movement there (among other things, leveling the capital of Grozny) and current President Vladimir Putin renewed the campaign in 1999, there were widespread international accusations the Russian government was terrorizing the Chechens and engaging in crimes against humanity (acts of state terrorism). So who is the terrorist here?

Having an agreed definition of terrorism would help answer this and similar questions about other potentially terrorist activities, but unfortunately, such an agreement does not exist. Rather, there are virtually as many different definitions as there are people and organizations making the distinctions. There are also some commonalities that recur across definers, which make it possible to adopt a definition for present purposes. A few arguably representative examples aid in drawing distinctions.

The U.S. Department of State offers the official governmental definition, which is applied in its annual survey of international terrorism. Its definition of terrorism is "premeditated, politically motivated violence perpetrated against noncombatant targets by subnational groups or clandestine agents, usually intended to influence an audience." In *Attacking Terrorism*, co-editor Audrey Kurth Cronin says terrorism is distinguished by its political nature, its nonstate base, its targeting of innocent noncombatants, and the illegality of its acts. Jessica Stern, in *Terrorism in the Name of God*, defines terrorism as "an act or threat of violence against noncombatants with the objective of exacting revenge, intimidating, or otherwise influencing an audience." Alan Dershowitz (in *Why Terrorism Works*) offers no definition himself but notes that definitions typically include reference to terrorist targets, perpetrators, and acts.

These definitions and similar ones from others in the field differ at the margins but have common cores. All of them share three common points of reference: terrorist acts (illegal, normally violent), terrorist targets (usually innocent noncombatants), and terrorist purposes (political persuasion or influence). The only difference among them is whether they specify the nature of terrorists and their political base: the State Department, Cronin, and Dershowitz all identify terrorist organizations as nonstate-based actors. Cronin in particular emphasizes that "although states can terrorize, by definition they cannot be terrorists."

The definition used here incorporates the three components of terrorist acts, targets, and purposes but not the criterion of terrorist organizations as nonstate actors. Historically, states have been leading terrorists either through the actions of government organizations like the secret police or by creating, commissioning, or controlling the activities of terrorists. In the contemporary setting, almost all terrorist organizations are nonstate based, and this fact is at the heart of the difficulty in dealing with them. Defining terrorism as a nonstate-based activity, however, removes an important category of past (and conceivably future) activity from the definitional reach of terrorism. The nonstate basis is a characteristic of modern terrorism, not a defining element.

Based on these distinctions, terrorism is defined as the commission of violent acts against a target group normally to gain compliance with some demands the terrorists insist upon. Terrorism thus consists of three related phenomena, each of which must be present in some manner for something to be considered an act of terrorism. If all three elements are present, so is terrorism. If one or more elements are missing, the phenomenon is not terrorism but something else. Discussing each helps enliven an understanding of what constitutes terrorism.

Terrorist Acts

The first part of the definition refers to *terrorist acts*, which are the visible manifestation of terrorism and the part of the dynamic of the phenomenon with which most people are most familiar. Several comments can be made about terrorist acts.

Terrorist acts are distinguished from other political expressions in that they are uniformly illegal. Terrorist acts are intended to upset the normalcy of life through destructive acts aimed at either injuring or killing people or destroying things. Regardless of the professed underlying motives of terrorists (normally couched in lofty political terms), the actions they commit—and especially their focus on noncombatants whose only "guilt" is being part of the targeted group—break laws and are subject to criminal prosecution. By raising the rhetoric of terrorist actions to acts of war (currently holy war, or *jihad*), terrorists may seek to elevate what they do to a higher plane ("one man's terrorist is another man's freedom fighter"), but the simple fact remains that terrorist acts are criminal in nature.

The general purpose of terrorist acts is to frighten the target audience: indeed, the word *terrorism* is derived from the Latin root *terrere*, which means "to frighten."

The method of inducing fright is through the commission of random, unpredictable acts of violence that seek to induce such fear that those who witness the acts (or learn of them) will conclude that compliance with terrorist demands is preferable to living with the fear of being future victims themselves. Acts of terrorism are not necessarily aimed at the actual victims themselves (who are often randomly selected and whose individual fate does not "matter" to the terrorist) but at the audience who views the actions. As Brian Jenkins once put it, *"Terrorists want a lot of people watching and a lot of people listening, and not a lot of people dead"* (emphasis in original). The dynamic of inducing this fright is the disruption of the predictability and safety of life within society, one of whose principal functions is to make existence predictable and safe. Ultimately, a major purpose of terrorism may be to undermine this vital fiber of society, a goal shared with fourth-generation warriors.

Beyond frightening the target audience, individual terrorist acts are committed for a variety of reasons, not limited to the normally expressed political goals of particular terrorist organizations. Al Qaeda, for instance, says that its most fundamental goal is the expulsion of the West (especially the United States) from the holy lands of Islam and that its acts (especially those serving bin Laden's *fatwa* calling for killing Americans everywhere) are intended to further that goal. But that is not the only motivation for particular actions.

Terrorists may also act for a variety of other reasons. Jenkins provides a list of six other, generally less lofty, purposes for terrorist actions. First, terrorist actions may be aimed at exacting special concessions, such as ransom, the release of prisoners (generally members of the terrorist group), or the publicizing of a message. The capture and threatened (or actual) beheading of foreigners by Iraqi resistance groups to force countries to withdraw their nationals from Iraq is a case in point in the use of terrorist actions for gaining concessions. In that case, the capture of foreign nationals was at the base of demands for prisoner release and to force foreign countries to withdraw from the international relief effort in that country. Jemaah Islamiyah carried out its 2004 attack on the Australian embassy in Jakarta, Indonesia, and promptly announced that it would perpetrate similar attacks if its leader Abu Bakar Bashir was not released from prison.

Second, terrorists may act to gain publicity for their causes. Before Palestinian terrorists kidnapped a series of airliners and then launched an attack on the Israeli compound at the Munich Olympics in 1972, hardly anyone outside the region had ever heard of the Palestinian cause; the terrorist actions got them global awareness of that cause. The publicity may be intended to remind a world that has shifted its attention away from a particular group and its activities that it is still active and that it is still pursuing its goals. One of the apparent reasons for the spate of Chechen violence in 2004 for which Chechen leader Shamil Basayev claims credit was to remind the world that the Chechen movement to gain independence from Russia is still alive.

A third, and more fundamental, purpose of terrorist acts is to cause widespread disorder that demoralizes society and breaks down the social order in a country. This, of course, is a very ambitious purpose and one that presumably can only be undertaken through a widespread campaign that includes a large number of terrorist acts, and it is the kind of objective most likely to be carried out by governments or semigovernmental actors. The suicide terror campaign by Hamas against Israeli civilians (and arguably the Israeli counterattacks against Palestinians) provides an example of terrorism for this purpose.

A fourth, more tactical use of terrorism is to provoke overreaction by a government in the form of repressive action, reprisals, and overly brutal counterterrorism that may lead to the overthrow of the reactive government. This was a favorite tactic of the Viet Cong in the Vietnam War and evoked the ironic analogy among Americans of building schools during the day (as a way to pacify the population) and then bombing those schools at night (because they became the source of Viet Cong actions after nightfall). It is not clear whether some of the acts committed against American forces in Iraq by the resistance have been to try to elicit American overreactions and thus fuel anti-Americanism among Iraqi citizens.

A fifth purpose of terror may be to enforce obedience and cooperation within a target population. Campaigns of terror directed by the governments of states against their own citizens often have this purpose and are often assigned to a secret police or similar paramilitary organizations. The actions of the KGB in the Soviet Union, the Gestapo and other similar organizations in Nazi Germany, and the infamous death squads in Argentina during the 1960s and 1970s are all examples of the use of government terror to intimidate and frighten their own population into submission. At a less formal governmental level, many of the actions of the Ku Klux Klan during the latter nineteenth and early twentieth centuries against Black Americans qualify as well.

Jenkins's sixth purpose of terrorist action is punishment. Terrorists often argue that an action they take is aimed at a particular person or place because that person or institution is somehow guilty of a particular transgression and is thus being meted out appropriate punishment for what the terrorists consider a crime. Although the Israeli government would be appalled at the prospect of calling its counterterrorist campaign to bulldoze the homes of the families of suicide terrorists (or to bomb the homes of dissident leaders) acts of terror, from the vantage point of the Palestinian targets of the attacks, they certainly must seem so.

Stern adds a seventh motivation that is internal to the terrorist organization: morale. Like any other organization, and especially terrorist groups in which the "operatives" are generally young and not terribly mature, it may be necessary from time to time to carry out a terrorist attack simply to demonstrate to the membership the continuing potency of the group as a way to keep the membership focused and their morale high. As Stern puts it, "Attacks sometimes have more to do with rousing the troops than terrorizing the victims." Improving or maintaining morale may also have useful spin-off effects, such as helping in recruiting new members to the group or in raising funds to support the organization's activities.

A final comment about terrorist acts is whether, or to what degree, they are successful. The answer is rather clearly a mixed one that has to do with the scale of the actions and their intended results. In some cases, terrorism has been highly successful, but usually in relatively small ways where the terrorists' purposes were bounded and compliance with their demands was not overly odious. To cite one example, terrorist demands to release what they view as political prisoners (usually jailed members of their group) have, on occasion, been complied with, although some countries are more prone to comply than others. Likewise, the Iraqi resistance's campaign of kidnapping and threatening to execute foreign nationals if the countries did not leave Iraq has been somewhat successful and will almost certainly be duplicated in the future by other asymmetrical warriors who include acts of terrorism in their operational repertoires.

It is when terrorists make large demands and follow them up with sizable actions that they tend to be less successful. When terrorists come to pose a basic perceived threat to the target country (often because of the audacity of what they have done or the perceived obnoxiousness of what they propose), the reaction by the target may be, and usually is, increased resolve rather than compliance. The September 11, 2001, attacks, after all, did not result in a groundswell of sentiment for the United States to quit the Middle East (especially Saudi Arabia) as bin Laden and Al Qaeda demanded; rather, they stiffened the will of the country to resist (by late 2005, American troops had in fact left the Saudi Kingdom). This poses something of a quandary to the terrorist: the more ambitious a group becomes, the more likely it is to increase opposition to achievement of its goals. On the other hand, sizing terrorist acts downward to levels that will not increase resolve may result in less positive, and less than satisfying, outcomes.

What this discussion of terrorist acts seeks to demonstrate is that, like virtually everything else about the subject, terrorists act for a variety of reasons. Some of these are more purposive and "noble" than others, but it is not clear what may motivate a particular action. Moreover, different reasons may motivate different groups at different times and under different circumstances. Knowing that a terrorist attack has occurred, in other words, does not necessarily tell one why it has been committed.

Terrorist Targets

Akin to the military objectives in more conventional war, the targets of terrorists can be divided into two related categories. The first is people, and the objective is to kill, maim, or otherwise cause some members of the target population to suffer, usually as an example for the rest of the population (in some cases, terrorists target and kill specific people whom they oppose to eliminate them, of course). The second category is physical targets, attacks against which are designed to disrupt and destroy societal capabilities and to demonstrate the vulnerability of the target society. The two categories are obviously related in that most of the physical targets worth attacking contain people who will be killed or injured in the process. As well, attacking either category demonstrates the inability of the target population to provide protection for its members and valued artifices, thus questioning the efficacy of resisting terrorist demands.

There are subtle differences and problems associated with concentrating on one category of target or another. Clearly, attacks directly intended to kill or injure people are the most personal and evoke the greatest emotion in the target population, including the will to resist and to seek vengeance. From the vantage point of the terrorist, the reason to attack people (beyond some simple blood lust) is to attack the target population's will to resist the demands that terrorists make. Snow and Drew refer to this as *cost-tolerance*, the level of suffering one is willing to endure in the face of some undesirable situation. In the case of terrorist targeting, the terrorist seeks to exceed the target's cost-tolerance by making the target conclude that it is less painful (physically or mentally) to accede to the terrorist's demands than it is to continue to resist those demands. The terrorist seeks to exceed cost-tolerance by maximizing the level of fear and anxiety that the target experiences because of the effects (often hideous) of attacks on other members of the target group. The terrorist wants the target group to become so afraid of being the next victim that they cave in and accept the terrorist demands. If cost-tolerance is exceeded, the terrorist wins; if the target remains resolute, the terrorist does not succeed (which may not be the same thing as saying the terrorist loses).

Recognizing that producing fright is the objective reinforces Jenkins's observation about the murderousness of those committing terrorist acts against targets. It is, after all, impossible to frighten dead people, nor can the victims of murder capitulate and accede to demands. Only survivors who view the carnage and wonder if they will be next can be so manipulated, and the terrorist has a vested interest in keeping enough around to buckle to terrorist demands.

Overcoming target cost-tolerance is not an easy task, and it usually fails. For one thing, terrorist organizations are generally small with limited resources, meaning that they usually lack the wherewithal to attack and kill a large enough portion of the target population to make members of that population become individually fearful enough to tip the scales (blowing up people on airplanes may be a partial exception). One of the great fears associated with terrorist groups obtaining and using weapons of mass destruction is that such a turn of events would change that calculus. For another thing, attacking and killing innocent members of a target group (at least innocent from the vantage point of the group) may (and usually does) infuriate its members and increase rather than decrease the will to resist. That was certainly the case during World War II in Germany, where constant aerial bombardment failed to destroy the German people's will to survive and may actually have strengthened their will to resist.

Standing up to terrorist attacks on human targets is not always easy, as the example of hostage taking in Iraq shows. In such cases, officials are placed in an obvious quandary. On one hand, when hostages are taken and their execution threatened if some demands are unmet, there is an obvious and understandable instinct to try to save the hostage(s); and in the absence of an ability to rescue them physically (which, in the Iraqi cases, was apparently impossible), the only means available is to accede to the terrorists' demands (have cost-tolerance exceeded). On the other hand, doing so means the terrorists succeed and are likely to be emboldened to do the same thing again, as was the case in Iraq when several countries pulled their workers out after some of their nationals were kidnapped and threatened with execution. The Americans and British refused to accede in these demands, and a number of their citizens were executed. In those cases, the terrorists did not prevail, but they also did not visibly lose, since (at this writing) none of them had been captured and brought

Amplification 12.1

THE MORALITY OF SAVING TARGETS

Dealing with terrorists always poses difficult moral dilemmas that different people and countries handle in different ways. One of the most difficult dilemmas is what to do in instances when terrorists capture hostages and demand concessions that, if not honored, will result in the execution of the hostages.

There are two ways to respond to such occurrences and demands. One, prominently associated with the American and British governments, is to refuse categorically to negotiate with terrorists. The rationale is that if governments do negotiate, and especially comply, with these demands, the terrorists are somehow legitimized and, at a more practical level, encouraged to repeat the kidnapping. The refusal also usually condemns the kidnapped to execution, bringing pain and grief to their families and friends, who are also fellow countrymen. As the Iran–Contra scandal of the 1980s revealed, this principle is sometimes ignored.

The other way to respond is to take notice of the terrorist demands, negotiate with them, and potentially agree to the demands the terrorists make. This solution has the likely humane outcome of saving a human life or lives, but it also represents capitulation to the terrorists and the success of their action. In the context of the war on terrorism, it arguably amounts to nearly a surrender to the terrorists.

In principle and in the abstract, the refusal to give in to terrorist demands has overwhelming appeal because it is a more virile response than negotiating with terrorists. At the same time, that refusal amounts to signing a death warrant for the victim(s), and that is not always politically or morally acceptable. Because of the moral dilemma, governments react in both ways on different occasions.

to justice for their deeds. This situation is difficult for policy makers, as discussed in Amplification 12.1.

When the targets are physical things rather than people per se, the problems and calculations change. When the target of terrorists is physically a whole society, the range of potential targets is virtually boundless. In attacking places, the terrorist seeks to deprive the target population of whatever pleasure or life-sustaining or life-enhancing value the particular target may provide. The list of what used to be called *countervalue* targets when speaking of nuclear targeting (things people value, such as their lives and what makes those lives commodious) covers a very broad range of objects, from hydroelectric plants to athletic stadiums, from nuclear power generators to military facilities, from highways to research facilities, and so on. Compiling a list for any large community is a very sobering experience. The problem is further complicated because acting to protect one class of targets may simply cause terrorists to move on to another class (a process known as target substitution).

It is unreasonable to assume that the physical potential target list for any country can be made uniformly invulnerable. There are simply too many possible targets, and the means of protecting them are sufficiently discrete that there is little overlap in function (protecting a football stadium from bombers may or may not have much carryover in terms of protecting nuclear power plants from seizure). As a result, there will always be a gap between the potential threats and the ability to negate all those threats, and the consequence is a certain level of risk remaining: realistically, protecting targets is an exercise in risk reduction, not elimination.

Terrorist Objectives

The final element in the definition of terrorism is the objectives, or reasons, for which terrorists do what they do. These objectives, of course, are directed against the target population and involve the commission of terrorist acts, so the discussion of objectives cannot be entirely divorced from the other two elements of what constitutes terrorism.

For present purposes, the discussion of terrorist objectives refers to the broader outcomes that terrorists seek (or say they seek) to accomplish. Objectives are the long-range reasons that terrorists wage campaigns of terrorism. In the short run, terrorists may engage in particular actions for a variety of reasons, as already noted (group morale or recruitment, for instance). What they seek ultimately to accomplish is the province of terrorist objectives.

It is useful to distinguish among types of goals terrorists pursue. The major objectives of terrorists, their ultimate or strategic goals, refer to the long-term political objectives to which they aspire. For Al Qaeda, for instance, the removal of Americans from the Arabian Peninsula is a strategic goal; for Chechen separatists, independence from Russia is the ultimate objective. At the same time, terrorists also pursue interim, or tactical, goals, which generally involve the successful commission of terrorist acts against the target population. The purpose, in the case of tactical objectives, is to demonstrate continuing viability and potency, to remind the target of their presence and menace, and to erode resistance to their strategic goals.

Because most terrorist groups are ultimately political in their purposes, terrorist objectives are political as well. To paraphrase the Clausewitzian dictum that war is politics by other means, so too is terrorism politics by other, extreme, means. Likewise, the objectives that terrorists pursue are extreme, at least to the target population if not to the terrorists themselves. Sometimes terrorist objectives are widely known and clearly articulated, and at other times they are not. Ultimately, however, campaigns of terror gain their meaning in the pursuit of some goal or goals, and their success or failure is measured by the extent that those goals are achieved.

As a form of asymmetrical warfare, terrorism is, of course, the method of the militarily weak and conceptually unacceptable. The extremely asymmetrical nature of terrorist actions arises from the fact that terrorists cannot compete with their targets by the accepted methods of the target society. Terrorists lack the military resources to engage in open warfare, at which they would be easily defeated, or in the forum of public discourse and decision, because their objectives are unacceptable, distasteful, or even bizarre to the target population. Thus, terrorists can neither impose their purposes on the target nor persuade the target to adopt whatever objectives they want. These facts narrow the terrorist group's options.

The fact that terrorist objectives are politically objectionable to the target sets up the confrontation between the terrorists and the target. Normally, terrorist goals are stated in terms of changing policies (Palestinian statehood or the right to repatriation within Israel, for example) or laws (releasing classes of unjustly detained people) in ways that the majority in the target state find unacceptable. Since the terrorists are in a minority, they cannot bring about the changes they demand by normal electoral or legislative means, and they are likely to be viewed as so basically lunatic and unrealistic by the target audience that it will not accord seriousness to the demands or those who make them. To the terrorists, of course, the demands make perfect sense, and they are frustrated and angered by the treatment their demands are given. The stage is thus set for confrontation.

Terrorists achieve their objectives by overcoming the will of the target population to resist, or by exceeding cost-tolerance. The campaign of terrorist threats and acts is intended to convince the target population that acceding to the terrorist demands is preferable to the continuing anxiety and fear of future terrorism. If the target population concludes that giving in to the terrorist demands is better than continuing to resist, cost-tolerance has been exceeded and the terrorist wins. If continuing resistance (even increased defiance) is the outcome, then cost-tolerance is not exceeded and the terrorists do not succeed.

The failure to achieve strategic objectives is not the same thing as total failure, however. The successful terrorizing of a large society by a small group of terrorists is a tall order, one for which the terrorists (almost by definition) do not have the resources to achieve. At its zenith, after all, Al Qaeda consisted of probably fewer than ten thousand active members, who could hardly bring the United States to its knees. Terrorism is, after all, the "tactic of the weak," and there are real limitations on the extent of the danger such groups can physically pose. The degree to which a target society inflates—even overinflates—the extent of the threat is, arguably, an indicator of terrorist success.

Determining whether terrorists achieve their goals or fail is complicated by the contrast between the tactical and strategic levels of objectives, making the compilation of a "score card" difficult. Modern terrorists have rarely been successful at the strategic level of attaining long-range objectives. Al Qaeda has not forced the United States from the Arabian Peninsula (although American presence has declined), Russia has not granted Chechnya independence, and Jemaah Islamiyah has yet to achieve a sectarian Islamic state in Indonesia. At the same time, the terrorist record at achieving tactical objectives (carrying out terrorist attacks) is, if not perfect, not a total failure either. As long as terrorists continue to exist and to achieve some of their goals, they remain a force against the targets of their activities. Thus, the competition between terrorists and their targets over the accomplishment of terrorist objectives continues to exist within a kind of netherworld where neither wins or loses decisively and thus both can claim some success: "We do not give in to terrorism," defined as resisting terrorist strategic objectives, versus "We succeed by killing the infidels," defined as the successful commission of acts of terrorism.

PERSPECTIVES ON AND CAUSES OF TERRORISM

For most people, terrorism is such an alien phenomenon that they have difficulty conceptualizing exactly what it is and why people would engage in acts of terrorism, up to and including committing terrorist acts that involve their own planned deaths (suicide). And yet the historical and contemporary public records are strewn with enough instances of terrorism as to make confronting the conceptual "beast" necessary for understanding and coping with the reality around us and devising strategies and policies that will combat it.

Terrorism is too complex a phenomenon to capture entirely in a single chapter, but it is possible to gain some insights into it by viewing it through two lenses. The first is by examining three perspectives that try to capture terrorism and its place in international politics. The second is to look at three of the explanations commonly put forward to answer the question, Why is there terrorism?

Three Perspectives

Where does terrorism fit into domestic and international politics? Is terrorism ever a legitimate enterprise, or is it always something outside the realm of legitimacy? Answers to these questions depend on one's perspective, as captured in a typecasting of terrorism as legitimate or illegitimate behavior. Two polar opposite perspectives are generally the basis for such a discussion: terrorism as crime and terrorism as war. To these two distinctions, a third, developed throughout the discussions, is terrorism as a specific kind of warfare, asymmetrical war.

The basic distinction serves two purposes. On the one hand, it speaks to the legitimacy of terrorism: a depiction of terrorism as crime clearly stamps it as illegal and thus illegitimate, whereas depicting it as war (of one sort or another) raises its status among actions of states and groups. The distinction also suggests the appropriate approach to dealing with terrorism either as a legal system or a military problem, which is also a contentious matter.

The *terrorism as crime* perspective focuses on terrorist acts and their acceptability, with an emphasis on their illegality. It is primarily the perspective of the victims of terrorism. All terrorist acts against people and things violate legal norms in all organized societies: it is against the law to murder people or to blow up things, after all, regardless of why one does so. If acts of terrorism are, at their core, criminal acts, then terrorists are little more than common criminals and should be treated as such. Terrorism thus becomes at heart a criminal problem, and terrorists are part of the criminal justice system subject to arrest, incarceration, trial, and, where appropriate, imprisonment or execution. This is the perspective that most European countries have toward terrorism.

Terrorists simultaneously reject and embrace this depiction. They reject the notion that what they do is criminal, because their acts—while technically illegal—are committed for what they believe to be higher political purposes. Terrorists kill people, but they do not murder them. Terrorists are not criminals; rather, they are warriors (in contemporary times, "holy" warriors). Thinking in this manner elevates the status of the terrorist from criminal to soldier, a far more exalted and acceptable position. At the same time, terrorists prefer for target societies to think of them as criminals in those situations in which they are captured and brought to justice (assuming the capturing society adheres to its own criminal procedures, which is not always the case). The reason is simple: at least in the West, criminal procedures are considerably more stringent in procedural and evidentiary senses than military law, affording terrorists greater protections under the law and making their successful prosecution more difficult. Attempts in the United States to relax criminal safeguards regarding terrorists seek to change that status but have created controversy in civil rights and liberties terms.

Terrorists prefer the second perspective, *terrorism as war*. This viewpoint emphasizes the political nature of terrorism and terrorist acts, in essence adopting the Clausewitzian paraphrase that "terrorism is politics by other means." If one accepts the basic premise of this perspective, then terrorist acts are not crimes but acts of war and, as such, are judged by the standards of war (broadly defined, since asymmetrical warfare commonly succeeds by ignoring conventional rules that disadvantage them) rather than by criminal standards. The interactions between terrorist organizations and their targets are thus warlike, military affairs. Killing outside situations of war is always illegal, but within war it is permissible, at least within certain bounds regarding who and in what conditions killing occurs.

The current global war on terrorism implicitly accepts this perspective, if not its implications. Within the GWOT, the term *war* is used rather loosely and almost allegorically rather than literally, and almost all apostles of the designation do not view terrorists as warriors but rather as wanton criminals to be brought to justice or their demise. Within the antiterrorism campaign in Afghanistan, for instance, members (or alleged members) of Al Qaeda were not treated as prisoners of war, which would have afforded them certain legal rights under the Geneva Conventions on War, but instead under the legally vague designation of "detainees," who the Bush administration apparently does not believe possess Geneva Convention protections.

The problem of treating terrorism as crime or as war is that, in most cases, it is both. Terrorists do engage in criminal acts, but they do so for reasons more normally associated with war. This suggests that there should be a third way of depicting terrorism, which can be called *terrorism as asymmetrical war*. Asymmetrical warfare is different from the conventional forms of warfare that are covered by the traditional laws of war; indeed, a major characteristic of asymmetrical warfare is the rejection of traditional norms and rules as part of the attempt to level the playing field of conflict. As noted in Chapter 11, for instance, the asymmetrical warrior does not distinguish between combatants and noncombatants, just as the terrorist considers all members of the target group equally culpable and thus eligible for attack.

Terrorism as asymmetrical war is a hybrid of the other two perspectives. The terrorists' rejection of accepted rules means they can treat their actions as acts of war while the target society rejects this contention and can continue to consider their actions crimes against mankind. The status of asymmetrical warriors as warriors may be ambiguous within the rules of war, but leaving their actions within criminal jurisdiction satisfies the target society's depiction while affording captured terrorists the legal protections they seek. This perspective also allows terrorism to be depicted as both a criminal *and* a military problem, which it is, and thus allows both law enforcement and military responses to terrorists. The only difficulty is in determining the appropriate mix of criminal justice and military responses generally and in specific situations.

Three Causes

The motivation to become a terrorist and to engage in the often gruesome and dangerous acts that typify terrorism is also the source of considerable speculation and disagreement among experts and lay observers. Much of the difficulty in making such assessments derives from the absolute inability most people have in imagining why anyone would become a terrorist and kill people who, from the victims' perspective, are innocent. Whatever leads people to become terrorists is so alien that people cannot draw analogies from their own experiences or those arising in society as they know it.

Three vantage points on what causes people and groups to adopt terrorism are often put forward, reflecting in some ways the disciplinary vantage points that various students of the phenomenon represent. Most of these explanations surfaced during the 1960s and 1970s, during the third or "New Left" wave of modern terrorism, according to David C. Rapoport (the first two were anarchism and anticolonialism; the fourth and present wave is religious). This is worth noting because the 1960s and 1970s tended to be more tolerant of, even sympathetic to, politically aberrant movements than is true today. At any rate, terrorism is typified as primarily a societal, a psychological, or a political problem. The three explanations are neither mutually exclusive nor agreed upon.

The *societal* argument is that social conditions provide the breeding grounds for terrorism. Societies that consistently underachieve, that fail to provide adequate material or spiritual advances or hope for their people, and in which the citizens live in an unending and hopeless condition of deprivation provide a kind of intellectual and physical "swamp" in which terrorism "breeds" a ready supply of potential terrorism followers who are willing recruits for causes that promise to bring meaning and direction to their lives. These "failed societies" may even oppress specific groups that are even more prone to the appeals of terrorism recruiters and may prevent other groups from achieving the goals to which they aspire (what Gurr calls "aspirational deprivation"). A variant of this argument also suggests that some societies' values may be better suited than others for producing terrorists. In the contemporary setting, for instance, some observers note that Islam has a more prominent, positive role for religious martyrdom than do other religions, making the terrorist path, and especially suicide terrorism, more acceptable than it would be in other places.

If this argument is substantially correct, it leads to a potential solution to the terrorism problem: if the wretched (or frustrating) conditions are removed and the society ceases to be a failed one, then the conditions that breed the terrorists may also be removed. These failed societies are not necessarily the poorest societies (which tend to produce criminals but not terrorists) but those where opportunities are limited or missing. This is the heart of the argument for "draining the swamp" as a way to combat terrorism. The tool for doing so is the infusion of (probably massive) amounts of developmental assistance to create the physical basis for greater prosperity and a sense of meaningful futures: people do not volunteer for potential self-immolation (such as suicide terrorist missions) if they have hope for a more positive, promising future. In the current debate, feeding resources into the Pakistani education system to create a peaceful alternative to the religious *madrassa* schools that teach anti-Americanism is a prime example of the application of the societal argument.

Critics point to a hole in this explanation of what creates terrorism. They argue that many modern terrorists are not the product of objective societal deprivation, but of aspirational deprivation. Sixteen of the nineteen September 11 terrorists, after all, were Saudi citizens who could hardly be accused of coming from abjectly deprived backgrounds. Such an observation is obviously true, but it does not completely negate the argument that inferior societal conditions produce terrorists. Rather, the observation conditions the argument by saying that *not all* terrorists come from physically deprived backgrounds. Most terrorist leaders, it appears, and some of their followers come from middle-, even upper-class backgrounds (bin Laden, for instance), but a lot of their followers indeed emerge from the "swamp."

The second explanation moves from the group to the individual. Rather than focusing on failed societies, the *psychological* argument shifts the emphasis from the failed society to failed peoples. The psychological argument is not entirely divorced from the societal argument in that it basically contends that certain traits in people, certain psychological states, make them more susceptible to the terrorist appeal and thus more willing to commit terrorist acts than is true in other individuals. Since not everyone who possesses these traits becomes a terrorist (lots of people are frustrated but do not react by blowing themselves up, for instance), there must be triggering societal conditions that activate these tendencies.

Terrorist profiling is a clear example of the psychological explanation of terrorism. In many contemporary arguments, for instance, it has been observed that many of the individuals who perpetrate religious-based terrorism from Middle Eastern settings share several characteristics. Most of the terrorist followers (as opposed to the leaders who recruit, train, and direct them) tend to be teenaged boys with high school educations who do not have jobs at all, or if they do, their jobs pay them sufficiently poorly that they have few prospects. They tend to be unmarried with few prospects of finding a wife (often because they cannot support them). They also tend to have low self-esteem intermixed with a high sense of helplessness and hopelessness about their futures. These perceptions lead to a high sense of humiliation, embarrassment, and impotence toward the future. Individuals with this kind of profile are believed to be especially vulnerable to recruitment by terrorist leaders who promise to restore meaning and purpose and thus a sense of self-esteem. A particularly troubling

Amplification 12.2

PROFILING SUICIDE TERRORISTS

The problem posed by terrorists willing to kill themselves to commit their terrorist acts burst on the scene during the clash between Israel and the Palestinians that erupted in 2000 (*Intifada* II) and has been given further publicity by the suicidal actions of some Iraqi car bomber members of the Iraqi resistance. Suicide/martyr terrorism is neither truly new nor unique to the present: Americans, for instance, encountered suicide bombers during the conquest of Okinawa in World War II, which was one reason they sought to avoid an invasion of the Japanese home islands. The whole idea of self-immolation, especially by the young people associated with Palestinian suicide terrorism, is, however, totally alien to most Americans.

The Israelis (as reported in Stern) have developed a profile of these terrorists. They tend to be young, often teenagers, and they are generally mentally immature. In nearly all cases, they are under pressure to get a job but, due to a lack of connections, are unsuccessful in doing so. As a result, they have no money or reasonable prospects to improve their situations. Among other things, they cannot afford girlfriends or fiancées, and marriage is not an option for them. They thus feel a profound sense of helplessness and hopelessness. For many, God and the Mosque are their only refuge.

Becoming a suicide terrorist remedies some of these problems. Being a member of a terrorist organization can restore a sense of purpose and self-esteem: the recruit (*shaheed*) is now an important person, and his willingness to make the ultimate sacrifice only adds to his social prestige and acceptance. Martyrdom reestablishes his worth.

What is frightening is that the population bulge in the Middle East means there are a large number of young men (and increasingly women) who meet the profile. Unless steps—whatever they may be—can be taken to reverse the conditions that give rise to suicide terrorists, more suicide terrorists can be expected in the future.

recent trend has been the emergence of females with similar profiles in terrorist roles. The terrorist profile is discussed in Amplification 12.2.

The implications of this profile are particularly disturbing because the Middle East has a population "bulge," which includes a large number of young males who meet the basic enabling characteristics described in the profile. Moreover, the societal conditions in most Middle Eastern states offer few prospects for reducing these conditions, notably for employment, that can turn the situation around. As long as life does not contain meaningful prospects that can prevent the triggering of psychological processes leading to terrorism, there will be fertile breeding grounds for new generations of terrorists. It might be added that far fewer studies suggest similar profiles for terrorist leaders, except that they come from higher socioeconomic situations.

The third explanation is *political*, that failed governments produce the societal and psychological conditions in which terrorism emerges or produce conditions in which terrorists emerge or are nurtured. Although it hardly exhausts the possibilities, state action can lead to terrorism in two ways. First, state oppression (indeed, including the use of terrorism *by* the government) may lead to political opposition that must be clandestine and must resort to terrorism as the only means of survival (terrorism as the tool of the asymmetrical warrior). The Chechen resistance would certainly view itself in this manner. In other cases, the government may be so inept or ineffective that it provides a haven for terrorists to exist without being able to do anything about it. The ineffectiveness of the Pakistani government in suppressing remnants of Al Qaeda and other sympathetic groups in the mountainous areas of Waziristan bordering Afghanistan is an example. In yet other cases, sympathetic governments may even provide refuge and sanctuary for terrorist organizations. The relationship between Afghanistan's Taliban regime and Al Qaeda is a frequently cited example.

As with the other explanations, the political model also suggests remedies. If it is bad governments that create, put up with, or consort with terrorists, then there are two ways to deal with the problem. One is to convince the government to abandon the terrorists, quit creating them, or apprehend them, using either positive inducements (military or economic assistance) or threats of some form of sanctions to induce compliance. This has been the basic American strategy with Pakistan. If those efforts fail, a second option may be to replace those governments with more compliant regimes. That is at least part of the rationale for the American invasion of Iraq. The effectiveness of these solutions is, of course, open to question.

As noted, these explanations are not mutually exclusive. Failed governments have failed societal conditions as one of their causes and consequences, and it is failure at these levels that may create the triggering conditions for psychological forces that activate terrorists. It may be, as well, that these explanations are not comprehensive but may be characteristic of the 1960s and 1970s variants of terrorism, which were, among other things, noticeably secular rather than religious. Strategies for dealing with the terrorism problem must sort out the influences of various explanations and how well they apply to the current and evolving forms of terrorism.

TERRORISM SINCE SEPTEMBER 11

The events of September 11 understandably focused national attention on a specific terrorist threat posed by Al Qaeda. The focus was natural given the audacity and shock value of the actual attacks, the novelty of an organization such as Al Qaeda, and the underlying hatred of Americans that they revealed. To the extent that Americans had much of an understanding of terrorism, it was associated with more "classical" forms such as highly politicized anticolonialist movements like the Irish Republican Army (IRA), with state terrorism in the form of suppression by totalitarian regimes like Hitler's Germany or Stalin's Soviet Union, or with isolated anarchist assassinations or individual acts like the bombing of the Murrah Federal Building in Oklahoma City.

Understanding the nature of the threat has been difficult for at least two reasons. First, the contemporary form of terrorism appears very different from anything encountered before. It is nonstate-based terrorism that does not arise from specific political communities or jurisdictions but instead flows across national boundaries like oil slipping under doors. It is therefore conceptually difficult to make terrorism concrete and to counter it. It is also religious, showing signs of fanaticism that are present in all religious communities (including our own, historically) but that are alien to our ability to conceptualize. Slaughter in the name of God goes beyond most people's intellectual frameworks. It is also fanatically anti-American and thus in sharp contrast to the general pro-Americanism that at least seemed to dominate the end of the twentieth century. It also employs methods such as suicide terrorism that, if not historically unique, are deviant enough to go beyond most people's abilities to conjure.

Second, understanding is made more difficult by the extremely changing nature of contemporary terrorist opponents. The Al Qaeda of 2001 was hard enough for us to understand, but it has evolved greatly since then. Partly this is because international efforts since 2001 were quite effective in dismantling the old Al Qaeda structure by capturing and killing many of its members. This success, however, has caused the threat to disperse and transform itself into newer and arguably more deadly forms. A discussion of organizational evolution is necessary to clarify the nature of the current terrorist threat.

Jessica Stern, in *Terrorism in the Name of God*, lays out the requirements for a successful terrorist organization. The effectiveness of a terrorist organization is dependent on two qualities: resiliency (the ability to withstand the loss of parts of its membership or workforce) and capacity (the ability to optimize the scale and impact of terrorist attacks). The larger the scale of operations the terrorist organization can carry out without large losses to its members through capture or death, the more effective the organization. Conversely, if an organization can carry out only small, relatively insignificant acts while having large portions of its membership captured or killed, it is less effective.

Resiliency and capacity are clearly related. For a terrorist organization to carry out large operations such as the coordinated attacks on Spanish commuter trains in 2004, it must devise a sophisticated, coordinated plan involving a number of people or cells who must communicate with one another to both plan and execute the attack. The Achilles' heel in terrorist activity is penetration of the organization by outsiders, and the key element is the interruption of communications that allows penetration into the organization and movement through the hierarchy to interfere with and destroy the organization and its ability to carry out attacks (in other words, to reduce its resiliency). The most effective way for the terrorist organization to avoid penetration is to minimize communications that can be intercepted, but doing so comes at the expense of the sophistication, coordination, and thus extent of its actions (reduction in capacity).

The result of the interplay of these contradictory factors is a dilemma that is changing the face of contemporary terrorist organizations. Historically, according to Stern and others, most terrorist organizations have followed an organizational form known as the *commander-cadre* (or *hierarchical*) model. This form of organization is not dissimilar to the way complex organizations are structured everywhere: executives (commanders) organize and plan activities (terrorist attacks) and pass instructions downward through the organization for implementation by employees (cadres). In order to try to maintain levels of secrecy that improve resiliency, terrorist organizations structure themselves so that any one level of the organization (cell) knows only of the cell directly above and below it (which, of course, distinguishes them from more conventional complex organizations).

Commander-cadre arrangements can coordinate activities maximizing capacity (the African embassy bombings, for instance); they can organize recruitment and absorb, indoctrinate, and train recruits; and they can carry out ancillary activities such as fund raising, dealing with cooperative governments, and engaging in commerce and other forms of activity. The disadvantage of these organizations is that they may become more permeable by outside agencies because of their need to communicate among units.

The result of the post–September 11 campaign against Al Qaeda has been to cause it to adapt, to become what Stern calls the "protean enemy" that has "shown a surprising willingness to adapt its mission" and to alter its organizational form "to make it more resilient." Al Qaeda is no longer a hierarchically organized entity that plans and carries out terrorist missions. Instead, it has adopted elements of the alternate form of terrorist organization, the *virtual network* or *leaderless resistance* model and has dispersed itself into a series of smaller, loosely affiliated terrorist organizations (Jemaah Islamiyah is a prime example) that draw inspiration from Al Qaeda. The announcement by Iraqi resistance leader Abu Musab al-Zarqawi of allegiance to bin Laden's goals in October 2004 (Al Qaeda in Iraq) is part of the resurgence of Al Qaeda that raised concerns about new levels of activity in summer 2007. Zarqawi himself, however, was killed in 2006. If it ever was a monolithic dragon, Al Qaeda has instead become a hydra-headed monster.

The core of the leaderless resistance model is the reduction of direct communications between the leadership and its members. Rather than planning operations and instructing operatives to carry out those plans, leaders instead exhort their followers to act through public pronouncements (for instance, through the use of Web sites). Leaders may issue general calls to action, but they have no direct communications with followers that can be intercepted or used as the basis for suppression or conspiracy indictments. The leader has no direct knowledge or control of individual terrorist acts, which he or she may inspire but not direct.

The authoritative source of terrorist organizational activity is the U.S. Department of State's list of designated foreign terrorist organizations, an annual publication. *Infoplease*, an on-line publication of Pearson Education, takes this list and annotates it with additional information about the nature, goals and targets, membership, year of formation, and alleged activities of each organization. This information can be used to describe the current pattern of terrorist activity in the world. The most recent list available at the time of writing was from 2006. Although the list changes marginally from year to year, it is representative of current activity.

Forty-two organizations made the list. They come from four of the Earth's continents (Asia, Europe, Africa, and South America), and a slight majority (23 of 42) are Islamic in membership and purposes, but a sizable minority are not. They are summarized by origin and membership in Table 12.1.

Table 12.1: Demography of Terrorist Organizations

Location	Muslim	Non-Muslim	Total
Middle East (excluding Turkey and Pakistan)	13	4	17
Other Asia	6	6	12
Africa	4	—	4
South America	—	4	4
Europe	—	5	5
Total	23	19	42

It is a diverse lot of organizations. The largest concentration is Muslim Middle Eastern organizations, with one-quarter (13 of 42) of the total, including prominently Al Qaeda and Al Qaeda in Iraq as separate organizations. Most Muslim organizations espouse the formation of an Islamic state as a goal, including groups in Iraq, Kashmir, Egypt, Algeria, Lebanon, the Philippines (which also has a Marxist group seeking to overthrow the government), Uzbekistan, Indonesia, Pakistan, Libya, and Morocco. Not all of these movements are anti-American, depending on whether the United States opposes or ignores their goals. Non-Muslim groups vary from an Israeli extremist group (Kahane Chai) to separatist groups in Europe (the Irish Republican Army splinter groups, the Basque Fatherland and Liberty—ETA) to Marxist groups supporting the narcotics trade in South America. The point is that the worldwide roster of terrorist organizations is far wider and more diverse than the current GWOT emphasis on international religious terrorists (principally Al Qaeda) would suggest, and that the United States is not the particular target of many of these groups. It also suggests that a "successful" GWOT against Al Qaeda and its affiliates might eliminate that source of terrorism in the world and come close to eliminating the American concern with terrorism but that it would not eliminate the practice of terrorism worldwide.

THE GWOT: DEALING WITH TERRORISM

Terrorism is a variant of the asymmetrical warfare problem already described as a—arguably *the*—prominent national security problem facing the United States, and the political reaction to the September 11 attacks has raised it to the highest priority for the country's security. Whether the rhetoric of the GWOT is more hyperbolic than factual is almost beside the point; the public commitment is that terrorism must and will be defeated: the country is committed to "winning the global war on terrorism."

But what does that robust rhetoric mean? Exactly what (or who) is the opponent in this "war"? There are three possibilities. One is that the opponent is terrorism (which the official rhetoric suggests), but terrorism is a method, a way to do things. How does one defeat and subdue a method, and specifically a method that has endured for over two thousand years? A second possibility is that the opponent is terrorist purposes, but these are ideas that can only be "defeated" by being discredited, an intellectual process. The third possibility is that the contest is against terrorists, those who actually commit terrorist acts. Terrorists are at least a concrete opponent, but can eliminating particular terrorists extinguish terrorism as long as the method works at least some of the time and there are adherents to terrorist ideas?

All of these are valid questions for which definitive, consensually agreed-upon answers do not exist, but which must be dealt with if a coherent strategy for dealing with the problem is to be devised. Examine each possibility. It is frequently argued that it makes no sense to talk about war against an abstraction, and the idea of terrorism is the application of a method, a means to accomplish a goal. Can you "kill" an idea in some concrete or abstract manner? If so, how do know you have accomplished the task? Where, quite literally, are the bodies or the surrendering enemies? Wars, at any level, are contests between members of different groups to assert control. People and their ideas are not the same thing.

The war analogy suffers even if one switches emphasis and says the GWOT is a war on global terrorists. Switching the emphasis at least has the virtue of making a war of people against other people (a conceptual improvement), but it still retains two problems in the current context.

First, warfare against terrorists is war against asymmetrical warriors, as already noted. That means that the countries seeking to defeat terrorism are militarily superior in conventional terms and that terrorism is the asymmetrical means by which terrorists seek to create a situation in which they have a chance to succeed. The problem here lies in the criteria for success for those seeking to snuff out terrorists and for the terrorists themselves. For the United States (or any other country engaged in terrorism suppression), the criterion is very exacting: the war cannot be won until terrorists everywhere specified by the war (the globe as currently defined) have been defeated. Those seeking to suppress terrorists must crush their opponents; in a phrase, they can only "win by winning."

The situation is different for the terrorists. Terrorists know that they cannot win in the traditional sense of crushing their enemies (win by winning), but equally, they know their enemies cannot validly claim victory as long as the terrorists can continue to operate. Thus, terrorists (much like guerrillas) realize that their criterion for success is to avoid being defeated and that the longer they remain a viable force, the more likely they are to become a sufficient enough irritant that their opponents conclude that acquiescence to their demands is preferable to continuing the frustrating struggle against them. The terrorists, in other words, can "win by not losing" or, at a minimum, prevent their opponent from declaring victory by avoiding losing.

The problem of defeating terrorists is made more difficult by a second problem associated with modern asymmetrical warfare: contemporary international terrorist organizations are nonstate actors. As already shown, the majority of the contemporary religious terrorists are Muslims who come from or have connections to parts of the Islamic Middle East. All Muslims in the Middle East do not support the terrorists or what they do (although enough do to provide safe haven in which terrorists can hide), and no state government has claimed association with major terrorist organizations since the overthrow of the Taliban in Afghanistan. To make matters worse, these nonstate actors generally imbed themselves within physical areas and among people sympathetic to them; they move around, including across international borders such as the Waziristan region along the Pakistan–Afghanistan border, and they rarely establish public physical symbols that can be identified with them (some Islamic charities that serve as fronts for terrorist activities such as recruitment and fund raising are partial exceptions).

The problem this creates for a "war" on terrorists is finding and specifying targets that can be attacked and defeated. When Al Qaeda was openly running training camps in Afghanistan, this was not so much of a problem, and occasionally, a military attack would be made on one of these facilities (for instance, cruise missile attacks on Al Qaeda training camps in 1998 in retaliation for the bombings of American embassies in Africa). Since the fall of the Taliban and the dispersal of Al Qaeda into greater nonstate anonymity, military actions directly against Al Qaeda or its associates have essentially ceased. The most important military limitation is the inability to find and target the most vital parts of the terrorist existence—the so-called centers of gravity on which the terrorists rely for their continued viability. The result, according to Audrey Kurth Cronin, is "that it is virtually impossible to target the most vulnerable point in the organization." Until (or unless) these problems are surmounted, military efforts are likely to remain frustrating.

The current dilemma regarding Al Qaeda illustrates the problem. It is widely known (or suspected) that the Al Qaeda leadership and infrastructure are located in the Pakistani "badlands" of remote Waziristan, a province over which the Pakistani government exercises only nominal jurisdiction, ceding effective control to tribal leaders in return for their allegiance to the regime. The tribal leaders, in turn, have working relationships with Al Qaeda that leave the terrorist group secure and allow it safe transit back and forth across the Afghan border. The Pakistani government does not dare conduct large-scale operations against Al Qaeda because it might alienate local tribes and because it lacks detailed knowledge of where Al Qaeda is located in the area. Additionally, Pakistan's conventionally oriented army has been badly bloodied when it has forayed into this territory.

In this case, how can the GWOT be brought to bear against Al Qaeda? Politically, American ally Pakistan can neither conduct effective ground operations in Waziristan nor permit the United States to do so because of sovereignty issues. Additionally, American intelligence capabilities are too limited to pinpoint Al Qaeda targets (such as bin Laden) for aerial bombardment. The result is a very frustrating situation for the United States and a major source of friction between the United States and Pakistan.

In some sense, the GWOT even requires a continuing Al Qaeda presence. As former CIA official Paul R. Pillar explains, "The existence of a specific, recognized, hated terrorist enemy has helped the United States retain its focus. As long as Al Qaeda exists, even in its current, severely weakened form, it will serve that function." Were we to capture or kill bin Laden and his cohorts, we would destroy a terrorist focus, but we would not destroy terrorism; someone else would pick up the gauntlet. Al Qaeda and bin Laden help us keep our attention focused.

The continuing role of Al Qaeda is illustrated by a terrorist incident that occurred October 7, 2004, at seaside resorts on Egyptian soil in the Sinai peninsula.

Bombs tore apart a series of resort hotels where many of the occupants were Israelis celebrating the end of the Yom Kippur holiday. The immediate question was who was responsible, and within a day's time, Al Qaeda had been identified as the likely culprit. While bin Laden has publicly condemned Israel for its suppression of the Palestinians, there are not publicly known instances of Al Qaeda attacks against Egyptian targets. So, was Al Qaeda really to blame directly (did, for instance, bin Laden order the attacks)? Or could the attacks have been carried out by an affiliate or franchise of Al Qaeda acting independently or simply deriving the inspiration to do so from bin Laden's general exhortations? For purposes of the GWOT, simply blaming Al Qaeda removed the need for such nuanced public judgments.

Terrorism Suppression: Antiterrorism and Counterterrorism

In conventional terrorism suppression circles, two methods for dealing with the terrorist problem are most often invoked: antiterrorism and counterterrorism. The two terms are sometimes used interchangeably, although each refers to a distinct form of action with a specific purpose. Any program of terrorist suppression will necessarily contain elements of each of them, but failing to specify which is which generally or in specific applications only confuses the issue.

Antiterrorism refers to defensive efforts to reduce the vulnerability of targets to terrorist attacks and to lessen the effects of terrorist attacks that do occur. Antiterrorism efforts thus begin from the premise that some terrorist attacks will indeed occur (or at least be attempted) and that two forms of effort are necessary to counter these efforts. First, antiterrorists seek to make it more difficult to mount terrorist attacks. Airport security to prevent potential terrorists from boarding airliners and the interception and detention of possible terrorists by border guards are examples, as is placing barriers around buildings so that terrorists cannot drive bomb-laden vehicles close enough to destroy the buildings. Second, antiterrorists try to mitigate the effects of terrorist attacks that do occur. This form of activity is also known as civil defense or crisis management and is largely the province of first responders such as police and firefighters.

At least four related difficulties hamper conducting an effective antiterrorist campaign. One is that antiterrorism is necessarily reactive; terrorists choose where attacks will occur and against what kinds of targets, and antiterrorists must respond to the terrorist initiative. A second problem is the sheer variety and number of targets to be protected. As suggested earlier, the potential list of targets is almost infinite, and one of the purposes of attacks is often randomness so that potential victims are always off guard and antiterrorists will have trouble anticipating where attacks may occur. The third problem is, as noted, target substitution: if antiterrorist efforts are sufficiently successful that terrorists determine their likelihood of success against any particular target (or class of targets) is significantly diminished, they will simply go on to other, less well-defended targets. Given the variety of targets available, finding places and things that have not been protected is not impossible. The fourth is the political economy of the enterprise: suppressing terrorism is much more expensive than terrorism, a dynamic described in Amplification 12.3.

Amplification 12.3

The Cost-Effectiveness of Suppressing Terrorism

The economics of terrorism and its suppression favors the terrorist. Generally speaking, it is cheaper to mount a terrorist attack against a target than it is to protect that target. The reason is simple: the terrorists know what particular target in a target set (urban skyscrapers, for instance) they plan to attack and need to expend resources only to destroy that target. Antiterrorists, on the other hand, do not know far in advance (if they know at all) which part of the set is being targeted and must plan to protect the whole set, since the failure to protect a particular target might make attacks against it more likely.

Protecting the whole target set is more expensive than protecting individual targets, and since most members of the set are not actually under threat, the additional costs of protecting them favor the terrorist. This advantage extends to sacrifices people make in protecting target sets. As Enders and Sandler put it, "Each additional sacrifice of freedom gains less security from terrorist attacks." Terrorists can amplify this unfavorable economic dynamic by threatening additional target sets that can only be protected by cost-ineffective measures.

The other form of terrorist suppression is *counterterrorism*, offensive and military measures against terrorists or sponsoring agencies to prevent, deter, or respond to terrorist acts. As the definition suggests, counterterrorism consists of both preventive and retaliatory actions against terrorists. Preventive acts can include such things as penetration of terrorist cells and taking action—including apprehension and physical violence against terrorists—before they carry out their acts. Retaliation is more often military and paramilitary and includes attacks on terrorist camps or other facilities in response to terrorist attacks. The purposes of retaliation include both reducing terrorist capacity for future acts and hopefully deterring future actions by instilling fear of the consequences. In addition, Special Operations Forces are sometimes used to penetrate terrorist staging areas for reconnaissance and intelligence purposes.

Counterterrorism is inherently and intuitively attractive (which may be why there is a tendency to lump antiterrorist and other activities under the banner of counterterrorism). Preventive actions are proactive, taking the battle to the terrorists and punishing them in advance of creating harm. If effective, they prevent terrorist operations from being carried out and weaken the terrorist organization by capturing or killing its members. In its purest form, preventive counterterrorist actions reverse the tables in the relationship, effectively "terrorizing the terrorists." Pounding a terrorist facility as punishment from enduring a terrorist attack at least entails the satisfaction of knowing the enemy has suffered for the suffering it caused the victim.

The problem with counterterrorism, like antiterrorism, is that it is insufficient on its own as a way to quell terrorism. Preventing terrorist actions requires a level of intelligence about the structures of terrorist organizations that is quite difficult to obtain, and it has been a central purpose of terrorist reorganization into protean forms, discussed earlier, to increase that difficulty. If one does not know the terrorist organization in detail, it is, for instance, difficult to penetrate, learn of its nefarious intentions, and interrupt those activities. The absence of a state base that can be attacked means it is more difficult to identify terrorist targets whose retaliatory destruction will cripple the organization, punish its members, or frighten it into ceasing future actions. The difficulty of finding targets against which to retaliate is particularly frustrating for the military in its counterterrorism role because it is denied the kinds of targets associated with more conventional military operations.

Ideally, antiterrorism and counterterrorism efforts act in tandem. Counterterrorists reduce the number and quality of possible attacks through preventive actions, resulting in less frequent and thus more manageable antiterrorist efforts to ameliorate the effects of attacks that do succeed. Counterterrorists' retaliation, then, can hopefully reduce the terrorists' capacity for future mayhem. In practice, however, these efforts sometimes come into operational conflict. The antiterrorist emphasis on lessening the effects of attacks may lead to publicizing the possibility of particular attacks as a way to alert citizens (the color-coded warning system, for instance), whereas counterterrorists prefer to keep operations as secret as possible to facilitate clandestine penetration and interruption.

International versus National Efforts

There has been considerable discussion since September 11 about the appropriate level at which to conduct operations aimed at suppressing this current wave of international terrorist activity. In the immediate aftermath of the attacks, there was an enormous international outpouring of sympathy for the United States and willingness to join a vigorous international effort to deal with terrorists around the globe. That resolve resulted in a good amount of international cooperation among law enforcement and intelligence agencies in various countries, much of which continues quietly to this day. The more visible manifestations of that internationalization have faded as the United States has "militarized" the terrorist suppression effort (the GWOT as primarily "war") and moved toward actions opposed by the major allies in the law enforcement and intelligence efforts through unilateral actions in places like Iraq.

As already reported, the post–September 11 international effort has experienced apparent successes in reducing the size and potency of Al Qaeda as it existed at the time. The nature and extent of that reduction has been a matter of disagreement, as has the extent to which Al Qaeda and its various constituent groups have regenerated since. The international problem has, however, clearly changed, and the question is how this change is and should be reflected in the degree to which ongoing terrorism should be treated as a national or international effort.

Within the United States, most of the visible activity on reforming the effort has been national. *The 9/11 Commission Report*, for instance, emphasized reform within the American government (principally in restructuring the intelligence community) as a way to respond to the evolving problem. One section in its recommendations chapter is titled "Unity of Effort Across the Foreign–Domestic Divide," but its primary function is to suggest improvements in the American ability to cooperate with foreign sources. Emphases on problems like border protection—port security, for instance—generally have a primarily national content.

Does the nature of the new threat suggest a greater inward or outward turning of efforts? Former CIA expert Pillar suggests that the evolving nature of the threat reinforces the need for greater internationalization. As he describes it, "In a more decentralized network, individuals will go unnoticed not because data on analysts' screens are misinterpreted but because they will never appear on those screens in the first place." Much of the added data on the successors to Al Qaeda can only be collected in the countries where they operate, but Pillar sees two barriers to sustained international cooperation. On the one hand, "an underlying limitation on foreign willingness to cooperate with the United States is the skepticism among foreign publics and even elites that the most powerful nation on the planet needs to be preoccupied with small bands of radicals." This leads to a second misgiving, which is the perceived "ability to sustain the country's own determination to fight" the terrorist threat.

There is also at least muted disagreement in the United States about proper emphases and relationships between parts and levels of government involved in the terrorism suppression effort. At the federal level, the emphasis tends to be on counterterrorism through intelligence and military actions aimed at foreign terrorists—defeating the terrorists overseas so they do not have to be defeated here, in President Bush's often asserted phrase. At the state and local levels, there is more emphasis on antiterrorism by the first responders. Those differences in perspective often result in failures to communicate between levels of government and in competition over priorities for federal funding.

Other Aspects of the Problem

A final problem of the conceptual nature of the GWOT is that it does not capture the entirety of the problem that it has been asked to solve. The GWOT, as suggested, is really an effort aimed at suppressing terrorists, as are the forms of dealing with terrorists discussed in the previous section. Somehow capturing or killing all the existing terrorists does not, however, destroy *terrorism*, which is the underlying purpose of the entire enterprise. As long as individuals and groups choose terrorism as the means to realize their ideas, terrorism cannot be wholly eradicated; only its current manifestations can be contained.

This other part of any effort to suppress terrorism is intellectual, a war of ideas that has two basic parts. The first is the intellectual competition between terrorists and their enemies—the underlying reasons terrorists emerge and the appeal they have among the populations that hide, nurture, sustain, and form the recruitment base for movements that employ terrorism as a method. In the current wave of religious terrorism, virulent anti-Americanism is the activator; the United States and the American way are portrayed as the major threat to Islam and the way of life that it promotes. As long as the United States (and the West generally) does not compete with this basic idea and assert and convince those in the Middle East that our ideas produce a superior existence *for them*, there will be an endless stream of recruits to the banner that no terrorist suppression efforts can even hope to overcome. The best chance of "defeating" these ideas may be that their millenarian goals will eventually be abandoned as unattainable—as has happened in the past.

The second part of the intellectual battle is over the use of terrorism as the method of those whose ideas Americans oppose. This requires competing in the forum of ideas that can lead to terrorism and also dealing with what causes people to become terrorists. Regardless of the level of causation at which one begins (societal, political, or psychological), one must persuade people that volunteering to be terrorists (in the most extreme case, agreeing to commit suicide to advance the terrorist cause) is not acceptable to them if the flow of recruits of terrorists intent on killing people is to be staunched. This problem, "draining the swamp" in which terrorists breed, is clearly a necessary part of any comprehensive strategy.

CONCLUSION: A TERRORISM STRATEGY?

One thing has not changed since the terrorist attacks of September 11: the United States did not have a comprehensive, encompassing strategy for dealing with the risks associated with international terrorism then, and it does not have such a strategy today. What it does have is a series of catchphrases and partial approaches to the problem, some of which may actually contradict one another (Iraq and the war on terrorism, for instance). The same can be said of the world at large, but the problem is most poignant for the United States because of its status as the self-appointed world leader in the GWOT and because of the overwhelming preponderance of American power and resources that can and must be applied to reducing the risk of terrorism. Until the United States gets its act together, in other words, neither will the rest of the world.

The dilemma presented by confronting terrorism is twofold. First, it is a very complex problem of the kind with which political institutions are loathe to deal. Declaring a GWOT is a great deal simpler than dealing with the incredible complexities only broadly suggested in these pages. Individuals *within* governments can deal with these problems comprehensively, but large, cumbersome organizations with diverse purposes and agendas have a harder time. Second, the suppression of terrorism is not a conflict that can easily be won, if it can be "won" at all. Terrorism as an idea has been around for a long time, and it will likely continue to persist for a long time. The goal of terrorism strategy is to contain terrorism, to reduce the risks arising from it, not to exorcise it from national and international existence. That is not as high-flown a goal as obliterating terrorism, but it is more realistic.

What then are the goals and elements of a terrorism strategy? What one can do is raise questions, because there are no agreed-upon answers (if there were and they worked, there would not be the problem there is). Thus, the purpose of this conclusion is to help organize and articulate questions about how a comprehensive strategy toward terrorism might be fashioned, not to provide the definitive answers to those questions.

The first and obvious step in devising a strategy is deciding what its goal should be. It is clearly not enough to say the goal is to "win" the struggle; one must specify what winning means. During the latter stages of the 2004 presidential campaign, the principal candidates effectively—if inadvertently—framed this question. Democratic nominee John Kerry, in a *New York Times Magazine* interview, argued the only realistic goal was to contain the problem, to reduce it to the status of a nuisance rather than a central, encompassing fixation; he drew an analogy with containing prostitution and gambling. George W. Bush replied fierily that Kerry was wrong and that the goal of the GWOT had to be to hunt down and destroy terrorism everywhere it existed; winning means eradicating terrorism.

Which of these goals should be adopted as the bedrock of strategy? Eradication of terrorism is clearly more emotionally attractive, but is it a realistic or attainable goal for policy and strategy? As noted, terrorism has been around as a more-or-less permanent force for at least two thousand years (many scholars date it back to the first century A.D. to groups like the Sicarii and the Zealots), and although it has ebbed and flowed in its prominence across time, it has never disappeared altogether. Similarly, terrorist movements, such as the current religiously based terrorism, come and go, but they seem always to be replaced by something else. In that case, is a strategy based in destroying terrorism (more properly, terrorists) bound to fail and frustrate those who pursue it? Or is it more realistic (if less emotionally satisfying) to aim to minimize terrorism?

Then there is the question of how to implement the strategy. Clearly, any terrorism suppression strategy must begin with elements of both antiterrorism and counterterrorism, but in what balance? The two thrusts can be and sometimes are at odds with one another. An example shows this tension.

In August 2004, the American government announced it had seized computer diskettes from a suspected terrorist that contained blueprints for schools in New York City, New Jersey, the District of Columbia, and elsewhere. Coming on the heels of the school hostage-taking and murders in Beslan, Russia, earlier that summer, homeland security officials extrapolated that the diskettes might be evidence of a similar intent.

How should the situation have been handled? Through a quiet, behind-the-scenes counterterrorism effort whereby the potential terrorists were kept unaware the government had the diskettes while counterterrorists observed, tried to penetrate, and then squelched any plans? Or through an antiterrorist approach that notified the public of the threat and urged them to take action that would make any attack less effective? The problem was that the two approaches contradicted one another. A counterterrorism approach meant the public would be uninformed and, if an attack occurred, would be comparatively unprepared to moderate the disaster. Should an attack succeed despite counterterrorism efforts, the government's actions would have been roundly condemned for not attempting to protect American lives by warning them of the peril. An antiterrorist approach meant any secrecy would be blown, making a counterterrorism effort much more difficult or impossible. It also meant that any terrorists plotting an attack would know the government was aware of their plans, would thus abort those plans, and would avoid arrest or worse. In the real case, of course, the antiterrorists won, and the potential plot was widely publicized. No attacks occurred, and no suspected terrorists were apprehended. Was that the right decision?

There is another structural concern in dealing with existing terrorists. How can the United States improve the effort to detect, penetrate, and frustrate terrorist activities? At the national level, for instance, the 9/11 Commission made some strong suggestions for reform and consolidation of governmental efforts, but all entail considerable change in how people go about their business. How much of the commission's efforts will or should be implemented?

Further, how much of the effort should be internationalized? Should the United States remain largely independent of others in efforts ranging from counterterrorism to cooperation with United Nations or other international efforts? Or should the United States encourage greater cooperation across borders, even if it disagrees with some of those efforts?

There is the further question of what else is to be done. At least two concerns can be raised in this regard. Clearly, one way to eliminate or lessen the problem of terrorism is to discourage or lessen its appeal to potential terrorists: fewer terrorists, by definition, would pose a smaller terrorism problem. Antiterrorism and counterterrorism efforts may influence the actions of current terrorists, but they apparently do little to discourage, and may actually encourage, the recruitment of future terrorists. Israeli destruction of the family homes of Palestinian suicide terrorists has rather clearly not discouraged others from signing up for that grisly mission, and it has been argued that the American military effort in Iraq—regardless of the merit of its stated aims—has the ancillary effect of increasing regional anti-Americanism and thus intensifying efforts to recruit terrorists to oppose Americans.

How can terrorism be made less attractive to potential recruits? One approach is to relieve the human conditions in which terrorism seems to prosper—to "drain the swamp" of terrorism-producing societal, psychological, and political conditions and thus make terrorism a less attractive alternative. Intuitively, such efforts appear to make sense, but they face objections. One is expense: uplifting societies to the point that terrorism is unappealing to the citizens would require extensive monetary and other resources. For instance, what would it cost to fund a Pakistani education system that would make the terrorist-producing *madrassa* system obsolete? Are Americans willing to pay for such an effort? In addition, the results are uncertain: as many analysts point out, the September 11 terrorists came from Saudi Arabia, not some wretched backwater "swamp," and all the developmental assistance in the world presumably would not have had a positive impact on these people and what they did.

A second possible thrust of strategy might be to make terrorist targets less appealing as targets. Current Middle Eastern religious terrorism is fueled by a virulent anti-Americanism that Americans find intellectually ludicrous and incorrect. Should the United States be mounting a much more comprehensive campaign to convince people in the region that the western model is superior to the worldview that fanatical religious spokespersons are propounding? Is the neoconservative plan

Challenge!

TERRORISM AND YOU

Terrorism is both a frightening and a confusing phenomenon. The attacks of September 11 established that all of us are potentially targets of terrorist actions, removing some part of our senses of safety and tranquility. Some of the resulting anxiety has abated as time has passed and renewed attacks have not occurred, but simultaneously people are warned of an ever-present, if virtually invisible, threat. The confusion is the result of trying to come to grips with this elusive, shadowy phenomenon. It makes reaching personal judgments all the more difficult.

What does the terrorism problem mean to *you*? Is it a "war," as it is advertised, or is it something else, something more or less frightening? Does it belong at the absolute top of the list of national security concerns, or is it somehow a lesser problem than that? Has the problem, in other words, been "hyped"?

And what about our efforts to deal with the problem? We are spending a large number of tax dollars on the problem, but are we getting our money's worth? Do we have a coherent approach to dealing with the problem? If you had the ability to change the policy, how would you do so? What do you think about terrorism and yourself?

of imposing democracy—as has been attempted in Iraq—the way to do this? Or is there some other, better way?

Finally, there is the question of exposure. One reason for the underlying anti-Americanism in parts of the Middle East is the level of supposedly corrupting American physical presence in the region (this has been a particular obsession of bin Laden for some time). The obvious reason for that presence is Middle East oil, and without that need, the reason for American presence is reduced greatly or disappears altogether. If that is the case, should national energy policy not be an important element in terrorism strategy? Some of the most vocal proponents of the GWOT in the United States simultaneously oppose higher fuel-efficiency standards for vehicles (the so-called corporate average fuel efficiency—CAFE—standards), standards updated and made more stringent in 2007. Since oil revenue has clearly been linked to private support for terrorists in Saudi Arabia and elsewhere, is it not inconsistent to support strong terrorism suppression while driving a large, gas-guzzling sport utility vehicle? All these questions suggest difficult personal choices, as the accompanying *Challenge!* and the discussion in Chapter 14 suggest.

This discussion, of course, only explores the tip of the iceberg of what a comprehensive terrorism strategy would include. The problem to date, reflected in the artificial designation of the effort as a war, has been to isolate terrorism and its suppression from other aspects of national and international concern. Terrorism, however, is a broader phenomenon that is part of a broader set of problems and international malaise that will not go away on its own.

STUDY/DISCUSSION QUESTIONS

1. How is terrorism defined? Why is it important to have an agreed-upon definition of terrorism? What elements can go into a definition?
2. What are terrorist acts? Why do terrorists commit them? When are they successful or unsuccessful?
3. What are the two kinds of terrorist targets? Distinguish one kind from the other. What different problems are associated with each?
4. Define terrorist objectives at both the tactical and the strategic levels. At which levels are terrorists most and least successful?
5. What are the three perspectives on terrorism? Compare and contrast them. Which do you find most persuasive?
6. What three causes are sometimes attributed to terrorism? Compare and contrast them. Which do you find most convincing?
7. Discuss post–September 11 terrorism in terms of the types of terrorist organizations and the current pattern of those organizations, with an emphasis on Al Qaeda.
8. Critically analyze the global *war* on terrorism (GWOT). Is the analogy of war a good one for describing efforts to suppress terrorism?
9. Discuss terrorism suppression, emphasizing and contrasting antiterrorism and counterterrorism and how they complement or contradict one another as approaches to the problem.
10. Does the United States have an effective terrorism strategy? What elements should such a strategy include?

SELECTED BIBLIOGRAPHY

Allison, Graham. *Nuclear Terrorism: The Ultimate Preventable Catastrophe*. New York: Times Books (Henry Holt & Company), 2004.

Atran, Scott. "Mishandling Suicide Terrorism." *Washington Quarterly* 27, 3 (Summer 2004), 67–90.

Atwan, Abdul Beri. *The Secret History of Al Qaeda*. Berkeley: University of California Press, 2006.

Bergen, Peter. *Holy War Inc.: Inside the Secret World of Al Qaeda*. New York: Simon and Schuster, 2001.

Betts, Richard K. "How to Think About Terrorism." *Wilson Quarterly* 30 (Winter 2006), 44–49.

Bloom, Mia. *Dying to Kill: The Allure of Suicide Terror*. New York: Columbia University Press, 2005.

Burke, Jason. "Think Again: Al Qaeda." *Foreign Policy* (May/June 2004), 18–26.

Cronin, Audrey Kurth, "Sources of Contemporary Terrorism." Pages 74–93 in Audrey Kurth Cronin and James M. Ludes (eds.), *Attacking Terrorism: Elements of a Grand Strategy*. Washington, DC: Georgetown University Press, 2004.

Dershowitz, Alan M. *Why Terrorism Works: Understanding the Threat, Responding to the Challenge*. New Haven, CT: Yale University Press, 2002.

Enders, Walter, and Todd Sandler. *The Political Economy of Terrorism*. New York: Cambridge University Press, 2006.

Gunaratna, Rohan. "The Post-Madrid Face of Al Qaeda." *Washington Quarterly* 27, 3 (Summer 2004), 91–100.

Gurr, Ted Robert. *Why Men Rebel*. Princeton, NJ: Princeton University Press, 1973.

Habeck, Mary. *Knowing the Enemy: Jihadist Ideology and the War on Terror*. New Haven, CT: Yale University Press, 2005.

Hoffman, Bruce. *Inside Terrorism* (2nd ed.). New York: Columbia University Press, 2006.

Hoge, James F., Jr., and Gideon Rose (eds.). *Understanding the War on Terrorism*. New York: Council on Foreign Relations (*Foreign Affairs* Books), 2005.

Jenkins, Brian. "International Terrorism." In Robert J. Art and Kenneth N. Waltz (eds.), *The Use of Force: Military Power and International Relations* (6th ed., pp. 77–84). New York: Rowman and Littlefield Publishers, 2004.

Juergensmeyer, Mark. *Terror in the Mind of God: The Global Rise of Religious Violence*. Berkeley: University of California Press, 2003.

Krueger, Alan B., and David D. Laitin. "'Misunderestimating' Terrorism: The State Department's Big Mistake." *Foreign Affairs* 83, 5 (September/October 2004), 8–13.

Mueller, John. "Is There Still a Terrorist Threat?" *Foreign Affairs* 85, 5 (September/October 2006), 2–8.

Nacos, Brigette L. *Terrorism and Counterterrorism: Understanding Threats and Responses in the Post-9/11 World*. New York: Penguin Academics, 2006.

Pape, Robert. *Dying to Win: The Strategic Logic of Suicide Terrorism*. New York: Random House, 2005.

Pillar, Paul R. "Counterterrorism After Al Qaeda." *Washington Quarterly* 27, 3 (Summer 2004), 101–113.

Powell, Colin L. "No Country Left Behind." *Foreign Policy* (January/February 2005), 28–35.

Rapoport, David C. "The Four Waves of Terrorism." In Audrey Kurth Cronin and James M. Ludes (eds.), *Attacking Terrorism: Elements of a Grand Strategy* (pp. 46–73). Washington, DC: Georgetown University Press, 2004.

Reidel, Bruce. "Al Qaeda Strikes Back." *Foreign Affairs* 86, 3 (May/June 2007), 24–40.

Simon, Jeffrey. *The Terrorist Trap: America's Experience with Terrorism*. Bloomington: Indiana University Press, 2001.

Simon, Steve, and Jeff Martin. "Terrorism: Denying Al Qaeda Its Popular Support." *Washington Quarterly* 28, 1 (Winter 2004–2005), 131–146.

Sloan, Stephen. *Beating International Terrorism: An Action Strategy for Preemption and Punishment*. Montgomery, AL: Air University Press, 2000.

Snow, Donald M. *September 11, 2001: The New Face of War?* New York: Longman, 2002.

———, and Dennis M. Drew. *From Lexington to Desert Storm and Beyond: War and Politics in the American Experience* (2nd ed.). Armonk, NY: M. E. Sharpe, 2000.

Stern, Jessica. *Terrorism in the Name of God: Why Religious Militants Kill*. New York: ECCO, 2003.

———. "The Protean Enemy." *Foreign Affairs* 82, 4 (July/August 2003), 27–40.

The 9/11 Report: The National Commission on Terrorist Attacks Upon the United States. Thomas H. Kean and Lee H. Hamilton, Chairs. New York, St. Martin's Paperbacks, 2004.

U.S. Department of State. *Patterns of Global Terrorism*. Washington, DC: U.S. Department of State (annual publication).

"U.S. Designated Terrorist Organizations." *Infoplease*. New York: Pearson Education, 2007. (http://www.infoplease.com/ipa/A0908746.html)

Whiteneck, Daniel. "Deterring Terrorists: Thoughts on a Framework." *Washington Quarterly* 28, 3 (Summer 2005), 187–199.

Whittaker, David J. *Terrorists and Terrorism in the Contemporary World*. New York: Routledge, 2004.

Zakaria, Fareed. "Beyond Bush." *Newsweek*, June 4, 2007, 21–27.

CHAPTER 13

Peacekeeping and State Building: The New Dilemma

PREVIEW

In modern warfare, the cessation of active fighting does not necessarily signal the end of hostilities or the onset of peace. Rather, domestic reconciliation and the building or rebuilding of societies torn apart by either internal war or international military action must be part of efforts to stabilize the military situation (peacekeeping) and to create conditions in these countries where stability and peace will be self-sustaining. In the 1990s, American involvement in situations where these problems were present was largely justified on humanitarian grounds; today, the rationale is suppressing terrorism. To address this problem, the chapter begins by identifying vulnerable societies, the so-called failed states. It then looks at why and how to intervene in the future. The possibilities for improving the situations, peacekeeping and state building, are then examined, and the chapter concludes with likely effects of these actions for the future, and particularly the impact of the state-building effort in Iraq as an influence.

One of the most lasting, indelible legacies of the Iraq War has been the failure of the Phase IV operation, chronicled in detail by a number of critics of the war effort (Chandrasekaran, Diamond, Glantz, Record, and Ricks, for instance). These failures have included efforts to establish security and end violence and to build or rebuild the country to the point that it can be (or return to being) a self-sufficient, peaceful society. The task of fully securing the peace is the necessary precondition to rebuilding the country and is known as *peacekeeping (PK)*. The second task, either building a country's infrastructure or rebuilding it (especially if one is responsible for destroying it in the first place), is known as *state building (SB)*. No contemporary war can be said to be ended completely successfully until both these tasks are accomplished.

The historical and contemporary records in regard to these tasks are mixed. The United States (and the rest of the world) encountered these problems in the NIWs of the 1990s and gained some understanding of them in places like the Balkans (Bosnia and Kosovo). The Bush administration came to power openly disdainful of these kinds of operations (notably PK operations) and professed no obvious interest in state building. As a result, there was virtually no consideration of the dynamics and complexities of PK and SB in what passed for Phase IV operations planning in Iraq, and the results have been almost entirely unsatisfactory and have arguably contributed to the unrest and instability in that country.

Iraq offers the primary rationale for why the United States must come to grips with the PK/SB "dilemma." It is a dilemma for two reasons. On the one hand, almost all the opportunities and temptations to use military force the United States will encounter in the upcoming years will be in countries where, like Iraq, the conflict will not be resolved until PK operations and state building are complete and successful. On the other hand, there is no proven international, and certainly no American, blueprint for SB success. Indeed, John Hulsman of the Heritage Foundation, drawing upon the experience of T. E. Lawrence, argues that each potential situation is sufficiently unique that one must "avoid a cookie-cutter approach to state-building." SB is hard work, and no one knows for certain how to apply it with guaranteed success in any particular situation.

This leads to the dilemma for future policy makers. When presented with a temptation to apply military force in the future, there will be two obvious choices. One will be intervention, but exercising that option may place the United States in another Iraq-style occupation/state-building quagmire. The other choice will be abstention from involvement, with potentially dangerous impacts on the national interest. The critical point of decision may well boil down to whether the United States can successfully engage in PK/SB and thereby gain a favorable outcome. Thus, understanding the situations where the opportunities for intervention exist and the dynamics for successful PK/SB are necessary parts of success are part of the Iraq legacy.

THE CONTEMPORARY SCENE

Contemporary, normally asymmetrical wars share three characteristics that endow them with their unique nature and that define the problems the United States and others must confront if they become involved in them. First, they share an important, sometimes exclusive, internal or civil component: at least part of the situation has elements within a state fighting one another, meaning that part of the military and political problem of ending the war and restoring the peace is reconciling formerly warring factions. This problem is exacerbated when the battleground is a failed state. Second, these wars occur essentially exclusively in the developing world, and so when outsiders like the United States involve themselves, there is inevitably some resentment about that involvement, at least partially the result of a less-than-perfect understanding of the local situation by the intervening party.

The third characteristic is the most consequential, most difficult, and least well understood: that these wars almost always have three distinct phases, all of which must be surmounted before success can occur. The first phase is the actual fighting phase—the normal concept of the totality of war—and the normal response is to bring that fighting to an end on some terms (what will be called *peace imposition*). The period after the fighting has ended is one of adjustment and unstable peace, and the problem is maintaining the peace and beginning to improve conditions in the target country (what will be called *peace enforcement*). Finally, the situation must be improved physically and politically (*state building*) so that outsiders can prepare for their exit (what will be called *peacekeeping*). In Iraq, peace imposition refers to the conquest of Iraq; peace enforcement and state building refers to the occupation.

This model of dealing with developing-world environments has evolved through American involvement in a number of new internal wars in the 1990s, which was a decidedly mixed experience and one which was largely discarded after September 11. It is, however, virtually the identical structure of problems that we face in Afghanistan and Iraq. Although historical progressions are seldom linear, these dynamics, interrupted by September 11, are likely to continue into the foreseeable future.

The question of American involvement with force in the developing world was skewed by the events of September 11, 2001. Prior to the terrorist attacks, there was a lively, partisan political debate about the degree of American activism in the developing world. During the 2000 election campaign, then candidate George W. Bush and close advisors such as current Secretary of State Condoleezza Rice actively derided American intervention and continuing involvement in Second Tier locales like Kosovo and Bosnia, maintained the United States should cut back its involvement by scaling back or withdrawing American troops where they were present, and publicly promised that the United States would no longer be "the world's 911." More to the point, the commitment of American forces to missions such as peacekeeping and American resources to state building was derided as a misapplication and overextension of scarce and valuable American assets.

During the 1990s, the United States became involved in a number of these developing-world conflicts and avoided others, with decidedly mixed results. In 1992, the United States joined the international response to suffering and atrocity in Somalia, which ended with American withdrawal after nineteen of its soldiers were slaughtered in an ambush in the country's capital, Mogadishu. In 1994, the United States launched an "intervasion" (part intervention, part invasion) to restore the elected government of Haiti but sat out the slaughter in Rwanda that same year. Operation Restore Democracy (the name of the Haitian operation) restored democracy only in the most generous sense of that term. President Clinton deemed U.S. failure to act in Rwanda as one of the worst mistakes of his foreign policy. In 1995, the

United States was a central player in negotiating and enforcing a ceasefire among the warring parties in Bosnia, an action it reprised in 1999 in Kosovo. The latter two involvements are notable because they required American military participation in ongoing, open-ended peacekeeping missions.

All these were low-priority operations that entailed relatively modest investments and risks for the United States. The United States, at least after Somalia, could indulge in the inclination to "do something" when faced with atrocity on national cable news, because the costs in blood and treasure was modest. In the Haitian, Bosnian, and Kosovar involvements, there have, for instance, been *no* American casualties from hostile action. That one cannot measure great benefit from these operations (how much difference does it make that Haitian democracy remains an elusive chimera?) has been less important than the absence of losses.

This whole question appeared to change fundamentally when the United States set its sights on Afghanistan in the fall of 2001 and Iraq in 2003. The United States had tolerated the repressive, virulently anti-American stance of the Taliban regime there since they came to power in 1996, on the grounds that no American interests were affected by their objectionable attitudes and actions. Their sanctioning of terrorism was, of course, regrettable, but until their refusal to hand over the terrorists dictated their removal from power, they were not very high on the American agenda.

The apparent need to change terrorist-prone societies altered the calculus of involvement in poor, unstable developing-world countries for the Bush administration. In the period between the fault lines, the motivation to become involved was primarily humanitarian, trying to alleviate great human suffering because it was, in President Clinton's justification for intervention in Bosnia, "the right thing to do." Terrorist-proofing similar societies became Bush's reason for involvement, a rationale applied first to Afghanistan and then to Iraq.

Are the Afghanistan and Iraq cases typical or atypical of what the future will hold? The answer largely depends on the lessons that other states take from the American response in Iraq and its effects. Countries assessing likely future American responses may conclude that the United States will respond when obviously vital matters are involved (suppressing terrorists but not humanitarian motives). They may also conclude that American resolution to root out evil in the world is now sufficiently aroused that provocation of the United States is unwise in any circumstance. Whether the United States has become selectively or generally activist will be partially revealed by its actions against other states accused of harboring terrorists in the name of the Bush Doctrine. The other side is the Iraq hangover as an inhibition to future activism.

Assessing the likely future of American activism requires making two judgments, both of which are controversial and both of which apply equally to terrorist-suppressing and humanitarian motivations. The first is what the United States and its *developed* world allies seek to accomplish in the developing world. The Bush administration has suggested the aggressive role of promoting democracy and incorporating the developing world—and especially its more troublesome members—into the globalizing economy and general prosperity in the hopes that will remove their troublemaking. The actual course of events in Iraq may counsel a less activist role.

The other judgment is about how much *can* be accomplished. The experience transforming developing states into modern or postmodern states is limited and spotty. We succeeded in South Korea but failed in Iran. Moreover, most of our experience has been in countries that were not among the most destitute; most of the candidates in the future will be in those difficult places. Afghanistan is almost a textbook case of the difficulties that will likely be faced more generally. Iraq magnifies the difficulties.

All these concerns apply equally well to potential terrorist-suppressing and humanitarian situations, because the West believes the same underlying set of circumstances breeds asymmetrical warriors in the form of terrorists and practitioners of new internal war. Those conditions are poverty, despair, and oppression, which we believe constitute the swamp that, once drained, will cease to be the breeding ground for future instability and violence.

To begin to come to grips with (if not conclusively to answer) some of these questions, the discussion proceeds in steps. First, it looks at the kinds of places where intervention is likely to occur. In examining the failed states, this entails looking at why they fail, what characteristics cause failure (and thus must be remedied), and how we might attempt to intervene. Second, questions are raised about intervention in terms of the purposes for which it may be undertaken and the forms that it may take in different situations. We then turn to the proposed solutions, notably peacekeeping and state building, two different but interrelated approaches and goals. All of this comes together in the context of the Iraq experience.

FAILED AND FAILING STATES: THE CONTEXT

Almost all the violence that currently plagues the developing world and boils over occasionally into the developed world, as the events of September 11 did, comes from parts of the developing world. For present purposes, the developing world can be divided into useful categories: those countries that are part of the globalizing economy and those that are not (for a more detailed discussion, see Snow and Brown, *International Relations*). Members of the globalizing economy include those countries that are part of the regional and global economic associations that became prominent during the 1990s: APEC, NAFTA, and the EU, for instance. Geographically, this encompasses the Western Hemisphere (other than Cuba), most of Europe (including Russia, a member of APEC), and most of East Asia and the Pacific. The areas outside this network are principally found in Africa and parts of Central and South (including Southwest) Asia.

Using these categories to understand where violence is occurring, we find that it is overwhelmingly located in those parts of the developing world outside the globalizing economy. Other than Indonesia and the Philippines (both members of APEC), there are hardly any exceptions to this rule. While not all states outside the globalizing economy are violent and unstable, almost all the violent and unstable states are outside the global economy.

To understand why this pattern exists and persists, one must look at the kinds of states where violence is the norm. We begin by defining the failed states and the characteristics they tend to have, using the author's distinctions to define failure and Ralph Peters's characteristics of that failure. While other characterizations may hold better or worse in some individual circumstances, these categories are generally useful for our purposes. These distinctions are particularly relevant because Iraq has always been considered a prime example of the kind of state these distinctions depict.

What Is a Failed State?

The term *failed state* was coined in the early 1990s to describe a phenomenon occurring in parts of the developing world. The prototype was Somalia, a state that had simply collapsed as a viable entity in 1991 following an overthrow of government and the inability of any other group to assume political control. Thus, Helman and Ratner provide a definition of Somalia and states like it as failed: "a state utterly incapable of sustaining itself as a member of the international community."

In most cases, failed states have legacies of authoritarian rule but possess unstable regimes in which authoritarian rule has eroded but no viable alternative has emerged. These states thus slide from a condition of authoritarianism to one of anarchy from which they are incapable of extracting themselves on their own. In the most notable and troublesome cases, this anarchy is manifested in inconclusive, but often spectacular and bloody, internal wars.

These kinds of conditions are particularly prevalent in so-called artificial states: countries that comprise several distinct ethnic, racial, religious, linguistic, or historical groups—often with traditions of intergroup rivalry and violence—that are put together in a single multinational state. When authoritarian rule by one of these groups breaks down, there is no obvious consensus around which to form an alternative government, and the result is often chaotic, even anarchic.

Iraq is a prime example of this dynamic. Multiple historical groups (Sunnis, Shiites, and Kurds) were thrown together into a wholly artificial Iraqi state by the British and French in 1919. The Sunnis emerged as the dominant group wielding authoritarian rule, epitomized by the regime of Saddam Hussein. When his rule was shattered, there was no obvious basis around which to form a legitimate government. As a result, the country descended into an entirely predictable (and predicted) political chaos internally after 2004, when sovereignty was nominally returned to the Iraqis despite a continued American occupation.

State failure has both a political and an economic dimension. The political dimension may include anarchy, or it may be manifested by a weak, venal, and corrupt political system that has little control over its population, cannot allocate societal resources or maintain a civil order, acts capriciously and oppressively toward at least some of its citizens, and thus is not accorded legitimacy by sizable parts of the population. In most cases, this ineffectiveness is structural as well as political in that important governmental institutions (law enforcement, courts, public services, etc.) are nonexistent, hopelessly corrupt, or unable to operate effectively. Probably the most important shortfall is the absence of a criminal or civil judicial and law enforcement community that the public believes treats all citizens equitably and that those citizens are therefore willing to support.

These countries, generally but not exclusively located as they are outside the globalizing economy, are typically economically poor as well. In a number of cases, the reason is structural and endemic: there are few human or physical resources on which to build a viable economic condition. Haiti, for instance, is poor because there is essentially nothing in the country around which to build wealth, and it is hard to imagine how Bangladesh, which essentially is a flood plain of the Ganges River system, can ever develop a viable economic base. In other cases, whatever economic base exists is systematically misused (the looting of the diamond fields of Sierra Leone) or else maldistribution of wealth leaves a tiny elite in possession of fabulous wealth, while the masses toil in abject, crushing poverty. In some cases, the ravages of war add to the misery; twenty-four years of war in Afghanistan have left that country's modest prewar infrastructure in absolute ruin. The Iraqi economy has been at a standstill at least since 2003.

Not all states that show signs of failure fall into the same category. The worst cases, such as Somalia, Haiti, and arguably Afghanistan, have failed on all dimensions and have little prospect of changing their situation by themselves. Other states have not quite achieved the status of full-scale failure but are demonstrably showing signs of failure. The most prominent example of the *potentially failing* state is post-Suharto Indonesia, as depicted in Amplification 13.1. In addition, other states have shown signs of potential failure and thus can be designated as *failure-prone*. North Korea is an example.

Ralph Peters provides an interesting and valuable, if unorthodox, methodology for identifying what he calls "noncompetitive states." These noncompetitive states are not exactly the same as the failed states as defined already. What he develops is a set of criteria that can be applied to states in terms of looking at their potential for useful participation in the international system and in determining stability within states and the potential for state failure.

Peters's attributes are highlights of a generally failed condition. Three underlying factors in these societies underpin the list: they typically do not have a reliable and fair rule of law that applies to all citizens; they are generally rife with corruption (which is both a consequence of and reinforcement for a preference for the absence of law); and their economies are usually overly managed, particularly to favor those in power. They do not, in other words, produce a uniform sense of justice and security around which the population can gravitate.

Peters's list is also a warning guide of places to avoid. It contains seven indicators that individually and collectively demonstrate noncompetitiveness and in effect raise red flags about involvement with those societies. The first is a restriction on the flow of information within the society. Control of the information available to a citizenry has historically been a major source of power, particularly restricting information that might indicate that other places have a better existence. Although the products of the information age such as computers and televisions make restriction more difficult, some states continue to try, and their effort is an indication of their backwardness.

Amplification 13.1

INDONESIA AS A POTENTIALLY FAILING STATE

Indonesia, the world's largest archipelago and the fourth most populous state in the world, has experienced a downward political and economic spiral since it was one of the countries hit by the East Asian financial crisis in 1997. In Indonesia, the financial crisis triggered a political crisis that brought down the government in 1998 and left observers speculating whether Indonesia might move through the categories of state failure.

The financial crisis revealed great weaknesses in the Indonesian economy, as banks failed, savings were destroyed, economic expansion halted, and inflation ran rampant. The Suharto regime, which had been in power since 1966 and was widely regarded as one of the most corrupt regimes in the world, bore the brunt of the criticism and charges of cronyism and nepotism as the economy's weakness was revealed. Suharto was forced to resign, and between 1998 and 2001, two successors struggled in an atmosphere of recriminations regarding corruption. Some calm was restored when Megawati Sukarnoputri, the daughter of Achmed Sukarno, who led the Indonesian movement for independence from the Netherlands in the 1940s, was elected in 1998. She was defeated and replaced peacefully by Susilo Bambang Yudhoyono (known simply as SBY) in 2004.

Beyond political crisis, two factors cloud the future. One is the continuing economic crisis, which includes an active element that wants Indonesia to withdraw from the globalizing economy, a prospect most observers believe would further harm the economy. The other is a series of separatist movements in the far-flung archipelago that began publicly in East Timor and includes the Free Aceh movement in the province of Indonesia where there are large deposits of natural gas crucial to the economy.

Source: Donald M. Snow, "Debating Globalization: The Case of Indonesia," Chapter 9 in *Cases in International Relations: Portraits of the Future* (2nd ed.). New York: Longman, 2006.

Second, noncompetitive states tend to subjugate women, restricting their rights in areas such as education and the workplace. This restriction may be a historic cultural artifact or it may be a means to ensure male control, but its practical impact is to remove half a country's talent from the productive process. Any society that creates such restrictions will, he argues, be uncompetitive with counterpart societies that do incorporate women.

Third, noncompetitive states are unable to accept responsibility for their own failure to compete in the world. Rather than recognizing they are the problem, the leaders are more likely to project their ills onto hostile others outside, using these outside forces as scapegoats. A society unwilling to bear this responsibility is particularly unlikely to reform itself and make progress in the world. The United States has been a particularly useful "whipping boy."

Fourth, noncompetitive states typically either the extended family, a clan, a tribe, or some similar entity as the basis of social organization. In many cases, this traditional social structure creates a crippling duality in terms of interpersonal dealings with societal consequences. In such settings, Peters argues, relations within the social unit may be very open and honest, but the structure creates an us-versus-them mind-set that makes relations between groups much less forthcoming and honest. The upshot is that this traditional form of social organization encourages corruption within the society as a whole and impedes formation and development of the kinds of societal mechanisms necessary for progress into the contemporary globalizing world.

Fifth, the dominance of a restrictive religion is often a characteristic of a noncompetitive state. Such a creed helps to reinforce the us-versus-them mentality and the denial of responsibility for the shortcomings of state performance. Restriction of religious belief not only binds the group together against others, but also makes more plausible the claim that hostile outsiders (infidels) are responsible for the group's own fate.

Sixth, tradition-laden religious restriction tends to create and reinforce a low valuation of education, and especially education that goes beyond the transmission of orthodox, and often fundamentalist, theology. States that devalue education dilute the potential value of their intellectual talent pool and thereby render themselves less competitive. Restriction of educational access and inequality only adds to this crippling effect.

Finally, noncompetitive states tend also to place a low value on work. In these generally male-dominated societies, menial tasks are generally assigned to women and children, and men gain prestige not because of what they produce but on the basis somehow of who they are. As long as this condition persists, the incentives to excel through productivity are largely missing.

What do these largely socioeconomic conditions have to do with American national security? The short answer is that these conditions represent the swamp that may produce terrorists and human rights–abusing insurgents, and alleviating them is prerequisite to possible stabilization in those cases. Application of American force to crush terrorists or human rights abusers that does not take these problems into account will likely fail in the long run. These are the problems that must be surmounted if the third phase of contemporary warfare is to be successful.

In contemporary terms, these factors also reflect state failure. Societies exhibiting these characteristics are likely to be either authoritarian or, where the coercive veil has been lifted, anarchical, lacking reliable political institutions. The human wastage created by restricting the role of women or downgrading education is clearly a contributor to the economic misery that typically marks the failed states.

Although Peters published *Fighting for the Future* in 1999, well before Afghanistan and Iraq were catapulted onto the world's center stage, it is remarkable how well his categories illustrate the deficiencies of Taliban-ruled Afghanistan and how rapidly the provisional government of Hamid Karzai tried to move to reverse these factors. While the early indications are positive, it is the longer-term implementation that is most important.

Information Flow Restriction. One of the major efforts of the Taliban was to shut the country off from the outside. A very visible symbol of Taliban rule was outlawing radios and televisions, often manifested in dramatic smashing of televisions and computers. One of the first images of Kabul and other cities after liberation was the marketing of replacements for those destroyed instruments of communication with the outside world.

Subjugation of Women. There was probably no country in the world that suppressed women as much as the Taliban. Women not only had to be fully covered (including wearing the most impenetrable head coverings, or *burkas*, possible), but also were systematically denied access to schools and the workplace. Within weeks of liberation, the *burkas* were virtually gone (although they have returned in modified form), and females were prominent in education and the workplace. On the other hand, when the first post-Taliban motion pictures were shown in Kabul after the liberation, only men were allowed to attend.

Inability to Accept Responsibility for Failure. This fairly common symptom of modern Middle Eastern Islamic states was especially pronounced in Afghanistan, where the fundamentalist rantings of Usama bin Laden and others were particularly filled with blaming the West, and especially the United States, for the region's ills.

Social Organization on an Extended Family or Clan Basis. Afghan society has always been based on clan membership. The Taliban came principally from the Pashtun tribe, which is the country's largest ethnic group and comprises about 38 percent of the population, according to the CIA *Factbook*. Not all Pashtuns, of course, were Taliban, but the majority of the Taliban were Pashtun. Sorting out tribal concerns in the attempt to form a broadly based, multitribal form of governance has been possibly the greatest challenge to establishing a legitimate government for Afghanistan and one that the history of tribal animosity and fighting suggests may not succeed for some time. The fact that Taliban military activity has returned suggests that tribally based animosities remain a potent force.

Dominance of a Restrictive Religion. A particularly fundamentalist form of Islam underlay the attractiveness and purpose of both the Taliban and bin Laden. According to Michael Doran in a *Foreign Affairs* article, this view sees outsiders and even some Muslim state leaders as defilers of Islam. As he puts it, "In bin Laden's imagery, the leaders of the Arab and Islamic worlds today are Hypocrites (people who extol but do not adhere to the faith), idol worshippers cowering behind America, the Hubal (the symbol of pre-Muslim polytheistic idol worship) of the age." These views are highly restrictive and intolerant. Since many Muslims share this view of the West's negative influence but do not endorse bin Laden's actions, transforming these beliefs will be a difficult issue to handle even though the outward forms of repression claimed necessary by the Taliban are removed.

Low Valuation of Education. Clearly, the education system suffered under the restrictive attitudes of the Taliban against women (including female teachers). One of the first institutions to be revived in post-Taliban Afghanistan was the schools, but war-gutted school buildings and the absence of even rudimentary educational materials handicapped the effort.

Low Prestige for Work. During the days of Taliban rule, the economy essentially did not function, some indication that work and progress were less important than piety within the hierarchy of Taliban priorities. Reviving the economy, which necessarily includes making hard work a valued trait, is also a major challenge for the post-Taliban rulers.

What this discussion suggests is that removal of many of the outward symbols of noncompetitiveness has been a major emphasis of Afghanistan after the Taliban. Much of this change arises from a very grassroots appeal—from women shedding their coverings and men shaving their beards to street vendors selling boom boxes to schools resuming as teachers (including women) and students simply return to their old buildings—that at once symbolizes the absolute lack of appeal of the Taliban's creed and the desire to embrace modernity. Whether washing away these vestiges of noncompetitiveness will result in removing the causes of state failure partly depends on the willingness of the Afghans to embrace fundamental change and the willingness and perseverance of the United States to provide the necessary resources on which to build change. A similar exercise applied to Iraq is probably premature as long as the Iraqi resistance disrupts that country.

The process of removing these obstacles to modernity has not been completely successful in Afghanistan, and progress there has been neither linear nor entirely positive. The growing of opium poppies and the resulting drug trade continue to dominate the economy, and the Taliban has returned as a significant politico-military challenge to the Karzai regime. To some degree, this resistance to change reflects the endurance and strength of tradition. At the same time, the United States promised considerable assistance to the Karzai regime to enhance modernization (state building) that has, by and large, never materialized.

Whether the causes are humanitarian (the 1990s) or traditionally geopolitical (the 2000s), the United States and other powers are and will continue to be drawn into developing-world conflicts. In some cases, a sober assessment of vital interests impels interventions (thus deployments of necessity); in other cases, the geopolitical need for involvement is less apparently compelling (deployments of choice). For whatever reasons, involvement in developing-world conflicts—often internal, almost always asymmetrical in one way or another—has become the norm. Since there is little reason to believe this pattern will not continue, it behooves us to better understand these situations and what we can do about them.

Concepts and Forms of Intervention

The Afghanistan effort by the United States and the U.N. peacekeepers (the International Security Assistance Force or ISAF) attracted more attention than previous peacekeeping missions because of the association of the mission with international terrorism. The missions in which the United States was involved in the 1990s—Somalia, Haiti, Bosnia, and Kosovo—generated some initial publicity when the

United States embarked on them and, in the case of Somalia, when the United States withdrew under less than ideal circumstances and with a less than favorable outcome. Interest, however, was never enormous, because these missions neither involved significant U.S. interests nor entailed significant costs in blood or treasure. In Afghanistan, interests were high and the costs moderate. Although Iraq has never been typified as a peacekeeping operation, the problems of dealing with an occupied Iraq are basically the same as those encountered in PK operations.

The 1990s missions had peacekeeping and, at least implicitly, state building as objectives. In Haiti, the mission involved restoring Jean-Bertrand Aristide to the elected presidency from which he had been removed by a military coup and creating the conditions for future stability. The first objective was achieved during the four years the United States remained in the country as the lead party of the Operation Uphold Democracy coalition. The second objective is hard to label a success because Haiti still lacks the basis of a stable, prosperous state.

In Bosnia and Kosovo, the United States was part of a U.N.-sanctioned peace-keeping mission with the purpose of restoring order and preparing the countries for postmission stability; in the case of Kosovo, the mission explicitly included state building. The Stabilization Force (originally Implementation Force) entered Bosnia in 1995, and the Kosovo Force was formed in 1999. Both are still in place (if reduced in size), and no one thinks they can be withdrawn without an almost certain return to violence.

Although the same terms, peacekeeping and state building, are used to describe Afghanistan and Iraq, these situations are sufficiently different as virtually to defy comparison. The efforts arise out of very different situations. In Kosovo and Haiti, re-pressive governments were suppressing the population, and the first goal was to end the suppression. In Bosnia, the problem was to separate warring parties as the first step in implementing the Dayton peace accords calling for a separation of factions. In Afghanistan, there was a conventional civil war going on between the Taliban government and its opponents, which the United States joined on the side of the in-surgents (although prior to the stimulus of the terrorist attacks, we had essentially ig-nored the war). In Iraq, of course, the United States overthrew the oppressive Hussein regime.

The structure and purposes of interventions are also different. The United Nations initially authorized the ISAF to restore and enforce order in Kabul, but its mission beyond that was not clear. The Afghans themselves expressed interest in a long deployment providing security for more of the country while the situation stabi-lized. The United States, meanwhile, established its own longer-term presence both by establishing and maintaining control of airfields and the like in Afghanistan itself and by establishing bases in adjacent former republics of the Soviet Union (e.g., Uzbekistan), while opposing the extension of the ISAF mission and declining to par-ticipate in it. Establishing bases outside Afghanistan was rather clearly a hedge against outliving the American welcome in Afghanistan itself. Meanwhile, international leaders were pledging support for rebuilding an Afghanistan ravaged by over two decades of war (in other words, state building), without being very specific about what that entailed.

Iraq is a unique situation not often described in PK/SB terms, but it arguably should be. After the United States successfully overthrew the Iraqi government, its first mission was to establish, maintain, and strengthen internal order and peace within the country (essentially peacekeeping). It also adopted a state-building role by declaring its intent to assist in the establishment of political democracy and the rebuilding of Iraqi society and the economy during Phase IV operations. What principally differs is that the United States *created* the need for such actions by starting the war rather than by reaching to preexisting conditions.

Basic Distinctions

Outside interference in the affairs of other states is always problematic. While the motives underlying interference may be noble and pristine (they may also not be), they are never going to be viewed by those in whose countries interference occurs in the same way they are by the intervening parties. The initial motivation during the 1990s among interveners (usually under the flag of the United Nations) was publicly humanitarian, and helping the suppressed and suffering is always part of the honest motives that impel the actions. This is as true in American-dominated missions like Iraq as it is in U.N. operations. Such efforts will always likely meet some initial opposition, which will increase the longer the operation lasts and the intervening parties stay. This is true because intervention always has the effect—if not the intention—of providing advantage to some internal factions at the cost to others, and the losers will eventually not appreciate the effort or view it as benign. How many Sunnis welcomed the American intervention in Iraq, for instance? At the same time, lengthy interventions, especially in the formerly colonized world, will almost certainly begin to look like recolonization and create rumblings of imperialism. No country's citizens long embrace being occupied by a foreign army.

This uncertainty of reception helps create the frame within which outside interference is contemplated. What outsiders propose to do really consists of two determinations. The first is what it will try to accomplish—its concept. To this end, the basic alternatives are between conflict suppression and state building. The other question is how it will accomplish the task—its form. This examination requires looking at a continuum of actions with peace imposition and peacekeeping as its poles.

The first distinction is between conflict suppression and state building. One of the frequent, recurring criticisms of American involvements in developing-world conflicts in the past has been the open-endedness of these missions. Part of this criticism is focused on the absence of establishing a clear initial objective to be accomplished. This criticism, in turn, leads to the more frequently alleged shortcoming, which is the lack of a clear point at which the mission is accomplished, sometimes called an end or exit strategy that tells Americans when to go home. The absence of such criteria causes us to remain apparently endlessly and even aimlessly in places such as Bosnia and Kosovo and is the main issue surrounding the deployment in Iraq and to a lesser extent Afghanistan. The longer the stay and the more seemingly ubiquitous the presence of the outsider, the greater the resentment of that presence will be among some groups, especially those that do not benefit from that presence, like the Iraqi Sunnis. This dynamic will occur regardless of how noble the outsider's personal intentions are.

When entering the chaos of a war-torn developing-world country that has been unable to terminate the violence itself (which is why a mission is called for in the first place), a state can have one of two missions. The first is conflict suppression, which involves either stopping the ongoing fighting (peace imposition) or making sure that a recently established but volatile ceasefire remains in place (peace enforcement). These actions do no more than cause the fighting and killing to stop; they do not in and of themselves assure postwar domestic tranquility. The simplest measure of success is whether the fighting is discontinued.

Conflict suppression does not, of course, address or solve the problems that led to fighting in the first place. A more ambitious definition of successful conflict suppression is that it results in continued peace after the force has been withdrawn. Unless the underlying causes of fighting are addressed, the reasons for fighting remain and are likely to be rekindled after the intervening parties leave. Conflict suppression deals, in other words, with the symptoms of violence, not the underlying disease. It is a bandage to staunch the wound, not a cure.

Since intervention usually occurs in failed or noncompetitive states, leaving behind a stable, nonviolent environment in which the return to violence will seem unappealing to the formerly warring parties is the clear requisite to success. As already noted, the societies that tend to collapse into violence generally require both political reform (institution building, political reconciliation, etc.) and economic development to create a sense of present or future tranquility and prosperity that is clearly preferable to war and that thus commands the loyalty of the population (in other word, results in the conferral of legitimacy to the regime). The collective actions taken to accomplish this goal compose state building.

Where both of these concepts are instituted, they are clearly sequential. A conflict must be terminated before any state building can begin. A country can engage in conflict suppression without engaging in state building, although the outcome is likely to be a reversion to war after the conflict-suppressing force withdraws. With the exception of interim actions, state building cannot be undertaken unless successful conflict suppression has occurred; it would not be safe to try to do so, and state building efforts would themselves be the object of future violence.

This leads to distinctions about what the intervening state attempts to do—the forms of intervention. In common terms, interventions are known collectively as peacekeeping, although the term is misleading in its generally accepted form and describes only a part of what is undertaken when intervention occurs.

The forms of intervention encompass three distinct activities that form a continuum paralleling the three phases of contemporary asymmetrical war already introduced. At one end of the spectrum is peace imposition, which refers to actions taken to stop the violence in a war zone. In most but not all cases, peace imposition is undertaken for neutral purposes to stop the fighting and killing, what may be called neutrality of intent. The effect of stopping the fighting will never, however, be neutral in effect, if for no other reason than stopping the fighting halts the military success of whoever was winning and ensures the likely failure of whoever was losing. The result is that some will congratulate and embrace the interveners (the winners, like the Iraqi Shi'a) and some will not (the losers, like the Iraqi Sunni). This is even more dramatically the case when those imposing peace have created the situation in the first place, such as the United States did by overthrowing governments in Iraq and Afghanistan.

At the other end of the continuum is peacekeeping. In its classic sense, peacekeeping consists of monitoring and observing an established ceasefire between warring parties when the peacekeepers' intent and effect is to oversee a temporary condition of peace conducive to discussions intended to produce a lasting, stable peace. In the terms introduced above, a peacekeeping setting is one where state-building activities can be undertaken with the relative assurance that the peacekeepers will not be the victims of violence while they build or rebuild the economic and political infrastructure of the target country.

Lying between these two extreme forms of activity is peace enforcement. It is an activity undertaken when the physical fighting has been concluded but wherein it is uncertain that peace would be sustained in the absence of the outside force. Whereas peace imposition and peacekeeping represent responses to concrete, finite situations (states of war, peace desired by all parties), peace enforcement constitutes a range of situations, from a near state of war in which few of the participants prefer war to its alternative, to a situation in which almost all the parties prefer peace. Most real situations into which outside forces are committed rightfully fall in the category of peace enforcement. Iraq, after "major combat" was declared ended in 2003, is a prime example.

These concepts can be applied tentatively to Iraq. The ultimate goal in Iraq, which may or may not be realized, is state building to produce a democratic, prosperous Iraq that will be a regional model. Within this neoconservative construct, the primary instrument for change has been U.S. military force. The conquest and the overthrow of the Hussein government can be thought of as peace imposition—although with the added step of destroying and then restoring peace. The occupation since has largely been an exercise in peace enforcement, since the "peace" is clearly fragile and would certainly break down if peace enforcers (the occupation troops) were withdrawn. The situation has not evolved to the point that the occupation is an exercise in peacekeeping, since that requires that all (or nearly all) groups prefer the peaceful status quo to continued violence. Since state building occurs best in a peacekeeping environment (where there is little violence to disrupt it), the absence of such an environment helps explain the relative lack of state-building progress. Whether continued American presence can move the situation from peace enforcement to peacekeeping is one way to couch the debate over withdrawal.

Peacekeeping

The term *peacekeeping* has its contemporary origins in a specific set of U.N. operations conducted during the Cold War that constituted one of the few notable successes of the world organization in the security area during that period. Those activities basically conform to the definition of peacekeeping described earlier and emphasize the observation and monitoring of ceasefires between formerly warring parties. In most cases, these peacekeeping forces were put in place between sovereign countries and had the passive purpose of making sure the terms of ceasefires were honored. Their success occurred when the parties truly preferred peace to war and thus preferred maintenance of the status quo to a return to violence. In those circumstances, peacekeepers could be neutral both in intent and in effect, thereby adding positively to the situation for all concerned. Peacekeeping works, in other words, when the parties want peace roughly in conformance with the conditions the peacekeepers are assigned to enforce.

That set of circumstances rarely holds in internal wars, as the United Nations learned in its two major Cold War intrusions into domestic fracases in the former Belgian Congo (later Zaire, now the Democratic Republic of Congo) and Cyprus. In the Congo in 1960, U.N. peacekeepers opposed the attempted secession of Katanga (now Shaba) province and found themselves in the position of partisans rather than neutrals, to the organization's discomfort and the mission's ineffectiveness. In Cyprus in 1967, the United Nations was so successful in imposing peace and a ceasefire line that the Greeks and Turks concluded there was no real need to settle their differences as long as UNFICYP (U.N. Forces in Cyprus) remained in place. The U.N. mission is still there, with no real prospect of being concluded and withdrawn.

When the Cold War ended, these distinctions and limitations were largely lost in the euphoria of the U.N.-sponsored Desert Storm coalition. The security role of the world body seemed to have been enhanced, and it appeared likely the U.N. role would become central to international security. In 1991, the Security Council instructed Secretary-General Boutros Boutros-Ghali of Egypt to draw up a blueprint for U.N. participation in the promotion of international peace in the post–Cold War world. In 1992, he produced *An Agenda for Peace,* which labeled almost any international intervention, regardless of whether it was in wars between states (which have been virtually nonexistent since the Persian Gulf War) or internal wars (which virtually all wars have been), as peacekeeping. The confusion over roles and missions has been ongoing ever since.

The problem, of course, is that the wake of internal wars or other interventions rarely resembles the tranquil situation for which traditional peacekeeping is designed. In most cases, missions are not contemplated until violence has been going on for some time and when the trigger for international action is the public revelation of hideous, often grotesque atrocity (such as in the Sudan). In those circumstances, the impulse for reconciliation will likely be overwhelmed by the desire for retribution, which peacekeepers can only interrupt (Albanian Kosovar reprisals against their Serbian former persecutors provides an example). The situation is normally tentatively one of peace enforcement—at best—wherein intervening forces must actively work to sustain the absence of violence rather than simply observe and monitor an established peace.

This situation has operational consequences as well. Classic, traditional peacekeepers are lightly armed forces (generally with only handheld weapons to be used only in personal self-defense) that require a minimum of physical or military support, since it is not anticipated they will be placed in harm's way. This also makes them relatively inexpensive, an attribute that makes them appealing to the United

Nations, which must rely on the often fickle collection of member-state contributions to support its activities. Peacekeeping is cheaper than fighting a war, making the characterization of situations as peacekeeping appealing to a perpetually financially strapped organization like the United Nations.

The problem is that few contemporary situations are peacekeeping in nature. The so-called U.N.-sponsored PK operation in Darfur, for instance, is there to *impose* and *enforce* a peace that not everyone (including the *janjaweed* "rebels" and the Sudanese government) wholeheartedly embraces. The classic passive peacekeeping model does not clearly apply. Similarly, American forces in Iraq would *like* the situation to become appropriate for a peacekeeping-type role, but that entails an internal political agreement all parties prefer to continued violence. Until that occurs, there will be no peace to keep, and the mission remains peace enforcement at best.

The tasks and complexities surrounding generic peacekeeping take on added meaning if we add two other dimensions to the peace imposition–peace enforcement–peacekeeping continuum, as shown in Figure 13.1.

In the figure, the situation and missions are as already described, with the addition of the term *unstable peace* to describe the range of situations in which peace enforcement is needed. Clearly, the peace is increasingly stable as one moves away from war and toward the consensus that peace is most desirable. The figure also shows the kinds of military skills required in various stages of the operation. When war is ongoing and peace must be imposed, the need is clearly for combat soldiers with all the equipment and other wherewithal necessary for self-protection and for imposing its will on a hostile enemy by brute force. When stable, self-sustaining peace is achieved, the monitoring function is largely a police function: the peacekeepers essentially make sure the "law" represented by the terms of the ceasefire is obeyed. The tools of their trade are light sidearms and aids to observation like binoculars. Combat soldiers may or may not be proficient at policing; police officers are typically not prepared for all-out combat.

The problem, of course, lies in the hybrid situation of unstable peace, which is the condition into which most outsider forces are in fact interposed (occasionally after imposing the peace in the first place) and where they are likely to be called upon to perform in the future. Clearly, when peace is fragile and fighting could resume, both combat and policing skills are needed, and in varying degrees of mixture as the situation changes. When the experience of war is still fresh, the combat soldier will still be needed to intimidate and coerce the parties not to begin fighting among themselves or to attack the peacekeepers. That role may provide a kind of shield behind which other, more positive and reconciling activities can take place, but in that role, soldiers do not

Figure 13.1: Situations, Missions, and Force Requirements

Situation:	War --------------------- Unstable Peace ------------Peace
Mission:	Peace Imposition ----- Peace Enforcement --------Peacekeeping
Force Required:	War Fighters -----------War Fighters/Police --------Police

contribute to the positive attainment of peace. The soldier, unlike the beat cop, does not befriend the neighbors where he patrols; doing so may get the soldier killed.

Ideally, the same people can fulfill both the combat and the policing roles, adapting chameleon-like to changing conditions and adapting their behaviors accordingly. Unfortunately, the character and skills that make a good combat soldier generally are not the same as those for a good police officer, and developing the second set of skills may degrade the primary skill: the soldier-cop becomes a less lethal soldier, and the cop-soldier becomes a less compassionate, more ruthless cop. This dynamic is explored in the caricature contained in Amplification 13.2. The bottom line is that real peacekeeping in the contemporary world includes a variety of roles

Amplification 13.2

THE TALK-SHOOT RELATIONSHIP IN PEACEKEEPING

The kind of troops that should be employed in peacekeeping has been a matter of disagreement since the United States began participating in these enterprises and is an especially difficult matter in situations where duties go beyond simple observation and monitoring to actual or potential combat operations. Should peacekeepers be lightly and defensively armed observers on the model of military police? Should they be fully armed combat troops ready to respond to any situation? Or should the same peacekeepers be used to fill both functions?

The official position of the American military is that regular combat forces can be trained to be peacekeepers as well as combatants, and the frequent assertion by official military sources is that "any good soldier can do peacekeeping." But is that assertion true?

One way to look at the roles of passive peacekeeper/police officer and combat soldier/peace imposer or enforcer is what can be called the "talk-shoot relationship." For the policeman confronted with a potentially dangerous situation, the procedure is to try to resolve the situation peacefully and to fire only as a last resort in self-defense (talk first, then shoot). For a combat soldier, the failure to attack in a dangerous situation may be to put his or her life in peril, and the appropriate response is to defend one's self (shoot first, then ask questions). The peacekeeper who fires first may be a murderer; the soldier who fails to shoot first may be dead.

Can the same personnel perform both functions, making the right decision in stressful situations? What does the combat soldier on patrol do when he sees someone about to throw something at him, not knowing if the object is a rotten tomato or a grenade? The decision is particularly difficult if the assailant is a child, as is increasingly the case and for which the military has few developed procedures (see the Singer article, listed in the "Selected Bibliography", for an assessment of this aspect of the problem). Also, can soldiers effectively make the transition back and forth from one role to another? If involvement in other people's internal conflicts is to become a common part of the future, answers to these kinds of questions must be found.

that shift over time, suggesting the need to alter and fine-tune the composition of the force across time and as progress is attained.

Even when the complexities of these situations are recognized and addressed, they only speak to part of the problem. Almost all the conditions that peacekeepers contribute to fall within the category of conflict suppression. As the situation moves toward the peace end of the continuum, the peacekeepers as police may make some positive contributions to restoring public confidence in the criminal justice system, but this will mostly occur when they are handing off their duties to natives recruited to replace them.

Moving the situation to one of stable peace requires restoring (or creating) confidence in and loyalty to the existing order in the country itself. The changing roles assigned to peacekeepers may contribute to that goal and even be a necessary condition for success. Peacekeepers cannot create the conditions necessary to build a stable political system and economic prospects of prosperity. Doing those things is the province of individuals and organizations engaged in state building.

State Building

The rationale for state building is a logical extension of the justification for conflict suppression. A state intervenes in the internal affairs of another for one of two reasons: either because the target state is engaged in a civil disagreement that it seems incapable of solving itself and that manifests itself in great suffering (the humanitarian argument) or because the intervening state has some interest in a particular outcome (the realist argument). The first justification underlay American involvement in places like Bosnia, Kosovo, and earlier Somalia. The second justification formed the basis for American involvement in Afghanistan and Iraq and may be extended to other places as part of the expanded "war" on global terrorism in the future.

State building is a logical part of these motives because simple conflict suppression will not by itself solve the root problems from which the violence has arisen in the first place—the conditions of the swamp. Somalia illustrates this problem. The roots of Somali anarchy lay in clan divisions that were deep-seated and historical and that had been magnified by several years of drought and starvation. The international effort there, however, was limited and shortsighted, at least partly because it was the first time the international community, with the United States in the lead, had tried to save a failed state. The initial effort was limited to conflict suppression designed to reinstate the flow of food supplies donated by the international community until the end of the drought began to result in crops being harvested.

The effort succeeded as far as it went, but it did not go far enough. Conflict suppression had eased the food crisis within weeks and had, by the estimates of American officials such as Chester Crocker, saved well over a hundred thousand lives that would otherwise have been lost to starvation. Unfortunately, staunching the wound did not address the real underlying problem—political chaos and structural economic misery—which the participants in UNISOM had no plans to address. Instead, they engaged in incremental acts of state building, including trying to disarm competing warlords who opposed the plan. The attempted disarmament of one clan leader's forces (those of Muhammed Farah Aideed) created such animosity that it produced the "Black Hawk Down" ambush in which nineteen Americans perished and which sent the United States scurrying away. The result has been that Somalia has largely remained in a state of desperately poor anarchy.

The idea of state building went into disrepute after Somalia, enshrouded as a form of hated mission creep (incremental, unplanned expansion of the mission that distorts its original intent) that had led to American failure in that campaign. The charge was always misinformed. The United States failed to produce a stable situation in Somalia not because of what it did but because of what it did not do, which was attempt to engage in state building. The effort might have failed anyway, in which case the United States would *truly* have failed. It was not until the end of the decade of the 1990s that the United States decided to try again, declaring the building of a stable state the goal in Kosovo, a promise reiterated for Afghanistan in 2001 and, at least implicitly, in Iraq in 2003.

Can state building turn a failed, noncompetitive state into a stable, contributing member of the international community? The answer is fundamentally unknown, because the United States has never systematically tried to do so before in the kinds of countries where attempts at state building are likely to occur in the present and future. It is sometimes suggested that state building was implemented in Germany and Japan after World War II, but the problems were not the same. In the former Axis countries, the problem was clearing the rubble and rebuilding the physical infrastructure. The price exacted was acceptance of democratic constitutions, the success of which we made highly likely with the generous influx of cash. If there is any parallel to the present, it may be the Republic of Korea, which became a priority after the Korean War. In Korea, resources were provided proportionately far in excess of the amounts that will be available in contemporary failed states.

The inability confidently to predict success, combined with the frank admission that it will be a long, expensive, and difficult process, makes selling state building difficult. Moreover, the places for which it is proposed—the failed and failing states—are simultaneously the most in need and, by definition, the most unprepared for the process. Just as the "great game" (Russo-British competition for influence) in nineteenth-century Afghanistan ultimately resulted in failure for both, American-led state building may also fail.

Having said all that, the last two American presidents (Clinton in Kosovo, Bush in Afghanistan and Iraq) have committed the United States to engage in state building. To help assess what lies ahead for these efforts, the author borrows three questions originally asked in *When America Fights* around which to organize the discussion: Where to go? What to do? And how to do it?

Where to Go? For the immediate future, that question has largely been answered. The United States is already part of the United Nations–led effort in Kosovo and is part of a similar effort in Afghanistan and Iraq. The "sample" has the virtue of representing the two motivations underlying intervention: humanitarianism in Kosovo, realism and geopolitics in Afghanistan and Iraq. The countries also represent the various levels of desperation state builders will encounter: Kosovo, as a province within European Yugoslavia, is much more developed than Afghanistan, whereas Iraq lies somewhere in between in developmental terms. At the same time, the outcome in Kosovo does not have the same urgency and thus priority that Afghanistan and Iraq have by virtue of being subsumed in the category of the war against terrorism.

The determination of places in which to intervene and engage in state building is only partially a matter of choice. There may be some other places like Afghanistan where an apparent deployment of necessity leads to a state-building mission of equal necessity, and where American initiatives trigger the need, as in Iraq. More opportunities are likely to present themselves in states where failure and noncompetitiveness have their primary, even whole, negative impact on the citizens of the country itself and where involvement and subsequent state building must be justified on humanitarian grounds, deployments and missions of choice (the Sudan). What they will all share is the enormous, even daunting, problems that state builders will encounter.

Recognizing how difficult circumstances are likely to be is crucial to determining whether to engage in state building. In most instances, there will be no functioning government (by design, in some cases, as in the criminal insurgencies) that has the loyalty of any sizable portion of the population. Instead, there are likely to be competing groups eager to ingratiate themselves with the state builders to benefit themselves but unable to cooperate or uninterested in cooperating among themselves (the internal political bickering in Iraq). Institutions are likely to be in ruin where they exist at all, and basic service providers are likely to be in short supply (during the Serb ethnic cleansing in Kosovo, public servants such as clerks and mail carriers were systematically targeted and killed to break down the Kosovars' ability to self-govern, for instance). Moreover, no regime or group is likely to have legitimacy in the eyes of the general population, a problem likely exacerbated by atrocities committed during the violent stage of the civil unrest or, in places like Iraq, afterward. Sometimes these problems will be structural and historical, as in the tribal, clan-based warlord systems in Afghanistan and Somalia; sometimes they will be the result of the excesses of the civil conflict, as in Bosnia and Sierra Leone. Other problems, like those in Iraq, may be the result of regime change that threatens the established ethnic power order.

Economic travail is likely to be present as well. It is generally true that political peace and stability accompany prosperity and economic improvement and not poverty and misery, but the lack of peace and prosperity contributes significantly to failed and noncompetitive status. Infrastructures are either nonexistent or destroyed by years of war (a central problem in Afghanistan) and neglect (Iraq) and must be built or rebuilt before other services can be addressed. In cold climates (Kosovo and Afghanistan) where winter is a problem and many homes have been destroyed, simply providing a warm space in which to live may be a top priority. In hot places like Iraq, turning the air conditioning back on is equally important.

What to Do? Although the generalized goals of state building are easy to articulate, getting there is difficult and is made more difficult by two problems, one discussed in this section, the other in the next. The first is what exactly needs to be accomplished and is made more difficult by the absence of any comprehensive list of characteristics or plan for achieving them. The second is a general lack of detailed knowledge about local conditions and people, creating a difficulty in knowing with whom to deal and how. Both were clearly present in phase IV planning in Iraq.

Building or rebuilding an internal war–ravaged country requires action on at least four dimensions, all of which must be accompanied by and must reinforce efforts by peacekeepers. The first dimension is *political,* somehow bringing a sense of order and eventually legitimacy into a setting that probably lacks both. Within this category, the first and most vital task is the simple establishment of order, creating the condition where citizens can expect peace and the absence of crime in their daily lives. Initially, this role will likely be assigned to peacekeepers, but if the situation is one of peace enforcement and the peacekeepers are in fact combat soldiers, they need rapidly to be replaced by police when conditions allow. This process is a key element of the evolving American mission in Iraq, and especially reaching the point where control is returned to the Iraqis and the Americans can leave.

A major first task is the recruitment of a police force, initially internationally and later from within the population. While this task seems obvious, it is not necessarily easy. Finding foreign police willing to serve in war zones is not easy; a force of thirteen thousand was authorized for Kosovo in 1999 and has never been achieved, even at premium salaries of over $90,000 for a one-year tour. Finding locals may also be hard; when the United States recruited a gendarmerie for Haiti in the mid-1990s, it turned out that many of the officers hired were former members of the terrorist *tonton macoutes* who wanted to be police so they could extract bribes from drug traffickers operating in the country. In Iraq, the resistance has targeted police recruits for assassination as a way to discourage volunteerism. At the same time, the criminal justice system must be revamped so that people view it as fair, and other governmental institutions must be created or restructured and personnel recruited to operate them. Simultaneously, preparations for turning governance over to citizens must be undertaken. In many cases, this entails helping to draft constitutional documents and finding the appropriate people to engage in a constitutional convention in a situation in which we know relatively little about the candidates and there is a long and well-established tradition of mistrust and noncooperation between groups in the political arena.

The second dimension of the problem is *economic.* When international interveners arrive on the scene, they are likely to encounter wretched economic conditions reflecting the destruction of the economy or the absence of developed economic structures. In some cases, what little economic activity does exist may be criminal, as in Afghan poppy and heroin production. In virtually all cases, conditions are likely to be sufficiently chaotic and unappealing that foreign investors are almost certain to be unwilling to come in, establish themselves, and create the kinds of jobs necessary for prosperity.

The first task is basic infrastructure development and rehabilitation. Where they exist at all, roads are in disrepair, bridges have been damaged or destroyed, railroad tracks are in disrepair, and airfields have been pockmarked or mined or both. All need attention for normal activities, including commerce, to resume. At the same time, electricity and water supplies have probably been disrupted; schools, hospitals, and other public buildings burned or bombed; stores looted; and private homes and apartments damaged. Until basic conditions of survival and living can be secured and the most basic services necessary for commerce and economic activity reinstated, little progress can be made on other fronts.

Military personnel attached to peacekeeping can be useful in alleviating some of these miseries. Just as soldiers (and especially military police) can help establish order and civic affairs units can aid in institution building, so too can soldiers and military engineers repair and secure runways, roads, and bridges. These personnel are unlikely to be available in sufficient numbers or for long enough periods of time to make more than a dent in the problems (many of the American service personnel with the requisite skills are reservists whose long-term availability is controversial), but they can contribute to getting the process started. Private contractors represent one alternative, but protecting them has been an added burden in Iraq, and the lucrative nature of many of the contracts has led to charges of corruption and bribery in the awarding of some contracts.

Longer-term economic success almost certainly requires attracting outside capital in the forms of foreign direct investment, location of manufacturing facilities, and the like, in the target country. In order for this to occur, however, the target country must make itself attractive to investors. In addition to overcoming a likely unsavory reputation from the past, this means the development of policies and laws friendly to investors, the development of financial and educational institutions to support business, and a condition of tranquility and peace to reassure potential investors that their investments will not literally blow up in their faces.

The third dimension is *social*. In most of the failed states, there is a social cleavage within the population that may be racial (Haiti), ethnic (Iraq and Sri Lanka), clan or tribal (Afghanistan and Somalia), religious (Indonesia), or some combination of those (Bosnia and Kosovo), wherein identification with one group and targeting of one or more of the other groups has been the basis for violence. The result of violence, often aimed at innocent noncombatants, inflames hatreds already present, leaving a postwar condition of animosity, distrust, and desire for revenge that must be overcome. Doing so is usually easier said than done.

These emotions often run very deep, especially in countries where there was physical mixing of communities before the conflict. When the violence pits neighbor against neighbor, reconciliation after the fact can be especially difficult to accomplish. In Rwanda, for instance, Hutu tribal members identified their Tutsi neighbors for slaughter. In Bosnia, after marauding "militias" had driven particular ethnic groups out of villages, members of the offending group would occupy or destroy their homes. The Bosnian government and international peacekeepers are still trying to return the dispossessed to their former homes. How Iraqi Sunnis, Shiites, and Kurds will finally reconcile is an ongoing question.

The residue of hatred and distrust in these communities will linger, in some cases for a generation or more. In some instances, it may be possible to partition the states in ways that leave ethnic or other groups together and secure. Cyprus is an example. In most cases, however, the partition solution is impossible or is more traumatic than not separating groups. In a country like Bosnia, or instance, commingling of population groups and the absence of natural physical boundaries (wide rivers, for instance) to create secure separation mean there are no easy ways to partition the country. At any rate, such solutions almost certainly involve uprooting and moving people to create ethnically pure communities. The history of such forced migrations does not commend partition as a method for broader application. The aftermath of partition of the Asian Subcontinent in 1947—when eight to ten million Muslims and Hindus were uprooted and forced to flee to countries where they were in the majority—is stark testimony to this problem.

The fourth dimension is *psychological.* Although many assessments of state building ignore or play down this dimension, it is clear that the atrocious conduct of many of these wars scars many of the survivors, often for life. People, especially children, see acts of gruesome violence committed before their eyes. When it is personalized—a child watching the gory execution of a parent—the result can be deeply traumatizing and require considerable counseling to assimilate. Even hardened soldiers experience debilitating mental problems.

It is almost universally true that in the countries that experience these traumas, there is an absolutely inadequate supply of doctors and psychologists to deal with the problem. It is also usually the case that the health care systems in these countries are among the first victims of war. Since the health care systems typically were fairly primitive before the violence, the result is that a bad situation becomes even worse. An ABC television report on January 17, 2002, for instance, revealed there were only *eight* psychiatrists and three mental health wards in all of Afghanistan to treat the psychologically disabled there. The ward in Kandahar was little more than an open courtyard in which patients were chained so they could not harm others.

How to Do It? The preceding discussion has touched on only the tip of the iceberg of substantive problems with which state builders must contend. This formidable list of tasks must be carried out in a situation in which multiple actors with very different perspectives and affiliations must cooperate with local officials in a place with which the state builders are only generally familiar. The environment is likely to be competitive and chaotic, and not all of the groups providing services will trust either one another or the target groups whom they are trying to assist. To add to the problem, there is no "guidebook" on organizing such operations, and the international system lacks enough experience to suggest comprehensive useful precedents.

The first concerted state-building exercise identified as such was mounted for Kosovo. As Amplification 13.3 indicates, it is not a model one would necessarily impose on other situations, such as the efforts in Afghanistan and Iraq. Creating a monolithic effort wherein all helping groups are operating together in a spirit of cooperation working toward commonly accepted goals is the obvious purpose. Accomplishing these goals is far from easy.

At a minimum, state building will have two different groups performing different tasks. On the one hand, there will be a military element engaged in peace enforcement or peacekeeping. The primary task of the military is, of course, keeping order and preventing the recurrence of violence, effectively acting as a shield behind which state building can move forward. Their secondary mission, which is sometimes

Amplification 13.3

KFOR AND UNMIK

At the end of the campaign to drive the Serbs out of Kosovo in 1999, the United Nations announced that the goal of the mission would be to build a stable, prosperous order in that province that could decide either to unite within a newly constituted Yugoslavia or to become independent. The mission is thus state building. The structure announced to implement the goal shows clearly the complexity and difficulty this kind of operation entails.

Although the entire effort is officially under U.N. control, this is not entirely the case in fact. Indeed, there are two separate entities operating in Kosovo, each part of a different command structure. The military peacekeeping element is the Kosovo Force (KFOR), which is a North Atlantic Treaty Organization (NATO) force commanded by a NATO general and reporting to NATO headquarters. The state-building element of the operation is the United Nations Interim Mission in Kosovo (UNMIK), which is headed by the special representative of the secretary general (SRSG) of the United Nations, and he or she reports to the United Nations. The SRSG, in turn, oversees the operations of four activities that constitute the major emphases of the state-building enterprise. Designated the four pillars, each function is administered by a different international organization. Civil administration is the responsibility of the United Nations itself; the development of political institutions is handled by the Organization of Security and Cooperation in Europe (OSCE); economic development is the job of the European Union (EU); and refugees are dealt with by the United Nations High Commission on Refugees (UNHCR). Each of these organizations has somewhat different memberships and reporting requirements. The relationship between KFOR and UNMIK is informal, based upon the personal ability of the KFOR commander and the SRSG to cooperate.

ignored by those planning or executing these missions, is self-protection, making sure their own members are not subject to lethal attacks from groups that suffer because of their presence.

The military component cannot be considered a single, monolithic entity, and it may have very different priorities than others. In most cases, the peacekeeping force will be a coalition of forces drawn from several countries under the auspices of either the United Nations or another organization, such as NATO (or, in Iraq, the United States). These countries will be present for a variety of reasons. Some have a philosophical commitment to this kind of mission (Canada and Norway as peace-keepers, for instance), while others will be there to collect the $100 per diem allowance provided by the United Nations (Ghana and Bangladesh, for example). While a commander will be identified for the mission, the individual country contingents generally report to their own governments, which instruct them on which orders from the command structure to carry out and which to ignore. When national and international orders contradict one another, national priorities prevail.

The United States has a unique position in these efforts. As the world's remaining superpower, the United States will almost certainly be involved at some level, usually including the provision of some troops. American presence is often at the insistence of the target government, and it may be the *sine qua non* for acceptance of a mission by the host country, as was the case in Bosnia. That participation will generally be some-what reluctant and come with at least two conditions. One is a maximum participa-tion by other states to demonstrate that the United States is not shouldering a disproportionate share of the burden. It will also insist that its forces remain under American command to avoid being placed in unnecessarily risky situations where ca-sualties may occur. Often the Americans are called upon to provide logistical support such as getting supplies and personnel to the locale (which means, at a minimum, some American soldiers will be on the ground to protect airfields and ports) and to provide satellite and other signal intelligence that only the United States has the physical capability to provide.

National control of peacekeeping forces and the mandate to limit exposure to danger mean the military side of the operation will be difficult and also virtually guar-antees some level of friction between the peacekeepers and the civilian state builders. The civilian element will also be a hodgepodge of different groups with different pri-orities. Representatives of governments providing developmental assistance will be on the scene identifying projects and making sure that the private contractors with whom they do business are fulfilling their obligations. Representatives from whatever international body is in charge of the state-building enterprise must try to coordinate national efforts to be certain the process is orderly and that vital priorities are being addressed. In addition, a multitude of nongovernmental organizations (NGOs) will be on the scene, either caregivers such as *Medicins sans Frontieres*/Doctors Without Bor-ders ministering to medical needs or monitors such as Amnesty International on the lookout for human rights violations. The media will also be present, at least in the early stages while the mission is still "news."

The ingredients for organizational chaos are clearly present and are made worse by two other factors. The first is dealing with the citizens of the country, who are the supposed beneficiaries of the effort. Who are their legitimate representatives? What do they want, and why? Will international efforts benefit one formerly warring group at the expense of others, thereby making things potentially worse rather than better? Do the state builders know enough about the country and its people to make valid independent judgments on any of these problems? The answers to these ques-tions are often less than absolutely clear to the state builders.

The U.S. effort in Iraq does not precisely reflect these circumstances (the U.S. government, for instance, has no real decision-making competitors), but the tasks and the difficulties of achieving them are not dissimilar (problems reflected in Afghanistan as well, as the *Challenge!* explores). In the Iraq case, most of the fissures have been internal—disagreement between the State Department and CIA and the Department of Defense over how to proceed, for instance—and have been compli-cated by the level of operational responsibility assigned to private contractors. At the same time, the fractiousness of internal elements within Iraq is quite similar to that encountered in more conventional state building missions.

Challenge!

WHAT SHOULD THE UNITED STATES DO IN AFGHANISTAN?

The removal of the Taliban government from power and its replacement by the Karzai government—supported by American and other foreign forces—represented the conflict-suppression phase of the international effort in Afghanistan (phase one). With the election of a permanent government in 2004 and the beginnings of international efforts to build and rebuild that war-torn country, an international state-building campaign began. The extent of that effort and its effects are not clear from the vantage point of 2008.

There has been clear rhetorical support for draining the Afghan "swamp" and building a stable country that will resist terrorist appeals and join the antiterrorism coalition in the future. As of the end of 2007, that rhetoric had not translated into the massive assistance program that most agreed was necessary to produce a stable and hopefully democratic Afghanistan.

All four dimensions of state building need attention. Progress in the military dimension is most advanced, as an Afghan armed force and constabulary have been initiated; the degree to which they run afoul of traditional Afghan tribal rivalries remains to be seen. The Taliban, for instance, have been reconstituted as a military force and effectively rule a good deal of the countryside. The economic dimension has hardly been addressed at all. There is wide agreement that massive amounts of money are necessary to build the Afghan economic infrastructure and to rebuild the country after so many years of war. Beyond more or less vague promises of assistance, the flow of resources has been slow to come, and Afghan patience is being tested. The social and psychological dimensions likewise suffer from years of privation and violence. Exacerbating the situation is official government repression of the one major cash crop that could pump money into the economy: heroin-producing poppies. Prior to the Taliban regime, nearly 70 percent of the world's heroin was grown in Afghanistan from poppies, and after the Taliban were overthrown, peasant farmers planted new crops that had been forbidden by the Taliban. At the prodding of Western governments, those crops were destroyed (with compensation) in 2002, but record crops have been harvested since. Efforts to control the situation have had mixed success.

What should the United States do for Afghanistan? How many American tax dollars should be spent on rebuilding the Afghan infrastructure and in building a prosperous society—especially since the results cannot be guaranteed? It is one thing to call for making an antiterrorist bulwark out of Afghanistan, but what budgetary sacrifices should Americans be forced to endure to produce such a state? Also, the degree to which the country responds to Afghanistan's plight will create a precedent for what other states may expect from the United States in the future. How seriously committed are Americans *in fact* to the continuing campaign against terrorism as it threatens to "attack" our own wallets? If Americans are not serious about state building in Afghanistan, will anyone believe Americans are any more serious about neoconservative dreams to build a stable, democratic Iraq that will act as a regional role model? What do you think?

CONCLUSION: THE FUTURE OF PEACEKEEPING AND STATE BUILDING

Contemporary military employments are very much unlike wars of the past. Traditional, symmetrical wars were more clear-cut and determinant, conforming to a *peace-war-peace* model that the present author described in *When America Fights* in 2000: "war is an interruption of peace, which is the normal and preferable condition. The function of military force is to repair a broken peace by going to war, subduing those who had breached the peace, and then returning to the normal condition, which is peace." In that structured environment, the last truly clear example of which was World War II, Iraqi-style Phase IV/peacekeeping and state building considerations are of far lesser concern, because the end of formal hostilities ushers in the reinstitution of peace and order. Had Iraq conformed to the peace-war-peace model, it would have been an unquestioned success. But it did not, because the model does not fit contemporary war.

In modern, asymmetrical warfare, the period after what the Bush administration called "major combat operations"—Phase IV—is easily as vital to the eventual outcome as are traditional military operations. Not only must the main body of the enemy—where it has one—be subdued, but also all active groups in the target society must be convinced to embrace the peace. Force has a role in nurturing that embrace, but it also entails the multiple dynamics described here as peacekeeping and state building. As the discussion has sought to convey, these tasks are far more formidable and problematical than overcoming organized armed forces (particularly given the tremendous weight of American conventional forces). Although the United States may not botch PK/SB operations in the future as spectacularly as it has in Iraq, there is clearly no proven American approach to peacekeeping, and especially to state building.

The requisites of peacekeeping and state building, in one form or another, will be part of the operational environment the United States will encounter when it contemplates the use of force in the post-Iraq world. It is a chastening realization, because factoring in these needs makes the planning and execution more complex and the prospects of success decidedly more difficult to project and achieve. In Iraq, these entirely predictable dynamics were ignored by those who made the decision to go to war, and the results are clear. If decision makers ignore this lesson and blithely proceed on the implicit assumption that the peace-war-peace model will hold, the results could be similar to Iraq. If one assumes, however, that peacekeeping and state building are integral parts of modern *war making* in the modern world, some decisions may be quite different in the future—another potential part of the Iraq legacy.

STUDY/DISCUSSION QUESTIONS

1. What three characteristics are shared by modern wars? How do these affect how to think about involvement in modern wars?
2. What is a failed state? What characteristics do failed states share? Apply Peters's notion of noncompetitive states to the failed states, using Afghanistan as an example.
3. What are peacekeeping and state building? What forms of activity can be included under the broad rubric of peacekeeping? Apply the distinctions to Iraq.

4. What was the original concept of peacekeeping? How has it been extended to deal with contemporary conflicts? Why? Explain the continuum from war to peace and the idea of unstable peace.
5. Briefly discuss the nature of state building and how it has evolved. Using the three questions posed in the text, discuss the nature and dictates of state building.
6. Why is an understanding of peacekeeping and state building critical to understanding the future of modern warfare?
7. Had decision makers understood the critical and difficult demands of Phase IV operations (peacekeeping and state building) before deciding to invade Iraq, would (or should) the decision have been different? If these alternatives had been presented to the American public before the invasion, how would they have responded? Why?

SELECTED BIBLIOGRAPHY

Atwood, J. Brian. "The Development Imperative: Creating the Preconditions for Peace." *Journal of International Affairs* 55 (Spring 2002), 333–349.

Barton, Frederick D., and Bathsheba N. Crocker. *A Wiser Peace: An Action Strategy for a Post-conflict Iraq.* Washington, DC: Center for Strategic and International Studies, 2003.

Bates, Robert H. *Prosperity and Violence: The Political Economy of Development.* New York: W. W. Norton, 2001.

Boutros-Ghali, Boutros. *An Agenda for Peace: Preventive Diplomacy, Peacemaking, and Peace-Keeping.* New York: United Nations, 1992.

Bynam, Daniel. "Insecuring Iraq." *National Interest* 76 (Summer 2004), 15–18.

Chandrasekaran, Rajiv. *Imperial Life in the Emerald City: Inside Iraq's Green Zone.* New York: Alfred A. Knopf, 2007.

Cordesman, Anthony H. *The Iraq War: Strategy, Tactics, and Military Lessons.* Washington, DC: Center for Strategic and International Studies, 2003.

Diamond, Larry. *Squandered Victory: The American Occupation and the Bungled Effort to Bring Democracy to Iraq.* New York: Times Books (Henry Holt and Company), 2005.

Doran, Michael Peter. "Somebody Else's Civil War." *Foreign Affairs* 81, 1 (January/February 2002), 23–40.

Durch, William (ed.). *The Evolution of UN Peacekeeping: Case Studies and Comparative Analysis.* New York: St. Martin's Press, 1993.

Eisenstat, Stuart, John Edward Porter, and Jerry Weinstein. "Rebuilding Weak States." *Foreign Affairs* 84, 1 (January/February 2005), 134–146.

Glantz, Aaron. *How America Lost Iraq.* New York: Jeremy P. Tarcher/Penguin, 2005.

Goldstone, Jack A., and Jay Ulfelder. "How to Construct Stable Democracies." *Washington Quarterly* 28, 1 (Winter 2004–2005), 9–20.

Gurr, Ted Robert. *Why Men Rebel.* Princeton, NJ: Princeton University Press, 1973.

Hanson, Victor Davis. *Between War and Peace: Lessons from Afghanistan and Iraq.* New York: Random House, 2004.

Helman, Gerald B., and Steven R. Ratner. "Saving Failed States." *Foreign Policy* 89 (Winter 1992–1993), 3–20.

Hulsman, John. "Lawrence of Arabia and the Perils of State Building." *Heritage Lecture* #900. Washington: Heritage Foundation, 2005.

Kemp, Geoffrey. "Losing the Peace?" *National Interest* 76 (Summer 2004), 46–48.

Krasner, Stephen D., and Carlos Pascual. "Addressing State Failure." *Foreign Affairs* 84, 4 (July/August 2005), 155–163.

Mueller, John. *Remnants of War*. Ithaca, NY: Cornell University Press, 2003.

Odom, William E. "Retreating in Good Order." *National Interest* 76 (Summer 2004), 33–36.

Peters, Ralph. *Fighting for the Future: Will America Triumph?* Mechanicsburg, PA: Stackpole Books, 1999.

Record, Jeffrey. *Dark Victory: America's Second War Against Iraq*. Annapolis, MD: Naval Institute Press, 2004.

Ricks, Thomas E. *Fiasco: The American Military Adventure in Iraq*. New York: Penguin Press, 2006.

Sachs, Jeffrey D. "The Development Challenge." *Foreign Affairs* 84, 2 (March/April 2005), 78–90.

Singer, P. W. "Caution: Children at War." *Parameters* 31, 4 (Winter 2001–2002), 40–56.

Snow, Donald M. *When America Fights: The Uses of U.S. Military Force*. Washington, DC: CQ Press, 2000.

——— and Eugene Brown. *International Relations. The Changing Contours of Power*. New York: Longman, (2000).

Tripp, Charles. *A History of Iraq* (2nd ed.). Cambridge, UK: Cambridge University Press, 2001.

CHAPTER 14

Extending Security in a Post-Iraq World

PREVIEW

While the environment in which national security policy is formulated will not necessarily change dramatically after the United States ends its involvement in Iraq, the way the United States views and interacts with that environment may well be different. One likely change will be in the degree of American military activism in the immediate post-Iraq years. Another is the likely extension of thinking about national security to include areas that do not have a heavy military content and that have not traditionally been thought of in national security terms. This chapter explores four of these policy areas that extend ideas of security in distinctly different ways: border security, natural resources security, environmental security, and health security. The chapter concludes with some discussion about how these extended applications will affect thinking about American national security in the future.

The environment in which national security policy is honed and in which threats to that security are mounted will not change completely after the Iraq War is over for the United States. The Middle East will, for instance, continue to be the most troublesome, unstable part of the world, and the continuing dependence of the United States on Persian Gulf petroleum will assure that American interests in the region will be sufficiently engaged to prevent total American disengagement from the region. The most spectacular aspect of that region's volatility will almost certainly continue to be international religious terrorism, the countering of which will remain a major focus of American security policy, if possibly with a different focus and employing different means. The most troubling potential problems in the

Middle East will be possible regional devolution into ethnic (e.g., Arab versus non-Arab) and communal (Sunni versus Shi'a) violence, possibly centering in and about Iraq. American response to such an occurrence or to the destabilization of a major ally such as Pakistan is problematical (the assassination of Benazir Bhutto highlights this possibility).

Although projecting into the future is an inherently risky and speculative business, at least two major trends are likely to become prominent about how the United States confronts the security environment of the next five to ten years. The first, resulting directly from the Iraq War experience extensively described in the preceding pages, will almost certainly be a lesser inclination toward military activism manifested in a reluctance to commit large-scale American military assets except under the most unambiguous conditions of need (a war of necessity). Large-scale, costly deployments of choice will be difficult to sell to a wary, war-weary public and to a depleted, rebuilding military, which would have to implement such a deployment. Arguments that particular situations constitute deployments of necessity rather than choice will be subject to much greater scrutiny than they were before Iraq, which was arguably a deployment of choice defended as one of necessity. The rejoinder of "no more Iraqs" will be a potent charge given the Iraq decision. Moreover, the opportunities to employ force will be in new variations of asymmetrical warfare situations about which both the American military and its civilian leadership have become appropriately wary. After the Iraq lesson that deployments against asymmetrical opponents are likely to result in frustrating and inconclusive outcomes, they will be difficult to justify or gain support for.

The second trend is likely to be a broadening of the matters on the national security agenda to include more concerns that either lack or do not prominently feature a traditional military component. Chapter 6 specifically indicated some of these concerns and hinted at but did not discuss such contingencies in detail. One such dimension is *economic security*, and in a world of increasing U.S. indebtedness to the rest of the world (accentuated by financing of the Iraq War), growing dependence on foreign manufactures and capital, and global economic volatility, economic security can only increase in salience. At the same time, international religious terrorism will continue to represent a semimilitary threat wherein the traditional tools of national security policy play an important, varying, but not determinant role. As noted earlier, one problem with the GWOT analogy is that the effort is not a war at all under common conceptions of what constitutes war.

These are not the only areas of concern that will likely be added to the security agenda in the upcoming years. To some extent, the list will expand because the Iraq hangover will discourage conceptualizing the world in terms of militarized situations and responses. At the same time, an expanded list will reflect a more complicated, variegated world where the real problems with which policy makers must deal can less and less be pigeonholed into traditional security and nonsecurity categories. Raising these concerns in a national security setting will be uncomfortable, even incongruous for many with a conventional view of national security. The contention here is that the failure to include these new areas within national security leaves an incomplete picture of the security environment of the future, and it is for that reason that this last chapter is devoted to these nontraditional security concerns that indeed extend thinking about national security.

There is no universal agreement about what a list of these concerns would contain or not contain, and there will be disagreement about the inclusion or exclusion of different concerns depending on individual interests and assessments: no list will please everyone. With no claims to inclusiveness, the author has chosen four areas for illustrative purposes. They all share the common characteristics of making Americans safe or feel safe (the heart of the definition of security) and of having both some conventional and some unconventional security aspects. They are presented in descending order of conventional (i.e., military) content.

The four areas are border security, natural resource security, environmental security, and health security. Problems associated with each—borders breached by terrorists, interruptions in the flow of oil, environmental catastrophes, the incursion of foreign deadly diseases—pose a threat to Americans (and everyone else), but each is unique in the threat it poses and how its risk can be reduced or eliminated. Border security seems the most obviously security-related issue, but it is a more complex issue than simply sanitizing or sealing the borders. Americans would clearly feel and be threatened by an interruption in the supply of natural resources to the country, but it is not clear whether or how, in different situations, the instrumentalities of national security apply to securing those resources. Environmental catastrophes of various kinds could represent the ultimate threats to security, even existence, but they lack obvious immediacy and thus tend to be consigned to future consideration even when current actions can accentuate or attenuate the threat. Although there have been both historical and contemporary examples where disease transmission has posed a threat to individual and national well-being, this prospect also tends to be consigned a lower order of priority not dissimilar to the attention denied terrorism prior to the major catastrophe represented by September 11.

Three of these issue areas were introduced in Chapter 6, if in a somewhat different context and with a different emphasis. Border security, energy security, and environmental security were all introduced in the context of additional problems the country faces, but not with the same emphasis on defining how and why they should be thought of as national security problems and as part of the broader definition of what makes the country feel or be safe. The purpose of reintroducing these areas—and adding the idea of health security—is to stimulate the reader to think about and consider more broadly what do and do not constitute legitimate items on the national security agenda.

BORDER SECURITY

In some important ways, the security of national borders is the oldest and most fundamental of all national security issues. Protecting and defending national, sovereign territory is, arguably, the most important and vital priority and task of government. National (or homeland) security is, at its most elemental level, about protecting the citizenry from hostile others who might breach those borders and do harm to the citizens. As noted in Chapter 4, preparing to repel armed hostile hordes has not been a prominent part of the American experience, but the task remains a fundamental part of the charge to government; it can be and often is, argued that a government that cannot protect its borders from hostile invasion can serve no other useful function.

The contemporary border security issue facing the United States is not so basic or dramatic as that. There is no equivalent, except in the most allegorical sense, of Genghis Khan's Golden Horde gathering on the country's boundaries. Thus, the answer to the question "Protection from what threat arising from an arguably insecure border?" is neither simple nor obvious, and the issue of border security also demonstrates the extremely diffuse, even loose, way in which the underlying concept of security is employed in describing the problem. Framing the border security problem and determining its security content require examining border security from two vantage points. These are the physical extent and dimensions of American borders and the nature and locales of threats to those borders.

The territorial boundaries of the United States are among the most extensive, complex, and difficult to secure of any country in the world. They can be divided into land and sea borders, each of which poses different priorities and problems that can be described in varying security terms. The land borders of the United States are shared with two contiguous neighbors, Canada and Mexico. The land border between Canada and the United States is slightly more than 5,500 miles long (the boundary between Canada and the contiguous 48 states is 3,987 miles, and that between Canada and Alaska is 1,538 miles). The border between Mexico and the United States is 1,933 miles long. Thus, the land borders of the United States and its foreign neighbors total 7,458 miles. Even this formidable total pales in comparison to that of Russia, the world's largest country, which is twice as big as the United States and has land borders approximately two-thirds longer than those of the United States, shared with fourteen countries.

Clearly, maintaining the absolute and inviolable sanctity of borders this long is physically impossible and would, for the most part, be unnecessary. Which parts of which borders will be secured (i.e., made inviolate) is a matter of risk assessment and risk reduction: where and what are the threats posed by permeable borders at different locations? Admitting that the principle of sovereignty suggests all borders should be secure, what priorities should be attached to making which borders more or less impermeable? Some of the answers are relatively simple: there is little reason, for instance, to expend major resources securing most of the border between remote areas of Canada and Alaska, because little threat is posed by allowing transit back and forth (which could probably not be prevented under any circumstances). Large urban crossings and the long border between the United States and Mexico may be different matters, however.

The sea borders of the United States are an even more daunting physical problem. Two measures are used to describe these dimensions: coastline and shoreline. The coastline refers generally to a line drawn along the intersection of the coast and the ocean, not allowing for bays, inlets, and other water features, whereas the shoreline measures the total topography of the coast, including the shores of bodies of water emptying into the oceans and seas. Using figures provided by the National Oceanic and Atmospheric Administration (U.S. Department of Commerce), the coastline of the United States is 12,383 miles, and the shoreline is 88,633 miles.

As with the land borders of the country, sealing access to American territory along the seas is a daunting task, probably beyond the physically possible. Once again, the problem is differential. Almost 42 percent (5,580 of the 12,383 miles) of coastline is between Alaska and the various bodies of water that touch it (the Pacific and Arctic Oceans, the Bering and Beaufort Seas), and 35 percent (31,383 of the 88,633 miles) of shoreline is Alaskan. Parts of the Alaskan coast were important during the Cold War, and the 1,350 miles of Florida's coastline and 8,426 miles of its shoreline have long been a source of concern regarding both drug (and other) smuggling and illegal immigration.

The answer to the general proposition of border security is thus a good bit more complicated than an atavistic call to "seal the borders." The physical dimensions of the problem are such that the task is probably impossible and certainly impracticable in terms of the resources necessary even to attempt it, and sealing great parts of the border would serve little justifiable national priority (most of the Alaska–Canada border and the Canada–U.S. border across much of the Great Plains and West).

These physical dimensions create enormous physical difficulties in trying to secure the country's borders. Clearly, continuously patrolling every inch of either the land or the sea borders goes beyond the capabilities of the various agencies assigned border protection tasks. The U.S. Coast Guard, for instance, is the agency primarily given the task of protecting the coastline and shoreline from unwanted foreign incursion, but it clearly lacks the number or quality of seacraft to prevent all intrusions that might be mounted. To argue that it should seek this capability would require a vast expansion of its capabilities (both sea- and air-based) that would go beyond any reasonable political expectations, and thus to argue that the entire coastline and shoreline will be sealed amounts to declaring a "paper blockade" of the coast. Similarly, the Border Patrol, which has comparable responsibilities for the land borders, cannot possibly seal every inch of the borders between the United States and Canada and the United States and Mexico. In both cases, it may be possible to provide a blanket protection of certain *parts* of the border or against particular intruders and intrusions (or both), but the attempt to guard comprehensively is feckless.

A couple of real examples may help clarify the magnitude of the problem of comprehensive border protection. According to Stephen Flynn, one of the country's leading experts in border and port security issues, in 2000 "489 million people, 127 million passenger vehicles, 11 million trucks, 2.2 million railroad cars, 829,000 planes, and 211,000 vessels passed through American border inspection systems." Given the limited resources available to border guards, it is physically impossible to inspect in any detail all of these entrants, and although most undoubtedly enter for legitimate and unimpeachable reasons, it is impossible to ensure that all undesirable people or things cannot enter. In addition, the border between the western extremity of Lake Superior and Boundary Bay, Washington, is only monitored at major crossing points; anyone who wants to walk across the border from Saskatchewan to

Montana or North Dakota where there are no roads can do so with a high likelihood of success. To make matters more complicated, Flynn adds that one-third of all the trucks (almost 4 million) entering the United States annually cross over one of four bridges from Canada into Michigan or New York State. If a real attempt to monitor the movement of goods across these bridges were attempted (as was briefly tried on the Ambassador Bridge between Detroit and Windsor, Ontario), the result would be massive gridlock. In the case cited, a number of Chrysler automobile assembly plants in the United States that depended on parts from Canada had to be shut down until the inspections were rescinded and normalcy returned. The problem is easily as great regarding the movement of vessels into the country's ports, where only a minuscule percentage of incoming freight is or can be inspected. Advanced technology is improving both these situations, but there remain barriers to an inviolable border.

To add to this problem, it is by no means obvious that essentially sealing the border from outside intrusion is desirable. A truly effective system of screening people and goods and services entering the country would, among other things, impede the flow of people, ideas, and goods across the border into the United States, a direct challenge to the dictates of globalization and free trade. In summer 2007, for instance, the Bush administration found itself in the incongruous position (although it did not admit the incongruity) of simultaneously promoting additional trade within the NAFTA trade area (which meant the increased flow of goods across the country's borders with Canada and Mexico) and arguing for increased border security that would have the effect of slowing and impeding rather than facilitating the very trade it was promoting. Which priority was thus to be served so that following one or the other did not have unintended consequences?

The question of border security must thus be made more specific, basically specifying who and what it is important to exclude from American soil and where that effort should be concentrated. An auxiliary question is to what agencies of the government different responsibilities should be assigned. This latter question is more complicated than it would seem on the surface, as the discussion will reveal. Moreover, attempts to create greater security may have undesirable, unintended consequences that must be taken into consideration when deciding the answers to any of these questions.

Because the United States is historically a country that has opened its borders to immigrants from around the world, the idea of secure borders in the sense of impermeable barriers to entry (or exit) from the country has not always dominated this aspect of the national security agenda. At the same time, it has also been true that the United States has always tried to keep what it viewed as undesirable people and unwanted things out of the country. The content of what or who is desirable and undesirable has changed across time: during Prohibition, for instance, it was a national priority to exclude alcoholic beverages from the country; at different times, the same exclusiveness has been aimed at different nationalities seeking to immigrate to this country (the Irish during the 1840s, for instance).

The current concern over border security must be placed in this context. Who and what does the United States seek to exclude from its sovereign territory? And how important is it that this exclusion succeeds? In the current context, border security has come to be associated with the 1,933-mile U.S.–Mexico land border, and the political cry has been to seal that border from undesired and presumably undesirable intruders. Even narrowing the problem to that level (thereby excluding the Canadian-American land borders and the protection of the coastline and shoreline), the problem is daunting and requires further elaboration.

The major question is against what threat border security is aimed. As Payan points out, there are three aspects to the U.S.–Mexico border issue, and each poses a different kind of problem, a different priority, and a threat of a differing security content. These three aspects are illegal immigration, drug trafficking, and terrorist penetration. Although they overlap some of the time (illegal immigrants may, for instance, carry drugs into the country, or they may also be terrorists), they are also distinct problems. Drug trafficking and illegal immigration may be primarily U.S.–Mexico border issues, but the penetration of the United States by terrorists can occur anywhere along the borders.

The illegal immigration issue has become the political hot-button topic because of the flood of Mexican citizens entering the country since the middle 1990s and the institution of NAFTA (for an explanation, see Snow, *Cases in International Relations*, Chapter 9). Although figures regarding illegal immigration are by definition unknown and unreliable, the number of Mexican citizens who are living in the United States but who have not entered the country through prescribed means of immigration has risen from about 1.5–2 million before NAFTA to 12–14 million today (some estimates are as high as 20 million).

What kind of problem does illegal immigration pose? That it violates the sanctity of the border is true by definition, but in and of itself, that raises the question, So what? Do illegal immigrants pose a security threat beyond the fact that they implicitly flaunt the sanctity of the border? Most of the arguments to stanch and reverse the flow are not made on traditional national security grounds (they pose no military threat, for instance), but on grounds such as the fact that these immigrants place additional demands on social services, they do not pay taxes, and they deprive American citizens of jobs. Placing these problems under the heading of "security" may have the implicit (or intentional) effect of elevating its perceived importance in the pantheon of national priorities, but it is not clearly a part of the national security agenda at all.

The second aspect of the border security problem is drug trafficking. Once again, precise determinations about the physical extent of the problem are probably unreliable, but Michael Shifter maintains, "Mexico is the transit route for roughly 70 to 90 percent of the illegal drugs entering the United States. . . . Along the U.S.–Mexico border, the kidnapping trade, clearly tied to the drug trade, is flourishing." Since the illicit drugs entering the United States have an impact on the criminal justice system designed to interrupt that commerce and to punish those who engage in it, it is also a domestic political problem rather than a national security problem on the face of it. It does, however, have strong indirect security implications: the deleterious effect of drug usage on Americans, and thus American society, and the political devastation to other countries (especially in but not limited to Mexico) created by the actions of drug traffickers.

The damaging effects of illicit drug usage on the United States have been sufficiently alarming that the Reagan administration declared it a national emergency during the 1980s (Nancy Reagan's "Just say no to drugs"), and George H. W. Bush upgraded the national effort to the "War on Drugs" during his term in office. The "war" analogy was always more symbolic than real, but it did include significant use of, for instance, military resources from the U.S. Southern Command (the military command whose mission covers Latin America) for identifying and destroying sources of drugs and processing facilities in South America and from the U.S. Air Force and Coast Guard for preventing transshipment of processed drugs through and over Central America and the Caribbean. While much of that effort has been scaled back, the interruption of drugs flowing into the United States, principally but not exclusively from Latin America, remains a high priority of the federal government.

Is the drug trade a national security problem? The argument that it is focuses on the negative impact that drugs have on the United States and Americans. Drugs are at the base of much crime (especially in inner-city areas), strain the criminal justice and penal systems, incapacitate and render socially less useful those Americans who use and abuse drugs, and even cripple the government's ability to conduct its business by denying it significant tax revenue from the illicit drug commerce. The contention is that the country would be stronger if drug use were sharply curtailed or eliminated.

If an argument can be made that drugs weaken America and thus are a legitimate national security concern, what solutions are there for the scourge they represent? Broadly speaking, there are two answers: demand side and supply side. Demand-side solutions are aimed at reducing demand for drugs so that the drug trade becomes progressively less lucrative and thus less appealing. Education is a prime example: teaching and convincing people that drugs are bad for them and should be avoided (the analogy with antismoking campaigns is often made). Supply-side efforts aim at reducing the availability of drugs for people. Such efforts include destruction of drugs at their source (the so-called Andean Initiative to destroy coca—the source of cocaine—crops and to destroy processing plants, mostly in Colombia) and interdiction of processed drugs coming into the country. As already noted, this latter effort has focused on the Mexican border, across which most of the drugs transit.

The transit of drugs through Mexico and across the border creates tremendous difficulties and strains in U.S.-Mexican relations. Drug smuggling is a big and very lucrative business, and it is very difficult to interrupt successfully. Peter Andreas, for instance, contends that "the amount of cocaine necessary to satisfy US customers for one year can be transported in just nine of the thousands of large tractor-trailers that cross the border every day." Given that the amount of commerce across the border—largely by trucks—is supposed to increase as the NAFTA-led integration of North American economies continues, monitoring this trade becomes increasingly difficult. At the same time, drug smuggling becomes intertwined with illegal immigration, as those seeking to enter the country illegally are recruited by drug smugglers to bring contraband across the border or, more insidiously, are required by agents who assist in illegal entry to engage in drug smuggling as part of the fee for assistance entering the

United States. Efforts to interrupt the flow of immigrants and drugs has an unintended effect here, as Andreas describes it: "adding thousands of new Border Patrol agents has had the perverse effect of enriching smugglers rather than deterring immigrants since the problem of breaching the border is more difficult" and requires help for some immigrants. Moreover, the dual goals of immigrant and drug interdiction bring both the Drug Enforcement Agency and the Border Patrol to the border with differing and occasionally conflicting priorities, hampering enforcement. The poverty of interdiction efforts is suggested by the fact that in recent years the street price of cocaine in the United States has dropped, indicating either that demand has dropped significantly or that supply has increased beyond past demand.

The drugs that enter the United States across the border must first transit across Mexico, and the result has been to corrode and corrupt the Mexican political process. Shifter lays out some of these problems. Governmental corruption is an endemic problem in Mexico, and "the astronomical revenues generated by the drug trade fuel the rampant corruption that eats away at already fragile institutions." Drug money to bribe officials to, at a minimum, ignore drug trafficking has attacked the system from top to bottom. At the local level, "the police are thoroughly corrupt, unreliable, and ill-equipped to handle increasingly violent traffickers," and the taint has extended to the top levels of the military and central government. The great danger is a general destabilization of the entire Mexican political system; Mexico in the throes of revolution would clearly pose a national security threat to the United States. At a minimum, it would almost certainly result in a flood of additional illegal immigrants across the border.

The third aspect of the problem is the penetration of the border by terrorists. This is clearly a problem that affects both the U.S.–Mexico and the U.S.–Canada borders, although one can argue that since it is more difficult to enter Canada than it is Mexico, the problem is more severe along the Mexican border. Conversely, it is easier for a potential terrorist to cross the Canadian than the Mexican border into the United States.

This aspect of the problem, as a part of the terrorism complex of problems, has the clearest national security content of any of the border issues. The difficulty is that border solutions to the terrorist entry problem are the most difficult to implement comprehensively. Current efforts by agencies like the Border Patrol and Immigration and Customs Enforcement (ICE) are necessarily concentrated at the points of greatest transit of goods and services—major crossing points on the borders and international airports and ports, for instance—and are totally inadequate to control or seal the entire border. Had, for instance, the terrorists who sought to attack Los Angeles International Airport in 2005 not tried to cross into the United States at the busy and well-controlled border crossing at Vancouver but instead have walked across the border into North Dakota, the chances are they would not have been identified or apprehended at that point. Moreover, the proposed (and congressionally authorized) 700-mile fence along the Mexican-American border will leave over 1,200 miles of border unfenced, including vast stretches along the Mexican border with Texas.

The border security issue is thus much more complicated and complex than is often argued in the general political debate. In the abstract, one can talk about the sanctity of the border as a general political value, but in an applied sense, the matter is by no means so simple. One must start with an observation similar to framing the terrorism problem in Chapter 12: what is the goal? In the terrorism case, the goal can be either elimination or control/reduction of the problem, with elimination as the ideal and reduction as the practical and attainable goal. The same is true of border security. It may, in an abstract sense, be desirable to make American borders impermeable to all undesirable outside intrusions, but the land and sea borders are simply too extensive for that to be practical. If one could construct an absolutely impenetrable boundary, it would greatly reduce or eliminate the movement of unauthorized immigrants, illegal drugs, and terrorists across the frontier, but such a restriction is almost certainly not possible. Moreover, it is not at all clear that building such a border would be desirable, a possibility explored in Amplification 14.1: An Impenetrable Border?

What one does, or proposes to do, about border security depends on national priorities, and particularly those surrounding what makes Americans safe or feel safe. Since absolute security cannot be guaranteed, the question thus becomes one of risk reduction, not risk elimination. Deciding what aspects of the border security problem should be accorded the greatest attention requires deciding what aspects of a permeable border

Amplification 14.1

AN IMPENETRABLE BORDER?

If it were possible, would sealing the border be desirable for the United States? Certainly, it would solve the problems of border penetration, as suggested in the text. But it might cause other problems that would be as bad or worse. First, it would be enormously expensive both to construct and to maintain. Electronic means of surveillance that might reduce human needs notwithstanding, such a system would require a large and expensive manpower commitment, and ironically the less manpower intensive the system might be to operate, the more expensive it would be to build. Are Americans really willing to incur such costs given other national priorities?

Second, such a system would, as already suggested, interrupt the flow of goods and services coming into the United States. In the most direct sense, the movement toward more secure borders runs directly counter to the greater globalization built into the full implementation of NAFTA as described in its provisions. NAFTA may be controversial, but if it is, it should be addressed specifically on its own merits. Increased border security is an indirect assault on NAFTA—and other aspects of globalization.

Third, there is the symbolism of greater border security. The United States has a long tradition of encouraging migration to this country, and relatively easy access is a part of that tradition. Fortifying the border—turning the Mexican-American border into something resembling the Great Wall of China, for instance—has symbolic importance. Does the United States still adhere to the Statue of Liberty's invitation to "give me your tired, your poor, your huddled masses yearning to breathe free," or does it prefer to build a wall to keep the barbarians out?

are most and least nettlesome and dangerous. What imperils American security the most: Is it the flow of illegal immigrants into the country? Do drug trafficking and its consequent impact on Americans and American society create the greatest threat? Or is the danger that porous border attract terrorist penetration the greatest threat? Until one reaches some consensus on the nature of the problem, it will be unlikely that border security will rise far above the level of a bumper-sticker entreaty.

NATURAL RESOURCE SECURITY

All countries are, to varying degrees, dependent on natural resources that do not exist in adequate supply within their own territory for their well-being and, in the most extreme cases, for their national existence. As pointed out in Chapter 4, resource dependency has not been an historic American problem because of the natural physical endowment of the North American continent. For most of American history—at least up to the end of World War II—the United States was essentially resource independent, and the problem of resource scarcity was largely an abstract concern that affected other countries. Three factors have changed that. First, adequate supplies of some resources at economic costs for extraction have been depleted, making foreign sourcing either necessary or economically preferable. Petroleum is the primary example. Second, modern technology requires some resources that are not present in adequate supply or at all on or under American soil. Titanium necessary for, among other things, jet engines is an example. Third, Americans now desire and demand some commodities that are not indigenous to the United States and that must be imported. Spices and exotic fruits and vegetables are examples.

Not all of the resources in inadequate supply for Americans (and others) are equally vital and thus the subject of security concerns. Americans, for instance, might not like being deprived of cinnamon from Southeast Asia, but the country would not collapse if cinnamon became unavailable. On the other hand, there are resources that are going to be clearly scarce and strategically important for the United States and much of the rest of the world. Some of these scarcities will (and do) have a direct impact on the United States: petroleum is the obvious example. Others will not affect the United States directly in the sense of creating shortages from which Americans will suffer but will affect the United States indirectly if the competition for those resources causes conflicts among countries and in regions of interest to the United States; water is the obvious example. Each will be explored as exemplary of the resource problem and how it is a concern of American security policy. Like border security, neither the statement of the problem nor its solutions is entirely and unambiguously part of the traditional domain of national security.

Petroleum Energy Security

For the United States, the continuing availability of reasonably priced petroleum from the international community is, and will continue to be, a highly salient national security concern. The problem is not, however, exclusively an American concern; it is part of a larger concern with energy security of which petroleum is one, if the largest, consideration, and its solution is only partly a matter of traditional national security. It is a dramatic and poignant security area both because of the heavy dependence of the American transportation system (including privately owned and operated vehicles) on petroleum and because of the obvious connection between petroleum and other more volatile aspects of national security policy, notably policy toward the Middle East. It becomes an emotional issue because it gets wrapped up in the overall debate over energy policy and thus the heated disagreement between energy producers and conservationists over expansion of energy sources and uses. As the price of oil passed $100 a barrel in early 2008, these concerns intensified.

The American petroleum problem is part of the global dilemma over the adequacy of this form of energy. The origins of the global problem go back to the end of World War II, when those rebuilding the ravages of the war made the dual decisions to reorient the rebuilding economies of Europe and elsewhere around petroleum as the primary energy source and to count on controllably affordable supplies from the Middle East—primarily the Persian Gulf littoral. When these decisions were made, there was a geographically limited level of demand, and the supplies were controlled by western interests whose purpose was to keep the oil flowing at favorable prices. Subsequent events—the expansion of markets for petroleum and the nationalization of oil supplies—have changed that calculation.

The global oil situation is easy to describe, if not to manipulate. Currently, global production is at about 85 million barrels of petroleum per day, with at least fourteen countries producing 2 million barrels per day according to 2004 figures. This production figure is balanced by current demands for oil of approximately 83 million barrels per day, of which the United States consumes about 11 million barrels per day of imported oil. This makes the petroleum market "tight" because demand and supply are so close that even marginal change in either supply or demand can upset the balance. As Leonardo Maugeri points out, this has been the result of a twenty-year trend: "Between 1986 and 2005, the world's spare oil production (the amount produced beyond current demand) dropped from about 15 percent to between 2 and 3 percent of global demand." The result is clearly a seller's market, as witnessed by the rising costs of petroleum exemplified most dramatically by the cost of gasoline at the pump in the United States and elsewhere.

This problem could get considerably worse in the future, for two reasons. The first is increases in global demand. The chief sources of increased demand are China and India. According to *Infoplease* data, China currently produces about 3.62 million barrels per day but consumes 6.5 million, meaning it must import about 45 percent of its production. According to David Zwieg and Bi Jianhai, China "accounted for 31 percent of global growth in oil demand" in 2004. The Chinese government has adopted a policy of greatly expanded automobile production for Chinese citizens, meaning the demand for petroleum will continue to increase. The Indian example is slightly less dramatic but nonetheless significant: India currently imports about 1.5 million barrels per day, and even though Indian production is supposed to reach about 3 million barrels per day by 2010, it will continue to be an increasing importer as the country undergoes growing economic development and enters the world automobile market.

The other side of the problem is supply. With a spare production capacity of only 2 million barrels per day and fourteen separate countries producing at least that amount, there are multiple countries that could, by suspending production, drive supply and demand into a tailspin. This provides the producing countries with enormous leverage in their relations with the oil consumers, creating phenomena like the "petrolist" phenomenon identified by Friedman earlier and the rise in power and influence of exporting states like Russia as described in Chapter 5. In addition, it makes countries like the United States extraordinarily sensitive to those parts of the world where petroleum is in great supply and creates interests in those regions that would probably not otherwise exist (or at least not be as intense). As suggested in Chapter 10, American interests in Iraq might be quite different if that country did not sit in the middle of the largest confirmed oil reserves in the world.

Energy consumption is the single most reliable indicator of economic activity and prosperity, and as a result, continuing, secure access to needed sources of energy is a vital interest of all states, including the United States. A dependency on foreign sources of vital resources over which less than total control can be exercised thus affects national security—defined both in traditional terms (since modern military systems rely critically on petroleum products) and in terms of the economic aspects of what makes people safe and life commodious. Finding a solution to the continuing problem that petroleum access represents thus is a critical matter of *energy* security, since petroleum energy is the largest source of energy production for many purposes (notably transportation).

Solutions to the petroleum energy problem can be thought of as discrete—how does the country guarantee the continuing flow of economical petroleum in adequate supply?—or as a supply-side problem. This approach to the problem is the easiest to couch in traditional security terms, because it falls within the geopolitical paradigm of threats to security for which military solutions seem applicable. Thus, one way to solve the problem of Middle East petroleum is to have a military presence in the region that can assure physically that the oil continues to flow. That paradigm has arguably been dominant since President Jimmy Carter issued the so-called Carter Doctrine as part of his 1980 State of the Union address, declaring that continuing access to Persian Gulf oil was a vital American interest. American leadership in the Persian Gulf War effort to expel Iraq from Kuwait, the continued presence of American military forces in the region after 1991, and the Iraq War can all be thought of as actions consistent with that approach.

The second way to look at the issue is as part of a broader energy policy, an orientation that brings both elements of supply and demand into the equation. Framing the question in the broader context of energy policy broadens the concern and moves it beyond the more conventional bounds of national security consideration because unlike petroleum, other alternatives sources of energy are neither controlled overseas (solar or wind energy, for instance) nor subject to determination on national security grounds (whether the country invests in additional nuclear plants to produce electricity, for instance, is not at heart a national security issue).

Subsuming the petroleum security question as part of energy policy opens additional strategic alternatives from both the supply and the demand sides of the energy equation. From the supply side, for instance, overall energy policy can view alternatives to imported petroleum as solutions to needs currently serviced by imported oil. These can include alternate sources of petroleum such as recovering hard-to-access petroleum in historical American oil fields, opening new domestic sources (the Alaskan wildlife reserves, for instance), tapping alternate sources of petroleum-based energy (Western oil shale or Canadian tar pits, for example), or developing entirely different sources of fuel (corn-based ethanol). There are arguments, based largely in resource adequacy or cost, to each of these alternatives, but they are at least potential ways to reduce foreign petroleum dependency and the additional costs (e.g., military actions) that current policy entails. A supply-side approach also looks at alternative sources of energy, from wind power to thermal energy to "clean" coal alternatives to nuclear power as strategic alternatives. All are aimed at reducing dependency on foreign oil and the baggage such dependency carries; all of them are also nontraditional approaches to a national security problem.

The other side is demand, and the key element in these approaches is conservation of energy. Clearly, for instance, if the United States burned less gasoline (or fuel oil), there would be the need for less imported petroleum. Reductions can be achieved by switching to alternate ways to power automobiles—electricity or ethanol, for instance—or by demanding higher efficiency in existing or new automobiles—increases in the Corporate Average Fuel economy (CAF) ratings—as has been proposed and recently updated and made more rigorous by the federal government.

This whole area evokes strong emotions when the question is expanded beyond petroleum to encompass broader energy policy, and especially when continued petroleum dependency is viewed as a *cause* of national security problems. The current Middle Eastern, including Iraqi, situation offers the clearest example. One can argue that the United States would have no reason for a major presence in or commitment to the Persian Gulf region in the absence of a need for secure access to the petroleum it contains. What would American policy in the region look like if the United States did not need *any* oil from there? From that assessment, it can further be argued that an obvious way to get the United States out of the harm's way that a visible presence in that volatile region entails would be to reduce, and preferably eliminate, that dependence, since it would remove the need particularly for a military role in regional politics. A chance for the reader to assess his or her feelings about this controversy is contained in the *Challenge!* Oil and Terror.

Water Security

Energy security has a direct and obvious impact on the United States that the question of water security at least currently lacks. It is, however, a pressing concern in at least one part of the world in which the United States is clearly entwined—once again, the Middle East. In that basically arid part of the world, water is in insufficient supply for current consumption in some areas both because the region is arid

Challenge!

OIL AND TERROR

There is an "urban legend" (a story said to be true but arguably not based in fact) that a group of Americans, armed with bumper stickers that say "I support Al Qaeda: Let Me Show You How," goes through Eastern urban areas placing those stickers on large, fuel-inefficient vehicles (e.g., Hummers, other large sport utility vehicles). The message is intended to assert two things. First, it argues that terrorist groups do receive part of their funding indirectly from gasoline purchases in the United States. Thus, the United States buys oil from Saudi Arabia, some of that revenue ends up in the hands of private Saudi citizens, and some of them make contributions to Al Qaeda (no one seriously disputes that this happens at some level). Second, it asserts that people who drive fuel-inefficient vehicles disproportionately contribute to the problem because they end up spending more on gasoline that trickles back in larger amounts to fund Al Qaeda than do those who drive less-gas-guzzling models. Thus, driving such a vehicle can be argued to provide more indirect support to Al Qaeda than driving a vehicle that gets higher gas mileage. Taken to its extreme, one can even argue that it is more patriotic to drive a gas "sipper" than a gas "guzzler" if patriotism and refusal to provide support—however indirect—for terrorism are equated.

What do you think of this argument? Does it reflect a deeper relationship between energy security and the larger issue of national security?

and because what water there is tends to be unevenly distributed. Water is in short supply in most of the region, and the problem is getting worse because the area has a growing population that will place even greater demands on the water supply in the future. This same dynamic can be projected in the future to other parts of the world; China is a particularly vexing prospect.

Water shortages are different than supplies of petroleum, in several ways. First, the problem of oil is not an inadequacy of supply (although that will become a problem sometime in the future) but a matter of distribution and availability at acceptable cost. The supply of water is a matter of finite amounts of the commodity where it is needed, and there are generally no feasible alternative sources of supply (a matter touched on below). Second, demands for water are inelastic in economic terms: the level of demand is based on what is required for human survival wherever scarcity occurs, and that demand cannot be greatly manipulated. Conservation is not as available a strategy as it is with petroleum, although it may be a partial solution in some cases (as the Turks argue with regard to the Tigris–Euphrates system). Third, there are no alternatives sources of potable water as there are with energy. The only alternatives to unpolluted fresh (potable) water are salt water and polluted fresh water, and these are only very limited alternatives. Salt water from the world's oceans and seas is certainly abundant, but economically viable methods of desalination have not been found despite decades of concerted effort; removing pollutants from otherwise potable water only solves a small part of the problem in selected areas that are least threatened by water shortages (e.g., part of formerly Communist Europe). Fourth, there are no means to import enough water from water-rich to water-deficient areas for that to be a remedy despite very inventive proposals (e.g., using boats to drag icebergs from the Arctic area to the Middle East).

The vitality and inelasticity of potable water supplies make access to water a particularly powerful source of conflict where scarcities are present. The two most obvious examples are in the Middle East and center around the two major river systems in that area (see Snow, *Cases in International Relations*, Chapter 14, for an overview). One involves the Tigris–Euphrates system that rises in Turkey and flows through Syria and Iraq (the Euphrates River) and directly into Iraq (the Tigris River) before joining and forming the Shatt al-Arab and flowing into the Persian Gulf. Both Syria and Iraq are water-deficient and rely on water from the system for survival; Turkey is water-independent, although it uses water from the system to assist development in its eastern, poor, and rebellious Kurdish region (notably the Greater Anatolia Project, GAP). Because it controls the headwaters of the rivers, Turkey also controls the flow of water to the downstream riparian countries, who demand that more of the water be released for their use. The Turks claim that they do allow adequate supplies to flow but that the Syrians and Iraqis waste water by using inefficient irrigation methods (letting water move through open trenches so that much of it evaporates) or by growing crops that require an excessive amount of water (cotton, for instance). Turkey has overwhelming leverage in this situation, both because the rivers begin within its territory and because Syria and Iraq lack the military or other power to compel Turkey to provide them with additional supplies.

The other dispute is over the water from the Jordan River, which flows out of the Sea of Galilee and is a major source of water for Syria, Lebanon, Jordan, and Israel. It becomes a matter of strategic concern depending on what country controls the headwaters of the river where it leaves the Sea of Galilee and begins its southward journey. The eastern bank of the river runs along the Golan Heights, a strategic part of the Israeli-Syrian border that was seized by Israel during the Six Days War of 1967. One reason that occupied territory has not been returned to Syria is that it historically provided high ground (the heights are low mountains) from which Syria launched artillery attacks on northern Israel; the other reason is that the Israelis fear that if Syria controlled the region, it might find a way to deprive Israel of Jordan River water on which the country depends.

These disputes fall generally below the international radar of major conflict problems, but that does not mean they can be ignored, for at least two reasons. One is that these particular problems are only going to get worse, due to skyrocketing population growth rates in the Middle East that can only make a serious problem critical. Once (or if) normalcy is reinstated in Iraq, for instance, the water question must be addressed; Turkey knows it holds all the cards in discussions, making negotiations difficult and conflict potential great.

The other reason is that these same kinds of problems may be visited in other parts of the world that are more significant in an immediate, geopolitical sense. The most obvious case is China where, according to a recent article by Elizabeth Economy in *Foreign Affairs*, "skyrocketing demand, overuse, inefficiencies, pollution, and uneven distribution have produced a situation in which two-thirds of China's approximately 660 cities have less water than they need and 110 of them suffer from severe shortages." This situation, part of a broader environmental crisis that China faces, has strong implications for the future of Chinese economic productivity, upon which the United States is heavily dependent in the consumer products sector.

These examples of water scarcity, particular when combined with the problem of petroleum energy security, demonstrate how resource scarcities are or can become an American security issue. The case of petroleum access is direct and compelling: as long as the United States is dependent on foreign sources of petroleum to fuel its economy, the prospect of petroleum scarcity (however immediate or distant) will require an American effort to ensure that petroleum access is continual and that interruptions can be avoided or corrected. In the immediate case, this means the United States will almost certainly have to maintain a physical, including military, presence in the Persian Gulf region for the foreseeable future despite its predilections to the contrary.

The water scarcity problem is more indirect, but each of the three instances cited demonstrates it cannot be ignored altogether. Regardless of how the United States finally extricates itself from Iraq, it will retain a residual interest in the condition of that country; to the extent the dispute over the Tigris–Euphrates system affects Iraq's future, it will represent an American concern as well. The United States' close relations with Israel and the American commitment to Israel's survival (at least an implicit pillar of American foreign policy) mean that the United States shares with the Israelis an interest in continued Israeli access to and control over water from the Jordan River basin. The economic interdependence of the United States and China creates an interest in assuring conditions in China that, in turn, assure the continuation of mutually beneficial economic relations and that do not force the Chinese to look outward—in a possibly antagonistic way—for alternative water sources. In combination, petroleum and water demonstrate the direct and indirect ways in which resource security affects the United States.

ENVIRONMENTAL SECURITY

The question about what aspects of the physical environment contribute to safety or a sense of safety is more abstract than either border or natural resource security and is thus more difficult to conceptualize within the normal structure of national security thinking. Partly, the reason is that the threat is more indirect: by and large, environmental catastrophes that could endanger people are either far into the future (projections about global warming, for instance) or the result of natural phenomena such as hurricanes or tornadoes over which there is little control. Environmental dangers lack immediacy, controllability, or both (who can know for sure, for instance, when the widely predicted massive earthquake will hit southern California?). Although environmentalists argue that many of the environmental threats faced by mankind are the result of human actions that are either creating future hazards or making them worse (global warming and the intensity of weather changes, for example), these are not clearly purposive acts of malevolent others that can be identified and their actions somehow stifled or reversed in the way that a physical invasion can be repulsed or terrorists frustrated or brought to justice. Moreover, environmental issues are not easy to specify in traditional national security terms—specifying who or what poses a physical *threat*, for instance—and their solutions are not within the obvious realm of traditional national security solutions.

Yet the term *environmental security* has entered the lexicon of applications of the term *security*, and the question is whether the designation is legitimate or whether it is more akin to the overextension and overuse of the term *war* to describe efforts aimed at phenomena as diverse as poverty, drugs, and terrorism. Environmental security is not a subject covered in most traditional treatments of national security and has indeed not been included in previous editions of this book. So why add environmental security to the present endeavor?

Beyond the attempt to broaden horizons about what constitutes security, two reasons will be suggested here. The first is that environmental factors, including those that may have consequences in a more-or-less nebulous future, do indeed have direct implications for the safety and well-being of people. If, for instance, the consequences of global warming are anything like those predicted by environmental scientists, they will have a major impact on the commodiousness and conditions of life for future generations, and thus actions or inactions today will make future generations more or less secure. The second is that some of these impacts are already present, and although it has not been customary to think about them in national security terms, it might be helpful to do so. The clear and compelling example in this regard is the impact of Hurricane Katrina.

To explore the notion of environmental security, two examples just suggested will be explored. The first is the question of global warming, a topic that is widely discussed and debated but rarely as a security issue. The second is Hurricane Katrina as an emblem for the kinds of threats to safety and security caused by natural disasters and as a symbol around which to explore whether it would be helpful to think of such occurrences and responses to them in security policy terms. Neither example is explored in substantive depth, which goes well beyond present purposes. The point of raising them is to explore whether it is helpful to think of either as a security problem.

Global Warming

Few issues in the contemporary political scene evoke as much emotion and disagreement as does global warming. The emotions tend to center around the severe consequences of unchecked carbon dioxide release (the source of most global warming along with several other gases like methane) for the environment.

If the trends projected by that part of the scientific community issuing warnings about global warming are (or will prove to be) true, the results could be cataclysmic across a range of environmental concerns. The disagreement centers on the accuracy of these projected dynamics. Although the vast majority of scientists who have studied the problem of global warming concur generally in issuing strong, even dire, warnings about the failure to curb the practices leading to global warming, a politically well-connected minority of scientists and others question the scientific bases of these dire projections and the policy implications that follow from those predictions. The disagreements are difficult to overcome because almost all the phenomena in question and all the predictions are in the future and thus not subject to current scientific observation and validation. The debate also tends to remain abstract and at the peripheries of the political debate because most people are not *currently* experiencing consequences that they attribute to global warming and thus demanding reform.

To make matters more politically difficult, proposed remedies for global warming center on potentially vast reductions in carbon dioxide emissions. The overwhelming majority of the carbon dioxide excess (that amount above the ability of the environment naturally to absorb and dissipate) comes from the burning of fossil fuels that provide most of the energy used for transportation and industry in the world. Thus, conservation efforts intended to reduce carbon dioxide emissions are aimed at practices that are at the heart of the productivity of societies. More perversely, if all members of the international system do not participate equitably in reducing these emissions, those who do not potentially can gain economic and possibly other advantages because their industrial and transportation bases are not tethered by environmental restrictions. This fear is most often expressed with regard to China, which, as Economy points out, is fast becoming one of the world's leading carbon polluters and is a major part of the Bush administration's objections to the Kyoto Protocols of 1997, which aim at carbon dioxide reductions but exclude China from reduction quotas (the United States is the only major industrialized country in the world that is not party to this international agreement, a position examined in Amplification 14.2: The United States and Kyoto).

Is global warming, as the leading emblem of worldwide environmental concerns, a legitimate national security issue that should be considered along with other, more conventional national security matters? With no claim to inclusiveness or exhaustiveness, three perspectives can be examined to help formulate the answer.

One way to think about the question is in terms of *threat*, since that is the normal framework within which national security is measured. Does global warming threaten Americans (or citizens of the world in general)? Answering that question is complicated, because the question is too simply put. Part of the answer is a matter of timing: global warming may pose some disquieting and inconveniencing short-term consequences (hotter summers, prolonged drought or rain-producing seasons, more violent weather generally), but it does not pose direct threats that people associate with the phenomenon. In the aftermath of unsettled weather that results in tornadoes ripping through the countryside, victims do not, after all, say, "If we had burned less gasoline in our cars, this tornado would not have happened." The longer-range consequence—the permanent flooding of low-lying coastal areas, making them uninhabitable—certainly affects the security of people who either live or want to live in those areas, but this consequence has not been experienced and lies

Amplification 14.2

THE UNITED STATES AND KYOTO

As noted, the United States is the major nonmember of the Kyoto Protocols of 1997 among major industrialized countries. The Clinton administration had negotiated participation but had not submitted the treaty to the U.S. Senate for ratification. On March 13, 2001, the Bush administration announced that it did not favor the treaty and would not transmit it to the Senate, thereby killing American participation.

The Bush administration stated two bases for its rejection of Kyoto. The first was that the United States would have to bear an unfair burden in implanting its provisions, since the United States was deemed the greatest contributor to greenhouse gas emissions (about 25 percent of all affected gases and 36 percent of carbon dioxide emissions worldwide) and would thus have to cut the most. Since compliance would require reduced fossil fuel burning beyond similar restrictions on other countries, the administration argued participation would harm the American economy disproportionately and unfairly. Second, the Kyoto Protocols excluded developing countries that had hitherto not made sizable contributions to the problem from its provisions, even if those countries were or were projected to become polluters in the future. As noted, the chief culprit was China, with India as a potential troublemaker as well.

These American objections, which have been rejected by most of the participating members, mean that implementation is less effective, since over one-third of the emissions are not regulated by the treaty's provisions. Fred Krupp, executive director of Environmental Defense, a private advocacy group, summarizes the concern: "It is bad for America's interests for the United States to be seen as a rogue nation of greenhouse gas pollution. By simply opposing the Kyoto Protocol, rather than seeking to improve it, the administration would have effectively blocked the only binding international agreement for fighting global warming, while offering no alternative path to protect the planet." American agreement in late 2007 to participate in follow-on efforts beyond Kyoto was expressed at the Bali, Indonesia summit and may ameliorate some international dissent.

somewhere in the future. Thought of in threat terms, global warming poses more of a *potential* than an immediate threat. (Global warming scientists would, of course, argue the consequences of that assessment, which can lead to inaction, making the long-term consequences worse than they would be if action were taken now.)

The security *consequences* of global warming are more difficult to specify, and thus it is more difficult to know who to punish or how to punish them. It is, for instance, very hard to specify how people will suffer specifically because of the consequences of global warming and, most importantly, to *personalize* the quality and nature of that future suffering in a way that motivates current actions that involve personal and societal sacrifice. If one could demonstrate that reducing the weight of automobiles by a certain number of hundreds of pounds would result in fuel savings (and consequent carbon dioxide emissions) that would mean that ocean levels would rise a concomitant number of feet less than without that reduction in automobile weight and thus not inundate a predictable amount of coastline (preferably including a part on which people live) within the lifetime of those people, the plea might be quite effective. It is not possible responsibly to issue such a threat, and thus the question of consequences tends to become more abstract and, as a result, less actionable.

If one moves the question to *solutions* to global warming, the issue becomes both more contentious and more directly security-oriented. All solutions to global warming hinge on carbon dioxide reduction, which, in turn, includes less burning of fossil fuels (principally petroleum). Such entreaties activate opposition to global warming solutions on traditional national security grounds: reduced energy production and its impact on economic productivity; the enormous dependency of modern military forces on petroleum for operational purposes; and the strategic leverage of petroleum possessors over those with dependencies, for instance. The impact is to bifurcate the argument into an either/or proposition: one can support traditional security *or* remedies to global warming, but since their consequences are incompatible (at least in the short run), one cannot support both.

The question remains, Is global warming a national security problem? (Alternatively, is it a national problem that can usefully be considered within the framework of national security?) The answer is not unambiguous. On one hand, categorizing global warming in these terms elevates its visibility and the extent to which it is taken seriously within the political process: the designation of national security, for better or worse, endows an issue with greater gravity in some circles than it possesses without it. Since those who are most interested in the global warming issue tend not to be participants in the traditional national security process, categorizing global warming as a national security issue probably raises its prominence and certainly broadens its audience. At the same time, inclusion of global warming on the broader national security agenda can result in dilution of its consideration (global warming as one of many problems) or contrary arguments not directly relevant to the issue (global warming is important, but other concerns like economic disadvantages are more important). The audience may broaden, but it will include more hostile voices.

Hurricane Katrina

Where does one place natural disasters within the priorities of national security? Clearly, the effects of natural disasters affect the security of those subject to them and are thus important national concerns. Formal federal jurisdiction over such incidents resides with the Federal Emergency Management Agency (FEMA), created by President Carter in 1979, and implementation of the Homeland Security Act of 2002 placed FEMA under the auspices (however reluctantly) of the new Department of Homeland Security (DHS), thus implicitly according it national security status. The federal response to Hurricanes Katrina and Rita, however, raised serious concern about the actual priority assigned to this function, and the unavailability of

National Guard units to aid in recovery efforts from subsequent natural disasters (because the units are on active duty in Iraq) has only added to this concern.

The ongoing response (or lack thereof) to Hurricane Katrina by the federal government has become something of an emblem for those critical of federal priorities. In terms of human devastation, for instance, official statistics indicate that as of August 2006, 1,464 people lost their lives as a result of the impact of Katrina on New Orleans and the Gulf Coast (in parts of Louisiana and Mississippi, and to a lesser extent Alabama), nearly half the number of people who lost their lives in the September 11 attacks. Much rhetoric has surrounded federal efforts to respond to the human and physical suffering that centered on New Orleans, but over two years later there were still large parts of the city (notably the Ninth Ward) that remained uninhabited and uninhabitable. Emergency supplemental funding for the area has been slow to get to the places where it is most needed, and the inevitable question of what priority disaster relief has in fact is routinely raised.

Should responses to natural disasters like Katrina be part of the national security equation? If so, where should they be placed in the hierarchy of national security concerns? Is, for instance, planning for and funding programs against the possibility of a major earthquake in southern California more or less important than continuing funding for the military effort in Iraq or funding for a missile defense system in Europe? Or are these areas of concern so unrelated that they cannot and should not fall under the same umbrella of consideration?

As noted, the federal government has implicitly elevated environmental disaster response to a national security concern by placing FEMA under the DHS, thereby making it difficult for the government to argue disaster relief is *not* part of national security, and the states concur in this judgment by making National Guard contingents under their control among the prominent first responders to national disasters within their jurisdictions. Yet National Guard units have been assigned to extended (and repeated) deployments to Iraq without apparent detailed regard to the effects of their absence from the resources available to deal with natural disasters, and FEMA resources originally intended for natural disaster relief have been diverted to priorities arising from the GWOT (some of the first responses to terrorist attacks resemble similar responses to natural disasters).

Would the response to Hurricane Katrina have been different if it had been considered a threat to national security rather than a response to a horrific but naturally caused disaster? Unlike global warming, it is difficult to assign human blame for the occurrence of Katrina. (An argument can be made that global warming has resulted in higher water temperatures in the Gulf of Mexico, making the hurricane *worse* than it would otherwise have been, but that effect is marginal.) The fact that there was no identifiable human enemy who caused Katrina did not make its effects any less severe to those who suffered them, yet patterns of response were noticeably slower and less intense (and certainly less effective) than they might have been had the event been viewed as a traditional national security disaster.

Where should priorities lie in the future? If the global warming theorists are substantially correct in their projections, one of the major impacts of continued neglect of global warming will be an intensification of weather patterns, including the severity of storms and their impact. If they are correct, Hurricane Katrina may only be the harbinger of things to come. At the same time, seismologists and other geologists maintain that a major shift in the Earth's crust is inevitable in southern California in the upcoming years. Depending on exactly how the resulting earthquake is centered and directed (at the Los Angeles basin or southward toward Mexico), the resulting devastation could make Hurricane Katrina or September 11 pale in terms of human and property losses. Is that a matter of high national priority on a plane with threats in the Middle East or elsewhere? Should these possibilities be thought of separately or together? What national priorities should attach to each prospect, and should they compete for national security resources? The answers are not simple, straightforward, or necessarily obvious.

HEALTH/DISEASE SECURITY

In 2000, the Clinton administration declared the acquired immuno deficiency syndrome (AIDS) pandemic in Africa a national security priority for the United States. The basis for this assertion was that AIDS was effectively decimating the African continent of a generation of young men and women who will not be available to assume leadership positions in their countries in the future, with the consequences that many countries may become dangerously destabilized and thus troublesome and that one reaction may be a massive migration of people from Africa to Europe and North America, a problem discussed several years ago by Robert D. Kaplan. Hardly anyone paid attention.

In January 2001, a Congolese woman entered Canada on a commercial airplane. She was coughing uncontrollably during the flight, and after she had deplaned and disappeared, a concern was raised that she might be carrying the incredibly deadly hemorrhagic Ebola virus, that she might have communicated the extremely contagious disease to other passengers in the enclosed (and almost ideal) incubating space of the flight, and that those passengers could further spread the disease (for which there is no known treatment) to others. When she was found, it turned out the woman was not infected, and the concern passed.

Is the threat of diseases a matter of national security concern? The recent pattern of outbreaks of diseases with the potential to spread misery and death broadly among populations (AIDS, Ebola, sudden acute respiratory syndrome, and avian flu, for instance) have raised the national consciousness on such matters, and there are historical precedents as well. The "black death" of bubonic plague raged through Europe in the 1300s and claimed nearly one-fourth of the population as victims. At the end of World War I, American forces returning to the United States were exposed to the so-called Spanish flu (so named because the first cases were observed in Spain), and the result was an epidemic in which 675,000 (out of 105 million) Americans died. Are there similar prospects in the future, and what can or should be done about them?

There are two ways to think about the dangers of disease as a national security matter. One is to think about the possible spread of diseases that originate elsewhere to the United States, where Americans could be infected and suffer or die. In the past several years, there have been numerous warnings about this possibility, normally associated with some form of influenza. The most recent threats came with the outbreak in China in February 2003 of sudden acute respiratory syndrome (SARS), which killed 8,098 people worldwide before it was declared eradicated in 2005 by the World Health Organization, and the avian or bird flu (technically H5N1 avian flu), which appeared in various parts of Asia in 2005. In both cases, the U.S. federal government issued warnings about the possibility the diseases could spread to the United States, and the Centers for Disease Control issued guidelines about the diseases but admitted that vaccines against them were either nonexistent or available in grossly inadequate supply. Like the Canadian Ebola incident, these dangers have not materialized, but that does not mean there are not others (particularly virulent and drug-resistant strains of tuberculosis, for instance) that will emerge as real threats on the scale of the Spanish flu (with today's population, about 2 million deaths) or even greater. One tantalizingly dire possibility comes from global warming scientists. Many of the most dangerous diseases come from the world's subtropical climates, and as global warming occurs, temperatures will rise enough that some of them can spread to places that formerly were too cold for them to survive and in which the populations have not evolved immunities to them.

The second problem is the impact the existence or spread of diseases can have on other parts of the world. The most obvious case in point, as suggested in the introduction to this section, surrounds the impact of AIDS. The most obvious and devastating effects have been and continue to grow in Africa and have been the subject of at least a handful of recent analyses (De Waal, Iliffe, and Patterson, for instance). Beyond the human tragedy associated with the loss of literally millions of victims, the shortening of life expectancies below forty years of age in several countries, and the prospects of continued ravages from more and more deaths, there are enormous geopolitical consequences that are only moderated for the most developed countries by the marginalization of Africa generally in world politics.

The AIDS problem is not, however, entirely isolated to Africa. Indeed, in recent years there have been reports of increased infection rates in China and India, to cite the most prominent cases. While neither country wants widely to publicize these outbreaks or their frequency (in some cases because they do not know, because they tend to occur in rural, outlying regions), a health crisis arising from an epidemic or pandemic could be severely taxing to the health systems of these two aspirants to major-power status and could form another layer of obstacles to a country like China that is already struggling with an environmental crisis, as noted earlier.

Protecting the public health is an obviously major obligation of the government, and protecting the populace from the intrusion of disease seeping across the country's borders is arguably a priority on a par with preventing other forms of alien invasion of American soil. In this sense, one can easily think of health and disease security as a form of national security, although one for which traditional national security instruments and strategies are inappropriate or irrelevant. Yet in times other than apparent or potential crisis like the avian flu potential epidemic, there is little concerted public attention to these matters parallel, for instance, to the emphasis on terrorism or illegal immigration. Why not?

There are, of course, numerous possible explanations for this lack emphasis, and three have been borrowed from the author's *Cases in International Relations* (Chapter 15) for mention. The first is the *seriousness and immediacy of the problem.* Despite the potential for catastrophic consequences from an outbreak of a hemorrhagic disease like Ebola in a large, metropolitan area or the spread of AIDS in the 1980s in this country, there have not been actual cases of a major disease-related national emergency since the Spanish flu nearly ninety years ago, and as a result, the prospects remain at a lower level of consciousness and thus demand for action than for more conventional threats. Having said that, the consequences of a disease for which there is no known cure or the supplies of curative medicines are in very short supply (and would thus have to be rationed) absolutely dwarf the consequences of the largest terrorist attack in human history (the September 11 attacks). It is sometimes suggested that terrorists might seek to attack the United States with pathogens in ways similar to alleged provision of smallpox-infected blankets to American Indians during the 1800s: would some credible evidence of such an intent raise awareness and concern?

The second problem is *lack of personalization* of the problems. The African pandemic is, after all, thousands of miles away, and even attempts to publicize it by people like former Secretary of State Colin Powell and countless entertainers do not drive home the suffering that occurs where diseases like AIDS wrack the human condition. President George W. Bush announced what he called a major initiative in his 2003 State of the Union address to help alleviate African AIDS through the President's Emergency Plan for AIDS Relief but it has languished at least in part because the general public has not demanded implementation in the face of other priorities. Will it require thousands of Americans dying hideous deaths from some incurable disease to make these problems seem real enough to attract concerted attention?

The third problem stems from the first two: *low prioritization of the problem.* There are, after all, no shortage of demands upon national resources and energies, and not all of them can have an equally high priority. That, after all, is the nature of risk management: to choose those areas where one will move to reduce and eliminate risk and, either by specific action or implicitly, to ignore others and accept whatever risk that ignorance entails. The calculation of those concerns to receive higher or lower priority depends on the immediacy and consequences of inattention: which matters *must* be dealt with, and which can be deferred? To date, dealing with the prospects of major diseases intruding on the United States has not been assigned a particularly high priority in the scheme of security concerns. As long as there is no national crisis arising from the outbreak of some deadly disease, the decision remains a viable one. But what if a new and deadly disease suddenly appears and the country is unprepared for it? Will national security be served?

CONCLUSION: EXPANDED SECURITY HORIZONS

The end of the Iraq War will, among other things, release some of the resources and energies that have been devoted to that endeavor for other purposes. It will probably not bring a "peace dividend" like that unfulfilled promise of the end of the Cold War (where it was predicted that resources previously spent on the military competition with the Soviets could be redirected to other priorities). The reason is that the war has been conducted almost entirely "off budget" (through supplemental appropriations) that will simply disappear after that spending ends, with no visible impact on the shape or priorities of the federal budget. Moreover, since most of these supplemental budgets have been financed through borrowing—particularly from foreign sources—the major effect will be that the country will decrease its rate of indebtedness to places like China. The expenditures are not inconsequential: the Bush administration had, by late August 2007, requested nearly $200 billion in supplemental appropriations for the upcoming 2008 fiscal year. These will never appear as part of the federal budget, and so their removal will reduce neither the budget nor the deficit the appropriations represent. If anything, there will be budgetary demands for additional funds to rebuild the armed forces to alleviate their depletion in Iraq. There will not be any noticeable amount of resources "freed up" for alternate spending.

There will, however, be the release of some intellectual energy, both inside and outside of government. The central argument of this book has been that a post-Iraq United States will turn its attention to concerns in addition to those national security problems for which military force is a solution, because there will be a reluctance—at least for a time—to employ military force to solve national problems. Periodic saber rattling by the Bush administration toward Iran demonstrates that the use of the military will be proposed, but in its current and post-Iraq condition, it is difficult to imagine how the United States could or why it would engage in another large-scale deployment of choice for the next few years.

Rather, militarized or semimilitarized efforts will likely be concentrated on the problem of terrorism, possibly conceptualized as something other than the GWOT. Government agencies not completely submerged in the terrorism campaign (the State Department, for instance) and analysts outside government will turn to other concerns that have been on the conceptual back burner since 2003, and these concerns will include the issues raised in this chapter and in Chapter 6.

Will these kinds of issues become a permanent part of the national security agenda? There is reason to believe both that they will and that they will not. Certainly, the kinds of problems discussed are likely to be enduring: global warming, natural disasters, infectious disease epidemics, petroleum dependency, and the control of the country's borders are long-term problems that will not disappear in the short or mid-term, and emphasizing them is a way to move the spotlight away from the military as it heals itself from the Iraq experience. At the same time, there will be resistance to thinking about these issues in national security terms. To some traditionalists steeped in the equation of security and military affairs, these nontraditional issues are "soft" in a geopolitical sense, important in their own right but not on a par with the military threats to national existence. Elevating environmental security, as an example, to national security status thus diverts and dilutes attention to what is truly important. At the same time, those people most concerned with the kinds of nontraditional issues discussed here are generally not sympathetic to more traditional, militarily oriented analysts (and vice versa), and it will take more than a little time and energy to bring both groups to the same conceptual page.

The brunt of the analysis in this volume has been that the Iraq War has, like the Vietnam War before it, had a traumatic effect on thinking and especially acting in the national security arena. The Vietnam hangover (the reaction to the war and its ending) sublimated active concern with national security matters for the bulk of the 1970s, as Americans were repulsed by Vietnam and did not want to consider national security matters until Ronald Reagan convinced them otherwise in the 1980 election. Will the Iraq hangover predicted in these pages be as great and encompassing as the reaction to Vietnam? From the vantage point of 2008, it is impossible to predict that impact with any confidence, but that the process of change in thinking about national security in a new era has been unleashed is close to a certainty.

STUDY/DISCUSSION QUESTIONS

1. Why does the text maintain that nontraditional security concerns could become more prominent in the next five to ten years? Do you agree?
2. Define the border security problem in historical perspective. Why has maintaining a secure border been simultaneously so difficult and of such low priority historically for the United States?
3. Define the various aspects of the country's current border security problem. Briefly describe each aspect and the extent to which it is or is not a national security problem. Is an impenetrable border a feasible or desirable goal (or both, or neither)?
4. Why is resource dependency a national security problem? Using petroleum as an example, define what problem that dependency creates for the United States, what the consequences of that dependency are, and what can be done about the problem.
5. Why is the availability of adequate potable water a national problem or potential national problem for some states? Use examples.
6. Define environmental security. Is it legitimate and/or helpful to think of environmental concerns like global warming and natural disasters like Hurricane Katrina in national security terms? Why or why not?
7. What kind of threat does the prospect of the intrusion of deadly diseases present to Americans? Should it be thought of as a national security problem? If not, what kind of problem is it?
8. Should the national security agenda of the United States in a post-Iraq environment be expanded to include nontraditional concerns like those discussed in the text? Why or why not?

SELECTED BIBLIOGRAPHY

Andeas, Peter. "Politics on Edge: Managing the U.S.–Mexico Border." *Current History* 105, 695 (February 2006), 64–68.

Anderson, Terry, and Harry I. Miller (eds.). *The Greening of U.S. Foreign Policy.* Stanford, CA: Hoover Institution Press, 2000.

Bijian, Zheng. "China's 'Peaceful Rise' to Great-Power Status." *Foreign Affairs* 84, 5 (September/October 2005), 18–24.

Browne, John. "Beyond Kyoto." *Foreign Affairs* 83, 4 (July/August 2004), 20–32.

Cashell, Brian W., and Marc Labonte. "The Macroeconomic Effects of Hurricane Katrina." Washington, DC: Congressional Research Service, September 13, 2005.

Castaneda, Jorge G. "Latin America's Left Turn." *Foreign Affairs* 85, 3 (May/June 2006), 28–43.

Das, Gurcharan. "The Indian Model." *Foreign Affairs* 85, 4 (July/August 2006), 2–16.

De Waal, Alex. *AIDS and Power: Why There Is No Political Crisis—Yet*. Amsterdam, Netherlands: Zed Books, 2006.

Diehl, Paul R., and Niles Peter Gleditsch (eds.). *Environmental Conflict*. Boulder, CO: Westview Press, 2001.

"Ebola." (http://nyu.edu/educational/mindsinmotion/ebola/htm)

Economy, Elizabeth C. "The Great Leap Backward." *Foreign Affairs* 86, 5 (September/October 2007), 38–59.

Elhance, A. *Hydropolitics and the Third World: Conflict and Cooperation in International River Basins*. Washington, DC: United States Institute of Peace Press, 1999.

Flynn, Stephen E. *America the Vulnerable: How Our Government Is Failing to Protect Us from Terrorism*. New York: Harper Perennials, 2005.

Garrett, Laurie. "The Lessons of HIV/AIDS." *Foreign Affairs* 84, 4 (July/August 2005), 51–64.

———. "The Next Pandemic?" *Foreign Affairs* 84, 4 (July/August 2005), 3–23.

Iliffe, John. *The African AIDS Epidemic: A History*. Athens: Ohio University Press, 2006.

Kaplan, Robert D. *The Coming Anarchy: Shattering the Dreams of the Post Cold War*. New York: Random House, 2000.

Kim, Richard. "The People Versus AIDS." *The Nation* 283, 2 (July 10, 2006), 5–6.

Krauze, Enrique. "Furthering Democracy in Mexico." *Foreign Affairs* 85, 1 (January/February 2006), 54–65.

Luterbacher, Urs, and Detlef F. Sprinz (eds.). *International Relations and Global Climate Change*. Cambridge, MA: MIT Press, 2001.

Lynn-Jones, Sean, and Stephen Miller (eds.). *Global Dangers: Changing Dimensions of International Security*. Cambridge, MA: MIT Press, 1995.

Maugeri, Leonardo. "Two Cheers for Expensive Oil." *Foreign Affairs* 85, 2 (March/April 2006), 149–160.

Patterson, Amy S. *The Politics of AIDS in Africa*. Boulder, CO: Lynne Reinner, 2006.

Payan, Terry. *The Three U.S.–Mexico Border Wars: Drugs, Immigration, and Homeland Security*. Westport, CT: Greenwood, 2006.

Pirages, Dennis C., and Theresa Manley DeGeest. *Ecological Security: An Evolutionary Perspective on Globalization*. New York: Rowman and Littlefield, 2004.

Rockenbach, Leslie J. *The Mexican-American Border: NAFTA and Global Linkages*. Abington, Oxford, UK: Routledge, 2001.

Rozenthal, Andres. "The Other Side of Immigration." *Current History* 106, 697 (February 2007), 89–90.

Shifter, Michael. "Latin America's Drug Problem." *Current History* 106, 697 (February 2007), 58–63.

Snow, Donald M. *Cases in International Relations: Portraits of the Future* (3rd ed.). New York: Pearson Longman, 2008.

Victor, David G. *Climate Change: Debating America's Options*. New York: Council on Foreign Relations, 2004.

Wirth, Timothy. "Hot Air over Kyoto: The United States and the Politics of Global Warming." *Harvard International Review* 23, 4 (2002), 72–77.

Yergin, Daniel. "Ensuring Energy Security." *Foreign Affairs* 85, 2 (March/April 2006), 69–82.

Zweig, David, and Bi Jianhai. "China's Global Hunt for Energy." *Foreign Affairs* 84, 5 (September/October 2005), 18–24.

Index

North Korea, 6, 22
    axis of evil designation, 34, 57,
        239, 241
    Nuclear Non-Proliferation Treaty
        (NPT), 175
    nuclear program, 175–76
Nuclear forces
    deterrence theories
        assured destruction, 231–32
        countervalue targeting, 232
        limited nuclear options
            (LNOs), 231, 232–33
        Single Integrated Operational
            Plan (SIOP), 233
    missile defenses
        Anti-Ballistic Missile (ABM)
            Treaty, 240–41
        appeal, 239–40
        China, 239
        cost, 240
        national missile defense
            (NMD) plan, 238–41
        Strategic Defense Initiative
            (SDI), 238
        workability, 240
    nuclear (horizontal) proliferation
        acquisition deterrence, 236
        China, 235
        employment deterrence, 236
        India and Pakistan, 235
        Iran, 235
        nonstate groups, 236–37, 238
        North Korea, 235
        nuclear weapon states, listed,
            235
    nuclear seminal events
        atomic (fission) bombs, 229
        ballistic missile defense
            (BMD), 231
        first atomic bomb, explosion
            of, 228–28
        hydrogen (fission-fusion)
            bombs, 229–30
        intercontinental ballistic missile
            (ICBM), 230, 231, 232, 233
        Manhattan Project, 228
        multiple independently tar-
            getable reentry vehicle
            (MIRV), 230
Nuclear Non-Proliferation Treaty
    (NPT), 175
Nuclear weapons, 103, 105, 113,
    114. See also Cold War, mili-
    tary competition
Nunn, Sam, 209
Nye, Joseph S., Jr., 37, 38

O

Office of Strategic Services (OSS),
    195
Office of the Coordinator for Secu-
    rity, Infrastructure Protection,
    and Counterterrorism, 215
Oil
    alternate sources of energy, 81, 154
    Caspian Sea pipeline, 154

dependence on foreign, 80, 81
exploration and opening up new
    reserves, 81
from Middle East, reliance on,
    80, 139
North Sea oil fields, 140
scarcity, 154
Oklahoma City bombing, 2, 336
On War (van Clausewitz), 84
Operation Desert Fox (1999), 66, 260
Operation Iraqi Freedom, 304
Operation Restore Democracy, 354
Operations Northern and Southern
    Watch, 66
Oppenheimer, Robert, 228
Organization of Petroleum Export-
    ing Countries (OPEC), 139
Organization of Security and Coop-
    eration in Europe (OSCE),
    376
Ottoman Turks, 78

P

Pakistan, 123, 125, 339, 341
PATRIOT (Provide Appropriate
    Tools Required to Intercept
    and Obstruct Terrorists)
    Act of 2001, 82, 222, 223
Patton, George S., 86
Peace enforcement, 354
Peace imposition, 354
Peacekeeping operations, 98, 353,
    354, 366–70
    talk-shoot relationship in, 369
Pearl Harbor, attack on, 20, 30, 43,
    50, 88
Perestroika, 119–20
Perestroika: New Thinking for Our
    Country and the World
    (Gorbachev), 120
Perle, Richard, 260
Persian Gulf War 1990–1991,
    57–58, 79, 93, 112, 281
Peters, Ralph, 358
Petroleum energy security, 392–95
Petropolitics, 126
Philippines, 79, 339, 356
Pillar, Paul R., 341
Planning, programming, budgeting,
    and spending (PPBS)
    system, 204
Policy Coordinating Committees
    (PCCs), 202
Political process, 58–61
Politics Among Nations (Morgen-
    thau), 53
Posse comitatus, 80, 215
Powell, Colin S., 67, 252
Power politics. See Realist paradigm
Pragmatism, 42
The Prince (Machiavelli), 52, 298
Principals Committee (PC), 202
Prisoners of war (POWs)
    versus detainees, 32–33
    Geneva Conventions of War,
        32–33

Guantanamo Bay (Gitmo),
    32–33, 196
information required of, 33
Taliban and Al Qaeda, 32–33
Privatization, 141, 144
Protectionism, 146
Putin, Vladimir, 7, 23, 122, 240, 322

Q

Quadrennial Defense Review
    (QDR), 167, 206, 249, 250,
    253

R

Radicalism, 42
Rapoport, David C., 333
Reactionism, 42–43
Reagan, Nancy, 389
Reagan, Ronald W., 50, 103, 119, 145
Reagan administration
    National Security Directive
        (NSD) 207, 215
    Strategic Defense Initiative
        (SDI), 238
Realism, 40–41. See also Cold War
    during Cold War competition, 52
    criticism of, 52, 53
    described, 40
    historical dominance of, 40
    as Hobbesian construct, 40
    realist-idealist axis, political
        alignment on, 41
    state-centricity, 41
Realist paradigm. See also Cold War;
    National security; Security
    anomalies
        Chechnya, Russian campaign
            in, 70–71
        international agreements, U.S.
            refusal to join, 70
        unilateralism, 71
    criticisms
        conflicts, emphasis on, 68–69
        humanitarian intervention, 68
        interest-threat mismatch,
            66–67
        state sovereignty, 64–66
    power politics
        cyberware, 62
        diplomatic power, 62
        economic power, 61–62
        informational power, 62
        instruments of power, 61–62
        international anarchy, 59
        measurement of power, 60
        military power, 62
        politics, defined, 58–61
        power relationships, 60–61
        self-help, 59
        situational specificity, 61
        Uganda example (Amin, Idi),
            61
    six propositions, listed, 51–52
    state sovereignty, 54–55, 64–66.
        See also Sovereignty
    vital interests

Realist paradigm   (cont.)
defined, 55–56
Iraq War, 56–58
and major interests, bound-
aries between, 57–58
national interest matrix
(Nuechterlein), 56
Persian Gulf War, 1990–1991,
57–58
power, defined, 56
scarcity, 58
September 11, 2001, 57
Reciprocal Trade Agreements Act
(RTAA), 135, 137
Rejectionists, 135, 151
Republic of Korea. *See South Korea*
Revolution in military affairs
(RMA), 39, 301–2
Ricardo, David, 146, 147
Rice, Condoleezza, 27, 127, 202,
261, 265, 354
Ridge, Tom, 11, 216, 220
Roosevelt, Franklin D., 136, 137,
195, 228
Rousseau, Jean Jacques, 172
Rubin, Robert, 145, 203
Rumsfeld, Donald, x, 28, 111, 112,
127, 199, 206, 249, 261, 282
Russia, 7, 23, 39, 322, 347
International Criminal Court
(ICC) and, 70
Rwanda, 354

S

Saudi Arabia, 125, 326
Savings and loan scandal of the
1980s, 144–45
Schmidt, Helmut, 321
Secretary of Defense (SECDEF),
196–97
Security. *See also National security;
Realist paradigm*
border security
American safety, 390–91
drug trafficking, 388–90
illegal immigration, 388–90
impenetrable border, 391
important exclusions, 387–88
land borders of the U.S., 385
national priorities, 390–91
physical dimensions, 386
resources available to border
guards, 386–87
risk assessment and reduction,
385
sea borders of the U.S., 385–86
contemporary environment
humanitarian vital interests,
183
Korean and Taiwanese scenarios, 175, 182
military threats, decrease in, 182
post-Afghanistan campaign
against terrorism, 182
realist paradigm, enforcement
of, 183

U.S. military strength, 182
use of armed forces, 183
defining terrorism as threat, 169
economic, 170
energy, 170
environmental security, 170
global warming, 399–400
Hurricane Katrina, 402–4
Kyoto Protocols, 401
health/disease security, 404–6
AIDs pandemic, 404, 405
avian flu, 404, 405
Ebola virus, 404
lack of personalization of
problems, 406
low prioritization of the
problem, 406
seriousness and immediacy of
problem, 406
sudden acute respiratory syndrome (SARS), 404, 405
Israel, Syria, the Golan Heights,
and water, 170
levels of
above and below the state, 172
Afghanistan *versus* Iraq, 173
The Holocaust, 173
individual security, 173
international security, 172, 173
national missile defense
(NMD) and China, 172
popular sovereignty, 173
security dilemma, 172
universal human rights, 174
levels of interest
during the Cold War, 178, 180
deployed *versus* employed
forces, 181
interest driven calculations,
178
interest-threat mismatch, 181
Nicaragua, Sandanista rule in,
180
realist paradigm, 178
Vietnam, 179–80
vital interests/less-than-vital
interests boundary, 178, 180
"long peace," 166
military elements
addition of during Cold War,
168
decrease in importance, 168
as only security concern
(pre-Cold War), 168
national resource security
petroleum energy security,
392–95
water security, 395–98
nonmilitary elements
addition of during Cold War,
168
economic security, 167–68
environmental security, 168
trade conditions, 168
risk and risk management
capability, 176
exposure, 174–75

increased capability, 177
modulation of risk, 177
notification of threats, 176
redefinition of threats, 176–77
risk, defined, 174
threat, 174
semimilitary elements
international terrorism, 168,
169
rise in importance, 168
weapons of mass destruction
(WMD), 168
Selective service, 286
September 11, 2001, *xi*
American symbols, attack on, 30
asymmetrical warfare, emphasis
on, 30–31, 293–96. *See also
Warfare*
as fault line, 6, 7, 8
fourth-generation warfare,
310–11
and geopolitics, 20, 30–31
homeland security, institutionalization of, 216–19
insecurity of Americans since, 77
military spending, 31
multilateralism *versus* unilateralism, 34
national security environment,
changes in, 3–5
neo-isolationism, crippling of, 50
nonstate actors (terrorist organizations), dealing with,
30–32
terrorism, difficulty defining, 2–3
vital interests/major interests
boundary, 57
Serbia, 78
Seven Sisters, 140
Seven Years' War, 84
Shalikashvili, John, 95
Shinseki, Eric, 267, 270
Sierra Leone, 67, 312, 313, 358
Single Integrated Operational Plan
(SIOP), 233
Smoot-Hawley Tariff Act (1930),
135
Soft power, 38, 44
Somalia, 67, 354, 362
South Korea, 12, 175
Sovereignty
anarchy, 55
defined, 55
domestic, 55
international agreements, U.S.
refusal to join
Convention on Genocide, 70
International Criminal Court
(ICC), 51, 70, 73
Kyoto treaty, 71, 401
Universal Declaration on
Human Rights, 70
international politics, effect
on, 55
Milosevic extradition, 73
partisan viewpoints, 71
political order, 55

418